New Essentials of
UNIFICATION THOUGHT
HEAD-WING THOUGHT

New Essentials of
UNIFICATION THOUGHT
HEAD-WING THOUGHT

UNIFICATION THOUGHT INSTITUTE

Published by Kogensha
37-18 Udagawa-cho, Shibuya-ku, Tokyo, Japan
First Published 2006
ISBN 4-87656-829-4 C0010
Copyright © Unification Thought Institute
All rights reserved.
Printed in Korea

UTI-KOREA
#381-7 Samyong Cheonan-si, Chung Nam, 330-150, Korea
Tel : 82-41-559-1230-4, 82-2-737-7467 Fax: 82-41-559-1239, 82-2-737-7468
E-mail: jslee@sunmoon.ac.kr

UTI-JAPAN
Seiyaku Bldg., 4F, 5-13-2 Shinjuku, Shinjuku-Ku, Tokyo, 160-0022, Japan
Tel: 81-3-3341-7811, Fax: 81-3-3341-7814
E-mail: utitokyo@nifty.com

UTI-USA
The Research Institute for the Integration of World Thought
708 Atlantic St., Bridgeport, CT 06604, USA
Tel : 1-203-366-2347, Fax: 1-203-366-2347
E-mail: RIIWT7899@hotmail.com

UTI-GERMANY
c/o IIFWF e.V., Marienstr. 19-20, D-10117 Berlin, Germany
Tel : +49-(0)211-786379, Fax: +49-(0)211-786379
E-mail: utuente@gmx.de

UTI-PHILIPPINES
32 Samar Avenue South Triangle, 1103 Diliman, Quezon City, Philippines
Tel : 632-924-1835, Fax: 632-924-1826
E-mail: pwpa@umphil.net

UTI-TAIWAN
Suite A, 4F, 273, Sec 3, Roosevelt Road, Taipei, Taiwan
Tel : 886-2-2363-7656, Fax: 886-2-2363-8410
E-mail: iifwp@cm1.ethome.net.tw

UTI-CZECH REPUBLIC
Na Jarove 11, 13000 Prague, Czech Republic
E-mail: ethics@tiscali.cz

UTI-INDIA
180, Satya Niketan, Moti Bagh II, New Delhi 110 021, India
Tel : 91-11-26118990, Fax: 91-11-26118991
E-mail: ffwpuindia@sify.com

UTI-RUSSIA
Kubanskaya St. 29-1 Moscow 109387, Russia
Tel: +7(095) 350-0588
E-mail: jackcorley@mtu-net.ru

UTI-BULGARIA
25, G. Benkoviski Str., Sofia 100, Bulgaria
E-mail: utibulgaria@mail.bg

UTI-MONGOLIA
Dr. Dashpurev, POBox 205, Ulaanbaatar Branch 46, Mongolia
Tel : 976-11-328681, Fax: 976-11-329450
E-mail: utimn@hotmail.com

The Reverend Dr. Sun Myung Moon

Foreword

The first English version of Unification Thought was published in 1973, entitled Unification Thought. Since that time, several editions have been published, including *Explaining Unification Thought* in 1981, *Fundamentals of Unification Thought* in 1991, and *Essentials of Unification Thought* in 1992. The reason why new books, with new titles, continued to be published over the years is because the Rev. Sun Myung Moon has continually revealed new content in the numerous speeches and sermons he has delivered to a great variety of audiences worldwide. In accordance with the changing world situation, his thought continually takes on new and different dimensions.

In the process of systematizing the Rev. Moon's thought, the author continually integrated this new content within the context of the existing system of thought, and published the result as a new book. Nonetheless, the essence, or core, of the Unification Thought perspective has remained unchanged. New content was added in order to supplement and enrich this basic perspective, and this would appear as a new book.

The final text by the author was published in Korean in 1993, under the title *Essentials of Unification Thought (Head-Wing Thought)*. That book served as the culmination of all of his writings. Its Japanese version was published in 2000, and its English version, *New Essentials of Unification Thought*, has now been published as the present text, which the reader holds in her/his hands.

The relevance of this text is no less today, in 2006, than it was when it first appeared in 1973. Today we live in a changed and changing world. The Communist system has collapsed, and yet Communist philosophy, the materialist dialectic, which denies God, still exists, in various forms and manifestations, thus continuing to confuse the world in a diverse number of ways. Furthermore, evolutionary theory, which would deny any idea of creation by a designer (God), is currently widely accepted, and promoted as the only viable scientific perspective, and is promoted as objective truth.

An even greater concern lies in the fact that ethnic, racial, and cultural conflicts and tensions, most, if not all, of which have a religious impetus in their background, continue as they have in the past, only now threatening ominously to explode in greater and greater violence. This, in spite of the fact that religions surely must all spring from one and the same ultimate reality as their fundamental ground. In the context of this extremely precarious cultural and social situation, this latest publication of *New Essentials of Unification Thought* is of the greatest significance.

Unification Thought is also called Head-Wing Thought or Godism. Head-Wing Thought seeks to unite both left-wing and right-wing ideas by overcoming materialism and humanism. Godism embraces and unites all religions by clarifying God's fundamental attributes, His basic principles and methods of designing and creating the universe, and the universal laws of science and morality which underlie all of natural and social reality. It sets forth a practical way by which a peaceful world might be realized, a world wherein all human beings might live together as one family, united in one heart, with God as the True Parent. Therefore, Unification Thought has the potential of accomplishing a truly historic task.

I sincerely hope that this book will serve as a beacon of hope to give the bright light of inspiration to a world presently mired in anxiety and confusion.

May, 2006

Sung-Bae Jin, Ph. D.
President, UTI of Korea

Preface

During the decade of the 1990s the world underwent great and unprecedented changes. An attempted coup by the conservative wing of the Soviet Communist Party provided the momentum for the astonihshing series of events that culminated in the demise of the Soviet empire—the powerful empire that had, for the better part of the twentieth century, shaken the world under the slogan of global communization.

In the wake of the flurry of events that witnessed the disintegration of the Communist bloc, the President of Russia, Mr. Boris Yeltsin, visited the United States and declared, to a joint session of the Senate and the House, that Communism had died and would never again be allowed to revive in his country.

Yet, the republics that comprised the former Soviet Union, freed from the shackles of Communism, are now at a loss as to where to go and have not yet recovered from social chaos and economic bankruptcy. Meanwhile, in China, and in other nations which still hold to Communism as their national policy, a contradiction persists between their endeavor to attain economic reform under an open-door policy and their adherence to the socialist system and to Communist dictatorship.

In the meantime, the situation has not fared much better in democratic countries. The United States, still the champion of the democratic world, for a brief moment basked in the glory of winning the Gulf War. But the glitter of that victory has quickly been dimmed by the staggering red ink of the U.S. economy and, as time goes on, the stature of the United States as a respected global leader is slowly declining.

Now that the ideal of Communism has faded, and there exists no strong leadership in democracy, the conflicts deriving from the opposition between nations and religions, and from economic friction, are erupting throughout the world, casting ominous shadows over the future of humankind. This situation is being further aggravated by the tragic spread of AIDS and by a losing battle against poverty and starvation in developing countries.

In such a state of disorder and unrest, the world is now earnestly seeking for new vision and new leadership to guide humankind. In such a situation, the Unification Movement, motivated by the Rev. Moon, is offering what seems to be the brightest light of hope in sight.

Unification Thought, which is the Rev. Moon's thought and the perspective (thought system) of the Unification Movement, is also called Godism or Head-Wing Thought. The term "Godism" indicates that this system of thought has God's truth and love as its nucleus; and the term "Head-Wing Thought" indicates that this system of thought is neither a part of the right wing nor of the left wing, but rather embraces both.

Only Godism, or Head-Wing Thought, or Unification Thought—with its spirit of promoting love for others from the perspective of a God-centered view of values—can overcome the hatred, hostility, and materialism of Communism, the left-wing ideology, and eradicate the egoism and self-centeredness of democracy, the right-wing ideology. This will go far to reconcile these two opposing wings and can guide people on both sides to advance together toward the realization of an ideal world, a long-cherished desire of both God and humankind.

Moreover, Unification Thought is the thought of God, and holds to the purpose of reconciling warring nations and conflicting religions through the true love of God, the supreme center who is the origin of all religions. The purpose of Unification Thought is thus to achieve the goal of creating a global family and to realize the everlasting ideal world of God's true love by solving—fundamentally and once and for all—all the numerous and difficult problems that afflict humankind. Therefore, no matter how difficult the problems may be, they can be resolved permanently and fundamentally once Unification Thought (Godism) is applied to them.

The author of the present text has been organizing, from a philosophical perspective, the teachings of the Rev. Moon. I, the author, experienced much suffering in my life and, like many people, have borne many of life's problems. Since joining the Unification Church in 1956, I carefully studied the teachings of the Rev. Moon and found in his teachings many astounding truths that could completely solve the problems of human life. The image of the Rev. Moon in my mind in those days was that he was a treasure house of truth and a fountain of thought. Once he started speaking, he could speak for hours and hours and, as if from a fountain, the water of his thought flowed out boundlessly. Many times I became completely intoxicated by the truth which filled his thought, and I would forget the passage of time. It was in this way that his words were so truly valuable and precious to me.

There is an old saying, that a bagful of gems can become a beautiful necklace if they are strung together on a thread; but if left as they are, they may easily get lost. Likewise, if the precious teachings of the Rev. Moon had been heard and then left as they were, part of each of those teachings might soon disappear from the realm of our memory, just like gems easily disappear if not strung together. I could not dispel such a fear. Moreover, I, who had suffered from many problems of human life and had been saved through these truths, wished to string them together into a necklace of truth and convey them to those who might also be suffering. This is why I undertook the task of organizing the large number of those teachings, as though I was organizing gems into a beautiful necklace.

In the meantime, I had an opportunity to participate in the Korea-Japan Professors' Friendship seminar held in Japan in the summer of 1972 in accordance with the Rev. Moon's instructions. During my stay in Japan, I presented lectures to the intellectual leaders of the Unification Movement in Japan, on some of the contents of the Rev. Moon's philosophical thought which I had systemized by that time. Their response was unexpectedly supportive. Upon my return to Korea, I reported this to the Rev. Moon. In response, he instructed me to publish a book based on the contents of the lectures, to establish a Unification Thought Institute with five to seven sections, and to promote an ideological movement, while continuing to organize his teachings. So, I further systemized the Rev. Moon's thought, and in 1973 published the first edition of *Essentials of Unification Thought* (in Korean)—the title of which was handwritten in Chinese calligraphy by the Rev. Moon—in the name of the Unification Thought Institute (The English translation of that first book was published under the title *Unification Thought*).

Since that time I have continued to systemize the Rev. Moon's thought, and various Unification Thought books have been published. The present work includes the heartfelt teachings that have been imparted by the Rev. Moon since the early days of the Unification Church, arranged under his guidance. It is proper that the book is published not under the author's name but under the name of the Unification Thought Institute, since the content of the book is entirely what the Rev. Moon has taught. This is similar to the case of the late President Hyo-Won Eu, of the Holy Spirit Association for the Unification of World Christianity (Unification Church) of Korea, who published *Divine Principle*, the content of which came from the teachings of the Rev. Moon, not in Mr. Eu's name, but in the name of the Holy Spirit Association for the Unification of World Christianity.

It should be noted here that, first, the way of systematization developed in the book is not a product of Unification Thought itself, but rather the Rev. Moon's thought itself is Unification Thought, and therefore, the system-atization by the author is but one expression of the Rev. Moon's thought; second, even though my intention was to accurately present the thought given by the Rev. Moon, it is always very difficult to ensure the absolute accuracy of expression, due to the limitations of my own ability. That is why the first edition contained so many points which were rather difficult to understand.

Since Unification Thought is the theoretical system of a profound thinker—namely, the Rev. Sun Myung Moon—it was felt necessary to make it available to scholars interested in philosophy. Accordingly, copies of the book were sent to several international professors. Shortly after that, there was an unexpected response: Some professors pointed out that, publishing a book without the author's name was an unfair and irre-sponsible attitude on the part of the author, because in doing so, he is evading responsibility for any controversies that might arise from the book.

Faced with such a criticism, I explained to the Rev. Moon that, since it was necessary to introduce his thought to world scholars, I felt compelled to publish future books in my own name, thus taking responsibility for any misinterpretations or mistaken wording. That is why the Japanese editions, and later the English editions (*Explaining Unification Thought* and *Fundamentals of Unification Thought*) were all published under my name.

Yet another unexpected result occurred: Quite a few scholars began to think that the content of those books was my own thought, even though I had clearly introduced it as the Rev. Moon's. That misunderstanding caused me to feel deep grief. Recently, however, quite a few Unificationist scholars have qualified themselves as Unification Thought lecturers and now can cope with arguments concerning Unification Thought. In this context, it has now become unnecessary to place my name on the book.

Yet, it seems equally inappropriate to place the Rev. Moon's name as the author. The reason is that, even though it is almost no longer necessary for me to bear responsibility for the wording of the book, the content of the book is but a part of the Rev. Moon's thought. Furthermore, and I could hardly assume that this book is a perfect rendition of the Rev. Moon's thought, I did not want even a small portion of it to cause any harm to Heaven's authority.

In organizing and systematizing Unification Thought, it is indispensable to make a comparison with the thoughts of other philosophers in various fields, in order to argue that Unification Thought is more complete than other, past, thoughts. Yet, I am not sure that this comparative effort has been done adequately or not.

Here I can sympathize with the predicament of the late President Eu, who likewise was unable to publish *Divine Principle*(1966) under the Rev. Moon's name, even though it contained the Principles taught by the Rev. Moon. Thus, just as *Divine Principle* was published under the name of the Holy Spirit Association for the Unification of World Christianity, likewise the books dealing with Unification Thought will, from now on, be published under the name of the Unification Thought Institute, whether in Korea or abroad, by permission of the Rev. Moon—just as the first edition was.

The present work, *New Essentials of Unification Thought*, is the English translation of the Korean edition published in 1993, which is, per the Rev. Moon's instructions, subtitled *Head-Wing Thought*. Also, this book is in fact the revised and enlarged edition of *Essentials of Unification Thought* (1992) published in English. Ever since the publication of the first Korean edition of *Essentials of Unification Thought*(1973), the Rev. Moon has continued to teach us more profound truths at every opportunity, and I have arranged his teachings and included them in the present text. Therefore, the content of the present edition has increased significantly, compared with previous editions.

Here, I would like to add another comment. I have introduced only the main points of certain traditional philosophies, those points which are relevant to each area of Unification Thought, in order to advocate the profound insights of Unification Thought. Some readers may have the impression that traditional philosophies are treated too simply. This is because the primary aim of this work is not to introduce these traditional philosophies, but to introduce Unification Thought, correctly and in the limited space of one book.

Unification Thought deals comprehensively with all areas of thought, and its way of arrangement, that is, the order in which the various areas unfold, is similar to the order of God's creation of the universe. In other words, since Unification Thought begins with God as the starting point of creation, it deals first with the theory regarding God, who created the universe. Thus, the first chapter is the Theory of the Original Image, which deals with God, the fundamental cause of the universe. Next, since in the order of creation by God all things were created ahead of human beings, Ontology is addressed, as a theory concerning all things. After the creation of all things, human beings were created; therefore, the third area is the Theory of the Original Human Nature, which concerns the original human being.

After creating Adam, God brought beasts and birds to Adam (Gen. 2:19-20). Upon seeing them, Adam gave them names. This means that, while observing all things with interest, Adam engaged in cognition and thinking. Therefore, the fourth and fifth areas are Epistemology which is the theory of cognition, and Logic which is the theory of thinking.

Adam and Eve were to perfect the three great blessings. This means that they should have perfected their character in order to realize the world of the ideal of creation. The world of the ideal of creation is a world where such people of perfected character live with values centered on true love. Therefore, the sixth area is Axiology, or the theory of value.

If Adam and Eve had perfected themselves by fulfilling their portion of responsibility, they would have taught their children their experiences during their growing period, and their children would have matured, through a relatively light portion of responsibility, to perfect the first blessing. Thus, the perfected Adam and Eve would have educated their children. Therefore, the seventh area is the Theory of Education. Since the first blessing is followed by the second and the third blessings to comprise the three great blessings, the theory of education also deals with the educational aspects of the second and third blessings. When human beings mature, they marry and form a family, as was originally intended; therefore, the eighth area to be addressed is Ethics, which deals with norms within the family.

The next area concerns the human dominion over all things. The human being is to have dominion over all things, and all things are to return beauty to the human being. Accordingly, the ninth area is the Theory of Art. Since dominion implies not only dominion over nature but also over all the different kinds of human activities, under the concept of dominion are included economics, politics, society, culture, and so on. Though Unification Thought does not address politics and economics as such, it does address the historical changes in those areas. Accordingly, the tenth area to be addressed is the Theory of History.

There exist invariable laws consistently at work in all fields of human endeavor; and the theory dealing with these laws is Methodology, which is the eleventh area to be addressed. Because of its all-encompassing nature, methodology should have been placed right after the theory of the Original Image; but since a comparative analysis must be made between Unification Methodology and traditional methodologies, it has been placed last.

It was in this manner that the eleven areas of Unification Thought originally came to be arranged. The areas of epistemology and logic, however, have been placed at the end of the book right before methodology, for the sake of convenience, since they deal with sophisticated traditional epistemological and logical theories. As mentioned above, the content of this book is an arrangement of the major aspects of the Rev. Moon's thought, covering, however, only the part of his thought that has been made available to the public. It is quite possible that new and deeper points of truth will become available to the public as time goes on. Accordingly, if the necessity arises, such new points will be added from time to time, according to the Rev. Moon's instructions.

Finally, I would like to express my sincerest wish that this book may be of help to all the readers who are seeking a deeper understanding of the thought of the Rev. Moon, who has been living a life of complete dedication, under inexplicable persecution.

April, 1993
The Author

Contents

Foreword VII

Preface IX

1. Theory of the Original Image 1

   I. Content of the Original Image 2
      A. Divine Image 2
         1. *Sungsang* and *Hyungsang* 2
         2. Yang and Yin 13
         3. Individual Image 19
      B. Divine Character 22
         1. Heart 23
         2. Logos 27
         3. Creativity 33

   II. Structure of the Original Image 39
      A. Give and Receive Action and Four Position Foundation 40
         1. Give and Receive Action between *Sungsang* and *Hyungsang* 40
         2. Subject and Object, and the Four Position Foundation 43
      B. Formation of the Four Position Foundation 47
         1. Constituents of the Four Position Foundation 47
         2. Inner Four Position Foundation and Outer Four Position Foundation 49
         3. Two-Stage Structure of the Original Image and Two-Stage Structure of Existence 50
      C. Kinds of Four Position Foundations 52
         1. Inner Identity-Maintaining Four Position Foundation 52
         2. Outer Identity-Maintaining Four Position Foundation 54
         3. Inner Developmental Four Position Foundation 56
         4. Outer Developmental Four Position Foundation 72
      D. Origin, Division, and Union Action 84
      E. Unity in the Structure of the Original Image 90
      F. Ideal of Creation 91

III. Traditional Ontologies and Unification Thought 97

2. Ontology: A Theory of Being 103

I. Individual Truth Being 105
   A. *Sungsang* and *Hyungsang* 105
   B. Yang and Yin 110
   C. Individual Image of the Individual Truth Being 113

II. Connected Being 118
   A. What is a Connected Being? 118
   B. Subject and Object 123
   C. Mode of Existence 133
   D. Position of Existence 144
   E. Law of the Universe 147

3. Theory of the Original Human Nature 151

I. A Being with Divine Image 155
   A. A United Being of *Sungsang* and *Hyungsang* 155
   B. A Harmonious Being of Yang and Yin 158
   C. A Being of Individuality 162

II. A Being with Divine Character 164
   A. A Being of Heart 164
   B. A Being of Logos 167
   C. A Being of Creativity 169

III. A Being with Position 172
   A. Object Position 172
   B. Subject Position 174
   C. "Connected Being Consciousness" and Democracy 176

IV. Conclusion 179

V. A Unification Thought Appraisal of the Existentialist Analysis of Human Existence 180
   A. Søren Kierkegaard 181
   B. Friedrich Nietzsche 185
   C. Karl Jaspers 188

D. Martin Heidegger 192
　　　E. Jean-Paul Sartre 195

4. Axiology: A Theory of Value 199

　I. Meaning of Axiology and Significance of Value 202
　II. Divine Principle Foundation for Axiology 204
　III. Kinds of Value 207
　IV. Essence of Value 208
　V. Determination of Actual Value and Standard of Value 210
　　　A. Determination of Value 210
　　　B. Subjective Action 211
　　　C. Standard for Determining Value 212
　VI. Weaknesses in the Traditional Views of Value 217
　　　A. Weaknesses in the Christian View of Value 217
　　　B. Weaknesses in the Confucian View of Value 219
　　　C. Weaknesses in the Buddhist View of Value 220
　　　D. Weaknesses in the Islamic View of Value 222
　　　E. Weaknesses in the Humanitarian View of Value ... 223
　VII. Establishing the New View of Value 224
　　　A. Theological Ground for the New View of Absolute Value ... 225
　　　B. Philosophical Ground for the New View of Absolute Value ... 226
　　　C. Historical Ground for the New View of Absolute Value 229
　VIII. Historical Changes in the View of Value 231
　　　A. Views of Value in the Greek Period 231
　　　B. Views of Value in the Hellenistic-Roman Period ... 233
　　　C. Views of Value in the Medieval Period 235
　　　D. Modern Views of Value 236
　　　E. Necessity for a New View of Value 238

5. Theory of Education 241

　I. Divine Principle Foundation for the Theory of Education ... 243
　　　A. Resemblance to God and the Three Great Blessings ... 243
　　　B. Process of Growth of Human Beings 247

C. Three Great Ideals of Education 249
   II. Three Forms of Education 250
      A. The Education of Heart 250
      B. The Education of Norm 258
      C. The Education of Dominion 260
   III. Image of the Ideally-Educated Person 263
   IV. Traditional Theories of Education 266
   V. An Appraisal of Traditional Theories of Education from the Perspective of Unification Thought 274

6. Ethics 279
   I. Divine Principle Foundation for Ethics 280
   II. Ethics and Morality 282
   III. Order and Equality 286
   IV. An Appraisal of Traditional Theories of Ethics from the Perspective of Unification Thought 290
      A. Kant 290
      B. Bentham 293
      C. Analytic Philosophy 295
      D. Pragmatism 297

7. Theory of Art 301
   I. Divine Principle Foundation for the Theory of Art 302
   II. Art and Beauty 304
   III. Dual Purposes of Artistic Activity: Creation and Appreciation 309
   IV. Requisites for Artistic Creation 311
      A. Requisites for the Subject in Artistic Creation 311
      B. Requisites for the Object in Artistic Creation 314
   V. Technique, Materials, and Style in Artistic Creation 315
   VI. Requisites for Artistic Appreciation 320

VII. Unity in Art 323
VIII. Art and Ethics 326
IX. Types of Beauty 327
  A. Types of Love and Beauty from the Perspective of Unification Thought 327
  B. Traditional Types of Beauty 330
X. A Critique and Counterproposal to Socialist Realism 331
  A. Socialist Realism 331
  B. Critique of Socialist Realism 333
  C. An Indictment of Communism by Notable Writers 335
  D. Errors in the Communist Theory of Art Seen from the Perspective of Unification Thought 336

8. Theory of History 339

I. Basic Positions of the Unification View of History 340
II. Laws of Creation 343
  A. Law of Correlativity 344
  B. Law of Give and Receive Action 344
  C. Law of Repulsion 345
  D. Law of Dominion by the Center 346
  E. Law of Completion through Three Stages 348
  F. Law of the Period of the Number Six 349
  G. Law of Responsibility 351
III. Laws of Restoration 352
  A. Law of Indemnity 353
  B. Law of Separation 353
  C. Law of the Restoration of the Number Four 355
  D. Law of Conditioning Providence 356
  E. Law of the False Preceding the True 358
  F. Law of the Horizontal Reappearance of the Vertical 359
  G. Law of Synchronous Providence 361
IV. Changes in History 363
V. Traditional Views of History 366

    VI. Comparative Analysis of Providential View, Materialist
        View, and Unification View 374

9. Epistemology 381

    I. Traditional Epistemologies 382
        A. Origin of Cognition 383
        B. Essence of the Object of Cognition 390
        C. Epistemologies in Terms of Method 392

    II. Unification Epistemology 399
        A. Outline of Unification Epistemology 400
        B. Content and Form in Cognition 404
        C. Protoconsciousness, Image in Protoconsciousness,
            and Category 407
        D. Method of Cognition 412
        E. Process of Cognition 417
        F. Process of Cognition and Physical Conditions 422

    III. Kantian and Marxist Epistemologies Seen from
        the Perspective of Unification Thought 432
        A. A Critique of Kantian Epistemology 433
        B. A Critique of Marxist Epistemology 434

10. Logic 437

    I. Traditional Systems of Logic 438
        A. Formal Logic 438
        B. Hegel's Logic 448
        C. Dialectical Logic (Marxist Logic) 455
        D. Symbolic Logic 456
        E. Transcendental Logic 457

    II. Unification Logic 458
        A. Basic Postulates 458
        B. Logical Structure of the Original Image 461
        C. The Two Stages in the Process of Thinking and the Formation of
            the Four Position Foundation 464

III. An Appraisal of Traditional Systems of Logic from
the Perspective of Unification Thought ········· 472

11. Methodology ········· 479

I. Historical Review ········· 479

II. Unification Methodology—Give and Receive Method ······ 490
  A. Kinds of Give and Receive Action ········· 490
  B. Scope of Give and Receive Action ········· 495
  C. Types of Give and Receive Action ········· 497
  D. Characteristics of the Give and Receive Action ········· 497

III. An Appraisal of Traditional Methodologies from
the Perspective of Unification Thought ········· 497

Appendix ········· 507

I. Principle of Mutual Existence, Mutual Prosperity and
Mutual Righteousness ········· 507
  A. Principle of Mutual Existence ········· 507
  B. Principle of Mutual Prosperity ········· 513
  C. Principle of Mutual Righteousness ········· 521

II. Three Great Subjects Thought ········· 524

III. Significance of the Four Great Realms of Heart and
the Three Great Kingships ········· 534
  A. Four Great Realms of Heart ········· 534
  B. Three Great Kingships ········· 543

Notes ········· 548

Bibliography ········· 596

1

Theory of the Original Image

As was stated in the Preface, Unification Thought is the thought which has appeared to lead humankind eternally by fundamentally solving all the difficult problems of humanity. Yet, the fundamental solution of all these difficult problems is possible only through a correct and full understanding of the attributes of God.

The theory concerning the attributes of God, in Unification Thought, is called the Theory of the Original Image. "Original Image" means the attributes of God, the causal being. The attributes of God consist of "form" and also of "function" including nature, character, ability, etc. We call the former aspect the "Divine Image" and the latter aspect the "Divine Character."

In such historical religions as Christianity and Islam, the attributes of God have been expressed in various ways: omniscience, omnipotence, omnipresence, supreme good, supreme beauty, supreme truth, righteousness, love, creativity, and so on.

Unification Thought certainly affirms such characteristics as these as included among the attributes of God. Yet, we can not solve actual problems fundamentally by limiting ourselves to this traditional way of understanding God's attributes.

Unification Thought considers such attributes as those mentioned as belonging to the Divine Character of God. A more important aspect of the attributes of God, however, is the Divine Image. The Divine Image consists of dual characteristics, as is explained in the Divine Principle. Only through a correct and full understanding of the Divine Image, as well as the Divine Character, will we be able to fundamentally solve the problems of human life, society, history, and the world.

The Divine Image of God in Unification Thought refers to the dual characteristics of *Sungsang* and *Hyungsang*, and Yang and Yin, and to the Individual Images. The Divine Character in Unification Thought refers to Heart (*Shimjung*), Logos and Creativity. In this Theory of the Original Image, the content of the Divine Image and the Divine Character will be explained in the section "Content of the Original Image," and the relationship between *Sungsang* and *Hyungsang* will be dealt with in the section "Structure of the Original Image."

I. Content of the Original Image

The content of the Original Image refers to the attributes of God. Here, the content of the Divine Image—*Sungsang* and *Hyungsang*, Yang and Yin, and the Individual Images—and the content of the Divine Character—Heart, Logos and Creativity—will be explained in detail.

A. Divine Image

Divine Image refers to the "form" attribute of God. We can not see God. Yet, He has definite forms. Strictly speaking, He has the potential to take definite forms, or He has a determinativeness. This is called Divine Image. Divine Image includes *Sungsang* and *Hyungsang*, Yang and Yin, and the Individual Images. First, I will explain *Sungsang* and *Hyungsang*.

1. *Sungsang* and *Hyungsang*

God has the dual characteristics of *Sungsang* and *Hyungsang* as His attributes. God's *Sungsang* and *Hyungsang* are also called Original *Sungsang* and Original *Hyungsang* in order to differentiate them from the *sungsangs* and *hyungsangs* of all creation. The relationship between God and all things is that of Creator and created, that is, cause and effect. Therefore, Original *Sungsang* is the root cause of the intangible, functional aspect of all created beings, and Original *Hyungsang* is the root cause of the tangible, material aspect of creation.

The relationship between God and human beings is that of father and children. We were created in the image of God according to the principle of "creation in likeness," Original *Sungsang* corresponding to the minds of human beings, and Original *Hyungsang* corresponding to their bodies. *Sungsang* and *Hyungsang* are not separate, different attributes, but are harmonized as one in a reciprocal relationship.[1] This is what is meant in the Divine Principle when it states that "God is the Subject in whom the dual characteristics of original internal nature [Original *Sungsang*] and original external form [Original *Hyungsang*] are in harmony" (*Exposition of the Divine Principle*, hereafter cited as *DP*, 19).[2] Thus, God is a being with the dual characteristics of Original *Sungsang* and Original *Hyungsang* harmoniously united.

From an ontological viewpoint, the concept of Divine Image is neither just spiritual nor just material: it can be described as a "Theory of Oneness" or "Unification Theory." It can be said that spiritualism, in limited perspective, regards only Original *Sungsang* as the cause of the universe, whereas materialism regards only Original *Hyungsang* as the cause of the universe. Let us consider the content of *Sungsang* and *Hyungsang*, and explain them in more detail.

a) *Sungsang* (Original *Sungsang*)

Original *Sungsang* and Created Beings

God's *Sungsang* corresponds to the mind of a human being. Therefore, Original *Sungsang* is the mind of God, and it is the root cause of the intangible, functional aspects of all created beings. Thus, God's *Sungsang* is the root cause of the human mind, animal instinct, vegetable life, and mineral physicochemical character. In other words, God's *Sungsang* is manifested in space and time on various levels, forming mineral physicochemical character, vegetable life, animal instinct, and the human mind; all according to the principle of "creation in likeness."

Even on the lowest level of the chain of being, God's *Sungsang* is manifested in inorganic materials and minerals as law. In plants, God's *Sungsang* manifests itself as life on a higher dimension (recently experiments have shown that plants have mental functions able to react to a human mind). In animals, God's *Sungsang* manifests itself in a still higher form of mental function as instinct. According to recent research by scholars, we can see that animals also have functions of intellect, emotion and will; they have consciousness as humans do. Yet, animals do not have the self-consciousness which humans have.

Inner Structure of the Original *Sungsang*

God's *Sungsang* has the duality of Inner *Sungsang* and Inner *Hyungsang*. Inner *Sungsang* refers to the functional, subjective part, and Inner *Hyungsang* refers to the objective part. I will explain God's Inner *Sungsang* and Inner *Hyungsang*, taking a human being as an example, inasmuch as the human mind resembles that of God.

Inner *Sungsang*

The Inner *Sungsang*, the functional part within the *Sungsang*, refers to the faculties of intellect, emotion and will. Intellect, which is the faculty of cognition, consists of perception, understanding and reason; emotion is the faculty of feeling joy, anger, sadness and happiness; and will is the faculty of desiring, intentionality, or determining. These faculties all work actively on the Inner *Hyungsang*. Inner *Sungsang* is the subjective part within the *Sungsang*.

The perception faculty of the intellect refers to one's ability to perceive external objects just as they are reflected on one's five senses, or one's ability to perceive intuitively; understanding refers to one's ability to perceive logically following cause and effect; and reason refers to one's ability to comprehend universal truths, and one's capacity for conceptualization.

These three functions can be explained by taking as an example the process of Isaac Newton's discovery of universal gravitation. First, Newton perceived as fact that an apple had fallen from an apple tree. Next, he reflected about the cause of the apple falling, and came to understand that the earth and the apple attracted each other. Finally, by studying, experimenting, and observing, he inferred that, in the universe, all material bodies with mass—aside from the earth and the apple—attract one another. In this process, the first stage in Newton's cognition is perception, the second stage is understanding, and the third stage is reason, which can be called universal cognition.

Inner *Hyungsang*

Inner *Hyungsang* refers to the objective part within the Original *Sungsang*, and contains elements that have form. These important elements include ideas, concepts, laws, and mathematical principles.

i) Ideas: Ideas are concrete representations or images of individual created beings within God's *Sungsang*. We human beings also have concrete pictures of individual created beings in the objective world within our minds as images, and those images are our ideas. Our ideas come from our experiences, but in God, the absolute being, ideas have existed within Him from the beginning.

ii) Concepts: A concept is an abstract and universal image, which arises from the common elements among a group of ideas. Common elements among the ideas of dog, chicken, cow, and pig include, for example, "movement" and "senses." These are collected into an image, and we obtain an abstract image of "animal," which is a concept. Concepts may be further differentiated as specific concepts and generic concepts.

iii) Laws (Principles): Laws or principles in the Inner *Hyungsang* are the original laws at the root of natural laws and norms (laws of value). In other words, it is in and through the numerous natural laws of nature and norms of human life that these original laws find their expression. It can be seen that, as the seed of a plant germinates, and its trunk and branches grow, and many leaves develop, these natural laws, and human norms as well, all derive from the original laws in God.

iv) Mathematical Principles: Mathematical principles are the ultimate cause for the mathematical phenomena inherent in the natural world. All numbers, mathematical values and formulas, which lie in mathematical phenomena, come ultimately from the mathematical principles in the Inner *Hyungsang*. Pythagoras (ca. 570–496) asserted that numbers are the root of all things. The British physicist Paul Dirac (1902–84), who contributed to the formulation of quantum mechanics, held that "God is a high-level mathematician using high-level mathematics in forming the universe." [3] The numbers and mathematics referred to here are the mathematical principles in the Inner *Hyungsang*.

Divine Principle and Biblical Foundation for the Inner *Hyungsang*

I would like to explain about the foundation for the Inner *Hyungsang* as it can be found in the Divine Principle and in the Bible.

i) Inner *Hyungsang*: In the Divine Principle it is written, "The inner quality, though invisible, possesses a certain structure which is manifested visibly in the particular outer form. The inner quality is called *internal nature*, and the outer form or shape is called *external form*" (*DP*, 17). This passage means that prior to the visible forms, there exists a form within the *Sungsang*. This refers to the Inner *Hyungsang*.

ii) Ideas and Concepts: The Bible says, "So God created man in His own image, in the image of God He created him; male and female He created them" (Gen. 1:27, Revised Standard Version) (hereafter Biblical quotations are from RSV). On each day, God said, "Let there be⋯." And it was so. And God saw that it was good (Gen. 1:3–31). This means that all things were created according to the ideas and concepts He had in His mind.

iii) Laws (Principles): In the Divine Principle it is written, "God made the world and carried out His providence according to the Principle" (*DP*, Korean version, 108)[4], "[God is] the Author of the Principle" (*DP*, 43), "Although God created human beings based on the Principle, He governs us through love" (*DP*, 66). Thus God first established the Principle and then He created human beings and all things.

iv) Mathematical Principles : In the Divine Principle it is written, "The universe unfolds and manifests God's original internal nature and original external form based on mathematical principles. Hence, we can infer that one aspect of God's nature is mathematical" (*DP*, 41), and "God exists upon His Principle, which has a numerical aspect" (*DP*, 294). We can, therefore, understand that all of the elements that constitute the Inner *Hyungsang* have a reference in the Divine Principle and in the Bible.

So far, I have explained about the functional part (Inner *Sungsang*) and objective part (Inner *Hyungsang*) in God's Original *Sungsang* through comparisons with a human mind. It is for the purpose of solving actual problems that I have explained God's Original *Sungsang* in some detail. For example, when we say that intellect, emotion and will are centered on Heart, this means that the values of truth, beauty, and goodness—the values which correspond to intellect, emotion and will, respectively—are based on love. Inner *Hyungsang* is objective to Inner *Sungsang* consisting of intellect, emotion, and will; and at the same time, together with Original *Hyungsang*, it is the cause of the tangible aspects of all created beings. From this, it may be concluded that, in our actual life, we should give priority to a life of value (truth, goodness, and beauty) over a material

life of food, clothing and shelter.
Next, I would like to explain about God's *Hyungsang* in more detail.

b) *Hyungsang* (Original *Hyungsang*)

Original *Hyungsang* and Created Beings

In terms of a human being, God's *Hyungsang* corresponds to the human body. It is the fundamental cause of the corporeal, material aspect of all created beings: the human body, the animal body, plant cells and tissues, and the atoms and molecules of minerals. In other words, God's *Hyungsang* was manifested in different forms in time and space. This, again, reflects the principle of "creation in likeness."

Thus, the fundamental cause of the corporeal aspect of all created beings is God's *Hyungsang*, and it has two characters. One is the material element, and the other is the potential for a limitless number of forms. (The origin of the actual forms of all things exists in the Inner *Hyungsang*.)

Here, I can explain the potential for a limitless number of forms by taking the example of water. Water itself has no definite shape of its own. However, it takes various shapes according to its container. In a circular container, it appears as circular; in a rectangular container, it appears rectangular; and in a tall container, it appears columnar. It is because water itself is shapeless and has the potential for a limitless number of forms that an accomodation into any shape is possible. In other words, water exists in countless shapes. In an analogous manner, God's *Hyungsang* has no specific form of its own, and yet it possesses the nature of adjusting itself to any image, or adapting itself to countless forms. Thus, the fundamental cause of the corporeal aspect of created beings has two characteristics: the material element and the potential for a limitless number of forms.

In human creative activities, visible materials (plaster or marble in the case of a sculpture, for example) are transformed in such a way as to conform to the design of the artist's mind. In other words, it can be said that the creative activity is the transformation of materials according to the artist's design. A similar thing can be said for God and His creation. God put the material elements of the Original *Hyungsang*, having the potential for a limitless number of forms, into the mold of the Inner *Hyungsang* in making all things with definite concrete forms. This was the manner of God's creation.

Original *Hyungsang* and Science

The fundamental material element, which is the fundamental cause of the corporeal aspect of created beings, is also the fundamental cause of the "matter" that science has been pursuing. Let us look more closely at the fundamental material element as seen by science.

According to today's science, the fundamental cause of matter is energy (physical energy) which gives rise to elementary particles: That energy has both particle and wave natures. However, since science only conducts its research within the parameters of the phenomenal, resultant world, the energy science is describing is not yet the fundamental and primary cause of matter. The Theory of the Original Image holds that the ultimate cause of matter lies in the Original *Hyungsang*. Thus, the Original *Hyungsang* is the stage just prior to the physical energy being described by science, and so it can be called "prior-stage energy" or simply "pre-energy."[5]

Original *Hyungsang* and Force

In God's creation, two kinds of energy—"forming energy" and "acting energy"—are generated from the pre-energy in the Original *Hyungsang* through give and receive action (which will be explained in the next section "Structure of the Original Image"). Forming energy is that energy which becomes particles and creates material. On the other hand, acting energy is that energy which acts upon all things and is manifested as the force that causes give and receive action (i.e., centripetal force and centrifugal force) among all things. This causal force is called "Prime Force" in Unification Thought. When Prime Force acts horizontally as the acting force among all things, it is called "Universal Prime Force."[6]

Forming energy and acting energy both appear from the Original *Hyungsang* when it is engaged in give and receive action with the Original *Sungsang*. Heart, the root of love, is the base of give and receive action and therefore, the two energies are both the unity of physical energy and the force of love. Thus, the force of love is contained in Prime Force, and in Universal Prime Force as well. (Since his New Hope Banquet speech in May, 1975, Rev. Sun Myung Moon has often mentioned that the force of love is acting in Universal Prime Force.)

Difference and Homogeneity between *Sungsang* and *Hyungsang*

The question of whether *Sungsang* and *Hyungsang* are essentially heterogeneous or homogeneous, that is, the question concerning the difference between *Sungsang* and *Hyungsang* should be considered. What position does the "theory of the dual characteristics of *Sungsang* and *Hyungsang*" occupy among the ontologies of traditional philosophies? Is the "theory of the dual characteristics of *Sungsang* and *Hyungsang*" a monism or a dualism? Is it materialistic or idealistic?

Here, monism refers either to monistic materialism, which asserts that the origin of the universe is solely matter, or to monistic spiritualism (idealism), which asserts that the origin of the universe is solely spirit. Marxist materialism is an example of the former, and Hegelian idealism is an example of the latter. Dualism holds that matter and spirit are separate entities, which gave rise to the universe. For example, Cartesian dualism recognizes the two distinct substances of thought (spirit) and extension (matter).

Given this, is the "theory of the dual characteristics of *Sungsang* and *Hyungsang*" in Unification Thought monistic or dualistic? Stating the question in different terms, are *Sungsang* and *Hyungsang* in the Original Image homogeneous or heterogeneous? If we say they are completely heterogeneous, God becomes a dualistic being, and so we must examine this issue closely.

We must ask whether the Original *Sungsang* and the Original *Hyungsang* are two heterogeneous elements, or if they are simply two expressions of one homogeneous element. Unification Thought holds that the Original *Sungsang* and the Original *Hyungsang* are two forms of expression of one homogeneous element.

As an analogy we can say that steam and ice are the two different forms of expression of one entity, water (H_2O). In water, the attraction and repulsion of molecules are balanced, but when it is heated, the repulsive force becomes predominant and water vaporizes into steam; when it is cooled, the attractive force becomes predominant and water turns into ice. Steam and ice are but two states of water; in other words, they are simply different expressions of the relative relationships between attraction and repulsion of water molecules. Therefore, they are not totally heterogeneous entities.

In the same way, the *Sungsang* and *Hyungsang* of God are the forms of expression of God's absolute attribute. This absolute attribute refers to mind possessing energy, or on the other hand, to energy possessing mind. That is to say, energy and mind are not totally different elements, but are originally united as one. This absolute attribute manifests itself as *Sungsang*, the mind of God, and as *Hyungsang*, the body of God.[7]

Sungsang consists primarily of mental elements, but there is some element of energy in it as well. In *Sungsang*, the mental element is predominant over the element of energy. Likewise, *Hyungsang* is made of energy, but there is some mental element included in it. Thus, *Sungsang* and *Hyungsang* are not totally heterogeneous elements. Both have the mental element and the element of energy in common.

In the created world, *Sungsang* and *Hyungsang* are manifested as the elements of spirit and matter. Yet, there are still some common elements between them. This can be understood from the following example. If an electrical impulse is applied to the nerve of a leg muscle removed from a frog, the muscle will contract. On the other hand, we can move the muscles of our hands and legs by our thinking (mind): Our thought stimulates our nerves and moves our muscles. This means that our mind has the same kind of energy as the physical electrical energy. The fact that there are people who can move another person's body through hypnotism also indicates that there is some energy in the mind.

On the other hand, we can say that there is some *sungsang* element in energy. According to recent scientific understanding, elementary particles are formed in a vacuum state through the vibration of energy. When the particles are formed, however, the vibration of energy is not continuous, but occurs at graded levels, or states. Just as there are scales in music, there are graded states in the vibration of energy and, as a result, different types of elementary particles come into being at graded states. It is concluded that a *sungsang* aspect exists behind energy which determines the stages of the vibration of energy, in the same way that scales in music are determined by our mind.

Thus, there is some *hyungsang* element in the *sungsang*, and likewise there is some *sungsang* element in the *hyungsang*. In the Original Image, *Sungsang* and *Hyungsang* are united into one. They are at the root one and the same absolute attribute, from which are engendered the different *sungsang* and *hyungsang*. When this absolute attribute is manifested in the created world through creation, it becomes two different elements. This is analogous to the drawing of two straight lines from a single point. One of the lines, in this case, corresponds to *sungsang* (or spirit), and the

Content of the Original Image / 11

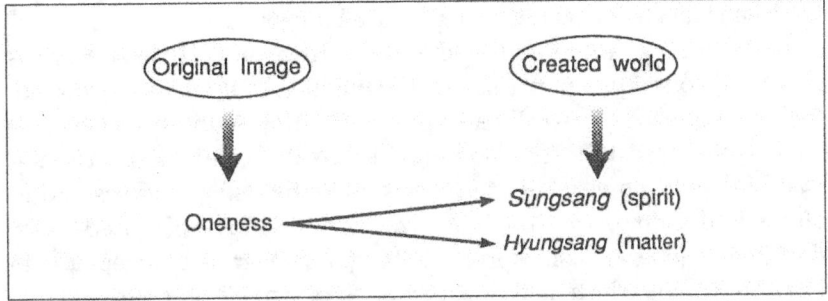

Fig. 1.1. Difference and Homogeneity between *Sungsang* and *Hyungsang* from the Viewpoint of the Theory of Oneness

other corresponds to *hyungsang* (or matter) (see fig. 1.1).

It is written in the Bible that one can understand the nature of God by observing created beings (Rom. 1:20). If we observe created beings, we will notice that they have the dual aspects of mind and body, of instinct and body, of life and body (which is made of cells and tissues), and so on. From this we can infer that God, who is the absolute causal being, is, likewise, of dual aspects. These are the dual characteristics of God. In God, however, the dual characteristics are essentially one. In reference to this point, the *Divine Principle* states that "God is the Subject in whom the dual characteristics of original internal nature [Original *Sungsang*] and original external form [Original *Hyungsang*] are in harmony" (*DP*, 19). We call this viewpoint "Unification Theory."[8] This is also called "Theory of Oneness,"[9] referring to God's absolute attribute.

For Aristotle (384–322 BC), substance consists of *eidos* (form) and *hylē* (matter). *Eidos* refers to the essence that makes a substance into what it is; and *hylē* refers to the material that forms the substance. Aristotle's *eidos* and *hylē*, which became two basic concepts in Western philosophy, correspond to *sungsang* and *hyungsang* in Unification Thought. There are, however, fundamental differences between the two views, as follows.

According to Aristotle, when we trace *eidos* and *hylē* back to their ultimate origin, we arrive at "pure *eidos*" (or prime eidos) and "prime *hylē*." Pure *eidos*, or God, is pure activity without any form; it is nothing but thinking itself. Thus, God was regarded as pure thinking, or the thinking of thinking. "Prime *hylē*," however, was considered to be entirely independent of God. Hence, Aristotle's ontology was dualistic and thus different from Unification Thought; it is also different from the

Christian view that God is the Creator of all things.

Incorporating Aristotle's thought into Christianity; Thomas Aquinas (1225–74) considered pure *eidos*, or the thinking of thinking, to be God. Just as Augustine (354–430) had done before him, Aquinas claimed that God created the world from nothing. God created everything, including *hylē*, and since no element of *hylē* existed within God, Aquinas had to affirm the doctrine of *creatio ex nihilo* ("creation out of nothing"). The doctrine that matter (energy) comes from nothing, however, is unacceptable to modern science, which holds that the universe is made of energy.

René Descartes (1596–1650) held that God, spirit, and matter are three different types of substance. He believed that God is the only real substance. Spirit and matter are totally independent from each other, though each of them is dependent on God. Hence, Descartes proposed a dualism. As a result, it became difficult for him to explain how spirit and matter can interact with each other.

The Flemish philosopher A. Geulincx (1625–69), succeeded Descartes in developing the doctrine of dualism. He sought to solve the problem of how mind and body interact with each other by explaining that God mediates between the two. In other words, the occurrence of a mental state gives God the occasion to cause a physical action corresponding to it; and the occurrence of a physical state gives God the occasion to cause a mental state corresponding to it. This was the essence of occasionalism.[10] This explanation, however, is unacceptable expediency, which no philosopher now takes seriously. The root of Descartes' problem was that he conceived of spirit and matter as totally heterogeneous entities.

It is clear from the above discussion that the concepts of *eidos* (form) and *hylē* (matter), as well as spirit and matter, as held in Western thought, have presented a difficult impasse. These difficult problems have been resolved by the Unification Thought theory of *sungsang* and *hyungsang*, namely, the theory that the Original *Sungsang* and Original *Hyungsang* are the two forms of expression of one and the same essential element.

This concludes my explanation of "*Sungsang* and *Hyungsang*" of the Divine Image. Next, I would like to explain "Yang and Yin," which is another aspect of the Divine Image.

2. Yang and Yin

Yang and Yin Are Also Dual Characteristics of God

Yang and Yin are also dual characteristics of God. However, the dual characteristics of Yang and Yin are different in dimension from those of *Sungsang* and *Hyungsang*, which were previously dealt with. *Sungsang* and *Hyungsang* are God's direct attributes, while Yang and Yin are God's indirect attributes; in other words, Yang and Yin are the attributes of both *Sungsang* and *Hyungsang*, respectively. To put it another way, God's *Sungsang* has Yang and Yin as its attributes, as does God's *Hyungsang*.

The dual characteristics of Yang and Yin are completely harmonized, as are the dual characteristics of *Sungsang* and *Hyungsang*. This is what the Divine Principle means in saying that "God, as the Subject partner, has dual characteristics of Yang and Yin in perfect harmony [*Chung-hwa*]" (*DP*, 18-19). The Korean term *Chung-hwa*, as used for Yang and Yin, as well as for *Sungsang* and *Hyungsang*, means harmony and unity. The dual characteristics were united into oneness before creation was designed. From this oneness, Yang and Yin attributes were separated at the time of creation. Looking at Yang and Yin from this perspective, *I Ching*, or *the Book of Changes*, is correct in saying that "The Great Ultimate, or T'aichi, generates the two primary elements of yin and yang."

The concept of yang and yin in Unification Thought looks similar to that in the *I Ching*, but they are actually different. In the Oriental concept yang means light or brightness, while yin means shade or darkness. These basic meanings are extended, and used in various ways. For example, yang is used to refer to the sun, a mountain, heaven, day, hard, hot, high, and so on, while yin is used as referring to the moon, a valley, earth, night, soft, cold, low and so on.

However, in Unification Thought yang and yin are the attributes of *sungsang* and *hyungsang*. This is why *sungsang* and *hyungsang* make up an individual or substance, while yang and yin only appear as the attributes of a substance. For example, the sun (an individual) is a union of *sungsang* and *hyungsang*, and the brightness of the sun is yang. In the same way, the moon itself is an individual (substance) consisting of *sungsang* and *hyungsang*, and the paleness of the moon is yin.

I would like to explain the concept of substance in Unification Thought. The concept of substance, as used in Unification Thought, originates in the Divine Principle. There, many terms with the word "substance" are

14 / THEORY OF THE ORIGINAL IMAGE

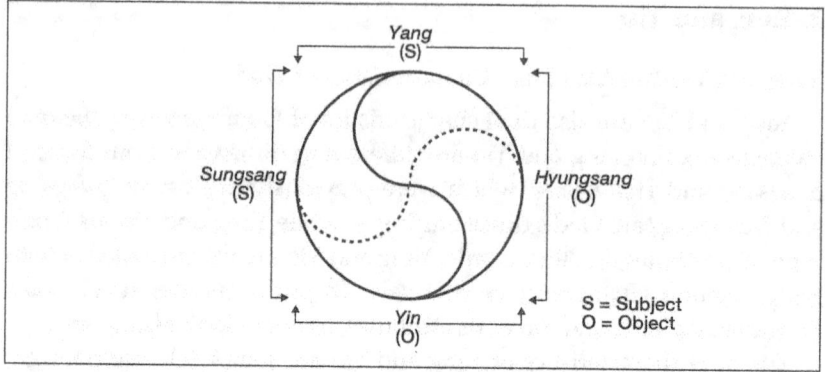

Fig. 1.2. Dual Characteristics of *Sungsang* and *Hyungsang* and Yang and Yin in the Original Image

used, such as "foundation of substance," "substantial offering," "substantial temple," "substantial world," "substantial embodiment," "substantial object," "substantial course" and so on, whereas the term "substance" traditionally refers to a created being, an individual, a human being with physical body, a material being, and so on.

Every created being, including human beings, is the united being of *sungsang* and *hyungsang*. In other words, in a created being *sungsang* and *hyungsang* are components of that individual (substance). Moreover, *sungsang* and *hyungsang* themselves each have the character of substance. It is like saying that an automobile is a product (substance) as are each of its parts, such as the tires, the transmission, and so on. Thus, especially in human beings, both *sungsang* and *hyungsang* are included in this general concept of substance in Unification Thought.

To be precise, Yang and Yin in the Original Image are called Original Yang and Original Yin, respectively (*DP*, 19). "*sungsang* and *hyungsang*" and "yang and yin" in a human being resemble the "Original *Sungsang* and Original *Hyungsang*" and "Original Yang and Original Yin" in the Original Image. As explained above, in the created world *sungsang* and *hyungsang* have the character of substance, while yang and yin are the attributes of *sungsang* and *hyungsang*; in other words, yang and yin are the attributes of an individual being which is the united being of *sungsang* and *hyungsang*. The unity of the dual characteristics of *Sungsang* and *Hyungsang* and the dual characteristics of Yang and Yin in the Original Image is shown in fig. 1.2.

TABLE 1.1 Yang and Yin as Attributes of *Sungsang* and *Hyungsang* (in a Human Being)

		Yang	Yin
Sung-sang	Intellect	Clarity, Good Memory Distinctiveness, Wittiness	Vagueness, Forgetfulness Unclear Ideas, Seriousness
	Emotion	Pleasantness, Loudness, Joy Excitement	Unpleasantness, Quietness Sorrow, Composure
	Will	Activeness, Aggressiveness Creativeness Carefreeness	Passiveness, Tolerance Conservativeness Carefulness
Hyungsang		Protuberant Parts, Protrusions Convex Parts, Front Side	Sunken Parts, Orifices Concave Parts, Back Side

In order to know correctly the relationship between *Sungsang* and *Hyungsang* and the relationship between Yang and Yin in the Original Image, we need to study the relationship between the *sungsang* and *hyungsang* of a person, and the relationship between yang and yin as his or her attributes. The relationship between *sungsang* and *hyungsang*, and that between yang and yin, in human beings are shown in table 1.1.

As shown in the table, the faculties of intellect, emotion and will of the *sungsang* (mind) have the attributes of yang and yin. The yang aspects of the intellect are clarity, distinctiveness, and so on. The yin aspects of the intellect are vagueness, unclear ideas, and so on. The yang aspects of emotion are pleasantness, joy, and so on. The yin aspects of emotion are unpleasantness, sorrow, and so on. The yang aspects of will are activeness, creativeness and so on. And the yin aspects of will are passivity, conservativeness and so on. Needless to say, the *hyungsang* (physical body) also has yang aspects (protuberant parts, protrusions) and yin aspects (sunken parts, orifices).

To clarify, what is explained in the above table applies only to human beings. God is the causal being centered on Heart. Prior to the creation, He has Yang and Yin, the attributes of *Sungsang* and *Hyungsang*, as potentials to realize harmonious interactions. Once creation starts, Yang and Yin as potentials become active and bring about harmonious changes to the faculties of intellect, emotion, and will, and also harmonious changes to *Hyungsang*.

Relationship between Yang and Yin, and Man and Woman

We will next examine the relationship between yang and yin with regard to man and woman. In the Orient, from ancient times, man and woman have been equated with yang and yin. In Unification Thought, however, man is considered as a "yang substantial being" and woman as a "yin substantial being." The oriental philosophical view and the viewpoint of Unification Thought concerning man and woman seem to be, but are not, the same.

In Unification Thought, man is the "union of *sungsang* and *hyungsang* with yang characteristics" and woman is the "union of *sungsang* and *hyungsang* with yin characteristics." Thus, man is described as a "yang substantial being" and woman as a "yin substantial being."

It should be noted here that the meaning of yang when used in calling man a yang substantial being and the meaning of yin when used in calling woman a yin substantial being are not identical with the meanings of yang and yin as described in table 1.1. In other words, the yang and yin in *sungsang* and in *hyungsang*, as described in table 1.1, are not related to man and woman. Let me explain this point more concretely.

First, let us consider the difference between yang and yin in the *hyungsang*, in man and woman. In the *hyungsang* (body), both man and woman have the yang protuberant parts and protrusions, and the yin sunken parts and orifices, but these characteristics are not the same in man and woman. Man has more defining protuberant parts than woman does, and woman has more defining sunken parts than man does. Also, there is a difference between man and woman in the average height, and in the average size of their hips. Thus, the difference between yang and yin in a man's and in a woman's *hyungsang* is a quantitative one. In other words, man has more defining yang elements expressed while woman has more defining yin elements expressed.

Then, how about the *sungsang* aspect? The difference between yang and yin in a man's and in a woman's *sungsang* is not quantitative but qualitative (There is no quantitative difference in this respect between man and woman). For example, man and woman both possess clarity (yang) in the intellectual faculty of *sungsang*, but the character is different as between man and woman. Generally, clarity in man is expressed more in terms of comprehensive thinking, while clarity in woman is oriented more towards details. A similar thing can be said for other aspects of the intellect.

TABLE 1.2 Qualitative Differences of Yang and Yin between Man and Woman

			Man	Woman
Yang	Intellect	Clarity	Comprehensive	Attention to Detail
		Wittiness	Boldness	Minuteness
	Will	Activeness	Hardness	Softness
Yin	Emotion	Sorrow	Painful Sorrow	Grieving Sorrow

Looking at the emotional faculty, man's sorrow (yin) tends to be of a painful kind, whereas woman's sorrow tends to be of a grieving kind. As for the activeness (yang) of will, man's activity generally gives an impression of hardness while woman's activity gives a softer impression to others. Such differences between man and woman are characteristic. This can be summarized in table 1.2.

Thus, between men and women there are characteristic differences between yang and yin in the *sungsangs* of both. Such differences can be likened to the differences found in vocal music. In the high vocal ranges there is a difference between tenor (male) and soprano (female), and in the low vocal ranges there is a difference between bass (male) and alto (female).

Given the above, we can understand that the yang and yin of the *sungsang* represent characteristic differences between man and woman, and so we express man's yang and yin as masculine, and woman's yang and yin as feminine. Thus, we have the concepts of "masculine yang and yin" and "feminine yang and yin."

Since the differences between man and woman in terms of *hyungsang* are quantitative, it is easily accepted that man is a yang substantial being and woman is a yin substantial being. In terms of *sungsang*, however, the differences between man and woman are characteristic. Then, why is man called a yang substantial being and woman a yin substantial being?

Concerning this point, it can be explained as follows: whether quantitative or qualitative, the difference in yang and yin between man and woman is the difference between subject and object. As will be explained below, the character of the relationship between subject and object is that of active and passive, initiating and responding, and so forth.

For example, in a yang aspect of the intellectual faculty, namely clarity, man's comprehensiveness and woman's orientation toward details are in the relationship of subject and object, and in a yin aspect of the emotional faculty, namely sorrow, the relationship between man's painful sorrow and woman's grieving sorrow is that of subject and object. Also, in a yang aspect of the volitional faculty, in other words, activeness, the relationship between man's hardness and woman's softness is that between subject and object. This concludes my explanation that the relationship between man and woman is that between yang and yin, and that man is called a yang substantial being and woman, a yin substantial being.

Solution of Actual Problems through Understanding that Yang and Yin Are the Attributes of *Sungsang* and *Hyungsang*

From the explanation above, it has been clarified that yang and yin are the attributes of *sungsang* and *hyungsang*. The reason why this is important is that this also becomes the standard for the solution of actual problems. Actual problems here refers to the problems between man and woman, such as degradation of sexual morality, disharmony between husband and wife, destruction of the family, and so on.

That yang and yin are the attributes of *sungsang* and *hyungsang* means that the relationship between '*sungsang* and *hyungsang*' and 'yang and yin' is one of substance and attribute. Between substance and attribute, substance is more important, for it is the attribute's foundation. Without substance attribute has no meaning. Hence, without *sungsang* and *hyungsang*, yang and yin have no meaning. Thus, *sungsang* and *hyungsang* are substances and so they are the foundations for yang and yin.

In human beings, the *sungsang* and *hyungsang* task is to realize unity between mind and body, or between spirit mind and physical mind; in other words, to attain the perfection of character. The yang and yin task, likewise, is to unite man and woman (husband and wife). Here, there are two tasks to achieve: the perfection of one's character and the unity between man and woman. According to the statement that "yang and yin are the attributes of *sungsang* and *hyungsang*" it is concluded that man and woman have to perfect their characters before they get married.

In the three great blessings (perfection of indivduality, perfection of the family, and the perfection of dominion) explained in the Divine Principle, the perfection of individuality (perfection of character) is placed prior to the perfection of the family, or the unity between husband and wife. The reason for this lies in the statement that "yang and yin are the attributes of *sungsang* and *hyungsang*."

In Confucius's Eight Articles of *The Great Learning*, it is written that

"Their persons being cultivated, their families were regulated. Their families being regulated, their States were rightly governed. Their States being rightly governed, the whole kingdom was made tranquil and happy."[11] Here, the cultivation of the person is placed prior to the regulation of the family. This is because the author of *The Great Learning* understood this pattern, even if unconsciously.

Today, there are many social problems, including degradation of sexual morality, disharmony and destruction of the family, divorce, and so on, which are all connected to the relationship between man and woman. These problems occur because the perfection of character is not achieved prior to the perfection of the family. In other words, the "cultivation of the person" is not achieved before the "regulation of the family".

In conclusion, the problem of man and woman, which is one of the most difficult of all actual problems today, can only be solved through the perfection of character in both man and woman before starting a family (before they get married); namely, through the cultivation of the individual prior to the regulation of the family. Thus, the statement that "yang and yin are the attributes of *sungsang* and *hyungsang*" is another way of viewing the standard for the solution of actual problems.

3. Individual Image

What Is the Individual Image?

Sungsang and *Hyungsang*, and Yang and Yin, are the dual characteristics of God, and these two correlative attributes are universally manifested in every being in the created world. What is meant here is explained in the Bible: Ever since the creation of the world his invisible nature, namely, his eternal power and deity [Divine Image and Divine Character] has been clearly perceived in the things that have been made (Rom. 1:20). Thus, since all things universally have *sungsang* and *hyungsang*, and yang and yin, both *sungsang* and *hyungsang*, and yang and yin are called the "Universal Image."

In addition to this, there are many kinds of minerals, plants and animals and all existing things have their unique individual natures. All heavenly bodies, whether fixed stars or planets, have their own characteristics. Especially in the case of human beings, each person has remarkably unique natures in his or her build, constitution, looks, character, disposition, and so on.

The origin of such individual characteristics of all things and human beings lies in the Inner *Hyungsang* within God's Original *Sungsang*, and it is called the "Individual Image." In other words, the Individual Images in God which are manifested in created beings are called the individual images of those created beings.

Since in human beings characteristics are different from person to person, the individual image of human beings is called the "personal individual image" and since all things (other than human beings) are different from species to species, the individual image of all things is called the "species individual image." Thus, in human beings, the individual image refers to the characteristics of an individual, while the individual image of all things (animals, plants, and minerals) refers to the characteristics of a species, which is the specific difference on the lowest taxonomic level. The reason for differences in individual images is that human beings are created as the object partners of joy for God, and as His children, while all things are created as the object partners of joy for human beings.

Individual Image and Universal Image

At this point, the relationship between the individual image and the universal image of created beings can be explained. The individual image, which is the unique characteristic of an individual, does not exist independently of the universal image; actually, the individual image is the universal image which has been individualized.

For example, the particular look of a person is the individualization or particularization of the universal image of the human body, and the unique character of a person is the individualization or particularization of the universal image of the human mind. In human beings, the individual image is the universal image which is individualized for each individual person, and in other created beings, it is the universal image individualized for each species.

The reason that the individual image is the individualized universal image is that the Individual Images (in the Inner *Hyungsang*), which are the cause of the individualization of created beings, are working through the give and receive actions between *Sungsang* and *Hyungsang*, and between Yang and Yin in the Original Image.

The Universal Image of God is also called the "Original Universal

Image," and the Individual Image within the Inner *Hyungsang* of God is also called the "Original Individual Image." The universal image and individual image of created beings derive from the Original Universal Image and the Original Individual Image, respectively.

Individual Image and Mutation

Let me now discuss the individual image and the gene. According to the theory of evolution, the appearance of the individual image of a living being, which is the specific difference, is understood as the appearance of a new character caused by mutation. Furthermore, the appearance of the individual image of a person is understood as having been caused by the mixing or combination of his or her parents' DNA.

However, as understood from Unification Thought, the theory of evolution is merely a phenomenological understanding of the process of creation. In fact, the appearance of a new character in a living being, seemingly caused by mutation, is instead the creation of a new being with a new individual image through gene recombination; that is, the appearance of a new character by the mixing of the parents' DNA is the creation of a new being with a new individual image achieved through the mixing of the hereditary information. To be precise, the creation of a new individual image in living beings or in human beings means that an Original Individual Image is given to a species or to a person.

Individual Image and the Environment

In order for an individual being, which has an individual image, to grow and develop, it must be continuously engaged in reciprocal relationships with its environment. In other words, an individual being changes, grows, and develops while being engaged in give and receive action with the environment. This is in accordance with the give and receive law that a new being or a change is caused by give and receive action.

As a matter of fact, the characteristic (individual image) of a being is, in principle, native, but some aspects of the individual image change through the influence of the environment. This is why some people misunderstand and think that characteristics are acquired a posteriori.

Also, there are different ways of change in the characteristics among people in the same environment. This means that the way one adjusts to the environment differs from person to person. This difference also derives from the individual image of a being. Such a character, which sometimes has the appearance of an a posteriori character, is the modification of an individual image, and it can be called a "transformed individual image."

Preciousness of Human Individuality

The characteristics of created beings thus derive from the Individual Images in God, and therefore they are precious. Especially human individuality is more remarkable than others and is far more holy and precious. This is because a human being is the lord of creation, and is at the same time a united being of spirit self and physical self, wherein the spirit self lives eternally even after the death of the physical self. Human beings have been created to pursue the ideal of creation while practicing love through their individualities; therefore, human individualities are very precious and holy. Humanism also asserts the preciousness of human individuality, but so long as it does not recognize that such human individuality has come from God, it is difficult to overcome the materialistic view of human beings, which regards humans as animal like beings. Thus, the theory of the Individual Image becomes the answer to another actual question, that is, why should human individuality be respected? This concludes my explanation of the Divine Image.

B. Divine Character

In addition to the aspect of form in God's attributes, there is the aspect of function, nature, or ability, which is called "Divine Character." Omniscience, omnipotence, omnipresence, supreme good, supreme truth, supreme beauty, righteousness, love, creatorship, logos, and so on, as taught in Christianity and Islam are attributes that belong to the Divine Character. Unification Thought also affirms these as belonging to the Divine Character.

However, such concepts, as given, are not so helpful in solving actual problems since they do not seem to be so related to the aspect of form (Divine Image), and they are not directly related to God's creation. Instead, Unification Thought proposes Heart, Logos, and Creativity, which are directly related to the solution of actual problems, as constituting the Divine Character. Among these, Heart is the most important aspect of the Divine Character, never before clearly taught in any other school of thought. Let me explain these three aspects of the Divine Character and clarify how they can help us in solving actual problems.

1. Heart

What Is Heart?

Heart, or *Shimjung*, is the core of God's *Sungsang*. It is the "emotional impulse to seek joy through love." In order to offer a correct and clear understanding of the concept of Heart, I will explain it using the convenient case of human beings.

Everybody seeks joy by their very nature. To be sure, there is no one who does not desire to be joyful. Everybody wants happiness, which is the same as seeking to be joyful. Although everybody always has the impulse to become joyful, it seems true that, until today, most people have been unable to obtain genuine and eternal joy. This is because people have tried to achieve happiness through the acquisition of money, power, and/or knowledge. But these can never bring true joy. Then, how can we obtain true joy? True joy can be obtained only through a life of true love. A life of true love means an altruistic life of service, a life lived for the sake of others, and a life lived by pleasing others with a warm heart.

Heart Is an Emotional Impulse

Let me explain the concept of emotional impulse. An emotional impulse is the irrepressible desire that wells up from within us: Normal desires might be repressed through one's will, but emotional impulses can not be so repressed.

We know, through our daily experiences, that it is difficult to repress our impulse to seek to be joyful. We want money, a high position, knowledge, and power, because we want to be joyful; children earnestly seek to learn everything, through their curiosity, because they want to be joyful; even criminals commit crimes according to their impulse to be joyful, but in this case, in the wrong direction.

Thus, it is not possible to repress the impulse to seek joy. One's desire will be satisfied when it is fulfilled. However, for most people the desire to seek joy remains unfulfilled. This is because they do not realize that joy can only be obtained through love. The reason why joy can be obtained only through love is that the foundation of joy lies in God.

God Is the God of Heart

God possesses Heart, or the emotional impulse to seek joy through love, and such an impulse of God was far more irrepressible than that of human beings. However incompletely, human beings have inherited the Heart of God according to the law of likeness. Accordingly, even though we are fallen and have lost true love, we still have the impulse to seek joy, and it is impossible to repress it.

In God, this emotional impulse to seek joy is grounded in the impulse to seek love, since true joy can not be obtained other than through true love. Thus, the impulse to seek love is stronger than the impulse to seek joy. The impulse to seek love is the desire one possesses wherein one can not help loving others. In other words, one can not help but seek partners of love.

The impulse to seek joy is triggered by this impulse of love: the impulse of love is primary, and the impulse of joy is secondary. Thus, love is an unconditional impulse, rather than the means for joy. The necessary result of love is joy. Thus, love and joy are two sides of a coin, and the impulse to seek joy is the impulse to seek love that has manifested.

Thus, God's Heart can also be expressed as the "emotional impulse to love infinitely." Love necessarily requires an object partner. Especially, the love of God is an irrepressible impulse and therefore, an object partner of love was absolutely necessary for God. Thus, creation was necessary, inevitable, and can never be considered as merely accidental.

Creation of the Universe and Heart

With Heart serving as the motive, God created human beings and all things as His object partners of love. Human beings were created as His direct object partners of love, and all things were created as His indirect object partners. The fact that all things are indirect object partners of God's love means that all things were created to be direct object partners of love for human beings. Seen from the motive of creation, human beings and all things are object partners of God's love, but seen from the result, human beings and all things are the object partners of God's joy.

This theory of the creation of the universe having Heart as the motive (which is called the "Heart Motivation Theory") is able to solve the philosophical problem of whether the creation theory or the generation theory is correct. In other words, the Heart Motivation Theory can resolve and bring an end to the controversy between the creation theory and the generation theory concerning the beginning of the universe. In generation theories, such as Plotinus' emanation theory, Hegel's theory of the self-development of the Absolute Spirit, Gamow's theory of the Big Bang, and

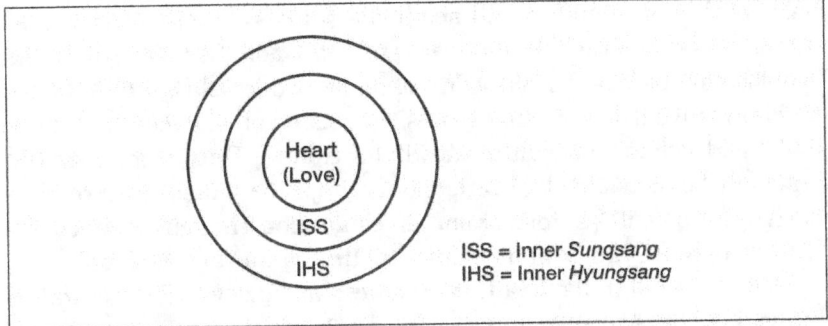

Fig. 1.3. Inner *Sungsang* and Inner *Hyungsang* centered on Heart

the Confucian theory of Heaven giving birth to all things, the negative aspects of crime, evil, and confusion in the world are considered to have occurred naturally and the way to solve these problems is closed. The creation theory presented here, on the other hand, holds that such negative aspects have a cause and are thus capable of being eliminated at their very root.

Heart and Culture

In Unification Thought, the relationship between Heart and culture is explained based on the proposition that "Heart is the core of God's *Sungsang*." God's *Sungsang* consists of Inner *Sungsang* and Inner *Hyungsang*, wherein the Inner *Sungsang* is more internal than Inner *Hyungsang*, and Heart is the core in the Inner *Sungsang*. Such relationships apply also to the *sungsang* of the original human being. This is illustrated in fig. 1.3.

This means that heart is the driving force behind human intellectual, emotional, and volitional activities. In other words, heart is the emotional impulse, which constantly stimulates the intellectual, emotional, and volitional faculties, resulting in intellectual, emotional, and volitional activities.

Such academic fields as philosophy and science are developed through human intellectual activity; artistic fields such as painting, music, sculpture and architecture are developed through emotional activity; and such normative fields as religion, ethics, morality and education are developed through volitional activity.

In a true human society consisting of original human beings, the motive force behind intellectual, emotional, and volitional activities is heart and love; therefore, all academic studies, artistic efforts, and normative behavior will be motivated by heart, and their aim will be the actualization of love.[12] The totality of all academic fields, artistic fields, and normative fields, in other words, the totality of all intellectual, emotional and volitional activities constitutes culture. Thus, culture should originally be motivated by heart, and its aim is the actualization of love. Such a culture will last forever and, in Unification Thought, is called the "culture of heart," the "culture of love," or the "culture of harmony."

Due to the fall of the first human ancestors, however, the cultures of humankind have become unprincipled, having various negative aspects, and such cultures have continued until today, all the while repeating the cycle of rising and falling. This is because heart, which should have been the core of the human *sungsang*, was blocked, and the impulse of heart was distorted into an impulse for egotism, or selfishness.

The best way to rectify present-day culture, which seems increasingly chaotic, is to eradicate egotism, and revitalize the impulse of heart in the core of the *sungsang* of human beings. Doing so can transform all the fields of culture so that they can be motivated by heart, and can pursue the actualization of love. In short, a new culture of heart and love can be established. The proposition that "Heart is the core of God's *Sungsang*" thus becomes a standard for solving yet another problem: how to salvage culture from its present-day crisis.

Heart and Prime Force

Let me now explain about Heart and Prime Force. All things of the universe continue to receive some force from God even after their creation. Based on this force, created beings give and receive some force among themselves. The former is a vertical force, and the latter is a horizontal force. In Unification Thought, the former is called "Prime Force," and the latter "Universal Prime Force." [13]

In fact, Prime Force itself is a new reality formed through the give and receive action within the Original Image, in other words, through the give and receive action between *Sungsang* and *Hyungsang*. To be more precise, Prime Force is a new force formed through the give and receive action between the impulse of Heart within the *Sungsang* and the pre-energy within the *Hyungsang*. When Prime Force works upon all things, it becomes the horizontal Universal Prime Force, which causes give and receive actions between all things. Thus, Universal Prime Force is an extension of Prime Force.[14]

The fact that Universal Prime Force is an extension of Prime Force, which is formed by the impulse of Heart and pre-energy, means that the force of love, as well as physical force (energy), is at work among all things in the universe.[15] Therefore, for human beings to love each other is more in accordance with the Way of Heaven, which everybody should follow, than for people to believe they can do just as they like. Thus, this theory concerning "Heart and Prime Force" becomes yet another standard for solving actual problems. It offers answers to such questions as "Should we love others without fail?," or "Is struggle or violence necessary at certain times?," or "Should we love our enemies or attempt to defeat them?"

2. Logos

What Is Logos?

According to the Divine Principle, Logos means "Word" or "reason-law" (i.e., "rational principle") (*DP*, 170). In the first chapter of the Gospel of John it is written that all things were created by the Word of God: "In the beginning was the Word, and the Word was with God, and the Word was God. He was in the beginning with God; all things were made through Him, and without Him was not anything made that was made" (John. 1:1-3).

In Unification Thought, Logos as "Word" means the thought, design, or plan of God, and Logos as "reason-law" means the unity of reason and law. Reason belongs to the intellectual faculty of the Inner *Sungsang* within the Original *Sungsang*. However, this reason in Logos, which created all things, is different from the capacity of reason in the human mind. Human reason, the character of which is freedom, is the faculty for conceptualization, and for pursuing universal truth. Reason in Logos, on the other hand, is merely a free intellectual faculty with the power of thought.

Law, which is the other aspect of Logos, is characterized solely by a mechanical and necessary nature, without any element of freedom or purpose. Law works with precision always and everywhere, transcending time and space. Just as the hour and minute hands of a watch, which is a mechanical device, keep time always and everywhere, law functions regularly and mechanically.

Logos Is Reason-Law

Logos as reason-law needs some explanation. Reason-law means the unity of reason and law. This concept is for the purpose of establishing another standard for solving actual problems. The problem at issue is that of how the collapse of values, which is causing great confusion in society today, can be stopped.

According to the Divine Principle, Logos is the object partner of God, and at the same time has dual characteristics (*DP*, 170–171). This means that Logos is a kind of created being, a new being which resembles the dual characteristics of God, and which can be regarded as similar to the union of *Sungsang* and *Hyungsang*.

Since Logos is the Word, or plan, of God, and since all things were created by and through it, Logos itself can not be a created being on the same level as all other beings. Logos, which is the object partner of God, and which resembles His dual characteristics, is a being resulting from His thinking. It is a comprehensive design, a blueprint formulated in the mind of God. When we make a building, we first make a detailed blueprint for that building. In the same way, when God created all things, He first made a comprehensive blueprint or plan for each created being, and this is Logos.

Though a blueprint is not yet a building or a product, it is a resultant created being. Therefore, Logos, which is a design or a blueprint, is a resultant being, a new being, and a created being. All things are created resembling the dual characteristics of God. Then, what dual characteristics of God does Logos, as a new being, resemble? It resembles the dual characteristics of Inner *Sungsang* and Inner *Hyungsang* within the Original *Sungsang*.[16] In other words, the unity between Inner *Sungsang* and Inner *Hyungsang* centering on purpose forms the dual characteristics of Logos, in the same way that the unity between Original *Sungsang* and Original *Hyungsang* forms the dual characteristics of God (Divine Image).

As mentioned above, Logos is "reason-law" as well as "Word." Then, what are the dual characteristics of Logos as reason-law? They are reason and law. The relationship between reason and law is the same as the relationship between the Inner *Sungsang* and Inner *Hyungsang*, which are subject and object; therefore, the relationship between reason and law is subject and object.

Logos Is the Union of Reason and Law

Since all things were created by Logos (reason-law), all created beings contain elements of reason and law. Accordingly, while all things exist and perform movements, these two elements work together. Yet, the lower the level of the created being, the more predominantly does the element of law operate; the higher the level of the created being, the more predominantly do we find the element of reason operating.

In minerals, which are the lowest level of created beings, it seems that only the element of law operates, and in human beings, who are the highest level of created beings, it seems to be only the rational element operating. In reality, however, law and reason operate in tandem in both cases.

Thus, freedom and necessity, purposefulness and mechanicalness operate in an integrated fashion in the existence and movement of all things. In other words, freedom functions in connection with necessity, and purposefulness operates together with mechanicalness. Until now, the relationship between freedom and necessity has often been understood as one of antinomy: freedom and necessity were regarded as opposite concepts in the same way that liberty and restraint might be understood to be in tension.

In Unification Thought, however, reason and law in Logos are seen not as being in a relationship of antinomy, but of unity. I can explain this point by using the example of a train running along a rail as an analogy. That a train should run on rails is a rule that must be observed by all means; once it derails, not only will the train be damaged, but it might also injure people and destroy buildings. Therefore, the train must run on its rails without fail and, in this way, a train obeys the law necessarily. Yet, it is the freedom of the locomotive engineer to make a train run fast or slow. It might seem that a train runs totally mechanically but, in reality, it operates under the united influences of freedom and necessity.

Let me offer a second example. A person can drive a car when the traffic light is green, but must stop when the traffic light turns red. This is a traffic rule that everyone must necessarily obey. Yet, once the traffic light has become green, the driver can accelerate freely, as long as the car is running properly. Thus, freedom and necessity are united in driving a car as well.[17]

Using the examples of a train and a car, I have explained that freedom and necessity operate in unison. We can thus understand that reason and law, as the dual characteristics of Logos, function not in a relationship of antinomy but in a relationship of unity.

Since Logos is the unity of reason and law, and since all things, from the astronomical bodies in the macroscopic world to atoms and subatomic particles in the microscopic world, are created through Logos, reason and law operate unitedly in all of them without exception. In this way all things exist, move, and develop through the unity of reason and law, freedom and necessity, or purposefulness and mechanicalness.

This idea is in full agreement with the current views of science. Consider, for example, the Backster Effect. This phenomenon has shown, through an examination of the reaction of a plant, to the leaves of which the electrodes of a lie detector have been attached, that even a plant has a kind of consciousness.[18] There is also the theory of complex relativity, proposed by Jean E. Charon (1920–), which claims that even electrons and photons are equipped with mechanisms of memory and thinking.[19] That a plant possesses consciousness and that an electron has a mechanism of thinking support the notion that reason and law, and freedom and necessity, are operating together in all created beings.

Logos, Freedom, and License

Let me now clarify the true meaning of freedom, and the problem of license, as related to Logos. Through a correct understanding of freedom and license significant actual problems can be solved. Today, various acts of delinquency that serve to destroy the social order are carried out in the name of freedom. What is an effective countermeasure against such acts that cause social confusion? In order to solve this problem, let us first clarify the true meaning of freedom, and the nature of license.

In the Divine Principle, it is written that "There is no freedom outside the Principle," that "There is no freedom without responsibility," and that "There is no freedom without accomplishment" (*DP*, 74). In other words, there are three conditions for freedom: "to be within the Principle," then "to bear responsibility," and then "to make accomplishment." Here, "to be within the Principle" means that one should not deviate from the Principle or law; "to bear responsibility" means to complete one's portion of responsibility; and "to make accomplishment" means to complete the purpose of creation and bring about good results. The completion of one's portion of responsibility, the completion of the purpose of creation, and bringing about good results are all principled acts in accordance with the Way of Heaven, or laws (norms).

These three requisites for freedom—"to be within the Principle," then "to bear responsibility," and finally "to make accomplishment"—can be expressed in a word, as being/acting "within the Principle." It can be concluded, therefore, that true freedom can only be achieved in full conjunction with law and necessity. Law refers here to the laws of value (norms) operating in human life as well as to the natural laws operating in nature. Norms, or values, are sustained only in the context of order. Therefore, in the original world, to disregard norms, or to destroy order, can never result in freedom.

Freedom in its strict sense means freedom of choice, and one's choice is determined through reason. Consequently, freedom starts with rational choice and then it is carried through into practice. The motivating power, that which expresses freedom in practice is one's free will, and when freedom is exercised together with one's free will, the result is free action. These are the concepts of free will and free action as found in the Divine Principle (*DP*, 74).

Thus, rational choice, the exercise of free will, and the resultant free action should never be done merely arbitrarily. They should only be carried out within the parameters of the Principle or law (laws of value), as necessary. In this way, freedom is the freedom of reason, and reason always operates within law. In other words, originally, true freedom can be realized only within reason-law, in other words, within Logos, and it can not be realized apart from the Logos. It is sometimes argued that laws tend to restrict freedom, but that is a misunderstanding arising from one's ignorance of the original meaning of law and freedom.

Originally, law and freedom were intended to function for the realization of love. That is to say, law and freedom only truly operate within the context of true love. True love is the source of our life and joy. Accordingly, in the original world, through observing laws one can joyfully enjoy freedom. This is because Logos is based on Heart.

Arbitrary thinking and arbitrary action which are apart from Logos are exercised through a false freedom, which is license. Freedom and license are absolutely different concepts. Freedom is an affirming and constructive concept that brings about good results, whereas license is a destructive concept bringing about evil results. Freedom and license must be strictly distinguished, but in reality they are often confused and misunderstood. This is because people do not have a proper understanding of Logos, which is the true foundation for freedom. Once one understands the correct meaning of Logos, and knows the true meaning of freedom, then all kinds of license masquerading under the name of freedom, can be abolished; it will finally become possible to end social confusion. Thus, the theory of Logos, again, becomes a standard for solving actual problems.

Logos, Heart, and Love

Here, the relationship between Logos, Heart, and love will be explained. As already defined, Logos is the Word or plan and at the same time it is reason-law. Word and reason-law are not two different things. Reason-law is included within the Word, as an internal part. The relationship can be compared to physiology being included within biology, as a subfield within it. In other words, physiology is one field of biology, which consists of the various fields of anatomy, biochemistry, ecology, embryology, physiology, and so on. In the same way, reason-law is a part of the Word, wherein limitless amounts and kinds of knowledge about God's creation are included. Reason-law, which is a part of the Word, is that part which deals specifically with the interactions and relationships among all things. Thus, Word and reason-law are not different things. Furthermore, Heart is the basis for both Word and reason-law. In the same way that the investigation of organisms is common to all the fields of biology, God's Heart is the common foundation for both Word and reason-law.

Heart is the emotional impulse to seek joy through love. The fact that Heart is the basis for both the Word and for reason-law in God's creation means that all phenomena, including existence, change, motion, and the development of created beings, are supported and permeated by the impulse of love. Accordingly, whether we are concerned with natural law or ethical law, love is necessarily operating, and must be operating, behind law. Generally, natural law is understood as solely physicochemical law, but this is an incomplete understanding; love is operating, without fail, behind all law, although the level of love may be different among different creatures. Clearly, love is operating in the ethical laws (norms) of human beings.

In my earlier explanation of Logos, I primarily discussed it in the sense of its being reason and law, or freedom and necessity. Yet, in the actual operation of reason-law, love is significantly more important than reason or law, and love often stands superior to them.

A life of reason-law, but without love, easily becomes like that of a cold and formal barracks, in which solders live according to strict rules, and this way of life easily withers like an immature ear of wheat. Only in a life of reason-law filled with warm love, can the peace of a spring garden, in which all kinds of flowers bloom, and bees and butterflies fly, realistically come about. This criterion of a life of warm love becomes another standard in solving actual problems. The question is: what is the true guideline for bringing peace into a family and society? The answer can only be the theory of Logos based on Heart.

3. Creativity

What Is Creativity?

Generally, creativity is defined as "the ability to create new things." In the Divine Principle, God's creativity is expressed as "God's creative nature" and "God's power of creation" (*DP*, 43).

Yet, we do not have an accurate understanding of God's creation with just these concepts alone. As already explained, the purpose in understanding the attributes of God is to arrive at a fundamental solution to actual problems. Accordingly, all our explanations about God must be as accurate and concrete and concise as possible. Our understanding of God's creativity is no exception. It is difficult to understand God's creativity accurately with mere commonsense explanations. Hence, the characteristics and requisites of God's creativity must be clarified.

God's creation was neither accidental nor spontaneous. It was accomplished based on an irrepressible, inevitable motive with a clear and purposeful intention. This may be called the theory of creation motivated by Heart or, simply, the Heart Motivation Theory.

In creation, the inner and outer four position foundations, and give and receive actions, which will be explained fully in the next section, "Structure of the Original Image," are all necessarily formed centering on the purpose of creation. Consequently, God's creativity can be described as "the ability to form the inner and outer four position foundations centering on purpose." In the case of human creative activity, such as the production of commodities, the formation of the inner four position foundation corresponds to planning, the development of an idea, making a blueprint, and so on; the formation of the outer four position foundation corresponds to the actual production of the commodity through the use of machines and appropriate materials, according to the blueprint.

In God, the formation of the inner four position foundation is the formation of Logos centered on purpose, and the formation of the outer four position foundation is the creation of all things, through the give and receive action between *Sungsang* and *Hyungsang* centering on purpose. Thus, God's creativity is the ability to form such inner and outer four position foundations, namely, the ability to form Logos and to create all things. The reason we seek to explain God's creativity in such detail is to establish a standard for the fundamental solution of the various actual problems that are related to creative activity, including such things as pollution, the reduction or abolition of armaments, how scientific and artistic endeavors should be carried out, and so on.

Human Creativity

Let me now explain about human creativity. Human beings have the ability to produce new things, in other words, they are creative. Human creativity is what God gave to human beings in accordance with the law of resemblance. Originally, human beings should have inherited God's creativity (*DP*, 43, 67, 167), and human creativity should have resembled God's creativity completely. Due to the fall, however, human beings have only incompletely inherited God's creativity.

It is because God was to bequeath His creativity to human beings (*DP*, 78, 167) that human creativity was to resemble God's creativity. Then, why did God want to give His creativity to human beings? It was in order to bless human beings as the lords of creation (*DP*, 78), and to give to them the qualification to enjoy dominion over all things (*DP*, 67, 78). Here, dominion over all things refers to one's treating all things as one wishes, while yet always regarding them as being precious. In other words, treating all things with a heart of love is truly one's dominion over all things, and all fields of human life are included. For example, economy, industry, art and so on, all are included in the concept of dominion over all things. Since human beings on earth live in their physical bodies, they are dealing with matter in all fields of their lives. Therefore, it is not too much to say that one's entire human life is a life of dominion over all things.

Dominion over all things, as originally intended, is possible only when human beings fully inherit God's creativity. Original dominion means to utilize things creatively, with a heart of love, in various activities, including cultivation, manufacturing, production, reforming, construction, invention, safekeeping, transportation, storage, artistic activity, and so on. Religious and political activities are also included, since material things and economic concerns are indispensable in these activities as well. New creative ideas, as well as love, are requisites for human beings to deal with things. In other words, God's creativity is required for the original dominion of things by human beings.

If human beings had not fallen their creativity would have completely resembled God's, and they would have been able to exercise their original dominion over all things. However, due to the fall of the first human ancestors, human beings lost their original nature. Hence, human creativity became distorted, and their dominion over all things became imperfect and non-principled.

Here, the following question may arise: "If God created human beings according to the law of likeness, they would have received original creativity from the very beginning, at their birth, and, accordingly, regardless of the fall, would that creativity not have remained until today? In fact, numerous scientists and technicians are today displaying a very high level of creative ability." How might we answer this question?

Creation in Likeness

I would like to explain specifically how creation in likeness applies in the world of time and space, since God's creation means that each created being has appeared in the world of time and space. After God's creation was carried out in His mind, and the Logos (or plan) was formed, transcending time and space, each created being then appeared in the world of time and space, starting from a small and immature, young stage, then passing through the process of growth, and finally reaching its full maturity.

After it has thus grown and completed itself, a created being completely resembles God's plan and His attributes. This period of time prior to its completion is its immature stage, during which time each created being is coming to resemble the image of God. According to the Divine Principle, this growing period is divided into three ordered stages of growth: the formation stage, the growth stage, and the completion stage (*DP*, 42).

The human ancestors fell at the top of their growth stage (*DP*, 43). Consequently, they inherited only "two-thirds" of their originally intended creativity. No matter how much scientists may display of their gifted creativity, it still falls far short of the degree God originally intended to bestow on human beings.

Among all created beings, only human beings fell. All things have grown to perfect themselves without falling, and thus they resemble the attributes of God at their own given levels. Here, the following question arises: Why did human beings, who are the lords of creation, fall? The fall occurred because, while all things are created to grow requiring only the autonomy and dominion of the Principle, human beings were given their own portion of responsibility for their growth, in addition to the autonomy and dominion of the Principle.

Creativity and the Portion of Responsibility

The autonomy of the Principle refers to the life force of an organism, and dominion refers to the influence of the life force over an organism's environment. For example, a tree grows in accordance with the life force within it, and dominion refers to the influence of the life force of the tree over the environment. During the growth of human beings, the autonomy and dominion of the Principle also operate. However, in human beings, only the physical self grows in accordance with this autonomy and dominion; the spirit self does not. The growth of the spirit self requires a different condition: fulfillment of the human portion of responsibility.

It should be noted here that growth of the spirit self does not mean the growth in its height. Since the spirit self is united with the physical self, it naturally grows in size along with the physical self. However, the growth of the spirit self referred to here is the maturation of its spirituality: the improvement of one's character, or of one's heart. In other words, the growth of the spirit self is the growth of the mind in such a way that we are able to practice God's love.

The growth of the spirit self can be achieved only through the fulfillment of one's human portion of responsibility. This fulfillment of the human portion of responsibility refers to the continuous practice of love, all the while holding fast to one's faith in God and firmly observing His commandments. In this way we can overcome the numerous trials that may come to us, through our own decisions and without any help from others.

It was not an easy matter for Adam and Eve to fulfill such a portion of responsibility, since God was unable to intervene, and they had no parents to teach them. Nevertheless, they were expected to fulfill such a responsibility. However, tempted by Satan, Adam and Eve failed to fulfill their portion of responsibility, and fell. Why did God give Adam and Eve such a heavy responsibility, one that they might fail to fulfill? Why could God not enable them to grow easily, like all other things? The reason is because God wanted to give human beings the qualification to have dominion over all things, and to make them the lords of creation (Gen. 1:28, *DP*, 78).

Dominion is, in principle, only the dominion over one's possessions or things that one has created, and one is not allowed to exercise one's dominion over the possessions of others or over things created by others. Since human beings were created after all things had been created, logically they can not be the possessors or creators of all things. Yet, since God created human beings as His children, He intended to endow them with the qualifications of being a creator, so as to make them the lords of creation. Hence, He intended to have human beings fulfill a certain extra condition; thereby, human beings would be recognized as having participated in God's creation of the universe.

Human Perfection and One's Portion of Responsibility

The extra condition required of Adam and Eve was to be responsible for their own perfection. That is, if Adam and Eve had perfected themselves without any help from others, God would have regarded them as having qualifications equal to His as the creator of the universe. As a matter of fact, the value of a person is the same as the value of the whole universe, as described in the Divine Principle: Every human being is an embodiment (or encapsulation) of all elements in the cosmos (*DP*, 30, 47), and a microcosm (*DP*, 47), and only when human beings have perfected themselves will the creation of the entire universe also be perfected. Along the same lines, Jesus said, "For what will it profit a man, if he gains the whole world and forfeits his life? Or what shall a man give in return for his life?" (Matt. 16:26) Thus, when Adam and Eve had perfected themselves, they would have been regarded as equal in position to the creator of the universe.

Creation will be carried out as the responsibility of the creator. Hence, God created the universe as His own responsibility; and Adam and Eve, who were to inherit creatorship, should have perfected themselves through their own responsibility. That is why God gave Adam and Eve their portion of responsibility.

Yet, God is a God of love, and He did not want to assign Adam and

Eve one hundred percent responsibility; rather, He retained most of the responsibility for their growth, and only gave them a very small portion —five percent figuratively speaking. God then intended, after their fulfilling their own five percent portion of responsibility, to regard them as having fulfilled the entire one hundred percent. In spite of such a great blessing from God, Adam and Eve failed to fulfill even their own small portion of responsibility, and fell. Thus, they became unable to fully inherit God's creativity.

If human beings had not fallen, what would have become of them? If they had perfected themselves without falling, first, they would have inherited God's Heart, the emotional impulse to seek joy through love, and they would have become loving persons just as God is a God of love, and second they would have inherited completely God's creativity centered on Heart.

This means that, from now on, all the activities of dominion over all things should become based on Heart and love. As already mentioned, politics, economy, industry, science, religion, and so on, all belong to the dominion over all things since they deal with material things, and activities in all these areas will become a dominion of love through creativity (perfect creativity) inherited from God.[20]

Original Creativity and Cultural Activity

Culture is the totality of the achievements of the intellectual, emotional, and volitional activities of human beings. Since intellectual, emotional, and volitional activities commonly deal with material things, cultural activity can be regarded as the activity of dominion over all things with creativity.

Today, the quality of cultures around the world is rapidly declining. In virtually every field, including politics, economy, society, science, art, education, media, ethics, morality, religion, and so on, there are whirlpools of confusion wherein people lack a true sense of direction. Unless some epoch-making proposal is introduced, salvaging the vanishing culture will become an almost hopeless task.

The Communist dictatorial system, which had solidified its formidable foundation with the iron curtain, began to collapse through the open door policy and, today, Communist countries are hastening to introduce the capitalist economic method. Seeing this trend, people in the capitalist camp may be tempted to become proud of the supremacy of the capitalist economic system, and of their scientific technology. This is, however, a shortsighted illusion. They are ignoring the chronic ills of capitalism that will surely lead to its decline and fall: labor disputes arising from structural contradictions within the capitalist economy, the increasing gap between the rich and the poor, degradation of values, rampant social crime, the advancement of criminal techniques accompanying the advancement of science and technology, increasing pollution accompanying industrial development, and so on.

Seen from the viewpoint of dominion over all things, we must seek to find the root cause of today's cultural crisis at the very beginning of human history. Due to the fall of the first human ancestors, human beings inherited not God's Heart, love, and creativity, but self-centeredness and egotism which have now spread worldwide. This is the fundamental cause of today's cultural crisis.

The only way to save contemporary culture from such a crisis is to eradicate egotism, and instead advance all human activities of creation and dominion centering on God's love. In other words, when all the leaders in various fields and at various levels begin to work centering on God's love, the complex and difficult problems in the various cultural fields such as politics, economy, society, education, science, religion, philosophy, media and so on, will finally come to be solved fundamentally and totally, thereby allowing a new and true culture of peace to blossom worldwide. Such a new culture will be neither Communist nor capitalist. It will be the culture of Heart, the culture of love, and the culture of harmony. This, I hope, clarifies that the theory of God's creativity can become a standard for solving actual problems. This concludes my explanation of the content of the Original Image. Let me now turn attention to its structure.

II. Structure of the Original Image

I will from this point discuss the structure of the Original Image. In the section "Content of the Original Image," each attribute of the Divine Image and the Divine Character was explained, while in this section, the relationships between the dual characteristics of the Original Image—mainly the relationship between *Sungsang* and *Hyungsang*—will be explained. The purpose of such an explanation is to set forth the standards necessary for solving, fundamentally, various actual problems, in this case, problems of relationship.

A. Give and Receive Action and Four Position Foundation

1. Give and Receive Action between *Sungsang* and *Hyungsang*

Reciprocal Relationship between *Sungsang* and *Hyungsang*

In the Principle of Creation of the Divine Principle, it is written that "All beings exist through the reciprocal relationships between their dual characteristics of internal nature and external form" (*DP*, 17). Furthermore, "[every living being] maintains its life through the reciprocal relationship of yang and yin elements within itself" (*DP*, 16). The reason for this is that, since God, the First Cause of all things, is the harmonious Subject of the dual characteristics of *Sungsang* and *Hyungsang*, and of Yang and Yin (*DP*, 19), all things were created according to the law of likeness and, without exception, resemble the dual characteristics of God. A reciprocal relationship means a relationship of two elements or two individuals that are facing each other. For example, when two persons seek to engage in conversation, or to engage in buying and selling, the situation wherein the two partners are facing each other first needs to be established before a conversation or trade takes place. The reciprocal relationship should necessarily be a mutually affirming relationship, and never a mutually negating one.[21]

When such a reciprocal relationship is established, something is given and received between the two partners. In human beings, people are giving and receiving words, money, power, influence, love, and so on. In the natural world, universal gravitation acts among heavenly bodies, carbon dioxide and oxygen are exchanged between animals and plants, and so on. The action of giving and receiving something between the two partners is called "give and receive action."

The establishment of a reciprocal relationship does not necessarily mean that a give and receive action will take place. In order for a give and receive action to take place, a "common base" must be established. This common base is a reciprocal relationship established centering on a common element, or a common purpose. Thus, correctly speaking, once two parties are engaged in a reciprocal relationship and a common base is formed, give and receive action will take place.

In God as well, give and receive action takes place between *Sungsang* and *Hyungsang* according to this principle. *Sungsang* and *Hyungsang* are engaged in a reciprocal relationship centering on a common element (Heart or purpose), and so a common base is formed, and a give and receive action does take place. *Sungsang* gives to *Hyungsang* ideas, emotional elements, and so on; and *Hyungsang* gives to *Sungsang* an energetic element (pre-energy). Through this give and receive action between *Sungsang* and *Hyungsang*, the attributes of God either form a harmony (union), or give rise to creation (new beings).

What Is the Give and Receive Action Between *Sungsang* and *Hyungsang*?

In the Original Image, when *Sungsang* and *Hyungsang* enter into a reciprocal relationship, give and receive action does take place. As mentioned above, however, a common base has to be formed centering on a common element. In God, the common element is Heart, or the purpose of creation, which is established by Heart. When give and receive action takes place, a result necessarily appears. Thus, a center and a result necessarily accompany a give and receive action. When Heart is the center, a union is realized as a result, and when purpose is the center, a new being or a multiplied being appears as a result. Union here refers to a unified state, whereas a new being refers to a created being. Accordingly, in the Original Image the appearance of new beings means the creation of all things.

Concepts of Union and New Being

Here, I will discuss the concepts of union, and of new being in the created world. In the created world, union connotes existence, survival, duration, unity, a spatial circular movement, maintenance, and so on, whereas new being refers to a newly born result or product, a new character, a new element, a new individual, or a new phenomenon. In other words, the appearance of a new being is a phenomenon of development in the created world.

The reason that all things maintain their existence, survival, and duration, and at the same time move and develop is that give and receive actions similar to those in the Original Image (between *Sungsang* and *Hyungsang*) are carried out among the myriads of individuals from heavenly bodies to atoms. In accordance with the law of resemblance, the natures of all things resemble the attributes of God, and the relationships and interactions among all things resemble the structure of the Original Image, namely, the relationship and give and receive action between *Sungsang* and *Hyungsang*. In other words, all created beings should necessarily resemble the give and receive action within the Original Image in order for them to exist, live, move, and develop.

Round, Harmonious and Smooth Nature of the Give and Receive Action

Whether it is centered on Heart or purpose, give and receive action in the Original Image is round, harmonious and smooth. Heart is the emotional impulse to seek joy through love, and Heart is the source of love. It is love that makes the give and receive action harmonious. Therefore, the give and receive action centered on Heart, from which love wells up, is harmonious. The same thing can be said when the give and receive action is centered on purpose, because purpose itself is established based on Heart.

There is no contradiction, opposition, or conflict in the round, harmonious, and smooth give and receive action within the Original Image. If there is no center or common element such as Heart or purpose, and there is no love, then contradiction, opposition, or conflict can appear. In other words, if the give and receive action is not centered on love, it may not be harmonious, but rather it easily becomes conflictive.

This round, harmonious nature of the give and receive action in the Original Image becomes another standard for solving actual problems. The great confusion of today's world has been brought about by the fact that most, if not all, relationships have a conflictual tendency. In other words, struggles have been developing in virtually all relationships, such as those between nations, those between ideologies, those between the Communist camp and the free camp, those between peoples, those between religions, those between political parties, those between managers and laborers, those between teacher and student, those between parents and children, those between husband and wife, those between persons, and so on. The result of the accumulation of such numerous conflicting relationships is the great confusion in today's world. Consequently, the way to remove such worldwide confusion is to transform all conflicts into round and harmonious relationships. This becomes possible once these relationships are established through the give and receive actions centered on God's love. Thus, the round, harmonious, and smooth nature of the give and receive action in the

Original Image becomes another standard for solving actual problems.

2. Subject and Object, and the Four Position Foundation

What Is the Four Position Foundation?

As already explained, give and receive action between *Sungsang* and *Hyungsang* is carried out centering on Heart or purpose, giving rise to union or to a new being. Hence, these four elements, the center, *Sungsang*, *Hyungsang*, and the result, always participate in a give and receive action.[22] The relationship of these four elements is the relationship of positions. The center, *Sungsang*, *Hyungsang* and the result, each occupy a position and, at the same time, they are related to each another. The foundation of these four positions, whereupon give and receive action takes place, is called a "four position foundation." Whether in the Original Image or in the created world, no matter what type of give and receive action it may be, without exception give and receive action takes place within the context of a four position foundation. Hence, the four position foundation is the fundamental foundation upon which all things and human beings exist. Give and receive action and the four position foundation in the Original Image is illustrated in fig. 1.4.

When *Sungsang* and *Hyungsang* are engaged in give and receive action, they are not in the same position. Position here refers to the position with the qualification to rule all things (*DP*, 78). In other words, position is related to the degree of activity: When we say that *Sungsang* and *Hyungsang* are different in position, it means that *Sungsang* is in a more active position than *Hyungsang*, or *Hyungsang* is in a more passive position than *Sungsang*. An element or an individual that is in a more active position is called "subject," and an element or an individual that is in a more passive position is called "object." Accordingly, when *Sungsang* and *Hyungsang* are engaged in give and receive action, *Sungsang* is subject, and *Hyungsang* is object.

The four position foundation consists of the four positions of center, subject, object, and result, and give and receive action always takes place based on the four position foundation. This means that the structure of the four positions of center, subject, object, and result is fixed and unchanging, whereas the actual element to be established in each position is different for each four position foundation.

For example, in the family four position foundation, the purpose (or the

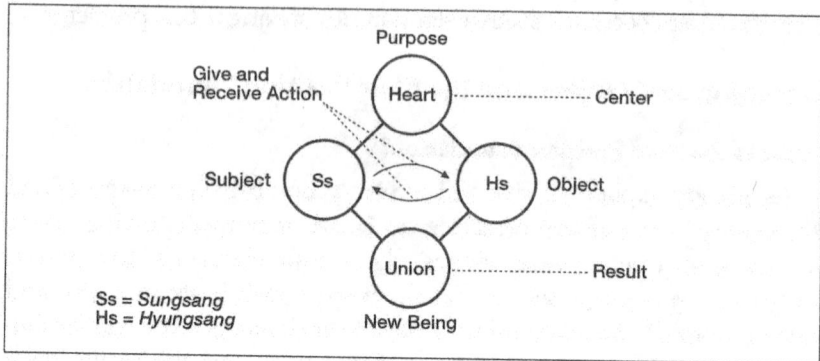

Fig. 1.4. Give and Receive Action and the Four Position Foundation

motto) of a family, or the grandparents who represent it, is in the center, the father is in the subject position, the mother is in the object position, and the peaceful environment of the family, or the multiplication of children is the result. In a four position foundation of dominion, such as in business activity, the goal or the ideal of an enterprise is in the center, various personnel (managers and employees) are in the subject position, material elements (machines and raw materials) are in the object position, and products (commodities) are the result. In the solar system, the center is the purpose of creation, the sun is in the subject position, the planets are in the object position, and the result is the existence of the solar system. In a human being, the center is the purpose of creation, mind is the subject, body is the object, and the result is an individual (union of mind and body). Thus, in the four position foundation, the elements or beings to be established (which may be called the "settled beings") are different depending on each four position foundation, but the structure, which consists of center, subject, object, and the result, are always fixed and unchanging.[23]

Concept of Subject and Object

Let me discuss the concept of subject and object more concretely. By doing so the character of give and receive action may be understood more concretely. As already explained, the subject is "active" in relation to the object, whereas the object is "passive" in relation to the subject. To explain in more detail, the relationship between a subject and an object is characterized as "central" and "dependent," "dynamic" and "static," "initiating" and "responding," "creative" and "conservative," "outgoing" and "modest" as well as "active" and "passive."

In the created world, from the heavenly bodies to atoms, there are various kinds of subject and object relationships. For example, the relationship between the sun and planets in the solar system, and the relationship between the nucleus and electrons in an atom are the relationship of central and dependent; the relationship between parent animals and their young, and that between a protector and the protected are relationships of dynamic and static; the relationship between an educator and the educated, and that between the giver and the receiver are relationships of initiating and responding, or activity and passivity. In a family, in many cases, the husband works hard to support his family and the wife keeps the house with affectionate care: the relationship between them is rather creative and conservative, or outgoing and modest.

It should be noted here that the concept of subject and that of object are not fixed, but relative, concepts. A subject being becomes an object being when it relates to a higher level being, and an object being becomes a subject being when it relates to a lower level being.

Subject and Object Occupy Different Positions

As explained above, the subject is central, dynamic, initiating, creative, active, and outgoing in relation to the object, whereas the object is dependent, static, responding, conservative, passive, and modest in relation to the subject. The cause of this difference between subject and object lies in the subject-object relationship within the Original Image.

Give and receive action takes place only between subject and object. That is to say, give and receive action takes place when there is a difference in position. When two elements occupy the same position, give and receive action does not take place, but rather a repulsion will appear between them. For example, repulsion appears between two positive charges.

When there is a difference in position between subject and object, a certain order is established. Thus, give and receive action takes place where there is order. This theory of subject and object becomes another standard for solving actual problems. As mentioned above, the world today is experiencing increasing chaos, which is very difficult to control. The reason for such increasing chaos is that most relationships are not based on harmonious give and receive action, so they have instead become conflicting relationships. In other words, the relationships are not those of subject and object, but rather, they have become those repulsive relationships of subject and subject.

The best way of solving our social chaos is to re-establish order. In order to establish order, conflictual relationships between subject and subject should be changed into harmonious relationships. Thus, it is necessary to explain the concept of subject and object, and the standard for the relationship between subject and object should be clarified. The theory of the four position foundation in the Original Image, or the theory of give and receive action between subject and object can meet this demand. Thus, the theory of subject and object in the Original Image becomes a standard for solving actual problems.

Correlatives and Opposites

I will now discuss the concepts of correlatives and opposites in relation to subject and object. The original relationship between subject and object centered on purpose is harmonious and never conflicting. When two elements or two individuals are engaged in a harmonious relationship, these two elements or individuals are called "correlatives" in Unification Thought. This differs from Marxist Thought, where two elements or individuals are "opposites," because they engage in struggle with each other. Development can be realized only through harmonious correlatives, whereas in the case of struggling opposites, development is blocked and can come to a complete deadlock. Communism has tried to reform politics, economy, and culture based on its materialistic dialectic —the theory of contradiction, or the theory of opposites—and, as a result, they have come to a deadlock which can never be controlled.

Development is achieved through the give and receive action of correlatives centered on purpose, and never through the conflict between opposites where there is no common purpose. The theory of correlatives is a theoretical method which today can provide a fundamental solution to the chaos of Communist countries, as well as of the free world. Thus, the theory of correlatives becomes yet another standard for solving actual problems.

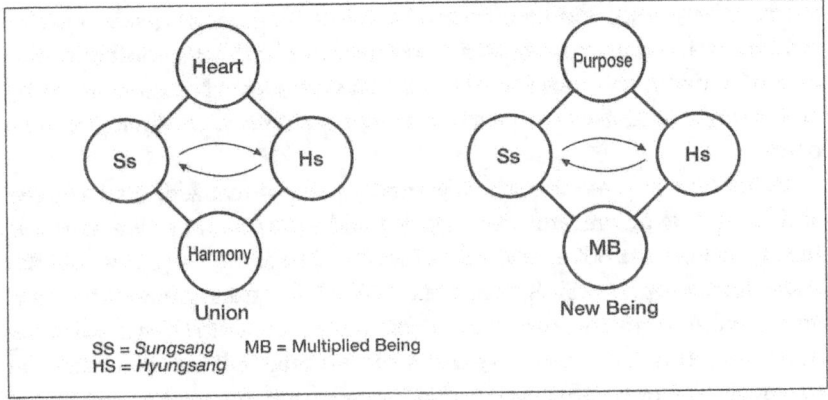

Fig. 1.5. Give and Receive Action Centered on Heart and that Centered on Purpose in the Original Image

B. Formation of the Four Position Foundation

1. Constituents of the Four Position Foundation

As already explained, give and receive action between *Sungsang* and *Hyungsang* in the Original Image gives rise to two different results, depending on the center. When the center is Heart, the result is union, and when the center is purpose (purpose of creation), the result is a new being. The same thing can be said about the give and receive action between created beings, since the give and receive action of created beings resembles that in the Original Image.

There are two kinds of give and receive action: One is the give and receive action centered on Heart whereby a state of unity is realized; the other kind is the give and receive action which is centered on purpose, whereby new beings are produced. The former is the give and receive action between *Sungsang* and *Hyungsang* which gives rise to harmony (union) (*DP*, 19) and the latter is the give and receive action between *Sungsang* and *Hyungsang* which multiplies substantial object partners (*DP*, 24), i.e., the creation of all things. This is illustrated in fig 1.5.

The characteristics of the give and receive action in the Original Image manifest themselves in created beings, especially in human beings. A human being is the union of mind and body, or the union of *sungsang* and *hyungsang*, which are engaged in give and receive action centering on purpose (purpose of creation). An artist makes a plan or has an idea in his or her mind, and then he or she paints a picture or carves a statue with his or her hands using artistic instruments. This is the multiplication of a new being through the give and receive action between *sungsang* and *hyungsang* centering on a purpose (the purpose of producing a work of art).

In the give and receive action whereby unity is realized, the *sungsang* and *hyungsang* before, and the *sungsang* and *hyungsang* after the give and receive action are not essentially different. The same *sungsang* and the same *hyungsang* have simply become unified. For example, when a man and a woman marry, the man is the same man before and after the marriage, and the woman is the same woman before and after the marriage. The only difference is that the man and the woman are united in oneness after the marriage. On the other hand, in the give and receive action whereby a new being is produced, the *sungsang* and *hyungsang* before give and receive action and the result (new being) which has appeared after give and receive action are different.

The give and receive action through which unity is realized, is called an "identity-maintaining give and receive action"; and the give and receive action through which a new being is produced, is called a "developmental give and receive action."

Seen from the viewpoint of change or motion, the former is called a "static give and receive action" since the *sungsang* and *hyungsang* undergo no change either before or after the give and receive action; and the latter is called a "dynamic give and receive action," since a new being appears as the result of the give and receive action. Seen from the viewpoint of position, give and receive action between *sungsang* and *hyungsang* is that between subject and object, whereby, together with the center and the result, a four position foundation is established. Accordingly, the identity-maintaining give and receive action gives rise to an identity-maintaining four position foundation, and the developmental give and receive action gives rise to a developmental four position foundation. Therefore, we have two kinds of four position foundation: the identity-maintaining four position foundation, in which a union is formed, and the developmental four position foundation, in which a new being is formed.

Structure of the Original Image / 49

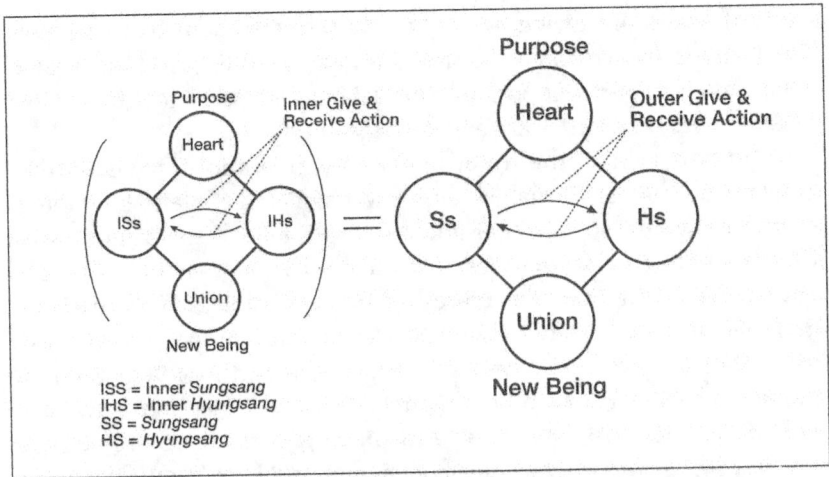

Fig. 1.6. Inner Four Position Foundation and Outer Four Position Foundation

2. Inner Four Position Foundation and Outer Four Position Foundation

There are another pair of four position foundations. These are the "inner four position foundation" and the "outer four position foundation." These two four position foundations arise from inner give and receive action and outer give and receive action, respectively.

I explained earlier, in the section on the "Content of the Original Image," that the Original *Sungsang* consists of the functional part and the objective part, or the Inner *Sungsang* and the Inner *Hyungsang*. In other words, there are another *Sungsang* and *Hyungsang* within the Original *Sungsang*.

Seen from just the position of the Original *Sungsang*, there are *Sungsang* (Inner *Sungsang*) and *Hyungsang* (Inner *Hyungsang*) internally within itself, and then there are this *Sungsang* (Original *Sungsang*) together with the *Hyungsang* (Original *Hyungsang*) externally. When *Sungsang* and *Hyungsang* enter into a reciprocal relationship centering on a common element, give and receive action necessarily takes place. Hence, give and receive action takes place both internal to the Original *Sungsang*, between Inner *Sungsang* and Inner *Hyungsang*, and externally between the Original *Sungsang* and Original *Hyungsang*. The former is called the inner give and receive action and the latter the outer give and receive action. In these give and receive actions, center (Heart, or purpose) and result (union, or new being) are involved necessarily, giving rise to the four position foundation: The inner four position foundation is formed through an inner give and receive action, and the outer four position foundation is formed through an outer give and receive action. These are illustrated in fig. 1.6.

In human beings, the inner and outer give and receive actions correspond to one's internal life and external life. The internal life refers to one's individual spiritual life, and the external life refers to one's social life wherein he or she associates with others. The internal life is the give and receive action that takes place within one's mind, and the external life is the give and receive action that takes place in one's relationship with other people. Such inner and outer give and receive actions in humans are modeled after the Original *Sungsang's* inner and outer give and receive actions. The inner and outer give and receive actions manifest themselves in every created being as well as in human beings.

As already explained, the relationship between *Sungsang* and *Hyungsang* is that between subject and object, and give and receive action between subject and object, with the involvement of the center and the result, result in the formation of a four position foundation. Accordingly, seen from the viewpoint of position, the inner give and receive action becomes an inner four position foundation, and the outer give and receive action becomes an outer four position foundation. Thus, the Original *Sungsang* is engaged in the formation of four position foundations both internally and externally. The Inner four position foundation together with the outer four position foundation in the Original Image is called the "two stage structure of the Original Image." Taking after this structure of the Original Image, four position foundations are formed internally and externally in each and every created being. This structure in created beings is called the "two stage structure of existence."

3. Two-Stage Structure of the Original Image and Two-Stage Structure of Existence

In all created beings, without exception, the inner and outer four position foundations, which are derived from the Original Image, are formed. In other words, in order for any created being to exist, it must necessarily form both the inner and outer four position foundations. The give and receive action in the Original Image is round and harmonious centered on Heart, or on the purpose of creation. Accordingly, in all

Structure of the Original Image / 51

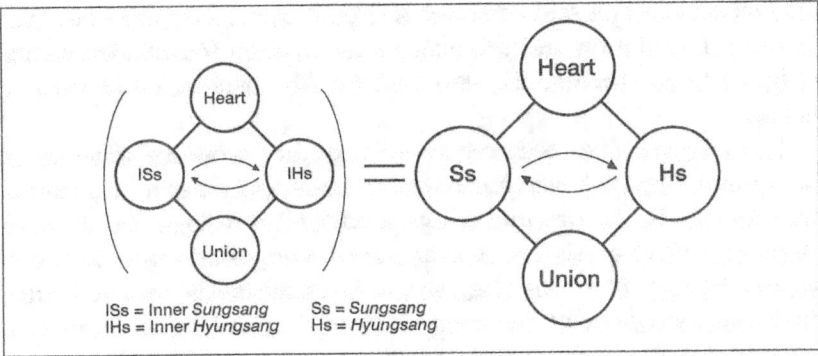

Fig. 1.7. Two-Stage Structure of the Original Image

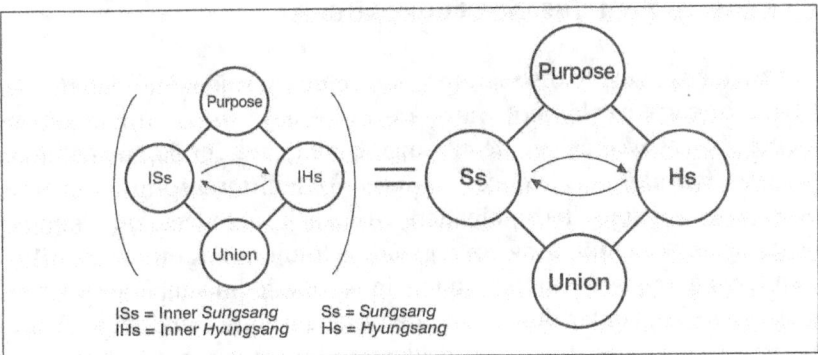

Fig. 1.8. Two-Stage Structure of Existence

things, the inner and outer four position foundations are to be formed, without exception, through round and harmonious inner and outer give and receive actions centering on the purpose of creation.[24] Human beings, however, failed to form the inner four position foundation and the outer four position foundation centering on Heart (love) or the purpose of creation, in their internal life (spiritual life) and external life (social life). Instead, they have deviated into self-centeredness, giving rise to such social dysfunctions as friction, conflict, opposition, struggle, and so on.

Therefore, the fundamental way of solving social problems (actual problems) is for human beings to re-establish original four position foundations internally and externally. Thus, the theory of the inner four position foundation and the outer four position foundation becomes another standard for settling actual problems. In this way, the inner four position foundation and the outer four position foundation in the Original Image become the standard for the existence of all created beings.

This discussion has been concerned with the "two-stage structure of the Original Image," which consists of inner and outer four position foundations in the Original Image, and the "two-stage structure of existence," which consists of inner and outer four position foundations in created beings. The "two-stage structure of existence" resembles the "two-stage structure of the Original Image" according to the law of resemblance. These structures are illustrated in figures 1.7 and 1.8.

C. Kinds of Four Position Foundations

I would like now to discuss the kinds of four position foundations. As I have already explained, there are inner and outer four position foundations as well as the identity-maintaining and developmental four position foundations. Hence, we have four different kinds of four position foundations. In combination we have the following foundations: inner identity-maintaining four position foundation, outer identity-maintaining four position foundation, inner developmental four position foundation, and outer developmental four position foundation. These are illustrated in fig. 1.9. I would like now to explain each of them in turn.

1. Inner Identity-Maintaining Four Position Foundation

The inner identity-maintaining four position foundation is the combination of the inner four position foundation and the identity-maintaining four position foundation. It is an inner four position foundation, within the Original *Sungsang*, which maintains itself and is unchanging.

The identity-maintaining four position foundation is formed when the *Sungsang* and *Hyungsang* are engaged in give and receive action, and unity is realized as a result. The identity-maintaining four position foundation is formed internally within the *Sungsang* and, at the same time, externally between *Sungsang* and *Hyungsang*. We human beings live our lives while thinking various things in our mind. Thinking is carried out internally through give and receive action between inner

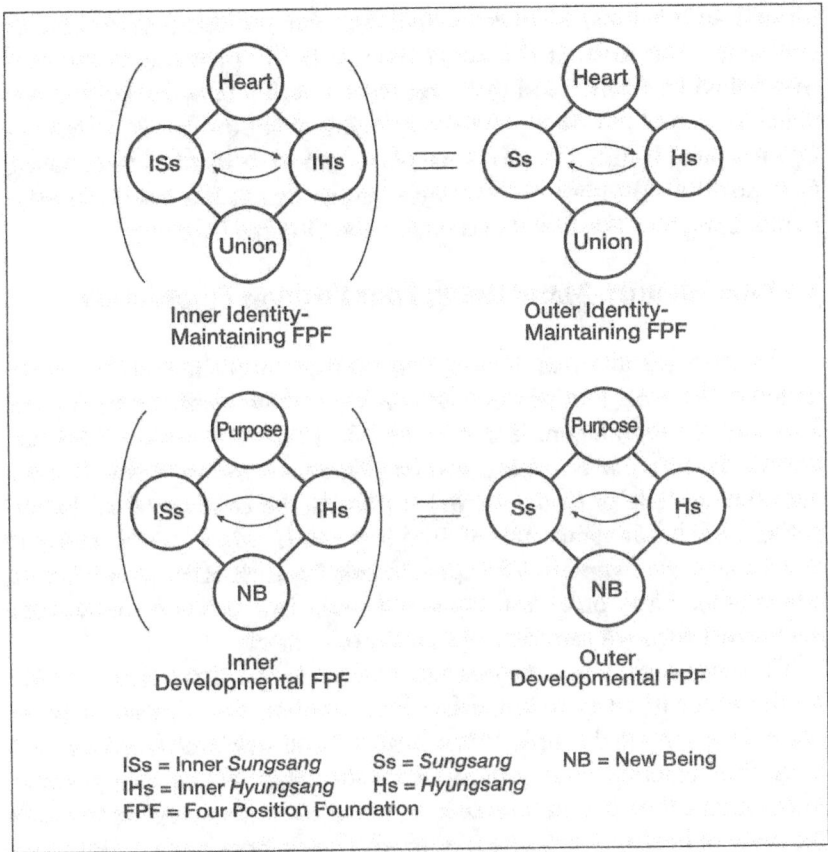

Fig. 1.9. Four Kinds of Four Position Foundations

sungsang and inner *hyungsang* whereby inner four position foundations are formed. We also live our lives externally through give and receive action with other people, whereby outer four position foundations are formed.

When one's thinking is reflective and quiescent, and the result of thinking is a certain state of mind; i.e., a union of inner *sungsang* and inner *hyungsang*, it is said that an identity-maintaining four position foundation is formed internally within one's mind; thus, an inner identity-maintaining four position foundation is formed.

Within every created being, give and receive action takes place, and thereby an inner identity-maintaining four position foundation is formed. In this inner identity-maintaining four position foundation, the center is heart and, at the same time, it is the purpose of creation established by heart,[25] and give and receive action between subject and object is carried out harmoniously, bringing about the result, which is a union (united being). The prototype of such an inner identity-maintaining four position foundation in created beings lies in the inner identity-maintaining four position foundation in the Original *Sungsang*.

2. Outer Identity-Maintaining Four Position Foundation

The outer identity-maintaining four position foundation is the combination of the outer four position foundation and the identity-maintaining four position foundation. It is an outer four position foundation formed outside the Original *Sungsang*, and its character is immutability. It is the harmonious state of God's attributes prior to the creation of all things, namely, the harmonious state of *Sungsang* and *Hyungsang*. In a family or in a society, we live with other people helping each other or relying on one another. Here, outer identity-maintaining four position foundations are formed between members of a family or a society.

The outer identity-maintaining four position foundation is accompanied by the inner identity-maintaining four position foundation. A good example is a married couple. While husband and wife each live their own lives, thus forming their own inner identity-maintaining four position foundations, they live in harmony and help each other, and in this way the unity of husband and wife is realized. This unity of husband and wife is the formation of an outer identity-maintaining four position foundation. Thus, an outer identity-maintaining four position foundation is inseparable from an inner identity-maintaining four position foundation. In other words, an outer identity-maintaining four position foundation is established on the basis of an inner identity-maintaining four position foundation.

Let me now explain the relationship between all things, taking the relationship between the sun and the earth as an example. The sun and the earth are engaged in the giving and receiving of universal gravitation (under the operation of the Universal Prime Force). The sun is the subject and the earth is its object; the sun is the center, while the earth is dependent on the sun.

In the created world, the give and receive action between subject and object gives rise to a circular motion in which the object revolves around the subject. This circular motion is the expression of the round and harmonious nature of the give and receive action between *Sungsang* and *Hyungsang* within the Original Image. In other words, where there is a circular motion, there is a give and receive action between subject and object.

In the relationship between the sun and the earth, the earth rotates around its own axis while revolving around the sun. This is to maintain both its own identity and the solar system: maintaining itself through rotation, and maintaining the solar system through revolution. In other words, a give and receive action is taking place internally within the earth in order to maintain the earth, and a give and receive action is taking place externally between the earth and the sun in order to maintain the solar system. The sun itself is maintaining its identity by its rotation. At the same time, in the solar system the sun is exercising its dominion over the earth, as subject and its center: the sun gives universal gravitation (under the operation of the Universal Prime Force) and light to the earth; thereby the sun helps the earth revolve around the sun while maintaining life on the planet. At the same time, the sun, as an object, revolves around the center of the galaxy, its subject. Thus, both the inner identity-maintaining four position foundation and the outer identity-maintaining four position foundation are established for the sun as well as for the earth. These inner and outer identity-maintaining four position foundations are inseparable.

Circular motion which manifests the inner identity-maintenance (namely, rotation) and the circular motion which manifests the outer identity-maintenance (namely, revolution) are also seen in the original way of human life. Yet, since human life is spiritual, circular motion in this case is not physical, but it is a round, harmonious, and smooth give and receive action centered on love, which is the same as in the Original Image. In humans, the inner identity-maintaining four position foundation is manifested as one's peaceful and loving personality. As for the object partner, the outer identity-maintaining four position foundation consists of its revolution around the subject, which means obedience and gratitude to the subject. As for the subject partner, the outer identity-maintaining four position foundation is manifested as its dominion over the object through truth and love: the subject continuously loves and educates the object.

So far I have explained the inner identity-maintaining four position foundation and the outer identity-maintaining four position foundation in the original world. Yet, in fallen society today we can hardly recognize such an ideal case. Instead, we witness only the over-all collapse of values and increasing social crimes. Thus, the theory of inner and outer four position foundations in the Original Image becomes another important standard for solving actual problems.[26]

3. Inner Developmental Four Position Foundation

The inner developmental four position foundation is the combination of the inner four position foundation and the developmental four position foundation; namely, it is the inner four position foundation, which has the character of development and movement.[27] Here, developmental four position foundation refers to the four position foundation which is established through give and receive action between subject and object, centering on the purpose of creation, whereby a new being is produced.

Internally and externally, developmental four position foundations are formed in the Original Image. Yet, unlike the case of the identity-maintaining four position foundations, inner and outer developmental four position foundations are not formed simultaneously, but rather successively: the inner developmental four position foundation is formed first, and then the outer developmental four position foundation is formed after that.

In the case of the production of a commodity or a work of art by human beings, an idea or a plan is made first and then a commodity or a work of art is produced or created using machines and tools. Thus, planning comes first and production is second. Planning, which takes place in the mind, is internal, whereas production, which is made with machines or tools, is external. Both planning and production are made through the formation of four position foundations. The result of planning is a new being, and the result of production is also a new being. The plan is not vague, and it is made with a clear purpose of producing a definite commodity. Needless to say, production is made with a clear purpose as well. Thus, four position foundations both in planning and in production are centered on purpose. Four position foundations accompanied by a purpose and a new being are developmental four position foundations. Developmental four position foundations are formed internally and externally; the inner developmental four position foundation for planning, and the outer developmental four position foundation for production.

The prototype of the process of planning in human productive activity is the structure of the Original Image. It is the inner developmental four position foundation (the formation of Logos) which is established through give and receive action between Inner *Sungsang* and Inner *Hyungsang* centering on purpose within the Original *Sungsang*. Thus, the inner developmental four position foundation in the Original Image is the prototype for all inner developmental four position foundations in created beings.[28]

Next, I will explain in detail about the inner developmental four position foundation in the Original *Sungsang*, under the topics: "purpose as the center," "Inner *Sungsang* as subject," "Inner *Hyungsang* as object," "inner give and receive action," and "a plan as the result."

a) Purpose as the Center

The center of the inner developmental four position foundation is purpose (purpose of creation), which is based on Heart, the emotional impulse to love. Since God's creation is motivated by Heart, the purpose of creation is to have object partners of love and to realize a loving world. God therein wanted joy and comfort. Human beings were created as God's object partners of love, and all things were created as human beings' object partners of love. Accordingly, the "purpose for being created" for we human beings is that we love each other and love all things, thereby giving joy and comfort to God. The "purpose for being created" for all things is that they give beauty and joy to we human beings, while at the same time realizing harmony with each other. Due to the fall, however, human beings became unable to love each other, and they became unable to fully love all things and appreciate their beauty. As a result they made God sorrowful and made all things groan in travail (Rom. 8:22).

Human beings were created after the pattern of God, according to the law of likeness. This applies also to their purpose of creation. Originally, the purpose of all human activities of creation (production, manufacturing, artistic creation, and so on) is to realize God's love according to the purpose of creation. Due to their fall, however, human beings became self-centered, and they became unable to realize God's love. As a result, they went against the Way of Heaven, and human societies have fallen into chaos. Accordingly, the way to settle the great confusion of today's world is for all people to bring the purpose of all their activities of creation into complete harmonization with God's purpose of creation. This theory concerning purpose at the center of the inner developmental four position foundation, thus becomes another standard for solving actual problems.

b) Inner *Sungsang* as Subject

What Is Inner *Sungsang*?

In the inner developmental four position foundation, Inner *Sungsang* is in the subject position. Inner *Sungsang* consists of intellect, emotion and will. These three faculties are not independent of each other, but rather they are connected to each other. In the intellect, emotion and will are included; in the emotion, intellect and will are included; and in the will, intellect and emotion are included. In other words, these three faculties function as one; and from their unity, the intellectual faculty works relatively strongly at one time, the emotional faculty works relatively strongly at another time, and the volitional faculty works relatively strongly at yet another time. It is necessary for us to understand the three faculties of the mind as such. These three united faculties of the mind were mobilized for the formation of the inner developmental four position foundation in God's *Sungsang*.

When we understand the three faculties of intellect, emotion and will in this way, we realize that the three values of truth, beauty and goodness, which correspond to these three faculties, respectively, also have some common elements between them. Furthermore, the three major fields of culture (the academic field, the artistic field, and the field of religion and morality), which correspond to the three values of truth, beauty and goodness, also have some common element between them. It should be noted here also that there are intermediate fields among the three major fields mentioned.

This point bears an important actual significance. Motivated by Heart, God established the purpose of creation, and He mobilized the three faculties of intellect, emotion and will centering on that purpose, whereby He invested all His power in His creation (Rev. Moon once said, "God invested all of Himself in His creation of heaven and earth"). In His providence of re-creation as well, He mobilized all His faculties of intellect, emotion and will. Furthermore, in the history of restoration, especially today, when the chaos of the Last Days prevails, the three great fields of culture—the academic field, such as science and philosophy; the artistic field, such as music, dance, painting, sculpture, poetry and so on; and the field of life norms, such as religion, morality and ethics—have to be mobilized for the purpose of the realization of God's ideal world, namely, the world of the unified culture, or the world of the culture of heart.

Nevertheless, today, almost all cultural fields have lost their proper direction, and they are sinking into degeneracy. In our time, pseudo-revolutionary thoughts such as Marxism and Kim Il-Sung's Juche Idea advocate proletarian art and folk art. In fact, however, they are vulgarizing and making sterile all the cultural fields, especially the arts.

It is evident, therefore, that intellectuals, and scholars who are engaged in the various cultural fields today, have an urgent mission to accomplish. They should understand God's purpose of creation and advance forward with firm determination to realize it, and construct the ideal world of creation, the world of the unified culture (culture of heart). Thus, the fact that the three faculties of intellect, emotion and will in the Inner *Sungsang* were mobilized, centering on purpose, in the formation of the inner developmental four position foundation in God's Creation, is also an important standard for solving actual problems.

Inner *Sungsang* Is the Union of Spirit Mind and Physical Mind

It should be noted here that the intellect, emotion and will of both the spirit self and the physical self are contained in the human mind. Since a human being is a dual being (united being) of spirit self and physical self, the human mind is the union of spirit mind and physical mind. Hence, the faculties of intellect, emotion and will of the spirit mind and those of the physical mind are combined and united in the human inner *sungsang*. The physical mind has an instinctive level of intellect, emotion and will. The intellect, emotion and will of the spirit mind is creative and developmental, whereas the intellect, emotion and will of the physical mind is not.

The intellectual faculty of the physical mind is capable of sensibility and perception with a low level of understanding, whereas the intellectual faculty of the spirit mind is capable of the functions of perception, understanding and reason, through which abstract and universal truths can be attained. The spirit mind thinks of, and reflects upon, oneself; namely, it possesses self-consciousness. When the neuro-physiologist

John Eccles and the biologist Andree Goudot-Perrot say that only human beings possess self-consciousness, they are referring to the spirit mind.

The emotional faculty of the physical mind is also of a lower level than that of the spirit mind. The emotional faculty of the physical mind has the ability to feel joy, anger, sorrow, and easiness, and to show an altruistic nature, to a lesser extent than does the spirit mind. The emotional faculty of the spirit mind is of a higher level, and with it we are able to engage in artistic activities, and to love our nation and humankind, often even at the risk of our lives.

The volitional faculty of the physical mind is also of a lower level than that of the spirit mind. The volitional faculty consists of desire, the power of practice, and the power of decision, with all of which the purpose of creation (the purpose for the individual and the purpose for the whole) can be realized. An animal's purpose of creation is achieved primarily through material life (food, shelter, multiplication, and so on), while the purpose of creation in human beings is achieved through one's spiritual life (a life of truth, goodness and beauty). Thus, in the volitional faculty as well, there is a distinction between animals and human beings. The volitional function of an animal is solely related to food, clothing, shelter, and sex; but the volitional function of human beings is a combination of that of the physical mind together with that of the spirit mind. In an original human being, the spirit mind is superior to the physical mind; therefore, we should put our priority on pursuing a life of value, and only then should we be concerned with our material life.

I have explained above that human intellect, emotion and will are the union of these faculties of the spirit mind with those of the physical mind: Intellect is the union of the intellect of the spirit mind with that of the physical mind, and the same thing can be said about emotion and will. Furthermore, these three faculties of intellect, emotion, and will are not separate from each other, but rather they are unified. In Unification Thought epistemology, this unified inner *sungsang* is called "spiritual apperception." Spiritual apperception is the unified faculty of cognition which is centered on the spirit mind. This concept of the inner *sungsang* as the union of intellect, emotion, and will can provide solutions to the historically unsolved problems concerning freedom.[29]

c) Inner *Hyungsang* as Object

What Is Inner *Hyungsang*?

Next, I will discuss the Inner *Hyungsang*, which is in the object position in the inner developmental four position foundation. As already explained, the Inner *Hyungsang*, the aspect of form in the Original *Sungsang*, consists of ideas, concepts, principles, and mathematical principles. An idea is a concrete image of each created being that will be created, or already has been created. A concept is a universal image of features abstracted from a group of ideas. Principles are the root cause of the natural laws of the universe and the norms of human life. Finally, mathematical principles are the ultimate cause of the numerical phenomena in the natural world.

Let me explain here about the elements of the Inner *Hyungsang* in relation with creation. What kind of role did the Inner *Hyungsang* play in God's creation? Figuratively speaking, it performed the role of a mold. A mold can be understood as a container into which molten metal is poured in order to make a certain metallic product. It can be said that the Original *Hyungsang*, or pre-energy, corresponds to this molten metal during the process of God's creation. In other words, in a manner analogous to that of making iron products by pouring molten iron into a mold, God created all things by pouring the spiritual molten metal (Original *Hyungsang*) into the spiritual mold (Inner *Hyungsang*).[30]

Inner *Hyungsang* Is a Kind of Mold

A mold of Inner *Hyungsang* is not simply a mold concerned with external appearances, as in the case of an artificial mold. A mold of Inner *Hyungsang* is vastly more detailed and includes internal structure as well. For example, the mold for the creation of a human physical body includes the intimately detailed structure of internal viscera, organs, tissues, and cells. A mold of Inner *Hyungsang* is made up of ideas, concepts, laws, and mathematical principles. Living beings which belong to a certain species have a common peculiar shape and a common character and they obey certain laws and mathematical principles. It is because of this that all things are created taking after the Inner *Hyungsang*, the spiritual mold, in a way analogous to that by which an iron product resembles its mold.

A spiritual mold of Inner *Hyungsang*, as just explained, is directly related to a created being. It should be noted, however, that there are many other ideas, concepts, laws, and mathematical principles which are the molds not for created beings but rather for abstract beings. For example, such ideas or concepts as "God," "I," "parents," "beauty," "ideal," "purpose," and so on are not molds for things that appear in the world of time and space; they take part in creation but they are not molds for created beings as such.

d) Inner Give and Receive Action

What Is Inner Give and Receive Action?

An inner developmental four position foundation is formed in the Original *Sungsang* through the inner give and receive action, centering on the purpose of bringing forth a new being. This inner give and receive action is carried out between subject and object in the Original *Sungsang*; namely, between the unified faculty of intellect, emotion and will, and Inner *Hyungsang*. The inner give and receive action centered on the purpose of creation, is the "thinking" or "planning" that takes place in God's mind.

Why do we regard "thinking" as a give and receive action? Thinking, as we commonly understand it, is constituted by such functions of the mind as memory, reflection, judgment, interest, planning, opinion, understanding, imagination, conjecture, inference, hoping, meditation, interpretation, and so on. To be honest, even an illusion can be included in the concept of thinking, since it is also a phenomenon in the mind.

Thinking can, in turn, be classified into three categories: thinking of the past, thinking about the present, and thinking of the future. Thinking of the past is related to memory, thinking about the present is related to opinion, inference, understanding, and so on, and thinking of the future is related to planning, hoping, and so on. It should be noted here that ideas (or images) are necessarily involved in any kind of thinking. These ideas in our mind were acquired through our past experiences. For example, we have the images of birds or flowers in our mind because we have seen and experienced them. Thus, thinking always includes ideas (images), with which give and receive action is made in our mind.

Operation of Ideas

What does the expression "thinking necessarily requires ideas" mean? It means that any kind of thinking we do—whether it is related to the past, the present, or the future—is possible only with the use of ideas acquired from our past experiences. The richer our experiences in the past, in other words, the more ideas we can have, the more thinking we can do. This is similar to being able to increase one's living expenses, when it is necessary, if one has saved money. Also, it is like our being able to use a necessary good at any time, if we have stored up a lot of goods. To deepen our knowledge is, in other words, to store up various ideas in the storehouse of our memory. Thus, ideas are drawn from the storehouse of memory and they are dealt with appropriately in our thinking, just as we select goods from the storehouse and use them fittingly, for example, in arranging a room. This process is called the "operation of ideas" in Unification Thought.

An idea is an image in the mind. An idea corresponding to a being is called a "simple idea," whereas an idea consisting of two or more simple ideas in combination is a "complex idea." Here, it should be noted that "simple" and "complex" are relative concepts. An operation, as in an operation of ideas, is something like the operation of machines. The operation of machines includes the following procedures: preparation of the machines and parts, construction of machines, overhaul of machines, assembly of parts into a machine, change of parts within a machine, assembly of a machine into a unified system, and so on.

Operation of Ideas is Give and Receive Action

The operation of ideas is carried out in a manner similar to the operation of machines. The "recollection" of an idea corresponds to the preparation of a machine. The "association" or "composition" of ideas corresponds to the construction of machines. The "analysis" of an idea corresponds to the overhaul of a machine. The "formation" of a new idea corresponds to the assembly of a new machine. "Conversion" corresponds to the exchange of parts within a machine. The "synthesis" of ideas corresponds to the assembly of machines into a unified system. There is another operation of ideas, which is called "obversion," during which an affirmative form of judgment is changed into a negative form of judgment. Thus, the operation of ideas refers to recollection, association, analysis, formation, conversion, synthesis, obversion, and so on, with which various ideas are dealt with.

Recollection is to retrieve a necessary idea from one's past experiences. Association of ideas means that one is reminded of an idea by the presence of another idea. For example, one is reminded of one's mother when one thinks of one's father. The formation of an idea refers to the operation with which several lower level ideas are combined to form a higher level idea. For example, an idea of a house is composed of the lower level ideas of foundation, cornerstone, pillar, crossbeam, beam, girder, rafter, roof, room, and so on. An analysis of an idea refers to the division of an idea into lower level ideas. For example, we analyze our body as consisting of the nervous system, digestive system, sense organs, circulatory system, respiratory system, muscular tissue, urinary organs, endocrine glands, lymph nodes, and so on. Synthesis of ideas refers to the operation in which various lower level ideas are united into a higher level idea. For example, the union of the ideas of the nervous system, digestive system, sense organs, circulatory system, respiratory system, muscular tissue, urinary organs, and so on makes the higher level idea of the human body. Conversion is the operation in which subject and object are exchanged while keeping the content of judgment. For example, the judgment "Every A is B" is changed into "Some B is A." Obversion is the operation of changing an affirmative form of judgment into a negative form of judgment (i.e., a predicate is changed into the negative form), while keeping the meaning: "A is B" is changed into "A is not non-B."

I have engaged in making a rather long explanation here in order to better help the reader to understand "thinking" as inner give and receive action.

Types of Give and Receive Action

As explained above, different kinds of thinking (recollection, judgment, opinion, imagination, understanding, inference, and so on) take place by operating with ideas in various ways. Give and receive action consists in the operation of ideas (see fig. 1.10). I can explain this point further. In order to understand that the operation of ideas is give and receive action, we first need to understand the types of give and receive action. There are five types: bi-conscious type, uni-conscious type, unconscious type, heteronomous type, and contrast type (or collation type).

A bi-conscious type of give and receive action is made when both the subject and the object have consciousness. A uni-conscious type is made when the subject has consciousness, whereas the object, which is an inorganic non-living being, does not. An unconscious type is one carried out unconsciously between subject and object. For example, the exchange

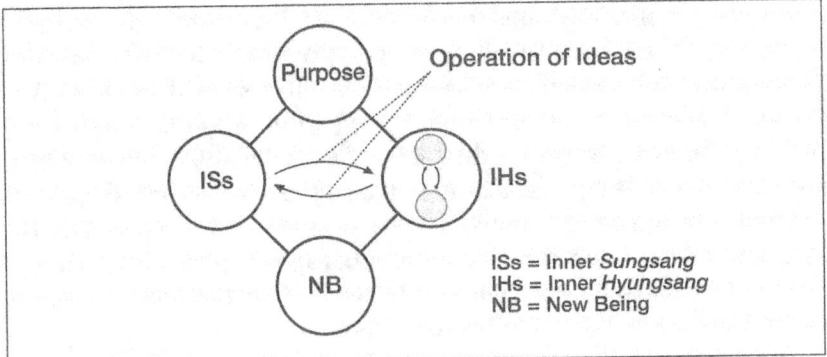

Fig. 1.10. Operation of Ideas

of carbon dioxide and oxygen between animals and plants is made unconsciously. A heteronomous type of give and receive action is made when two parties, which are non-living beings, are induced by the will of a third party to engage in give and receive action. For example, the various parts of a machine engage in give and receive action with one another according to the will of the engineer who made the machine.

A contrast type of give and receive action is made during the process of cognition, or in a judgment. In this type, only the subject has consciousness, as in the uni-conscious type. In this type, however, the subject purposefully brings into contrast two or more objective beings or elements within an object. For example, when we see a man and woman walking on the street we recognize them as husband and wife by making a comparison of their ages and gestures. Or, again, when we see commodities in a store, we select a good one by making a comparison of their qualities. Also, when we see a house with a red tile roof in a green forest, we can appreciate beauty by sensing harmony between them. In a contrast type of give and receive action, a judgment or comparison is made unilaterally by the subject. Yet, a judgment or comparison is possible only when the object manifests its appearance to the subject, who takes an active interest in the object. This is why this is also considered to be a give and receive action.

Thinking Is a Contrast Type of Give and Receive Action

I have explained that thinking is made by give and receive action. The spiritual apperception, or the subject of cognition, which is the union of intellect, emotion and will in the mind, contrasts various ideas obtained from one's experiences and these ideas are then stored in the inner *hyungsang*. When the spiritual apperception contrasts the two elements, it recognizes one element as subject and the other element as object. The focus of interest of the spiritual apperception goes back and forth between the two elements within inner *hyungsang*. Thus, two elements are regarded as being engaged in a give and receive action, which is a contrast type of give and receive action in a narrow sense. Thus, both the give and receive action between the spiritual apperception and the inner *hyungsang* and that between the two elements within the inner *hyungsang* are contrast types of give and receive action.

What is the result of the give and receive action (or collation) between any two elements? Sometimes, two elements are regarded as being completely the same, and at other times they are regarded as resembling each other, and at still other times they are regarded as being different from each other. There are even cases in which they might be regarded as opposites. In other words, they can be seen as being in a relationship of correspondence in some cases, and as not being so in others. Since give and receive action takes place centering on purpose, the result may be different depending on the purpose. Anticipating a certain result, our spiritual apperception carries out give and receive action toward a definite direction. This is the act of thinking. It is because of the difference in the purpose of give and receive action and the way of collation that we come to have such various kinds of thinking as recollection, understanding, judgment, inference, hope, and so on. Thus, various ways of thinking are made successively in the same way that water flows in a river.

A flow of thinking can come to a conclusion at a given point. Then, an idea (either simple or complex) which can serve as a mold for the created being is formed. This idea might be called an "idea-mold." An idea-mold is a new being that has been formed through the contrast type of give and receive action. It is a "new idea," a mold for creation. However, this is not yet a Logos (plan), but rather it is a stage prior to a Logos, which might be called a "pre-Logos" or "pre-plan." A new idea, or an idea-mold is something concrete, in which concepts, laws, and mathematical principles are included. In other words, it is a concrete idea for a created being with its detailed internal structures. This new idea, or pre-Logos (pre-plan) is formed in the initial stage of the inner give and receive action. The Logos (plan) of a created being is established in the second, following stage.

Purpose Is the Center

Thinking is an inner give and receive action taking place in the mind, and the give and receive action is centered on purpose. In humans, however, thinking is often vague, not having a definite purpose. In contrast, in God, the Creator, thinking is based on purpose from the very beginning. This is the purpose of creation (purpose for the whole, and the purpose for the individual), which is based on Heart.

Prior to God's thinking of creation, the four position foundation centered on Heart, or the identity-maintaining four position foundation, was formed in God. Since Heart is an irrepressible emotional impulse, He could not help but establish the purpose of creation. The developmental four position foundation was formed on the basis of this identity-maintaining four position foundation. In other words, the identity-maintaining four position foundation (the unchangeability and absoluteness of God) remains as the basis of the developmental four position foundation, even after His creation.

Thus, God's planning or thinking was made centered on purpose and Heart. This is a very important point, since it becomes yet another standard for settling actual problems. Originally, it is not that we were allowed to be engaged in just any kind of thinking, but rather, we were meant to think solely motivated by Heart, and for the realization of the purpose of creation. Hence, in order to settle today's social confusion, we need to abandon our self-centered, arbitrary ways of thinking and return to the original way: to think and act in order to realize the purpose of creation, in other words, to realize the Kingdom of Heaven.[31]

e) A Plan as the Result

What Is the Result?

What is the plan that is to be established as a result of the formation of the inner four position foundation? In the previous section, "inner give and receive action," I explained planning as thinking, or as inner give and receive action. Now, I will explain the plan as being the result of thinking. The plan refers to the Word, or Logos, as is written in the Bible (John 1:1), an aspect of the Divine Character in the Original Image. Though I have already explained Logos as plan and as reason-law, I have explained it mainly as reason-law, and I have yet to explain it in detail as plan. Thus, some explanation should be added here. I can first summarize what has already been explained.

According to the Divine Principle, Logos is the Word or reason-law. The Word refers to idea, plan, and thought, and reason-law refers to the union of reason and law. Reason is characterized by freedom and purpose, whereas law is characterized by necessity and mechanicalness.

Accordingly, freedom and necessity are united and purpose and mechanicalness are united in the reason-law. Since the universe was created by reason-law, this reason-law is at work in all things. The reason-law at work in the natural world takes the form of natural laws, whereas the reason-law at work in human life, manifests as behavioral norms.

The fact that freedom and necessity are united in reason-law means that freedom is the freedom within necessity, or the freedom within law (principle). In other words, freedom is the freedom of selection by reason within the principle. Freedom outside the principle or law is license. Also, as already explained, Logos is the Word, or reason-law. Since reason-law, or the Word, is the object partner of God, resembling His dual characteristics (*DP*, 170), it is a new being and a created being. Besides these points, I have explained the following: Since creation is motivated by Heart, reason-law is also based on love. Love is at work behind both natural laws and values (or norms). In our daily life reason-law must be observed without fail. Only in a life of reason-law filled with love, can the peace of a spring garden, in which all kinds of flowers bloom, actually come.

Logos as Pre-plan

In the summary above I explained Logos mainly as reason-law, but I have not yet explained it as Word or plan in much detail. I will do so now.

Earlier I referred to planning when I discussed the inner give and receive action. Planning is not a plan, in the strict sense of a new being (resultant being). Rather, it is an action of thinking, namely, a give and receive action, or an operation of ideas. I have also referred to the concept of a "pre-plan." This is a concrete spiritual mold, a model for a creature, or a "new idea" (an "idea-mold"), which is formed through a contrast type of give and receive action, and which contains concepts, laws, mathematical principles, and exact internal structures

The plan (pre-plan), however, is not the plan in the sense of being the Word with which God created the universe. It is the prior stage Logos, which is a static image, similar to a photo; it is not a dynamic and living image as can be seen in a movie. In contrast, the Logos, or Word, with which God created the universe, is a new living being, or a living plan. This explanation is supported by the Biblical passage: In the beginning was the Word, and the Word was with God, and the Word was God. He was in the beginning with God; all things were made through him, and without him was not anything made that was made. In him was life, and the life was the light of men (John 1:1-4).

Logos as Plan

The Word with which all things were created is a plan possessing life and vigor. It is a new idea with exact structures, an idea-mold, or a new being (formed through the operation of ideas), which is given life and has assumed a dynamic character. Then, how does a new idea, which before had a static character, come to assume a dynamic character? It does so by making the passage from the first stage to the second in the inner give and receive action. There are two stages in the inner give and receive action between the spiritual apperception (union of intellect, emotion and will) and the inner *hyungsang*. In the first stage, a new idea (pre-plan) is formed through the operation of ideas. And in the second stage, the faculties of intellect, emotion and will are injected into the new idea centered on Heart (love), and then the new idea becomes vigorous and dynamic, and it becomes a perfected plan.

It must be clarified here that Yang and Yin, which exist as potentials within intellect, emotion and will, surface in the second stage, and harmonize the manifestation of the three faculties. The perfected plan in the second stage is Logos, the object partner of God, or Logos with dual characteristics (*DP*, 171). This is Logos as the Word with which God created the universe, or it is the plan as the result of the inner developmental four position foundation.

The dual characteristics of Logos refer to the fact that the necessary elements of both the inner *sungsang* and the inner *hyungsang* are contained in the Logos, in accordance with its level and its kind. In other words, the faculties of intellect, emotion and will which are in the inner *sungsang*, and ideas, concepts, laws, and mathematical principles, which are in the inner *hyungsang*, are contained in the Logos according to the level and kind of created being intended. Thus, in the second stage of inner give and receive action, the faculties of intellect, emotion and will, which are motivated by Heart, are injected into the pre-plan—which had been formed through the operation of ideas—to vitalize it.³²

This concludes my explanation of the inner developmental four position foundation. Let me briefly summarize what has been said so far.

f) A Summary of the Explanation of the Inner Developmental Four Position Foundation

Center of the Inner Developmental Four Position Foundation

The inner developmental four position foundation is formed prior to the outer developmental four position foundation in God's creation. The purpose, which is the center of the four position foundation, and which is established on the basis of Heart, is to create human beings as God's object partners of love, in other words, to realize love through human beings. Accordingly, for humans, the purpose of being created is to love one another, to love God and all things. Due to the fall, however, human beings have lost their original nature and have brought about today's great confusion. Hence, one way to settle this confusion is to redirect all the purposes guiding human beings toward the original purpose of their being created.

Subject of the Inner Developmental Four Position Foundation

The three faculties of intellect, emotion, and will are united, and are in the subject position in the inner developmental four position foundation. The values of truth, beauty and goodness are pursued through the faculties of intellect, emotion and will, respectively, and three cultural fields can be established through realizing these three values. In His creation of the universe, to realize the purpose of creation, God invested His whole energy and all of His intellect, emotion and will. Hence, in order to restore fallen human culture, presently in crisis, and to create a new one, intellectuals and scholars in various cultural fields should come forth with a unified ideal. In the human mind the faculties of intellect, emotion and will of both the spirit mind and the physical mind are unified, and intellect, emotion, and will are also unified. This union of intellect, emotion, and will is called the "spiritual apperception." Their spiritual apperception is what makes humans spiritual beings, and beings possessing self-consciousness. The spirit mind pursues a life of truth, goodness, beauty, and love, namely, a life of value, whereas the physical mind pursues a life of food, clothing, shelter, and sex, namely, a material life. In an original human being, priority is put on a life of value, pursued through the spirit mind, and a material life, as pursued through the physical mind, has a secondary priority.

Object in the Inner Developmental Four Position Foundation

The Inner *Hyungsang*, in which ideas, concepts, laws, and mathematical principles are included, is in the object position in the inner developmental four position foundation. In the Inner *Hyungsang* concepts, laws, and mathematical principles are united and included in an idea. This idea plays the role of a mold (spiritual mold) in creation. At times, a simple idea becomes the mold, and at other times a complex idea becomes the mold. The spiritual mold has an exact internal structure. The molten metal (spiritual molten metal) is pre-energy or the Original *Hyungsang*. There are countless spiritual molds used in creation, all different from each other. In other words, each mold corresponds to an individual image. Since in humans the individual image is different for each person, the role of each mold is completed when once used. In contrast, the individual image for all things is for one species, and therefore, a single mold can provide for the many creatures that all belong to that one species.

Inner Give and Receive Action

In the inner developmental four position foundation a give and receive action between Inner *Sungsang* and Inner *Hyungsang* is carried out centering on purpose. This is thinking or planning. Thinking is classified into three categories: thinking of the past (memory, recollection, and so on), thinking of the present (opinion, judgment, inference, and so on), and thinking of the future (plan, hope, ideal, and so on). The most fundamental element in thinking is an idea, or an image in the mind, and thinking is the process of working with ideas in various ways. The operation of ideas includes recollection, association, analysis, formation, conversion, synthesis, obversion, and so on.

Inner give and receive action, which takes place in the inner developmental four position foundation is, in short, the operation of ideas. The Inner *Sungsang* (spiritual apperception), the subject, and the Inner *Hyungsang*, the object, engage in give and receive action whereby the operation of ideas is carried out in various ways. The operation of ideas is made through a comparison of ideas. In other words, inner give and receive action consists of a comparison of ideas. This is a uniconscious type of give and receive action, and at the same time, a contrast type of give and receive action.

Result of the Inner Developmental Four Position Foundation

Finally, I can summarize my explanation of a plan, which is established in the position of "result." A plan, as a result, is different from the planning in the inner give and receive action. The latter means thinking or an activity, whereas the former means a new being which appears as the result of give and receive action. The plan as a new being is Logos, or the Word with which God created all things.

Inner give and receive action consists of two stages. In the first stage, a new idea is formed through the operation of ideas in the Inner *Hyungsang*. A new idea is a pre-plan, an early stage of a plan, which is a static image lacking vitality or dynamism. The plan, as the Word with which God created the universe, is a new being endowed with vitality, which is formed in the second stage of inner give and receive action. The faculties of intellect, emotion, and will, or the spiritual apperception is injected into a new idea, and the idea is thereby activated, becoming a perfected idea. The plan formed in the second stage is the Logos, with dual characteristics, and reason-law is an integral part of it. Reason-law is the union of reason and law, wherein freedom and necessity are united. I have already discussed this point in detail in my explanation of the Logos in the section on the Divine Character.

4. Outer Developmental Four Position Foundation

a) What Is the Outer Developmental Four Position Foundation?

This foundation is a combination of the outer four position foundation and the developmental four position foundation. In other words, it is the outer four position foundation that has been formed through give and receive action outside the Original *Sungsang*, namely, between the Original *Sungsang* and the Original *Hyungsang*, and which has assumed a developmental or dynamic nature.

As explained previously, development means the appearance of a being with a new character, namely, a new being (development is a concept arising when creation is seen from the perspective of the result). The developmental four position foundation is formed when the subject and object are engaged in give and receive action centering on the purpose of creation, thus giving rise to a new being.

The developmental four position foundation is formed inside and outside the Original *Sungsang*, in the same way as is the identity-maintaining four position foundation. However, with the developmental four position foundation, the inner and outer four position foundations are not formed simultaneously. The inner developmental four position foundation is formed first, and then the outer developmental four position foundation is formed second.

b) **Outer Developmental Four Position Foundation Is formed on the Basis of Inner Developmental Four Position Foundation**

The four position foundation is a spatial understanding of the give and receive action, between subject and object, that is centered on Heart or purpose, and giving rise to a result. Accordingly, we can discuss the inner and outer developmental four position foundations from the viewpoint of give and receive action. Since development is a concept arising when creation is seen from the result, we can best understand the developmental four position foundation if we examine how the creation is made.

In creative activity, we first have an idea or plan in our mind. When we build a house, for instance, we first have a purpose and a plan in our mind and then we make a blueprint, or specifications, which is a plan written on paper. The formation of a plan is inner give and receive action, which takes place in the first stage of creation.

In the second stage of creation, a house is actually built using materials according to the plan. After a certain period of time, the building of a house is accomplished. Building a house with materials in accordance with the plan is give and receive action which takes place outside the mind; it is an outer give and receive action.

The plan is a new being that has not existed before, and the house is also a new creation that has not existed before. The appearance of a new being is creation when seen from the cause or motive, whereas it is development when seen from the result. In the outer give and receive action, the subject is a plan (to be exact, the person who made the plan or who keeps the plan), and the object is the various construction materials. The give and receive action between them is the construction work, and the result of the give and receive action is a completed house.

For another example, when a painter wants to draw a picture, he or she first sets up a purpose and makes a plan, which is a sketch. This is the first stage. When the plan is finished, the second stage starts. The painter paints a picture just as he or she planned, using materials such as a canvas, brushes, paints, an easel, and so on, until finally the actual picture is accomplished. The planning in the first stage, and the painting in the second stage, are both carried out through give and receive actions. Both the plan in the first stage and the picture in the second stage are new results, or new beings, which have not existed before. Thus, painting is creation, and at the same time is development.

c) All Creative Activities are Made Through the Two-Stage Developmental Four Position Foundations

I have clarified the following points. First, creation is always carried out in two stages. Second, the first, internal stage is planning, and the second, external stage is building or production. Third, both first and second stage give and receive actions are made centering on the same purpose, bringing about new beings as results. Here, the first stage is the inner developmental give and receive action, while the second stage is the outer developmental give and receive action.

These same principles are applied to all kinds of creative activities, including production, manufacturing, invention, art, and so on. The prototype of such activities is the inner and outer developmental give and receive actions within the Original Image. God first set up a purpose, and planned the creation of all things, and then He created all things as He planned by making use of the materials of the *Hyungsang* (pre-energy). Planning is carried out by the inner developmental give and receive action, while the creation of all things is carried out by the outer developmental give and receive action.

I have explained that in human creative activity, creation or production is always accompanied by planning. In other words, inner developmental give and receive action always accompanies outer developmental give and receive action. The prototype of give and receive action in human creative activity is the give and receive action within God's Original Image.

Give and receive action always takes place on the basis of the four position foundation. Therefore, another name for the four position foundation is give and receive action, and another name for give and receive action is the four position foundation. Hence we may conclude: Since

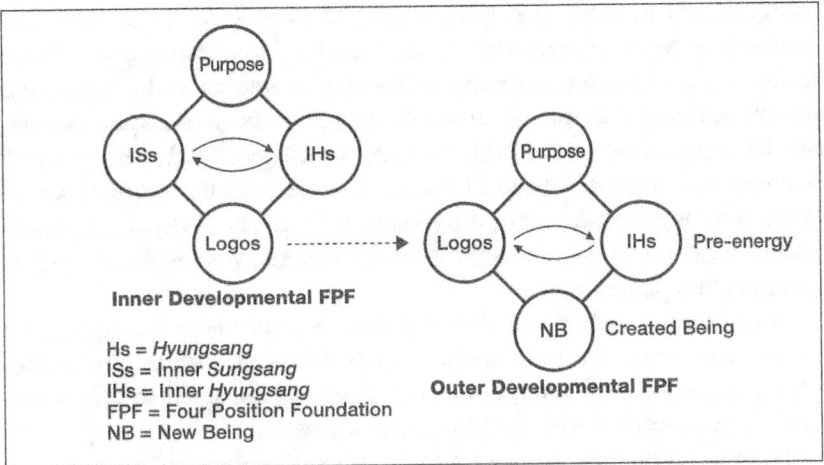

Fig. 1.11. Two-Stage Structure of Creation

inner developmental give and receive action precedes outer developmental give and receive action, the inner developmental four position foundation precedes the outer developmental four position foundation. In other words, the inner developmental four position foundation and the outer developmental four position foundation are formed successively in God's creation. This structure is called the "two-stage structure of creation of the Original Image," which is illustrated in fig.1.11. In actual human creative activity as well, inner and outer four position foundations are formed successively; in this case the structure is called the "two-stage structure of actual creation."

Here the following question may arise. Why is there a need to use such awkward terms as "inner developmental four position foundation," "outer developmental four position foundation," "two-stage structure," and so on, in Unification Thought? Would it not be more understandable if we explained using such simple expressions as, "The plan is made first in creative activity"? Are sophisticated terms preferred over easy terms in Unification Thought? The primary reason why we use such technical terms is that Unification Thought is addressing the fundamental principles of the cosmos.

Fundamental principles or fundamental reasons should apply to all phenomena, whether in the spirit world or in the physical world. Fundamental principles cover a profound and broad sphere. Yet, the terms related to these principles should be as concise as possible. One example is "dual characteristics," or "*sungsang* and *hyungsang*." These terms apply to the human mind and body, as well as to the correlative attributes of animals, plants, minerals, and even those of a spirit person, and all things in the spirit world. Thus, the meaning of "dual characteristics" is broad and comprehensive. However, the term "dual characteristics" is difficult to understand as it is; therefore, it is necessary to explain it plainly and in more detail. Sometimes it becomes necessary to explain using an example or a metaphor.

Furthermore, such a way of explanation of Unification Thought terms is necessary since the fundamental principles dealt with in Unification Thought are mostly having to do with God and the spirit world, which can not be perceived with the physical five senses.

However, one must realize that an explanation using an example or a metaphor is merely an expedient way of clarifying a fundamental principle, and not the explanation of a fundamental principle in itself. A concept related to a fundamental principle is God's "dual characteristics" or "*Sungsang* and *Hyungsang*." Also, "give and receive action," "four position foundation," and "two-stage structure" are basic concepts related to fundamental principles. Thus, these terms can not be neglected. "Inner developmental four position foundation," "outer developmental four position foundation," and "two-stage structure of creation" are also such concepts.

Concerning this point, it may be asked: "In this busy time, when we have to live sparing just a minute or so, why is it necessary to have to learn such involved concepts?" The reason is that the standard with which to solve various complex problems can be clarified only through a correct understanding of such basic concepts.

d) Constituent Elements of the Outer Four Position Foundation

Let me return now to my explanation of the outer developmental four position foundation. As already mentioned, in human creative activity the outer developmental four position foundation is always formed after the formation of the inner developmental four position foundation, and this two-stage process is called the "two-stage structure of actual creation." Likewise, in God's creation, a similar two-stage structure is formed: an inner developmental four position foundation and an outer develop-mental four position foundation are formed inside and outside of the Original *Sungsang*. This structure is called the "two-stage structure of creation of the Original Image," since these four position foundations are formed within the Original Image at the time of creation.

I have already discussed the inner developmental four position foundation within the Original Image in detail. Hence, I will omit its discussion here except to mention the following points which we should keep in mind. First, the inner developmental four position foundation consists of the four positions of center, subject, object, and result, where purpose, Inner *Sungsang* (spiritual apperception), Inner *Hyungsang*, and a new being, respectively, are set up. Second, the give and receive action between the subject and object is the process of thinking, or the process of operating with ideas.

The outer developmental four position foundation also consists of the four positions of center, subject, object and result. In this case, the center is the purpose of creation based on Heart (the very same purpose of creation as in the inner developmental four position foundation), the subject is the Original *Sungsang*, the object is the Original *Hyungsang*, and the result is a new being (created being) formed through the give and receive action between them. I will explain more specifically about each of these positions of the developmental four position foundation. The purpose as the center is the same as in the inner developmental four position foundation. Thus, I will omit an explanation about the purpose as center, and will only explain here about the Original *Sungsang* as subject, the Original *Hyungsang* as object, the outer give and receive action between them, and the new created being as a result.

Original *Sungsang* as Subject

The outer developmental four position foundation in the Original Image is the foundation for give and receive action between Original *Sungsang* and Original *Hyungsang*. What actually is the content of the Original *Sungsang* in the subject position? It is the plan which was formed as the result of the inner developmental four position foundation. In other words, it is the Word, Logos, or plan, that is, a new being formed through the inner give and receive action between the Inner *Sungsang* and Inner *Hyungsang*. Inner give and receive action is thinking, or the process of thinking.

As already explained there are two stages in the process of inner give and receive action. In the first stage, an operation of ideas is made, whereby a pre-plan is formed. In the second stage, the faculties of intellect, emotion and will of the spiritual apperception are put into the pre-plan through the operation of Yang and Yin, which are the attributes of intellect, emotion and will, and the pre-plan then becomes a completed plan with vitality, which is the Logos with dual characteristics. Thus, the Logos is formed as a new being within the Original *Sungsang*. Logos, to which the spiritual apperception refers, is engaged as the subject in the give and receive action with the object (Original *Hyungsang*).

Here, I must clarify the following: Even if the spiritual apperception (the union of intellect, emotion and will), which is the Inner *Sungsang*, is put into a "new idea" in the Inner *Hyungsang* through the inner give and receive action, the spiritual apperception remains as it is; it retains its integrity and its function as the unity of intellect, emotion and will, since its function is essentially of an infinite and permanent nature. Thus, the Original *Sungsang*, which is engaged in the give and receive action with the Original *Hyungsang*, is the Logos to which the spiritual apperception refers.

Original *Hyungsang* as Object

As explained in the section on the Divine Image, the Original *Hyungsang* is the fundamental material element with the potential for a limitless number of forms. The material element refers to the fundamental cause of the corporeal aspect of all created beings, and the potential for a limitless number of forms refers to the possibility of taking any shape, in the same way that water does.

Since the material element is the fundamental cause of matter, and is thus beyond the sphere of science, it is called in Unification Thought "prior-stage energy," or simply "pre-energy." When water is put into a container, it conforms to the shape of the container. Likewise, when the Original *Hyungsang* is put into the mold (spiritual mold) of the plan in the Original *Sungsang*, a creation appears, as an actual being with a definite shape.

Outer Give and Receive Action

Next, I will explain outer give and receive action. With such an explanation we will be able to confirm the validity of the viewpoint of Divine Principle and Unification Thought that all things were created through give and receive action between the *Sungsang* and *Hyungsang* of

God.³³ Outer give and receive action also takes place based on the four position foundation. I can explain outer give and receive action as follows: subject and object, separated from each other, are united and give rise to new beings (all things). It must be realized that this kind of explanation is an expedient explanation designed to help our understanding. Since God transcends time and space, there is no actual inside or outside, up or down, far or near, or wide or narrow in God. There is no large, medium, small, and no infinity or infinitesimal. There is no before or after, and no past, or present, or future; thus, infinity and temporality are the same.

In this way, give and receive action in God transcends time and space. For the convenience of our understanding, however, we explain give and receive action in God using a spatial concept: subject and object, which are occupying the same space and overlap each other, are engaged in give and receive action. As a matter of fact, in a human being, who is the union of spirit self and physical self, spirit self and physical self are engaged in give and receive action, while they are overlapping each other; in other words, they are not spatially separated, but occupy the same space. From this point of view, I will explain outer give and receive action within the Original Image: subject (Original *Sungsang*) and object (Original *Hyungsang*) are engaged in give and receive action, giving rise to a new being (a creation), whereas the new being, the subject, and the object are occupying the same space, all overlapping each other.

As already explained, the subject in the outer developmental four position foundation is Logos (a new being to which the spiritual apperception refers) in the Original *Sungsang*, and the object is pre-energy, the potential for a limitless number of forms, in the Original *Hyungsang*. When subject and object are engaged in the give and receive action, while occupying the same space overlapping each other, a new being is created. The created being also occupies the same space, overlapping them. Thus, the four positions of the four position foundation are not four separated positions, but are rather united in one position where the four "settled beings" exist, overlapping each other.

Let me now explain concretely the give and receive action between Original *Sungsang* and Original *Hyungsang* that overlap in one position. It is the injection of pre-energy into the mold (spiritual mold) of the plan (Logos). As already explained, a mold of an idea (idea-mold), or a new idea with fine internal structure is formed in the first stage of give and receive action within the Original *Sungsang*, and when it is given life by the impulsive force of Heart, it becomes a completed plan. This completed plan is a living idea-mold, or, a living mold.[34] In other words, an idea-mold with fine internal structure in the first stage, is given life in the next stage. However, as much vitality as it may have, and as fine an internal structure it may be, it is still only a mold (spiritual mold). In making an iron product, molten iron is injected into a mold which has a spatial structure. Likewise, in God, the material element of the Original *Hyungsang* (pre-energy), which corresponds to molten iron, is injected into an idea-mold which has a spatial structure.

The spatial structure of a mold accepts and is filled by the molten metal. The injecting which takes place between the Original *Sungsang* and Original *Hyungsang*, is give and receive action. In other words, it is give and receive action whereby the material element in the Original *Hyungsang* permeates into and fills the fine spatial structure of an idea-mold within the Original *Sungsang*. At this moment Yang and Yin, the attributes latent within the Original *Hyungsang* as potentiality, surface and bring about a harmonious variation to the stream of permeated matter of the Original *Hyungsang*. We can regard such a phenomenon as give and receive action, since the Original *Sungsang*, with its spatial structure, offers the Original *Hyungsang* an opportunity to permeate, and the Original *Hyungsang* fulfills the purpose of the spatial structure by filling it.

I have now explained outer give and receive action using the spatial expression of a model of mold to assist our understanding: Give and receive action between subject and object is carried out while they are occupying the same position overlapping each other. This is the content of the outer developmental give and receive action which takes place within the Original Image when God creates. We may add that this give and receive action is a uni-conscious type, wherein the subject is the spiritual apperception (with an idea-mold) and the object is the Original *Hyungsang* (matter).

Created Being as Result

A created being, as the result, is a new being formed through the give and receive action between the Original *Sungsang* and the Original *Hyungsang*, centering on the purpose of creation. It is the "substantial object partner" or the "individual truth being" explained in the Divine

Principle. *Explaining the Divine Principle* [35] states as follows: "God, who is the subject of the dual characteristics of Original *Sungsang* and Original *Hyungsang*, manifests Himself as the substantial object partner in image, and as the substantial object partner in symbol in accordance with the principle of creation" (p. 25). Also, it is written that every creation is "the individual truth being in the image of the dual characteristics of God" (ibid., 25), and "the substantial manifestation of the dual characteristics of subject and object" (ibid., 24). *Exposition of the Divine Principle* notes: "Every creation is God's substantial object partner, formed in His likeness as a discrete projection of His dual characteristics" (*DP*, 19), and "These object partners are called individual embodiments of truth [individual truth beings], in image and symbol" (*DP*, 20).

The concepts of "substantial object partner" and "individual truth being" in the Divine Principle have slightly different meanings. This difference is a difference in viewpoint when seeing a created being. "Substantial object partner" is a concept wherein the focus is on the objective, material aspect of a being: it refers to the objective, material object in three dimensional space, rather than to the idealistic being in the mind. "Individual truth being," on the other hand, is a concept wherein the focus is on the dual characteristics of a being, which resemble those of God. Since every being, without exception, is created in accordance with the law of resemblance, it is an individual truth being.

Resemblance and Outer Give and Receive Action

When we say that all things were created in the image of God's dual characteristics, wherein, concretely, lies the resemblance? As already explained, a creation is a new being that has appeared as the result of give and receive action between Original *Sungsang* and Original *Hyungsang* centering on the purpose of creation. Here, Original *Sungsang* is the spiritual apperception with a living idea-mold, and Original *Hyungsang* is the material element. The living idea-mold is the Logos with dual characteristics.

The dual characteristics of Logos refers to the duality of Inner *Sungsang* and Inner *Hyungsang*, where Inner *Sungsang* refers to the faculties of intellect, emotion and will, and Inner *Hyungsang* refers to an idea-mold, namely, a new idea formed through the operation of ideas. Thus, Logos is a new being in which the faculties of intellect, emotion and will, and an idea-mold are united. A part of the spiritual apperception (Inner *Sung-*

sang) and an idea-mold (Inner *Hyungsang*) from the Original *Sungsang* are embodied in a created being (a final-stage new being). The material element from the Original *Hyungsang* is embodied as it is in a created being. This is what is stated in the following: The material element of the Original *Hyungsang* permeates into the fine spatial structure of an idea-mold. Thus, the elements of the Original *Sungsang* and the elements of the Original *Hyungsang* together give rise to a creation through the outer give and receive action between them.

It should be noted here that the Original *Sungsang* and the Original *Hyungsang* create all things through the operation of Yang and Yin. Thus, all things assume the elements of Yang and Yin, as well as the elements of the Original *Sungsang* and Original *Hyungsang*.

An idea-mold within the Original *Sungsang* is the same as an individual image. Finally, we can conclude that a creation has inherited all the attributes of God (Original *Sungsang* and Original *Hyungsang*, Original Yang and Original Yin, and Individual Image). Such a creation (an individual) is called an "individual truth being." This is what is meant in the Divine Principle when it states that a creation is an individual truth being in the image of the dual characteristics of God.

Relationship between Logos and All Things

Next, I will discuss the relationship between Logos and all things. In the Bible it is written that God made all things with the Word (John 1:1–3). According to the Divine Principle, the Word is Logos (*DP*, 170). Also it is written that "Since God, the subject partner of the Logos, exists with dual characteristics, the Logos as His object partner should also be composed of dual characteristics. If the Logos were without dual characteristics, all things made through it would not be composed of dual characteristics" (*DP*, 170–171). This means that the dual characteristics of a creation resemble the dual characteristics of Logos, and that the dual characteristics of Logos resemble the dual characteristics of God. Hence, we might be inclined to believe that the dual characteristics of Logos and the dual characteristics of God are precisely the same. From the perspective of Unification Thought, however, the dual characteristics of Logos are the duality of Inner *Sungsang* and Inner *Hyungsang*, whereas the dual characteristics of God are the duality of Original *Sungsang* and Original *Hyungsang*. In other words, the dual characteristics of God and the dual characteristics of Logos are not precisely the same. Thus, the resemblance of all things to the dual characteristics of God means a resemblance to the Original *Sungsang* and Original *Hyungsang* of God, whereas the resemblance of all things to the dual characteristics of Logos means a resemblance to the Inner *Sungsang* and Inner *Hyungsang* of Logos. Then, what aspect of Inner *Sungsang* and Inner *Hyungsang* do all things resemble?

As stated before, Logos is a perfected plan, or a living plan, formed at the second stage of the inner developmental give and receive action, by means of the injection of a part of the spiritual apperception into a new idea (an idea-mold), which was formed in the first stage of the inner developmental give and receive action. Thus, the Inner *Sungsang* of Logos is a part of the faculties of intellect, emotion and will which is put into an idea-mold, and the Inner *Hyungsang* of Logos is that idea-mold itself.[36] This is what is meant by the dual characteristics of Logos as Inner *Sungsang* and Inner *Hyungsang*. These are the dual characteristics of Logos which the Divine Principle says the dual characteristics of a created being resemble.

It should be noted here that a created being in the spatio-temporal world, does not resemble the dual characteristics of Logos as such. Logos is a living plan, an idea with vitality. It is something like a picture in a movie, or an image in our dream. When it is said that actual humans and other creations resemble the dual characteristics of Logos, it means that they resemble those living and moving images. In other words, humans and other creations existing as living images (i.e., in Logos) resemble actual humans and other creations except for the fact that they do not have tangible bodies. In order for them to become beings with tangible bodies, they must resemble the dual characteristics of God. In other words, they must resemble the Original *Sungsang* and Original *Hyungsang* of God.

Then, how do they come to resemble the Original *Sungsang* and Original *Hyungsang* of God? They do so when the material element (pre-energy) within Original *Hyungsang* permeates into the fine spatial structure of a living mold within Original *Sungsang*, the process whereby outer give and receive action takes place. Through this outer give and receive action, a moving image comes to have a tangible body and it becomes an actual substantial being. Thus, a creation becomes that which resembles the dual characteristics of God.

I hope that I have now clarified how the dual characteristics of God and the dual characteristics of Logos are different from each other. I hope, too, that I have clarified the difference between them when we say that a creation resembles the dual characteristics of God, and when we say that it resembles the dual characteristics of Logos. I will now discuss origin, division, and union action, or *Chung-Boon-Hap* action, which is related to the give and receive action.

D. Origin, Division, and Union Action

What Is Origin, Division, and Union Action?

As already explained, give and receive action takes place on the basis of the four position foundation. In other words, in order for give and receive action to take place, the four positions of center, subject, object and result should necessarily be established. Every phenomenon takes place in time and space. Give and receive action seen from the viewpoint of space is the four position foundation. Give and receive action can also be seen from the viewpoint of time, and the temporal perception of give and receive action is "origin, division, and union action" (or *Chung-Boon-Hap* action). In other words, give and receive action as the process of the formation of the four position foundation is origin, division, and union action. First, the center is established, next, subject and object are established, and finally, the result is established. Thus, give and receive action in terms of three stages is the origin, division, and union action (see fig. 1.12).

In the Divine Principle, it is written that "the four position foundation is realized by God, husband and wife, and children; they complete the three stages of origin, division, and union action. Hence, the four position foundation is the root of the principle of three stages" (*DP*, 25). This passage indicates that the four position foundation is give and receive action when seen from the viewpoint of space, and origin, division, and union action when seen from the viewpoint of time.[37] Hence, the content of origin, division, and union action is entirely the same as that of give and receive action. That is, centering on the purpose based on Heart, subject and object engage in harmonious give and receive action thereby forming a union or a new being. Therefore, the types of origin, division, and union action correspond with those of give and receive action. Hence, there are four kinds of origin, division, and union action: inner identity-maintaining origin, division, and union action, outer identity-

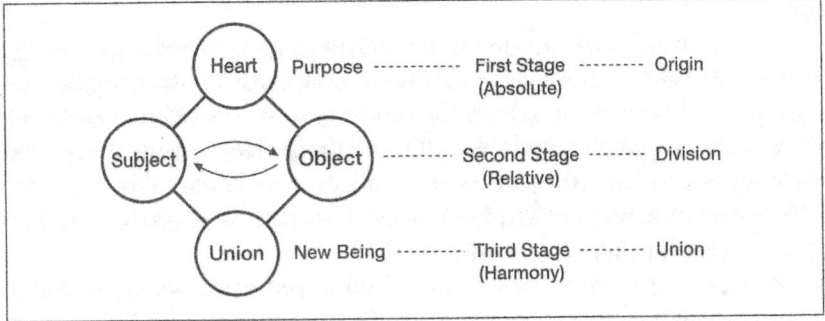

Fig. 1.12. Origin, Division, and Union Action

maintaining origin, division, and union action, inner developmental origin, division, and union action, and outer developmental origin, division, and union action.

Origin-Division-Union and Thesis-Antithesis-Synthesis

The temporal concept of origin, division, and union action has special significance when compared with the Communist materialistic dialectic. Communism is based on the materialistic dialectic, which is a theory of the development of nature that consists of the following three laws: the law of contradiction (or the law of the unity and struggle of opposites), the law of transformation from quantity to quality, and the law of the negation of the negation. It is well-known that Marx inherited the concept of the dialectic from Hegel's idealistic dialectic, and that he connected it to materialism. Hegel introduced the basic form of dialectic development: thesis, antithesis, and synthesis, or affirmation, negation, and negation of negation.

Marxism critically inherited this dialectical form from Hegel, and made use of it in explaining the development of nature and history. According to the materialist dialectic, in development, a thing (affirmation, or thesis) necessarily comes to have an element within itself (antithesis) that negates the thing, and they come to oppose each other (this state is called opposition or contradiction). This opposition (contradiction) is negated again (negation of negation), and is transcended to a higher stage (synthesis). This is the three-stage dialectical form of development. Here, transcendence refers to the fact that when a thing is negated (and again negated), the affirmative elements within the thing are retained and the thing is elevated to a new stage.

Let us consider the process of the hatching of a chicken egg. An egg (thesis) contains within itself an embryo (antithesis), which negates the egg and, as the embryo grows, the opposition or contradiction between them becomes greater, and finally this contradiction is transcended, and the egg is negated. At this time, the yolk and the white, which are the affirmative elements, are absorbed (in other words, preserved) as nutrition into the embryo, bringing about a chick.

Marxism also applied this form of thesis, antithesis, and synthesis to its explanation of social development. For example, the development of capitalist society into socialist society is explained as follows: Capitalist society (thesis) necessarily has within itself the proletarian class (antithesis), which negates the capitalist society. With the growth of the proletarian class, the class struggle intensifies, and finally the capitalist society collapses. At this time, the affirmative elements of the capitalist society—economic development, technical development, etc—are preserved and they are inherited by socialist society, which is a higher stage of society (synthesis).

Critique of the Theory of Thesis-Antithesis-Synthesis

Here, I will discuss the dialectic of thesis, antithesis, and synthesis, and clarify whether it is correct or incorrect. Its correctness depends on whether development in nature and society are actually in accordance with the process of thesis, antithesis, and synthesis, or not. In other words, what should be clarified is whether or not the dialectic form of development is in accordance with actual processes. This must be analyzed, since Marxism has claimed that the materialist dialectic is science, and that Marxism is a philosophy which has appeared in order to solve actual problems—the structural problems and ills of capitalism. In fact, neither the materialist dialectic nor the dialectic form of development is in accordance with actuality, and neither has been successful in solving actual problems. The materialist dialectic and the dialectic form of development are false. Let me analyze them more concretely to support this contention.

Let me first critique the dialectic form of thesis, antithesis, and synthesis, taking the hatching of an egg as an example. First, the embryo within an egg is not something which appeared afterwards as a negative element whereby hatching is accomplished, but rather it was a part of the egg from the very beginning, together with the shell, white and yolk. The embryo, which is part of an egg, can not negate the egg. If the embryo were to negate the egg, it would have to have been something that did not originally exist within the egg, but would have to have appeared as a negation within the egg sometime afterwards. This is in accordance with the process of thesis, antithesis, and synthesis. In reality, however, the embryo existed as a part of the egg from the very beginning. Second, it is unreasonable to say that the yolk and white are negated in the hatching, since they are simply absorbed as nutrients by the embryo. This is actually an affirmation. Third, it is not true that the embryo becomes a chick, a new being, when the shell is broken, whereby the egg is negated. The fact is that the chick, which has already developed into a chick (a new being), comes out by pecking the shell open. Thus, the hatching of an egg does not follow the dialectic form of development—thesis, antithesis, and synthesis.

Next, I will critique the dialectic development of thesis, antithesis, and synthesis as it is applied to social development. According to this theory, capitalist society (thesis) is negated by the proletarian class (antithesis) existing within itself, whereby it is changed into a socialist society (synthesis), which is a society at a higher stage, and the achievements of capitalist society are preserved in the socialist society. However, this scenario was not the case in reality.

It was to be expected that the advanced capitalist countries, such as Great Britain, the United States, France, and Japan would first be changed into socialist countries. But this was not the case. On the contrary, socialism was established in the underdeveloped countries, to which this formula could not be applied. Second, when socialism was established in the underdeveloped countries, the early capitalistic achievements in their countries prior to revolution were not preserved, but were rather damaged, and the economy actually regressed to a still earlier stage. That is why Lenin had to carry out the New Economy Policy (NEP) after the revolution, and Deng Xiaoping, after the Cultural Revolution, acknowledged the failure of the Chinese economy.

Thus, the dialectic form of development, or thesis, antithesis, and synthesis, which was applied to social development, proved discordant with actual historical facts. The former Eastern European socialist countries, along with the former Soviet Union, the suzerain socialist country, which were supposed to be economically more developed than capitalist countries, came to an economic deadlock, and as a result, they finally collapsed. This fact proves beyond any doubt the falseness of the materialist dialectic form of development: thesis, antithesis, and synthesis. Thus, the materialist dialectic theory of development totally failed in solving actual problems, since it was not in accordance with natural phenomena or with historical facts.

Theory of Thesis-Antithesis-Synthesis and its Failure in Solving Actual Problems

Then, why did the theory of thesis, antithesis, and synthesis fail in solving actual problems? We should make an analysis of its failure. The first reason for its failure is the absence of purpose in the form of thesis, antithesis, and synthesis. Development without purpose has no direction; in other words, it is aimless. In a chicken egg, the purpose to become a chick is determined, and once the egg is warmed at the appropriate temperature, development takes place in time, realizing its purpose. Where there is no purpose, there can be no development. The same thing can be said about social development. If there were only the opposing thesis and antithesis, without any purpose, social development would be aimless. In a capitalist society, capitalists seek to maximize their profit, laborers seek to increase their wages and improve their labor conditions; and only a small number of professional revolutionists would have the purpose of realizing socialism. In such a conflicting society, where two classes are opposed to each other without any common purpose, social development to a new stage, which is supposed to take place according to the three stage dialectic, could not be expected from the very beginning.

A second reason for the dialectic's failure is that the theory of thesis and antithesis, which are regarded as being in opposition, contradiction, or conflict, necessarily leads to the neglect of cooperation and harmony. Social development can only be achieved through a harmonious and cooperative relationship between members of a society. Yet, in this theory, the law (dialectic) and form (thesis, antithesis, and synthesis) of development are based on a relationship of opposition, contradiction, or conflict. Consequently, it has become almost commonsense to regard all human relationships as contradictory or in opposition, where harmony and cooperation are rare and abnormal. In such a conflictive society, how can there be development? If there were a person in such a society, with the philosophy that development comes through cooperation, he would be alienated because of his philosophy which defies that very society.

The proposal that development is made through harmonious and cooperative relationships can also be applied to development in nature. As explained already in the example of the hatching of a chicken egg, a chick is born through the cooperative interaction between the embryo on one hand, and the yolk, white and shell on the other hand. Thus, development in both nature and society is made through harmonious and cooperative relationships between elements or between persons centering on a common purpose (or goal). In the Marxist theory of thesis, antithesis, and synthesis, however, purpose or cooperative relationships are neglected, and so it became a false theory having failed to solve actual problems.

Here, it may be understood that the counterproposal to the form of thesis, antithesis, and synthesis is the form of origin, division, and union. The theory of origin, division, and union action is, in other words, the theory of give and receive action, or the theory of the four position foundation. Only through the three-stage process of origin, division, and union, is a harmonious and cooperative relationship established, and as a result, a new being appears. This is development.

It should be noted here that the three stages of thesis, antithesis, and synthesis and the three stages of origin, division, and union do not correspond to each other at all. These theories are similar only in the fact that they each have three stages. In fact, thesis and origin are different, antithesis and division are different, and synthesis and union are different. The thesis in "thesis, antithesis, and synthesis" refers to a thing, whereas origin in "origin, division, and union" refers to purpose or Heart. Antithesis in "thesis, antithesis, and synthesis" refers to a negative element which opposes the thing, whereas division in "origin, division, and union" refers to the two elements of subject and object which exist in a correlative relationship. Finally, synthesis in "thesis, antithesis, and synthesis" refers to that which appears through the transcendence of the opposition between thesis and antithesis, whereas union in "origin, division, and union" refers to a new being that appears through the give and receive action between subject and object.

Thus, it becomes very clear that the theory of origin, division, and union action, which is the temporal perception of give and receive action, is the only successful counterproposal to the Marxist theory of thesis, antithesis, and synthesis, which has failed to solve actual problems of development. With this I conclude my explanation of the main points of the theory of the Original Image. Let me now move on to explain some points related to the structure of the Original Image: the unity in the structure of the Original Image and the ideal of creation.

E. Unity in the Structure of the Original Image

As explained earlier, the structure of the Original Image is the correlative relationship between *Sungsang* and *Hyungsang* in the Divine Image. Through clarification of this structure, it has become possible to arrive at standards for solving various actual problems, since most problems are those of relationships, and they are caused by improper relationships. In other words, once the structure of the Original Image is clarified, thus clarifying the original structure of relationships in all things, then all kinds of problems have the possibility of being fundamentally and eternally solved. What should be added here, concerning the structure of the Original Image, is why the concept of structure is necessary and what the Original Image is when seen from the viewpoint of structure.

Traditionally, the word "structure" has been used in explaining the interrelations between such things as materials in a building, or in a machine. It has been used when we analyze the mechanics of material beings: the structure of the human body, the structure of the economy, the structure of a molecule, the structure of an atom, and so on. Thus, when we investigate things we commonly use the concept of structure. If the concept of structure is extended, we may use it in analyzing immaterial things such as consciousness, spirit, and so on. In fact, such terms as the "structure of mind," "spiritual structure," and so on have also been used.

Coming from this perspective, I used the concept of structure in treating the attributes of the invisible God. We can understand the attributes of God in detail, especially *Sungsang* and *Hyungsang*, by using the concept of structure. However, even when doing so and, indeed, when classifying the various kinds of give and receive action between *Sungsang* and *Hyungsang*, we must not forget that in reality the Original Image transcends time and space. Then, what is the reality of the Original Image which we discuss here using concepts of structure or time and space?

In a word, the Original Image is a oneness. Since there is no space, there is no position, no front or back, no right or left, no up or down, no inside or outside, no wide or narrow, no far or near, and there is no shape, such as triangle or square. Infinity and the infinitesimal are the same. The Original Image is the multidimensional world in which all spaces are overlapping in one point. At the same time, it is the world from which up and down, front and back, right and left, and inside and outside are extended infinitely.

Moreover, there is no time in the Original Image. However, if we must use a temporal concept, past, present, and future are all united in a "now." This can be compared to a reel of motion picture film in which past, present, and future are all contained. Time is united in one point. In other words, there is eternity in a moment, and a moment is in eternity. Thus, a moment and eternity are the same. This means that the Original Image is the world of "pure continuance" (the state in which *Sungsang* and *Hyungsang*, Yang and Yin are united). In other words, "pure continuance" characterizes time in the Original Image.

In short, the Original Image is "pure oneness." Not only time and space, but the causes of all other phenomena (except for the non-principled phenomena related with the human fall) are united in a single point. In other words, all phenomena in the universe including time and space appeared from this oneness. Just as an infinite number of infinitely long lines can be drawn above and below, front and back, right and left from a single point, the world of time and space expands infinitely from this oneness into the directions of above and below, front and back, and right and left.

No matter how vast and boundless the universe may be, and no matter how complex the phenomena and movements in the universe may be, the fundamental principles which rule time and space and all phenomena in the universe lie in this single point, namely, oneness. In other words, the principle of unification, the principle of give and receive action, and the principle of love lie in this single point. Hence, space was developed from the single point of the four position foundation, and time was developed from the single point of origin, division, and union action.

F. Ideal of Creation

What Is the Ideal of Creation?

The ideal of creation is related to the structure of the Original Image since it is directly related to the purpose of creation, which is the center of the four position foundation. Generally speaking, an ideal refers to a state wherein our hope or desire is fully realized. Why do we have hope and desire? Because we want to obtain joy. How is joy produced? Joy arises when love is realized, since the basis of joy is the impulse of Heart, namely, the impulse of love. Concerning the question of how joy is produced, Divine Principle explains as follows:

> God wanted His creations to be object partners embodying goodness that He might take delight in them (*DP*, 32).

> Joy is the purpose of creation, and joy can only be attained when desire is fulfilled (*DP*, 70).

> Joy arises when we have an object partner in which our internal nature and external form are reflected and developed (*DP*, 33).

> The three great blessings are fulfilled when the whole creation, including human beings, completes the four position foundation with God as the center. This is the Kingdom of Heaven, where ultimate goodness is realized and God feels the greatest joy. This is, in fact, the very purpose for which God created the universe (*DP*, 32–33).

In sum, the purpose for which God created the universe is to seek joy, and joy is attained when an object partner embodies goodness, when one's desire is fulfilled, when an object partner resembles the subject, and when the purpose of goodness is realized. In other words, God's joy is attained first when a creation becomes the object partner of goodness, resembling God, whereby God's desire is fulfilled, and second, when a reciprocal relationship between God and a creation is established. The fulfillment of God's desire is, in other words, the fulfillment of His hope or wish. It is the realization of God's ideal. The object partner of goodness is the object partner of love, since the basis of goodness is love. The resemblance of a creation to God refers to its resemblance to the harmonious give and receive action between God's *Sungsang* and *Hyungsang*, and its resemblance to God's act of love. This is in accordance with what is written in the *Divine Principle*: "God's purpose of creation can be achieved only through love" (*DP*, 59). Hence, the meaning of God's ideal becomes clear. It is the state where God's intention (or hope) at the time of creation is fully realized, and the state where God's love is fully realized through human beings who resemble God.

Difference between Purpose of Creation and Ideal of Creation

Let me clarify the difference between the purpose of creation and the ideal of creation. The purpose of creation is to attain joy as is written in the Divine Principle. Joy is attained when desire is fulfilled. The fulfillment of desire is the fulfillment of hope or wish. The fulfillment of God's wish is none other than the realization of the ideal of creation. Therefore, it is concluded that the fulfillment of God's desire as well as the attainment of God's joy can be achieved when the ideal of creation is realized. Ultimately, God's purpose of creation is the realization of the ideal of creation. This is in accordance with what the Divine Principle states: "Had God's purpose of creation been realized in this way, an ideal world without even a trace of sin would have been established on the earth" (DP, 36).

Here, I will clarify, for the purpose of aiding our understanding, the difference between the purpose of creation of human beings and the purpose of creation of all things. The purpose for which God created human beings and all things was to seek joy by seeing them. Yet, direct, exciting, and deep loving joy can be felt only through human beings. God also feels joy from all things. God's joy from all things, however, can not be as exciting as that from human beings. Nevertheless, God's joy from all things was to be attained indirectly through human beings who had perfected themselves. In fact, human beings are God's embodied object partners in image, while all things are God's embodied object partners in symbol (DP, 28). This means that all things were created as the direct object partners of joy for human beings. Concerning this point, Divine Principle writes as follows: "The natural world is an object partner which exhibits human internal nature and external form in diverse ways. Hence, ideal human beings receive stimulation from the world of nature. Sensing their own internal nature and external form displayed throughout the creation, they feel immense joy" (DP, 35).

Since the individual images for all things are different from kind to kind, the purposes for their creation are supposed to be different, respectively, from kind to kind. However, nothing is mentioned about this in the Divine Principle. For example, the purposes of creation for flowers and the purposes of creation for birds are not the same; however, there is no explanation about this. There is no explanation because there is no real need to clarify each individual purpose of creation. The purpose of creation for flowers is to make human beings joyful when seeing the beauty of flowers, and the purpose of creation for birds is to make human beings joyful when hearing the singing of birds. In the Divine Principle, the purpose of creation for all things refers to the common aspect among the various purposes of creation for all things.

In addition to the original meaning explained above, the purpose of creation in the Divine Principle sometimes refers to the purpose for being created, and the ideal of creation. The original meaning of the purpose of creation is that "God seeks joy through created beings." In other words, the purpose of creation is "the purpose established by God, the Creator," and at the same time "the purpose established in His creation." In the Divine Principle, however, the purpose of creation is used also in the sense of the purpose for being created. For example, "a person who has realized the purpose of creation" (*DP*, 112, 167) means "a person who has realized the purpose for being created." To be precise, the purpose of creation is the purpose of God, the Creator, to seek joy, and the purpose for being created is the purpose of human beings to return joy to God.

Our purpose in making a watch is "to know time," and a watch is made "to tell us time," which is the purpose of a watch being made. The purpose of making and the purpose for being made are different. Likewise, the purpose of creation and the purpose for being created are different. What we should do for God is not "to feel joy" (like God's purpose of creation), but rather "to return joy" (the purpose for being created). Let me examine the purpose of creation in the following statement: "God could not accomplish His purpose of creation due to the human Fall" (*DP*, 155). The purpose of creation here clearly means that "God seeks joy," and it is different from the purpose of creation in "a person who has realized the purpose of creation" mentioned above.

Consider an example in which the purpose of creation is used in the meaning of the ideal of creation. Divine Principle says that "God's providence to have fallen people establish the foundation upon which they could receive the Messiah, and thence complete the purpose of creation, began with Adam's family" (*DP*, 181). It is unnatural to interpret "the purpose of creation" in this statement as "to seek joy." Rather, it is more natural to interpret it in the sense of meaning the ideal of creation, which is "the state in which God's love is fully realized." This point also becomes clear if we examine the following statement: "This foreshadowed that when Christ comes again, he will surely be able to realize God's ideal of creation, which will never again be withdrawn from the earth" (*DP*, 202). The meaning of "ideal of creation" in this sentence and "purpose of creation" in the previous sentence are the same. It is not natural to interpret "ideal of creation" in this sentence in the sense of the original meaning of the purpose of creation, namely, to seek joy. Therefore, we should interpret "purpose of creation" in the previous statement in the sense of the "ideal of creation."

Thus, in the Divine Principle, the purpose of creation is often used in the sense of the purpose for being created, or in the sense of the ideal of creation. In Unification Thought, however, a distinction is made between these concepts. When there is no need to distinguish between them, in other words, when either the purpose of creation or the purpose for being created can be used, or when a specific purpose is mentioned, we simply use "purpose."

I have clarified the difference between the ideal of creation and the purpose of creation. In sum, the ideal of creation refers to "the state in which the goal is realized," and the purpose of creation refers to "the goal" which will be realized in the future. In fact, as already stated, the ideal of creation is "the state in which God's love is fully realized through human beings who resemble God." On the other hand, the purpose of creation is "to seek joy through the object partner," which is the goal to attain in the future. If we speak in grammatical terms, the ideal of creation is expressed in the future perfect tense, while the purpose of creation is expressed in the future tense. Hence, the ideal of creation is "the state in which the purpose of creation has been realized," and the purpose of creation is attained when the ideal of creation is realized.

Ideal of Creation Is the State in Which God's Love Is Fully Realized

Then, what is "the state in which God's love is fully realized"? To state the conclusion, it is "the state in which the ideal person, the ideal family, the ideal society, and the ideal world are realized." Here the ideal person refers to the ideal man or woman who has realized the unity between mind and body, resembling God's harmony of *Sungsang* and *Hyungsang*; the ideal man or woman who can realize God's love to all human beings and all things; and the ideal man or woman who can serve God as the True Parents." Such a person is one who has realized Jesus' Words: "You, therefore, must be perfect, as your heavenly Father is perfect" (Matt.

5:48). Hence, such a person is "unique in all the cosmos," "the lord of the entire natural world," and the possessor of "the value of the cosmos" (*DP*, 166).

An ideal family is formed through the marriage of such an ideal man and woman, resembling the harmony of God's Yang and Yin. Such a loving family will love their neighbors, society, nation, world, and all things and it will attend God as True Parents. When ideal families congregate to form a society, that society will be filled with love, resembling the image of God, and attend God as the True Parents, while realizing harmony with other societies. That is the ideal society. As ideal societies expand to form the world, this will become the world resembling the image of God, where all humankind enters into the relationship of brotherhood, while attending God as the True Parents of humankind, and they will live a life of eternal peace, prosperity and happiness. This is the ideal world, the utopia about which saints, sages, righteous people, and philosophers have dreamed since the beginning of history.

Love is realized by people living lives centered on the values of truth, goodness and beauty. Hence, the ideal world is a world of values, and will be a unified world characterized by the three major spheres of true life, ethical life and artistic life, and at the same time it will be a society of "mutual existence, mutual prosperity and mutual righteousness," wherein God's love is realized in politics, economy, and religion (ethics). This is the Kingdom of Heaven on earth. The ideal of creation refers to the state wherein such an ideal human being, ideal family, ideal society and ideal world are realized. Once such a state is realized, once the ideal of creation is realized, then God's purpose of creation, namely, His original desire to seek eternal joy will be fulfilled. This concludes my explanation of the ideal of creation.

Now, let us consider the theme, "Traditional Ontologies and Unification Thought." I would like to briefly introduce an outline of some traditional ontologies along with short comments about them in order to highlight the limitations they faced in solving actual problems. In this way, it will become more evident that Unification Thought can serve as a standard for solving actual problems.

III. Traditional Ontologies and Unification Thought

The theory of God, or the theory of the origin of the universe, that is, ontology, has traditionally been held to be the basis of a philosophical system. Hence, the way one addresses problems is generally determined by one's ontology. Let me here introduce the fundamental ideas of past ontologies, and their impact, or lack thereof, in solving actual problems.

View of God in Augustine and Thomas Aquinas

Affirming that God is spirit, Augustine asserted that God produced matter from nothing and created the world. Likewise, Thomas Aquinas inherited Aristotle's principle of matter and form and regarded God as the supreme "pure form," in which there is no matter. Like Augustine before him, Aquinas maintained that God created the world out of nothing.

How does such an understanding of God relate to actual problems? Since these views regard the spirit as primary and matter as secondary, there developed the tendency to deny the physical world and to attach importance only to the spiritual world. This resulted in the view that the only thing that is important is salvation in the world after death. Such a view dominated the Christian world for a long time. Nevertheless, matter is necessary in our actual life; hence, the Christian's life has remained in a contradictory state, with one pursuing material goods in actual life while, at the same time, holding material things to be of little value in the realm of one's faith. Consequently, with Christian theology, the solution of actual problems on earth was impossible from the beginning, since many problems of our life on earth are related to material things.

The fundamental reasons that Christian theology could not but fail in solving actual problems are: first, it regarded God as purely spiritual, matter originating from nothing; and second, it did not clarify the motivation and purpose of God's creation.

Li-Ch'i Theory

During the Sung dynasty, the Neo-Confucianist Chou Tun-i (Chou Lien-hsi, 1017–73) asserted that the origin of the universe is the Great Ultimate (or *T'ai-chi*). Chang Tsai (Chang Hêng-ch'ü, 1020–77) called it the

Ultimate Vacuity (or *T'ai-hsu*). Both spoke of *Ch'i* as the unity of yin and yang. Since *Ch'i* can generally be equated with matter, these theories were close to materialism.

In contrast, the *Li-Ch'i* Theory advocated by *Ch'eng I* (Ch'eng Ich'uan, 1033–1107) stated that all things are composed of *Li* and *Ch'i* together. This theory was perfected by Chu Hsi (1130–1200). *Li* was seen as an intangible substance existing behind phenomena, and *Ch'i* was matter. Chu Hsi asserted that *Li* was more essential than *Ch'i*, and that *Li* was not only the law of heaven and earth but also the law within humanity. Accordingly, he saw that the law followed by heaven and earth and the ethical law of human society are manifestations of this same *Li*.

In daily life based on this thought system, one strove to maintain harmony and to live in accordance with the law of heaven and earth. Eventually, people came to focus on maintaining order and observing social ethics. Moreover, since everything was attributed to law, people became prone to taking a bystander's attitude with regard to change and/or crisis in nature and society. It became unlikely for such people to opt for a creative and active way of life leading to dominion over nature and development of society. As a result, those who lived by the *Li-Ch'i* theory were not able to deal effectively with actual problems. The fundamental limitation of this thought system is that the motivation and purpose for which all things appeared from the Great Ultimate or from *Li-Ch'i* were never clarified.

Hegel's Absolute Spirit

According to G.W.F. Hegel (1770–1831), the origin of the universe is God, who is the Absolute Spirit, Logos, or Notion. Notion develops by itself through contradictions according to the dialectical form of development, i.e., the three stages of thesis, antithesis, and synthesis. When Notion self-develops and achieves the level of Idea, it alienates itself (or negates itself) to become nature. Idea appears as spirit in human beings, and in human beings Idea recovers itself and, after passing through many stages of development, it finally realizes itself as the Absolute Spirit. In other words, it returns to itself (Absolute Spirit) which was/is the starting point. Thus, Hegel regarded human history as the process wherein Logos actualizes itself, and he maintained that human society, through the actualization of a rational state, would ultimately take on a rational form in which freedom would be realized to the highest degree, and human society would realize its most rational form.

In Hegel's philosophy, the world and history are the processes of the self-actualization of Logos; therefore, human society would naturally become a rational form according to the dialectical form of development. He believed that this rational state would be actualized in Prussia. In this view, we are relegated to the status of being onlookers in the face of irrational reality, since we should entrust the actual development of society to the law of necessity.

In addition, Hegel's view that nature is Idea, in the form of otherness, could be regarded as a type of pantheism,[38] with which the solution of any actual problems becomes quite difficult. Hegel's philosophy, moreover, could easily lead one into atheistic humanism or materialism. His perspective would also provide a foundation for the later rise of the Marxist theory of struggle, since it regarded contradiction as the impetus for development. In other words, Hegel's philosophy failed to solve the actual problems of Prussian society; instead, it provided the basis for the appearance of atheistic philosophies like Marxism. All these consequences stem from the fact that Hegel regarded God as Logos, and the dialectical self-development of Logos as God's creation.

Schopenhauer's Blind Will

A. Schopenhauer (1788–1860), in opposition to Hegel's rationalism, asserted that the essence of the world is irrational. In his view, the essence of the world is the will working blindly, without any purpose, which he called a "blind will to life" (*blinder Wille zum Leben*). The human being is moved by this blind will to life, and is reduced to living merely for the sake of living. Human beings thus live without any kind of satisfaction, always seeking after something. Satisfaction and happiness are merely temporary experiences; what exists more enduringly is just dissatisfaction and pain. He regarded this world essentially as a "world of pain." What arises from the philosophy of Schopenhauer is pessimism. He advocated salvation from the world of pain through artistic contem-plation and religious asceticism; nevertheless, what he actually offered was no more than a theory of escape from reality—hardly a solution to any actual problems.

The reason why Schopenhauer failed in solving actual problems is that he did not know the reality of God's creation and His providence of salvation, and he did not realize that the world is dominated by evil.

Nietzsche's Will to Power

In contrast to Schopenhauer, who assumed a pessimistic attitude toward life and said that the essence of the world is the blind will to life, Friedrich W. Nietzshe (1848–1900) stated that the essence of the world is a "will to power" (*Wille zur Macht*), and assumed an attitude of thoroughly affirming life. The will to power is the will to seek to be strong, and to control. He established the concept of the "superman" (*Übermensch*) as an ideal image embodying the will to power, and asserted that the human being must endure any fate and must be ready to suffer any pain which life presents in the process of striving to achieve the status of a superman. Moreover, Nietzsche radically denied Christianity and proclaimed that God was dead. He asserted that Christian morality sympathizes with the weak, denies the strong, and opposes the essence of life and is, in effect, a slave morality.

Consequently, Nietzsche's view represents a denial of all the traditional views of value. Furthermore, his concept of the will to power led to the adoption of force as a way of solving actual problems. Hitler and Mussolini would later make use of Nietzsche's thought as a means of maintaining their power. In short, Nietzsche also failed in solving actual problems.

Needless to say, Nietzsche's failure is that he denied the true God. What he should have denied is only the false God. Yet, the only God he knew was the false God, and in his denial he came to deny even the true God. Hence, he was destined to fail from the beginning.

Marx's Materialism

Based on the materialist dialectic, Karl Marx (1818–83) asserted that the essence of the world is material and that the world develops through the struggle of opposites, or contradictory elements. Social transformation, according to Marx, can not be accomplished by means of religion or justice, but only through class struggle, violently changing the material relations of production (i.e., the economic system). His revolutionary theory, based on the materialist dialectic, was another method of solving actual problems.

The human being was held to be a class-bound being, belonging either to the ruling class or to the ruled class. A person was recognized to have value as a human being only when he or she participated in revolutionary activity by joining the struggle on the side of the ruled class (i.e., the proletariat). Marx's ideas contained no value perspective that would respect an individual's personality as something absolute. This is why Marxists have been able, without any guilt of conscience, to carry out massive massacres of those people who were of no utility value to the revolution, or who opposed the revolution.

Today, those Communist regimes based on Marxism, have collapsed in East Europe and in Russia. The revolutionary theory based on Marx's dialectical materialism failed completely in solving actual problems. The reasons for its failures are: first, it unconditionally denied God without knowing the true God; and second, it advocated social reform through violence, disregarding the heavenly principle that violence necessarily gives rise to violence.

Ontology of Unification Thought

As we have seen from the above discussion, the way in which one understands the origin of the universe, and the attributes of God,[39] determines the way one understands the essence of the human being and the nature of society and history—and this will ultimately determine the method to be used in solving the actual problems of human life and society. Logically, then, achieving a correct view of God, or a correct ontology, can lead to a correct and fundamental solution to the actual problems of human life, society and history.

According to the ontology of Unification Thought, namely, the Theory of the Original Image, the core of the attributes of God is Heart. Within the Original *Sungsang*, centering on Heart, Inner *Sungsang* (i.e., intellect, emotion, and will) and Inner *Hyungsang* (i.e., ideas, concepts, etc.) are engaged in give and receive action, and Original *Sungsang* and Original *Hyungsang* (pre-matter) are also engaged in give and receive action. This is the way in which God exists. When purpose is established by Heart, give and receive action becomes developmental, and creation takes place.

Traditional ontologies are centered on reason, or on will, or on an idea, or on matter itself. Moreover, some traditional ontologies are monistic (asserting either that the spirit alone is substantial or that matter alone is substantial), whereas others are dualistic (asserting that spirit and matter are substances that are mutually independent from each other), and so forth. From the perspective of Unification Thought, it can be said that traditional ontologies have not fully succeeded in correctly understanding the reality of God's attributes nor the relationships among those attributes.

On the other hand, the ontology of Unification Thought clearly and concretely explains the motivation and purpose of creation, the content of the attributes of God, and the structure among those attributes. Hence, a standard for the fundamental solution of actual problems can be established. The only need now is for the world's leaders to understand this and to strive to live life and to guide their societies based on this standard.

2

Ontology: A Theory of Being

The word ontology, as it has been used in philosophy, originates from the Greek word *Ontologia*, which consists of onta (what exists) and *logos* (logic). Ontology is that field of philosophy which deals with the fundamental matters of existence. Likewise, in Unification Thought, ontology deals with the common attributes of all created beings, the way they exist, their movements, and so on, all based on the Divine Principle view of God's creation.

Hence, Unification Thought ontology deals with all created beings, including human beings. However, since the human being is the lord of dominion over all things and occupies a position different from that of all other created beings, the human being will be discussed in more detail in a separate chapter, the "Theory of the Original Human Nature." We can note that, whereas the Theory of the Original Image deals with God, ontology in Unification Thought deals primarily with all things.

In this ontology, we will ascertain whether or not the attributes of God, as they are explained in the Theory of the Original Image, are actually manifested in all things and, if so, how. If it can be shown that the attributes of God are universally manifested in all things then the veracity of the Theory of the Original Image becomes more certain and persuasive. Therefore, ontology, which deals with the attributes of all things, can be described as a theory that confirms, in visible terms, the attributes of the invisible God. In other words, Unification ontology is a theory that supports the Theory of the Original Image, which itself, is a deductive theory based on the Divine Principle.

Today, the natural sciences, which deal with all things, have made rapid progress. Yet, in most cases, scientists have been observing the natural world from a purely objective point of view, without giving any consideration to God. Since all things were created according to the law of likeness, the scientific facts as observed by scientists can be expected to be in accordance with the attributes of God, and so the natural sciences will come to support the Theory of the Original Image. In fact, in Unification ontology it will be clarified that the achievements of the natural sciences today are indeed supporting the Theory of the Original Image.

According to the Divine Principle, human beings were created in the image of God (Gen. 1:27), and all things were created in the image of the human being. Prior to creating the universe, God first envisioned the image of the human being, which resembles God's own image. Then, using the human image as the prototype, and in likeness to it, God formed the ideas of all things. This is called "creation in likeness."

Because of the human fall, however, human beings, and their societies, lost their original nature and fell into an unprincipled state, even though all things of creation have remained as originally created. For this reason, we can never find in actual human beings or societies the way to solve our problems, in other words, the problem of existence, and the problem of relationship. This is why many saints and sages of the past have sought to understand the way for people to live, not by observing humanity but by observing the movements of the stars, the growth and decline of living beings, the changes of the four seasons, and so on. They were unable, however, to clarify why it is possible to obtain from the natural world, the truth for people and society. They obtained only a merely intuitive realization of the truth.

Unification Thought, on the other hand, maintains that since all things were created in the likeness of human beings, it is possible to know the original characteristics of human beings and society through observing the natural world. In the Theory of the Original Image, it was explained that a correct understanding of the attributes of God is the key to solving the problems of individuals and society. Yet, creation was made in likeness; therefore, if we correctly understand the attributes of all things, then this can help us secure the key in solving actual problems. Consequently, ontology becomes another standard for solving existing questions.

In the ontology laid out here, each created being is called an "existing being." Hence, ontology is the theory of existing beings. An existing being is examined from two points of view, namely, as an "individual truth being" and as a "connected being."

An individual truth being refers to an individual being resembling the attributes of God, namely, the content of the Original Image, and it refers to an existing being considered as such, independently and without regard to any of its relationships with other beings. In actuality, of course, all existing beings have mutual relationships with one another, and when a being is seen in terms of these relationships it has with other beings, then that being is called a "connected being." A connected being thus refers to the same individual truth being, but in this case we are seeing it from the viewpoint of its relationships to other beings.

Since all existing beings were created in the likeness of God, the image of each being resembles the Divine Image. The Divine Image includes the universal image and the individual image; therefore, an existing being has both a universal image and an individual image. Here, the universal image refers to *sungsang* and *hyungsang*, and yang and yin, whereas the individual image refers to those peculiar characteristics which each individual being possesses. Let us first discuss the universal image of an individual truth being, namely *sungsang* and *hyungsang*, and yang and yin.

I. Individual Truth Being

A. *Sungsang* and *Hyungsang*

First of all, every created being possesses the dual characteristics of *sungsang* and *hyungsang*. *Sungsang* refers to the invisible, immaterial aspect of created beings, such as their faculty and nature. *Hyungsang* refers to the visible aspect of created beings, such as mass, structure, and shape. In minerals, *sungsang* is physicochemical character, and *hyungsang* is structure, shape, and so on, composed of atoms and molecules.

Plants have their own peculiar *sungsang* and *hyungsang*. The *sungsang* peculiar to plants is life, and the *hyungsang* peculiar to plants is their cells and tissues, which compose their structure and shape—in other words, the body of a plant. Life is the consciousness latent within the body, and it possesses purposefulness and directiveness. The function of life is the ability to grow while maintaining itself as an individual being. Therefore, it can be said that life has autonomy. While plants possess their own peculiar *sungsang* and *hyungsang*, they also contain the elements of *sungsang* and *hyungsang* of the level of minerals. In other worlds, plants contain mineral matter.

In animals, there are aspects of *sungsang* and *hyungsang* that are peculiar to animals and so they exist on a level higher than that of plants. The *sungsang* peculiar to animals is instinct, and the *hyungsang* peculiar to animals is their structure and shape which includes sense organs and nerves. Animals have both mineral matter, which contains the *sungsang* and *hyungsang* of the mineral-level, and they also possess plant-level *sungsang* and *hyungsang*; all the cells and tissues of animals exist on this level.

The human being is a two-fold being of spirit self and physical self. Therefore, the *sungsang* and *hyungsang* of the human being are unique and are of a still higher level than those of the animals. The *sungsang* unique to the human being is the "spirit mind," which is the mind of the spirit self, and the *hyungsang* unique to the human being is the spirit body. In a human physical self, the *sungsang* is the physical mind and the *hyungsang* is the physical body. Mineral matter is contained in the physical body, and in this sense the human being has mineral-level *sungsang* and *hyungsang*. The human physical body is also composed of cells and tissues, and therefore has plant-level *sungsang* and *hyungsang* as well. Like animals, the human being has sense organs and nerves, and hence the *sungsang* and *hyungsang* corresponding to animals. The animal-level *sungsang* in human beings, namely, the instinctive mind, is called the "physical mind." Thus, the human mind consists of the physical mind (instinctive mind) and the spirit mind. While the spirit mind pursues the values of truth, goodness, beauty, and love, the physical mind pursues a life of food, clothing, shelter, and sex. The original human mind ("original mind") is the union of the spirit mind and physical mind.

Let us now discuss the spirit self of a human being. The physical self consists of the same elements as those of the natural world and has only a certain period of time for its existence. In contrast, the spirit self is made of spiritual elements, which can not be perceived with our physical senses; yet, the spirit self has an appearance no different from that of the physical self. When the physical self dies, the spirit self discards it—in much the same way as when we discard an article of clothing when it is old and worn out. Having discarded the physical self, the spirit self goes on to the spirit world, where it exists forever.

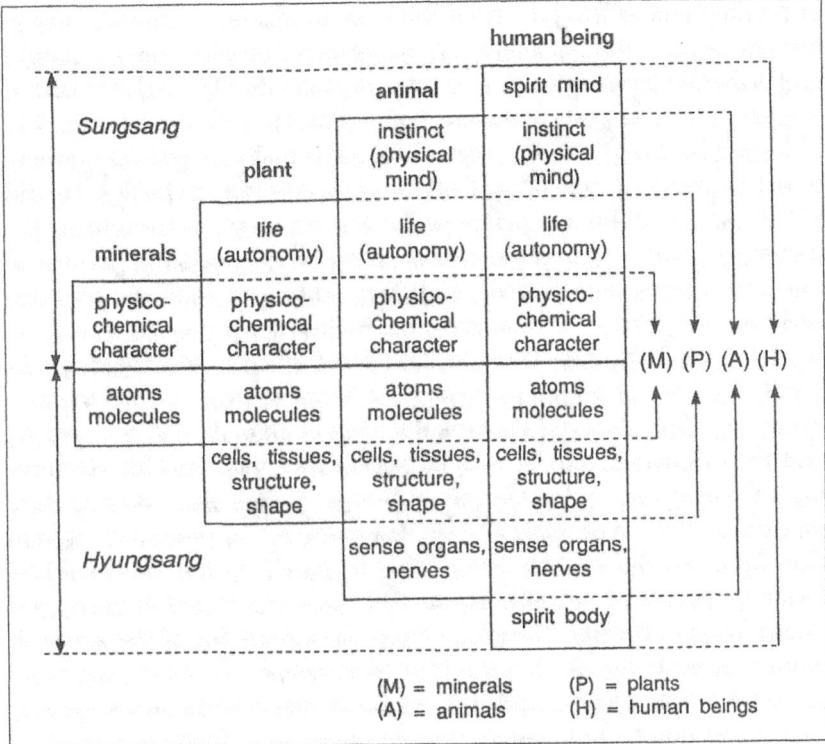

Fig. 2.1. Layered Structure of *Sungsang* and *Hyungsang* in Existing Beings

The spirit self is composed of the dual characteristics of *sungsang* and *hyungsang*. The *sungsang* of the spirit self is the spirit mind, and its *hyungsang* is the spirit body. The sensibilities of the spirit self are nurtured in its mutual relationship with the physical self. In other words, the sensibilities of the spirit self develop on the basis of the physical self. Therefore, when an individual dies after having practiced God's love during life on earth, that individual's spirit self will lead a life of joy filled with love in the spirit world. In contrast, those who commit evil acts while on earth can not but experience a life of suffering after death.

It is evident that human beings possess the *sungsangs* and *hyungsangs* of minerals, plants, and animals and, in addition, they possess a *sungsang* and *hyungsang* of a still higher level. When seen in this way, the human being can be regarded as the integration of all things, or as a microcosm of the universe. From this explanation, it becomes clear that, as the levels of existing beings ascend—from minerals to plants, to animals, and to human beings—the *sungsangs* and *hyungsangs* become more substantial and elaborate layer by layer. This may be called the "layered structure of *sungsang* and *hyungsang* in existing beings," and it is illustrated in fig. 2.1.

It must be noted, however, that when God actually created the universe, in the sequence of minerals, plants, animals and human beings, He did not simply create human beings at the end by merely accumulating the previously existing and respective *sungsangs* and *hyungsangs* peculiar to minerals, plants, and animals, and then, adding to them the *sungsang* and *hyungsang* unique to human beings. Rather, in the process of creation, according to Unification Thought, God first formed or visualized, in His mind, the idea of a human being as a being of united *sungsang* and *hyungsang*. Only then did He form the ideas of animals, and then plants, and then minerals, one by one, by subtracting their specific elements from the *sungsang* and *hyungsang* of human beings and lowering their dimension. It must be realized then, that in the actual process of creation God followed the reverse order—that is, based on the ideas He had formed, He created actual minerals first, then plants and animals, and finally human beings. Therefore, from the viewpoint of the result, it would, indeed, appear that the human *sungsang* and *hyungsang* were made by simply accumulating the respective layers of the *sungsangs* and *hyungsangs* unique to minerals, then to plants, and finally to animals—but this is just a matter of appearance. That the human *sungsang* and *hyungsang*, diagrammatically, possess a layered structure, as was described earlier, has the following important implications.

First, such a layered structure implies that there is a certain continuity among the various layers within the *sungsang*. Specifically, the human mind, which consists of spirit mind and physical mind, possesses continuity between these two minds; hence, a human being can control the physical mind through the spirit mind. Furthermore, the human mind is connected to life, or autonomy. Even though, through the conscious mind, one can not usually control the autonomous nerves, it is well known that such control can become possible through training. Yoga practitioners, for example, can, through meditation, change the pace of their heartbeats.[1] In addition, the human mind is connected with the *sungsang* of minerals within the body. Also, the human mind is externally connected to the *sungsang* of animals and plants. It is known that a human being with his or her power of mind can influence even material beings, as well as animals and plants, outside themselves without using physical means.[2]

In addition, it is said that animals, plants, and minerals respond to the human mind. In the case of plants, the Backster Effect, observed by Clive Backster, an American lie-detector technician, testifies to this fact.[3] Furthermore, it has been reported that there may exist a certain perceptive ability even in the realms of minerals and elementary particles.[4]

Second, the layered structure of human *sungsang* and *hyungsang* provides important insights with regard to the question of life. Theists and atheists have continually argued about the existence or non-existence of God. Theists have always disagreed with atheists, claiming that life can not be created by humans, that only God can create life. No matter how much progress natural science may have made, it had not been able to present a reasonable scenario for the origin of life. Hence, for a long time the question of life had been the sole foothold on which theism could base its position. Today, however, that foothold is being threatened by atheists, since scientists now assert that they have reached the point where they can create life.

Can scientists then, indeed, create life? According to contemporary biology, the DNA (deoxyribonucleic acid) within the chromosomes of a cell contains four kinds of nitrogenous bases, which are adenine, guanine, cytosine, and thymine. The way in which these four different bases are arranged form the genetic information of a cell, which can be called the blueprint of a living organism. The structure and functions of a living organism are determined by this genetic information. Therefore, it can be said that living things, ultimately, are made through their DNA. Scientists today have become capable of synthesizing DNA. Therefore, materialists have come to conclude that God is quite unnecessary in explaining the phenomenon of life. They assert that it is not necessary to hold that God has existed from the beginning.

But, is the synthesis of DNA by scientists the same phenomenon as the creation of life? From the viewpoint of Unification Thought, it is not. Even if scientists are capable of synthesizing DNA, they will merely have succeeded in producing the *hyungsang* aspect of life phenomena. Life is, in essence, the *sungsang* aspect of life phenomena. Therefore, what scientists have become able to produce is not life itself, but simply the carrier of life. In a human being, the physical self, which is *hyungsang*, carries the spirit self, which is *sungsang*. One's physical self comes from one's parents, while one's spirit self comes from God. Likewise, even if

DNA does come from scientists (that is, even if science may synthesize DNA), life itself comes from God.

Figuratively, this point may be elucidated by using the example of a radio. A radio receiver is a device that converts electrical waves into sound waves. It receives the electrical waves coming from a broadcasting station and converts them into sound waves. Therefore, the fact that scientists have made a radio does not mean that they have made sound, since sound comes from the broadcasting station, being carried by the electrical waves. Likewise, the fact that scientists have synthesized DNA does not mean they have created life itself; it means, simply, that they have made a device that is capable of catching life.

The universe is a life field; it is permeated with life, which originates from God's *Sungsang*. Once there appears a device that is capable of receiving life, then, and only then, can life appear. The device in question is precisely the special molecule called DNA. Such a conclusion can be derived from the concept of the layered structure of *sungsang* and *hyungsang*.

B. Yang and Yin

Yang and Yin Is Another Dual Characteristic

We shall now discuss the yang and yin characteristics of the individual truth being. As stated in the Theory of the Original Image, Yang and Yin, another pair of dual characteristics in God, are the attributes of *Sungsang* and *Hyungsang*. This means that there are Yang and Yin characteristics in *Sungsang* and Yang and Yin characteristics in *Hyungsang*.

Let us first examine the yang and yin characteristics of the human *sungsang* and *hyungsang*. The human *sungsang* is the mind, which possesses the faculties of intellect, emotion, and will. There are yang aspects and yin aspects in each of these faculties of the mind. The yang aspects of the intellect are clarity, good memory, distinctness, wittiness, and the like. The yin aspects of the intellect are vagueness, forgetfulness, unclear ideas, seriousness, and so on. The yang aspects of the emotion are pleasantness, loudness, joyfulness, excitement, and the like. The yin aspects of the emotion are unpleasantness, quietness, sorrow, composure, etc. The yang aspects of the will are activeness, aggressiveness, creativeness, carefreeness, and other such qualities. Finally, the yin aspects of the will are passiveness, tolerance, conservativeness, carefulness, and so on.

TABLE 2.1. Yang and Yin as Attributes of *Sungsang* and *Hyungsang* (in Human Beings)

		Yang	Yin
Sung-sang	Intellect	Clarity, Good Memory Distinctiveness, Wittiness	Vagueness, Forgetfulness Unclear Ideas, Seriousness
	Emotion	Pleasantness, Loudness, Joy Excitement	Unpleasantness, Quietness Sorrow, Composure
	Will	Activeness, Aggressiveness Creativeness Carefreeness	Passiveness, Tolerance Conservativeness Carefulness
Hyungsang		Protuberant Parts, Protrusions Convex Parts, Front Side	Sunken Parts, Orifices Concave Parts, Back Side

With regard to the *hyungsang*, or the physical body, protuberant parts, protrusions, convex parts, the front side, and so on, are the yang aspects; whereas sunken parts, orifices, concave parts, the back side, etc., are the yin aspects. These points are systematically arranged in table 2.1.

In a similar way, in animals, plants, and minerals there are yang and yin in the *sungsang* as well as in the *hyungsang*. Animals sometimes behave actively and sometimes they do not. Plants sometimes grow and sometimes they wither; sometimes plants open their flowers, and sometimes they close them; trees grow upward into the sky and their roots grow downward into the soil. In minerals, physicochemical functions sometimes proceed intensely and at other times do not. These are yang and yin characteristics of the *sungsang*. As for yang and yin characteristics of the *hyungsang*, these include protuberances and orifices, high and low, front and back, light and dark, hard and soft, dynamic and static, pure and impure, hot and cold, day and night, summer and winter, heaven and earth, mountain and valley, and so forth. This is how we can understand yang and yin in the *sungsang* and *hyungsang* of the individual truth being.

An individual truth being is equipped with yang and yin as the attributes of *sungsang* and *hyungsang*. Further, each type of created being consists of a pair of individual truth beings, i.e., a yang substantial being and a yin substantial being: the former is equipped with relatively more yang characters than its partner and the latter is equipped with relatively more yin characters than its partner. We can find pairs of yang substantial being and yin substantial being at each level of beings. These are man and woman in human beings, male and female in animals, stamen and pistil in plants, cation and anion in minerals, and protons and electrons in atoms. It is said that there are male and female even in single-cell bacteria.[5]

Yang Substantial Being and Yin Substantial Being in Human Beings

Yang substantial being and yin substantial being are concepts often used to refer to man and woman. Then, concerning human beings, in concrete terms what are a yang substantial being and a yin substantial being? Since this issue has already been explained in detail in the Theory of the Original Image, I will merely summarize the content here.

In the *hyungsang* (body), the difference between man and woman in terms of yang and yin is very clear. It is a quantitative difference: man's body has more yang elements than woman's, and woman's body has more yin elements than man's. On the other hand, in the *sungsang*, the difference between man and woman in terms of yang and yin is a characteristic difference.

As explained earlier, man and woman both have yang and yin in each faculty of intellect, emotion, and will. There are, however, characteristic differences between man and woman with regard to yang and yin. For example, man and woman both have clarity, which is a yang character of the intellect, but the character of this clarity differs between man and woman. Generally, clarity in man has a more comprehensive character, whereas clarity in woman is more analytic and is oriented more toward details. As for sadness, a yin character of emotion, man's sorrow tends to have a more painful character, while woman's tends to have a grieving character. As for activeness, a yang character of the will, the character of a man's activeness gives an impression more of hardness, whereas the character of a woman's activeness gives more an impression of softness. Such differences between man and woman are characteristic differences.

For the sake of better understanding, let me cite the case of vocal music. In vocal music, the male tenor and the female's soprano are both high sounds, and so correspond to yang, but they are characteristically different. Likewise, masculine bass and feminine alto are both low sounds, and so correspond to yin, but they are characteristically different. As shown through this comparison, the differences between yang and yin in the *sungsang* is a characteristic difference and, therefore, masculinity appears in man and femininity appears in woman.

Let us now consider how the functions of yang and yin operated in the process of the creation of the universe. God's creation can be compared to the creation of a great work of art in which yang and yin are in harmony. That is, it can be said that God has been conducting a grand symphony entitled "The Creation of Heaven and Earth." God started with the "Big Bang," [6] and then created the galaxies, the solar system, and the earth. On the earth, He created plants, animals, and finally human beings. In the playing of a symphony, various yangs and yins are operating, such as high and low tones, strong and weak notes, long and short sounds, as well as yang instruments and yin instruments. In a similar way, in the process of the creation of the universe, various yangs and yins are considered to have been at work.

In our galaxy there are perhaps about 200 billion stars, arranged in a spiral. The areas of the galaxy where the stars are in dense concentration are yang, and the areas where the stars are sparse are yin. On the earth, lands and oceans were formed; the land is yang, and the ocean is yin. Mountain and valley, day and night, morning and evening, summer and winter, and so forth, are all expressions of yang and yin. Through the various yangs and yins operating in this way, the universe was created, the earth was formed, living things came into being, and humankind appeared. Human activities, also, are carried out through the operation of yangs and yins. Through the harmony between husband and wife, a family is formed. In artistic creation, harmonies between curved and straight lines, light and dark colors, big and small masses, and so on, are required.

In this way, both in the creation of the universe and in the activities of human society, yang and yin are operating in *sungsang* and *hyungsang*. The harmonious action and interaction of yang and yin is an indispensable factor in variety and development, as well as in the expression of beauty. Thus, we can come to a conclusion: God made yang and yin as the attributes of *sungsang* and *hyungsang* in order to express harmony and beauty through yang and yin.

C. Individual Image of the Individual Truth Being

In addition to the universal image of *sungsang* and *hyungsang*, and yang and yin, each individual truth being has unique attributes of its own. These unique attributes are the individual image of the individual truth being, and it goes without saying that this individual image originates from the Individual Image of the Original Image.

Individualization of Universal Image

The individual image is not an image separate from the universal image; rather, it is the universal image specialized, or individuated. Since the universal image is composed of *sungsang* and *hyungsang*, and yang and yin, the manifestation of these attributes in a different and unique way in each individual being is precisely the individual image of that particular individual being.

In the case of human beings, the personality (*sungsang*) and physical appearance (*hyungsang*) of individuals differ from one another. Furthermore, the yang and yin of the *sungsang* and the yang and yin of the *hyungsang* of individuals differ from one another. For example, joy (a yang emotion) is expressed differently by different individuals, as is sorrow (a yin emotion). The nose (a yang part of the body) differs in size and shape from individual to individual. The ear canal (a yin part of the body) also differs in size and shape from individual to individual. Thus, the individual image can be understood as an individualization of the universal image.

Specific Differences and Individual Image

Those characteristics which a group of beings has in common are called taxonomic characteristics (Merkmal), and those taxonomic characteristics peculiar to a certain specific concept are referred to as the "specific difference" of that being. For example, "human being," "dog," and "cat" are all specific concepts, and are grouped together, under the more generic concept of "animal." The specific difference then, of human beings is "reason" since it is unique to the human being. (From the viewpoint of Unification Thought, both taxonomic characteristics and specific differ-ences are connected to the individualization or the particularization of the universal image.)

The taxonomic characteristics of a particular living being are a combination of the specific differences of the different levels. Consider, for example, the case of a human being. As a living being, the human being has the specific difference of an animal rather than that of a plant. Furthermore, as an animal, the human being has the specific difference of a vertebrate rather than that of an invertebrate. As a vertebrate, the human being has the specific difference of a mammal rather than that of a fish or a reptile. As a mammal, the human being has the specific difference of a primate rather than that of a carnivore or a rodent. As a primate, the human being has the specific difference of *Hominidae* rather than that of a long-armed ape. As *Hominidae*, the human being has the specific difference of *Homo* rather than that of an ape-man. Finally, as *Homo*, the human being has the specific difference of *Homo sapiens* rather than that of a primitive man.

In this way, the taxonomic characteristics of a human being include the specific differences from seven different taxonomic levels, namely, kingdom, phylum, class, order, family, genus, and species. Upon the foundation of the specific differences from each of the seven levels, the special and unique characteristics of an individual, namely, one's individual image is established. Thus, it might be said that the individual image of a human being consists of those characteristics determined based on the set of specific differences taken from seven different levels.

In actual fact, however, the specific differences of each of these seven levels in human beings are only classifications created by biologists for the sake of convenience; God did not create human beings by successively piling up layer after layer of these various specific taxonomic differences. It is written in the Divine Principle that "Prior to creating human beings, God created the natural world by expressing partial reflections of the internal nature and external form He had conceived for human beings" (*DP*, 34). Thus, in creating the universe, what God first thought about was the complete and unified human being; yet, the human being was the last to actually be created.

Taking the image of the unitary human being, which He had envisioned in the very beginning, as the standard, God subsequently formed the conceptions of animals, plants, and minerals. In other words, in the process of conceptualization, God first developed the conception of human beings, and then that of animals, then plants, and finally minerals and heavenly bodies, proceeding downward. Then, with regard to the actual creation, the order followed was the exact opposite: God first created minerals and heavenly bodies, and then plants, animals, and finally human beings, proceeding in an upward fashion.

In conceptualizing, the way in which God visualized the conception of a human being was not by separately collecting together specific differences; rather, He immediately and comprehensively formed the conception of a human being as a complete, unitary whole, with all the relevant attributes (i.e., *sungsang* and *hyungsang*, and yang and yin).

Moreover, the conception that came to God's mind was not that of a man and a woman in the abstract, but rather that of a specific man (Adam) and a specific woman (Eve), with their concrete individual images, namely, the very ideas of Adam and Eve. Next, God subtracted, or abstracted out, certain pertinent qualities and elements from the unitary conception of the human being and transformed them, whereby He could create the conceptions of the various animals. In like fashion He subtracted certain qualities and elements from the conception of animals and transformed them, whereby He could create the conceptions of the various plants. Subsequently, He subtracted certain qualities and elements from the conception of plants and again transformed them, whereby He developed the conceptions of the various heavenly bodies and minerals.

At the animal stage, furthermore, in God's downward formation of conceptions, God started from the conception of the higher and most complex animals and, by eliminating certain qualities and elements from it, and transforming it, gradually developed, step by step, the conceptions of lower and simpler animals. The same can be said of plants. Accordingly, if one observes human beings only from the phenomenological point of view of the actual creation, one may be left with the impression that the specific differences of progressive animal orders have simply been accumulated, layer upon layer; but it is important to realize that this is just an appearance. One needs to understand God's conceptualization process, which preceded the actual creation process.

With regard to the microscopic world (e.g., molecules, atoms, and elementary particles), it should be noted that the individual image in this case is the same as the specific difference of the species to which the individual belongs. For example, every water molecule has the same shape and the same chemical character. The same thing can be said about atoms and elementary particles. Thus, in the microscopic world, the individual image is identical to the specific difference. The reason for this is that atoms and molecules exist as component elements of beings of higher levels. In the case of non-living beings, each being made of minerals (e.g., a mountain, a river, and a heavenly body) has its own individual image; with regard to the mineral elements, however, the individual image of each element is the same as its specific difference.

The same thing can be said for plants and animals. Their particular characteristics are their individual images. For example, the characteristics of a Rose of Sharon become the individual image of all Roses of

Sharon, and the characteristics of a certain kind of chicken become the individual image of all chickens of the same kind. Thus, the individual image of all things differs from species to species, whereas the individual image of a human being differs from individual person to individual person.

Individual Image and Environment

The individual image of a human being is that special and unique character that each person possesses by nature, but included in it there is also an aspect of being able to change according to one's environment. This is so because in every being—just as in the Original Image—there is an identity-maintaining aspect and a developmental aspect, in its existence and development. In other words, a human being exists and grows as the united being of an unchanging aspect and a changing aspect. Of these two, the unchanging aspect is essential, and the changing aspect is secondary. From the viewpoint of genetics, it can be said that the individual image corresponds to one's inherited hereditary traits. In the course of growing, the individual image of a human being undergoes partial changes through its continual give and receive action with the environment. That portion of one's individual image that is changed is called the "changed individual image." That portion of the individual image that is changed can be regarded, in genetic terms, as one's acquired character.

T. D. Lysenko (1898–1976) conducted experiments to transform autumn wheat into spring wheat through a process called vernalization, and claimed that the characteristics of living beings could change with the environment. Furthermore, he dismissed as mere metaphysics the genetic theories of Mendel and Morgan, according to whom there exists in living beings an unchanging character, which is inherited through genes. Lysenko ignored the unchanging aspect of living beings and emphasized only the aspect of being able to change through interaction with the environment. Lysenko's theory was received with favor by J. V. Stalin (1879–1953), so much so that in the Soviet Union the Mendelist-Morganian scholars were ostracized. Later, however, Lysenko's theory, through further experiments by scholars abroad, was found to be in error, and the Mendel-Morgan theory was reinstated as the correct one. In the end, it became evident that Lysenkoism had been a theory fabricated under the banner of the Soviet government, and had been intended simply to justify the materialist dialectic. Therefore, we can discount that point of view and confidently confirm that every thing exists as a unity of unchangeability and changeability.

With regard to one's individual image, there still remains the question of whether or not the environment determines human nature. Communism claims that the human being is a product of the environment and insists, for instance, that a leader such as V. I. Lenin (1870–1924) could have been born only in the circumstances of the Russia of his time. From the perspective of Unification Thought, however, the human being is the subject and ruler of the environment. In this view, a person who has been endowed at birth with an outstanding individual character can emerge as a leader (i.e., a subject) in order to bring the environment under control. Therefore, in the case of the Russian Revolution, it should be understood that Lenin, who was endowed at birth with an outstanding ability, appeared when the conditions inside and outside the country matured, and he led Russia to the Communist revolution, bringing the environment under control. If we understand the concept of the individual image, we can say that the environment influences only the changeable aspect of the individual image, but not the whole individual image.

II. Connected Being

A. What Is a Connected Being?

A Connected Being Seen from the Viewpoint of Structure

As stated earlier, each individual truth being contains within itself the correlative elements of subject and object centered on purpose, and these two elements are united through give and receive action. In addition, an individual truth being can also form a relationship of subject and object with other individual truth beings, whereby they can engage in give and receive action. In such a relationship, the individual truth being is called a "connected being." In other words, when an individual being which has formed an inner four position foundation enters into a relationship with another individual being to form an outer four position foundation, this individual being (an individual truth being) forms a structure which resembles the two stage structure of the Original Image, and is called a connected being.

A Connected Being Seen from the Viewpoint of Purpose

When an individual being is seen as a being with dual purposes, namely, the "purpose for the individual" and the "purpose for the whole," it can be called a connected being. Its purpose for the individual is to maintain its existence and development as an individual, and its purpose for the whole is to live for the existence and development of the whole.

As examples of dual purposes, let us consider the system of the created world, which extends from the level of elementary particles all the way up to the level of the universe. Elementary particles exist for the purpose of forming atoms, but at the same time, they maintain their own existence as elementary particles. Atoms exist for the purpose of forming molecules, but at the same time, they maintain their own existence as atoms. Molecules exist for the purpose of forming cells and matter, but at the same time they maintain their own existence as molecules. Cells exist for the purpose of forming tissues and organs, but at the same time they maintain their own existence as cells. Atoms and molecules also exist for the purpose of forming minerals, which form all material bodies, such as the earth. The earth exists for the purpose of forming the solar system, but at the same time, it maintains its own existence as the earth. The solar system exists for the purpose of forming the galaxy, but at the same time, it maintains its own existence as the solar system. The galaxy exists for the purpose of forming the universe, but at the same time, it maintains its own existence as the galaxy. Furthermore, the universe exists for the sake of humankind, but at the same time, it maintains its own existence as the universe.

Human beings are minute beings compared to the vast universe, but their value is greater than the totality of the whole universe. That is why the universe exists for the sake of human beings. In this way, all created beings have dual purposes, namely, their purpose for the individual and their purpose for the whole. Among the various purposes for the whole, which one is the highest purpose? In the created world, the highest purpose is to exist for the sake of human beings. For example, the earth has the purpose of forming the solar system, but at the same time it has the purpose of serving as the dwelling place for human beings. In the case of electrons, they revolve around the atomic nucleus in order to form an atom, but they also do this for human beings by forming all things, which exist for the sake of human beings, since things are objects of human dominion. Thus, each level of created beings—from elementary particles

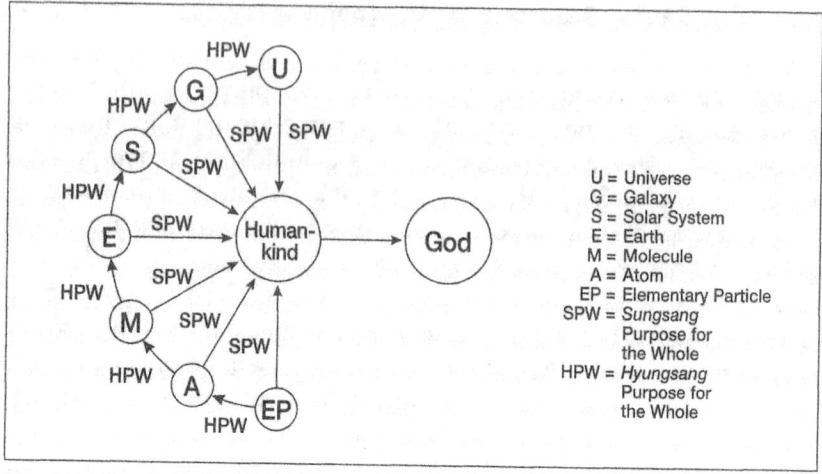

Fig. 2.2. The System of Purposes for the Whole in Created Beings

to the universe—exists both for the purpose of being part of a higher-level being and, at the same time, for the sake of humankind. The former purpose is called the *"hyungsang* purpose for the whole," and the latter purpose is called the *"sungsang* purpose for the whole."

For human beings, the purpose for the whole is to exist for the sake of God. Thus, all created beings, from elementary particles to the universe, and to human beings, exist as connected beings with dual purposes. Fig 2.2 illustrates a series of connected beings with dual purposes.

A Connected Being Seen from the Viewpoint of Relationship

We saw previously that the Original Image exists in a two-stage structure, namely, the inner four position foundation and the outer four position foundation. In the created world (including humans), all existing beings exist in a similar two-stage structure: they maintain inner four position foundations as individual truth beings, while at the same time forming outer four position foundations with other individual truth beings. Based on these inner and outer four position foundations, all existing beings are engaged in inner and outer give and receive actions. This structure is the two-stage structure of existence.

In forming an outer four position foundation, a person enters into give and receive action with other persons in six directions, namely, above and below, front and back, and right and left. Taking oneself as the center,

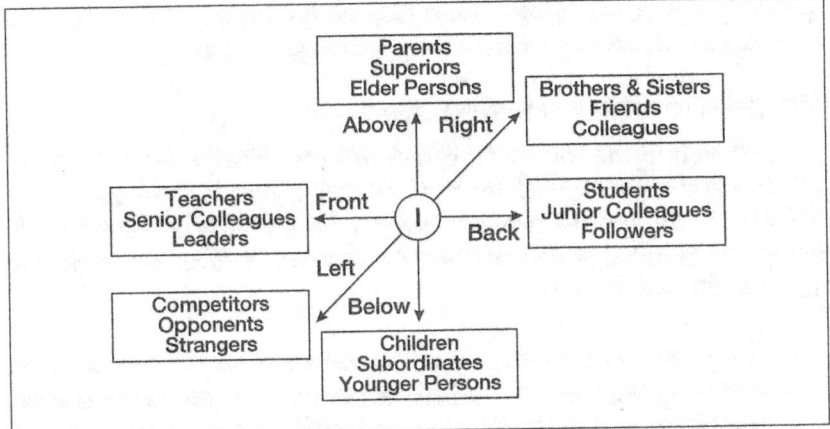

Fig. 2.3. The Six Directions of Human Relationships of a Connected Being

above there exist one's parents, superiors, and elder persons; below there exist one's children, subordinates, and younger persons; to the front, there are teachers, senior colleagues, and leaders; to the back, there are students, junior colleagues, and followers; to the right, there are brothers and sisters, intimate friends, and intimate colleagues; and to the left, there are competitors, opponents, and strangers. The original way of human life is to form harmonious relationships in all six directions. In this way, a person is related to other persons in six directions. The same thing can be said about all things as well. An individual being, related to other beings in six directions, is a connected being. The six directions of human relationships are illustrated in Fig. 2.3.

Human beings also stand in a relationship with the natural environment. They are susceptible even to the influence of the stars; that is to say, it is commonly held that cosmic rays exert a certain influence on human physiological functions. Needless to say, human beings have a close connection to minerals, plants, and animals. In this sense as well, a human being is a connected being.

A Connected Being Seen from the Viewpoint of Position

In order for an individual being to exist, it necessarily has to be engaged in subject-object relationships with other beings. Hence, an individual being exists standing either in a subject position or in an object position in relation with another being. An individual truth being with such a "position of existence" is also called a connected being. I will explain this topic more in detail when I discuss the "position of existence."

Materialist Dialectic and Interconnectedness

In relation to the connected being, one can critique the concept of "interconnectedness," which is one of the main concepts in the materialist dialectic. Stalin, for instance, emphasized the interconnectedness of all things and branded as metaphysical the position of those who regarded things as separate beings:

> Contrary to metaphysics, dialectics does not regard nature as an accidental agglomeration of things, of phenomena, unconnected with, isolated from, and independent of, each other, but as a connected and integral whole, in which things, phenomena, are organically connected with, dependent on, and determined by, each other.[7]

From the perspective of Unification Thought, all beings are created in the likeness of God's dual characteristics, and therefore they exist not only as individual truth beings, but also as connected beings, whereby they are connected, directly or indirectly, with other individual truth beings. From this perspective, we regard the universe as one huge, organic body. The materialist dialectic explains this in terms of interconnectedness. Nevertheless, the materialist dialectic merely acknowledges the interconnectedness of all things; it does not and can not offer any adequate explanation as to why things are interconnected. Furthermore, for a long time Communists asserted, on the basis of this theory of interconnectedness, that the world laborers must unite for the sake of revolution. Such an assertion is a jump in logic.

In contrast, Unification Thought maintains that each being is interconnected with other beings centering on a purpose. Interconnectedness is something inevitable because every existing being is related to other beings in six directions, above and below, front and back, and right and left. From this perspective, the entire universe can be regarded as an immense, organic body consisting of innumerable individual beings, all of which are mutually interconnected.

B. Subject and Object

I have already explained that an individual truth being has the universal image, which consists of *sungsang* and *hyungsang*, and yang and yin. *Sungsang* and *hyungsang*, and yang and yin, exist in the relationship of subject and object. An individual truth being, which is a created being, is involved in yet another type of subject and object pair besides *sungsang* and *hyungsang*, and yang and yin. This pair consists of principal element and subordinate element (or principal being and subordinate being). This situation results from the fact that the created world is temporal and spatial in nature.

For example, the relationships between parents and children in a family, between teachers and students in a school, between the sun and the earth in the solar system, and between the nucleus and the cytoplasm in a cell are neither a relationship of *sungsang* and *hyungsang* nor a relationship of yang and yin. These are relationships of principal element and subordinate element, or principal being and subordinate being.

This shows that there are three kinds of subject and object relationship in any individual truth being, namely, *sungsang* and *hyungsang*, yang and yin, and principal element (being) and subordinate element (being). All of these resemble the relationship of subject and object as seen in the dual characteristics of God.

The characteristic features of the relationship between subject and object are those of central and dependent, active and passive, dynamic and static, creative and conservative, initiating and responding, outgoing and modest, and so forth. This does not mean that a particular principal element and a particular subordinate element must have all of these characteristics at any given time; they may sometimes be in the relationship of central and dependent, sometimes in the relationship of active and passive, or outgoing and modest, and so forth. Generally speaking, the relationship between the subject and the object is that between one exercising dominion over the other and one receiving dominion from the other.

System of Individual Truth Beings in the Created World

Every existing being contains a correlative relationship of *sungsang* and *hyungsang*, yang and yin, and principal element (being) and subordinate element (being). This will be explained through a few selected examples of individual truth beings on different levels, extending from the cosmos (macrocosm) down to the smallest elementary particles (microcosm).

The cosmos, however big it may be, is nevertheless an individual truth being. It consists of the spirit world and the physical world (the earthly world). The spirit world is the invisible world, and the physical world is the visible world. These two worlds exist in a relationship of subject and object, which is the relationship between *sungsang* and *hyungsang*, as in the relationship between spirit self and physical self in a human being.

The universe (i.e., the physical world), in turn, is an individual truth being as well. The universe has a center, and around that center, about 200 billion galaxies (or nebulae) are revolving. In this particular relationship, the center of the universe is the principal element, and each galaxy is a subordinate element. These elements are in the relationship of subject and object. A galaxy, also, is an individual truth being. The galaxy in which we live, for instance, consists of a nucleus and about 200 billion stars. The galactic nucleus is the principal element, and the stars are subordinate elements; these two kinds of elements exist in the relationship of subject and object.

Our sun is one of the stars in our galaxy. The solar system, also, is an individual truth being. The solar system consists of the sun and nine planets. The sun and the planets are in the respective positions of principal element and subordinate elements, forming a relationship of subject and object. The earth, one of the planets in the solar system, is an individual truth being as well. The earth has a core, on one hand, and a surface and crust, on the other. These are the principal element (core) and the subordinate element (surface and crust), forming a relationship of subject and object.

The surface of the earth can, likewise, be regarded as an individual truth being. The earth's surface consists of natural things, and is inhabited by human beings. Human beings are the principal beings, and natural things are the subordinate beings. Human beings form nations, which are individual truth beings, consisting of a government and people, where the government is the principal element and the people collectively are the subordinate element.

A family, a unit of a nation, is also an individual truth being, consisting of parents and children, or husband and wife. Parents and children are principal and subordinate individuals, whereas husband and wife are yang and yin individuals; both of these are in the relationship of subject

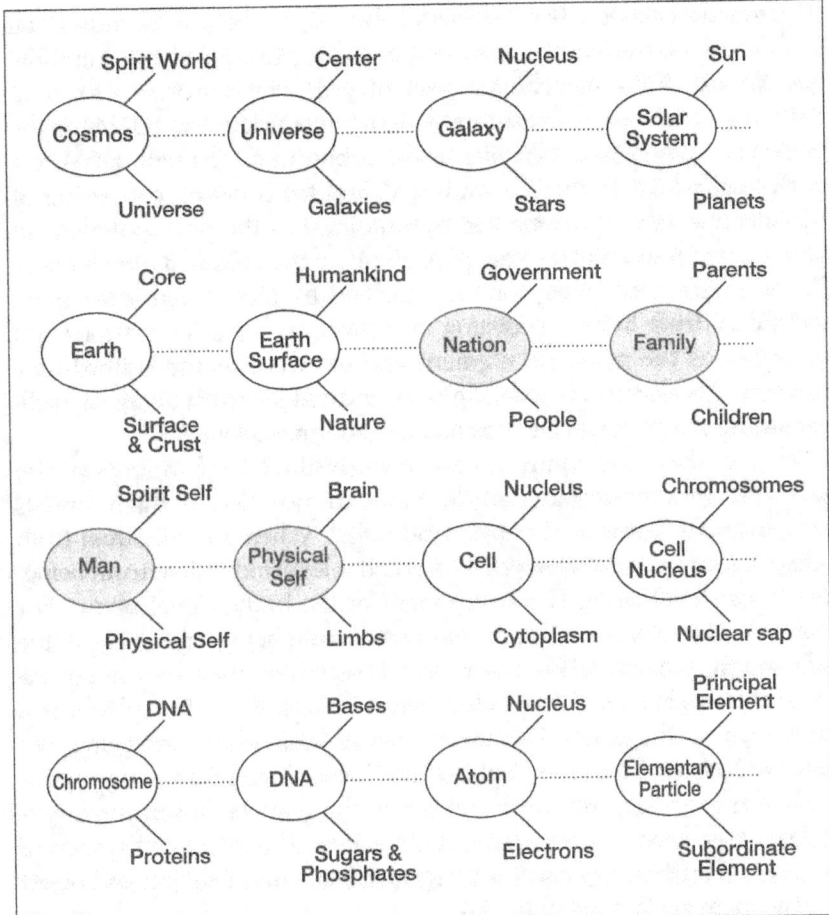

Fig. 2.4. The System of Individual Truth Beings and the Correlative Elements Within Each Individual Truth Being on Each Level

and object. An individual person, also, is an individual truth being, consisting of spirit self and physical self. In this case, spirit self and physical self are *sungsang* and *hyungsang* and they are in the relationship of subject and object.

If we now direct our attention to the physical self, it consists of principal and subordinate elements, the brain and the limbs. Within the human body (physical self), each cell is an individual truth being, consisting of a nucleus as the principal element and the cytoplasm as the subordinate element. The nucleus of the cell, in turn, is an individual truth being, consisting of chromosomes as the principal element and the nuclear sap as the subordinate element. Each chromosome, also, is an individual truth being, consisting of deoxyribonucleic acid (DNA) as the principal element and proteins as the subordinate element. DNA is a molecule, which in itself is an individual truth being, consisting of nitrogenous bases (purines and pyrimidines) as the principal element and sugar (deoxyribose) and phosphate as the subordinate element. Bases, sugar, and phosphate are formed by atoms. An atom is an individual truth being, consisting of elementary particles: protons and neutrons as the principal element and electrons as the subordinate element. An elementary particle is an individual truth being as well, consisting of a principal element and a subordinate element.

Hence, there are many levels of individual truth beings in the universe, from elementary particles to the cosmos. Each of them consists of correlative elements of subject and object. When an individual truth being is seen from the viewpoint of a higher-level individual truth being, the lower-level being is a component of the higher-level being. For example, the solar system is an individual truth being, consisting of the sun and the planets; when, however, it is seen from the viewpoint of the galaxy (a higher-level individual truth being), the solar system is a component of the galaxy. This means that an "individual truth being" is a relative concept. Moreover, "subject" and "object" are relative concepts as well. For example, the sun is subject to the planets, but in the larger galaxy, it is object to the nucleus of the galaxy. The integrated system of individual truth beings and the correlative elements of subject and object within them are laid out in fig. 2.4.

Types of Subject and Object

The concept of subject and object in Unification Thought differs in important ways from the concept of subject and object in traditional philosophy. This difference must be explained. From an epistemological perspective, a "subject" in traditional philosophy refers to that which cognizes, that is, the consciousness, or the self, whereas an "object" refers to that which is cognized. Thus, an object refers to something which exists either within the consciousness (as an idea or concept) or outside the consciousness (a thing). From an ontological perspective, or in a practical sense, a subject in traditional philosophy refers to an existing being with consciousness (i.e., a human being), whereas an object refers to a being with which the subject is faced. In short, in traditional philosophy subject and object refer to the relationship between consciousness (or the human being) and the thing with which it is faced.

In Unification Thought the concepts of subject and object carry a different meaning. These concepts refer not only to the relationship between a human being and a thing, but also to the relationship between one human being and another human being, and to that between a thing and another thing. These relationships are of four types, as follows:

(1) *Original Type*: The original type refers to a relationship that is everlasting and universal from the perspective of God's creation. Examples of such an original type are the relationships between parents and children, husband and wife, teacher and students, star and planets, cell nucleus and cytoplasm, and atomic nucleus and electrons. These relationships never change.

(2) *Temporary Type*: Relationships that last for only a limited time are of the temporary type. These relationships frequently occur in day-to-day life. One example is the relationship between a lecturer and the audience, which is established when a lecture is being given. Even in relationships of the original type, the positions are sometimes reversed to create a relationship of the temporary type. In a family, for instance, should the husband become absent or sick, the wife will temporarily take on the responsibility of her husband, and when the parents are sick or become old, the children will take on the responsibility of the parents. Such relationships can be regarded as being of the temporary type. But even in such cases, the original type does not totally disappear; thus, they are simply relationships of a temporary type based on the original type.

(3) *Alternating Type*: When the subject alternates with the object, the relationship is of the alternating type. An example of this is a dialogue between two persons: the one who speaks is the subject, and the one who listens is the object. In a dialogue, however, the person speaking and the person listening alternate with each other—hence, this is a relationship of the alternating type.

(4) *Undetermined Type*: In certain relationships, the human being freely decides which element is the subject and which is the object. These are called relationships of the undetermined type. In this case, subject and object are not determined objectively. For example, in the relationship between animals and plants, animals discharge carbon dioxide, which is

used by plants, and plants, in turn, discharge oxygen, which is used by animals. From the perspective of the flow of oxygen, plants can be regarded as the subject; but, from the perspective of the flow of carbon dioxide, animals can be regarded as the subject. The relationship of subject and object changes depending upon which being a person emphasizes, namely, according to the will of the person. The subject and object in such a case fall under the undetermined type.

Give and Receive Action

When a correlative relationship of subject and object is formed centering on a common purpose, either between two elements within a being or between one being and another being, there comes about an action of giving and receiving a certain element or force. This kind of action between subject and object is called the "give and receive action." Through this action, the entities involved maintain their existence and are able to move, change, and develop.

For example, when students enroll in a school, a correlative relationship is established between students and teachers. Based on this correlative relationship, the teachers provide instruction, and the students gain new learning. This is a give and receive action. Through this action, knowledge and techniques are transmitted, and also the students' personality and character are nurtured. Thus, students will feel grateful to the teachers and the teachers will feel satisfied with their vocation.

The following example can more concretely explain the meaning of a correlative relationship. When a man and a woman become acquainted with each other, whether by some chance opportunity or by special arrangement, they form what is called a "correlative relationship." If, subsequently, they get married, create a family, and live a life of love, they are engaging in what is called "give and receive action." The solar system is another example: the sun and the planets have existed in a correlative relationship for 4.6 billion years, giving and receiving through universal gravitation whereby the planets are revolving around the sun, and in this way they maintain the solar system.

In God, there are the identity-maintaining and the developmental aspects. In the identity-maintaining aspect, Original *Sungsang* and Original *Hyungsang* engage in give and receive action centering on Heart, forming a union or harmony. This is the identity-maintaining aspect of God, the foundation for His eternity and self-existence. Also, Original *Sungsang* and Original *Hyungsang* engage in give and receive action centering on purpose (i.e., the purpose of creation), engendering multiplied beings, or new beings. This is the developmental aspect of God. The first relationship is described as an "identity-maintaining give and receive action," and the second one is described as a "developmental give and receive action."

In a similar fashion, there are identity-maintaining give and receive actions and developmental give and receive actions in the created world, which is created in the image of God. For instance, in our galaxy give and receive action takes place between its nucleus and about 200 billion stars. The shape of our galaxy has the form of a convex lens and is constant, and all the stars perform revolving motions while keeping their own particular orbits. From this perspective, the galaxy has an unchanging aspect. On the other hand, it is said that in the beginning the galaxy revolved slowly, but as time went on, it came to revolve faster and faster. Also, it is well known that old stars die and new stars are born. Thus, the galaxy has the aspect of change as well. Hence, there are aspects of both identity-maintaining give and receive action and developmental give and receive action in the galaxy.

Furthermore, within God's *Sungsang*, the correlative elements of the Inner *Sungsang* and the Inner *Hyungsang* are in the relationship of subject and object, and they are engaged in give and receive action centering either on Heart or on purpose, whereby they form either a union or produce a new being, respectively. This is called "inner give and receive action." On the other hand, Original *Sungsang* and Original *Hyungsang* are also engaged in give and receive action centering either on Heart or on purpose, whereby they form either a union or produce a new being, respectively. This is called "outer give and receive action."

This two-stage action, namely, inner give and receive action and outer give and receive action, forms the two-stage four position foundation, which is called the "two-stage structure of God." This two-stage structure as found in God applies also to the created world. Hence, every being internally has correlative elements of subject and object within itself, and at the same time, it is externally related to other beings in a correlative relationship of subject and object. For example, in the relationship between a human being and all things, the human being, through the inner give and receive action, engages in thinking, and then, through the outer give and receive action, cognizes things and exercises dominion over them.

There are five different types of give and receive action, which I will explain next. What distinguishes one type from another is whether or not the subject and/or object possess consciousness. The five types of give and receive action are as follows:

(1) *Bi-Conscious Type*: In a classroom, a teacher is the subject and the students are the objects, and they engage in a give and receive action wherein both sides are conscious of that action. This is called a give and receive action of the bi-conscious type. The subject and the object both have will and they are both conscious, not only in cases like this, between one human being and another, but also in such cases as those between a human being and an animal, and even between one animal and another. Such relationships as these are of the bi-conscious type.

(2) *Uni-Conscious Type*: When a teacher writes words on a blackboard with chalk, a give and receive action takes place between the teacher and the chalk. In this case, the teacher acts consciously, whereas the chalk does not. One side alone (the subject) has consciousness while the other side (the object) does not. This is called a give and receive action of the uni-conscious type.

(3) *Unconscious Type*: Animals inhale the oxygen emitted by plants and exhale carbon dioxide. On the other hand, during the daytime plants absorb the carbon dioxide emitted by animals and release oxygen through photosynthesis. In this instance, animals do not consciously exhale carbon dioxide for the sake of plants, nor do plants consciously release oxygen for the sake of animals. Both sides act unconsciously in this exchanging of carbon dioxide and oxygen. Such a case in which both parties engage in a give and receive action unconsciously, even if one or both parties may have consciousness, is called a give and receive action of the unconscious type.

(4) *Heteronomous Type*: When neither the subject nor the object possesses consciousness, and both are induced heteronomously by the will of a third party to engage in a give and receive action, the relationship is called a give and receive action of the heteronomous type. For example, the sun and the earth engage, according to natural law, in give and receive action according to God's purpose of creation, even though they are not conscious of it. This is a give and receive action of the heteronomous type. In another example, the various parts of a watch engage in give and receive action with one another according to the will of the person who made the watch. Such kinds of give and receive actions are of the heteronomous type.

(5) *Contrast Type (Collation Type)*: When we human beings contrast two or more things and therein discover harmony between them, we regard them as engaging in a kind of give and receive action. This is called give and receive action of the contrast type, or collation type. In this relationship, the human observer establishes (consciously or unconsciously) one element as the subject and another as the object, contrasts them, and thus regards them, subjectively, as engaging in give and receive action.

Creation or appreciation of artwork is a typical example of a give and receive action of the contrast type, in which a human subject intentionally contrasts the objective elements. In creating a work of art, the artist adjusts and contrasts colors, shades of light, sounds, and so forth, in order to harmonize these elements. In art appreciation, the appreciator, when contemplating a work of art (a painting, a musical piece, etc.) will also contrast the various elements within the artwork in order to find harmony in them.

Give and receive action of the contrast type can also be found in the process of thinking. For example, the judgment "this flower is a rose" is made by regarding "this flower" as the subject and "a rose" as the object, and then contrasting them. In the process of cognition, contrast takes place between the sense content (such as shapes, colors, and fragrances) coming from the outside world and the prototypes (ideas) within the human subject. In Unification Epistemology, these processes are called "collation," and are instances of a give and receive action of the contrast type.

Correlatives and Opposites

As stated earlier, in each individual truth being there always exist paired elements of subject and object. These paired elements are called "correlatives." The correlative elements of subject and object form a correlative relation centering on a purpose and engage in harmonious give and receive action, forming either a union or a multiplied being. In Unification Thought, this is called the "law of give and receive action," or simply, "give and receive law." This understanding contrasts with that of the materialist dialectic, which asserts that within every being there exist "opposites," or "contradictory elements," and that things can develop only through a struggle between these opposites.

Do things exist and develop through a harmonious give and receive action between correlatives (as Unification Thought asserts), or do they exist and develop through a struggle between opposites (as the materialist dialectic asserts)? It should be noted, first, that Unification Thought and the materialist dialectic agree on one point, and that is that in every being there are always two elements. In actual development, however, the two positions are diametrically different. In order to determine which one is correct, we need only to compare the nature of the two elements in both cases. If there is a common purpose, we can say that the two elements are correlatives; if there is no common purpose between them, we must say that the two elements are opposites. Another way is to examine whether the interaction between the two elements is harmonious or conflictive. If we find the interaction to be harmonious, then it is give and receive action; if, instead, we find it to be conflictive, then it is dialectical action. Also, we can determine which one is correct if we examine the positions of the two elements; in other words, if they are different in position (subject and object) they are correlatives, and if they are equal in position (subject and subject, for example) they are opposites.

Marx asserted that things develop through the dialectic, but he only dealt with social problems, and did not cite a single example that could indicate that natural phenomena develop through the struggle of opposites. Thus, in order to compensate for this weakness in Marx's thought, Engels studied the natural sciences and compiled his conclusions in the books *Dialectics of Nature* and *Anti-Dühring*; thereby, Engels announced that he had reached the conclusion that "nature is the proof of dialectics." [8] In other words, he asserted that all natural phenomena, without exception, follow the dialectic.

If, however, one carefully examines the natural phenomena cited by Engels, one finds that what is actually occurring in those phenomena are not struggles but rather harmonious actions centered on a common purpose. A more detailed explanation of this point is given in *The End of Communism* by Sang Hun Lee,[9] and it is omitted here for lack of space. To conclude, nature can not be said to be the "proof of dialectics"; instead, nature is the "proof of give and receive action." Struggles do exist, but only among human beings in society; these struggles are a result of the human fall.

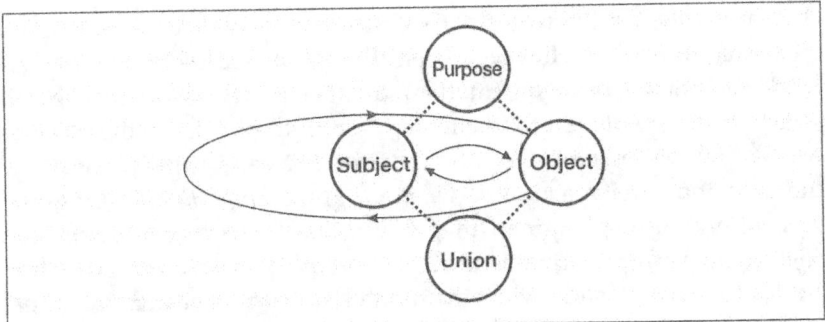

Fig. 2.5. Circular Motion Through Give and Receive Action

C. Mode of Existence

Now, I will explain the manner in which all created beings exist, that is, their mode of existence. The mode of existence of created beings is their motion in time and space. Hence, "mode of existence" is a spatio-temporal concept applicable only in the created world. Since God is the absolute being, God does not literally perform such motion. Therefore, there is no concept of a mode of existence in the Original Image. There is, however, a prototype within the Original Image, which corresponds to the mode of existence in the created world.

1. Circular Motion

When, in the created world, two elements or beings in the relationship of subject and object engage in a give and receive action, centering on a common purpose, then the result is that both union and motion appear simultaneously. Purpose itself is not an existing being, and the union is merely a state that arises as a result of give and receive action; therefore, the actual participants in the motion of give and receive action are the two elements (beings) in the roles of subject and object. The center of the give and receive action lies not in some intermediary position between the subject and the object, but within the subject itself. Accordingly, the motion of this give and receive action can not but become a subject-centered circular motion. This circular motion is illustrated in fig. 2.5. In an atom, for instance, electrons revolve around the nucleus; and, likewise, in the solar system, planets revolve around the sun.

What, then, is the reason why created beings necessarily engage in circular motion? In the world of God there exists no time or space and, therefore, no motion. However, even though in God there is no actual mode of existence, or circular motion, still there must exist in the Original Image some prototype of the circular motion that exists in the created world. This prototype is the round, harmonious and smooth nature of the give and receive action between Original *Sungsang* and Original *Hyungsang*. In the Original Image, Original *Sungsang* and Original *Hyungsang* perform harmonious give and receive action centering either on Heart or on purpose. When the round and harmonious nature of the give and receive action in God is expressed (symbolically) in terms of time and space, it becomes circular motion.

The world of created beings is the symbolic expression of God. For instance, the vastness of the ocean symbolizes the vastness of God's mind; the heat of the sun symbolizes the warmth of God's love; and the light of the sun symbolizes the brightness of God's truth. Likewise, circular motion in the created world symbolizes something in God, namely, the round and harmonious nature of the give and receive action within God. Harmonious give and receive action is the expression of love centered on Heart. In other words, circular motion symbolizes the roundness and, at the same time, the love in God. Love has no corners or angles, and is expressed in a circular form. Thus, if we were to express the Original Image in a diagram, such a diagram would be of a circular, or spherical, form.

God is formless and has no definite appearance; yet, God has the potentiality to appear in any form. In other words, God, who is formless, has a limitless number of forms. Compare this to the phenomenon of water. If placed in a rectangular container, water takes a rectangular shape; if placed in a triangular container, water takes a triangular shape; and if placed in a round container, it takes a round shape. In other words, water can take on any form, depending on its container. Therefore, it has a limitless number of forms. Of all these forms, however, the one most typical of water is the spherical form. We can know this from the fact that when a drop of water falls, it assumes a spherical form.

Similarly, God can manifest Himself in the form of waves, in the form of wind, in the form of fire, and so forth, but if we were to choose a typical form of God, it would be a spherical form. In this sense, the Original Image can be expressed in a circular or a spherical form. This is why all things, in resemblance to the Original Image, basically have a spherical form. Atoms, the earth, the moon, the sun, stars, and so on, all have a spherical form. Even plants and animals can be said to have a spherical form since the starting point of the growth of a plant is a seed, and the starting point of the growth of an animal is an egg. These have an essentially spherical form. As explained above, circular motion in all things originates from the roundness of the give and receive action in the Original Image. At the same time, it originates from the representative circular or spherical shape of the Original Image.

There is yet another reason why the motion performed when a subject and an object engage in give and receive action is circular. Circular motion is a necessary representation of the give and receive action. If the object did not revolve around the subject, but instead moved in a straight line, then the object would ultimately depart from the subject. If that were to occur, subject and object would become unable to perform give and receive action, and if they could not perform give and receive action, the created being could not exist, for it is through such give and receive action that the forces for existence, multiplication, and action come into being. Accordingly, in order for subject and object to engage in give and receive action, the object must maintain a continuous relationship with the subject—and in order for that to happen, the object must go around the subject.

2. Rotation and Revolution

Next, let me explain rotation and revolution. Any individual being engaged in circular motion is simultaneously performing two kinds of motion, namely, rotation and revolution. The reason for this is that every individual being is simultaneously both an individual truth being and a connected being. This is so because each individual being engages in internal give and receive action as well as external give and receive action. As a result of these two kinds of give and receive action, two kinds of circular motion come into being. The circular motion produced through the internal give and receive action is rotation, and the circular motion produced through the external give and receive action is revolution. For example, the earth revolves around the sun while rotating itself; an electron revolves around the atomic nucleus while rotating itself. Rotation and revolution, then, are the results of the internal and external motions of things, and the reason these two types of motion exist is that they resemble the round and harmonious nature of the inner give and receive action and the outer give and receive action within the Original Image.

Through these inner and outer give and receive actions, inner and outer four position foundations are formed centering on purpose (unlike in the Original Image, where the center can be Heart, in created beings the center is always purpose, in any kind of four position foundation). In the formation of the inner and outer four position foundations, the result is either a union or a new being. Here, let us examine the case in which the result is a union.

In the Original Image, when the result is a union, an inner identity-maintaining four position foundation and an outer identity-maintaining four position foundation are formed through the inner give and receive action and the outer give and receive action, respectively. That is the "two-stage structure of the Original Image." In resemblance to this structure, every created being forms an inner identity-maintaining four position foundation and an outer identity-maintaining four position foundation, which together constitute the "two-stage structure of existence." Give and receive action takes place on the basis of the four position foundation, and when give and receive action takes place, circular motion always appears. Accordingly, in the formation of inner and outer four position foundations, inner and outer give and receive actions take place and, at the same time, inner and outer circular motions take place. The inner circular motion is rotation, and the outer circular motion is revolution.

3. Forms of Circular Motion

In actuality, spatial circular motion can be seen, in the created world, only in astronomical bodies such as stars and planets and in elementary particles and atoms. In other cases, we do not see literal circular motion. Plants, for example, are fixed in certain positions, and animals, though they are moving, are not performing circular motion. In these cases, although the basic mode of their existence is circular motion, it has been modified to take other forms. The reason the circular motion is modified is because each created being must achieve its particular purpose of creation, that is, its purpose for the whole and its purpose for the individual. There are three categories of circular motion: basic circular motion, transformed circular motion, and spiritual circular motion.

a) Basic Circular Motion

There are two types of basic circular motion, namely, "circular motion in space" and "circular motion in time."

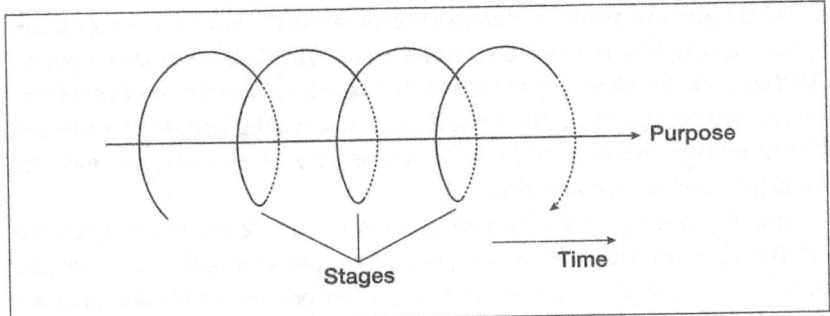

Fig. 2.6. Spiral Motion (Circular Motion in Time)

i) Circular Motion in Space

Spatial circular motion is physical, repetitive circular motion, and examples are the rotation and revolution of celestial bodies and elementary particles. These are the spatial representation of the identity-maintaining give and receive action within the Original Image. They are circular motion in the literal sense, and since they nearly always maintain the same orbit, this can be called "repetitive motion."

ii) Circular Motion in Time (Spiral Motion)

The repetition of life cycles, or the succession of generations of living beings, can also be regarded as a kind of circular motion, that is, a spiral motion. Let us consider the growth of plants. A seed puts forth a new sprout, which grows into a plant; the plant blooms, bears fruits, and produces numerous new seeds. The new seeds, greater in number than the initial one, again sprout, grow, and bear new fruits. A similar process occurs in the development of animals. A fertilized egg grows; the young are born; the young grow to maturity, engage in reproduction, and again new fertilized eggs are made. The new fertilized eggs, greater in number than the initial one, again grow; the young are born; the young grow to maturity and engage in reproduction. Thus, both plants and animals preserve their species by repeating life cycles, or life histories.

This succession of generations, intended for the preservation of the species, is a kind of circular motion, having the following characteristic features: (1) it possesses purposefulness, (2) it develops through time, and (3) it has the nature of proceeding in distinct stages. This is called a "spiral motion," and it is illustrated in fig. 2.6.

Let us consider now the significance of the fact that living beings make spiral motion, that is, the preservation and multiplication of their species. All things are the objects of joy and at the same time the objects of dominion for human beings. Thus, the preservation and multiplication of species in living beings corresponds to the succession of generations and the multiplication of human beings.

The physical self of the human being is not an eternal being. Only the spirit self, which matures on the basis of the physical self, lives eternally. When the spirit self becomes perfected, the physical self dies, and the mature spirit self goes on to live eternally in the spirit world. (Yet, because of the human fall people went to the spirit world with their spirit selves still unperfected.) The perfection of the spirit self is the realization of the purpose of creation, which means that human beings grow, perfect their individuality, get married, multiply, and have dominion over all things—in other words, they fulfill the three great blessings (Gen.1:28). Thus, human beings are created to live during a certain period of time on earth and they maintain their species through a succession of generations. Also, all living beings, which exist as objects to human beings, preserve their species through a succession of generations, and multiply in order to continue as the objects of dominion for human beings on earth. Such circular motion in time is the temporal manifestation of the developmental give and receive action within the Original Image.[10]

b) Transformed Circular Motion

There are two kinds of transformed circular motion, namely, motion with a fixed nature, and motion with an alternative nature.

i) Motion with a Fixed Nature

This refers to the situation wherein the circular motion is fixed in place in order for an existing being to achieve its specific purpose of creation. For example, a stationary radio satellite is fixed at a certain position in space for the sake of achieving its purpose. In the case of the earth where humans live, if the immeasurable atoms forming the earth were to move about randomly, then the earth would take on a more gaseous state, and humans would not be able to live on it. If the earth is to be a dwelling place for humans, the atoms that constitute it must be fixed firmly in place, united with each other in order to form solid ground. Therefore, the atoms forming the earth perform transformed circular motion (rigid chemical bonding), maintaining their fixed positions in order to form an appropriate dwelling place for human beings, in other words, to realize their purpose for the whole.

Similarly, the cells forming the tissues of living beings are positioned and fixed unitedly with respect to one another. For example, the cells forming the heart of an animal are fixed in place and united with one another, which enables the heart to contract and expand in performing its function. If the heart cells were to move about independently, the heart would not be able to perform its proper function.

ii) Motion with an Alternative Nature

In animals, instead of the cells performing circular motion, the blood and lymph circulate throughout the body, connecting the cells, thereby bringing the same result as if the cells themselves were performing circular motion. In plants, also, water and minerals are absorbed by the roots and circulate throughout the body of the plant through the vessels and tracheids of the xylem. The nutrients which have been manufactured in the leaves travel through the sieve tubes of the phloem, connecting all cells. The overall result of this is the same as if the cells themselves were making circular motion. In this way, blood and lymph, water and nutrients circulate, in place of the circular motion of cells. This is called circular motion with an alternative nature, or simply, motion with an alternative nature.

In the earth, also, there are the convective currents in the mantle, the movement of the plates (called plate tectonics), and so on, which manifest the effects of circular motion. They are also regarded as motion with an alternative nature. The circulation of goods and money in the economy are also examples of motion with an alternative nature.

c) **Spiritual Circular Motion (*Sungsang* Circular Motion)**

The give and receive action between the spirit mind and the physical mind in human beings is not a physical kind of circular motion, but rather a spiritual kind of circular motion in the sense that the physical mind responds to the desires of the spirit mind. Accordingly, this is spiritual circular motion, or circular motion on the *sungsang* level. Also, in the sense that the object behaves as the subject desires, the harmonious give and receive action between one person and another in a family or in society is circular motion on the *sungsang* level, or spiritual circular motion. For example, when parents love their children and instruct them well, the children obey their parents well. This, too, comes in the category of spiritual circular motion.

4. Growth and Developmental Motion

Development from the Viewpoint of Unification Thought

Now I will explain the concepts of growth and development in order to clarify the Unification view of development. Living beings are endowed with life. Life refers to the autonomy and dominion of the principle, or the conscious energy (in other words, the consciousness with energy) latent within living beings. The growth of living beings is guided by this life, the autonomy and dominion of the principle, which is the unity of consciousness and energy latent in living beings; thus, this motion of conscious energy is none other than the motion of life.

Autonomy is the ability to direct one's own motion without any influence from other beings. The earth revolves around the sun, but it does so by following natural law in a merely mechanical manner. Living things, however, do not just follow laws mechanically. They are able to control themselves as they grow, while coping with various kinds of situations in their environment. This is the meaning of "autonomy of the principle." On the other hand, "dominion of the principle" refers to the function or ability of exerting an influence on an existing being's surroundings. For example, when the seed of a plant is sown, a sprout emerges, a trunk grows, and leaves come out. This force of growing is the action of the autonomy of the principle. At the same time, plants have an influence on their surroundings[11]; they provide animals with oxygen, and attract bees and butterflies by blooming. This aspect is the dominion of the principle. Life, then, when viewed from the aspect of growth, is autonomy, and when viewed from the aspect of influencing its surroundings, is dominion.

The growth of living beings, due to the life inherent within them, is developmental motion. All created beings are endowed with the purpose of creation (the purpose of being created). To say that living beings are endowed with the purpose of creation means that the life force within living beings is conscious of that purpose. Accordingly, the growth of a living being is a movement aiming towards a goal (purpose) from the very beginning.

Development thus has a definite purpose, and a direction determined by its inner life force. That is to say, there is life within the seed of a plant, and it is this life which causes the seed to grow (develop) toward the goal of becoming a tree bearing fruits. Also, there is life within the fertilized egg of an animal, and it is this life which causes the egg to grow (develop) toward the goal of becoming an adult animal.

Let us now consider the particular case of the development of the universe as a whole. According to the Big Bang theory, about fifteen billion years ago the universe started out as a mass of energy, of extremely high temperature and density, all concentrated in one point. A "great" explosion took place, and the universe began to expand. After the initial explosion, the hot, swirling gases eventually cooled and condensed to form the many galaxies. In each galaxy, numerous stars came into being, some of which were surrounded by planets. One of the stars with planets was the sun, and one of its planets was the earth. Life came into being on the earth, and finally human beings appeared.

This is the essence of today's scientific view of the development of the universe. Considering this, we may ask if the development of the universe is much different from the growth (development) of living beings? And, if it is different, then how is it different? Is it simply development based on physicochemical laws? Or, is it a development of life, in the same way as living beings?

If, when considering the development of the entire universe, we look at that process over a comparatively short period of time, we may only be able to discern physicochemical laws at work. If, however, we look at that process over a much longer period of time—say, several billion years—we would be able to discern that the universe, while certainly following physicochemical laws, has yet been developing in a definite direction. This tells us that there has been a goal in the development of the universe. That goal is the appearance of human beings, who are intended to have dominion over the universe. In other words, the universe has been developing, seemingly in the expectation of the appearance of human beings. What has given this kind of direction to the development of the universe is the consciousness latent within the universe. This can be called "cosmic consciousness," or "cosmic life."

Just as in the development of a plant there is at first a seed which sprouts, grows and finally bears fruit, so too, in the development of the universe we can consider it to be the case that, in the beginning, the universe began as a seed, which has been growing until today. The human being is the ultimate fruit of the universe. Accordingly, just as bearing fruit is the goal of a plant, so also the human being was the goal of the development of the universe. It was stated earlier that growth is a phenomenon that exists only in living things, but seen from the perspective of so vast a period of time as fifteen billion years, one can realize that the entire universe has, in fact, been growing.

Communist Perspective on Development

Next, let us examine the Communist perspective on development. Development is an irreversible, purposeful movement that proceeds toward a definite goal. Yet, Communists never described development as a motion proceeding toward a goal. Communists maintain that development takes place through the contradiction inherent within a thing, and it only admits to lawfulness and necessity, denying any sense of purpose. Why do they deny purpose (or goal)? The reason is that only will or reason can establish a purpose; and if there were reason that established purpose at the beginning of the universe, that could be none other than the reason of God. From this it follows that God has established the purpose of the universe. If God were accepted, atheistic Communism would inevitably fall, which is why Communists never admitted purpose.

In contrast, Unification Thought, in addition to describing development in terms of necessity and lawfulness, asserts that there is purpose in development. This is because the motive force of development is life, and life is purposive and conscious energy. Necessity and lawfulness in development are all for the sake of the realization of this purpose. In other words, all created beings are endowed with necessity and lawfulness so that they realize their purpose, that is, the purpose of creation.

As stated in the Theory of the Original Image, within God's *Sungsang*, centering on purpose, the Inner *Sungsang* (reason) and the Inner *Hyungsang* (law) are engaged in give and receive action whereby Logos is formed. Logos is the union of reason and law. Law already existed within God's Inner *Hyungsang*, prior to His creation of the universe, and it existed for the realization of the purpose of creation. In other words, law had been prepared, from the very beginning, for the realization of purpose.

Communist materialism denies purposefulness in the development of the universe. This view implies that human beings are purposeless, born through the necessity of law. If this were the case, humans become accidental beings, without purpose. For such humans, there is no place for values or morality. A world without values or morality can not but become a world where the strong prey upon the weak and only the strong can survive.

Communist Perspective on Motion

Communists comprehend matter as "matter in motion." Friedrich Engels (1820-95) said, "*Motion is the mode of existence of matter.* Never anywhere has there been matter without motion, nor can there be···. Matter without motion is just as inconceivable as motion without matter."[12] For what purpose do Communists assert that motion is the mode of existence of matter? Their purpose is to deny the existence of God. Newton considered the universe as essentially an enormous machine and recognized God as the Being who had made the machine and had caused it to start moving. From that perspective, if we think of matter and motion as separate realities, then we must concede that motion must have derived from something other than matter itself—ultimately, by some being like God. Thus, in order to prevent such a metaphysical interpretation of motion, Communists defined motion as the mode of existence originally inherent in matter.

From the Unification Thought viewpoint, things exist and move through give and receive action between subject and object. Accordingly, motion is the mode of existence of all things. However, motion is not the mode of existence of an individual being itself, but rather it is a phenomenon that appears when subject and object engage in give and receive action. Give and receive action between subject and object is an action intended for the realization of the purpose of creation. Ultimately, then, motion exists for the realization of the purpose of creation. For example, the earth engages in give and receive actions internally and externally in order to realize its purpose of creation—that is, to provide the environment for human beings to live in—and therefore engages in rotation and revolution.

Communists assert that motion is the mode of existence of matter, but they say nothing at all about the reason why matter has such a mode of existence or about the kinds of motion it performs. Communists merely want to assert that things move through the struggle of opposites.

D. Position of Existence

Every individual being has its own place for existence. The place that a being possesses is called its "position of existence" in Unification Thought. When two individuals engage in a subject and object (namely, give and receive) relationship, there is a difference between the position of the subject and the position of the object.

Position of Existence Seen from the Viewpoint of a Connected Being

A being exists as an individual truth being and, at the same time, as a connected being. As a connected being, a being is simultaneously both in the position of object and in the position of subject. As a result, numerous beings become connected upwards and downwards, in front and back, and to the right and left, forming a system of positions, namely an orderly system. Such a system of positions of subject and object is simply a reflection of the positions of subject and object in the Original Image, which are projected into the three dimensional spatial world.

There are numerous stars in the universe which, as connected beings, engage in give and receive actions from their different respective positions, all forming an orderly system. Such order in the universe comes about through the accumulation of the two-stage structures of existence, all of which are modeled after the two-stage structure of the Original Image. As connected beings, which are beings with dual purposes, all the beings in the universe are related to each other. Hence, the universe is a giant organic body. Human beings exist in the highest position of the organic orderly system, and God exists above human beings.

Vertical Order and Horizontal Order

The order of the universe is of two kinds, namely, vertical and horizontal. An example of the vertical order of the universe is as follows. The moon (a satellite) and the earth (a planet) engage in give and receive action, with the earth as the subject and the moon as the object. The earth, in turn, engages in give and receive action with the sun (a star), forming a part of the solar system. Here the earth is the object and the sun is the subject. Next, the sun engages in give and receive action with the galactic center and, together with many other stars, forms the galaxy. Here the sun is the object, and the galactic center is the subject. Furthermore, the galaxy, in unity with many other galaxies, engages in give and receive action with

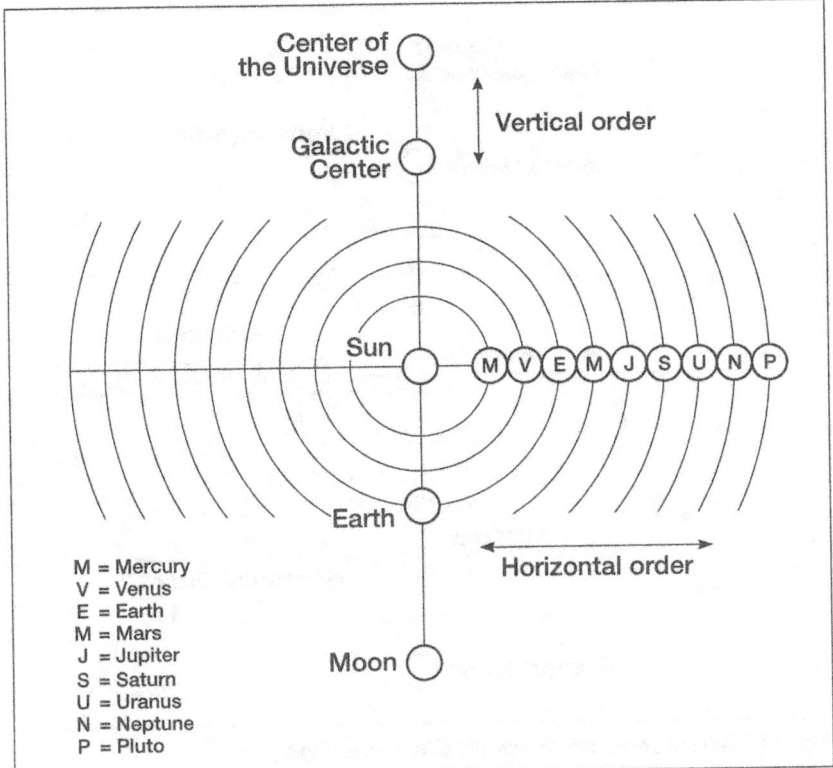

Fig. 2.7. Vertical Order and Horizontal Order in the Universe

the center of the universe, forming the universe. In this case, the galaxy is the object, and the center of the universe is the subject. This thread of connection—running from satellite to planet, to star, and to galactic center, all the way to the center of the universe—makes up the vertical order of the universe.

We can also consider the horizontal order of the universe. If we look at the nine planets of the solar system, we can see that they form an orderly, horizontal arrangement of Mercury, Venus, Earth, Mars, Jupiter, Saturn, Uranus, Neptune, and Pluto. This planetary system, centering on the sun, is an example of horizontal order in the universe. Also, this kind of horizontal order can be seen in other fixed stars which have planets. The vertical order and the horizontal order of the universe are illustrated in fig. 2.7.

146 / ONTOLOGY: A THEORY OF BEING

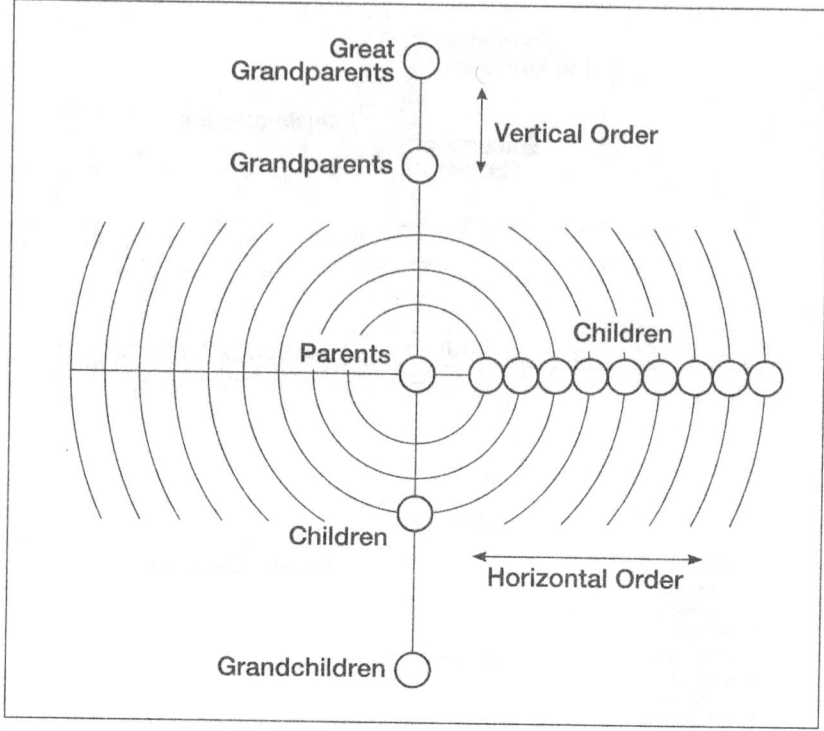

Fig. 2.8. Vertical Order and Horizontal Order in a Family

Order in the Universe and Order in the Family

A human family, in its original form, should also have had an orderly system like that of the universe. In a family there is vertical order, which consists of grandchildren, children, parents, grandparents, great grandparents, and so on; and there is horizontal order, which consists of brothers and sisters centered on the parents. The vertical order and the horizontal order of a family are illustrated in fig. 2.8.

From the perspective of composition the human being is a microcosm, or a miniature of the universe. Considered from the aspect of order, the family is a miniature of the universe, and the universe is an expanded image of the family. It is well known that in a galaxy there are innumerable planetary systems similar to the solar system, and that in the universe there are innumerable galaxies. Therefore, we can assert that the universe is an ordered assemblage of innumerable families of heavenly bodies.

In the universe, perfect order is maintained through harmonious give and receive action. In the solar system, the nine planets are engaged in give and receive action with the sun and, centering on the sun, they maintain a collective disc shape while moving along their specific individual orbits around the sun. In the Milky Way galaxy, approximately 200 billion stars are engaged in give and receive action with the galactic center, and they maintain, as a whole, the shape of a convex lens while remaining in their respective established orbits. In the universe, upwards of 200 billion galaxies are engaged in give and receive action with the center of the universe, and they maintain the harmony in the universe as a whole while yet remaining in their respective established orbits.

This order of the universe is reflected in the family. In the universe, order and peace are maintained through harmonious give and receive action (the Way of Heaven) among all heavenly bodies. Similarly, in a family order and peace are to be maintained according to the law of harmonious give and receive action, that is, the principle of love, among the family members. The principle of love is ethics, the norm of the family, which corresponds to the Way of Heaven. Due to the human fall, however, the family has lost its original state of existence. Thus, family ethics has collapsed, and family members have become disunited. Society, which is an extension of the family, has also become extremely disorderly.

E. Law of the Universe

The law that governs the universe is called the Way of Heaven. This law refers to the harmonious give and receive action between subject and object. This universal law of give and receive action has the following seven characteristics, or seven principles:

(1) *Correlativity*: Every being not only has correlative elements of subject and object within itself, but also externally forms correlative relationships of subject and object with other beings. Without such correlativity, no being can exist or develop.

(2) *Purposefulness and Centrality*: The correlative elements of subject and object always possess a common purpose and perform give and receive action centering on that purpose.

(3) *Order and Position*: Every being has its own existing position whereby it maintains a certain order.

(4) *Harmony*: The give and receive action between subject and object is spherical and harmonious, without any opposition or struggle in the relationship, for God's love is always at work there.

(5) *Individuality and Connectedness*: Every being is an individual truth being and, at the same time, exists as a connected being. Each being, while maintaining its own inherent characteristics (individuality), has certain relationships with other beings and interacts with them.

(6) *An Identity-Maintaining Nature and a Developmental Nature*: Every being maintains its own unchangeable essence (identity-maintaining nature) throughout its life, and, at the same time, has aspects that change and develop (developmental nature) as it grows and develops.

(7) *Circular Motion*: In the give and receive action between subject and object, the object revolves around the subject and performs circular motion in time and space.

It can be said that the law of the universe is the work of Logos. Logos is law, but at the same time it contains reason, based on Heart. Thus, behind Logos there is love at work. In other words, when God created the universe through Logos, the motivation of its creation was Heart and love. Therefore, Rev. Sun Myung Moon has stated that in the universe there is not only physical force, but also the power of love.

Applied to the human individual, the law of the universe manifests itself as morality, and applied to the family, it manifests itself as ethics. Hence, the law of the universe, and moral and ethical laws are in a relationship of correspondence. A society is the extension of a family. Accordingly, social ethics is to be established, in correspondence to the Way of Heaven.

When an individual being violates the law of the universe, that being becomes unable to maintain its own existence. Indeed, if one of the planets of the solar system were to deviate from its orbit, not only would that planet be unable to maintain its own existence, but great calamities in the solar system would also ensue. Likewise in a family and in a society, if people violate ethical laws, that can only give rise to destruction and disorder. Accordingly, in order to help a confused society, the most urgent task, which should be pursued before anything else, is to re-establish ethical laws.

Yet, moral and ethical theories based on traditional religions and thought systems do not have sufficiently developed logical explanations, and because of that they are not persuasive for present-day analytical and rational people. This is why these laws are all but neglected today. In contrast, in Unification Thought we provide a sound logical basis, so that moral and ethical laws may be strengthened with the understanding that they (moral and ethical laws) correspond to the law of the universe.

Thus, Unification Thought is able to provide a firm foundation for the practice of morality and ethics. This point will be explained in further detail in the chapters on "Axiology" and "Ethics."

My final point in this chapter will be an analysis, from the viewpoint of Unification Thought, of the views of Communism concerning the law of the universe. Communism is based on a dialectical view of the universe; therefore, it asserts that phenomena of motion, change, and development in the universe take place through the contradiction, or the struggle of opposites, inherent in all things. Communism also claims that in order for human society to develop, struggle (i.e., class struggle) is necessary. On this matter, Lenin wrote, "The unity (coincidence, identity, equal action) of opposites is conditional, temporary, transitory, relative. The struggle of mutually exclusive opposites is absolute, just as development and motion are absolute."[13] Lenin went so far as to definitively affirm that "Development is the 'struggle' of opposites."[14]

Communism asserts that things develop through the struggle of opposites but, in reality, we can not find such phenomena anywhere in the universe. It is only through harmony that the universe has been developing. If one observes the universe, one may find certain phenomena, such as the explosion of a star, which appear destructive. However, this is not a destructive phenomenon of the universe as a whole, but only a limited destructive phenomenon. These phenomena are not different from what happens to a living being. When the cells of a living being become old, they are replaced by new ones. Likewise, when stars become old, they disappear, and new ones are born.

At this point, someone might argue that in the animal kingdom, where the stronger prey upon the weaker, the theory of the struggle of opposites holds true. For example, snakes eat frogs, and cats eat mice. Communism attempts to justify the theory of struggle in human society on the basis of such observations of nature as these. It should be noted, however, that the struggles between snakes and frogs, or between cats and mice, are struggles between animals of different species.

In taxonomy, living beings are divided into the categories of kingdom, phylum, class, order, family, genus, and species. In the case of cats and mice, cats are in the order Carnivora, and mice are in the order Rodentia. Cats and mice are different from each other on the level of order. In the case of snakes and frogs, snakes are in the class Reptilia, and frogs are in the class Amphibia. Snakes and frogs are different from each other on the class level. In other words, when one animal preys upon another, the preying animal is usually different from its prey at least on the level of species. In nature, we do not see animals belonging to the same species fighting to the death. A cat does eat mice, but it does not eat other cats. A snake does eat frogs, but it does not eat other snakes of the same species.

In marked contrast, human beings, who all belong to the same species (namely, *Homo sapiens*), plunder from one another and kill one another. Therefore, the fact that human beings struggle with one another can not be justified on the basis of the natural phenomenon that the stronger prey upon the weaker.

As an illustration, consider the case of struggle among lions. When a new lion is placed into a pride of lions, a struggle takes place between the new lion and the leader of the pride. This kind of struggle is intended to determine which lion should be the leader—in other words, it is intended to establish order. Once a new leader is determined, the weaker lion surrenders to the stronger one and the fight is over. Such a fight is essentially different from the struggles in which human beings kill each other. Thus, we can not find any phenomenon which justifies struggles in human society.

It is only because humankind fell away from God, and became self-centered, that human beings came to plunder from, and kill, one another. Accordingly, if humankind returns to its original state, such struggles will no longer be seen in human society. Furthermore, if humankind had not fallen, people would have become the rulers of all things, and would have exercised dominion over nature through love.[15]

Thus, we come to the conclusion that, in the development of the natural world the law of contradiction, or the law of the struggle of opposites, is never at work, but rather there is the law of the harmonious give and receive action between correlatives (subject and object).

3

Theory of the Original Human Nature

The theory of the Original Human Nature is a study concerning the image of what the original human beings would have been like, if the human fall had not happened. As stated in the Theory of the Original Image and in Ontology, throughout the long period of history human beings have struggled to solve the fundamental problems in human life and the universe. Especially today, after the collapse of Communism, new confusion has appeared worldwide. Faced with such problems as the north-south problem, racism, religious conflicts, injustice, corruption, the spread of various kinds of crime due to the collapse of traditional values, and the subsequent struggles and wars, the world is in the midst of a whirlpool of confusion. These problems all can be classified into "problems of existence" and "problems of relationship." How can these problems be solved?

Throughout human history there have been people who questioned the reality of human beings, and looked for answers about the original state of human beings, which they believed, even if vaguely, to exist. They were religionists and philosophers. They seriously grappled with the question, "What is the human being?" and looked for the way to recover the original way of life.

Gautama Buddha, who was born in the middle of the fifth century BC in the Kapilavastu castle, now in Nepal, spent several years of his life practicing strict asceticism, and finally immersed himself in deep meditation. As a result, he came to realize that human beings originally possessed Buddhahood, but that through ignorance, came to be bound by worldly desires, and fell into suffering. Buddha taught that the way to recover one's original nature is through a life of spiritual discipline.

Jesus inquired deeply into the problems of human life prior to starting his public ministry at the age of thirty, and he taught that human beings are sinners and that everyone must be born again by believing in the Son of God, that is, in Jesus himself. He proclaimed to the Jewish people, "Repent, for the kingdom of heaven is at hand" (Matt. 4:17). He traveled around Palestine, spreading his teachings, but he was unable to move the hearts of the politicians and religionists who were in power and, in the end, he was crucified.

Socrates observed the decadent chaos of the polis (city-state), and taught that the true way of human life is to love true knowledge. He encouraged people to "know thyself," to make an effort to bring one's inner self into the light. For Plato, the supreme ideal of human life is to recognize the idea of the Good. For Aristotle, reason is what makes a person human. He said that virtue is best realized in the communal life of the polis, and that the human being is a social animal (or *polis*-animal). Greek philosophers, generally speaking, held the view that reason is the essence of human nature, and that if a person's reason is allowed to operate fully, that person will become an ideal human being.

During the Middle Ages of Western society, Christianity reigned over the human spirit. The Christian view of human nature at the time was that human beings are sinful and can be saved only by believing in Jesus. In this view, reason was regarded as ineffective. In the modern period, however, currents of philosophy that emphasize human reason have again come to appear.

Descartes considered human beings to be rational beings, and said that correct knowledge can be obtained only by reason. He coined the well-known proposition "*Cogito, ergo sum*" (I think, therefore I am).

Kant claimed that human beings are persons of character who obey the inner voice of moral obligation, ordered by practical reason, and he argued that human beings should live according to their reason, without succumbing to any temptations or desires.

Hegel, too, regarded human beings as rational beings. According to him, history is the process of the self-realization of reason in the world. Freedom, the essence of reason, was to be realized along with the development of history. According to Hegel's theory, human beings and the world should have become rational with the establishment of the modern state (i.e., the rational state). In reality, however, people still remain deprived of their human nature just as they always had been, and the world has continued to be as irrational as it was before.

Kierkegaard opposed extreme types of rationalism such as that offered by Hegel. Kierkegaard did not agree that humankind would become increasingly rational as the world progresses, as Hegel had claimed. In actual society, he said, human beings are no more than average people, whose true nature had been lost. Accordingly, only when a person carves out life independently as an individual, apart from the public, can that person's true human nature be regained. Thus, the conceptual framework for dealing with people in actual society, who have lost their original nature, and for seeking to restore human nature independently, was subsequently developed as the thought of existentialism. This will be further explained later in this chapter.

Feuerbach, in opposition to Hegel's rationalism, regarded the human being as a sensuous being. According to Feuerbach, humans are species-beings possessing reason, will and heart (love), which is their species-essence, but they have alienated themselves from their species-essence, objectified it, and have come to revere it as God. Therein, he argued, lay the loss of human nature. Thus, Feuerbach asserted that human beings must recover their original human nature, and that this can only be done through denying religion.

Departing from Hegel's idea of actualizing freedom, Karl Marx called for the true liberation of human beings. In the early capitalist society of Marx's time, the lives of laborers were indeed miserable. They were forced to endure long hours of labor, and were given wages that could barely sustain their lives. Disease and crime were rampant among laborers, who were deprived of their human nature. In contrast, Marx said capitalists were living in great affluence gained from their merciless exploitation and oppression of laborers. In his view, the capitalists themselves were also deprived of their own original human nature.

Determined to liberate humankind, Marx first adopted Feuerbach's humanism as the way to restore human nature; later, however, he came to realize that human beings were not only species-beings but also social, material, and historical beings engaged in productive activity. This led him to the view that the essence of humankind is the freedom of labor; however, in capitalist society, laborers were deprived of all the products of their labor, and they labored not by their own will, but by the will of the capitalists. Therein, precisely, lay the laborers' loss of human nature, according to Marx.

Thus, Marx concluded that in order to liberate laborers, what must be done is to overthrow capitalist society, wherein laborers are exploited. When such liberation occurred, capitalists could also regain their own human nature, Marx thought. Furthermore, based on the materialist view, Marx concluded that human consciousness is determined by the relations of production, which are the basis of society, and that the capitalistic economic system must be changed violently by force. Nevertheless, the Communist countries, in which revolutions took place in accordance with Marx's theory, have become dictatorial societies wherein freedom is suppressed, and human nature is violated and neglected. Those are the societies in which people have increasingly been losing their original nature. This implies that Marx made a great error in his understanding of the cause of, and in his method for solving the problem of, human alienation.

Human alienation, however, is not the problem of Communist society alone. In capitalist society as well, individualism and materialism are rampant, and a self-centered way of thinking—whereby people think they are permitted to do anything they please—has become pervasive. As a result, in capitalist society, too, human nature is increasingly being lost.

Max Scheler (1874–1928), who considered anthropology to be the foundation of all studies, classified human beings into three categories in his *Philosophical Perspective*: the intellectual person (*Homo sapiens*), the worker who uses symbols and tools (*Homo faber*), and the religious person (*Homo religiosus*). There were other views, also, about the human being advocated by other thinkers: the economic man (*Homo economicus*), the liberal man (*Homo liberalis*), the national man (*Homo nationalis*), and so on. None of these views of the human being, however, has touched on the essence of being human.

In this way, throughout human history numerous religious people and philosophers have attempted to find answers to the questions of what the human being is, and what human life is. Yet, their efforts have never been completely successful. Therefore, many people, who strive diligently to live correctly, but still can not find the meaning of human life, become pessimistic. In the Orient, for example, sincere young persons like Yoon Shim-dok of Korea and Misao Fujimura of Japan are among those persons and tragically, they became so desperate as to commit suicide.

One person who has devoted his entire life to providing fundamental solutions to such unresolved questions in human history is Rev. Sun Myung Moon, whose thought is contained in this book. He has proclaimed, as is revealed in the Divine Principle, that originally human beings are children of God, even though, having lost their original nature, they have become miserable.

Human beings were created in the image of God, but due to the fall of the first human ancestors they have become separated from God. They can restore their original nature, however, by living in accordance with God's Word, thus coming to receive God's love. In this chapter, the problems of the human fall and the way to restore the original human nature will not be discussed (these topics are dealt with in the Human Fall and in the Principle of Restoration of the Divine Principle); our focus here will be on describing the original human nature itself.

From the original standpoint, each human being exists as a being with Divine Image, which means we resemble the Image of God, and as a being with Divine Character, which means we embody the character of God. We are also beings occupying a certain position, which means we assume positions taking after the subject-object relationship in the Original Image. Each of these characteristics will be discussed below.

I. A Being with Divine Image

In the Original Image (God), there are the Universal Image, which consists of *Sungsang* and *Hyungsang*, and Yang and Yin, and the Individual Image. Resembling the Original Image, an original human being possesses the universal image of *sungsang* and *hyungsang*, and yang and yin, and also an individual image. Such a being is called a "being with Divine Image." First, we will examine the aspect of *sungsang* and *hyungsang*.

A. A United Being of *Sungsang* and *Hyungsang*

The resemblance of a human being to God's *Sungsang* and *Hyungsang* means that a human being is a dual being of mind and body, namely, a united being of *sungsang* and *hyungsang*. There are four kinds of *sungsang* and *hyungsang* in a human being. First, each person is an integration of the universe, or the encapsulation of all the elements of the universe. Hence every person has all the *sungsang* elements of animals, plants, and minerals, in his or her *sungsang*, and all the *hyungsang* elements of animals, plants, and minerals, in his or her *hyungsang*. Second, each person is a dual being of spirit self and physical self. Third, each person is a united being of mind and body. Finally, each person is a being with a dual mind consisting of the united spirit mind and physical mind.

Now, when we consider a human being from the perspective of having lost the original human nature, the relationship between the spirit mind and the physical mind (the fourth kind of *sungsang* and *hyungsang* mentioned above) is especially important. Thus, a "united being of *sungsang* and *hyungsang*" refers to a "united being of spirit mind and physical mind." I can explain the relationship between spirit mind and physical mind as that between *sungsang* and *hyungsang*, in spite of the fact that both spirit mind and physical mind belong to the mind. The reason is that the spirit mind is the mind of the spirit self (*sungsang*) and the physical mind is the mind of the physical self (*hyungsang*), and, therefore, the relationship between the spirit mind and the physical mind is the same as the relationship between the spirit self and the physical self. Next, let us consider the functions of the spirit mind and the physical mind.

The function of the spirit mind is to guide us in pursuit of a life of truth, goodness, beauty, and love, namely, a life of value. Love is the origin of life and at the same time the foundation for truth, goodness, and beauty. Therefore, a life of truth, goodness and beauty, centered on love is a life of value. A life of value includes the aspect of pursuing one's own joy by seeking values for oneself; nevertheless, the more essential aspect of a life of value is the effort to please others through realizing values. Therefore, a life of value is a life of love, of living for the sake of others, namely, a life of love in which one lives for the sake of the family, tribe, nation, humankind, and ultimately for God. In contrast, the function of the physical mind is to guide us in pursuit of a life of food, clothing, shelter, and sex, namely, a material life. Material life is a life centered on the individual.

In the original order of things, the spirit mind and the physical mind exist in the relationship of subject and object, since the spirit self is subject and the physical self is object. Accordingly, the physical mind should be subservient to the spirit mind. The union of the spirit mind and the physical mind constitutes the "human mind." The human mind in which the spirit mind functions as subject and the physical mind as object is called the "original mind." That the physical mind obeys the spirit mind means that a life of values (namely, a life of pursuing and realizing values) should be given priority and a material life (a life of pursuing material satisfaction) secondary. This means that a life of truth, goodness, beauty, and love is the ultimate purpose, or goal, and a life of food, clothing, shelter, and sex serves as the means to achieving that goal. Once the physical mind obeys well the spirit mind and fulfills its proper function, the spirit self and the physical self can resonate well with each other. This is the state in which one's human character is perfected. This is the way in which human beings should originally have lived.

Due to the human fall, however, human beings failed to actualize the original relationship between the spirit mind and the physical mind. As a result, the physical mind, which should have functioned in a subservient position, came instead to stand in the subject position; and the spirit mind, which should have been in the subject position, came to stand in an object position. As a result, a life of food, clothing, shelter, and sex became people's primary objective, whereas a life of truth, goodness, beauty, and love became no more than a means to that end. Love for others and deeds of truth, goodness, and beauty came to be carried out for such purposes as one's gaining wealth and obtaining position. This does not mean that there are no values in the fallen world: values do exist there, but in many cases these values have meaning only in the context of a self-centered, material life. The reason for this is that the physical mind has become the subject, and the spirit mind has become the object.

Thus, in the actual life of human beings the original relationship between the spirit mind and the physical mind has been reversed. Therefore, in order to recover the original state of human life, this relationship must be returned to its original state. This is the reason why human beings should necessarily lead a life of spiritual discipline, and why, throughout history, the various religions of the world have taught and encouraged people to win victory in their battle against their own selves.

Confucius, for instance, spoke of a "return to the observance of the rites through overcoming the self." Jesus said, "If any man would come after me, let him deny himself and take up his cross and follow me. For whoever would save his life will lose it, and whoever loses his life for my sake will find it" (Matt. 16:24-25), and "Man shall not live by bread alone, but by every word that proceeds from the mouth of God" (Matt. 4:4). In order to achieve a victory over themselves, people have often chosen a monastic way of life, which includes such practices as asceticism, fasting and vigils.

Thus, unity between the spirit mind and the physical mind refers to a way of life in which one places priority on living a life of truth, goodness, and beauty, and makes the life of food, clothing and shelter secondary, through having the physical mind subservient to the spirit mind. However, due to the fall, human beings have come to lead a self-centered, material life in which their physical mind dominates their spirit mind, and it is from this that all the pains, suffering, and unhappiness of human beings have come into being.

The original mind, in which spirit mind and physical mind are united through give and receive action, resembles the inner four position foundation within God's *Sungsang*. The primary function of the original mind is to guide us in living a life of love, pursuing the values of truth, goodness, and beauty based on the spirit mind. Thus, the human being can be characterized, fundamentally, as *Homo amans*, or a loving person. A life of value refers to a true life, a moral and ethical life, and an artistic life. The secondary function of the original mind is to guide us in living a life of food, clothing and shelter, namely a material life, based on the physical mind.

B. A Harmonious Being of Yang and Yin

Yang and yin in the Theory of the Original Human Nature refer to a husband and wife as a yang substantial being and a yin substantial being, respectively. The problems of how a husband and wife should live and what a family should be like have been important issues since ancient times. Animals, plants, and minerals all exist and multiply through the union between yang and yin. Yet, to regard the union between yang and yin in human beings, namely, the union between husband and wife, simply as a physical union would be equivalent to regarding it simply as a biological union. In advanced nations today, men and women easily get married and easily get divorced; as a result, the sacredness and eternal character of marriage are being lost. This is not the original way for the relationship of husband and wife.

No satisfactory answers have yet been given to such questions as why a man and woman exist or for what purpose they get married. Hence, people many times prefer not to get married at all. To these problems, Unification Thought offers clear solutions.

First, a husband and wife each, originally, represents one of God's dual characteristics of Yang and Yin; accordingly, their conjugal union signifies the manifestation of God. When a husband and wife love each other horizontally, centering on God, His vertical love dwells there, and life is created through the multiplication of love.

Second, the union of a husband and wife represents the final stage of God's creation of the universe; therefore, the unity of husband and wife signifies the completion of the creation of the universe. If Adam and Eve had not fallen away from God, the creation of the universe would have been completed upon the occasion of their perfection. Since Adam and Eve did not perfect themselves, however, the creation of the universe was never completed. For that reason, God has been conducting the dispensation of re-creation. To re-create fallen human beings means to lead them to become perfected individuals, and further to become perfected husband and wife couples. Human beings were created to be the rulers of all things, but neither a man alone nor a woman alone can become a ruler. Only by being perfected as a couple, that is, as a husband and wife, can they become the rulers of all things. Only then will the creation of the universe be completed.

Third, since a husband and wife each, originally, represents one half of humankind, their union signifies the unity of humankind. To explain further, the husband represents all the men of humankind, and the wife represents all the women of humankind. The population of the world today is over six billion people. Therefore, a husband and wife each possesses the value of representing over three billion people.

Fourth, a husband and wife each, originally, represents one half of the family; therefore, their union signifies the perfection of the family. The husband represents all the men and the wife represents all the women of the family.

From the above perspective, that a husband and wife love each other signifies the manifestation of God in their family, the completion of the universe, the unity of humankind, and the perfection of the family. We can see that the union of a husband and wife is, indeed, a sacred and precious union.[1]

The harmony of a husband and wife is accomplished through the formation of the family four position foundation. The formation of the family four position foundation refers to the completion of the second blessing given to human beings by God when He created them. This is achieved when a husband and wife, who have perfected their personalities, centering on God, establish a correlative standard and engage in give and receive action of love and beauty. The unity of the husband and wife resembles the harmony of subject and object within the Original Image; in other words, it resembles the identity-maintaining four position foundation within the Original Image, while the multiplication of children by a husband and wife resembles God's creation of human beings; in other words, it resembles the developmental four position foundation within the Original Image. Through these accomplishments, a husband and wife realize harmony, while living in accordance with their original mind.

When one lives fully in accordance with one's original mind one resembles the inner four position foundation within the Original Image, and when he or she lives in complete harmony with another person they come to resemble the outer four position foundation within the Original Image. When a man and woman grow and mature as persons of character, resembling the Original Image, and then marry and perform a give and receive action of love, centering on the purpose of creation, God's love dwells in them. Thus, a family is the place where the horizontal love of a husband and wife and the vertical love of God are completely united. When such families, which are based on God's love, converge to form a society, then a nation, and then a world, this will be the Kingdom of Heaven on earth, a world wherein God's ideal of creation has been fulfilled.

The world in which God's ideal of creation is realized is a world of love that has been realized through the original order. Here, let me explain about order and love. A human being is a miniature of the universe, but so too, is the family. More specifically, a human being is a miniature of the universe seen from the viewpoint of constituent elements; in other words, a human being is the integration of all the elements of the universe. On the other hand, a family is a miniature of the universe, seen from the viewpoint of order.

To say that the family is a miniature of the universe in terms of order means to say that just as there is vertical and horizontal order in the universe, so too there is vertical and horizontal order in a family, only in a more compact form. Vertical order in a family refers to the orderly positions of grandparents, parents, children, grandchildren, and so on, and horizontal order in a family refers to the orderly positions of husband and wife, and brothers and sisters. Love is realized through such order. Thus, there is a vertical love and a horizontal love. Vertical love refers to the downward flow of love from parents toward children, and the upward love from children toward their parents. Horizontal love refers to the love between husband and wife, and the love between brothers and sisters.

Based on these forms of love, family ethics, which is the foundation for both vertical value and horizontal value, can be realized. Vertical value refers to the affection of parents toward their children, and the filial piety of children toward their parents. Horizontal value refers to the conjugal harmony between husband and wife, and friendship among brothers and sisters. Thus, ethics is the norm of behavior that is to be observed by each member of the family. (The details will be discussed later in the Theory of Ethics.) By extending family ethics to a society, an enterprise, or a school, social ethics, business ethics, and school ethics can, in turn, be established. Love for one's neighbors, love for one's nation, love for one's enemy, the conservation movement, and so on, all will be based on family ethics.

In sum, if we were to describe an original human being in one word, it would be that of a person of love (*Homo amans*). Due to the fall, however, Adam and Eve failed to perfect their personalities. Hence, they could not become the husband and wife that they should originally have become. They could not become united, centering on God's love, and so they lost God. Thus, until today, the creation of the universe has remained unfinished.

Today, family problems and social problems abound everywhere. The cause of all of these problems is due to the fact that husband and wife do not have a proper relationship. This is why families break down, societies are in disarray, nations become disorderly, and the world is chaotic. Therefore, for husband and wife to harmonize and unite through conjugal love is an indispensable prerequisite for world unity. Stated succinctly, the harmonious union of husband and wife is a key to solving social and world problems.

C. A Being of Individuality

In creating the universe, God first envisioned the image of a perfected human being, and then, with that image as the standard, He created all things as substantial objects. Accordingly, all things are individual beings that symbolically resemble the Original Image of God, the causal being, while human beings are individual beings that directly resemble the Original Image. An individual being refers to an individual truth being that resembles the individual image in the Original Image.

An individual truth being refers to an individual being that has the universal image and the individual image. When we emphasize the individuality of the individual truth being, we call it a "being of individuality." The individual image of a human being is, unlike that in the case of animals and plants, peculiar to each individual person. That is the reason why the faces and characteristics of human beings are clearly distinguishable from one another. Thus, in the case of animals and plants, the individual image differs according to each species, while in the case of human beings, the individual image differs according to each individual person.

God endowed each human being with such a particular individual image so that He might obtain, from him or her, a unique, stimulating joy. Therefore, a human being is a being of supreme value who gives supreme joy to God through his or her unique individuality. This individual image is another aspect of the original human nature, and it is manifested as unique human characteristics in three aspects as follows.

The first manifestation of human individuality is the uniqueness in a person's appearance; though there are over six billion people in the world, no two individuals have exactly the same face. The second manifestation is in behavior, which is different from person to person. If we regard appearance as the unique characteristic feature of one's *hyungsang*, then one's behavior can be regarded as the unique characteristic feature of one's *sungsang*, because behavior is a direct manifestation of the mind. The third manifestation is creative activity. Not only artistic creation, but any activity in which one's creativity is expressed is included in the concept of creation. This creative expression will differ from person to person. In this sense, if one lives one day to its fullest, expressing his or her creativity in everything they do, the footprints of that day become a work of art. Furthermore, the footprints of one's entire life course become a life work of art.

Hence, God feels pleased when looking at the face, behavior, and creative activity of each human being with original human nature. That God becomes pleased by looking at each human being means that he or she gives unique beauty to God through his or her appearance, behavior, and creative activity. That is the beauty of a person's individuality, which includes the beauty of appearance, the beauty of behavior, and the beauty of creative activity.

When parents look at their children, they perceive each child with his or her character as so beautiful and lovely, since children are the manifestation of their parents. In the same way, when God looks at human beings, He feels that the appearance, behavior, and creative activity of each human being is so beautiful and lovely, and He becomes pleased. Human indi-viduality originates from God, namely, it is God-given; therefore, it is very precious. This is why we should pay people the highest regard, and offer our utmost respect to their individuality.

Because of the human fall human individualities have largely been crushed or ignored, and human rights trampled upon, until today. This has been especially true in dictatorial societies. The paramount example of this is society under Communist rule. The reason for this is that Communism denigrates human individuality, regarding it as no more than a product of the environment—a viewpoint derived from materialism. In contrast, humanism put emphasis on the importance of human individuality. However, humanism had no philosophical answer as to why human individuality must be respected; therefore, humanism could not contend with Communism, which is an influential philosophy.

In this respect, Unification Thought offers a clear and much-needed theological and philosophical foundation. Viewed from the perspective of Unification Thought, human individuality is neither something accidental nor a product of the environment; rather, it is derived from the Individual Image of God. In other words, it is something that comes from God and, therefore, is very precious.

II. A Being with Divine Character

The human being resembles the Divine Character of God. God's Divine Character includes omniscience, omnipotence, heart (love), omnipresence, life, truth, goodness, beauty, righteousness, logos, creativity, and so on. Among these, the three most representative characters will be addressed here, as they are especially important for the solution of actual problems. These characters are heart, logos and creativity. Thus, the human being who resembles these three Divine Characters is a being of heart, logos, and creativity. These will be explained in the following section.

A. A Being of Heart

As explained in the Theory of the Original Image, Heart (*Shimjung*) is the "emotional impulse to seek joy through love." It is the "source of love," the "emotional impulse that can not but love," and the core of the Original Image. Thus, Heart is the core of *Sungsang*, and therefore the core of God's personality. Jesus said, "You must be perfect as your heavenly Father is perfect" (Matt. 5:18). In other words, Jesus taught that human beings should reflect God's personality centered on God's Heart.

In human beings as well, heart is the core of the personality. Accordingly, the perfection of one's personality becomes possible only when one experiences the Heart of God. A person who has perfected his or her character by experiencing the Heart of God is, indeed, a being of heart.

When people continuously experience God's Heart, they eventually come to inherit God's Heart completely. Such people naturally come to feel like loving everyone and everything. Not to do so would cause their heart to feel a great deal of pain. Fallen people find it difficult to love others, but once they become one with God's Heart, their life as a whole is transformed into one of love. Also, if love is present, those who have many possessions can not but want to share with those who have less. This is because love is not self-centered. Consequently, the gap between the haves and have-nots, between the rich and the poor, namely, exploitation in the world, will naturally disappear. Such a phenomenon is manifested due to the equalizing function of love. That human beings are beings of heart means that they live a life of love. Therefore, one can conclude that the human being is *Homo amans*, a loving person, or a person of love.

Heart is the core of the human personality. Therefore, the fact that human beings are beings of heart means that they are beings of personality. Such a person's spirit mind and physical mind engage in harmonious give and receive action centering on heart, and their faculties of intellect, emotion, and will are all equally developed in a balanced way, centering on heart.

In a fallen person, the functioning of the spirit mind is often very weak and is dominated by the functioning of the physical mind. Also, in many cases a person may have a well-developed faculty of reason (intellectual ability) but lack the emotional maturity, or sufficient will power to do what is good or right. On the other hand, once a person is able to inherit God's Heart and become a being of heart, then that person's intellect, emotion, and will can develop in a well-balanced manner, and their spirit mind will have the power to take dominion over their physical mind, whereby they can properly engage in harmonious give and receive action.

Furthermore, as the core of *sungsang*, heart is the motivating force that stimulates or empowers the faculties of intellect, emotion, and will to seek the values of truth, beauty, and goodness, respectively. Intellect is the faculty to cognize, and it pursues the value of truth; emotion is the faculty to feel joy, anger, sorrow, happiness, and so forth, and it pursues the value of beauty; and will is the faculty to determine one's mind, and it pursues the value of goodness. Originally, all three faculties should function with heart as their primary motivation. When one pursues truth through intellectual activity, the result will be the knowledge of science, philosophy, and so on. When one pursues beauty through emotional activity, the result will be art. When one pursues goodness through volitional activity, the result will be morality, ethics, and so on.

Politics, economics, law, media, sports, etc. are also the results of intellectual, emotional, and volitional activities. Accordingly, heart becomes the driving force behind all cultural activities based on intellect, emotion and will. Particularly, it becomes the driving force of artistic activities. The totality of these intellectual, emotional, and volitional activities is culture. In the original world, persons of heart (persons of love) play the main role in cultural activities. This is illustrated in fig. 3.1.

In this way, heart is the driving force behind all cultural activities. Therefore, the culture which human beings should originally have actualized would be a culture of heart. Heart is the essence of what a true

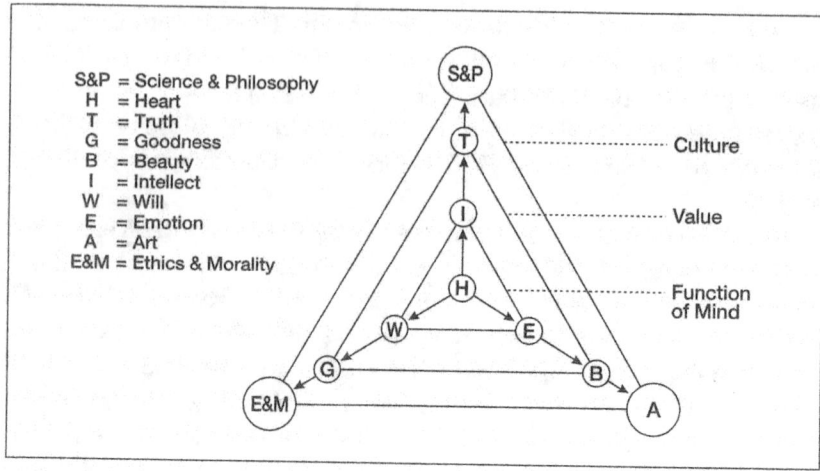

Fig. 3.1. The Relationship between Mind, Value, and Culture, centered on Heart

culture should be. The culture of heart, which God originally intended to realize through Adam, would have been the "Adam culture." Due to Adam's fall, however, a culture of heart was not realized; instead, until today cultures based on self-centeredness, or cultures in which the intellect, emotion, and will are separated from one another, have been established.

For example, in economic activities, in many cases, making money has, until today, been considered as the supreme purpose. In the original world, however, if someone were to live in isolated affluence while others lived in poverty, that person could never live comfortably, but would feel stricken by pain in his or her heart. Thus, those who earned a great deal of money would naturally want to share it with their neighbors or with society. In other words, people would feel like actualizing God's love through their economic activities. Not only in the economy, but also in other fields, people would want to actualize God's love. Thus, the culture of heart, or culture of love, will certainly be established, wherein intellectual, emotional and volitional activities will be united, centering on love. Hence, a culture of love is a unified culture.

To date, humankind has tried in many different ways to actualize the true culture, but all attempts ended in failure. The reality that, in human history various cultures have aisen and declined, illustrates this fact. The reason for this is that people did not understand what a true culture is like. The Great Proletarian Cultural Revolution in China is one example. The leaders of that revolution attempted to build a culture based on labor, in accordance with the materialist dialectic, but their efforts resulted only in the oppression of human nature and the delay of modernization. The true culture is a culture centered on heart. The New Cultural Revolution advocated by Rev. Sun Myung Moon aims precisely at the establishment of the culture of heart.

At this point, it may be opportune to elaborate on the concepts of culture and civilization. The sum total of the results of intellectual, emotional, and volitional activities, when considered from their material or external aspects, is called, "civilization"; and when those results are considered from their spiritual or internal aspects (especially in religion, art, and so on), they are called "culture." Since it is difficult to clearly distinguish the spiritual aspect from the material, however, these two terms are generally used with the same meaning. Therefore, in Unification Thought as well, culture and civilization are often used interchangeably.

B. A Being of Logos

As explained in the Theory of the Original Image, within the Original Image, Logos refers to a product or a new being appearing through inner give and receive action, centering on the purpose of creation. Here, the purpose of creation is based on Heart; therefore, Logos is based on Heart.

The universe was created through Logos and performs its movements in accordance with Logos; in other words, the universe is supported by Logos. Human beings also were created through Logos, and their lives should be in complete accordance with Logos. Thus, the human being is a being of logos.

Logos came into being within the *Sungsang* of the Original Image through the give and receive action between the Inner *Sungsang* and Inner *Hyungsang*, centered on purpose. Since "reason" plays a particularly important role in the Inner *Sungsang*, and "law" plays an equally important role in the Inner *Hyungsang*, Logos is referred to as "reason-law," the unity of reason and law. Thus, a human being, as a being of logos, is a being of reason-law. Since the characteristic feature of reason is freedom and the characteristic feature of law is necessity, a being of logos refers to a being in which freedom and necessity are united. This means that human beings are both normative beings, living according to laws (or norms), and rational beings, behaving according to their free will.

It is commonly held today that since human beings are free, they should not be restricted by any laws or norms. True freedom, however, consists in obeying certain laws—or, more precisely—in willingly observing certain laws. People may think that "freedom" allows them to ignore laws, but this becomes license, rather than freedom, and results in nothing but chaos and destruction. For example, a train, as long as it remains on its tracks, can run rapidly or move slowly, go forward or move backward. If, however, it leaves the tracks, it will not move at all. In other words, the train has freedom only insofar as it remains on the tracks. If it derails, it will destroy itself and may cause damage to people and property.

In like manner, people can enjoy genuine freedom as long as they live in accordance with certain (moral and ethical) norms. Confucius said in The Analects, "At seventy I followed my heart's desire without overstepping the line."[2] He meant that at the age of seventy he was able to become a perfected being of logos, in which free will and law are united.

Since human beings are beings of logos, their original nature is to try and follow the law. The law that they should follow is the same law that operates throughout the entire universe; specifically, it is the law of give and receive action. When Logos was formed in the Original Image, it was motivated by Heart, which is the root of love. Therefore, originally, the law of the universe is motivated by Heart, and the purpose of the law is the actualization of love.

As mentioned in Ontology, a family is a miniaturization of the orderly system of the cosmos. Therefore, just as the universe exhibits vertical and horizontal order, so too, the family is, likewise, endowed with vertical and horizontal order. The norms (values) that correspond to these two dimensions of order are the vertical norm and the horizontal norm. The vertical norm in the family is the norm for the relationship between parents and children. The horizontal norm in the family is the norm for the relationships between brothers and sisters, and between husband and wife. Furthermore, in human beings there is a norm for an individual to observe, namely, an individual norm, which is the norm prerequisite to perfecting the personality of each person. The vertical norm, horizontal norm, and individual norm will be explained in detail later in Axiology and Ethics.

The norms of the family, as mentioned above, can be extended directly to the society and nation. Ultimately, the norms of the family become the foundation of the norms to be observed on all the levels of the society and nation. Because of the human fall, however, people failed to become beings of logos. As a result, the breakdown of the family is becoming increasingly noticeable today, and societies and nations are in a chaotic situation. When people restore their original nature as beings of logos, then families, societies and nations will be able to return to their original, orderly status.

C. A Being of Creativity

God created the universe by virtue of His creativity, namely, His ability to create. He then endowed human beings with creativity through which they have been developing science and technology. What, then, is the essential nature of this creativity?

God's creativity is the ability to create, based on Heart. As was made clear in the Theory of the Original Image, at the time of creation a two-stage give and receive action takes place within the Original Image. The first stage is the inner give and receive action and the second stage is the outer give and receive action. In the first, Logos is formed through the inner give and receive action between Inner *Sungsang* and Inner *Hyungsang* centering on the purpose which is established by Heart. In the second, all things are created through the give and receive action between the Logos and the Original *Hyungsang* centering on the same purpose. Through this two-stage give and receive action, the two-stage developmental four position foundations are formed. Therefore, we can say that God's creativity is the ability to form these two-stage developmental four position foundations, namely, the inner developmental four position foundation and the outer developmental four position foundation.

In human creative activities, likewise, we first establish a purpose and then make a design or a plan with which to implement that purpose. In other words, an inner give and receive action is first carried out. Then, on the basis of that design or plan, we produce things through carrying out an outer give and receive action. God endowed human beings with creativity in order to empower them to have dominion over the creation with love, centered on heart. Dominion refers to dealing with or controlling material objects (all things in nature, and manufactured properties) and human object partners. The notion of dominion incorporates the meaning of managing, processing, preserving, and so on. Hence, various kinds of activities involving matter, such as primary, secondary, and tertiary industries, as well as the activities to govern society, including politics, art, and science, fall under the activities of having dominion over creation. It was the original nature of dominion that people carry out such varied activities of dominion with God's love. If, from the beginning human beings had completely inherited God's creativity, they would have been carrying out all of these activities centering on God's love.

God created human beings and said to them "Have dominion over creation" (Gen. 1:28). In order for human beings to have dominion over the creation in accordance with God's Words, however, human beings should have responsibly acquired the qualification to be the lord of creation. God, the Greatest Lord, has creativity as the qualification to have dominion over human beings; therefore, human beings were to have been given God's creativity in order to have dominion over creation. Hence, God intended to endow human beings with His creativity on the condition that they would have fulfilled their portion of responsibility for their perfection throughout their growth period. Thus, human beings could have received God's creativity and the qualification to have dominion over creation once they had perfected themselves "by accomplishing their own portion of responsibility until the end of their growing period" (*DP*, 78).

In its original meaning, dominion may be exercised over something only by the person who made that thing; thus, we can not, by our own will, exercise dominion over something made by someone else. Therefore, human beings can not, by their own will, exercise dominion over the creation, since human beings were created after all things had been created by God. However, human beings were created as God's children, and therefore, they should be allowed to inherit their parent's property and rights once they have grown up. Accordingly, God desired that Adam and Eve establish a condition to inherit His dominion: God directed them to grow, while accomplishing their portion of responsibility. The condition set for them was that they should perfect themselves through fulfilling their responsibility, whereby the condition would be regarded as equivalent to their having participated in God's creation of the universe.

Human beings are the integration of all things, a microcosm: the value of one human being is equivalent to that of the entire universe. Therefore, if human beings had perfected themselves, it would have been regarded as having the same value as if they themselves had created the universe. That is why God directed Adam and Eve to fulfill their portion of responsibility. In sum, God bade them fulfill their portion of responsibility in order for them to establish the condition that they had participated in God's creation. For this purpose, relevant to the process of growth of Adam and Eve, God gave them the commandment not to eat of the fruit of the tree of knowledge of good and evil, which meant they were not to engage in sexual love before the proper time (*DP*, 60). After God gave them this commandment, He did not interfere with their behavior. The reason for this is because, if God had interfered, then God Himself would have ignored the human portion of responsibility, which would have resulted in the contradiction that He would be allowing an unqualified Adam and Eve to exercise dominion over creation. As it happened, Adam and Eve did fail to comply with God's commandment, and humankind ever since has been unable to obtain the qualification necessary to exercise dominion over all things.

As a result, human beings have become unable to inherit God's creativity and, instead, have come to engage in creative activities based on their self-centered reason. Thus, in the case of creative activity on the individual level, people have come to place priority on personal interests; a family places priority on its own family interests; on the national level, each nation places priority on its own national interests, etc. Thus, for the most part, creative activities have become self-centered. Moreover, people have also become quite unconcerned about what happens to the environment or to other people. This has resulted in diverse problems, such as the destruction of nature, pollution, the development of weapons of mass destruction, and so on.

In order to solve these problems, people must become able to acquire the original creativity, which is centered on heart. That heart becomes the center of creativity means that creative activities should be made with love as their motivation, and on the basis of proper values. Therefore, scientists must first be persons of values, or persons of character, before being scientists. In other words, ethics must become the basis of natural science.

In this modern age, however, scientists have limited themselves to the pursuit of objective facts, disregarding values of any kind. The result is the chaotic situation we see today. To solve this problem, Rev. Sun

Myung Moon sponsored the International Conferences on the Unity of the Sciences (ICUS) and encouraged scientists to deal with values, so that they might restore true creativity. In other words, he encouraged scientists to manifest true creativity under the ethic which requires us "to love nature, to reconsider the dignity of human beings, to seek love among all humankind, and to search for God as the origin of love." [3]

III. A Being with Position

Resembling the relationship of subject and object in the Original Image, human beings exist in the positions of subject and object. When people are born, they start out as children in the position of object to their parents. After growing, they become parents themselves and stand in the position of subject to their children. In social life, too, people start out from a lower position and gradually rise to a higher position. Thus, human beings stand first in the object position, and then gradually grow to stand in the subject position.

A. Object Position

The object position is the position from which to receive the dominion of the subject figure, and at the same time it has its significance in being the position from which to return joy to the subject figure. The human being was created as the object partner of joy before God. Accordingly, the primary significance of the life of a human being, who is in the object position to God, is to please God.

Human beings stand first in the position of an object before God; therefore, they come to stand in the object position to those who stand in a position representing God. Those who stand in a position representing God are, for example, the president or king (to the people), parents (to their children), teachers (to their students), superiors (to their subordinates), the whole (to the individual), and so on. In other words, just as human beings are the object partners to God, so too the people are the object partners to their president or king, children are the object partners to their parents, students are the object partners to their teachers, subordinates are the object partners to their superiors, and individuals are the object partners to the whole.

A human being lives engaged in relationships with various subject figures. Since a person in the object position is to receive the dominion of his or her subject figure, a certain mental attitude, an "object consciousness" toward the subject figure is necessary. Object consciousness toward God is a heart of attendance and loyalty. Object consciousness toward the sovereign or chief of state is loyalty. Children's object consciousness toward their parents is filial piety. Students' object consciousness toward their teachers is a respectful heart and obedient mind. Subordinates' object consciousness toward their superiors is obedience. The object consciousness of an individual to the whole is having a mind of service. What these various types of object consciousness have in common is a heart of meekness and humility and an attitude of living for the sake of others.

In the fallen world, many dictators have appeared throughout history. They took advantage of people's object consciousness by behaving as though they were the true subject figures before the people, and thus they came to receive people's respect and support. Hitler, Stalin, Mao Zedong and Nicolae Ceausescu were major examples of this type of person. Yet, although false subject figures may be welcomed and prosper for a certain time, in the end they inevitably lose the support of the people. This is a fact proven by history.

Since human beings were created as the children of God, they have in the depth of their hearts, consciously or unconsciously, the object consciousness of attending, being loyal to, and pleasing God. Such object consciousness can lead them even to the point of sacrificing their lives for God's will. The spirit of martyrdom possessed by many religious people is a prime example. There is often the case in which some followers are even willing to offer their lives for the sake of their leader. This is a case in which the object consciousness is expressed to the extreme.

Unfortunately, people are often mistaken about who their true subject figure is; thus, they have often been deceived by false subject figures such as dictators, and have sometimes followed them blindly, bringing disastrous social results. Therefore, for people to meet a true subject figure is a very difficult, but very important, matter.

Object consciousness is an essential element in ethics. In today's society, however, object consciousness has almost become paralysed, and there is a growing tendency for people to ignore the authority of subject figures. As a result, the order of subject and object is neglected, throwing society into confusion. Therefore, in establishing an ethical society, what needs to be done first, and foremost, is a reform of consciousness in order to establish true object consciousness.

B. Subject Position

The subject position refers to the position of the subject figure in exercising dominion over the object. Originally, as human beings grew and became perfected, they were to come naturally to stand in the position of subject, or the "subject position," from which they were to have dominion over all things. However, the subject position referred to here is the position of subject in the various relationships among human beings. As already stated, examples of a subject figure in human life are as follows: In a family, parents are in the subject position to their children; in schools, teachers are in the subject position to students; in business, executives are in the subject position to subordinates; in a nation, the government is the subject to its people; furthermore, the whole is the subject to the individual. In exercising appropriate dominion over the object, it is necessary for the subject to have a certain mental attitude. The mental posture required of the subject toward the object is "subject consciousness."

First, the subject figure must have a genuine concern for an object partner at all times. Human alienation, which is a serious problem today, results from the fact that the subject figure is not sincerely concerned for every aspect of life of their object partner. A lack of concern means that the subject figure does not assume responsibility for their object partner. When that happens, the object partner can easily come to distrust and disobey the subject figure. Therefore, on the part of the subject figure, there can be no excuse for neglecting an object partner.

Second, the subject figure must love the object partner. Traditionally, ruling over the object partner, or giving orders to him or her may have been considered the way of showing subject consciousness, but in reality that is not the proper way. True dominion over an object partner is to actively love him or her. Love is the source of happiness, ideals, joy, and life. Therefore, when a subject figure loves an object partner, he or she becomes loyal and obedient to the subject. Therefore, just as God loves humankind, the object partners of God, so too must every subject figure love his or her object partners.

Third, a subject figure must exercise proper authority. The subject figure should love the object partner, but if a leader is always lenient when dealing with subordinates, authority can not easily be established. If the leader does not exercise authority, the subordinate will lose his or her seriousness and willingness to work. Therefore, it is necessary for the subject figure to maintain proper authority while loving the object partner. This means that love has not only a warm aspect, like spring, but also a strict aspect, like winter. Such a strict love, integrated with authority, enhances the trust, the sense of belonging, and the heart of obedience of the object partner toward the subject figure, and their desire to work. "Strict love with authority" is, in other words, an "authority with love."

Thus, the subject figure needs a certain authority, and yet it is not good for him or her to have an excessive consciousness of such authority. Love can not dwell in such authority. If authority is exercised too strongly, the subordinate will be intimidated and thus become unable to exhibit creativity. True authority makes those in the subordinate position feel thankful, even when they might be reprimanded by their superiors. This kind of authority is true authority, namely, an authority with love.

This is certainly true of God. God is a being of love, while at the same time, a being of authority. For example, we see in the Bible the classic case that when Abraham failed in his attempt to offer a heifer, a ram and a she-goat, a dove and a pigeon, God ordered him to offer his son Isaac as a sacrifice. But when Abraham, in obedience to God's order, was about to make the offering of Isaac, God stopped him and said, "Now I know that you fear God" (Gen. 22:12). This has the same meaning as, "since you ignored my authority, I asked you to offer your son as a sacrifice, in order to let you acknowledge it." In this way, God never wishes us to look upon Him easily as the God of love, or to call on Him without good reason. Rather, He wishes us to fear Him, as He is the God of authority.

As a final point, let us consider the subject position of human beings toward all things. As mentioned before, once human beings perfect themselves and inherit God's Heart, they will exercise dominion over all things by expressing their creativity based on heart. In other words, with God's love they come to have dominion over all things. When that happens, human beings will stand in the subject position over all things, in a true sense. This is in sharp contrast with the Marxist assertion that, when the means of production are nationalized and a planned economy is put into practice, then "[man] becomes the real, conscious lord of Nature."[4]

According to Marxism, human beings come to stand in the subject position of dominion over all things by implementing a planned economy. In other words, human beings come to stand in the position of dominion over all things through reforming the economy, not by means of love. In the past few decades, however, in the former Soviet Union, in China, and in other Communist countries, the economies collapsed due to unsuccessful economic policies and the resulting industrial stagnation. This tells us that Communism totally failed in its attempt to achieve dominion over all things. This highlights the limitation of the Marxist materialistic view of human nature; in other words, with such a materialistic view, people can not, in the true sense, stand in the subject position toward the creation.

C. "Connected Being Consciousness" and Democracy

Every person exists as a connected being in social life; so, everyone is both subject and object at the same time. In other words, every person is a being of both subject and object positions, or a being with a dual position. This fact can be summed up by the phrase, every person is in a "connected being position." The connected being position possesses dual purposes, namely the purpose for the whole and the purpose for the individual. For example, in a working place, a person is in the subject position to his or her subordinates while, at the same time, in the object position to his or her superiors. Though someone may be in the highest possible position, that person still is in the object position to God. Therefore, in a strict sense, everyone is always a connected being. The mental attitude that a connected being should take is that of possessing both object consciousness and subject consciousness: this is called "connected being consciousness."

As mentioned earlier, every person first stands in an object position, and then stands in a subject position. Therefore, in the connected being consciousness, priority should be given to one's object consciousness. In other words, subject consciousness should be established only on the basis of object consciousness. This is what was originally intended. In fallen persons, however, when one stands in a subject position, he or she easily forgets the importance of object consciousness and, instead, gives priority solely to subject consciousness. Dictators are typical examples of this tendency. They consider themselves supreme, and then seek to do everything according to their own will. In contrast, in the original society, leaders would be very conscious that they are always in an object position before God—even if they might be occupying the highest social position—and so would never lose their humble attitude.

Next, let us give some consideration to the connected being consciousness in a democracy. The fundamental principles of democracy are majority rule and the equality of rights. These principles are based on natural rights, as proposed by John Locke (1632–1704). Contrary to Thomas Hobbes (1588–1679), whose view was that the natural state of human beings is "the war of all against all" (*bellum omnium contra omnes*), Locke argued that, since natural law exists in the natural state, people are free and equal by nature. He held that in the natural state people have natural rights, i.e., the power to preserve one's life, liberty and estate.[5]

The concept of natural law, upon which the concept of natural rights is established, originated from the Stoics in the ancient Greek period. One's natural rights, under natural law, became the model for the establishment of the principles of modern democracy. Needless to say, natural rights here refers to those of the individual.

The theory of the equality of rights was originally derived from the Christian concept of "equality before God." In other words, the equality of the rights of people is given by God, not by the state. The theory of the equality of rights is also the foundation upon which modern democracy was established. Equality before God refers to the "equality of all people as objects before God, the Subject." Therefore, the theory of the equality of all people was originally based on object consciousness and, therefore, a consciousness of order.

Thus, democracy originally arose based on object consciousness. Yet, as it developed, the consciousness of God gradually faded in peoples' minds and, with an excessive emphasis on individual rights, object consciousness gradually disappeared. Today, people are mostly interested in subject consciousness alone. As a result, human relations have generally developed among those with a strong sense of subject consciousness; in other words, relationships between subject and subject. This is an age in which any sense of order has largely been lost. A relationship between subject and subject is essentially that of mutual repulsion.

For a time, after its beginning, democracy achieved a comparatively sound development. The reason for this is that people maintained an object consciousness before God, in virtue of their Christian spirit. As time passed, however, Christianity gradually became more secularized, influenced by scientific developments and materialistic ideas, and lost its ability to guide the human spirit. In addition, along with the rapid industrialization of society, value perspectives were gradually shaken.

Along with these changes in the social environment, the foundation for the equality of rights was transformed from that of "equality before God" into that of "equality before the law." As a result, the repulsive action between subject and subject, which has its seeds in democracy, surfaced, and various kinds of social confusion appeared. As stated above, the relationship between subject and subject is that of conflict. An example, from the natural world, is the repulsive action between positive electrical charges.

Therefore, equality of rights inevitably gives rise to conflicts, unless there is a buffering agent, like Christian love. Such disharmonies as conflicts, clashes, wars, and hatred occur in all parts of the world today. These are all manifestations of the repulsive action between subject and subject.

In other words, democracy, which claims an equality of rights, was imbued with elements of conflict from its very beginning. Consequently, the repulsive action was destined to surface eventually. Today, this latent conflict has fully surfaced: Murder, burglary, arson, terrorism, destruction, narcotics, injustice, corruption, deterioration of sexual morality, increase in divorce, collapse of the family, the AIDS epidemic, and sexual crimes are spreading to every democratic society. These are all phenomena arising from the collapse of values caused by the repulsive actions within democracy.

The key to solving this problem of the collapse of values in democratic societies lies in reviving a sense of object consciousness. In order to do so, we need to bring a sense of God, the true subject of humankind, back into peoples' daily experience. We must also return to the original spirit with which modern democracy started, namely, the idea that all people are equal before God. To achieve these objectives, the first and most important step is to provide reasonable proof for the existence of God, so that people in our contemporary age can believe in and embrace Him.

If people come to genuinely believe in and embrace God, they will naturally come to respect their superiors in society as well. Also, those in superior positions will come to guide their subordinates with love. The government will love its people, and the people will become loyal to their government. When democracy, which has lost God, returns to being a democracy truly centered on God, the ills of today's democratic society will be fundamentally resolved. Unification Thought refers to God-centered democracy as "Fraternalism centered on the Heavenly Father," or simply "Heavenly Fatherism," or "Fraternalism." There can be no brothers and sisters without parents, nor parents without children (i.e., brothers and sisters).

Finally, let me explain about human dominion over all things. As His third blessing God ordered human beings to dominate all things. Therefore, if human beings had not fallen but had perfected themselves, they would have stood in the position of the rulers of all things. Dominion over all things, here, does not simply mean that human beings, as the lords of creation, dominate other things of creation. All human economic and technological activities, including primary, secondary, and tertiary industries belong to this dominion over all things. If so, then what should be the mental attitude of human beings who are enjoying dominion over all things? They should have a heart of love for all things, and take care of all things with warm care and concern; in other words, they should deal with, and manage, all things with love. This kind of dominion is in accordance with the Way of Heaven: if there is love, then all things will be very happy to receive the dominion of human beings.

IV. Conclusion

As explained earlier, human beings, originally, are beings with Divine Image, beings with Divine Character, and beings with position. This is the response of Unification Thought to the age-old philosophical question, "What is a human being?" In conclusion, the original human nature can be summarized as follows:

(1) An original human being is a united being of *sungsang* and *hyungsang* resembling the Divine Image.

(2) The harmony of a man and woman together, as an original couple, is a harmonized yang and yin, resembling the Divine Image.

(3) An original human being is a being of unique individuality, resembling the Divine Image.

(4) An original human being is a being of heart resembling the Divine Character, that is, a person of character who practices love; in other words, a loving person, or a person of love (*Homo amans*).

(5) An original human being is a being of logos, resembling the Divine Character, that is, a being of norm, who lives according to the Way of Heaven, or the law of the universe.

(6) An original human being is a being of creativity, resembling the Divine Character, that is, a heart-centered ruler of all things.

(7) An original human being is a being with position, oriented toward dual purposes and having a connected being consciousness.

This is the image of the original human being, a valuable and sacred being, possessing inner content of the greatest value. If any one of these human characteristics were to be chosen as the most essential, it would be that of the human being as a "being of heart." Traditionally, the human being has been portrayed as "the knower" (*Homo sapiens*), with reason as the essence of human nature; or as "the maker" (*Homo faber*), with the ability to use tools as the essence of human nature, and so forth. Greek philosophy and modern rationalist philosophy would hold the former view, whereas Marxism and pragmatism would hold the latter. In contrast, Unification Thought advocates the concept of the human being as a "loving being" (*Homo amans*), asserting that the essence of human nature is heart, or love.

V. A Unification Thought Appraisal of the Existentialist Analysis of Human Existence

Existentialists are representative of those philosophers who have searched for the original state of human beings, or how they believe human beings should be. According to existentialists, human beings, existing in society, but having become alienated from their essential self, find themselves caught in a state of despair and dread. These thinkers have seriously considered how human beings may be delivered from that despair and dread. In this section, the views of five existentialists will be briefly discussed and compared with the Unification Thought view of human nature. Through this comparative analysis, it is hoped that the reader's understanding of the Unification Theory of the Original Human Nature will be deepened.

A. Søren Kierkegaard (1813–55)

1. Kierkegaard's Analysis of Human Existence

Søren Kierkegaard asked himself the question, "What is the human being?" His answer was, "A human being is spirit. But what is spirit? Spirit is the self. But what is the self? The self is a relation that relates itself to itself."[6] Then, who is it that establishes such a relation? It must be a third party, a reality other than one's own self, and that reality is none other than God Himself. Therefore, Kierkegaard concluded, the original self is the self that stands before God.

Yet, human beings, who should thus live in a relationship with God, have become separated from God. Kierkegaard explained the nature of that separation, in his analysis of Genesis outlined in his book, *The Concept of Dread*, as follows: In the beginning, Adam was in a state of peace and comfort, but at the same time, he was in a state of dread (*Angst*). When God told Adam, "of the tree of the knowledge of good and evil you shall not eat" (Gen. 2:17), the possibility of freedom was awakened within Adam. This possibility of freedom caused Adam an extreme sense of dread. As Adam looked into the abyss of freedom, he became dizzy and clung to his own self. That was the precise moment when the original sin first came into being.

As a result, a division arose in the "relation that relates itself to itself," and human beings fell into despair (*Verzweifelung*). People tried to remove this despair, regarding it as something that has come from the outside, but they can never remove it with such an understanding. Only through faith, by rediscovering their relationship to God, can they restore their original relationship to themselves, and escape from despair.

Kierkegaard criticized the public for its irresponsibility and lack of conscience, saying, "A public is everything and nothing, the most dangerous of all powers and the most insignificant."[7] He asserted that, in order for people to actualize their true human nature, they must depart from the world of the public and stand before God all by themselves—each as an individual. He explained the stages through which people return to their original selves in terms of three stages of existence.

The first stage is the stage of "aesthetic existence." Persons in this stage simply follow their sensual desires exactly as they are, and live just as they please. The purpose of this kind of life is pleasure. The position of someone in the stage of aesthetic existence is that of a seducer, a pursuer of erotic love. But since the moment of pleasure is not something that can be maintained continuously, persons in the aesthetic stage are trapped by fatigue and dread. They become frustrated and fall into despair—but, through their making a decision they proceed to the next stage.

The second stage is that of "ethical existence." Persons in this stage seek to live according to their conscience, with good and evil as their standard of judgment. They seek to live as good citizens with a sense of responsibility and duty. Yet, no matter how hard they may try, they can not live totally in accordance with their conscience. So, they become frustrated and fall into despair. Again, through making a decision they can proceed to the next stage.

The third stage is that of "religious existence." Here, each person stands alone, with faith in the presence of God; only by doing so can the person become a true existential being. In order to enter this stage, a leap of faith is required. Such a leap is possible if one believes in a paradox that can not be understood with the intellect. It is to believe that which is irrational, such as Abraham's obedience to God's commandment to offer his son Isaac as a sacrifice, or the irrational statement that the eternal God became incarnate in the finite time spectrum and became a man (Jesus). Only by such a leap of faith can people truly recover their relationship to God. Kierkegaard considered

Abraham's obedience to God's commandment to offer his son Isaac as a sacrifice, which seems contrary to any sense of human ethics, as a typical model of the religious life.

This being the case, when individuals who have become true existences centered on God—in other words, who have become their original selves—come to love one another, through the mediation of God, by following Jesus' words to "love your neighbor as yourself," only then, said Kierkegaard, through such "works of love," can a true society be established.

2. A Unification Thought Appraisal of Kierkegaard's View of the Human Being

According to Kierkegaard, as people separated from God, a division arose in the "relation that relates itself to itself," causing people to fall into despair. From the perspective of Unification Thought, this "relation that relates itself to itself" can be regarded as the relation between one's mind and body or the relation between one's spirit mind and physical mind.

This means that, as human beings are separated from God, our mind and body have become divided. This implies that the mind and body, in an original being, are united, centering on God. Then, how can one's mind and body become one? This is possible once the spirit mind and the physical mind restore their proper relationship of subject and object, and perform harmonious give and receive action.

Søren Kierkegaard said that "when someone stands before God as an individual," that person stands in an absolute relationship to the Absolute Being (or God). This corresponds to the concept of a "being of individuality" referred to in Unification Thought. Yet, Kierkegaard did not explain why this individual can be considered to be absolute. From the Unification Thought perspective, the reason why a human being, as a "being of individuality," can be considered as absolute is that a human being resembles an Individual Image in God, the Absolute Being. Thus, Kierkegaard's views of a human being as a "relation that relates itself to itself" and as an "individual" correspond easily to the "united being of mind and body" and the "being of individuality," respectively, as found in Unification Thought.

Nevertheless, this is not all there is to the original human nature. The most essential aspect of the original human nature is that of heart. Moreover, it would only be a partial understanding to say that a person stands before God alone as an individual, namely as a being of individuality. When man and woman get married and stand before God as husband and wife, they truly become perfect as human beings, namely as a harmonious couple of yang and yin. They are also beings of logos and creativity. Moreover, they are beings with position, endowed with both the nature of a subject and the nature of an object. An "individual" standing before God, as proposed by Kierkegaard, although sincere, is but a solitary and lonely figure.

Why have human beings become separated from God? Unless the cause of this separation is clarified, it will be impossible for one to return to one's original self, that is, to the person of the original ideal of God. Kierkegaard said that Adam fell into sin through the dread that arose from the possibility of freedom. Can this be true? According to the Divine Principle, neither freedom nor dread was the cause of the human fall. The first human ancestors, Adam and Eve, did not observe God's Word, but followed the temptation of the Archangel instead, thus misdirecting their love. The force of the non-principled love that arose as a result is what made them fall away from God. As Adam and Eve began to deviate from the right path, in violation of the Word of God, the freedom of their original mind is what gave rise to their dread, the dread of having violated God's Word. Thus, freedom and dread worked, instead, in the direction of trying to prevent them from deviating. Yet, the power of their non-principled love suppressed this feeling of dread, making them cross the line of the fall. As a result, human beings became separated from God, and dread and despair came into being due to the guilt they experienced as a result of their disobedience to God's Word, and their separation from the love of God. Accordingly, unless the problem of the fall is correctly solved, it is impossible to fundamentally solve people's dread and despair.

Kierkegaard's concept of God's love is also ambiguous. God's love arises from Heart, which is the limitless emotional impulse to warmly give everything to His object partners. When God's love appears on earth, it manifests as various directional loves. In a family, it manifests as the directional, divisional loves of parents' love for children, husband's and wife's mutual love, brothers' and sisters' love, and children's love for parents. When these basic loves are extended or expanded in various ways, they manifest as one's love for humankind, one's love for one's nation, one's love for one's neighbors, one's love for animals, one's love for nature, and so on. Thus, God's love is not an ambiguous love, but rather it appears as various concrete and directional expressions of love.

Kierkegaard asserted that in order for us to recover our authentic state we must fight against the falsity of the crowd and return to God. This reflects his own personal path in seeking to encounter God, a path which he walked while enduring persecution and ridicule from his contemporaries. It was, moreover, his appeal to the religious people of his time to become true persons of faith. His efforts should be deeply appreciated.

At the age of twenty four Kierkegaard fell in love with, Regina Olsen, who was fourteen, and three years later became engaged to her. The next year, however, out of fear that he might plunge her into unhappiness through marriage, he unilaterally broke off the engagement and began looking for a love of a higher dimension than mere romantic love. Because of this, he was criti-cized by his society. From the viewpoint of Unification Thought, we can understand that his desire was to realize a true love between man and woman centered on God, after having perfected his character. It can be said that the original image of the human being pursued by Kierkegaard was basically in accord with Unification Thought in terms of its direction.

B. Friedrich Nietzsche (1844-1900)

1. Nietzsche's View of the Human Being

In contrast to the view of Kierkegaard, who held that only by standing before God can people become their original selves, Friedrich Nietzsche claimed that it is only when they free themselves from faith in God that they can become their original selves.

Nietzsche deplored what he saw as the leveling and demeaning of people in the European society of his time, and he attributed that to the Christian view of the human being. Through its preaching of asceticism, Christianity denied life in this world and, instead, placed ultimate human value in the next world. Moreover, it preached that all people are equal before God. For Nietzsche, such views deprived human beings of their vitality, pulled talented human beings down, and tended to equalize everyone.

In response, Nietzsche proclaimed that "God is dead," and vehemently attacked Christianity. He felt that it was Christian morality which oppressed human life and the physical body, by means of such concepts as "God" and "soul," and as a result of its negative view of the reality of life, blocked the way toward the development of stronger people. He felt that Christian morality aided only the weak and the suffering, and he called it a "slave morality." He also rejected the Christian life of love and spirituality, wholeheartedly affirming, on the contrary, one's instinct and life.

For Nietzsche, life is the force to grow, or the force to develop. He argued that behind every human action there exists a "will to power" (*Wille zur Macht*), a will which seeks to increase the individual's strength. In his words, "Where I found the living, there I found will to power; and even in the will of those who serve I found the will to be master." [8] He thus rejected Christianity's "slave morality" and promulgated instead a "master morality," which made power itself the standard of all values. Nietzsche described the standard of good and evil as follows:

> What is good? Everything that heightens the feeling of power in man, the will to power, power itself. What is bad? Everything that is born of weakness. What is happiness? The feeling that power is *growing*, that

resistance is overcome···. The weak and the failures shall perish: first principle of *our* love of man. And they shall even be given every possible assistance. What is more harmful than any vice? Active pity for all the failures and all the weak: Christianity.⁹

The ideal of the human being, according to master morality, is the "superman" (*Übermensch*). The superman is a being that has realized all human potentiality to the utmost limits, and is the embodiment of the will to power. The possibility of the superman lies in the endurance of any kind of pain in life and in the absolute affirmation of life itself. The absolute affirmation of life comes about through one's acceptance of the idea of "eternal recurrence," which Nietzsche expresses as, "Everything goes, everything comes back; eternally rolls the wheel of being."¹⁰ This is the idea that the world repeats itself forever, without any purpose or meaning. The absolute affirmation of life means the endurance of any kind of fate. He said that this becomes possible through "regarding the inevitable as beautiful" and through "loving one's fate"; thus, he preached the "love of fate" (*amor fati*).

2. A Unification Thought Appraisal of Nietzsche's View of the Human Being

Nietzsche asserted that Christianity's extreme emphasis on life after death crippled people's ability to value their actual everyday life, and so weakened it. His sincere effort in endeavoring to understand the original human nature merits our esteem. His views were an accusation towards, and a warning to, Christianity, which he regarded as having deviated from its original spirit. Nietzsche saw the God of Christianity as a judgmental and otherworldly being, sitting on the high throne of heaven, promising resurrection after death to those who did good, and meting out punishment to those who did evil. What Nietzsche was denouncing, however, was not the teachings of Jesus himself, but rather the teachings of Paul, who had transformed Jesus' teaching into a teaching that placed too much emphasis on life after death.¹¹

From the perspective of Unification Thought God is not an otherworldly being who denies reality, while situated in a high place somewhere in heaven. God's purpose of creation is not only the realization of the Kingdom of Heaven in the world after death, but, more importantly, the prior realization of the Kingdom of Heaven here on earth. Once the Kingdom of Heaven is established here on earth, those who have experienced life in the Kingdom of Heaven here on earth will subsequently build the Kingdom of Heaven in the spirit world. Jesus' mission, originally, was the realization of the Kingdom of Heaven here on earth. Therefore, Nietzsche's assertion is reasonable in that Jesus' teaching was changed by Paul into a teaching placing too much emphasis on one's life after death. Nevertheless, it is also true that, since Jesus was crucified, as a result of the chosen people's disbelief in him, the extent of the salvation that he was able to accomplish was limited to spiritual salvation, which means that people here in the real, day-to-day world of the flesh continue to live under the yoke of Satan, the subject of evil. Therefore, it was a serious misjudgment for Nietzsche, beyond criticizing Paul, to go so far as to deny Christianity itself, even declaring the death of God.

We can next examine Nietzsche's assertion that all living beings have a "will to power." According to Genesis, God gave human beings the blessing to "have dominion over all things" (Gen. 1:28). In other words, God gave human beings the way to become qualified to rule. This implies that the desire to rule (or desire to dominate) is one of the characteristics of the original human nature as endowed by God. The "position" to rule corresponds to the "subject position" among the characteristics of the original human nature, according to Unification Thought. With regard to the subject position, however—as mentioned earlier—true dominion is based on love rather than power. The condition for a human being to exercise dominion is that they must first perfect their personality, centering on God's Heart, and practice the ethics of love in family life. It is upon that basis, and that basis only, that true dominion can be expressed. Nietzsche, however, was not able to understand about that basis, and thus he stressed only the "will to power." This is another part of his misunderstanding.

Nietzsche asserted that Christian morality is the morality of the weak, which denies the strong—but this view is misleading. Christianity taught true love in order for people to come to exercise true dominion. People must first fight against the evil forces coming through the instinctive desires of the physical body. These instinctive desires of the body are not evil in themselves, but if fallen people, whose spiritual level of heart is not yet perfect, live according to the instinctive desires of their body, they tend to be dominated by evil forces. Only when the level of heart of the spirit person is raised, whereby the spirit mind comes to have dominion over the physical mind, can the activity of the body be considered good in the true sense.

Emphasizing only the values of the body, instinct and life, Nietzsche neglected the aspects of spirit, love, and reason. In other words, he disregarded the human spirit self. If the spirit self is disregarded, what will remain of the human being? What will remain is nothing but the animal-like physical self. This would certainly drag people down to the level and position of animals. Therefore, even though Nietzsche may be calling on people to become strong, in reality he is actually encouraging them to become animalistic. That is definitely not the level for which God created human beings. Nietzsche's effort to try to guide people back to their original image should be respected, but the method he proposed for doing so was wrong. A human being is a united being of *sungsang* and *hyungsang*, with the *sungsang* as the subject and the *hyungsang* as the object. Nietzsche, however, emphasized only the *hyungsang* aspect, neglecting the *sungsang* aspect. Still, Nietzsche is to be respected for having issued a warning against those Christians who, because of their ignorance of Jesus' original purpose of realizing the Kingdom of Heaven on earth, had a tendency to think too lightly of the importance of our human life on earth.

C. Karl Jaspers (1883-1969)

1. Jaspers' View of the Human Being

For Karl Jaspers, existence refers to the state of a human being truly awakened to oneself as an individual. He says, "Existence is the never objectified source of my thoughts and actions····. It is what relates to itself, and thus to its transcendence." [12] This way of thinking is basically the same as Kierkegaard's.

An existence that is in the process of attaining the original existence, having not yet encountered Transcendence, or the Comprehensive (*das Umgreifende*), is called a "possible existence." Usually, human beings are only possible existences that live in various circumstances; but by acting upon their given circumstances, they can live positively. Jaspers points out, however, that there exist certain situations beyond which we can not go, and which we can not change, including "death," "suffering," "struggle," and "guilt." These he calls "boundary situations." [13] Even though people may wish to live eternally, yet not a single person can escape death.

Death is the denial of one's own existence. Also, human life involves various kinds of suffering, such as physical pain, disease, senility, and starvation. As long as people live, such struggles can not be avoided. Moreover, people live with the unavoidable guilt that their own existence can not but reject others.

In the face of such boundary situations, people can not but despair and eventually become frustrated, becoming aware of their own limitations. At such times, the way people experience and respond to that frustration will determine what will become of them. If they face their frustration head-on, and endure it silently, honestly, and without trying to escape from the situation, then they will come to experience the reality that "originally exists, transcending the world of existence."[14]

In other words, they will come to realize that behind nature, behind history, behind philosophy, and behind art—all of which seemed meaningless until then—there is Transcendence, or God, who embraces us and speaks to us. On that occasion, Transcendence will appear to us, not directly, but by means of coded messages. In the form of such codes, Transcendence reaches out to us through nature, history, philosophy, art, and so on. Those who have experienced frustration in boundary situations will be able to interpret those coded messages. This he called the "reading of ciphers"(*Chiffredeutung*). By interpreting or reading such coded messages, a human being, alone, comes to stand face to face with Transcendence. This is what he means by awakening to one's true self.

After encountering God in this way, a human being engages in the practice of love in their communication with others. The original way of life for human beings is to stand in an equal position with one another, loving one another, while yet recognizing one another's independence. Through fellowship with others, existence is perfected. Jaspers said, "The purpose of philosophy, which alone gives a final ground to the meaning of all purposes, that is to say, the purpose of perceiving existence internally, elucidating love, and perfecting comfort, is only attained in communication."[15] Communication is the relationship of loving struggle.[16]

2. A Unification Thought Appraisal of Jaspers' View of the Human Being

Jaspers said that human beings are normally only possible existences that are unable to perceive Transcendence, but that once they pass through boundary situations, they can become existences that relate to

Transcendence, that is, original selves.

But why do human beings normally remain only as possible existences, separated from Transcendence? And why do they become connected with Transcendence only after going through such boundary situations? Jaspers is quiet concerning these questions. Yet, unless these questions are answered, we can not understand concretely what the original self is, or how to recover it.

According to the Divine Principle, human beings were created to fulfill the purpose of creation. The fulfillment of the purpose of creation means fulfillment of the three great blessings (Gen. 1:28), that is, perfection of one's personality, perfection of one's family, and perfection of one's dominion. However, Adam and Eve, the first human ancestors, failed to keep the Word of God during their growth period, and while their personalities were still imperfect they fell, becoming separated from God, becoming husband and wife centering on non-principled love and giving birth to sinful children. As a result, all humankind came to be separated from God. Therefore, the true path for recovering the original self is for people to separate themselves from non-principled love and return to God, thereby fulfilling the purpose of creation centering on God's love.

The original human nature is meant to manifest itself fully once people fulfill their purpose of creation. Like Kierkegaard, Jaspers said that existence is to become a being that relates to Transcendence, while at the same time relating itself to itself. In saying this, Jaspers was referring to the perfection of one's personality, which is the first among the three great blessings. Among the various different aspects of the original human nature discussed in Unification Thought, Jaspers was concerned only with the "united being of *sungsang* and *hyungsang*," while neglecting the others. Jaspers does say that we must practice love in our communication with others, but just as with Kierkegaard, his concept of love is vague.

True love (God's love) is an emotional impulse, in accord with which one can not help but giving, with a warm heart, what one has to others. This love is manifested divisionally through the family, as different ways of loving one's object partner: children's love for their parents, conjugal love for one's spouse, parental love for one's children, and siblings' love for one's brothers and sisters. Truly harmonious love in one's communication with others can be realized on the foundation of these four types of love. Jaspers said that communication among existences is a relationship of loving struggle. According to Unification Thought, however, the essence of love is joy. Original love is not something that can be described as any kind of struggle.

Another question is why human beings become connected with Transcendence only by passing through boundary situations. Jaspers said that people encounter God by facing the frustration of a boundary situation head-on and by honestly accepting it. Yet, among those who have, indeed, faced the frustration of the boundary situation head-on and have, indeed, honestly accepted it, there are some who, like Nietzsche, became further separated from God and some who, like Kierkegaard, became even closer to God. Why do such different results come about? The reason for this difference is not clarified in Jaspers' philosophy.

In contrast, Unification Thought provides a clear rationale behind these different results. In failing to observe God's Word, human beings became separated from God and fell under the dominion of Satan, the subject of evil. Because of this, they can not go back to God unconditionally. Only by establishing some condition of compensation, that is, some condition of indemnity, can human beings return to God. Accordingly, what Jaspers described as the despair and frustration experienced in boundary situations corresponds to a condition of indemnity. Once that condition is successfully fulfilled, human beings come to be in a position closer to God. To achieve this, however, one must, while enduring the pain inherent in the boundary situation, remain humble and must maintain an attitude of object consciousness in seeking the absolute subject, as is taught in the Bible, "Ask and it will be given to you; seek, and you will find; knock, and it will be opened to you" (Matt. 7:7). Those who maintain an attitude reflecting a self-centered subject consciousness, or who continue to harbor a spirit of revenge, can never encounter God, even though they may experience such boundary situations. Jaspers believed that we can meet Transcendence through reading the cipher of frustration; but the God we come to know in this manner is merely a symbolic God. We can not comprehend or appreciate the true image of God through such means alone. We must learn about the human fall and God's purpose of creation, and must endeavor to realize the three great blessings through a life of faith. When we do these things, we will be able to experience the Heart of God and become a true human being with a genuine existence.

D. Martin Heidegger (1899-1976)

1. Heidegger's View of the Human Being

Unlike much of modern philosophy, the philosophy of Martin Heidegger did not regard the human being as a self facing the world. For him, the human being is "*Dasein*." *Dasein* refers to a being (*Sein*), an individual human being, who lives in the world. A being relates to other beings, attends to the environment surrounding itself, and cares for other people. This is a being's fundamental way of existence, which Heidegger described as "being-in-the-world" (*In-der-Welt-sein*). Being-in-the-world means that human beings have been cast into the world without being informed as to the origin from which they came or the destination towards which they are going. Such a state Heidegger calls "thrownness" (*Geworfenheit*), or "facticity" (*Faktizitat*).

Normally, people come to lose their subjectivity (or independence) when they strive, through their daily lives, to adjust themselves to their external circumstances or to other peoples' opinions. This is the situation of the "they" (*Das Man*) who has lost the original self, according to Heidegger.[17] Such a "they" spends its daily life indulging in idle talk, distracted by curiosity, and living in peaceful ambiguity. This is called the "falling" of *Dasein*.

This *Dasein*, which has been thrown into the world, seemingly without any reason, exists also in anxiety (*Angst*). If we inquire deeply into the nature of this anxiety, we eventually reach the fundamental anxiety one experiences concerning death. When, however, a person does not simply spend time waiting, in anxiety, for some vague future, but rather positively accepts the fact that he or she, as a human being, is a "being-towards-death" and, with that in mind, lives with a serious determination toward the future, that person can progress toward the original self. In this way, human beings project themselves toward their future; in other words, they put stake in their future. Heidegger calls this "projection" (*Entwurf*). This nature of the being he calls "existentiality."

At such a time, based on what do people project themselves? They project themselves based on the "call of conscience." The call of conscience is that inner voice that calls people to abandon their fallen selves and go back to their original selves. Heidegger speaks of the call of conscience as follows: "The call undoubtedly does not come from someone else who is with me in the world. The call comes *from* me and yet *from beyond* me."[18]

Heidegger grasps the meaning of being in terms of temporality (*Zeitlichkeit*). When being is seen from the perspective of casting itself, it can be grasped as "ahead-of-itself," and when seen from the aspect of having already been cast, it can be grasped as "being-already-in"; and when seen from the aspect of tending the environment and caring for others, it can be grasped as "being-alongside." Human beings do not proceed toward a solitary self, separate from the world. If these aspects are seen in the light of temporality, they correspond, respectively, to the future, the past, and the present. Human beings proceed toward the future potentiality by listening to the call of conscience, in order to save the self from present falling, while taking on the burdens of the past. This is Heidegger's view of the human being seen from the viewpoint of temporality.

2. A Unification Thought Appraisal of Heidegger's View of the Human Being

Heidegger asserted that the human being is a being-in-the-world, a "they" who has lost the original self; he also said that the characteristic feature of that situation is anxiety. He did not, however, clarify why human beings have lost their original selves, or what the original self is like. He speaks of projecting oneself toward one's original self, but if the image of the self to be attained is not clear, there is no way we can verify that we are indeed proceeding toward the original self. Heidegger said that the call of conscience guides human beings to go back to their original selves, but this is not an adequate solution to the problem. Actually, this is little more than a philosophical expression of the common knowledge that people ought to live in obedience to their conscience. In a world that does not recognize God there can be only one of two possible ways of life, namely, living according to one's instinctive life, as proposed by Nietzsche, or according to one's conscience, as Heidegger proposed.

From the perspective of Unification Thought, however, it is not sufficient merely to live in accordance with one's conscience. Instead, people should live in accordance with their "original mind." Conscience may be oriented toward what each individual person regards as good and, therefore, the standard of conscience and of what is good, will vary according to each individual. Hence, when people live according to their conscience, there is no guarantee that they are indeed moving toward their original selves. Only when people live in accordance with their original mind, which possesses God as its standard, will they indeed be moving toward their original selves.

Heidegger said that human beings can be saved from anxiety when they become seriously determined to accept the future, instead of aimlessly waiting for the future to come to them. But, again, how can we be saved from anxiety when the original image of the self is not clearly defined? Seen from the viewpoint of Unification Thought, the cause of anxiety lies in our separation from God's love. Therefore, when human beings go back to God, experience the Heart of God, and actually become beings of heart, only then will they be delivered from anxiety and be filled with peace and joy.

Heidegger also argued that the way for human beings to transcend the anxiety of death is for them to accept death positively as part of their destiny. This, however, is not really a true solution to the problem of the anxiety of death. Unification Thought sees the human being as a united being of spirit self and physical self, or a united being of *sungsang* and *hyungsang* in such a way that the maturation of the spirit self is based on the physical self. When human beings fulfill the purpose for which they were created, during their physical lives on earth, their perfected spirit selves, after the death of their physical selves, will go on to the spirit world, where they will live eternally. Therefore, a human being is not a "being-towards-death," but rather a "being-towards-eternal-life." Therefore, the death of one's physical self corresponds to the phenomenon of ecdysis as found among insects. The anxiety one has of death originates from the ignorance of the meaning of death not to mention the feeling, either conscious or unconscious, that one has not yet perfected oneself.

Heidegger further stated that the human being (*Dasein*) has temporality. In other words, he said that they must take on the past, must separate themselves from the present falling, and must project themselves toward the future. But, why should they do so? Heidegger did not clarify the reason for all this. According to the Divine Principle, ever since the fall of Adam and Eve, human beings, in addition to inheriting the original sin, have also received through heredity the sins committed by their ancestors; They also have collective sin for which the nation or humankind as a whole bears responsibility, as well as committing their own personal sins. Therefore, fallen people have been given the task of restoring their original selves, and the original world, through establishing conditions of indemnity which can pay for these various sins.

Such a task can not generally be accomplished in only one generation; it is accomplished after being passed on from generation to generation. Specifically, in the present generation, we are entrusted with those conditions of indemnity that were not completed by our ancestors. Hence, we attempt to establish those conditions in our own generation, thus bearing responsibility for the future and for our descendents. This is the true meaning, seen from Unification Thought, of the fact that human beings have temporality.

E. Jean-Paul Sartre (1905-80)

1. Sartre's View of the Human Being

Dostoevski said, "If God did not exist, everything would be possible." [19] The denial of the existence of God is the very starting point of the philosophy of Jean-Paul Sartre. In contrast to Heidegger, who asserted his existentialism without any reference to God, Sartre went further and advocated an existentialism that altogether denied God's existence. He explained that, in human beings, "existence precedes essence," as follows:

> What is meant here by saying that existence precedes essence? It means that, first of all, man exists, turns up, appears on the scene, and, only afterwards, defines himself. If man, as the existentialist conceives him, is indefinable, it is because at first he is nothing. Only afterward will he be something, and he himself will have made what he will be. Thus, there is no original human nature, since there is no God to conceive it.[20]

The use or purpose of a tool, that is, the essence of that tool, is already determined by its manufacturer even before it is produced. In this case, essence precedes existence. In the same way, if God exists, and if He has created human beings based on His idea, then it must be that, in the case of human beings, essence precedes existence as well. But Sartre denied the existence of God; therefore, for him, the essence of the human being is not determined from the very beginning. According to him, people appeared not from essence, but rather from nothing.

Moreover, Sartre says that "existence is subjectivity." Human beings are accidental beings that appeared from nothing. They are not defined by anyone. Therefore, they themselves plan what they will be like. They choose themselves. This is what Sartre means by "subjectivity." In other words, human beings choose what they will become—whether they will be Communists or Christians; whether they will choose to marry or remain single.

The fundamental feature of such an existence is "anguish," according to Sartre. Man chooses himself, which means, at the same time, that "in making this choice, he also chooses all men." [21] Therefore, to choose oneself means to take responsibility for the whole of humankind—a responsibility that incorporates anguish, according to Sartre. Anguish, however, does not prevent human beings from acting; on the contrary, it is the very condition for their action, and it is a part of that action itself.

In Sartre's view, human beings are "free" beings. Since existence precedes essence, they are not determined by anything, and are allowed to do anything. Being free, however, implies that the entire responsibility for their deeds lies with themselves. In that sense, being free is a kind of burden for them; therefore, human beings are "condemned to be free." In other words, human beings experience anguish because they are free. Sartre explained it this way:

> Man is free, man is freedom. On the other hand, if God does not exist, we find no values or commands to turn to which legitimize our conduct. So, in the bright realm of values, we have no excuse behind us, nor justification before us. We are alone, with no excuses. That is the idea I shall try to convey when I say that man is condemned to be free.[22]

A human being, who is subjectivity, will exercise his or her subjectivity. In order for a human being to exercise subjectivity, there must exist an object that can receive dominion from him or her. Among the types of beings, there are the "being-in-itself" and the "being-for-itself." The being-in-itself refers to all things and the being-for-itself is the being which is conscious of itself, namely, the human being. When a person exercises subjectivity, there is no problem so far as he or she deals with a being-in-itself as his or her object. But, once a person faces another person (i.e., a being-for-itself), problems arise. The reason for this is that in such a relationship both will assert their subjectivity.

When one person faces another, their human existence becomes a "being-for-others"; that is, a being that is opposite to another being, according to Sartre. The fundamental structure of the being-for-others is the relationship in which one is either a "being-looking-at" or a "being-looked-at"—that is, a relationship in which "the Other is an object for me" or "I myself am an object-for-the-Other." [23] This means that human relationships are in constant conflict. As Sartre explained it,

> It is therefore useless for human-reality to seek to get out of this dilemma: one must either transcend the Other or allow oneself to be transcended by him. The essence of the relations between consciousnesses is not the *Mitsein* [co-existence]; it is conflict. [24]

2. A Unification Thought Appraisal of Sartre's View of the Human Being

Sartre said that "existence precedes essence," and that human beings create themselves. Along this same line, Heidegger contended that people must project themselves toward the future. For Heidegger, the "call of conscience," though vague, guides people toward the original self. For Sartre, however, the original self is totally denied. According to Unification Thought, the absence of the original self is a natural consequence of the fact that human beings have become totally separated from God. If we were to accept Sartre's views, we would be left without any standard at all to judge between good and evil. In that situation, no matter what people did, they would always be able to rationalize their actions by saying that they had acted on their own volition. That would necessarily create a society without ethics.

Sartre also said that the human being is subjectivity. In contradistinction to that, Unification Thought asserts that the human being is both subjectivity and objectivity, at the same time. In other words, a person of original nature is both in the subject position and in the object position. What Sartre calls subjectivity refers to the fact that human beings are free to choose themselves and to objectify others; in contrast, what Unification Thought calls subjectivity refers to the human ability to have dominion over an object being, with love. In order to exercise true subjectivity, people must first establish their own objectivity. In other words, they must first have object consciousness in an object position. Going through the experience of being in an object position, they grow and are promoted to stand in a subject position, and thus become able to exercise subjectivity.

Furthermore, according to Sartre, the characteristic of a mutual relationship between human beings is that of conflict between subjectivity and subjectivity, or a conflict between freedom and freedom. This is similar to Hobbes' concept of a "war of all against all." Needless to say, such concepts of subjectivity and freedom are mistaken. Unless such mistaken views regarding subjectivity and freedom are corrected, the confusion now existing in democratic society can not be resolved. Only when people learn to establish both subjectivity and objectivity, whereby harmonious give and receive action between subject and object takes place in every sphere, can a world of love and peace be actualized.

Moreover, Sartre says that human beings are "condemned to be free." From the viewpoint of Unification Thought, however, freedom is anything but such a sentence. Freedom can not exist apart from the principle, and the principle is the norm for actualizing true love. Accordingly, true freedom is freedom for the sake of actualizing true love.

4

Axiology: A Theory of Value

Our contemporary age is an age of great confusion and turmoil. Wars and conflicts continue unabatedly, and innumerable alarming and tragic phenomena, including terrorism, destruction, arson, kidnapping, murder, drug abuse, alcoholism, sexual immorality, family breakdown, injustice, corruption, oppression, conspiracy, and slander, are occurring worldwide. At the vortex of this turmoil, humankind's most valuable assets are now almost obliterated. I am referring to the loss of personal human dignity, the loss of time-honored traditions, the loss of the dignity of life, the loss of mutual trust among people, the loss of the authority of parents and teachers, and the list goes on.

The fundamental cause of such confusion and turmoil is the decline of traditional values. That is to say, the traditional values of truth, goodness, and beauty are being lost sight of. Among these, the value of goodness in particular, is disappearing, and existing ethics and morals are rapidly collapsing. What is causing this ominous collapse of traditional values?

First, in virtually every field, including economics, politics, society, education, and art, a sense of God is being excluded as religion is neglected. Since many traditional values are based on religion, those values which are losing their religious basis can not but decline.

Second, materialism, atheism, secularism, and especially the viewpoints of Communism, are infiltrating everywhere, undermining traditional values. Communism has been working to divide people into opposing classes and then to foment conflicts between those classes by increasing mistrust and instigating hostilities everywhere. In so doing, it has been very critical of traditional values, attempting to destroy them by claiming that such values are feudalistic, intended solely to maintain existing social systems.

Third, conflicts among religions and philosophies themselves are hastening the collapse of values. Values are established on the basis of religions and philosophies; therefore, if disagreements among religions and philosophies exist, many people will come to regard these values as merely relative in nature. As a result, an increasing number of people are coming to believe that it is no longer necessary for them to respect such values.

Finally, the virtues extolled by traditional religions (such as Confucianism, Buddhism, Christianity, and Islam) are losing their power to persuade modern people, who are inclined to think more scientifically. The teachings of traditional religions often have contents which contradict scientific facts. Accordingly, they become unacceptable to modern people, who have come to place great confidence in science.

When we analyze the causes of the collapse of traditional values in this way, we come to realize that there is an urgent need for a new and fresh value perspective. Without such a fresh, new perspective, we may not be able to adequately prepare ourselves for the ideal world to come in the future. Then, what should such a new value perspective be like? First of all, it must be able to embrace the fundamental teachings of all religions and thought systems. Also, it must be able to overcome materialism and atheism. Furthermore, it must be able to embrace and even guide science. Ultimately, it must be a value perspective centered on the true love of God. It is precisely such a value perspective as this that is so urgently needed today so that we may prepare for the future society.

Then, let us examine as concretely as we can what the future society we should be preparing for might be like. This future society will be created by original human beings, people of integrity who experience God's Heart and who have perfected their characters. A person of character is one in whom intellect, emotion, and will have developed fully and harmoniously, centering on heart. Accordingly, the future society will be established by people whose intellect, emotion, and will are developed harmoniously centering on God's Heart. Here, implicitly, the idea of new values refers to those values sought after by the original faculties of intellect, emotion, and will.

The faculties of intellect, emotion, and will seek the values of truth, beauty and goodness, respectively, and through these, a true, artistic, and ethical society will inevitably be actualized. A true society is a society realized through one's pursuit of truth; an artistic society is a society realized through one's pursuit of beauty; and an ethical society is a society realized through one's pursuit of goodness.

To empower one's pursuit of such values as these, a theory of education is necessary for the realization of a true society; a theory of art is required for the realization of an artistic society; and a theory of ethics is required for the realization of an ethical society. Since axiology is a theory which addresses the values of truth, goodness, and beauty in general, it is a comprehensive theory serving as a basis for these three more particular theoretical viewpoints.

The future society will thus be a society wherein the values of truth, goodness, and beauty will be fully realized; in this society, the economy will achieve the highest level of development through the progress of science, completely solving, once and for all, all of society's economic problems. People's lives will come to be focused primarily on the enjoyment of values, even as they are realizing them. The society wherein the values of truth, goodness, and beauty, centered on heart, are realized is a society of heart, creating a culture of heart; this is a society with a unified culture.

I have so far explained that a new value perspective is necessary in order to prepare for the future society. Yet, this new value perspective is necessary not only for preparing for the future society, but perhaps even more importantly, it is necessary in order to clear the confusion of our present world. As mentioned, in today's world values are generally collapsing due to various factors. In order to solve this problem, there exists an urgent need to re-establish a proper value perspective.

A new value perspective is also essential in the effort to unify cultures. That is, in order to fundamentally solve the world's present-day confusion, it will be necessary to bring various traditional cultures into harmony. Cultures are based on certain religions or thoughts, and those religions and thoughts all advocate certain values. Therefore, in order to unite cultures, it is necessary to unite the various value perspectives such as the Christian view of value, the Buddhist view of value, the Confucian view of value, and so on. Also, it is necessary to unite the views of value of the East and the West. Therefore, once again, it is necessary to present a new view of value which can genuinely embrace all value perspectives.

I. Meaning of Axiology and Significance of Value

Before outlining the new view of value, let me first explain about the meaning of axiology, and the meaning of value.

Meaning of Axiology

Value theory is dealt with in economics, in ethics, and in various other disciplines. In philosophy, axiology refers to the philosophy of value. In other words, it is that field of philosophy that deals with value in general. The content of axiology, even fragmentarily, can already be found in ancient times. But, it is in modern times, especially after Kant made his well-known distinction between fact and value, that axiology became an important field of study in philosophy.

Particularly, Rudolph H. Lotze (1817–81), who made a distinction between value and existence, whereby value is regarded as being in contradistinction to existence, argued that existence is comprehended with the intellect, while value is comprehended with the emotion. He became the founder of axiology by introducing the clear concept of value into philosophy.

What Are Values?

Since the term "value" was originally derived from economic life, it refers mainly to economic value. Today, however, the term has become more generalized, being used in almost all areas of human activity, including society, politics, economics, law, morality, art, learning, religion, etc. In the Unification Thought view, there are both material values and spiritual values. Material values are connected with the daily necessities of human life, such as commodities; on the other hand, spiritual values refer to those values corresponding to the faculties of intellect, emotion, and will, namely, the values of truth, beauty, and goodness. Of these two kinds, Unification Axiology deals primarily with the spiritual values.

It has generally been thought difficult to define the concept of value and that there was no other way to deal with it than to analyze it through those phenomena related to it.[1] In the theory of axiology presented here, however, value is defined as that quality of an object that satisfies the desire of the subject. That is, when an object has a certain quality that satisfies the desire or wish of the subject and which is recognized as such by the subject, then that special quality of the object can be called value. In other words, value is something that belongs to an object; yet, unless it is recognized as valuable by the subject, it does not become actual value. For example, even though there may exist a flower, unless someone (the subject) perceives the beauty of that flower, the actual value (beauty) of the flower does not manifest. In this way, in order for value to become actual, there is a need for a process in which a subject must recognize the quality of an object and must appraise that quality as valuable.

Desire

As explained above, value refers to the quality of an object that satisfies the desire of a subject. Therefore, in order to discuss values, we need to analyze the desire of the subject. Philosophical attempts to deal with questions of value (including material value) have generally focused on objective phenomena alone, excluding consideration of human desire. They have, therefore, been inadequate, like a tree without roots. A tree without roots withers. Accordingly, existing thought systems are revealing their insufficiency today as regards solving various social problems.

For example, economic theories, which deal with material values, have become relatively useless in solving the phenomena of the current economic confusion. Many complex problems, which even many economists did not anticipate, are also emerging, such as the impact that labor-management relations can have on business results. Why is this? The primary reason is that economists have not correctly analyzed human desire itself. Although they know that the motivation of economic activity is human desire, they have not engaged in any serious analysis of this desire. In order to understand such phenomena correctly, we should begin by analyzing human desire. Prior to this, however, let us first address the Divine Principle foundation of axiology, so that we may begin with the proper context.

II. Divine Principle Foundation for Axiology

According to the Divine Principle, the human being, as a united being of *sungsang* and *hyungsang*, has both purpose and desire. Desire is part of the original human nature given by God (*DP*, 70). Furthermore, purpose and desire both have a dual nature. Unification Axiology is formulated on the basis of these fundamental ideas.

Sungsang and *Hyungsang* and Dual Purposes

As a created being, a human being is endowed with a certain purpose for being created (namely, God's purpose of creation). A human being, endowed with such a purpose is, at the same time, a united being of *sungsang* and *hyungsang*, namely, a dual being of spirit self and physical self, or a dual being of spirit mind and physical mind. To say that a human being has a purpose for being created means that *sungsang* and *hyungsang* both have a purpose. The former is called the *sungsang* purpose and the latter is called the *hyungsang* purpose. Together we may call them the "dual purposes," and they correspond to the dual characteristics of *sungsang* and *hyungsang*.

Here, *sungsang* refers to the spirit mind, and *hyungsang* refers to the physical mind. Thus, the *sungsang* purpose is the purpose of the spirit mind, which is to guide us in leading a life emphasizing truth, goodness, beauty, and love, and the *hyungsang* purpose is the purpose of the physical mind, which is to guide us in leading a life emphasizing food, clothing, shelter, and sexual fulfillment.

Sungsang and *Hyungsang* and Dual Desires

A human being is, as just noted, a united being of *sungsang* and *hyungsang*, namely, a being with a dual mind (spirit mind and physical mind). Therefore, human desire functions in these two modes, namely, there is a *sungsang* desire and there is a *hyungsang* desire. The *sungsang* desire is the desire of the spirit mind which seeks after truth, goodness, beauty, and love, whereas the *hyungsang* desire is the desire of the physical mind which seeks after food, clothing, shelter, and sexual fulfillment. These are "dual desires."

TABLE 4.1 The Duality of Desire, Purpose, and Value

		Purpose		Desire		Value	
Dual Characterstics	Dual Mind	Dual Purposes	Dual Purposes (corresponding to the whole and the individual)	Dual Desires	Dual Desires (corresponding to the whole and the individual)	Dual Value	Dual Values (corresponding to the whole and the individual)
Sung-sang	Spirit Mind	Sung-sang Purpose	Purpose for the Whole	Sung-sang Desire	Desire to Realize Value	Sung-sang Value	Realized Value
			Purpose for the Individual		Desire to Seek Value		Sought-after Value
Hyung-sang	Physical Mind	Hyung-sang Purpose	Purpose for the Whole	Hyung-sang Desire	Desire to Realize Value	Hyung-sang Value	Realized Value
			Purpose for the Individual		Desire to Seek Value		Sought-after Value

Dual Purposes, Dual Desires and Dual Values

According to the Divine Principle, a human being is a connected being with dual purposes: the purpose for the whole and the purpose for the individual (*DP*, 33). Thus, the *sungsang* and the *hyungsang* of the mind are connected to the purpose for the whole and the purpose for the individual, respectively. Accordingly, both *sungsang* purpose and *hyungsang* purpose have the purpose for the whole and the purpose for the individual.

A desire is an impulse of the mind to achieve a certain purpose. Accordingly, desire seeks to achieve both the purpose for the whole and the purpose for the individual. The former is called the "desire to realize value," and the latter is called the "desire to seek value." Together these are called the "dual desires for value." This means that both the *sungsang* desire and the *hyungsang* desire are for realizing the dual purposes. In other words, both the *sungsang* desire and the *hyungsang* desire have the desire to realize value and the desire to seek value.

Dual values can be explained in connection with dual purposes and dual desires. In the same way that there are dual purposes and dual desires, so too, there are dual values: the "value to be realized" and the "value to be sought." "The value to be realized" refers to the value that is to be realized or that has been realized. "The value to be sought" refers to the value that is to be sought or that has been sought. Dual purposes, dual desires, and dual values all correspond with one another. An arrangement of the duality of desire, purpose, and value in relation to dual mind (spirit mind and physical mind) is shown in table 4.1.

Origin of Desire and Purpose of Creation

For what purpose do human desires exist? They exist in order that we might realize the purpose of creation. God's purpose of creation is for God to receive joy through loving His object partners (human beings and all things). For created beings, however, their purpose of creation is the purpose for which they were created. Particularly for human beings, the purpose for being created is to return beauty and give joy to God. Accordingly, the purpose for which human beings were created can be fulfilled through their realization of the three great blessings, namely, to be fruitful, to multiply, and to have dominion over all things (Gen. 1:28). Therefore, the purpose of creation for human beings is none other than their completion of the three great blessings.

If, at the time of the creation of human beings, God had given them only this purpose but had not given them desire, then the most they would have been capable of doing would be to come up with the mere thought, "There is a purpose of creation," or "There are the three great blessings." They would not have felt any necessity for putting such thoughts into action. If this had been the case, then the purpose of creation and the three great blessings could never have been realized. Therefore, God also needed to give human beings the impulsive will to actualize that purpose, the impulse of the mind to do or obtain something. This impulse to do so, is desire. Accordingly, driven by an innate impulse to achieve the purpose of creation, namely, to fulfill the three great blessings, human beings gradually grow to maturity. This desire, with which human beings have been endowed by God, is centered on heart.

A human being is a connected being possessing dual purposes, namely, the purpose for the whole and the purpose for the individual. Accordingly, the purpose of creation is to fulfill the purpose for the whole and the purpose for the individual. The purpose for the whole, for human beings, is to realize true love, namely, to serve one's family, society, people, nation, and world, and ultimately God, the Parent of humankind: the purpose for the whole is to give joy to humankind and to God. On the other hand, the purpose for the individual is to live for one's own growth and to seek one's own joy. Not only human beings, but also all things, have a purpose for the whole and a purpose for the individual. This is the two-fold nature of the purpose of creation, or the purpose for being created.

The way in which the purpose of creation is accomplished by all things non-human is different from the way in which human beings accomplish their purpose. Inorganic substances fulfill their purpose of creation following natural law; plants, by following the autonomy of the principle (life) within them; and animals, by following their instinct. Human beings, however, must in addition accomplish their purpose of creation by following and satisfying the desire given to them by God, using their own free will, and fulfilling their own responsibility. As mentioned already, desire is the impulse of the mind to attain a certain purpose. Just as purpose has duality, namely, the purpose for the whole and the purpose for the individual, there are also dual desires, the desire to realize value and the desire to seek value. Corresponding to the dual purposes and dual desires, value itself also has a duality, namely, realized value and sought-after value, as shown in table 4.1.

III. Kinds of Value

Sungsang Value

Value is that quality in an object that satisfies the desire of the subject. As desires of a dual being of *sungsang* and *hyungsang*, human desires can be divided into *sungsang* desire and *hyungsang* desire; as a consequence, there exist also *sungsang* value and *hyungsang* value. *Sungsang* value is a spiritual value which satisfies the *sungsang* desire: it consists of truth, goodness, beauty, and love. To be precise, love is the basis for the values of truth, goodness, and beauty. Truth, beauty, and goodness are the values corresponding to the three faculties of the mind, namely, intellect, emotion and will. That is to say, when the subject appraises an element of the object as being valuable, the subject appraises it as truth, beauty, or goodness, according to the faculties of intellect, emotion, or will, respectively.

Hyungsang Value

Hyungsang value, which satisfies the *hyungsang* desire, includes those material values (commodity values) of daily necessities, such as food, clothing, and shelter. Material value is the value necessary for maintaining physical life, or that value which satisfies the desire of the physical mind. Physical life is the condition for the growth of the spirit self and for the fulfillment of the three great blessings; thus *hyungsang* value is a prerequisite for the realization of *sungsang* value.

Love is the basis for the values of truth, goodness and beauty. Let me explain this in more detail. The more a subject loves an object, and the more the object loves the subject, the truer, the better, and more beautiful the object comes to appear to the subject. For example, the more parents love their children and the more children love their parents, the more beautiful the children will appear. When children look more beautiful, the parents will feel like loving them even more. The same thing can be said of truth and goodness. The more parents love their children and the more children love their parents, the truer and the better children will appear. In this way, truth, goodness and beauty come into being on the foundation of love. Of course, there are many cases wherein truth, goodness and beauty can be felt without love. Strictly speaking, however, in such cases the subject unconsciously has love within his or her subconsciousness.

In this way, love is truly the source and foundation of value. Without love, true value will not appear. Accordingly, the more we experience the Heart of God and lead a life of love, the more we will experience and actualize brilliant value. As mentioned already, value consists of *sungsang* values and *hyungsang* values. Unification Axiology deals primarily with *sungsang* values.

IV. Essence of Value

Essence of Value and Actual Value

There are two ways in which to understand value: one is to consider the very essence of value, some quality which is possessed by the object, and the other is to consider the actualization of value, which takes place in the relationship between subject and object. The former is called "potential value," and the latter, "actual value." When it is said that value is that quality of an object which can potentially satisfy the desire of a subject, the value being referred to is potential value. Actual value is something that is necessarily appraised in our actual life, and such appraisal is actually carried out during the give and receive action between a subject and an object. The value determined by such an appraisal may be called actual value.

Potential value, then, is the quality of an object, or the essence of value, which refers to the contents, attributes, conditions, and so on of the object. The values of truth, goodness, and beauty themselves are not realized in the object itself, but are only latent in the object as the essence that can be realized as actual only through a relationship with the subject. Through that relationship they become actual values.

Potential Value

Then what, concretely, is the essence of value? The essence of value consists of the object's purpose of creation and the harmony existing between paired elements in the object. Every created being has a purpose for which it was created, namely, its purpose of creation. For example, a flower has the purpose to give joy to people through its beauty. Not only in the beings created by God, but also in things produced by people (e.g., art works and commodities) there are always purposes for which they were created.

The harmony between paired elements refers to the harmony between subject element and object element. Since all things are individual truth beings, they have within themselves correlative elements of subject and object, such as *sungsang* and *hyungsang*, yang and yin, and principal element and subordinate element. Harmony is realized through the give and receive action between these correlative elements. The give and receive action here referred to is that of the comparison type. In this way, the situation wherein the paired elements are harmonized centering on the purpose of creation is a situation wherein the essence of value, or potential value, exists.

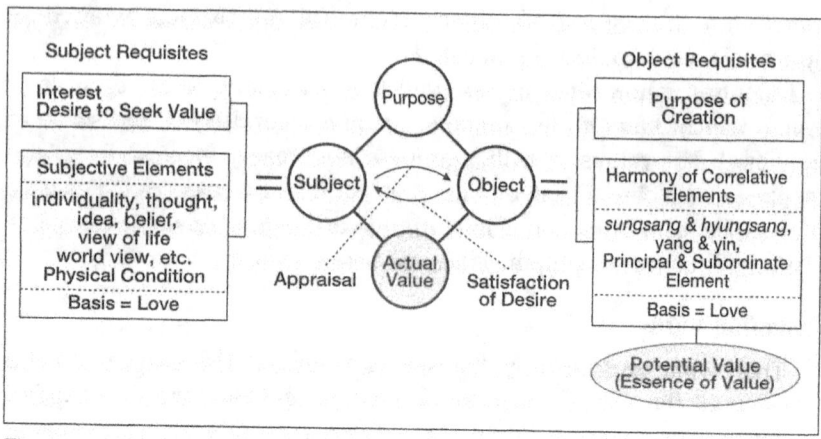

Fig. 4.1. The Determination of Value

V. Determination of Actual Value and Standard of Value

A. Determination of Value

Value is determined, or appraised, through a give and receive action between a person (subject) and an object. The condition that must exist in the object, the "object requisite," is, as mentioned above, a harmony between its paired elements, centering on its purpose of creation. On the other hand, there are also certain conditions that must exist in the subject (human being), the "subject requisites," in order for value to be determined. First, the subject must possess the desire to seek value; next, the subject must have a concern for, or interest in, the object. Moreover, one's philosophy, taste, individuality, education, view of life, outlook on history, world view, and so on, which one (as subject) possesses as subjective elements are all conditions that will influence any determination of value. These subjective elements, including the desire to seek value and an interest in the object, are the "subject requisites" which the subject necessarily must have. Actual value is determined through the correlative relationship between these subject requisites and object requisites (see fig. 4.1).

When both the subject requisites and the object requisites are present, give and receive action will take place between the subject and the object, and this is how value is determined. Determining concrete value means determining the quantity and quality of value. The quantity of value refers to the quantitative appraisal of value, such as "very beautiful," or "not so beautiful." There are also qualitative differences in value. For example, in beauty there are various nuances, such as graceful beauty, awesome beauty, solemn beauty, comic beauty, and so on. These are qualitative differences in value.

B. Subjective Action

As mentioned already, subjective elements significantly influence the determination of value. That is to say, the particular actual value which an individual subject will feel is determined when such subjective elements as one's own philosophy, taste, individuality, education, view of life, outlook on history, world view, and so on, are projected upon the object (or added to the objective requisites), and reflected back once again.

For example, when the moon is observed by different people, it may appear sad to one person but happy to another. Even when the same person looks at the moon, if the person is sad, the moon may look sad, but if the person is happy, the moon may look happy. Differences in beauty arise depending on the mood of the subject. This can be said not only about beauty, but about truth and goodness as well; the same applies to the value of commodities. Thus, quantitative and qualitative differences in value arise because the subject's subjectivity is projected onto the object, and reflected back. In other words, the subject conditions significantly influence the determination of value. This effect is called "subjective action." It refers to the action through which a subject's subjectivity is projected upon an object, and reflected back.

This idea corresponds to the idea of "empathy" in aesthetics as mentioned by T. Lipps (1851–1914). Empathy means that when one looks at natural scenery, or appreciates a work of art, one projects one's feeling or idea upon the object, and appreciates it. Let me cite a few examples of subjective action. While speaking about heart, Rev. Moon said,

> Suppose the Son of God gave you a handkerchief. That handkerchief is worth more than gold, more than life, more than anything else in the

world. If you are a real Son of God, whatever humble place you may lay yourself, it is a palace. Then our clothing is no problem, and the place we sleep is no problem, because we are already rich. We are the princes of God.[2]

The meaning here is that if one is aware that he is the son of God, even a shabby hut would seem like a luxurious palace. This is an appropriate example of subjective action. There is a passage in the Bible: "The kingdom of God is in the midst of you" (Luke 17:21), which is also an example of subjective action. In Buddhism also, there is a saying, "The three realms are only manifestations of the mind." This means that all the phenomena of the three realms (i.e., the entire world) are manifestations of the mind.[3] This is also an example of subjective action.

C. Standard for Determining Value

Relative Standard

As a result of subjective action, the determination (or appraisal) of value will differ according to different individual subjects. Yet, when there are many commonalities in the subject conditions, there will also be many points of agreement in the appraisal of value. Among people who believe in the same religion or philosophy, the way they feel about values will be almost the same. For example, "filial piety toward parents," which is a virtue of Confucianism, is always highly appraised and is universally held as good in Confucian societies.

This means that among people who have the same religion or thought, the unification of values is quite possible. For example, during the period of the Pax Romana, the Stoic spirit of self-control and cosmopolitanism were the dominant, unifying values. During the Tang period in China and the period of Unified Shilla on the Korean peninsula, when Buddhism was the state religion, Buddhist morality was the central value system. In the United States, a Christian nation, the Christian (especially Protestant) moral view has been the unifying value system of the people.

Differences in the views of value do arise, however, among different religions, different cultures, and different philosophies. For example, in Hinduism, eating beef is prohibited, whereas in Islam, eating beef is allowed, but one is not allowed to eat pork. Another example is when Communists talk about peace; in so doing they mean something quite different from what that same term means in the free world.

Thus, in those regions and societies where people have the same religion or thought, their views of value become almost identical. Between different religions or thought systems, however, the views of value are not identical. In such cases, the agreement in the view of value is limited to a certain sphere. In this way, when standards for value judgment apply only to a limited sphere, we can call them "relative standards."

Absolute Standard

Humankind's values can not be unified on the basis of such relative value standards, nor will the conflicts and struggles resulting from differences in values come to an end if we base ourselves on relative standards alone. In order to realize true peace for all humankind, a standard for value judgment must be established such that it can apply to all people in common, transcending all differences in religion, culture, thought, nationality, and so on. This standard of value appraisal would be an absolute standard.

Then, is it possible to establish such an absolute standard and, if so, how can it be done? In order to show that it is possible, we must first clarify that the causal being of the universe, the being who gave rise to all religions, cultures, thought systems, and all ethnic groups, is only one, and is an absolute being. Furthermore, we must discern the various commonalities which originate from this causal being.

As was explained in detail in "Ontology," all things in the universe exist in innumerable ways, but they all move in a specific order and according to certain laws. Also, all things have common attributes. The reason for this is that all things in the universe were created in resemblance to the causal being, or God. Likewise, although there are many religions, cultures, philosophies, and ethnic groups, all of them being different from one another, if there is one causal being that gave rise to all of them, then there must be certain commonalities shared by all of them, which originate from that causal being, or fundamental being.

Numerous religions have emerged throughout history, but they were not just arbitrarily established by their founders. In order to save all of humankind, ultimately, God established specific founders in specific regions and at specific periods of time, seeking to save the people of each region and in each period. This is because God has been carrying on the dispensation of salvation for peoples of different languages, different customs, and different environments, and He has established religions in such a way that each was most suitable for a particular age, and for each region.

Thus, in order to discover the commonalities among the different religions, it is necessary to clarify that the causal being, who established all religions, is one and the same being. The causal being of all things in the universe is variously called *Jehovah* in Judaism, *Allah* in Islam, *Brahman* in Hinduism, *Tathatā* in Buddhism, and *Heaven* in Confucianism. According to Unification Thought, all of these terms refer to the same being as the term *God* in Christianity.

Yet, the attributes of this causal being, or fundamental being, have not been clearly stated in any of these religions. For example, in Confucianism, the concrete nature of *Heaven* is not sufficiently explained, nor is there a sufficient explanation given about *Tathatā* in Buddhism, or about *Brahman* in Hinduism. The same thing can be said about *God* in Christianity, *Jehovah* in Judaism, and *Allah* in Islam.

Beyond this, the reason why the causal being has created humankind and the universe has not been clearly explained by these various religions; nor is it explained why this causal being has not been able to more quickly save suffering humanity. Accordingly, this causal being, as understood in the various religions, has been vague, as if hidden by a veil. Furthermore, since each religion grasps only certain aspects of this causal being, this being appears to be different in the different religions.

In order to show that the causal being of these different religions is, ultimately, one and the same being, we need to understand correctly the attributes of God, His purpose of creation, the laws (or Logos) of the creation of the universe, and so on. If we were to acquire such an understanding, we could quickly come to realize that the people of all religions are brothers and sisters originating from one and the same God. We would also be able to put an end to the long-lasting conflicts and struggles among religions, and could come to reconcile with one another and love one another. Thus, we will find that a correct knowledge of the nature of God is the key to the solution of actual problems. The same thing can be said with regard to cultures, philosophies, and peoples. Once we understand that the fundamental being that gave rise to all cultures, philosophies, and peoples is one and the same being, then the commonalities among them can also be clarified.

Then, what, concretely, are the commonalities that can become an absolute standard in the appraisal of values? They are God's love (absolute love) and God's truth (absolute truth). God created humankind in order to obtain joy through love. The love of God has been expressed variously, as *agape* in Christianity, mercy in Buddhism, *jen* (benevolence) in Confucianism, compassion in Islam, and so on. The teachings of love in all religions were inspired from the love of the one God. God's love is especially manifested among human beings in the form of the three object partners' loves, namely parents' love, love of husband and wife, and children's love. (If children's love is further differentiated into their love for their parents and love they share among themselves, namely brotherly/sisterly love, we arrive at four object partners' loves.) The practice of love for one's neighbor in Christianity, the practice of mercy in Buddhism, the practice of *jen* in Confucianism, the practice of compassion in Islam, and so on, have all been emphasized in order to actualize these three object partners' loves.

Since the eternal God created the universe, the truth or law through which God created the universe and which governs all the movements of the universe, is also eternal and universal. The fundamental law of the universe is that all beings exist, not for their own sake, but for the sake of others, for the sake of the whole, and for the sake of God. That is to say, they are beings for others. Accordingly, the universal standard of good and evil is whether one lives for other people (humankind) or lives for oneself in a self-centered way.[4]

Absolute Standard and Human Individuality

As explained above, an absolute standard for the appraisal of values comes to be established only through God's true love and truth, and this appraisal can become identical among all humankind. Then, what about a person's unique individuality? Since a value judgment is influenced to some extent by the subjective elements of individual persons, certain differences in value judgment necessarily arise, depending on different individualities. Then, the question may be raised: "If value judgments should become identical in view of an absolute standard, won't human individuality be disregarded?"

Fortunately, even if the value judgment does become identical in the context of an absolute standard, individuality will neither be disregarded nor abolished, but rather it will be preserved as it is. Let us look at the reason for this.

Since human beings are individual truth beings, they resemble God's Universal Image (commonality), and His Individual Images (particularity). Also, since they are connected beings, they exist with both the purpose for the whole and the purpose for the individual. Accordingly, an absolute standard for value judgment is connected to the universal image and the purpose for the whole, while one's subjective action is connected to the individual image and the purpose for the individual. These are always united.

Thus, even if absolute values are determined by an absolute standard, naturally there will still exist individual differences due to subjective action. In other words, absolute value is a universal value which includes individual differences, in the same way as when one finds that in an individual truth being the universal image includes the individual image. Human beings, through their individual image, pursue the purpose for the whole; they thus express their individual image while maintaining the universal image.

Therefore, the appraisal of value, though based on an absolute standard, can not be done apart from one's subjective action based on one's individuality. Nevertheless, individual differences must still be based on commonality. As long as there is a common base, there will be no confusion in value perspectives. This is because the differences in such cases are not qualitative but quantitative.

For example, in the case of the appraisal of goodness, "to help the poor" is judged as good regardless of religion and thought. In the ideal world, there will be no one who judges it as evil (qualitative judgment). However, depending upon persons, there can be quantitative differences such as judging it as "very good," or "moderately good," or "ordinarily good." The same thing can be said of the judgments of beauty and of truth. In sum, an absolute standard in the appraisal of value refers to the agreement of the qualitative judgment. In fallen egoistic society, however, qualitative differences have arisen and, as a result, a confusion of values has also emerged.

Here, with Unification Thought, the establishment of a new view of value and the unification of existing views of value become possible. It is possible to unite the various standards of value appraisal, centering on absolute love and absolute truth, while yet preserving individuality in the value appraisal. This new view of value is one based on the absolute love and truth of God. This new view of value is none other than the view of absolute value.[5] Absolute value can harmonize and embrace all value systems. This can bring the unification of various views of value. In order to unify systems of value in this way, the correct understanding of God's attributes, His purpose of creation, Heart, Love, Logos, and so on are required as prerequisites. The unification of religions and the unification of thought systems becomes possible through such a unification of the views of value.

VI. Weaknesses in the Traditional Views of Value

As already stated, one of the causes of the collapse of values today is that traditional systems of value—primarily religious systems—have lost their persuasive power, their ability to persuade people. Why have the traditional views of value lost their persuasive power? Let us look at some representative cases.

A. Weaknesses in the Christian View of Value

Christianity promotes excellent virtues, as expressed in the following biblical passages:

> "You shall love your neighbor as yourself" (Matt. 22:39).
> "Love your enemies and pray for those who persecute you" (Matt. 5:44).
> "Whatever you wish that men would do to you, do so to them" (The Golden Rule, Matt 7:12).
> "Blessed are the poor in spirit, for theirs is the kingdom of heaven.
> Blessed are those who mourn, for they shall be comforted.
> Blessed are the meek, for they shall inherit the earth.
> Blessed are those who hunger and thirst for righteousness, for they shall be satisfied.
> Blessed are the merciful, for they shall obtain mercy.
> Blessed are the pure in heart, for they shall see God.
> Blessed are the peacemakers, for they shall be called sons of God.
> Blessed are those who are persecuted for righteousness' sake, for theirs is the kingdom of heaven" (Matt. 5).

"So, faith, hope, love abide, these three; but the greatest of these is love" (1 Cor. 13:13).
"The fruit of the Spirit is love, joy, peace, patience, kindness, goodness, faithfulness, gentleness, self-control; against such there is no law" (Gal. 5:22-23).

Although in Christianity there are many other virtues, it is stated that "love builds up" (1 Cor. 8:1), which means that the basis for all virtues is love. It is also stated that "Love is of God···. God is love" (1 John 4:7-8), which means that the basis of love is God.

Yet, in our modern age the existence of God came to be denied by Nietzsche, Feuerbach, Marx, Russell, Sartre, and many others. Christianity has not been able to respond effectively to such God-denying philosophies. That is to say, in the confrontation between theism and atheism, Christianity has lost ground. As a result, a great number of people have become influenced by atheism.

Furthermore, a challenge has been issued by Communism against the Christian view of value. Communists deny the concepts of absolute love and love for humankind, as asserted in Christianity, and insist that real love is class-centered love, or love for one's comrades. In a society where there are conflicts of interest, there can be no love beyond one's own social class. One simply has to choose to stand either on the side of the proletariat or on the side of the bourgeoisie. It is impossible to practice a love for humankind in an actual class society. Ultimately, say the Communists, love for humankind is an empty phrase that can not be put into actual practice.

To hear such assertions, certainly class-centered love sounds more actual, whereas Christian love sounds merely conceptual. Especially for those who are not convinced of the existence of God, it is quite natural that Christian love does not seem to be so convincing.

It is also not surprising that Liberation Theology and Dependency Theory have emerged today in the Third World. According to Liberation Theology, Jesus was a revolutionary who came to save the oppressed and the poor of his age. Therefore, Liberation Theology preaches that those who are true Christians must fight for social revolution. Thus, sympathy for the poor agrees well with the Communist view of class-centered love, and eventually this kind of sympathy becomes aligned with Communism in working to solve actual problems.[6]

According to Dependency Theory, poverty in the third world arises from structural contradictions between advanced countries and the third world, and is unavoidable. This theory asserts that in order for the third world to be liberated from poverty, the third world must confront advanced capitalist nations. Dependency Theory attempts to align itself with Communism in much the same way as Liberation Theology does.[7]

Neither Liberation Theology nor Dependency Theory possesses a coherent philosophy, a coherent theory of history, or a coherent economic theory when compared to Communism. Therefore, eventually they can not but be absorbed by Communism. Christianity has been unable to take an effective course of action to resolve this situation.

B. Weaknesses in the Confucian View of Value

In Confucianism there are such virtues as the following:

(1) *The Five Moral Rules Governing the Five Human Relationships*: The five moral rules, since ancient times, have been described as follows: "Affection should mark the relations between father and son; justice and righteousness should mark the relations between sovereign and subject; distinction should mark the relations between husband and wife; order should mark the relations between elder and younger brothers; trust should mark the relations among friends." These have been regarded as the basis for human relationships, and were especially emphasized by Mencius.

(2) *The Four Virtues*: Mencius preached four virtues, namely, *jen* (benevolence), righteousness, propriety, and knowledge. Later, Tung Chung-shu, of the Han dynasty, added "faith," establishing the Way of the Five Cardinal Virtues (*jen*, righteousness, propriety, knowledge, and faith).

(3) *The Four Beginnings*: According to Mencius, the feeling of commiseration, the feeling of shame and dislike, the feeling of modesty and complaisance, and the feeling of approving and disapproving, are the Four Beginnings. Each of these was thought to be the beginning of one of the Four Virtues, *jen*, righteousness, propriety, and knowledge, respectively.

(4) *The Eight Articles*: In order to govern the world peacefully, an official must do the following: (a) investigate many things; (b) extend his knowledge; (c) be guided by sincere thoughts; (d) rectify his heart; (e) cultivate his personality; (f) regulate his own family; (g) govern the state well; and

(h) bring peace to the world.[8]

(5) *Loyalty and Filial Piety*: Loyalty and filial piety are the virtues with which one serves one's superiors and one's parents.

The basis for all these virtues is *jen*, and the basis for *jen* is Heaven.[9] However, Confucianism does not explain clearly what Heaven is. Communists have criticized Confucianism by applying the Communist theory of "basis and superstructure," saying that the Confucian teaching is nothing more than a means of justifying the existing rules. They argue that Confucian values were coined by the ruling class during the feudal period in order to make the people follow obediently and that, therefore, Confucian teachings are not appropriate for a modern, democratic society, which follows the principles of equal rights and majority rule. Consequently, Confucian virtues are all but neglected today. Furthermore, as communities have become urbanized and families have divided into nuclear families, the Confucian view of value is increasingly collapsing and, as a result, there has been an acceleration of disorder and confusion in many communities.

C. Weaknesses in the Buddhist View of Value

The fundamental virtue of Buddhism is mercy (*maitri*), and in order to practice mercy a life of training is required. Through such a life of training, one reaches *Srāvaka* (one who is awakened by hearing the teachings, or one who wishes to become a disciple of the *arhat*, the enlightened one), *Pratyeka-buddha* (one who awakens by oneself, or the one who has realized the principle of no generation or destruction and attained the state of freedom), *Bodhisattva* (the one striving for enlightenment, or the one who strives for Buddhahood and tries to lead people to Buddhahood) and finally Buddhahood (the enlightened one, or the one with perfect personality). Mercy, a virtue, becomes possible at the levels of *Bodhisattva* and Buddhahood. One is not yet ready to practice mercy at the levels of *Srāvaka* and *Pratyeka-buddha*.

Human beings are not aware of the fact that all things in the world change, or are transitory; accordingly, they are overly attached to their present life, and that is the cause of their suffering. In order to end suffering one must get rid of such attachments through a life of training. Deliverance from attachments and liberation from suffering are understood as "salvation" (*vimukti*) in Buddhism. Through salvation, one enters a state of selflessness and acquires the ability to practice true mercy, according to Buddhism.

The fundamental thought of the Buddha has been systematized in the teachings of the Four Noble Truths and the Noble Eightfold Path. The Four Noble Truths consist of (1) the Truth of Suffering, (2) the Truth of the Cause of Suffering, (3) the Truth of the Cessation of Suffering, and (4) the Truth of the Noble Path to the Cessation of the Cause of Suffering. The Truth of Suffering tells us that human life is full of suffering. The Truth of the Cause of Suffering teaches that the cause of this suffering is attachment. The Truth of the Cessation of Suffering teaches that in order to get rid of suffering and attain *Nirvana* (Perfect Tranquility), one must give up attachment. The Truth of the Noble Path to the Cessation of the Cause of Suffering is that, in order to make one's suffering disappear and to attain *Nirvana*, one must be trained in and walk according to the Noble Eightfold Path.

The Noble Eightfold Path is the following: (1) Right View, (2) Right Thought, (3) Right Speech, (4) Right Behavior, (5) Right Livelihood, (6) Right Effort, (7) Right Mindfulness, and (8) Right Concentration.

Right view refers to one's having correct knowledge about the essence of the world without any prejudice. Through right thought, a person decides to walk the correct path. Right speech includes not lying or criticizing others unjustly. Right behavior includes abstaining from killing and stealing. To follow right livelihood, a person must live a righteous life in accordance with the right law. To practice right effort, a person must conquer all evil thoughts, and strive to dwell only on good thoughts. To attain right mindfulness, a person must seek truth, freeing his or her mind from earthly thoughts. Finally, through right concentration, a person engages in deep meditation and attains a tranquil state of mind without worldly desires.

The system of twelve points was established through an enquiry into the cause of the emergence of human pain. That cause is the teaching of the twelve causations. According to this teaching, the root cause of human suffering is desire or greed, but more fundamental than that, there is ignorance of *Tathatā* (the source of the universe), and of the state of not realizing that pain and suffering are not essential. From this ignorance, all kinds of suffering arise.

In Mahayana Buddhism, the perfection of the following six practices (*pramit*) is necessary for one to become a *Bodhisattva*: (1) Offering, (2)

Keeping precepts, (3) Endurance, (4) Endeavor, (5) Concentration of mind, and (6) Wisdom. Offering means giving to others unconditionally, with benevolence. Keeping precepts is for the perfection of morality. A person must endure sufferings. Endeavor refers to one's practice of the teachings of Buddha with diligence and courage. Concentration of mind is the perfection of meditation, and wisdom is the knowledge and ability to judge good and evil, or right and wrong.

The root of the above virtues of Buddhism is mercy, and the basis for mercy is *Tathatā*, which is the source of the universe.[10] Today, however, the Buddhist view of values has lost its ability to persuade people. This is because the Buddhist doctrine has the following problems:

(1) The exact nature of *Tathatā*, the source of the universe, is not explained.

(2) The way the *dharmas* (all phenomena) have come into being is unclear.

(3) A fundamental explanation of how ignorance came about is not given.

(4) A fundamental solution of actual problems (of human life, society, and history) is impossible merely through training.

Moreover, Communism has served as a challenge to Buddhism. The Communist assault can be summarized as follows: "Actual society is filled with exploitation, oppression, the gap between rich and poor, and other social ills. The cause of these vices lies not so much in personal ignorance as it does in the contradictions within the system of capitalist society itself. Buddhist training is for the salvation of the individual, but is not that just a way of escaping from reality, a way of avoiding a real solution to the problems? Engaging in training without solving actual problems is nothing but hypocrisy." Thus confronted, Buddhists have been unable to counter with an appropriate response.

D. Weaknesses in the Islamic View of Value

Islam regards Muhammad as the greatest of all prophets and the Qur'an as the most perfect of all scriptures, but it also believes in Abraham, Moses, Jesus, and the prophets, and regards the five books of Moses, David's Psalms, and the Gospel of Jesus, as its scriptures. Therefore, Islamic virtues have many points in common with Judeo-Christian virtues.[11]

The Islamic teachings of faith and practice are summarized in the Six Articles of Faith and the Five Obligatory Practices. The six articles of faith are that one must believe in God, in angels, in the scriptures, in the prophets, in the Day of Judgment, and must believe that human destiny is in the hands of Allah. The five obligations, or pillars, are prayer, confession of faith, fasting, almsgiving, and pilgrimage.

The object of faith is Allah, who is absolute, the only one, the Creator, and the Ruler. To the question of who Allah is, Islamic theologians offer ninety-nine attributes, among which "compassionate" and "merciful" are the most fundamental.[12] Therefore, we can say that the most fundamental and representative virtue of all Islamic virtues is compassion, or mercy.

In this way, Islamic values have many points in common with the values of other religions, and can exist in harmony with them. However, there have been many cases of serious conflicts, including wars, among Islamic sects, and between Islam and other religions. Taking advantage of such conflicts, Communism has been challenging Islam. The Communist criticism could be summarized as follows: "There can be no love for humankind, as Islam advocates. The struggles among Islamic sects verify our assertion. In a class society, there can be only class-centered love." Thus, by taking advantage of existing conflicts, Communists have attempted to make Islamic countries Communistic, or at least pro-Communistic.

As mentioned, Islam has experienced internal conflicts among its sects and externally with other religions. Above all, the conflict between Islam and Judeo-Christianity has been particularly sharp since the Crusades. The serious conflicts among its sects, and with other religions, all having in common a belief in God's creation and providence, rendered Islamic values virtually impotent as far as having a persuasive influence on people.

E. Weaknesses in the Humanitarian View of Value

The term humanitarianism is often used as having the same meaning as humanism. Yet, in a strict sense, there are important differences. Humanism is a perspective that aims to achieve the liberation of human beings by fostering the independence of the human personality. On the other hand, humanitarianism has strong ethical overtones, advocating respect for people, philanthropy, universal brotherhood, and so on. Unlike animals, human beings possess humanity; therefore, all people should be respected. This rather vague perspective is characteristic of humanitarianism. Nevertheless, it does not explain clearly what a human being is.

Consequently, humanitarianism has inevitably been vulnerable to attacks from Communism. Let us suppose for example, that there is a humanitarian business person. A Communist might approach that person with the following reasoning: "You are exploiting your workers without knowing it. Why do not we build a society where all people live in affluence?" Also, suppose there is a humanitarian youth who believes that acquiring knowledge is the most important thing in life. A Communist might say to that person, "What are you studying for? You should not always be thinking only of your own success. That will, after all, serve only the bourgeoisie. Do you not think we should live for the sake of the people?" Thus confronted, a conscientious humanitarian would find it difficult to respond. Even if the person did not become a Communist, he might be left with a favorable impression of Communism, and harbor good reasons to support it. Accordingly, those with a humanitarian view of value have been unable to deal with Communist admonitions, and therefore many humanitarians have been deceived by Communism. Today, however, Communism having declined, many humanitarians have come to realize that Communism is wrong.

Through the examples given above, it should have become clear that traditional systems of value have lost their ability to persuade people. Therefore, one way of restoring traditional values is to establish a new view of value on the firm foundation of a belief in the existence of God.

VII. Establishing the New View of Value

As mentioned earlier, by this new view of value is meant an absolute view of value. Today's value decline makes it urgent that a new view of value be established. It would be impossible, however, to prevent the phenomenon of the collapse of values by means of any relative view of value. Therefore, an absolute view of value must be established. This absolute view of value must be established on the basis of a clarification of the kinds of attributes God, who is absolute, possesses, and for what purpose (purpose of creation) and through which laws (Logos) God created human beings and the universe.

God created we human beings as object partners of His love, seeking to obtain joy through loving us. In order to please us, He created all things as object partners of love for us. Absolute values are the values of truth, goodness, and beauty based on God's absolute love, that is, absolute truth, absolute goodness, and absolute beauty. Thus, this new view of value is established on the basis of absolute love.

The unification of the views of value means the unification of the various standards for the judgment of value (especially the value of goodness), making it clear that all virtues are simply diverse expressions of absolute value, and that ultimately, all virtues exist in order to actualize absolute love.

Clearly, then, it would be erroneous to think of this new view of value as an entirely new system, established at the cost of denying traditional views of value as found in Christianity, Confucianism, Buddhism, Islam, and so on. Rather, this new view of value is established on the basis of traditional values. Since the foundations upon which traditional values stood are collapsing, we need to rebuild those foundations and revive and strengthen traditional values so that they are invested with new vitality and persuasive power. That is how we can establish a new view of value. Next, in order to explain the absoluteness of this new view of value, I will present the theological, philosophical, and historical grounds upon which it stands.

A. Theological Ground for the New View of Absolute Value

A theological ground involves the question of whether or not the Absolute Being in the universe, referred to as *God* in Christianity, *Heaven* in Confucianism, *Tathatā* in Buddhism, *Allah* in Islam, and so on, truly exists, as well as the question of the nature of the relationship among these different appellations and their referents.

In order to address such questions, what must first be clarified are those questions of significant import in the traditional religions, such as why the Absolute Being created human beings and the universe in the first place. As already explained in the Theory of the Original Image, the reason why God created human beings and the universe is that God is a being of Heart. Heart is the "emotional impulse to seek joy through love." Because of this impulse of His Heart, God created human beings as His object partners of love, and the universe as the environment in which human beings could live. Thus, understanding that God is a God of Heart, the reason for God's creation can be explained very reasonably. Moreover, this becomes an important basis for affirming the existence of God.

God's desire was for a human being to grow as the image of God. This is because, once we become an image of God, God's joy can be realized to the highest degree. It is for this reason that God gave human beings the three great blessings, which meant that God directed man and woman to perfect their character, to perfect their family, and to perfect their qualifications for dominion over all things. Thus, God's purpose of creation would be attained by human beings' realizing the three great blessings. Seen from this point of view, we come to understand that the various virtues of the different religions can come into agreement with one another on the point of accomplishing the three great blessings as the way of realizing God's purpose of creation.

B. Philosophical Ground for the New View of Absolute Value

The value systems of Christianity, Confucianism, Buddhism, and Islam emerged in the period from the sixth century BC to the seventh century AD. During that period of history, people tended to accept unconditionally the rule of authority figures, such as their king. In order for them to live, they had no other choice. Moreover, people in those days were not knowledgeable enough to offer theoretical criticisms of those teachings. Accordingly, it was natural for people to unconditionally obey the rule of authority: they accepted the teachings of Confucius, Buddha, Jesus, or Muhammad unconditionally, and followed them. In modern times, however, it has become more difficult to convey such values to people, because people now have a more rational, analytical, and logical way of thinking. Hence, it is necessary to modernize those values by providing them with rational explanations acceptable to present-day intellectuals.

Then, what kind of explanation is acceptable to twenty-first century people? It is the natural-scientific method. Even ethical virtues could be accepted easily by present-day intellectuals, if they are supported by scientific laws.

It was customary in ancient Greece, and in the Orient, to study nature and thereby to determine a view of value or a view of life. In China, for example, Chu Hsi asserted the correspondence between natural law and ethical law, and said that natural law becomes the ethical law of human society. In modern times, even Marxism took a similar position, although it had a mistaken concept of natural law. Marxism emphasized the identity between natural law and social law (norms in social life) and thus asserted that both nature and society develop according to the dialectic.

As thus evident, in establishing a new view of value it is important to observe nature and the universe, ascertain the fundamental law at work therein, and incorporate it into a view of value. That is, we can clarify that the law inherent in the universe, namely, the Way of Heaven, becomes the standard for ethics and morality. This is what is meant by presenting the philosophical ground for absolute values.

Here arise such questions as whether or not natural law and ethical law correspond to each other, and whether or not natural law can be applied directly to ethical law. From the viewpoint of Unification Thought, all beings are equipped with the dual aspects of *sungsang* and *hyungsang*. Therefore, we are naturally led to the conclusion that ethical law, which is a *sungsang* law, and natural law, which is a *hyungsang* law, are in a relationship of correspondence.

The important point here is how we can obtain a correct understanding of nature. As mentioned in Ontology, Marxist dialectics took, as its point of departure, an inaccurate understanding of nature and then concluded, also incorrectly, that nature develops through the struggle between opposites. As a result, the way of life derived from that wrong interpretation of nature became an incorrect way of life as well.

Seen from the viewpoint of Unification Thought, the fundamental law at work in the universe is not the dialectic, but rather it is the law of give and receive action, which, as stated in Ontology, has the following characteristics: (1) correlativity, (2) purposiveness and centrality, (3) order and position, (4) harmony, (5) individuality and relatedness, (6) identity-maintaining nature and developmental nature, and (7) circular motion. Thus, on the basis of these characteristics of the law of the universe, I will discuss the new Unification View of Value.

The universe has both a vertical order and a horizontal order. The moon revolves around the earth; the earth revolves around the sun; the solar system revolves around the nucleus of the galaxy; and the galaxy revolves around the center of the universe. This is the vertical order of the universe. On the other hand, centering on the Sun, the planets Mercury, Venus, Earth, Mars, Jupiter, Saturn, Uranus, Neptune, and Pluto all revolve in specified orbits. This is one of the horizontal order systems of the universe. These are all harmonious systems of order. There is no contradiction or conflict in these systems. A miniature of this order system of the universe is the family order. Therefore, in the family, too, both a vertical order and a horizontal order are established.

Corresponding to the vertical order of the family, vertical values come to be established. In the family the parents show benevolence to the children, and the children practice filial piety toward the parents. These are vertical values on the family level. When these values are applied to society and the nation, various kinds of vertical values can be derived. Clemency and good governance by the ruler toward the people; loyalty of the people toward their ruler; the teachers' duty to their students; respect and obedience of students toward their teachers; protection of the junior by the senior; respect of the junior for the senior; the authority of superiors over their subordinates; the obedience of subordinates to their superiors; and so on.

Corresponding to the horizontal order of the family, horizontal values come to be established. In the family there is harmonious love between husband and wife and love among brothers and sisters. These, in turn, will expand as values toward colleagues, neighbors, compatriots, community, humankind, and so on. Accordingly, such values as reconciliation, tolerance, duty, fidelity, courtesy, modesty, mercy, cooperation, service, sympathy, and so on, come into being.

If such vertical and horizontal values are maintained well in society, then the society will remain peaceful and develop in a wholesome way. If not, society falls into disorder. Unlike what Communists often assert, these values are not merely relics from feudal society; rather, they are universal norms of conduct that human beings should observe eternally. This is because, just as the law of the universe is eternal, the law of human society is eternal, corresponding to the law of the universe.

Furthermore, the law of the universe has individuality, corresponding to which there are individual values as well. All individual beings in the universe participate in the universal order while maintaining their own unique characteristics. In human society as well, each person engages in mutual relationships with other people while maintaining his or her own character. Individual values include purity, honesty, righteousness, temperance, courage, wisdom, self-control, endurance, independence, self-help, autonomy, fairness, diligence, innocence, and so on. All of these are values for an individual's self-cultivation.

Such vertical, horizontal, and individual values are not particularly new as virtues. They were taught by Confucius, Buddha, Jesus, Muhammad, and others. Today, however, these values have lost their power to persuade people because their philosophical ground has been ambiguous. For that reason, we seek to revive these traditional values by providing them with a firm philosophical basis.

C. Historical Ground for the New View of Absolute Value

Can this new view of value be justified historically? Communism asserts that just as natural phenomena develop through struggle, so too, has human history been developing through struggle (i.e., class struggle). As will be explained in the chapter "Theory of History," however, history has not been developing through struggle. Historical development can be attained only through harmonious give and receive action between subject and object (i.e., leaders and people in society).

Struggles have indeed occurred in history, but they can not be classified simply as class struggles. More precisely, they have been struggles between the forces of relative good and the forces of relative evil. From the perspective of values, it can also be said that they were conflicts between different systems of value. In other words, they were struggles between, on one side, a party with a value perspective that was more in accord with the Way of Heaven (the side of relative goodness) and, on the other side, a party with a value perspective that was more in discord with the Way of Heaven (the side of relative evil). There were some cases in which the relatively good side suffered a set-back, being temporarily defeated by the relatively evil side, but in the long run, the relatively good side always prevailed. As Mencius said, "Those who follow Heaven, survive; those who do not, perish." More importantly, however, struggles between good and evil were not for the purpose of developing history, but rather for the specific purpose of turning history toward a better direction (see chapter 8, "Theory of History").

This can be substantiated by a simple review of history. Secular powers have risen and fallen, but religions, which advocate the cause of goodness, have managed to survive continuously until today. Also, the teachings and achievements of saints and righteous men and women have served as exemplary models for people in later periods, even though many of those saints and righteous people fell victim to evil forces in their own time. These historical facts strongly reinforce the notion that the Way of Heaven has been working in history. In other words, they show that the Way of Heaven should not be rejected by someone in a position of power and that those who do reject it will eventually face a tragic fortune.

Another law of history provides that there was a goal already set up, even at the starting point of history. The universe was created according to an ideal (Logos), centering on purpose (the purpose of creation). In living beings, there is an idea already inherent within a seed or an egg (imprinted in the genetic structure), and the seed or egg grows according to that idea. Likewise, in human history there was an ideal at the outset, and history has been developing toward that ideal. That is to say, at the starting point of history there already was a goal toward which history was to develop. That was the ideal of a nation, the founding idea of a country, or the ideal of humankind recorded symbolically in mythology, legends, and in the holy scriptures of religions.

Human history started as a sinful history as a result of the fall of the first ancestors. Nevertheless, God, by making use of symbols and figures in mythology and in scriptures, has presented the image of the ideal world as envisioned in the original ideal of creation, the ideal world that was lost and which should be restored in human history. The incident in the Garden of Eden as recorded in Genesis, the prophetic records in the Book of Isaiah and in the Revelation to John, and the *Tangun* mythology of the Korean nation are such examples. The ideal pursued until today by humankind is the bright world of goodness, peace and happiness. It is the world that exists in accordance with the Way of Heaven. God has been teaching through mythology and prophecy that the goal of history was already been set up at the outset of history. Therefore, the future world that history aims to attain can be expressed as a world in complete accord with the Way of Heaven, a world wherein the true view of value is firmly established.

VIII. Historical Changes in the View of Value

In this section, let us consider the changes that have taken place in Western views of value from a historical perspective. Through this we can grasp the historical process through which the views of value of Greek philosophy and Christianity, both of which sought absolute values, became overwhelmed by relative views, and eventually became powerless. That will again bring us to the point where it is evident that the confusion in today's world can not be solved without a new view of value (that is, an absolute view of value).

A. Views of Value in the Greek Period

Materialistic View of Value

A materialistic natural philosophy arose in Ionia, an ancient Greek colony, in the sixth century BC. Before that time, Greece had been a tribal society, guided by an age of mythology, but Ionian philosophers were not satisfied with mere mythological explanations and tried to explain the world and human life from a viewpoint based on nature. In the Ionian city of Miletus, foreign trade thrived and merchants were engaged in trade activities throughout the Mediterranean Sea area. They were realistic and active, and in that environment, people gradually discarded their mythological ways of thinking.

In the trading city of Miletus, materialistic philosophers appeared from the sixth century BC. They were known as the Miletus school, whose representatives are Thales, Anaximander, Anaximenes, and others. They discussed ideas mainly with regard to the root cause (*arche*) of all things. Thales (ca. 624–546 BC) advocated that the *arche* was water; Anaximander (ca. 610–547 BC), that it was the boundless (*apeiron*); Anaximenes (ca. 585–528 BC), that it was air; and Heraclitus (ca. 535–475 BC), that it was fire. Influenced by these naturalistic philosophies, objective and rational ways of thinking were fostered.

Arbitrary (Sophistic) View of Value

During the fifth century BC, democracy developed in Greece centering on Athens. Young people sought to acquire knowledge for the purpose of success in life. To be successful, the art of persuasive speech (rhetoric) was especially important. Scholars were paid to instruct young people in the art of persuasion; those scholars came to be called sophists.

Until then, Greek philosophy had dealt primarily with nature. Philosophers became aware, however, that human problems could not be solved through natural philosophy alone. They gradually turned their attention to the problems of human society and soon realized that, whereas natural laws were fixed and objective, the laws and morality of human society differed from country to country and from age to age, with no apparent objectivity or universality. For that reason, the sophists came to take a relativistic, skeptical position on values in order to find solutions to social problems. Protagoras (ca. 481–411 BC) said, "Man is the measure of all things," meaning that the standard of truth differs depending on the person—which clearly indicated relativism.

The sophists, at first, had an enlightening effect on the public. Gradually, however, they came to take a more and more skeptical position, asserting that truth does not exist at all. They attached importance only to the art of persuasion, and attempted to win arguments at any cost, even by resorting to false reasoning, or sophistry. Soon they began to use fallacies in their arguments. That is why the word "sophist" has come to mean a person who uses clever but misleading reasoning.

Absolute View of Value

Socrates (470–399 BC) appeared when sophism was rampant in Greece. He deplored the situation. For him, the sophists pretended to know, but in reality they knew nothing. Of himself, he said, "One thing only I know for sure, and that is that I know nothing." Such was the starting point of reaching true knowledge. He sought the basis of morality in the god (*daimon*) inherent within the human being, and asserted that morality is absolute and universal. Virtue, as taught by him, was a loving attitude of seeking knowledge for the purpose of living truthfully. "Virtue is knowledge" was his fundamental thought. He also advocated the unity of knowledge and action, saying that once one knows virtue, one should, without fail, put it into practice.

How can one obtain true knowledge? True knowledge is not to be poured into a person by others, nor can it be known by an individual alone. Socrates held that it is only through dialogue (questions and answers) with others that one can acquire true knowledge (the universal truth) which satisfies all people. He then sought to save Athens from its social disorder by establishing absolute, universal virtues.

Plato (427–347 BC) thought that there is an unchangeable world of essence behind the changing world of phenomena, and called it the world of Ideas. Yet, since the souls of human beings are trapped in their bodies, they usually think that the phenomenal world is the true reality. The human soul previously existed in the world of Ideas, but when it came to dwell in the body, the soul was separated from the world of Ideas. Accordingly, the soul constantly longs for the world of Ideas, which is the true reality. For Plato, the awareness of the Ideas was but a recollection of what the soul knew before coming into the body. Ethical Ideas include the Idea of Justice, the Idea of Goodness, and the Idea of Beauty. Among these, the Idea of Goodness is supreme, according to Plato.

Plato enumerated four virtues: wisdom, courage, temperance, and justice, as the virtues which everyone must possess. He asserted that particularly those who rule the state must be philosophers possessing the virtue of wisdom. They alone had an understanding of the Idea of Goodness. For Plato, the Idea of Goodness was the source of all values. Inheriting Socrates' spirit, Plato sought absolute value.

B. Views of Value in the Hellenistic-Roman Period

The Hellenistic-Roman period refers to the approximately three centuries, from the time Alexander the Great defeated Persia until the time Roman forces conquered Egypt and unified the Mediterranean world. During this era a trend of individualism, seeking one's own safety and peace of mind, was predominant. The fall of the city-state (*polis*) rendered useless the values centered on the state. The Greeks began to emphasize more individualistic ways of living under increasingly unstable social conditions. At the same time, cosmopolitanism, transcending the bounds of nationality, was enhanced. The representative schools of thought of this era were the Stoic, the Epicurean, and the Skeptic.

With this individualistic tendency, people came to feel a sense of powerlessness. As a result, in the Roman period people sought a way to be elevated above such a vulnerable human situation, and gradually developed religious aspirations. Neoplatonism was one of the fruits of this trend.

Stoic School

The founder of the Stoic school was Zeno of Citium (ca. 336–265 BC). The Stoics held that Logos (law, reason) dwells in all things in the universe, and that the universe moves in an orderly fashion according to law. Moreover, Logos dwells in human beings as well. Therefore, we can know the law of the universe through our reason, and should "live according to nature." That was the basic position of the Stoic school.

The Stoics held that people feel pain because of their passions. To solve this, people should rid themselves of passions and reach the state of *apathy* (the absence of passion) or the perfectly peaceful state of the mind that will not be tempted in any way. Thus, the Stoic school advocated asceticism in which the supreme virtue was *apathy*.

All people, whether they were Greek or Oriental, ought to obey the law of the universe. For the Stoics, the Logos was God, and all people were brothers and sisters as God's children. Thus they established a cosmopolitanism.

Epicurean School

In contradistinction to the Stoic school, which advocated asceticism, the Epicurean school, which originated with Epicurus (341–270 BC), advocated pleasure as the supreme good. Epicurus thought that the pleasure of individual persons in this world was directly in accordance with virtue. By pleasure he did not mean physical pleasure, but rather "having no pain in one's body and giving calm and repose to one's soul." Epicurus called this peaceful state of mind *ataraxia*, or the state of separation from pain, and regarded it as the supreme state of being.

Skeptic School

Pyrrho (ca. 356–275 BC) taught that human beings experience pain because they pass judgment on things one way or another. He urged people to seek calmness of mind by suspending all judgment. This was called *epoche*, or "suspension of judgment." The Skeptic school asserted that since knowledge of the truth can not be attained by human beings, it is best for them to abstain from any form of judgment whatsoever.

The absence of passion (*apathy*) of the Stoic school, the pleasurable peace of mind (*ataraxia*) of the Epicurean school, and the non-judgment (*epoche*) of the Skeptic school were all attempts to find a calmness of mind in the individual. Thus, they regarded as questionable the absoluteness of value pursued by Socrates and Plato.

Neo-Platonism

Greek philosophy continued into the Roman period, which succeeded the Hellenistic period. The philosophical culmination of the Hellenistic-Roman period was Neo-Platonism, a philosophical view-point whose most eminent proponent was Plotinus (205–270).

Plotinus advocated an "emanation theory," according to which everything flows out of God. Specifically, he asserted that *nous* (reason), which is the reality closest to the perfection of God, and then next the soul, and finally matter, the most imperfect level of creation, all emanated from God, stage by stage. Formerly, Greek philosophy had propounded a dualism that regarded God and matter as opposing each other. In contrast, Plotinus advocated monism, claiming that God is everything.

The human soul flows out into the sensual material world, and at the same time seeks to return to *nous* and to God. Therefore, people should avoid being caught up in physical things, and their souls should ascend to the level of perceiving God, thereby becoming united with Him. Such an achievement was regarded as the supreme virtue. Plotinus said that the human being becomes completely united with God in "ecstasy," which he regarded as the highest state of mind. Hellenistic philosophy culminated with Plotinus, and Neo-Platonism had a profound impact on Christian philosophy, which was soon to emerge.

C. Views of Value in the Medieval Period

Augustine

Augustine (354–430) provided a philosophical basis for faith in Christianity. According to Augustine, God is eternal, unchangeable, omniscient, omnipotent, the being of supreme goodness, supreme love, and supreme beauty, and the Creator of the universe. In contrast to Plato, who regarded the world of Ideas as independent in itself, Augustine held that such Ideas exist within the mind of God, and asserted that everything was created with the Ideas as prototypes. In contrast to Neo-Platonism, which held that the world necessarily emanated from God, Augustine advocated creation theory, saying that God freely created the world from nothing, not utilizing any material. Then, why is the human being sinful? For Augustine, the reason is that Adam, the first human ancestor, misused freedom and fell, thus betraying God. Fallen people can be saved only through God's grace. Augustine said that faith in God, hope for salvation, and love for God and one's neighbors are the way to true happiness, and recommended the three virtues of faith, hope, and love.

Thomas Aquinas

Thomas Aquinas (1225–74), who firmly consolidated Christian theology, divided virtues into the religious and the natural. Religious virtues refer to the three primary virtues of Christianity, namely, faith, hope, and love, while natural virtues refer to the four primary virtues of Greek philosophy, that is, wisdom, courage, temperance, and justice. Religious virtues, among which love is supreme, can lead to bliss, and people can experience bliss through loving God and their neighbors. On the other hand, natural virtues are in accordance with one's obedience to the directives of reason. Natural virtues were regarded as a means of reaching religious virtues.

D. Modern Views of Value

In the modern period, little of significance has emerged with regard to views of value. Modern views of value can basically be understood as extensions or transformations of the Greek philosophical and Christian views of value.

René Descartes (1596–1650) began by doubting all established traditional values. He was not a skeptic, however. Rather, he attempted to find something steadfast through his doubt. As a result, he reached the fundamental principle of "I think, therefore, I am." He held human reason to be the basis for one's judgments. That gave rise to Descartes' moral teaching that human beings should act with a resolute will while controlling their passions through reason.

Blaise Pascal (1623–62) regarded the human being as a contradictory being, possessing greatness as well as silliness. He expressed this by saying that "Man is a thinking reed." Human beings are the weakest of all beings in nature, but they are the greatest by virtue of their ability to think. Still, he held, their true happiness consists not in using reason but rather in reaching God through faith, namely, through heart.[13]

Immanuel Kant (1724–1804) discussed, in his *Critique of Pure Reason*,

Critique of Practical Reason, and *Critique of Judgment*, how truth, goodness, and beauty might be established, and asserted that we should seek after these values. Especially with regard to goodness, or morality, he asserted that we should act according to the unconditional moral imperative, for example, "be honest"—that is, the categorical imperative, which comes from practical reason.

Jeremy Bentham (1748–1832) thought that happiness is the state of the absence of pain. Thus, on the basis of the principle of "the greatest happiness for the greatest number" he advocated utilitarianism. He reasoned that the value of human behavior can be determined by calculating pleasure and pain quantitatively. Bentham's utilitarianism was a theory of value that came into being in the context of the Industrial Revolution. It can be regarded as a *hyungsang* view of value.

Søren Kierkegaard (1813–55) advocated three stages of existence, saying that people should pass through the "aesthetic stage" and the "ethical stage" in order to reach the "religious stage" of existence. He asserted that people should not live merely for pleasure; in his view, it is not sufficient merely to live conscientiously by observing ethics; rather, people should live in faith, standing before God. Kierkegaard tried to revive the true Christian view of value.

Friedrich Nietzsche (1844–1900) regarded Europe at the end of the nineteenth century as being in an era of nihilism, in which all values were collapsing. He described Christianity as a "slave morality," that is, as a morality that rejects the strong and equalizes human beings. He regarded Christianity as the greatest cause of the rise of nihilism. So, he presented a new theory of value with the "will to power" as its standard. "Live strongly in this godless world," was Nietzsche's assertion.

Wilhelm Windelband (1848–1915), of the Neo-Kantian school, dealt with values as the central issue of philosophy, taking up the values of truth, goodness, and beauty in a united way. Following Kant, who had distinguished matters of fact from matters of right, Windelband distinguished judgments of fact from judgments of value, and said that the task of philosophy was to deal with judgments of value. A judgment of fact is an objective proposition about a fact, whereas a judgment of value is a proposition in which a subjective appraisal of a fact is made. For example, such propositions as "this flower is red" and "the man built the house" are factual judgments; whereas such propositions as "this flower is beautiful" and "that man's conduct is good" are value judgments.

Ever since, fact and value have been dealt with as quite separate issues, in the sense that factual judgments are dealt with in the natural sciences, whereas value judgments are dealt with in philosophy.

The twentieth century saw the rise of analytical philosophy, which employs the "logical analysis of language" as the most appropriate method of philosophy. With regard to axiology, analytical philosophy took the following position: (1) One can not know values except through intuition; (2) Judgment of value is but an expression of the speaker's feelings about moral approval or disapproval; (3) Axiology is significant only for the analysis of value language. Thus, analytical philosophy generally sought to exclude axiology from philosophy.

Pragmatism, represented by John Dewey (1859–1952), based value judgments on usefulness for life. Such value concepts as truth, goodness, and beauty were regarded as means, or tools, for processing things effectively. From this standpoint, what is perceived as valuable differs from person to person. Even the same person may differ in the way he or she perceives value from time to time. Dewey's standpoint was a relative pluralism as far as value was concerned.

Lastly, I will mention the Communist view of value. This view of value was defined by B. P. Tugarinov as follows: "Value is a phenomenon of nature or society that is useful and necessary for those people who belong to a particular society or class in history, as something actual, as a purpose, or as an ideal."[14] In Communism, usefulness for the proletariat class is the standard of value. A postulate of the Communist view of value was that all the established religious values, which were regarded as bourgeois views of value, had to be denied and destroyed. For Communism, a moral act is an act that is useful in promoting collective life for constructing Communist society. It includes such virtues as dedication, obedience, sincerity, love for comrades, and mutual help.

E. Necessity for a New View of Value

As seen above, many different views of value have appeared throughout history; in fact, history can be seen as a continuous succession of failed attempts to establish absolute values.

In ancient Greece, Socrates and Plato attempted to establish absolute values by pursuing true knowledge. With the collapse of the Greek city-state society, however, the views of value of Greek philosophy also collapsed. Next, Christianity attempted to establish absolute values, centering on God's love (*agape*). The Christian view of value ruled medieval society, but with the collapse of medieval society, it gradually lost its power.

In the modern period, Descartes and Kant established views of value centered on reason, as in Greek philosophy; yet, their understanding of God, which was the basis for their views of value, was ambiguous. As a result, their views of value fell short of becoming absolute. Pascal and Kierkegaard attempted to revive true Christian values, but they fell short of establishing a firm system of value.

The Neo-Kantian school dealt with value as one of the main issues in philosophy, but they completely separated philosophy, which deals with values, from natural science, which deals with facts. As a result, today many problems have come into being. As scientists have continued to analyze facts in complete disregard of values, they have brought about weapons of mass destruction, destruction of the natural environment, pollution, and so forth.

Utilitarianism and pragmatism are materialistic views of value, which make values completely relative. Analytical philosophy is a philosophy without value. Nietzsche's philosophy and Communism can be described as anti-value philosophies, opposing traditional views of value.

Traditional views of value based on Greek philosophy and Christianity are no longer regarded as effective today. Traditional views of value have become weak and separated from the natural sciences. Currently, they have been almost completely eliminated even from the field of philosophy. As a result, society today is in extreme confusion. The appearance of a new view of value that can establish absolute values while revitalizing traditional values is seriously needed. This new view of value should be able to overcome materialism and to guide science with its correct view of value.

This is the case because value and fact are in a relationship of *sungsang* and *hyungsang*, and just as *sungsang* and *hyungsang* are united in existing beings, value and fact are originally united. Unification Axiology has appeared on the scene to meet this demand of our times.

5

Theory of Education

Education in today's democratic societies is in crisis, as can be seen from the increase in juvenile delinquency, the degradation of the sexual morality of the youth, the frequent occurrence of school violence, and so on. Yet, a proper theory of education, able to overcome this confusion, is difficult to find anywhere, and present-day education seems to have lost its sense of direction. Appropriate relationships between teachers and students are diminishing. That is to say, students do not respect their teachers, and teachers have lost their sense of authority and enthusiasm. In consequence, the relationship between teachers and students has largely become one wherein the teachers are merely selling knowledge, very often based largely on "political correctness," and the students are buying it, so that schools have turned into places for buying and selling knowledge. Communist ideology has infiltrated these circumstances, turning schools into places teeming with disturbances.

The democratic idea as regards education is to cultivate democratic citizens who observe such principles of democracy as the sovereignty of the people, majority rule, equality of rights, while at the same time respecting the rights of others, fulfilling their own responsibility, and claiming their own, legitimate rights.

Against this democratic ideal of education, however, Communists lodge the following charge: "In a class society, can the ruling class ever truly respect the rights of laborers and farmers? To fulfill one's own duty and mission in class society means to be a loyal servant to the ruling class, does it not? That is not true democracy. True democracy is a democracy for laborers and farmers, in other words, a people's democracy. Therefore, a true democratic education should be one for the sake of the people.

Thus, in order to offer a true education, we should overthrow capitalist society and construct a socialist society." Many people have been persuaded by such an argument.

This Communist challenge against capitalism will not lose its persuasiveness as long as social structures of exploitation, oppression, injustice, corruption, and so on remain in capitalist society. Therefore, these social evils must be eliminated. To do this, a movement for a new view of value based on God's true love must be launched and, along with it, a new theory of education must be established.

Such a new theory of education should be established based on the standard that God originally intended human beings to achieve as they grew. Such a theory can then give proper direction to today's educational institutions, which are in confusion, and can provide a vision of education for the future society. In other words, it is a theory of education that enables us to prepare for the future ideal society. The Unification Theory of Education presented here is just such a new theory of education.

Theories of education usually have two aspects. One is concerned with the ideals, goals, methods, and so on, of education, and corresponds to what is called the philosophy of education. The other aspect deals with education as an objective, observable phenomenon, and is called the science of education. The science of education inquires into educational curricula, student evaluation, learning techniques, student counseling, school administration, educational management, and so on.

These two aspects in education stand in the relationship of *sungsang* and *hyungsang*. The philosophy of education is the *sungsang* aspect of education, whereas the science of education is the *hyungsang* aspect of education. Unfortunately, while the science of education has made admirable progress up to the present time, propelled by our modern tendency to hold science in high esteem, the philosophy of education has been relatively neglected, and so is in steady decline. The fact that education today has lost its direction implies the absence of a sound philosophy of education. Therefore, what is urgently needed today is the establishment of a new philosophy of education. The Unification Theory of Education presented here is offered in order to meet that precise need.

I. Divine Principle Foundation for the Unification Theory of Education

A. Resemblance to God and the Three Great Blessings

God created man and woman in His image (Gen.1:27). When creation was finished, God gave them His blessings (the three great blessings), saying, "Be fruitful and multiply, and fill the earth and subdue it; and have dominion over the fish of the sea and over the birds of the air and over every living thing that moves upon the earth" (Gen. 1:28). This is the very foundation for education. Based on this foundation, education can be described as the process of raising children to attain resemblance to God. In other words, education is an effort to guide children so that they come to resemble God. To resemble God means to resemble His Divine Image and Divine Character. A human being is born with a Divine Image (*sungsang* and *hyungsang*, yang and yin, individual image), but it is in an immature state. Accordingly, human beings gradually come to resemble the Divine Image of God as they grow. This is even more true for the Divine Character. For a human being to resemble God's Divine Image means to resemble God's *Sungsang* and *Hyungsang*, Yang and Yin, and Individual Image, and to resemble God's Divine Character is to resemble God's Heart, Logos, and Creativity.

Among the blessings God gave to human beings, to "be fruitful" means to grow and perfect one's individual character; to "multiply and fill the earth" means to become husband and wife and multiply children; and to "subdue it [the earth]" means to have dominion over all things. Through their realizing these three great blessings, man and woman come to inherit God's Divine Character, namely, His Heart, Logos, and Creativity, and they also come to resemble God's natures of perfection, multiplication, and dominion (see fig. 5.1) as well as inheriting God's Divine Image.

Next, I will give a concrete explanation about the meaning of perfection, multiplication, and dominion, since the idea for education is established on the basis of these three great blessings.

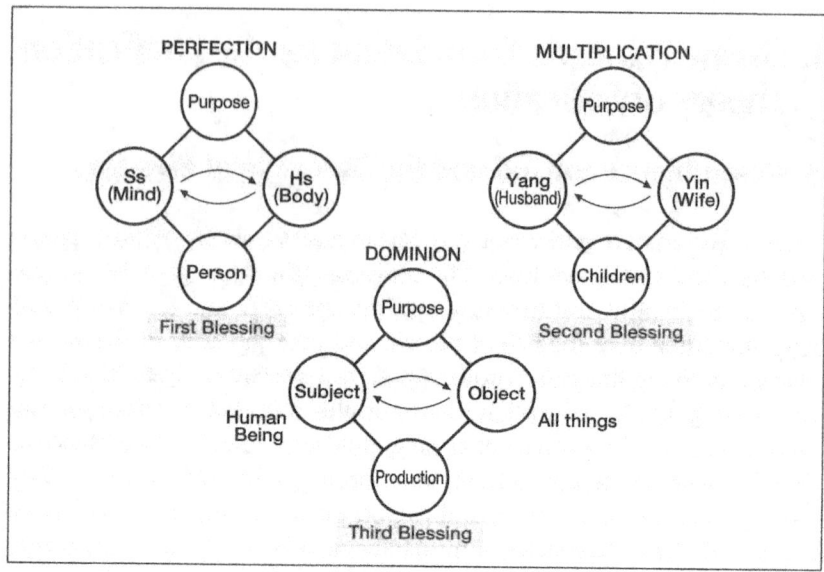

Fig. 5.1. Resembling God and the Three Great Blessings

Perfection

Jesus said, "You must ⋯ be perfect, as your heavenly Father is perfect" (Matt. 5:48). This is a call for people to resemble the perfection of God. Perfection refers to the unity of *sungsang* and *hyungsang*. In God, the *Sungsang* and *Hyungsang* are in harmonious give and receive action in the relationship of subject and object centering on Heart, and are united in oneness. This state is perfection.

Accordingly, for human beings to resemble God's perfection means that their *sungsang* and *hyungsang* are united in oneness, centering on heart. In a human being there are four categories of *sungsang* and *hyungsang*, as mentioned in the Theory of the Original Human Nature, but here I refer specifically to the spirit mind as *sungsang* and physical mind as *hyungsang*. In order for the spirit mind and physical mind to be united, the spirit mind must function as the subject, and the physical mind must function as the object; that is, the spirit mind must have dominion over the physical mind. The spirit mind is concerned with the pursuit of the values of truth, goodness and beauty, whereas the physical mind is concerned with the pursuit of food, clothing, shelter, and sexual fulfillment. Thus, in order for the spirit mind and physical mind to be united, a life in pursuit of truth, goodness, and beauty must take priority, and a life in pursuit of food, clothing, shelter, and sexual fulfillment must become a secondary means to that end.

The center of give and receive action between the spirit mind and the physical mind is heart and love. In summary, a life in pursuit of food, clothing, and shelter must be led centering on a life in pursuit of truth, goodness, and beauty, based on love. This is what is meant by resembling God's perfection. When people are young, they do not understand well the values of truth, goodness, and beauty; but as they mature, their hearts gradually develop and they come to lead—centering on love—a true life, a good life, and a beautiful life. Thus, they gradually come to resemble the perfection of God.

Since the human being is a dual being of spirit self and physical self, human growth involves the growth of both spirit self and physical self. The first blessing, "to grow," refers not only to the growth of the physical self, but primarily to the growth of the spirit self, namely, the improvement of a person's spiritual level. Yet, the spirit self grows on the foundation of the physical self, namely, through give and receive action with the physical self. If human beings grow to maturity in this way, they inherit God's perfection. Therefore, this is the first blessing, given as a promise to human beings.

Multiplication

Next, human beings must resemble God's nature of multiplication; namely, they must develop to the point where they can multiply their children. God is the harmonious being of Yang and Yin. Therefore, man and woman are supposed to resemble this harmony of God's Yang and Yin. The harmony of yang and yin in human beings refers to the harmony of husband and wife. Human beings were created through God's nature of multiplication; namely, through the harmony of God's Yang and Yin as well as through the unity of God's *Sungsang* and *Hyungsang*. Therefore, in human beings as well, they will create (multiply) their children through their harmony between yang and yin, as well as through the unity of their mind and body.

The call to resemble God's nature of multiplication is a call for man and woman to grow to the point where they are qualified and able to be engaged in harmonious give and receive action in the same way as the Yang and Yin in God are engaged in harmonious give and receive action.

To accomplish this, man and woman must mature in such a way that they become qualified to get married and have children. That is to say, a man should become perfectly equipped with all the qualifications requisite to being a man, and a woman should become perfectly equipped with all the qualifications requisite to being a woman. Thus, the call is for them to become capable of fulfilling a man's duty as a husband and a woman's duty as a wife, respectively. When they come to possess such qualifications and abilities, they are to get married and have children. Therefore, this is the second blessing, given as a promise to human beings.

Dominion

Furthermore, human beings must resemble God's nature of dominion. To resemble God's nature of dominion means to inherit God's creativity, which is the ability to create object beings (new beings) centering on Heart (love). God created human beings and all things with His creativity, and intended to have dominion over them. Since human beings were originally endowed with this creativity, they were created to have dominion over all things, centering on heart. In other words, human beings were created to possess this ability once they mature. This is the third blessing, given as a promise to human beings.

All industrial activities are activities of dominion exercised by human beings over all things. For example, farmers cultivate the land, which is a form of dominion over the land. In a factory, workers produce goods out of raw materials by using machines. This is a form of dominion over raw materials and machines. Fishing is a form of dominion over the fish and the water, and forestry is a form of dominion over trees and mountains.

To have dominion over all things is to manifest one's creativity. Seen from the viewpoint of the formation of the four position foundation, creativity refers to the ability to form an inner four position foundation and an outer four position foundation.

Accordingly, in agriculture, farmers cultivate the fields making creative efforts, based on their ideas, to obtain a greater harvest. In commerce, too, people will not be successful without ideas and creative will. In short, by manifesting creativity, all human industries, including agriculture, mining, manufacturing, commerce, forestry, fishing, and so on, are forms of human dominion over things. Science and art, also, come into the category of dominion over all things. Dominion over society, namely, participation in politics, also lies in the category of dominion over all things.

Yet, due to the fall, human beings became unable to inherit God's Heart-centered creativity. Instead, they came to manifest a self-centered creativity, often inflicting damage on people and nature, through, for example, producing weapons for war and causing pollution. Therefore, in this new theory of education, teachers must guide students to manifest heart-centered creativity by resembling God's nature of dominion.

B. Process of Growth of Human Beings

Human beings were created to resemble God. This resemblance, however, does not occur instantaneously from the moment of birth. In order to come to resemble God, they need time to develop themselves, since the created world is a world of time and space. Thus, human beings have the need to grow through the three stages of formation, growth, and completion, and then come to resemble God in perfection, multiplication, and dominion. Human growth, therefore, is the process of coming to resemble God in terms of His personality, harmony of Yang and Yin, and creativity.

The three great blessings, given by God to human beings, imply that it is after their growing completely that they will be able to fully inherit God's perfection, multiplication, and dominion. Therefore, these three great blessings are, in fact, three great promised blessings. Due to the fall, however, these three great blessings, or commandments, were not fulfilled. As written in Genesis, these three great blessings were commandments in the form of "Do⋯." Even though human beings fell away from God, these commandments given by Him have not been annulled, but remain valid even now, today. This means that the will of Heaven has been urging human beings, through their subconscious mind, to fulfill the three great blessings or commandments.

This is why human beings have ceaselessly been endeavoring to fulfill the three great commandments, even if unconsciously. Accordingly, even in fallen society, people have endeavored, according to this will of Heaven, to mature themselves in personality, to find a good spouse and form a family, and to improve society and rule nature. It is for this reason that human beings have the desire to grow, the desire to get married, the desire to rule, the desire to improve oneself, and so on. Yet, these desires have not been completely fulfilled, even until now, because of the fall of the first ancestors of humankind.

Thus, a human being must grow for the purpose of completing the three great blessings. All things grow through the autonomy and dominion of the principle. This means that they naturally grow as the life force within them propels them to growth. The autonomy and dominion of the principle refer to the activity of life. In the case of human beings, however, although the physical self grows through the autonomy and dominion of the principle, like all creatures, the human spirit self does not. In order for the spirit self to grow, a certain condition is required. This is why human beings are given a "portion of responsibility." This means that human beings perfect their personality only through their own responsibility and effort. Thus, they must make efforts to grow by experiencing God's love while observing the norm (the principle) with their own free will.

The first human ancestors, Adam and Eve, should have grown by observing God's commandment, should have become husband and wife after having experienced God's Heart, and should have actualized God's love. Since Adam and Eve were to have become the first ancestors of humankind, as the representatives of all humankind they were responsible not only for themselves, but also for their descendants. For that reason, God totally refrained from interfering with their responsibility.

If Adam and Eve had fulfilled such a serious responsibility by observing God's Word, their descendants would have been able to grow through fulfilling a much lighter condition. In other words, in the case of Adam and Eve, they had to fulfill the three great blessings solely on the basis of their solemn responsibility; in the case of their descendants, however, they would have been able to perfect the three great blessings through a lighter responsibility, that is, simply by following obediently the teachings of their parents. For this reason, Adam and Eve should have achieved the three great blessings by fulfilling their own responsibility solely by themselves without receiving any help from others. Thus, after Adam and Eve had perfected themselves, their children were supposed to obey their parents' teachings; namely, children should receive education from their parents.

This is the origin of the need for parents to teach their children, or the need for education: education by parents is necessary for children to fulfill their portion of responsibility. Therefore, in its most fundamental form education is the guidance that parents give to their children so that their children may fulfill the three great blessings. Thus, we arrive at an ideal for education: parents teach and guide their children so that the children may be able to perfect the three great blessings. Therefore, the original place of education must be the family where parents and children live. Along with the development of culture, however, the amount of information and learning has increased, and it has become impossible for parents to convey the entire scope of education in the family. Naturally, therefore, the place of education was extended from the family to the school, the professional place for education, where teachers educate students on behalf of parents. Therefore, teachers, as the representatives of parents, must instruct students with a parental heart. This is the original way of education.

C. Three Great Ideals of Education

In the Unification Theory of Education, the purpose of education is to empower human beings to achieve resemblance to God's perfection, to God's nature of multiplication, and to God's nature of dominion. Based on these goals, the ideals of education can be established.

First, based on the idea of resemblance to God's perfection, the perfection of one's individuality is established as an ideal of education. This perfection of one's individuality, or the perfection of one's character, is the completion of the first blessing.

Second, based on the idea of resemblance to God's nature of multiplication, the perfection of one's family is established as an ideal of education: man and woman grow up, get married, manifest conjugal harmony, and build a harmonious family. This perfection of one's family is the completion of the second blessing.

Third, based on the idea of resemblance to God's nature of dominion, the perfection of one's dominion is established as an ideal of education: human beings inherit God's creativity in order to exercise dominion over all things. This perfection of one's dominion becomes the completion of the third blessing.

Thus, in the Unification Theory of Education, the ideal of education consists of three ideals: perfection of one's individuality, perfection of one's family, and perfection of one's dominion. In sum, one's completion of the three great blessings.

II. Three Forms of Education

Based on the ideas described above, what kind of education is required? For the perfection of the individual, an education of heart is required; for the perfection of one's family, an education of norm is required; and for the perfection of one's dominion, an education of dominion is required, including a technical education, an intellectual education, and a physical education. Each of these forms of education will now be discussed in turn.

A. The Education of Heart

1. An Education for the Perfection of the Individual

An education which enables an individual to grow to the point where he/she resemble God's perfection is an education of heart. To resemble God's perfection is to resemble the unity of *sungsang* and *hyungsang*, which in human beings refers to the state in which one's spirit mind and physical mind, as subject and object, engage in give and receive action centering on heart and are completely united. Therefore, in order for spirit mind and physical mind to become united, heart must be the center of their give and receive action. In order for the heart to become the center of the human spirit mind and physical mind, it is necessary for human beings to experience God's heart and be united with it. Thus, an education of heart refers to the education through which one's heart becomes united with God's heart. Accordingly, an education of heart turns out to be an education for the perfection of the individual.

An education of heart refers to the education necessary to nurture children so as to become persons who love all people and all things in the same way that God loves all people and all things. In order for children to become such people, it is necessary to guide them in experiencing God's heart. Then, how do children come to experience God's heart? The first step is for them to have a clear understanding of God's heart.

2. Forms of Expression of God's Heart

God's heart has been expressed in three ways during the process of creation and the dispensation of restoration. These three forms of God's heart are His heart of hope, His heart of sorrow, and His heart of pain.

God's Heart of Hope

God's heart of hope is the heart God experienced during the time of creation. It refers to God's joyful feelings, full of expectation and hope, in anticipation of begetting Adam and Eve, His first, most beloved children, to whom He could devote His unlimited love. When His heart of hope is finally fulfilled God will be filled with indescribable, limitless joy. In reality, God's heart was filled with indescribable, incredible joy at the moment when Adam and Eve were actually born.

According to modern physics, the universe began to be formed about 15 billion years ago. From the perspective of Unification Thought, God began to create the universe at that time. What was everything for? It was all for the sake of creating Adam and Eve, His most beloved children. In the hope of seeing the moment when His children would be born, God spent much time creating the universe, in spite of the grueling character of the effort necessary in making a total investment. God, being filled with hope, however, did not feel the process of creating the universe as too long or too arduous, its length and difficulty notwithstanding.

We can realize through our own experiences that this is true. When we work for something joyful, we do not feel the work to be so grueling, no matter how many hardships are experienced. We even forget about the time, because we know that joy awaits us in the future. God's expectation of joy was far greater than any kind of joy we may experience. Moreover, the joy God felt when Adam and Eve were actually born was so profound that it can not be easily compared to anything else.

God's Heart of Sorrow

God's heart of sorrow refers to the heart of God at the moment when Adam and Eve fell away from Him into the realm of death, which came to be under the control of Satan. It is analogous to the grieving heart of parents who lose their children. In the early days of the Unification Church, when speaking about the heart of God at that time, Rev. Sun Myung Moon would weep bitterly when he spoke about the fall of Adam and Eve.

God commenced the providence of restoration immediately after the fall of Adam and Eve. Ever since that time, God has been advancing His providence in hope of seeing the world of joy realized in the future when His will is finally accomplished. Yet, fallen people have been painfully indifferent to God's providence, continually indulging in corruption and violence. Whenever God saw this, it brought profound grief to His heart. God, who has thus been advancing His providence in history, became a God of *han*, or deep mortification, as well as a God of unfathomable sorrow. Since His expectation and hope at the time of creation were so great, His sorrow and disappointment due to the human fall, was all the greater.

Even among human beings, when a child whom the parents dearly love is dying, they, the mother in particular, will feel unfathomable sadness and grieve deeply. Even when a child's illness is very serious and the parents are told that the child will die, they will still try everything in their power to keep the child alive, by any means available. This is what the parental heart is like. So, when the child does eventually die, even though the parents knew it would happen, they still feel as though their hearts have been cut to pieces, and they are completely at a loss as to what to do. This is the heart of parents, especially the heart of a mother.

The sorrowful Heart of God at the time of the fall of Adam and Eve and the sorrowful Heart of God, who has had to watch Adam and Eve and their descendants suffering in the world under Satan's dominion, which is like a prison, was too great to be compared with anything, even with the heart of human parents who have lost their children. Since the beginning of history, there has been no person who has ever grieved as much as God. This is one aspect of God's Heart, as described by Rev. Moon.

Heart of Pain

God's heart of pain refers to the bitter feelings God has experienced, having had to endure watching the central figures in His providential history being persecuted by Satan and his agents. God did not abandon fallen human beings, but continually sent prophets, saints and sages in order to bring them to life again. Nevertheless, people did not easily follow the teachings of God's people but rather persecuted them, and sometimes even killed them. Every time God witnessed the saints and sages suffering from persecution, God would feel as though a nail was being driven into His chest, or His side was being pierced by a spear.

Those saints and sages were righteous men whom God sent to save human beings in the fallen world. Accordingly, God felt as if He Himself had received contempt, ridicule and persecution. This reveals another heart which God has endured in the course of the providence of restoration: the heart of pain.

3. Understanding God's Heart

Through an education of heart, children should come to understand the three kinds of God's heart as described above, especially the heart of God in the course of the providence of restoration. Therefore, I will introduce an understanding of God's heart as it was during the courses of Adam's family, Noah's family, and Abraham's family, as well as in Moses' course and Jesus' course. What follows is an introduction to God's heart according to the teachings of faith of Rev. Moon.

God's Heart as Experienced in Adam's Family

When God created Adam and Eve, He was filled with boundless expectation, hope and joy, but when Adam and Eve fell away from Him, God's grief knew no limit. Therefore, in order to save Adam's family, God encouraged Cain and Abel, their children, to make offerings. God, of course, very much hoped that they would succeed in their offerings.

There may be those who suspect that, since God is omniscient and omnipotent, He might have known from the very beginning that Adam and Eve, and later Cain and Abel, would fail. If this were the case, then how could God have grieved in the true sense? This, however, is not a correct understanding.

God was, of course, aware that there was a possibility of the human fall. Even so, since God is the God of heart and hope, His desire for human beings to succeed and not to fall was incomparably stronger than his fear that they might fall.

The same thing can be said of the offerings by Cain and Abel. Since God's expectation for their offering was so great and His hope was so strong, He virtually ignored the possibility of their failure in the offering. Here we can distinguish a difference between heart and reason. God's impulse of heart is so strong as to override reason.

At the time of Adam and Eve, and also at the time of Cain and Abel, God was a God of expectation and hope, who wished, absolutely, for nothing less than their complete success. Sadly, however, Adam and Eve, and also Cain and Abel, failed. Because of that, God's sorrow and disappointment were incomparably intense. However, even at such sad moments as these, God could not simply break down in tears, losing His dignity, no matter how sorrowful He felt, because Satan was watching. If God had openly expressed His deep sorrow, He would have seemed to Satan as miserable, and lacking dignity and authority. That is why all God could do was leave, silently, with His head bowed and tragedy etched on his face, having to suppress the sorrow welling up from within. This is what Rev. Moon revealed about God's heart in Adam's family in the early days of his ministry.

God's Heart as Experienced in Noah's Family

After God left Adam's family He walked a wilderness path for the long period of 1,600 years, looking for someone on earth with whom He could work. In all this time, no one welcomed God: everyone turned away from Him. There was not a single home where God could dwell, not a single square meter of land for Him to stand on, nor a single person whom He could relate to. God walked the lonely path of a miserable God, literally all alone in the world. In that condition, God finally found Noah. God's joy at that moment was beyond comparison. Yet, due to the providential situation, God had to give Noah a very difficult direction, which was to build the ark. Noah accepted God's direction and faithfully devoted himself in building the ark, for 120 long years, all the while suffering ridicule and contempt from the people.

Noah was not a "son of God." He was established merely as a "servant of God" and a righteous man. Yet, God was so pleased to meet such a man as Noah that He walked the path of suffering in the position of a servant together with Noah.

However, after the flood, since Noah's son Ham did not fulfill his portion of responsibility, Noah's family, which had been saved from the flood, was invaded by Satan. When that happened, God again felt heartbreaking pain and sorrow. Deeply disheartened, God had to leave Noah's family.

God's Heart as Experienced in Abraham's Family

Four hundred years later, God found Abraham and established him within the providence. The most serious time for Abraham in his providential course was when he was required to offer Isaac, his only son, whom he had begotten at the age of one hundred years (Gen. 21:5). God directed Abraham, who had failed in his symbolic offering of a dove and a pigeon, a ram and a goat, and a heifer, to offer Isaac as a sacrifice. Abraham's heart at that point was unimaginably painful. He was at a loss as to whether he should keep Isaac alive, according to human ethics, or offer him, according to Heaven's demand. In his heart, at that moment, Abraham would much rather have sacrificed himself than he would his son.

Nevertheless, he ultimately determined in his mind to sacrifice Isaac, in accordance with God's order: he decided to follow Heaven's direction, thus sacrificing his own heart. He wandered around Mount Moriah for three days. This three day period was a long, painful path for Abraham. During that time, God did not merely watch from afar; but having issued such a strict order to "sacrifice your own son," God suffered along with Abraham, suffering even more as He watched Abraham's suffering. When Abraham was about to sacrifice his beloved son, Issac with his sword, on Mount Moriah, God stopped his act of killing and said, "Now I know that you fear God" (Gen. 22:12).

Abraham's heart to follow God's will, his absolute faith, obedience, and loyalty established the condition of having killed Isaac, even though in fact he had not. That is why God was able to stop Abraham just before killing Isaac, and He provided him with a ram to offer as a burnt offering, instead of his son. "Now I know that you fear God" was an expression of His joy in seeing Abraham's loyalty, being willing to offer even his son Isaac as a sacrifice, as well as His regret at Abraham's failure in the earlier symbolic offering.

God's Heart as Experienced in Moses' Course

Moses was raised as a prince in the palace of the Pharaoh of Egypt. After he witnessed the suffering of his people, the Israelites, however, he decided to lead them to the land of Canaan according to the will of God. After many difficulties and setbacks, he led them out of Egypt and into the wilderness. The Israelites, however, revolted against him, their leader, each time they encountered difficulty. When Moses came down from Mount Sinai, after having completed forty days of fasting on the mountain and receiving from God the two tablets of stone, he found the Israelites worshipping a golden calf. Seeing such an act of faithlessness and blasphemy, Moses, in anger, dashed the tablets to the ground, thus smashing them into pieces. At that moment, God said, "Behold, it is a stiff-necked people; now therefore let me alone, that my wrath may burn hot against them and I may consume them" (Exod. 32:9–10).

How did Moses feel at that moment? Faced with God's wrath to the extent that He even wanted to destroy the Israelites, Moses' love and loyal heart for his people welled up within him at that moment. No matter how difficult it might be, Moses felt that he had to save his people by any means, even at the cost of his life. He appealed to God, saying, "Turn from thy fierce wrath, and repent of this evil against thy people" (Exod. 32:12). In the face of Moses' fervent appeal, God refrained from destroying the Israelites.

After the Israelites had wandered in the wilderness for 40 years and finally arrived at a place called Kadesh Barnea, the Israelites complained to Moses yet again, saying, "There is nothing to eat here." Out of frustration and anger at the Israelites, who were demonstrating utter faithlessness toward God, Moses struck the rock twice, thus going against God's will. God later called Moses to the top of Mount Pisgah. Showing him the promised land of Canaan, which Moses had labored so hard to reach, God said, "You shall not go there, into the land which I give to the people of Israel" (Deut. 32:52). God had no choice but to speak this way to the 120-year-old Moses, who had twice-fasted for 40 days and had suffered greatly for 40 years in the wilderness, all in order to lead the Israelites. In fact, it was God's desire to allow Moses, the leader of the Exodus, to enter the land of Canaan. However, due to Satan's accusation (based on Moses' having struck the rock twice), God had to take such an extreme measure, even unwillingly. In so addressing Moses, God felt deep sorrow and pain.

God's Heart as Experienced in Jesus' Course

As prophesied in the Old Testament (Isaiah 9:6), Jesus was born on earth as the Messiah. The entire world should have welcomed him wholeheartedly, but even from childhood he experienced heart-breaking rejection. His family rejected him; his religion (Judaism) rejected him; and his nation (Israel) rejected him. In the end, there was virtually no place wherein he could find any acceptance.

For 33 years, including his three years of public ministry, Jesus spent most of his days by himself, experiencing a life of loneliness. He expressed his lonely heart, saying, "Foxes have holes, and birds of the air have nests; but the Son of man has nowhere to lay his head" (Luke 9:58). When he looked at the temple at Jerusalem, he tearfully rebuked the Israelites, saying, "The days shall come upon you, when your enemies ··· will not leave one stone upon another in you; because you did not know the time of your visitation" (Luke 19:43-44).

As he walked along the shores of the Sea of Galilee in order to divert his mind from his loneliness, he once spoke with a woman of Samaria, who was not one of the chosen people (John 4:7-26). He expressed his mortified mind to the leaders of Judaism, saying, "Truly, I say to you, the tax collectors and the harlots go into the kingdom of God before you" (Matt. 21:31). God walked with this lonely Jesus through such a lonely path.

In the end, when Jesus was crucified, how deep the grief in the heart of God as He watched His beloved son, Jesus, miserably dying! Deploring that he could not save Jesus from the cross, God could not even bear to watch, but had to turn His face away. Seeing Jesus on the cross, God suffered even more than Jesus himself.

4. Introducing God's Heart

All of the above episodes are accounts described by Rev. Moon in his tearful sermons during the early days of his ministry. From him we come to know the heart of God in the courses of Adam, Noah, Abraham, Moses, and Jesus. Furthermore, behind the tribulations of the saints, sages, and righteous people of other religions and other nations, there was the heart of God constantly guiding them. Through an education of heart, teachers and parents should introduce the heart of God to children. In addition to talking to them about God's heart, they can teach them through TV, radio, movies, videos, novels, plays, paintings, and various other means of communication.

5. Education of Heart through Practice

It is necessary not only to teach God's Heart through words, but especially to manifest it directly through the practice of love. To do this, parents must first seriously love their children in the family. While parents raise their children by feeding, then clothing, then sheltering, then teaching them propriety, and so on, more importantly parents must always love their children with a warm and sincere heart. This is the true love of parents for their children. If parents consistently give such a quality of love to their children, the children will naturally come to sincerely respect their parents and practice filial piety. Furthermore, the children themselves would come to love each other. This is because

God's heart is conveyed through the parents' practice of true love towards their children.

The same thing can be said of school education. Teachers must express the true love of God through their words and actions. Needless to say, teachers should competently and sincerely teach their students each subject. Not only that, but since school education is basically an extension of family education, teachers must guide their students wholeheartedly, and with a parental heart, regarding them as their own children.

God's love should be conveyed through the teachers' daily words and deeds, since the teachers' every word and deed, private or public, become the material content for the students' learning, and for the formation of their character. When students receive such a school education filled with love, their heart will be moved, and they will come to respect and willingly follow their teachers. Furthermore, they will want to practice true love in the same way that their teachers do. This is an education of heart through one's practice in the family and in the school.

B. The Education of Norm

An Education for the Perfection of the Family

An education for the perfection of the family refers to the education necessary for the nurturing of a man and a woman; at the time of their marriage they should have fulfilled the conditions for becoming an original husband and wife by resembling the harmony of God's Yang and Yin.

Since the human fall involved a failure to observe the norm (commandment of God), this education is, first of all, an education of norm designed to lead human beings in such a way that they observe God's commandment. It is the education necessary to a man and a woman in order for them to gain the qualifications to become a principled husband and wife and form a family. A man must be fully equipped with the way of a husband; and a woman, with the way of a wife. The education of norm also includes learning the proper behavior expected of parents, the proper behavior expected of children, and the proper relationships necessary among brothers and sisters in the family.

Through this education of norm, the sanctity and mystery of the sexual relationship should be communicated with special care. A sexual relationship is something to be experienced only through marriage, and should never be violated at anytime, before or after marriage. According to the Bible, God told Adam and Eve, "of the tree of the knowledge of good and evil you shall not eat" (Gen. 2:17). This means that the sexual relationship is sacred, and must never be violated.

That commandment was intended not only for Adam and Eve, but for everyone, and it still maintains its validity today. This commandment is a supreme directive which will continue to be valid in the future as well. This supreme directive holds also that, after marriage, husband and wife can never, under any circumstances, have an illicit sexual relationship, that is, a sexual relationship with any person other than their spouse. Thus, the education of norm is, first of all, an education designed to nurture man and woman to the point of resembling God's harmony of Yang and Yin, all the while observing the commandment of God. In other words, it is the education necessary for one to achieve the qualification to become a husband or a wife.

An Education for Becoming a Being of Reason-Law

Since human beings were created through Logos (reason-law), the education of norm, at the same time, refers to the education through which one becomes a being of reason-law, who lives according to the Way of Heaven. Education of norm, therefore, is also called education of reason-law. The Way of Heaven is the law permeating the universe. It refers to the law of give and receive action. Two kinds of laws derive from the Way of Heaven: the law of value and the law of nature. Of these two, the law of value form the norm. As there are both vertical order and horizontal order in the universe, so there are vertical order and horizontal order in the family. Accordingly, in the family there are vertical values and horizontal values which correspond to those two orders. In addition, there are individual values. The topic of values has already been treated in some detail in the chapter on "Axiology."

The education of norm must be accompanied by an education of heart, since an education of norm per se necessarily has an obligatory nature, as can be seen in such normative directives as "You must not do this"; "You ought to do that"; and so forth. If such norms are not imbued with love, they can easily become excessively formal and legalistic. Therefore, an education of norm must be conducted in an atmosphere of love.

Love without norm is usually called blind love. Should parents or teachers express such love to children, they may become unreflective individuals, and end up with a despising heart. Parental love and the love of teachers must have some form of authority and dignity. In order to be of that nature, their love must be in accordance with Logos. In case there is too little love with too much emphasis on norms, the children will come to feel restricted and may revolt against their parents or teachers. Love should transcend norms, and should not be dominated by them. Even in the case where children may fail to obey norms once or twice, still they must be forgiven with warm love.

Love forgives and accepts everything, whereas a norm has the nature of strict regulation. Love is harmonious and round, whereas a norm is, so to speak, linear. Love and norms must be united. Since love is round and a norm is linear, a person in whom love and norm are united becomes a person of character in whom a circle and a straight line are united. In other words, a person of character refers to a person who, in a unified way, possesses the aspect of being the most harmonious, and at the same time possesses the aspect of being the strictest. A person with this kind of character can sometimes be very kind and at other times be very strict, and yet they can always assume the most appropriate attitude according to the time and place.

Therefore, an education of norm must be united with an education of heart. In other words, an education of norm must be given to children in a warm atmosphere of love both in the family and at school. If love becomes cool or cold, norms become formal and oppressive.

C. The Education of Dominion

An Education for the Perfection of the Nature of Dominion

An education of dominion refers to that education we receive which prepares us to manifest our dominion over the creation. In order to perfect one's nature of dominion, one must first acquire knowledge about the objects over which one is to have dominion. Intellectual education, or the education of knowledge, is necessary for that purpose.

Next, one needs to be educated in those techniques through which one can express the creativity necessary to have dominion over objects. That purpose is served by technical education. Furthermore, in order for us to become the subjects of dominion, our physical strength must be developed. That purpose is realized through physical education. Thus, intellectual education, technical education, and physical education, together, are all included in the education of dominion.

Through an intellectual education we obtain the knowledge necessary for us to have dominion. Intellectual education comprises various fields including the natural sciences, politics, economics, social studies, cultural studies, and so on, according to the field of dominion. All of these are included in the concept of dominion over all things.

Since technology is a direct means of exercising dominion over all things, technical education serves as the core in the education of dominion. Finally, needless to say, physical education and the promotion of physical ability is important for a dominion over all things. In technical education and physical education as well, there are various specialized fields. For example, the education of art, particularly education in the performing arts, may be regarded as a kind of technical education.

In short, the purpose of an education of dominion is to become well-versed in the various methods of developing one's creativity. Creativity is inborn; everyone is naturally endowed with a creative potentiality. An education of dominion, however, is necessary in order to actually manifest it.

Development of One's Creativity and Formation of the Two-Stage Structure

The development of one's creativity refers to the cultivation of one's ability to form an inner four position foundation and to enhance one's skill in forming an outer four position foundation, thus resembling God's two-stage structure of creation.

The ability to form an inner four position foundation refers to one's ability to form a logos, or to construct a plan. In order to be able to develop a logos, one must acquire a great deal of knowledge through intellectual education, and thus enhance the contents of the inner *hyungsang* (ideas, concepts, etc.) qualitatively as well as quantitatively. The more knowledge (information) one obtains, the richer and deeper one's ideas become. To form a logos means to develop a new idea. Technical innovations in industry are also developed through the repetitive creation of ever-new kinds of logos.

Following this, the cultivation of one's ability to form the outer four position foundation refers to the enhancement of one's ability to substantiate ideas through the use of tools and materials according to a certain plan—in other words the development of skills in conducting outer give and receive action. Here, technical education is required. Of course, good physical condition is required as well. Therefore, improving one's physical strength through physical education is also necessary.

One's Education of Dominion must be Based on a Universal Education

An education of dominion must be carried out on the basis of, and in conjunction with, an education of heart and an education of norm. Only when based on heart (love) and norm can one's intellectual, technical, and physical education become wholesome, and one's creativity be fully manifested.

An education of heart and an education of norm constitute a "universal education" since they must be given universally to all people. On the other hand, an education of dominion should be given to people according to their abilities, interests, and desires. Some may major in natural science, others in literature, and still others in economics, and so forth. Thus, the field a person chooses varies depending on that person's preference and aptitude. In this sense, an education of dominion becomes, in principle, an "individual education."

It can be said that universal education and individual education are in the relationship of *sungsang* and *hyungsang*. The reason is that an education of heart and of norm are a more spiritual education, that is, an education of the mind, whereas an education of dominion is a more material education since it is for exercising dominion over all things. Accordingly, a universal education (an education of heart and of norm) and an individual education (an education of dominion) must be carried out together in a relationship of subject and object. That is what is meant by a "balanced education" (see fig. 5.2).

In ancient Greece, in the Middle Ages, and in the Modern Age, there was always an effort to provide an education of love and an education of ethical and moral principles, even though the teachings provided were not perfect. Today, however, these kinds of education are being almost totally neglected. In many cases what can be called an "unbalanced education," with an excessive emphasis on knowledge and technique, is being practiced. As a result, the healthy growth of human nature is being severely hampered. Therefore, a new theory of education must be advocated, whereby an education of true love and of ethics and morality can be conveyed on an entirely new level. It will be on this new basis that an intellectual and technical education can most appropriately be

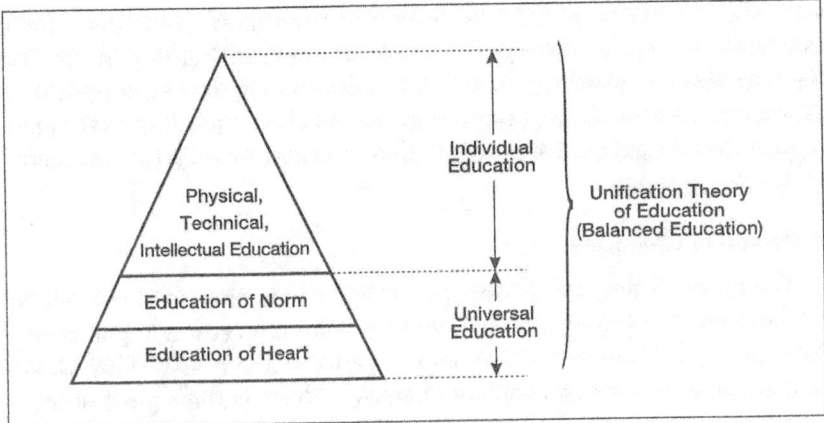

Fig. 5.2. Universality and Individuality in Education

conducted. Only through such a balanced education can science and technology be guided in the proper direction. Then, such problems as pollution and the destruction of nature will naturally be solved. Moreover, through this kind of education, teachers will once again be able to regain their authority as teachers.

It should be re-emphasized here that the starting point of education lies in family education. School education is primarily an extension and development of family education. Accordingly, family education and school education must be closely united. Otherwise, it would be difficult for an education of heart and of norm, as universal education, to be carried out. Unity in education could hardly be expected if family education and school education were not united.

III. Image of the Ideally-Educated Person

Since the beginning of history, many scholars have advocated various kinds of theories of education, each with its own image of the ideally-educated person. The Unification Theory of Education also has an image of the ideally-educated person. In the Unification Theory of Education this image is as follows: first of all, a person of character; second, a good citizen; and third, a genius. These are the images of an ideal man and woman corresponding, respectively, to the education of heart, the education of norm, and the education of dominion. Therefore, when education is seen in terms of the image of the ideally-educated person, the education of heart may be called an education to develop a person of character; the education of norm may be called an education to develop a good citizen; and the education of dominion may be called an education to develop a genius.

A Person of Character

The image of the person ideally educated concerning heart is a person of character. Accordingly, the education of heart is an education necessary for guiding children so that they may experience and practice God's love, and become persons of excellent character. Heart is the source of love, and it is the core of one's personality. Those who are lacking in heart—regardless of how much knowledge they may have, or how strong their physical power may be, or how much political or economic power they may have—will never be persons of character. From a secular perspective, a person with a certain degree of virtue, knowledge, and health is often considered to be a person of character, but in Unification Thought, a person of character is one who has internalized God's Heart and who practices love.

What, then, is an ideal person of character? A person of character is someone who has perfected his or her personality, having developed the faculties of intellect, emotion, and will in a balanced manner on the basis of heart (love). A person of character lives, above all, experiencing God's Heart; therefore, such a person always makes efforts to practice true love towards all people and all things. A person of character, with a sincere heart of loyalty, always seeks to console God for His sorrow and pains; this person, in tears, will forgive God's enemies with Divine love, even though he or she may feel public indignation against them. A person of character always practices vertical and horizontal values with a meek and humble mind, and with a warm heart. Since this person embodies both law and love, in practice he or she is most tender toward others and most strict toward himself or herself: love and law are united in his or her life. Love without law can make children weak and law without love may merely give them a sense of cold restriction. In sum, a person of character is able to practice God's true love towards all people and all things.

A Good Citizen

The image of the person ideally educated concerning norm is a "good citizen," a good citizen with a good personality. An education of norm may be given in schools, but its basis must be in the family. Since the family represents a miniature of the order of the universe, it can rightfully be said that the society, nation, and world are expansions of the system of order in a family. Therefore, a person who has received and internalized a good standard of education of norm in his or her family can easily observe norms in the greater society, nation, and world as well. As a result, that person becomes a good member of his or her family, a good member of their society, a good member of their nation, and a good member of the world. In other words, if one can become a good member of his or her family through an education of norm, one can naturally behave properly in conformity with the norms of their society, nation, and world.

Furthermore, a person who has lived as a good citizen on earth will naturally become a good spirit person in the spirit world as well. Leading a good life both on earth and in the spirit world, such a person can be called a good member of the cosmos. Cosmos here refers to the combination of the physical world and the spirit world. Living as a good citizen in the family, society, world, and cosmos is the same as living as a good citizen in the Kingdom of Heaven.

A Genius

The image of the person ideally educated concerning dominion is a "genius," which here means a person with rich and profound creativity. Originally everyone has the talent of genius, since human beings were originally created to become beings with creativity, inheriting God's creativity. As a matter of fact, the Chinese characters for "genius" indicate a person with talent which is given by Heaven. Creativity is given to a person at birth as an endowed potential. Therefore, all people have the potential to become a genius once they manifest their creativity one hundred percent. In order to actualize such creativity, however, a proper education is necessary. The kind of education necessary for this purpose is an education of dominion.

As mentioned above, an education of dominion should be based on the foundation of both an education of heart and an education of norm. In other words, an education of dominion must be carried out as one component of a balanced education; only then can true creativity be fully manifested. If an education of heart and an education of norm are insufficient or lacking, one's creativity can not be fully manifested. For instance, suppose there is a child with unusual musical potential who is trying to learn to play the piano. If the parents of that child are always quarreling with each other, or often strike or abuse the child, then the child will go to school with a wounded heart. In this case, when playing the piano, the child will not be able to move his or her hands smoothly, because of his or her disturbed emotions. Even though the child may have superior creative potential, the development of that creativity will be hindered due to the discord in his or her family environment.

Since human beings have been given individuality, each person's creativity, likewise, has unique characteristics. Some people are endowed with musical creativity; others, with mathematical creativity; someone else may have political creativity, while others have business creativity. If the creativity one possesses is fully manifested, that person may become a musical genius, a mathematical genius, a political genius, or a business genius. This is to say, based upon one's individuality, each person can become a unique genius.

Due to the fallen environment, however, people have become unable to manifest their God-given creativity to the fullest extent, and it has become very difficult for them to develop into geniuses. In fact, there may be only one person out of tens of thousands who can reach the level of a genius, while all the rest remain in mediocrity. That is the reality of an education of dominion in this fallen society.

Moreover, we should realize that cooperation from the spirit world is also involved in the education leading to one's becoming a genius. When a well-balanced education is provided, on the basis of a God-centered family, many good spirits can provide spiritual assistance and, as a result, children's God-given talents can develop rapidly.

IV. Traditional Theories of Education

In this section, I will introduce the main points of certain traditional theories of education. By comparing the Unification Theory of Education with these theories, it will be possible to more clearly understand the historical significance of the Unification Theory of Education.

Plato's View of Education

According to Plato (427–347 BC), the human soul consists of three parts, namely, the "appetitive part," the "spirited part," and the "rational part." The virtue required in the appetitive part is temperance; the virtue required in the spirited part is courage; and the virtue required in the rational part is wisdom. The virtue that manifests itself when these three virtues are harmonized is justice. There are three social classes in the nation corresponding to these three parts of the soul. The mass of citizens, including farmers, artisans, and tradesmen who form the lower class, correspond to the appetitive part of the soul. Public officials (guardians) form the middle class, corresponding to the spirited part of the soul. Finally, rulers form the upper class, corresponding to the rational part of the soul.

When those capable men who have gained knowledge of the "Idea of the Good" rule the nation, an ideal nation is realized. For Plato, the purpose of education is to bring people closer to the world of Ideas. Specifically, this aims at the education of the "philosopher-king" who is the educated ruler. Plato's image of an ideal person was that of "one who loves wisdom" (a philosopher) and that of "one who is harmonized," namely, a person whose mind and body are harmonized, possessing the four virtues of wisdom, courage, temperance, and justice. The ultimate purpose of education would be to realize an ideal nation, where the Idea of the Good is embodied.

The Christian View of Education in the Middle Ages

Whereas in the age of ancient Greece, education served the goal of developing good people who would serve the society, in the Christian society of the Middle Ages, education served to cultivate people who would realize the Christian ideal. The image of the ideal person was that of a "religious person," a person who would love and respect God, while loving his neighbors. With the purpose of cultivating such ideal persons, a strict education was given, particularly in monasteries. This was an education to attain a perfect spiritual life, with the virtues of purity, honest poverty, and submission. The purpose of this education was to cultivate people to become ideal Christians and to prepare them for life after death.

The View of Education During the Renaissance

In the age of the Renaissance, a human-centered world view, which valued human dignity, came into being, displacing the God-centered world view which had regarded obedience and abstinence as virtues. Desiderius Erasmus (1466–1515) was the main representative of this new, humanistic view of education. He asserted that the purpose of education is to teach people, who are originally free, to attain the complete development of their human nature and to acquire a culture rich in individuality. He emphasized the humanistic aspects of culture, such as literature, the fine arts, and science. Emphasis was also given to physical education, which had been neglected in the Middle Ages. The image of the ideal person in the Renaissance Age was an "all-round man of culture," whose mind and body are harmoniously developed. Erasmus' idea of the return to the original human nature was inherited by Johann A. Comenius and Jean Jacques Rousseau.

Comenius' View of Education

For Johann A. Comenius (1592–1670), the ultimate purpose of human life was to become united with God and obtain eternal bliss in the life after death, with life here on earth being the preparation for life after death.

For that purpose, everyone should (1) know all things, (2) become a person who can control things as well as oneself, and (3) become like the image of God. He advocated the necessity of three kinds of education: intellectual education, moral education, and religious education. To teach "all things to all men" was the theme of Comenius' theory of education, which was called *pansophia*.[1]

According to Comenius, the character to be achieved through education is naturally inherent in human beings, and it is the role of education to draw out this natural gift, namely, "nature." Comenius said that originally parents are responsible for education, but should they become unable to do it, schools would become necessary to replace them.

The image of the ideal person, according to Comenius, was that of a "*pansophist*," or a person who has learned all knowledge concerning God, nature, and human beings. The purpose of education is to raise practical Christians who have learned everything knowable, and to realize the peaceful unification of the world through Christianity.

Rousseau's View of Education

Jean-Jacques Rousseau (1712–78) in the Enlightenment Age wrote an educational novel entitled *Émile*, in which he said, "God makes all things good; man meddles with them and they become evil."[2] Thus, he insisted on educating children in a natural way. He asserted that since man possesses an inherent "natural goodness," his "nature" should be developed as it exists originally. Education, as advocated by Rousseau, should aim to develop people naturally through eliminating the factors that obstruct the development of their natural gifts, such as indoctri-nation by the established system of culture and by moral and religious teachings. Yet, in reality, "natural man" in the state of nature would not be well-suited to the existing fallen society. Concerning this point, he said that in the ideal republican society, the individual as a "natural man" and the individual as a citizen of society would get along well. Thus, he also advocated the necessity for educating people so that they can become full-fledged members of society.

The image of the ideal person in Rousseau's theory of education was that of a "natural man," and the purpose of education, in his view, was to nurture this "natural man" and realize an ideal republican society, in which this "natural man" would become a citizen. Rousseau's theory of education was inherited by Kant, Pestalozzi, Herbart, Dewey, and others.

Kant's View of Education

Immanuel Kant (1724–1804) said that "man is the only being who needs education"[3] and that "man can only become man by education,"[4] advocating the importance of education. Kant's view of education was influenced by Rousseau.

According to Kant, the mission of education is to develop people's natural gifts in a harmonious way, and to cultivate those who can act freely while following moral laws. Also, Kant asserted that education should not aim at adjusting to any particular society, but rather it should aim, more generally, at the perfection of humankind. Thus, he said, education must become cosmopolitan.

On the other hand, Kant recognized that there is in human nature a fundamental evil. According to him, evil comes into being when the moral law is subordinated to self-love. Therefore, Kant said that through inner conversion, one should come to place the moral law above self-love, and that duty so orders it. Respect for morality, trust in science and reverence for God characterize his view on education and on humankind. For Kant, the ideal image of a human being is that of a "good man," and the purpose of education is to perfect one's human nature as a cosmopolitan person, thereby establishing everlasting international peace.

Pestalozzi's View of Education

Under the influence of Rousseau, Johann H. Pestalozzi (1741–1827) advocated an education in conformity with "nature" and sought to liberate human nature, the noble nature inherent in all people. He held that when people based themselves upon something simple and pure, they come to do good by intuitively understanding fundamental principles. He also held that education starts from maternal love in the family, and asserted that family education forms the basis of education.

Pestalozzi said that there are three fundamental forces forming human nature, namely, mental power, heart power, and technical power; these three, he held, correspond to mind, heart, and hand. According to him, an education of mind is an education of knowledge, an education of heart is a moral and religious education, and an education of hand is technical education (including physical education). The internal power that unites these powers is love. Love is the basis of heart power and the driving force of moral and religious education. Accordingly, he advocated that these three types of education can be harmoniously united, centering on moral and religious education.[5]

The image of the ideal person advocated by Pestalozzi was that of a person in whom the three fundamental powers are harmoniously developed—namely, a "whole man." He advocated the education of the "whole man" centered on love and faith. The purpose of education was to cultivate human nature and build a moral and religious nation and society.

Froebel's View of Education

Friedrich Froebel (1782–1852) followed Pestalozzi and further systematized Pestalozzi's view of education. According to Froebel, nature and human beings are unified by God and move according to God's law. Divine nature constitutes the essence of all things, and the mission of all things is to express, reveal, and develop such a nature. Therefore, people should manifest in their lives the divine nature inherent within them, and education should guide people in that direction. He wrote, "The free and spontaneous representation of the divine in man ⋯ is the ultimate aim and object of all education, as well as the ultimate destiny of man."[6]

Froebel especially emphasized the importance of the education of children and family education. Froebel's basic position concerning education was that the place to develop children in a natural way is at home, where the parents are the teachers. Like Pestalozzi, he emphasized the role of the mother. He asserted that kindergarten is necessary as a supplement to family education and became the founder of the kindergarten.

The "natural man" with good nature, advocated by Rousseau was, for Pestalozzi, a "whole man" with noble human nature, and, for Froebel, the image of the ideal person was that of a "whole man with a divine nature."

Herbart's View of Education

Johann F. Herbart (1775–1841) attempted to systematize pedagogy as a science. In doing so, he incorporated ethics and psychology into pedagogy, as its basis, whereby he established ethics as the aim of education, and psychology as the means of education.

First, following Kant, Herbart considered a "good man" to be the image of an ideal person; and the "cultivation of a moral character" as the goal of education. Next, he outlined the method of education, proposing that what forms the foundation of human spiritual life are the presentations in one's mind; therefore, by cultivating one's circle of thought, or one's collection of presentations, a person's moral character can be cultivated. In other words, he advocated building moral character through teaching knowledge.

Herbart pointed out the importance of instruction in the formation of representations, and explained the process of instruction. According to the Herbartian school, which later revised Herbart's theory, the process of instruction consists of five stages: (1) prepare the students to be ready for the new lesson, (2) present the new lesson, (3) associate the new lesson with what was studied earlier, (4) use examples to illustrate the lesson's major points, and (5) test students to ensure they had learned the new lesson.

Dewey's View of Education

In the late nineteenth century, a pragmatic view of life, which placed behavior at the center of human life, was born in the United States. John Dewey (1859–1952) advocated instrumentalism, asserting that intellect is a tool useful for behavior and that thinking develops in the process of human efforts to control the environment.

Stating that "education is all one with growing; it has no end beyond itself,"[7] Dewey argued that no sense of purpose should be fixed in advance for education, but that instead, education should be regarded as growth. According to him, "education consists primarily in transmission through communication,"[8] and "education is a constant reorganizing or reconstructing of experience."[9] This transmission should be achieved through the medium of the environment rather than directly from adults (teachers) to children. Through such an education, society develops. What Dewey intended to achieve was a kind of practical, technical education aimed at the reconstruction of society. The image of the ideal person in Dewey's view of education was that of an "active man."

Communist View of Education

Marx and Lenin sharply criticized the kind of education conducted in capitalist society. According to Marx, in capitalist society educational policies are intended to keep people in ignorance.[10] Teachers are productive laborers who belabor children's heads and work to enrich the school proprietor.[11] According to Lenin, capitalist education is an "instrument of the class rule of the bourgeoisie,"[12] the goal of which is to raise "docile and efficient servants of the bourgeoisie" and "slaves and tools of capital."[13]

In contrast to the education in a capitalist society, in socialist society, Lenin asserted, "The schools must become an instrument of the dictatorship of the proletariat."[14] He also said that teachers must become the soldiers who instill the spirit of Communism into the masses of workers.[15]

The purpose of a Communist education was stated in the preamble of the "Fundamentals of National Education Act" (1973) of the Soviet Union: "The objective of national education in the U.S.S.R. is to raise a highly-cultivated, all-round, fully developed, and active architect of Communist society who has been raised under Marxist-Leninist thought, with respect for Soviet law and the socialist order, and with Communistic attitude toward labor."[16] In other words, the purpose of Communist education is to raise people dedicated to the construction of a Communist society. The image of the ideal person is the "all-round, fully developed human being."[17]

Then, what are the contents of a Communist education? First, it attaches importance to general technical education (or "polytechnism"), as opposed to individual technical education. It then asserts that general technical education should be carried out in connection with labor. Furthermore, it asserts that, in a socialist society, there are no conflicts of interest between individuals and groups, and that there is no individual apart from a group, calling for the necessity of collective education. The general technical education was systematized by N. K. Krupskaya (1869–1939), and collective education was systematized by A. S. Makarenko (1888–1939).

Democratic View of Education

The idea of education in democracy is based on democratic thought. Dewey's view of education played a major role throughout the first half of the twentieth century. I will quote here from the "Report of the United States Education Mission to Japan"[18] as to what represents the democratic idea for education after World War II. The report begins with the following definition of democracy:

> Democracy is not a cult, but a convenient means through which the emancipated energies of men may be allowed to display themselves in utmost variety. Democracy is best conceived not as a remote goal, however radiant, but as the pervasive spirit of every present freedom. Responsibility is of the essence of this freedom. Duties keep rights from canceling each other out. The test of equal treatment is the taproot of democracy, whether it be of rights to be shared or of duties to be shouldered.[19]

The report then describes the nature of democratic education, as follows:

> A system of education for life in a democracy will rest upon the recognition of the worth and dignity of the individual. It will be so organized as to provide educational opportunity in accordance with the abilities and aptitudes of each person. Through content and methods of instruction it will foster freedom of inquiry, and training

in the ability to analyze critically. It will encourage a wide discussion of factual information within the competence of students at different stages of their development. These ends can not be promoted if the work of the school is limited to prescribed courses of study and to a single approved textbook in each subject. The success of education in a democracy can not be measured in terms of uniformity and standardization. Education should prepare the individual to become a responsible and cooperating member of society.[20]

The ideal of democratic education is to nurture democratic citizens, who, while observing the principles of democracy, such as the sovereignty of the people, majority rule, and equality of rights, will respect the rights of others and will fulfill their own responsibility, and upon that basis will claim their own rights and will make effort to perfect their own personality.

The purpose of democratic education, therefore, is the perfection of character and the nurturing of responsible members of society. Its image of the ideal person is that of a "person of respectable individuality."

V. An Appraisal of Traditional Theories of Education from the Perspective of Unification Thought

Let us now briefly appraise these traditional theories of education from the standpoint of Unification Thought.

For Plato, the image of the ideal person is that of a philosopher who has recognized the "Idea of the Good." Plato thought that if such a philosopher were to govern the state, an ideal state would come about. In the Age of ancient Greece, however, no such philosopher ever emerged who could govern the state, and the Idea of the Good was not realized in the city-state (*polis*). Moreover, after the coming of the Age of Hellenism, the Idea of the Good collapsed together with the city-states. That was because the Idea of the Good was too ambiguous. Unless God's purpose for creating the universe and humankind is well clarified, the standard of goodness will remain ambiguous, and therefore, the Idea of the Good can not be actualized.

Christianity in the Middle Ages advocated a kind of education that could raise people to love God and their neighbors. Yet, that love was "agape," that is, the sacrificial love that was displayed in Jesus' crucifixion.

Such questions as to why God's love must be such a sacrificial love, and why human beings must love one another were not clarified. Accordingly, it was difficult for such a Christian view of education to guide people of the modern period, who were more awakened to actual human nature.

Education in the Renaissance period can be highly esteemed in that it liberated human nature, which had been oppressed; but from the mid-sixteenth century on, it gradually became formalized into a mere study of the classics. It also leaned toward human-centeredness and gradually lost its religious morality.

Comenius said that the role of education was to draw out the natural gift (nature) inherent in every person. It is not clear, however, what that gift was. There is also a problem with his concept of *pansophia*, according to which the acquisition of true knowledge would lead to virtue and faith. From the viewpoint of Unification Thought, true intellectual education can be established only on the basis of being educated about heart and norm. Still, the three kinds of education advocated by Comenius have something in common with the education of heart, the education of norm, and the education of dominion in the Unification Theory of Education.

Rousseau also advocated raising people in a natural way, but his concept of "nature" within the individual was too ambiguous. Furthermore, there is a problem in his definition of human nature as unconditionally good. He advocated bringing up children in a natural way, but without the education of heart and the education of norm centered on God's love (Heart), it is impossible to raise children as they naturally are and to lead them to become human beings as originally intended.

Kant attached importance to moral education. But his moral education had no solid foundation because God, who should be the foundation of morality, was conceived by him as an entity that is merely requested to exist, but of whose actual existence Kant himself was uncertain. Also, Kant dealt with morality only as a norm for individuals, but that is insufficient. Ethics, which is the norm for mutual relationships among human beings, is just as important as morality.

Pestalozzi asserted that three kinds of education, namely, an education of knowledge, a moral and religious education, and a technical education, should be unified through love. This assertion resembles the idea in Unification Thought of the education of norm and the education of dominion based on the education of heart. (Pestalozzi's education of knowledge and technical education correspond to the education of dominion in Unification Thought, and his moral and religious education corresponds to the education of norm in Unification Thought.) His idea for education with an emphasis on the "whole man" and his assertion that family education should be the foundation of education are also in accord with the Unification Theory of Education. Nevertheless, the point that the purpose of education is the fulfillment of the three great blessings was not clarified in his theory of education. Also, his understanding of God, who is the foundation for moral-religious education, was not sufficient. For these reasons, Pestalozzi's theory of education never became solidly established.

A similar comment can be made about Froebel, who inherited Pestalozzi's theory of education. For Froebel, the "whole man with a divine nature" was the image of the ideal person. This is in perfect accord with the viewpoint of the Unification Theory of Education, which says that the essence of education is to teach children to grow to resemble God.

Herbart considered representations and their mutual relationships to be the origin of all spiritual activities, such as emotion and will, and asserted that moral character can be built by cultivating a circle of thought. From the viewpoint of Unification Thought, however, it is not by cultivating one's thinking that morality is actualized. Morality can be actualized when people pursue the value of goodness and observe proper norms, centering on heart (love).

Dewey did not recognize any purpose in education, but emphasized only growth and progress. Emphasis on growth and progress, however, without clarifying purpose, can not solve human alienation and social problems. In fact, today, as science and civilization develop, many social ills have emerged in societies in the United States of America where Dewey's method of education has been practiced. Wholesome persons and societies can not be formed through the method of practical technical education proposed by Dewey, unless such education is based on an education of heart and an education of norm.

Marxism-Leninism regarded capitalist education as the "bourgeoisie's tool for class rule" and advocated Communist education as the "proletariat's tool for dictatorship." That is simply a view of education from the perspective of regarding human society in terms of class struggle. Since such Communist theories as dialectical and historical materialism have been found erroneous, the Communist view of education based on these theories is likewise wrong. Marxism-Leninism asserted that the aim of education was to raise an "all-round, fully developed person," but this did not refer to the personality of an individual whose faculties of intellect, emotion, and will are developed in a well-balanced manner; instead, it referred simply to a laborer with fully developed skills, so that he or she can engage in any kind of labor. Moreover, Marxism-Leninism insisted on general technical education, but since it placed emphasis on labor, this general technical education was no more than education in working skills. Moreover, collective education has come to oppress the dignity of human individuality and freedom.

Finally, a democratic education is based on the value and dignity of the individual. Yet, too much emphasis on the rights of the individual has given rise to a tendency toward individualism and egoism. Also, since it upholds human nature on the basis of humanism, its views on values have become relativistic. As a result, social disorder has become unavoidable. Only when an education of heart and an education of norm, based on God's absolute love, are practiced, can the value and dignity of the individual be firmly established, and social harmony and order maintained.

6

Ethics

When we observe the world today, we can not help but feel appalled by the rapid disappearance of any sense of moral and ethical consciousness. At the same time, antisocial ways of thinking are rapidly increasing. It is now becoming quite common for people to think that they are free to do whatever they wish and, as a result, many kinds of social crimes are committed repeatedly, social order becomes chaotic, and society falls into great confusion. One underlying cause of this social confusion is that the human pattern of thinking has become more materialistic; another cause is the collapse of traditional values and norms of ethical behavior. In order to free society from this chaos and to reestablish the correct order in society, a new perspective on ethics must be presented.

Furthermore, in order to prepare for a future ethical society, a new theory of ethics is required. In such an ethical society to come, the values of truth, goodness, and beauty will be actualized, centering on God's love. It will be a world of eternal love where truth, art, and ethics are united in harmony. Accordingly, the future society will be an artistic and ethical society, as well as a truthful society.

An ethical society is a society wherein good people, those who practice goodness, live. In order to realize such a society, wherein goodness is practiced, a new theory of ethics must be in place. More fundamentally, it is necessary to establish a new thought system, from which a new perspective of ethics, capable of correcting the defects of traditional ethics, and realizing a new ethical life, can be formulated.

In the coming ethical society, all human beings will live as brothers and sisters centering on God as the parent of humankind, and people will love one another centering on God's love. In that society it is ethics that will provide the guidelines for the practice of love. Since a human being is the center of harmony between the physical world and the spirit world, this coming ethical society will apply not only to this earthly world but also to the spirit world. Accordingly, the norms presented by this new theory of ethics must be able to solve not only the confusion of this earthly world, but also the confusion of the spirit world. This Unification Theory of Ethics has been formulated in order to play just such a role.

I. Divine Principle Foundation for Ethics

With in the Divine Principle there are three foundational points upon which this theory of ethics is established. The first is God's true love; the second is the family four position foundation; and the third is the three object purpose. Let me explain each of these.

The first foundational point is God's true love. As the subject of love, God created human beings as His substantial object partners of love so that, after they had perfected themselves, they could inherit God's Heart and love, and practice love through their daily lives.

God's love is the source of the values of truth, goodness, and beauty. Therefore, God's love is the very foundation for the theory of education, the theory of ethics, and the theory of art, which are theories concerned with truth, goodness, and beauty, respectively. This is especially the case with the theory of ethics; thus, the true love of God is the basic foundation for the establishment of a theory of ethics.

The second foundational point is the family four position foundation. In order for God's love to be realized perfectly, it is necessary to establish the family four position foundation (the four positions refer to God, father, mother, and children). In fact, God's love is manifested through the family four position foundation divisionally, namely, as parents' love, husband and wife's love, and children's love. Seen from the perspective of God's position, man and woman as parents, man and woman as husband and wife, and children are His object partners. Parents are His first object partners; husband and wife are His second object partners; and children are His third object partners. Thus, the love of parents, the love of husband and wife, and the love of children are together called the three object partners' loves. Hence, the Unification Theory of Ethics deals with the overall relationships of love centered on the family four position foundation.

The third foundational point is the three object purpose. When perfected man and woman become husband and wife and love each other, centering on God's vertical love,[1] children resembling God will be born. At that time, a family four position foundation, which consists of the four positions of God (center), father (husband), mother (wife), and children is established. Since grandparents stand in the position of God in a family, a family four position foundation can also be seen as consisting of father, mother, and children, all centering on grandparents.

In the family four position foundation centered on grandparents, the person in each position of the family four position foundation has, as just mentioned, three object partners. The grandparents have the father, the mother, and the children (grandchildren) as their object partners; the father has the grandparents, the mother (wife), and children as his object partners; the mother has the grandparents, the father (husband), and the children as her object partners; and the children have their grandparents, their father, and their mother as their object partners.

Thus, the person in each position of the family four position foundation faces three object partners. For human beings, the purpose for being created is fulfilled within the family by one's loving these three object partners. Therefore, the purpose of creation (or the purpose for being created) can be understood as fulfillment of the three object purpose. When a person in one of the positions loves the persons in the other three positions (object partners), the three object purpose becomes realized.[2]

The fulfillment of the three object purpose brings about the realization of God's love toward the three object partners. God's love is an absolute love, but when it manifests itself, it does so in a differentiated manner, according to the position and direction within the four position foundation. Divisional love refers to the three kinds of divine love expressed in the family, namely, parents' love, conjugal love, and children's love, namely, the three object partners' love. (As already mentioned, God's three object partners are the parents, His first object partners, husband and wife, His second object partners, and the children, His third object partners.)

Parents' love is a downward love, from parents to children; conjugal love is a horizontal love between husband and wife; and children's love is an upward love, from children to parents. In this way, divisional love is love with a directional nature. More precisely, love has twelve directions, because the person in each of the four positions has a different kind of love for each of the three object partners, respectively. Consequently, various kinds of love, with different nuances, come to appear. In order to realize these various kinds of love, various kinds of virtue are required, since with each kind of love there is a corresponding virtue.

To summarize, God's ideal of creation is for human beings to realize God's love through the family and to complete the family four position foundation. Therefore, the aim of the Unification Theory of Ethics is to fully explain the virtues of love, based on the family four position foundation.

II. Ethics and Morality

Definition of Ethics and Morality

As an individual truth being, each member of a family forms an internal four position foundation through the give and receive action between their mind and body or between their spirit mind and physical mind. This is an inner four position foundation. On the other hand, various outer four position foundations are formed through the give and receive action among the members of the family.

In the inner four position foundation, the spirit mind should take the subject position, and the physical mind, the object position. Since the fall of the first ancestors of humankind, however, the relationship between the spirit mind and the physical mind has been reversed. In other words, the physical mind has taken the subject position and has come to control the spirit mind. As a result, the activities related to the physical mind, that is, a life seeking food, clothing, shelter, and sex, are generally given first priority, whereas the activities pursued by the spirit mind, that is, a life seeking values, are relegated to a secondary status. This is why it has been necessary, throughout history, to make efforts to rectify the relationship between the spirit mind and the physical mind. For example, many saints and sages have emphasized the importance of living a disciplined life and have conducted training for cultivating one's character.

In this way, human beings have been seeking the perfection of their personality as individual beings. On the other hand, on the family level, they have been making constant efforts throughout history to perfect the family, namely, to perfect the family four position foundation.

At this point, then, let me define ethics and morality. Ethics is the norm of human behavior to be observed in the family by its members. In other words, it is the norm of human behavior in family life; the norm of human behavior that is in accordance with the law of give and receive action centered on love in the family; the norm for the family four position foundation. Therefore, ethics is the norm for a connected being to follow: the norm for the perfection of the family, which is the second blessing.

On the other hand, morality is the norm of human behavior to be observed as an individual. In other words, it is the norm of human behavior in one's individual life; the norm of human behavior that is in accordance with the law of give and receive centered on love in the individual's inner life; the norm for the individual four position foundation. Therefore, morality is the norm for an individual truth being to follow: the norm for the perfection of one's individuality, which is the first blessing. Consequently, ethics is an objective norm, whereas morality is a subjective norm.

Ethics and Order

Ethics is the norm of behavior of a person occupying a certain position of the family four position foundation and directed toward a certain goal—the three object partners. Needless to say, this norm of behavior is to be motivated by love.

Therefore, ethics is established in the context of a specific position and according to the order of love. This means that ethics can not be established apart from order. In a family today, however, order between parents and children, husband and wife, and brothers and sisters is often neglected or ignored. As a result, the family has become disordered or dysfunctional. This is the main cause of the collapse of social order. The family, which originally should have been the very foundation of social order, has become instead the starting point of the collapse of social order.

Order in love is closely related to order in sexual expression. Therefore, ethics is the norm for the order in love, and at the same time, the norm for the order in sexual expression. The order in sexual expression refers to the order in the sexual relationship between a man and a woman. It goes without saying that there must be order between parents and children's couples, and also between the elder brother's couple and the younger brother's couple. That is to say, the younger brother must not love his elder brother's wife sexually, and the elder brother must not love his younger brother's wife sexually.

Today, however, the proper order in sexual behavior has largely collapsed, and random and illicit relationships between a man and a woman have become commonplace. Along with that, the collapse of ethics is rapidly accelerating. One of the primary causes of the destruction of the sexual order is the animal-like view of human beings brought about by the collapse of traditional values. Another important cause is that society is being inundated by the sensual culture of sex, brought about by the media. Today, the sense of the sacredness of sex has almost been lost, and sex has become degraded nearly beyond recognition.

This situation is not at all different from the situation in the Garden of Eden, where Eve, tempted by the Archangel, had an illicit sexual relationship with him, and as a result, the order of love and sex was shattered. What is needed today is a new view of value that can bring the family back to its original state. Such a view of value must be able to re-establish the proper order in love and the proper order in sex. This is one reason why the Unification Theory of Ethics is presented.

Ethics, Morality, and the Way of Heaven

The human being is a substantial being that integrates the universe, that is, a microcosm miniaturizing the universe, and the family is a microcosmic system miniaturizing the system of the universe. The law that interpenetrates the entire universe is the "Way of Heaven," which is also called "reason-law." Accordingly, the norm for family life, or ethics, is the manifestation in a miniature form of the Way of Heaven (reason-law). Therefore, the family norm is exactly the Way of Heaven within the condensed scope of the family.

Just as we can find in the universe vertical order (e.g., the moon—the earth—the sun—the center of the galaxy—the center of the universe) and horizontal order (e.g., Mercury—Venus—Earth—Mars—Jupiter—Saturn—Uranus—Neptune—Pluto), so too, in the family we can find vertical order (e.g., grandchildren—children—parents—grandparents—great grandparents) and horizontal order (e.g., husband and wife, brothers and sisters). The various ethical virtues corresponding to such ordering are vertical virtues, such as the benevolence of grandparents and parents, and the filial piety of children, and horizontal virtues, such as the conjugal love between husband and wife, brothers and sisters' love between brothers, between sisters, and between brother and sister.

As already mentioned, ethics is the norm which family members observe toward one another as connected beings. On the other hand, morality is the norm of behavior for an individual to observe as an individual truth being. Morality also correlates with the law of the universe, or the Way of Heaven. Every heavenly body in the universe exists in a certain position, forming an inner four position foundation through the harmonious give and receive action between the subject and object elements within it. By the same token, internally within a human being, harmonious give and receive action must be made between the spirit mind and the physical mind, thus forming an inner four position foundation. The norm of behavior in forming this inner four position foundation is morality. Therefore, morality is also in accord with the Way of Heaven. Needless to say, the give and receive action between the spirit mind and the physical mind must be centered on God's Heart and the purpose of creation. Moral virtues include such virtues as purity, honesty, righteousness, temperance, courage, wisdom, self-control, endurance, independence, self-help, fairness, diligence, innocence, and so on.

Social Ethics as an Extension of Family Ethics

From the perspective of Unification Thought, human relationships in the wider society are simply an extension of the relationships carried out among family members at home. For example, in relationships where people's ages differ by thirty years or so, the senior individual should love the younger person as their child, and the younger individual should respect the senior individual as their parent. If the difference in age is ten years or less, the elder person should love the younger person as a younger brother or sister, and the younger person should respect the elder person as an elder brother or sister.

From this viewpoint, family ethics is the basis of all ethics. If family ethics is applied to society, it becomes social ethics; if applied to corporations, it becomes corporate ethics; if applied to the state, it becomes state ethics.

Accordingly, the following values (virtues) come to be established. In a country, the president and public officials should love the people while standing in a parental position, and the people should respect the president and public officials in the same way as they respect their parents. In a school, teachers should educate students well while standing in the position of their parents, and students should respect their teachers in the same way as they respect their parents. In a society, senior members should care for junior members, and junior members should respect senior members. In a business organization, superiors should guide their subordinates, and subordinates should follow their superiors. These are a few examples of the social extension of the vertical values (virtues) of the family.

When the fraternal love experienced among brothers and sisters is extended to one's colleagues, neighbors, society, nation, and the world, one should also actualize such horizontal values (virtues) as reconciliation, tolerance, obligation, fidelity, courtesy, modesty, compassion, cooperation, service, and sympathy.

Our societies, our nations, and the world today are all experiencing unprecedented chaos. The reason for this is that family ethics, which is the basis of all ethics, has become weakened. Therefore, the fundamental way of reviving society is to establish a new kind of family ethics, a new perspective on ethics. By doing so, we can progress toward saving families from collapse, and ultimately we can save the world.

It has been more than two hundred years since industrial capitalism emerged. During that entire period of time, labor-management relations have been a constant issue. It might even be said that Marx and Lenin appeared for the sole purpose of solving that particular problem, which they tried to do through their theory of violent revolution. In the end, their attempt proved to be a complete failure. Moreover, Communism is declining worldwide. It is the position of the Unification Theory of Ethics that in order to provide fundamental solutions to the problems of exploitation and labor-management problems, one must first establish corporate ethics on the basis of family ethics.

III. Order and Equality

Order and Equality Until Today

Modern democracy has superseded the medieval status system and the privileges existing under that system, and has attempted to realize an equality under the law. As a result, equality in political participation, that is, the system of universal suffrage, has been realized under the democratic system. Yet, even though this area of equality has been realized under the law, economic equality has not been realized yet, and the gap between the classes has been further widened. Unless this gap between the rich and the poor is solved, equality under the law is nothing more than an equality in name: genuine equality can not be realized substantially. In order to realize economic equality, Karl Marx advocated the establishment of a classless society, the Communist society, through the abolition of private property. In spite of the Communist experiment for over seventy years following the Russian Revolution, however, economic equality was not realized. Instead, a new privileged class appeared, bringing about a new form of gap between the rich and the poor. Thus, true equality has not yet been realized, even though people continue to try to achieve it, and have been trying ever since the beginning of human history.

In the democratic world, equality generally means equality of rights and this is one of the basic principles of democracy. Yet, the concept of equality is generally considered to be incompatible with the concept of order. In other words, if equality is emphasized, order is apt to be lost, and if order is emphasized, equality is apt to be lost. This has been the general view of order and equality up until today.

The fundamental question here concerns the relationship between order and equality. If all people were completely equal in their rights, there would be no difference between those who govern and those who are governed. Such a society would still become disordered and would exist in a situation of anarchy. On the other hand, if order is overemphasized, certain aspects of equality are bound to be lost. Thus, we must enquire as to the true nature of equality, namely, that equality for which human beings are sincerely searching in the depths of their original mind. We must also find a meaningful solution to the problem of the appropriate balance of order and equality.

Divine Principle Way of Order and Equality

Viewed from the perspective of Unification Thought, the Divine Principle way of equality is an equality of love and an equality of personality. In other words, the equality for which people are truly seeking is the equality possessed as children under the love of their Father, God. This is the equality in which God's love is given equally to all people, just as the light of the sun shines equally on all beings. Accordingly, the Divine Principle way of equality is an equality given by God, the Subject, rather than an equality that people, the objects, can establish as they so please.

God's love is manifested divisionally through order in the family. Therefore, an equality of love is an equality realized through order. An equality of love realized through order refers to an equality in the degree of the fullness of that love. In other words, true equality is realized when there is a fullness of love in everybody in such a way that is suitable to each person's position and individuality. Such fullness of love brings satisfaction, joy, and gratitude. Therefore, the Divine Principle way of equality is an equality of satisfaction, an equality of joy, and an equality of gratitude.

The experience of this kind of fullness of God's love comes to be felt only by those who have perfect object consciousness—that is, the heart to attend God and to be thankful to God. No matter how sublime God's love may be, those who lack a sense of object consciousness will never feel a sense of fullness; instead, they will continually feel dissatisfaction.

The rights in "equality of rights" refers to natural rights, such as those advocated by Lock (right to protect life, freedom, and property), by the Declaration of the Rights of Man (1789) at the time of the French Revolution, by the Declaration of Independence (1776) of the United States of America, and by the International Declaration of Human Rights (1948) adopted at the General Assembly of the United Nations. Here, let us consider for a moment the problem of rights and equality in the workplace. Needless to say, the rights accorded to each position can not be literally equal, since a given position usually carries with it appropriate responsibilities and obligations. In the original world, however, in spite of the difference between positions, there must be some aspect of equality transcending those differences, and this is an equality in love, an equality in personality, and an equality in satisfaction.

Let us consider the problem of equality between a man and a woman. Ever since the beginning of human history, women have been regarded as being inferior to men in positions, rights, opportunities, and so on. Not only that, women have nearly always been placed under the control of men. Today, women have become fully aware of the unfairness of this situation. Since the French Revolution, the movement for women's liberation emerged and has gained momentum and now women have come to demand that they be afforded equal rights along with men. Since an equality of natural rights (a right to life, freedom, and property) is a basic principle of democracy, women's demand for equal rights has been considered quite reasonable.

Side by side with various other social movements, the movement for women's liberation has steadily developed. After World War II, the demands of the women's liberation movement came to be reflected in the legislation in free nations to a considerable extent. The primary demands were an equality of position, an equality of rights, and an equality of opportunity. In the various Communist countries as well, such demands by women were guaranteed by law.

Since the late 1960's, the women's liberation movement has heralded a new development. Before that time, equality between men and women was guaranteed only nominally; in reality, equality was realized only partially. In many areas, unequal relationships between men and women persisted.

As a result of legal guarantees of the equality between men and women, the idea that men and women are equal in rights has spread, and a certain discord between husband and wife has become almost an everyday affair. Consequently, various tragedies and family breakdown, generally, have come to be frequent occurrences. What is the reason for this?

Basically, there can not be a perfect equality between men and women as far as rights are concerned. One's rights is a prerequisite for accomplishing one's life's task. Physiologically men and women have different roles in life. The fact that a man has a well-developed musculature, narrow hips, and broad shoulders indicates that a man's task lies in strength as it is related to external activities. On the other hand, a woman has a weaker musculature, broad, well-developed hips and breasts, and narrow shoulders, indicating that a woman's task is to give birth to children and raise a family. Insisting on an equality between men and women while neglecting these physiological conditions, is the same as saying that men and women should have the same role. This can not be the case, since a man can not give birth to a child, nor can his breast feed a baby, and a woman can not carry out the power-requiring tasks which a man is able to. This might remind us of the proverb that "the crow which tries to imitate a cormorant will be drowned."

There is one important sense in which an equality between a man and a woman must absolutely be realized. This equality, however, is not a mere equality of rights but, more importantly, an equality of love, an equality of personality, and an equality of joy. When a husband and a wife give and receive God's love, any sense of discrimination or inequality will completely disappear. They will become aware that they stand in an equal position internally and feel joy to the fullest extent.

Then, what about an equality in external position? A woman can possess or occupy the same social status or position as a man. As a woman, she can become a school principal or a company president. This is not because a man and a woman are the same, however, but because schools and companies are simply expansions of the family. Just as in a family the mother can serve as the head of the family on behalf of the father, so too, in a company a woman can serve as the company president, that is, as the mother of the company, and in a school, a woman can serve as the school principal, that is, as the mother of the school.

Particularly, in order to realize world peace it is highly desirable for women to take the lead, since the primary force for peace in a family is the mother. In other words, in order to realize true peace, it is necessary for women, who are peaceful by nature, to take the lead, rather than men, who are strong and aggressive by nature. This is a principled perspective with regard to the problem of the equality between men and women.

IV. An Appraisal of Traditional Theories of Ethics from the Perspective of Unification Thought

In this section, representative theories of ethics will be appraised from the perspective of Unification Thought. From the modern period, some major aspects of the theories proposed by Kant and Bentham will be discussed, and from the contemporary period, highlights of the theories of analytical philosophy and pragmatism will be examined.

A. Kant

Kant's Theory of Ethics

In his *Critique of Practical Reason*, Immanuel Kant (1724–1804) asserted that the true moral law should not be a "hypothetical imperative," which simply tells us to "do something as a means to achieve some purpose," but rather it should be a "categorical imperative," which straight-forwardly tells us to "do something," unconditionally. For example, we should not "be honest merely as a means of being regarded as a nice person," but instead we should "be honest," unconditionally. The categorical imperative is established by practical reason, and it gives our will an imperative, or an order. (Practical reason is called the "legislator".) The will that has received the imperative of practical reason is a good will, and a good will urges us to action.

Kant described the fundamental law of morality as follows: "So act that the maxim of your will could always hold at the same time as a principle in a giving of universal law." [3] "Maxim" here refers to a principle of practice determined subjectively by a person's individual will. According to Kant, an action undertaken should be such that the subjective principle, or maxim, directing it could be applied universally. Kant regarded as good that which holds true universally, with no contradiction, just like natural law; that which can not hold true universally, he regarded as evil.

Kant said that the moral law within us, present as the voice of duty, presses us into action. He stated, "*Duty!* Sublime and mighty name that embraces nothing charming or insinuating but requires submission, ··· but only holds forth a law that of itself finds entry into the mind and yet gains reluctant reverence." [4] The morality asserted by Kant was a morality of duty

Kant also stated that in order for a good will not to be regulated by anything, freedom must be postulated; and that, as long as imperfect persons seek to realize goodness perfectly, the immortality of the soul must be postulated; and that, when one seeks perfect goodness, or the supreme good, virtue should be connected with happiness, and in order for virtue to properly correspond with happiness, the existence of God must be postulated. Thus, Kant recognized the existence of the soul and of God as postulates of practical reason.

Unification Thought Appraisal of Kant's Perspective of Ethics

Kant distinguished pure reason (i.e., theoretical reason) from practical reason. Pure reason is for the purpose of knowledge, and practical reason regulates the will and guides it to action. Since pure reason is separate from practical reason, there can not but arise the question of why action required by the categorical imperative is good. In deciding whether or not a certain action is good, one must ascertain the result of that action. Yet, according to Kant, an action that is directly impelled by the categorical imperative to do a certain thing, irrespective of the results of that action, is good.

Suppose a person A happens to encounter a wounded person B, and the categorical imperative "you must help this person" is issued. Suppose, further, that A, receiving the categorical imperative, tries to take the wounded B to a hospital. Now, B may not want to be taken to the hospital, and he may refuse to be helped and want to go to the hospital by himself. A is satisfied with the situation because he followed a categorical imperative issued by practical reason. In this case, A will regard his action as a good deed unconditionally, but B will feel it to be disturbing and not want to regard it as good.

In this way, without taking into account the result, Kant is only concerned with the motivation. His position does not necessarily accord with the common sense of goodness. Such a difficulty can arise because Kant separated pure reason from practical reason, or knowledge from practice. In fact, pure reason and practical reason are not separated from each other: reason and act are one. We act while taking into account the result of our action, according to one and the same reason.

Kant's notion of moral law raises certain questions: what is the standard according to which subjective maxims are to be universalized, and in what way does such universalization become possible? Kant said, on the one hand, that if all people became perfectly moral happiness would be realized; on the other hand, however, that since an act aiming at happiness is merely a hypothetical one, it can not be regarded as good. Although he knew that people seek happiness, he held that they should not aim at happiness. In this context, he postulated God, and affirmed that if we practice goodness perfectly, we will necessarily be happy.

The problems in Kant's view are derived from the fact that he did not know about God's purpose of creation. For him, all purposes were self-loving and selfish. From the perspective of Unification Thought, however, human beings have dual purposes, namely, a purpose for the whole and a purpose for the individual, and originally they were to pursue the purpose for the individual while placing priority on the purpose for the whole. In contrast, what Kant referred to as "purpose" was nothing but the purpose for the individual. As a result, he denigrated every kind of purpose, and his moral law became a law with an ambiguous criterion.

Furthermore, Kant asserted that, in order for the moral law to be established, the immortality of the soul and the existence of God must be postulated. On the other hand, in his *Critique of Pure Reason*, Kant excluded God and the soul saying that it is impossible to cognize them since they lack any kind of sense-content. Here, also, there is a difficulty in Kant's philosophy. He postulated God, but his postulated God is only a hypothetical God, not the true or existing God. As such, his God was not the God whom we can believe in and rely on.

Kant attempted to establish the standard of goodness of his moral law based only on duty, which is given to us by practical reason. This is merely a cold world of duty, a world of regulations like those followed by a platoon of soldiers. Seen from the Unification Thought point of view, duty and behavioral norms can not be a purpose in themselves, since the purpose of our action is ultimately to realize true love. Duty and behavioral norms are merely the means for actualizing true love.

B. Bentham

Bentham's View of Ethics

Jeremy Bentham (1748–1832) starts with the following premise: "Nature has placed mankind under the governance of two sovereign masters; *pain* and *pleasure*. It is for them alone to point out what we ought to do, as well as to determine what we shall do."[5] Thus, he advocated the "principle of utility," according to which, pleasure and pain are the standards of good and evil.

Bentham calculated pleasure and pain quantitatively, regarding as good any act that brings the greatest pleasure, thus advocating "the greatest happiness of the greatest number" as the guiding principle of his moral philosophy. As to what it is that brings pleasure or pain to people, he stated that "there are four distinguishable sources from which pleasure and pain are in use to flow, ··· the *physical*, the *political*, the *moral*, and the *religious*."[6] Among these, he regarded the physical source as the most fundamental one, for only physical pleasure and pain can be calculated objectively. He considered it desirable for as many people as possible to obtain portions of material wealth in an equitable manner.

Contrary to Kant, who argued that pure goodness is not determined by purpose or material interests, Bentham asserted that human conduct can be considered good only when it realizes the greatest happiness for people. Thus, he argued that material happiness must be pursued directly. The Industrial Revolution of England served as the background for Bentham's thought.

Bentham's philosophy influenced many thinkers; one of these was

Robert Owen (1771–1858), a socialist reformer. Owen incorporated into his thought Bentham's belief in "the greatest happiness of the greatest number." Based on this, and under the influence of the French Enlightenment and materialist philosophy, Owen advocated a movement for social reform. Since people are the products of their environment, he thought that if the environment is improved, they will be improved as well, and a happy society can be realized. In order to actualize that ideal, Owen moved to the United States and constructed a *New Harmony* society of cooperatives in Indiana. This effort, however, ended in failure due to internal divisions among co-workers.

Utilitarians, influenced by this socialist movement, engaged in various activities for social reform. They promoted movements for the reform of electoral laws, the reform of laws concerning the poor, the simplification of legal proceedings, the abolition of crop regulations, the liberation of slaves in colonies, the expansion of suffrage, the reform of the living conditions of working people, and many others, and thus contributed significantly to the impetus to find solutions to the problems in capitalist society.

Unification Thought Appraisal of Bentham's Perspective of Ethics

Unlike Kant, who advocated goodness as a duty, Bentham asserted that a good act is one which leads to happiness. In this respect, Bentham's view is more in agreement with Unification Thought. The problem, however, is that Bentham understood happiness as having to do with material pleasure. According to Unification Thought, true happiness for human beings can not be obtained through material pleasure alone. In advanced countries today many people have come to enjoy material prosperity; yet, there are not so many people who regard themselves as truly happy, for many people are affected by the increase in social disorder and crimes in advanced countries. This indicates that utilitarianism is not an effective way to achieve true happiness.

From the Unification Thought viewpoint, Bentham's thought was proposed for the sake of restoring the environment. In order to realize the ideal society, human beings have to be restored; at the same time, a suitable environment must be prepared. So, from the providential viewpoint, it can be said that such philosophies as Bentham's utilitarianism become necessary as the Second Advent of Christ approaches. Kant, in contrast to Bentham, can be said to have advocated a philosophy for the sake of restoring human beings.

As pointed out above, utilitarianism was insufficient and fell short of realizing the happiness of humankind. Communism, which appeared later, was, like utilitarianism, a thought for the sake of restoring the environment. Communism moved in the wrong direction, however, in advocating violent revolution. As a result, far from realizing a happy society, Communism created one even more miserable. True human happiness must be realized in terms of both spiritual and material aspects. This is possible only when a standard of goodness is established that can present a unified and harmonious solution for both the spiritual aspects and the material aspects of human nature.

C. Analytic Philosophy

View of Ethics in Analytic Philosophy

According to analytic philosophy, the task of philosophy is not to establish any specific world view, but rather to make philosophy itself a scientific discipline by engaging in a logical analysis of language. The Cambridge Analytic School, with such scholars as George E. Moore (1873–1958), Bertrand Russell (1872–1970), and Ludwig Wittgenstein (1889–1951); the Logical Positivism of Vienna School, with such scholars as Moritz Schlick (1882–1936), Rudolph Carnap (1891–1971) and Alfred J. Ayer (1910–71); and the Ordinary Language School of Britain—all of these are referred to as schools of analytic philosophy. Among the representative ethical theories of analytic philosophy, we can include the "intuitionism" of Moore and the "emotive theory" of Schlick and Ayer.

According to Moore, goodness can not be defined. He argued: "My point is that 'good' is a simple notion, just as 'yellow' is a simple notion; that, just as you can not, by any manner or means, explain to any one who does not already know it, what yellow is, so you can not explain what good is." [7] Moore said further, "If I am asked 'What is good?' my answer is that good is good, and that is the end of the matter." [8] He stated that good can only be grasped by intuition, and argued that value judgments are entirely independent from factual judgments.

According to Schlick and Ayer, goodness is no more than a word expressing a subjective feeling and a quasi-idea that can not be verified objectively. Accordingly, an ethical proposition such as, "It is bad to steal money," is nothing but the speaker's expression of a feeling of moral disapproval and can not be regarded as either true or false.

Unification Thought Appraisal of Analytic Philosophy's Perspective of Ethics

The characteristic feature of analytic philosophy's view of ethics is its separation of factual judgments from value judgments. From the viewpoint of Unification Thought, however, factual judgments and value judgments are both objective, and they can be seen as the two sides of a single coin. Yet, since a factual judgment is a judgment concerning phenomena that can be recognized by anyone, it is characterized by an objectivity that can easily be grasped. In contrast, a value judgment is advocated by a limited number of, for example, religious people or philosophers, and is not necessarily understood by everyone—which gives the impression that a value judgment is purely subjective. If the spiritual level of human beings becomes enhanced, and the law of value operating throughout the entire universe comes to be understood clearly by all people, then value judgments would also come to be recognized as universally valid.

Natural science has been dealing only with factual judgments, and has been pursuing cause-and-effect relationships in things. Today, however, science has reached the point where it is no longer possible to thoroughly understand natural phenomena solely through the pursuit of cause-and-effect relationships. Scientists are now seeking the meaning behind, or the reason for, natural phenomena. This means that scientists have come to the point of pursuing value judgments in addition to factual judgments. It is the view of Unification Thought that fact and value, or science and ethics, must be approached as one united theme.

Another characteristic feature among the proponents of analytic philosophy is that they have regarded goodness as something undefinable, a quasi-idea. From the Unification Thought perspective, however, goodness can be clearly defined. In sum, human beings have the clear purpose of realizing God's love through the family four position foundation; thus, behavior in agreement with this purpose is good. Since such goodness is evaluated in actual life, value and fact can not be separated.

D. Pragmatism

Pragmatism's View of Ethics

Pragmatism and analytic philosophy stand on the same basis, in that both exclude metaphysics and attach importance to empirical scientific knowledge. Pragmatism, which was advocated by Charles S. Pierce (1839-1914), was popularized by William James (1842–1910).

According to James, "whatever works" is true. Suppose, for example, that someone comes to your home and knocks on the door, and you assume it must be your friend John. Only when you open the door and find that it is, indeed, John, can your thought be considered as true. In other words, only that knowledge which is verified through action is true knowledge. This means that the truth of an idea is determined by whether or not it has "working value." James said,

> The truth of an idea is not a stagnant property inherent in it····. It *becomes* true, is *made* true by events. Its verity is in fact an event, a process: the process namely of its verifying itself, its veri-*fication*. Its validity is the process of its valid-*ation*.[9]

This criterion of truth, also serves as the criterion of value and the criterion of goodness. Thus, an ethical proposition is not something to be proven theoretically, but is regarded as true and good, so long as it provides some satisfaction or peace to the mind. Therefore, goodness is not considered as something absolute or unchangeable, but rather something which is altered and improved upon, day by day, through the experience of humankind as a whole.

The philosopher who perfected pragmatism was John Dewey (1859–1952). Dewey advocated the theory of instrumentalism, saying that the intellect is something that works instrumentally toward future experiences, or a means for processing problems effectively. Contrary to James, who admitted religious truth as well, Dewey dealt only with everyday life, excluding completely any metaphysical thought.

Dewey's way of thinking derives from a view of humans as living beings, that is, as organic beings. A living being is in constant mutual relationship with its environment; when a living being comes into an unstable condition, it seeks to free itself from that condition and return to a stable state. It is intelligence, according to Dewey, that is utilized as the instrument effective for this. Good conduct is that which, based on intelligence, is effective toward creating an affluent and happy society.

For Dewey, scientific judgments and value judgments were regarded as being of the same quality. He believed that a good society would surely come if only people were to act rationally by using their intelligence. He saw no schism between fact and value in such a society. For him, goodness is something to be realized step by step through the increase of knowledge, responding to the requirements of life and bringing about the satisfaction of desires. Thus, Dewey denied the existence of any such ultimate goodness instantly recognizable. The concept of goodness, too, was simply an instrument, or a means, for coping with problems effectively. He said, "A moral principle, then, is not a command to act or forbear acting in a given way: *it is a tool for analyzing a special situation*, the right or wrong being determined by the situation in its entirety, and not by the rule as such."[10]

Unification Thought Appraisal of the Pragmatic Perspective on Ethics

James considered whatever works, or whatever is useful, as true and valuable. This means that he subordinated knowledge and values to one's everyday life. From the perspective of Unification Thought, however, it would be a reversal of the original way of thinking if we were to subordinate knowledge and values to one's everyday life consisting in the pursuit of food, clothing, and shelter. One's everyday life in pursuit of food, clothing, and shelter should rather be based on the values of truth, goodness, and beauty; and in turn, the values of truth, goodness, and beauty should be based on the purpose of creation. The purpose of creation is to actualize true love (God's love).

Therefore, an act in accord with the purpose of creation is good. An act that is merely useful to life, on the other hand, is not necessarily good. Of course, if an act that is useful to life is also in accordance with the purpose of creation, it becomes good. James based truth and goodness on their usefulness for life; instead, however, he should have looked for the purpose for which life exists and the purpose for which human beings live.

According to Dewey, intelligence, including the notion of goodness, is an instrument. Is the idea that the intelligence is an instrument correct? From the perspective of Unification Thought, logos (a thought) is formed through the inner *sungsang* and inner *hyungsang* engaging in give and receive action centering on heart (love) or purpose. Inner *sungsang* includes the faculties of intellect, emotion, and will, and inner *hyungsang* includes ideas, concepts, laws, and mathematical principles. Since inner *sungsang* and inner *hyungsang* are in the relationship of subject and object, the inner *hyungsang* may be regarded as an instrument of the inner *sungsang*. On the other hand, the faculties of intellect, emotion, and will, which constitute the inner *sungsang*, can be regarded as instruments for the realization of love. According to Dewey, however, intellect and concepts are instruments for social reform.

Dewey's instrumental theory is not wrong if it is centered on God's purpose of creation. But, as long as it is aimed merely at the attainment of affluence in one's everyday life, it is not correct. For, among concepts, there are some which may become the purpose of life but they can not become the means of life. The concept of goodness is not a means (of life); rather it is a concept having to do with the very purpose of one's life.

Dewey also considered that, if science develops in the direction of improving society, it will be in perfect accord with values. The progress of science, however, does not necessarily correspond with values. Only when science aligns itself with the realization of the purpose of creation —that is, the realization of God's love—will fact and value come to be unified.

7

Theory of Art

Culture, in a broad and general sense, refers to the totality of the various kinds of human activity, including economy, education, religion, science, and art, among which the most central is art. In other words, art is the essence of culture. However, art today is showing signs of a global tendency towards decadence. This is the case whether one considers democratic or former Communist nations, or whether one examines developed or developing nations. Decadent art can only generate a decadent culture. If today's decadence continues, world culture will face a serious crisis. Accordingly, in order to reverse this decadent trend, and even to create a new culture, a true art movement must be promoted, and for this purpose, it is necessary to propound a new theory of art.

The dawn of new eras in the past was always preceded by a new spirit in art. During the Renaissance period, for instance, artists played a leading role. In Communist revolutions as well, artists made a substantial contribution. It is well known that Maxim Gorky's works in the Russian Revolution and Lu Xun's works in the Chinese Revolution greatly contributed to those revolutionary movements. Therefore, in creating a new culture in the days to come, true art activities must be developed.

Communist art, centered on the Soviet Union, was called "socialist realism." Communists regarded art as a very important weapon in their revolution. Through art, they sought to expose the contradictions of capitalist society and to motivate people toward revolution. Socialist realism was a theory of art based on the materialist dialectic and historical materialism and it easily eclipsed theories of art in free societies, theories whose philosophical grounds were weak. Whereas socialist realism once dominated artistic society in Communist countries, with the fall of

Communism—or rather, since before its fall—it began to fade away.

Nevertheless, even though socialist realism has faded away, there is a possibility that it may reappear, inasmuch as it faded away without a substantial theoretical critique and, therefore, its disappearance was only superficial. In order to preclude its reappearance, it is necessary to critique it with a new theory of art.

It is in this context that I present the theory of art of Unification Thought, or the Unification Theory of Art, as just such a new theory of art. The Unification Theory of Art seeks to reverse today's trend towards decadence in art. Also, being based on a new philosophy it is presented as a critique of socialist realism, and as its counterproposal. This theory is for the purpose of contributing to the creation and establishment of a new cultural society. From the viewpoint of God's providence, the future society is not only true and ethical, but also artistic; therefore, it is all the more necessary to present a new theory of art.

I. Divine Principle Foundation for the Theory of Art

This new theory of art is based on the Divine Principle. The most important foundational concepts to be utilized are: (1) God's purpose of creation and His creativity, (2) joy and creation in resemblance, and (3) give and receive action.

First, let me explain God's purpose of creation and His creativity. The purpose for which God created the universe was to actualize joy through love. In other words, God created the universe as His object of joy. This means that God is a great artist and the universe is His work of art. To explain more concretely, God created human beings to be His object partners of joy and He created all things to be the object partners of joy for human beings.

For human beings, God's purpose of creation refers to the purpose for their being created: their purpose for the whole and their purpose for the individual. Their purpose for the whole is to give joy to the whole (namely, humankind, nation, tribe, and so on) whereas their purpose for the individual is to obtain joy for themselves from other individuals and the whole. God gave desire to human beings so that they could fulfill their purpose for being created. Accordingly, human beings always have a desire to obtain joy while they are pleasing God and the whole. Artistic activity is derived from God's creation of the universe. The activity of creation starts with the purpose for the whole, that is, it starts with an intention to please others. The activity of appreciation, on the other hand, starts with the purpose for the individual, that is, it starts with the intention of obtaining joy for oneself.

God's creativity is His ability to form the two-stage structure of creation, namely the inner developmental four position foundation and the outer developmental four position foundation within the Original Image. Forming the inner developmental four position foundation means to form Logos (plan); and forming the outer developmental four position foundation means creating all things by using *hyungsang* (material) in accordance with Logos. This process of creation by God is manifested as the two-stage structure of creation in human artistic activities. First, a plan is made; and second, a work of art is made by substantializing the plan through the use of materials.

Next, I will explain joy and creation in resemblance. God created human beings and all things as His object partners of joy. The joy of the subject is obtained through receiving the stimulation coming from an object whose *sungsang* and *hyungsang* resemble those of the subject.[1] Accordingly, God created human beings in such a way that they resemble in image the dual characteristics of God, and created all things in such a way that they resemble Him symbolically.[2] Applied to the theory of art, this means that an artist produces a work of art in resemblance to his or her own *sungsang* and *hyungsang* in order to obtain joy. Also, it means that an appreciator feels joy when sensing his or her own *sungsang* and *hyungsang* in and through a work of art.

Finally, I will explain give and receive action. In God, *Sungsang* and *Hyungsang* engage in give and receive action in a relationship of subject and object, and either form a union or produce a multiplied being.[3] To produce a multiplied being means to create a new being. When this give and receive action within God's Original Image is applied to the theory of art, it follows that the artistic activity of creation is performed through the give and receive action between the subject (the artist) and the object (materials), and that the appreciation of artistic work is performed through the give and receive action between the subject (the appreciator) and the object (art work). Accordingly, in both artistic creation and appreciation there are certain requisites for both subject and object to possess, since value (truth, goodness, and beauty) is determined by the correlative relationship between a subject and an object, as explained in Axiology.

II. Art and Beauty

What is Art?

The human mind possesses the three faculties of intellect, emotion, and will, corresponding to which there are different fields of cultural activity. Through intellectual activity, such fields as philosophy, science, and so on are developed; through volitional activity, such practical fields as morality and ethics are formed; and through emotional activity, the diverse areas of art come into being. In this way, art can be defined as "the emotional activity of creating and appreciating beauty."

Then, connected with this, what is the purpose of art? The purpose for which God created human beings and the universe was to obtain joy through loving object partners. Likewise, it is for the purpose of obtaining joy that works of art, which are artists' objects, are created. Therefore, art can also be described as the "activity of creating joy through creation and appreciation."

The British art critic Herbert Read (1892–1968) held that, "All artists have this same intention, the desire to please; and art is most simply and most usually defined as an attempt to create pleasing forms."[4] This sentiment is in solid agreement with the definition of art in Unification Thought.

Art and Joy

As already stated, art is the creation of beauty, namely, the creation of joy. Then, what is joy? According to the Divine Principle, "Joy arises when we have an object partner in which our internal nature and external form are reflected and developed. Our object partner helps us to feel our own internal nature and external form through the stimulation it gives. This object partner may be intangible or it may be substantial" (*DP*, 33). Thus, joy arises when the *sungsang* and *hyungsang* of an object partner resemble those of the subject.

As explained in Ontology and Epistemology, the human being is an encapsulation of the universe; therefore, all the *sungsang*s and *hyungsang*s of the universe exist in latent form within the human body. Consequently, when we recognize a flower, for example, we are already equipped with the prototypes of the color, form, softness, etc. of the flower. When we experience, through give and receive action, that the prototype is in full accord with the color, form, softness, etc, of the actual flower, we recognize it as a certain flower. The feeling of joy arises from that accordance. Therefore, if we want to appreciate the beauty of an object, we must first have the prototype in our mind.

Then, how does a prototype arise? The first requisite is one's purity of mind. If one's mind is pure, prototypes will come to the surface naturally. The second requisite is education. Through a theoretical study and appreciation of the various forms of beauty, the prototypes within one's sub-consciousness are more easily stimulated and come to surface awareness.

Resemblance in *Sungsang*

A resemblance in *sungsang* refers to the instance wherein subject and object resemble each other, either totally or partially, in terms of their thought, plan, individuality, taste, education, heart, and so on. Among these, a resemblance in thought is particularly important. When one finds within one's object a thought similar to one's own thought, the object appears beautiful. Therefore, if one's thinking is broad and penetrating, he or she will be able to appreciate a broader scope of joy, commensurate to that, and be deeply moved.

Thus, resemblance in *sungsang* refers to the resemblance between the artist's *sungsang*, which is contained in an art work, and the appreciator's *sungsang*: namely, the resemblance in their heart, thought, and so on.

Resemblance in *Hyungsang*

The *hyungsang* of an object refers to its physical elements, which we perceive with our five senses: the form, color, sound, odor, etc. of a thing. When these elements come into accord with the prototypes within us, we can appreciate beauty and feel joyful.

As will be explained in epistemology, the external world is an extension of the human mind. Accordingly, a human being has all the elements of the external world as prototypes in his or her mind. That is, the *hyungsang* elements such as form, color, sound, odor, etc. of all things or art works already exist within us as prototypes in contracted forms.

That is what is referred to as resemblance in *hyungsang*. When those elements—the physical elements of an object and the prototypes within us—come into accord, and our emotion is stimulated, we obtain joy.

Complementarity

Another aspect of resemblance, which is also a cause of joy, is complementarity. This refers to the instance wherein the subject feels joy by finding within the object some aspect which is absent within the subject. For example, a man is pleased to find grace and beauty in a woman, qualities which he lacks.

There are two reasons for this kind of joy. First, a human being alone can not become a complete being. Human beings were created in pairs: man, who has God's Yang characteristics, and woman, who has His Yin characteristics. When man and woman unite, they come to resemble the harmony of God's dual characteristics. This accords with how human beings were originally created.

This complementary nature can be regarded as a kind of resemblance. Every one has within one's sub-consciousness an image of what one lacks and which one wishes to be supplemented with. When one actually faces an object which matches that image, one feels joy, since the element one lacks is then supplemented. In this case also, the object resembles the image within the mind of the appreciator. Thus, complementarity is a kind of resemblance.

Second, God created human beings in such a way that they possess one of God's Individual Images; therefore, a man or a woman feels joy through engaging in give and receive action with others and finding within them that which is lacking in himself or herself. The beauty felt in this case is based on complementarity, which is a kind of resemblance, in a broader sense. God, the One, manifests Himself as paired beings of yang and yin, and as innumerable beings of individuality. Hence, we feel joy when we unite, becoming more perfect beings.

As another example, two separate things, a desk and a chair, become a perfect being (set) by complementing each other. To become a perfect being means that the purpose of creation is fulfilled, bringing about satisfaction and joy. In order for complementarity to be established, there must be resemblance in a deeper dimension, at the root. No beauty or joy can arise from mere differences without commonality, namely, a common purpose or resemblance.[5]

What is Beauty?

According to the Divine Principle, love is "the emotional force that the subject partner gives to the object partner" (*DP*, 38), and beauty is "the emotional force that the object partner returns to the subject partner" (*DP*, 38). In cases where the object is a mineral or a plant, what comes from the object is a material force, but the subject (human being) can still receive it as an emotional stimulation. However, there are cases where, even though the object gives stimulation (force) to the subject, the subject does not receive it emotionally. In such cases, the stimulus can not become an emotional stimulation. The question, therefore, is whether the subject receives the stimulus coming from the object emotionally or not. If the subject receives the stimulus emotionally, then that stimulus becomes an emotional stimulation. Therefore, beauty can be defined as "the emotional force, or the emotional stimulation that the object gives to the subject." Since beauty is one of the primary values—along with truth and goodness—beauty can be expressed in another way as well, namely, as "the value of an object that can be felt as an emotional stimulation."

I have described the emotional force which the subject gives to the object as love, and the emotional force which the object returns to the subject as beauty. In reality, however, in the case of human relations, both subject and object mutually give and receive love and beauty. In other words, the object also gives love to the subject, and the subject also gives beauty to the object. The reason is that, "when the subject partner and object partner become completely one in harmony, love is found within beauty and beauty is found within love" (*DP*, 38). When an emotional force is sent either from the subject to the object or from the object to the subject, it is sent as love, and it is received as an emotional stimulation, in other words, as beauty.

In the discussion above, I have given the definition of beauty as understood in Unification Thought. In the past, beauty was defined by philosophers in various ways. Plato, for instance, explained the essence of beauty in terms of beauty itself, namely, the Idea of beauty existing in an object. Concerning beauty, he said, "Fineness is auditory and visual pleasure." [6] Kant explained beauty as the "subjective purposiveness of an object," or the "form of purposiveness of an object." [7] What he means is: An object in nature has no intentional purpose. Yet, if a human being subjectively considers it as having purposiveness and receives a pleasant feeling from it, then that which gives that pleasant feeling to the human being is beauty.

Determination of Beauty

How is beauty determined? About this point, Divine Principle explains as follows:

> The value of an entity intended at its creation is not fixed as an inherent attribute. Rather, it is established through the mutual relationship between the purpose of the entity according to God's ideal of creation, and people's original desire to treasure it and bring out its true worth····. Consider a rose; how is its original beauty determined? It is determined when the purpose for which God created the flower and the divinely given human desire to appreciate and bring out its beauty are fulfilled together. To put it another way, an ideal person feels the fullness of joy when his desire to pursue beauty is satisfied by the emotional stimulation that the flower gives him. At that moment, the flower manifests its original beauty (*DP*, 36–37).

Beauty, then, is not something which exists objectively, but is something that comes to be determined through a give and receive action between the subject, which has the desire to seek value, and the object. In other words, beauty is determined when the subject, engaging in give and receive action, emotionally and subjectively judges the emotional stimulation coming from the object as beauty.

Elements of Beauty

Beauty is not something that "exists" objectively but is something that "is felt." Some element existing in the object gives the subject an emotional stimulation that is felt by the subject as beauty. Then, what is this element that stimulates the subject emotionally, in other words, what is this ele-ment of beauty? It is the combination of the purpose for which the object was created (the purpose of creation) and the harmony of the physical elements within the object. That is to say, when the physical elements, such as lines, shapes, colors, and spatial patterns in paintings, high and low sounds, long and short sounds in music, are well harmonized centering on the purpose of creation, and they give to the subject an emotional stimulation, the subject recognizes and feels it subjectively as beauty. When beauty is recognized as such by the subject, it becomes actual beauty.

Harmony refers to both spatial harmony and temporal harmony. Spatial harmony refers to the harmony in spatial arrangement, and temporal harmony refers to the harmony that is produced through the passage of time. Art forms expressing spatial harmony include paintings, architecture, sculptures, handicrafts, and so on, and can be called spatial art. Art forms manifesting temporal harmony include literature, music, and so on, and can be called temporal art. There are other art forms including drama, dancing, and the like, which manifest both spatial and temporal harmony, and these can be called spatio-temporal art or comprehensive art. In any case, it is the expression of harmony that gives rise to a feeling of beauty.

Aristotle said in his *Metaphysics*, "The chief forms of beauty are order and symmetry and definiteness." [8] Read said, "The work of art has an imaginary point of reference (analogous to a center of gravity) and around this point the lines, surfaces and masses are distributed in such a way that they *rest* in perfect equilibrium. The structural aim of all these modes is harmony, and harmony is the satisfaction of our sense of beauty." [9] Both agree that the element of beauty exists in harmony.

III. Dual Purposes of Artistic Activity: Creation and Appreciation

Artistic activities consist of two aspects, namely, creation and appreciation. These two aspects are not separate activities; rather, they are the two aspects of a united activity. This means that while one engages in creation, one engages in appreciation at the same time, and while engaging in appreciation, one creatively adds to the work of art one's own subjective perspective (called "subjective action," which will be explained below). In short, creation and appreciation are inseparably related.

Why are creation and appreciation so closely related? What are these two aspects of art necessary for? From the viewpoint of Unification Thought, creation and appreciation are practical activities carried out in order to fulfill the dual desires to realize value and to seek value. Specifically, creation is performed so that one may fulfill one's desire to realize value, and appreciation is performed so that one may fulfill one's desire to seek value. Then, for what purpose do human beings have these two desires? Human beings are given the desire to realize value in order to fulfill the purpose for the whole, and they are given the desire to seek value in order to fulfill the purpose for the individual. In other words, God gave human beings such desires as a driving force or impulsive force, so that they might act to fulfill the purpose of creation.

The purpose for the whole, even when not in one's conscious awareness, is nevertheless latent in the subconscious of a human being. At the same time, there exists in the human subconscious the desire necessary to fulfill the purpose for the whole. For this reason, everyone, consciously or subconsciously, strives to live a life of truth, to do good deeds, to create beauty, to serve humankind, and to please God. In this way, creation in art is based on the desire to realize value, namely, the desire to fulfill the purpose for the whole. Furthermore, human beings live for their own sake as well. This means that everyone seeks to obtain joy by finding value in an object based on their desire to seek value. The appreciation of art is based on this desire. Hence, the appreciation of art is a quest to fulfill the purpose for the individual.

The purpose for the whole and the purpose for the individual come from God's purpose of creation. God created human beings in order to obtain joy; this is the purpose of creation from the standpoint of God. From the standpoint of human beings, however, it is their purpose of being created, which is both to please God and the whole, and to find joy for themselves: the purpose for the whole and the purpose for the individual.

In this way, creation in art is the activity whereby an artist, in the position of object, manifests value (beauty) for the subject, namely, God and humankind, whereas appreciation is the activity whereby an appreciator, in the position of subject, finds and enjoys value (beauty) in an object, namely, a work of art. Both actions are ultimately derived from God's purpose of creation. Today, however, it is often the case that artists have deviated from the original proper position and have fallen into self-centered art. This has become a deplorable situation. If the true meaning of creation and appreciation becomes clear, artists will come to see their activities with more of a sense of purpose, and will pursue artistic activities as intended in the original ideal.

IV. Requisites for Artistic Creation

In order to understand creative activity in art, it is necessary to clarify the requisites for artistic creation. In creation, there are certain requisites for the subject (artist) as well as requisites for the object (work of art). Also, one's techniques, materials, and styles of creation are important requisites in creation. Each of these points will be discussed below.

A. Requisites for the Subject in Artistic Creation

Requisites for the subject in artistic creation refer to motif, theme, conception, object consciousness, individuality, and so on.

Motif, Theme, and Conception

In creating a work of art, there must first be a motif, a motivation for creation, and based on that motif, a purpose for creating a specific work is established. Next, the theme and the conception are established. The theme refers to the central content to be developed in the work, and the conception is the concrete plan for the content and form of an art work that is to be created based on the theme.

For example, suppose a painter, upon seeing an autumn landscape, is moved emotionally by its beauty and decides to paint it. The emotion thus aroused becomes the motif, and the purpose is set up of creating a painting of an autumn scene. Based on that purpose, a theme is established. If, for instance, there are especially strong feelings evoked by maple trees, the artist may decide to express the motif centering on maple trees, and a theme such as "Maple Trees in Autumn" may be decided. Once a theme is decided, the artist forms a concrete conception of how mountains, trees, rivers, sky, clouds, etc. will be arranged, what colors will be used, and so on.

The creation of the universe by God can be described in a similar way. First of all, a motif served as the motivation for creation. This motif had to do with His Heart, namely, His emotional impulse to "be joyful through love." Next, God established the purpose of creation, that is, the purpose of creating object partners of love resembling Him. Based on that purpose, the theme was determined: the human beings, "Adam and Eve." Then, a concrete conception of human beings and all things,

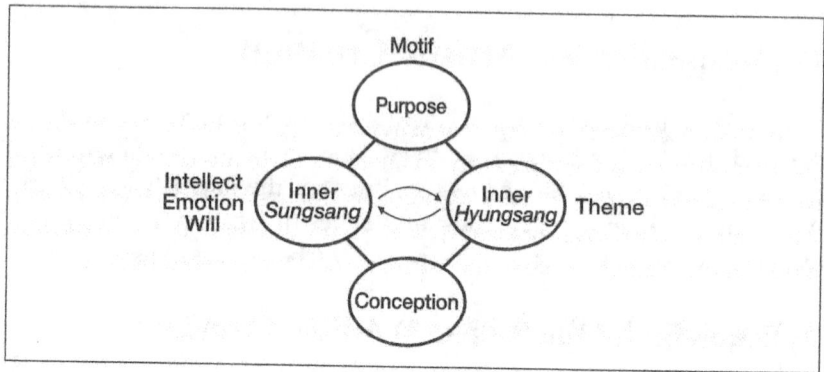

Fig. 7.1. Formation of the Inner Four Position Foundation in Artistic Activity

namely, Logos, was established. That is how we can explain the creation of the universe by God.

In God's creative act, His Inner *Sungsang* (intellect, emotion, and will) and Inner *Hyungsang* (ideas, concepts, laws, and mathematical principles) within God's *Sungsang*, engaged in give and receive action, centering on Heart (purpose), and the conception (Logos) was formed. The formation of this four position foundation can be applied directly to artistic creation. To explain, an artist establishes a theme, centering on a motif (purpose), and makes a conception through give and receive action between inner *sungsang* and inner *hyungsang* in the direction of actualizing the theme. This corresponds to the formation of the inner four position foundation in the process of creation by God (see fig. 7.1).

Let us consider the example of *The Thinker*, by Auguste Rodin (1840–1917), which is the statue of a poet sitting in the center of the upper level of the *Gate of Hell*, and was conceptualized on the basis of the first part of Dante's *Divine Comedy*, "Hell." The statue portrays a poet engaged in meditation while watching the people in hell, who are groaning in fear, anxiety, and pain. Rodin's motif in creating *The Thinker* may have been the deep emotion he felt upon reading Dante's *Divine Comedy*, realizing that every one must live a life of goodness in order to avoid suffering in hell. His theme was *The Thinker*, and the figure of a man sitting, engaged in meditation, was his conception.

There is another well-known statue whose theme is the same as with Rodin's work: the statue of the thinking Maitreya-Bodhisattva from the Shilla dynasty in Korea. However, it is quite different from Rodin's work.

The statue of the thinking Maitreya-Bodhisattva has as its motif the heart of the people waiting for the Maitreya, who was said to have been the most excellent disciple of Buddha and is to come again in order to save all humankind. The statue has a smile filled with self-confidence in his ability to save humankind. Rodin's statue displays a strong intellectual aspect, whereas the statue of Maitreya is centered on purified emotions, and, as a result, manifests itself as a very noble and holy statue. The difference between these statues, which have the same theme, derives from differences in motif and conception.

Object Consciousness

Creation is an activity whereby an artist, in the position of object, gives joy to the subject, namely, God and the whole (humankind, nation, tribe, etc.), by manifesting the value of beauty. To do so appropriately, the artist must first establish a sense of object consciousness. The attitude of wanting to give joy to God, the highest subject, and to manifest the glory of God, is the culmination of object consciousness. The content of such object consciousness will now be addressed.

First, an artist should have the attitude of wanting to comfort God, who has been grieving with sorrow throughout human history. God created human beings and the universe to obtain joy, and even endowed human beings with creativity. Therefore, the original purpose of human life was, above all, to give joy to God. Accordingly, all human creative activity should first be carried out in order to please God. However, human beings separated themselves from God and lost the consciousness of wanting to give joy to God. That has been the sorrow of God, even until now. Therefore, an artist should, above all, seek to comfort God for His historical sorrow.

Second, an artist should have the attitude of wanting to comfort the many sages and righteous people, especially Jesus, who walked the path of restoration with God. To comfort them leads to giving God comfort, who shared pain and sorrow with them.

Third, an artist should have the attitude of wanting to express the deeds of the good and righteous people of the past and present. That is, the artist should have the attitude of cooperating with God's providence by portraying the deeds of those people who were, and still are, persecuted by the people in the sinful world.

Fourth, an artist should herald the coming of the ideal world.

Therefore, an artist should create works of art which express hope for and confidence about the future. Through such works, God's glory can be manifested.

Fifth, an artist should have the attitude of wanting to praise God, the Creator, by expressing the beauty and mystery of nature. God created nature for humankind's joy. Due to the fall, however, people came to obtain less joy from the beauty of nature. Therefore, while having a feeling of awe toward nature, which is the manifestation of God's attributes, the artist should discover the profound and mysterious beauty of nature, praise the mystery of God's creation, and give joy to others.

Artists who have such an object consciousness and invest all their energy into their creative work, can receive blessings from God and assistance from the spirit world. This is the way in which truly great works of art can be produced. Such works may be considered to be the fruit of a co-creative effort between God and the artist.

Among the artists of the Renaissance period there were many who created their works of art with just such an object consciousness as this. For example, Leonardo da Vinci (1452–1519), Raffaello (1483–1520) and Michelangelo (1475–1564) were such artists. Beethoven (1770–1827), who perfected classical music, composed music with such an object consciousness.[10] This is why the works of these artists have become immortal masterpieces.

Individuality

Each person is a being with individuality, created in resemblance to one of the Individual Images in God. Accordingly, in artistic creation, the artist's individuality is expressed in a work of art because artistic creation is an expression of the artist's individuality, which is an individual image of divine origin. The artist gives joy to God and to others by manifesting his or her individuality. Actually, in great masterpieces the individuality of the artist is fully manifested. This is why the artist's name is usually attached to the work of art (e.g., Beethoven's Sixth Symphony and Schubert's "Unfinished" Symphony).

B. Requisites for the Object in Artistic Creation

The work of art, as an object of artistic creation, should reflect the artist's *sungsang* conditions, such as motif (purpose), theme, and conception (plan). For that purpose, the artist must use materials that are most appropriate to manifest these *sungsang* conditions. Moreover, those physical elements (components) themselves should be arranged in such a way that they express complete harmony. These are the *hyungsang* conditions.

As previously mentioned, many artists and aestheticians say that the physical elements (components) should be harmonized well in an art work. Harmony of the physical elements refers to such things as the rhythm of lines, the harmony of shapes, of spaces, of light and shade, of color, of tone, of massing in painting, of the segments in a line, of movement in dancing, and so on.

As for the harmony of the segments in a line, consider the so-called "golden section," which has been known since ancient times. The golden section is achieved by cutting a line in such a way that the ratio of the shorter segment to the longer segment is equal to the ratio of the longer segment to the total length of the line. This is achieved by dividing the total segment in proportions of approximately 5 to 8. When this proportion is employed, the end result is felt as stable in shape and beauty. In a painting, for example, if the relationship between the space above and that below the horizon or the relationship between the foreground and the background is made according to this proportion, harmony can be obtained. This golden section has also been applied to the pyramids and to Gothic cathedrals.

V. Technique, Materials, and Style in Artistic Creation

Technique and Materials

The two-stage structure in the Original Image refers to the two-stage structure in which, first, the Inner *Sungsang* and Inner *Hyungsang* engage in give and receive action, centering on purpose, to form Logos, and next, the Logos and *Hyungsang* engage in give and receive action, centering on purpose, to form a created being. All human creative activities are performed through this same process. For example, activities such as manufacturing, farming, scholarly research, and industrial research, are carried out according to this two-stage structure of creation.

This holds true also in the creation of artistic works. I have already

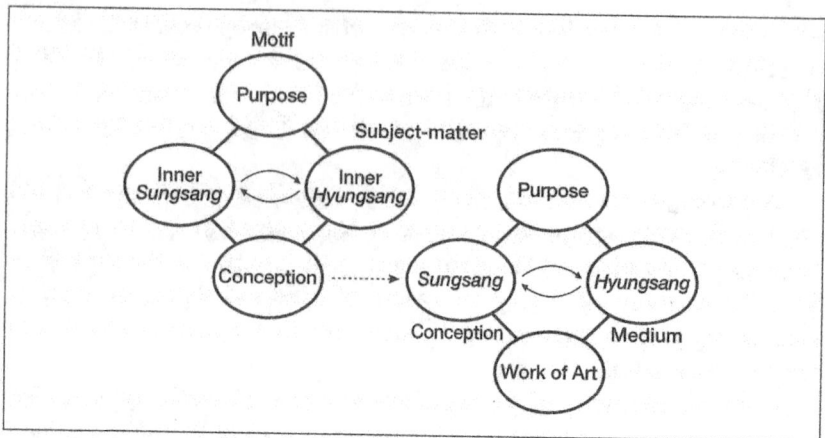

Fig. 7.2. Two-Stage Structure of Artistic Creation

explained the formation of the inner four position foundation in terms of the requisites for the subject. To repeat, centering on the motif (purpose), the inner *sungsang* (intellect, emotion, and will) and inner *hyungsang* (theme) engage in give and receive action and produce a conception (plan). This is the formation of the inner four position foundation. Next, based on this conception (plan) which has been formed through the inner four position foundation, the artist brings into being a work of art, using materials. In other words, the outer four position foundation is formed through give and receive action, centering on the motif (purpose), between the *sungsang* (conception) and the *hyungsang* (materials). In the formation of the outer four position foundation, the actual creation of a work of art, special techniques or abilities are usually required.

Next, I will explain about the materials necessary in creating a work of art. The materials required consist of the *sungsang* materials (i.e., the object of expression) and the *hyungsang* materials (i.e., the means of expression). The *sungsang* materials are called the "subject-matter." In writing, actions and events, whether they are real or fictitious, are the subject-matter. In painting, the people, landscape, and other images are the subject-matter. Thus, the subject-matter means the content of the theme.

The *hyungsang* materials (i.e., physical materials) are called the "medium." In a sculpture, such materials as chisels, marble, wood, and bronze are necessary. In painting, paints, canvasses, and so on are necessary. In producing a work of art, the artist determines the required quality and quantity of these physical materials and then utilizes them in concrete creative actions.

In this way, the artist first produces a conception (plan), and then completes the work by using specific materials. This process is called the two-stage structure of artistic creation,[11] which is illustrated in fig. 7.2.

Various Styles, and the Schools of Artistic Creation

The style of artistic creation refers to the method through which one manifests one's artistic expression, which is the particular way in which the two-stage structure of artistic creation is actually formed. Of particular importance here is the manner in which the inner four position foundation is formed, that is, the style of conception. The inner four position foundation is formed through the give and receive action between the inner *sungsang* (intellect, emotion, and will) and inner *hyungsang* (theme), centering on the motif (purpose).

Therefore, when there are differences in the motif, these will be reflected as differences in the finished works as well. Even with the same motif, with differences in the inner *sungsang*, works will differ. Also, with differences in the inner *hyungsang*, works will likewise differ. In the instance of variations or differences in any of the elements in any of the three positions in the inner four position foundation, the results (conceptions) will differ, and the works, also, will differ. This is the origin of the various styles of artistic creation. Based on these various styles, different schools of art have appeared historically. A few of the schools of art in history are described as follows:

(1) *Idealism*: Idealism is a style that seeks to express ideal beauty by idealizing human beings and the world. Many of the sixteenth century Renaissance artists were idealists. Raphael is a representative painter of this school.

(2) *Classicism*: Classicism refers to the artistic tendency in the seventeenth and eighteenth centuries to follow the examples of the forms of expression of Greco-Roman art. It attached importance primarily to form, seeking to achieve unity and balance. A representative literary work is Faust by Johann W. von Goethe (1749–1832). Among the painters, we can mention Jacques L. David (1748–1825) and Jean A. D. Ingres (1780–1867).

(3) *Romanticism*: As a reaction to classicism's focus on form, romanticism (eighteenth and nineteenth centuries) sought to give expression to the

passions. Among romanticists, we can mention the writer Victor Hugo (1802-85), the poet Lord Byron (1788-1824), and the painter Eugene Delacroix (1798-1863).

(4) *Realism/Naturalism*: Realism is a tendency to depict reality as it is. This style emerged as a reaction against romanticism, during the period from the mid to the late nineteenth century. Representatives of this school are such painters as Jean B. C. Corot (1796-1875), Jean F. Millet (1814-75), and Gustave Courbet (1819-77), and the writer Gustave Flaubert (1821-80). The style of realism developed a tendency toward positivism and scientism which led it to naturalism. A representative writer of the school of naturalism is Emile Zola (1841-1920). In the area of the fine arts, there was no distinction between realism and naturalism.

(5) *Symbolism*: Symbolism arose from the late nineteenth century to the early twentieth century as a reaction against realism/naturalism. As a school of literature, it sought to express feelings with symbols, abandoning the traditions and forms of the past. A representative of this school is the poet Arthur Rimbaud (1854-91).

(6) *Impressionism*: The school of impressionism considered the image caught in a single instant to be the true image of things, and sought to express individual and momentary impressions of shapes and colors. This movement was born and developed in France in the late nineteenth century. Edouard Manet (1832-83), Claude Monet (1834-1917), Pierre A. Renoir (1841-1919) and Edgar Degas (1834-1917) are representative painters of this school.

(7) *Expressionism*: Contrary to impressionism, which depicted impressions coming from the outside, expressionism sought to express internal human feelings. It arose as a reaction against impressionism in the early twentieth century. The painters Vasily Kandinsky (1866-1944) and Franz Marc (1880-1916) and the writer Franz Werfel (1890-1945) are representative artists of this school.

(8) *Cubism*: Cubism, a fine-arts movement of the early twentieth century, sought to disassemble objects into simple shapes and then reassemble them according to the artist's subjectivity. A representative painter of this school is Pablo Picasso (1881-1973).

(9) *Unificationism*: Finally, how could we characterize the artistic style of the Unification Theory of Art? It is a style in which idealism and realism are united, centering on the purpose of creation. As such, it is called Unificationism (see fig. 7.3).

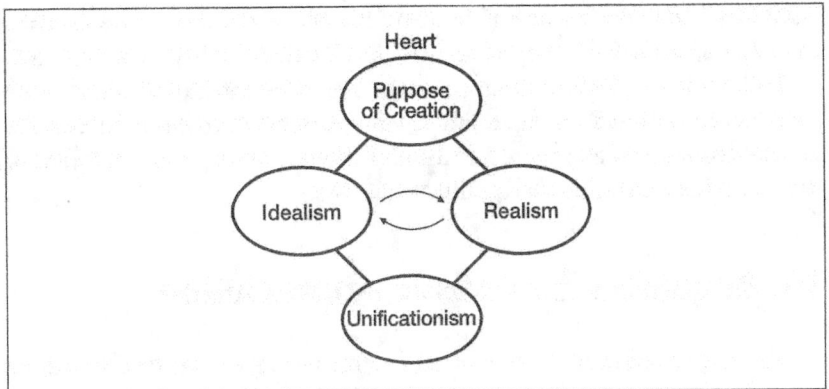

Fig. 7.3. Artistic Style of Unificationism

Since Unificationism seeks to realize the Kingdom of Heaven on earth, it regards reality as important. Accordingly, Unificationism has a pronounced sense of realism. At the same time, however, it strives, even while living in the real world to return to the original ideal world. So, the unification style includes idealism as well. Therefore, the unity of reality and the ideal becomes the Unificationist attitude of creation. For example, Unificationism would depict the image of a human being motivated by hope, seeking to overcome all hardships in the actual sinful world, all the while longing for the original ideal world. Unificationism is "Heartism," that is, a theory centered on God's Heart. Thus, Unificationism seeks to express ideal love centered on God, which naturally contains romantic elements as well. However, this is not like the romanticism of the past. When dealing with the love between a man and a woman, it will depict the ideal and realistic love between a man and a woman centered on God's love and on the love of the True Parents of humankind.

The various styles and schools of art mentioned above can be divided, in a broad sense, into realism and idealism, whereby realism is understood not in the sense of "a style that depicts reality as it is," but in the sense of "a style that is considered currently fashionable in a specific period," and whereby idealism is understood not in the sense of "a style that depicts ideal human beings and ideal reality," but in the sense of "a style that attempts to give rise to something new, and is oriented toward the future, in contradistinction to what might be currently fashionable in a specific period." In this broad sense, each of the past styles started out as an "idealism," but later became a "realism." It can be said that Unificationism as a style of art is the "unity of realism and idealism" in this sense as well.

This style of Unificationism, which is a style patterned after God's creative act centered on Heart and on the purpose of creation, is basically unchangeable and eternal, even though there may be some differences based on the individualities of different artists.

VI. Requisites for Artistic Appreciation

The appreciation of a work of art is a form of give and receive action; accordingly, in appreciation, as well, there are certain requisites for the subject and for the object. Those requisites will be explained here.

Requisites for the Subject in Appreciation

First, as a *sungsang* requisite, an appreciator must have a keen interest in the art work. Based on that interest, the appreciator must assume the correct attitude with which to enjoy the beauty in the work, namely, the attitude of intuition and contemplation. In other words, the appreciator must view the art work with a clear state of mind, freeing himself or herself from worldly, or impure thoughts. To do this, it is necessary to harmonize the spirit mind and the physical mind, such that the spirit mind and the physical mind are in the relationship of subject and object centering on Heart. This means that the appreciator should make the pursuit of the values of truth, goodness, and beauty primary, and the pursuit of the physical values secondary.

Next, the appreciator must have attained a certain level of culture, taste, philosophy, individuality, and so on. It is also necessary to understand as much as possible the *sungsang* aspect of the artist who created the work, namely, the motif (purpose), theme, conception, philosophy, historical and social environment, and so on. Understanding a work of art is a process of bringing into correspondence the appreciator's *sungsang* and the *sungsang* of the art work. Through this process of matching, the appreciator can enhance his or her resemblance to the art work.

For example, in order to deeply appreciate the works by Millet, it helps for one to understand the social environment of those days. At the time of the February Revolution of 1847, a heavy atmosphere of socialist reform had descended over France. It is said that Millet disliked that atmosphere and was more attracted to the simple life of the countryside. While living among farmers, he was inspired to portray their life-style as it was.[12] If one understands Millet's frame of mind, one can more deeply feel the beauty in his paintings.

In order to feel greater resemblance to the art work, the appreciator simultaneously engages in additional creative activity through "subjective action." Subjective action means that the appreciator adds his or her own subjective elements to the object (art work), thus adding new and additional value to the value already created by the artist. The appreciator then enjoys the enhanced value as the value of the object. Subjective action corresponds to the notion of "empathy" as defined by Theodore Lipps.[13] For example, in a play or a movie, an actor may break down in tears, and the audience may then weep along with the actor, thinking that the actor is really feeling sad. They project their own feelings on to the actor, judging the object subjectively. This is an example of subjective action, or empathy. Through subjective action, the appreciator becomes more closely united with the art work and obtains deeper joy.

Furthermore, the appreciator synthesizes the various physical elements discovered through contemplation and combines their overall unified harmony with the *sungsang* (conception) of the artist, contained in the work. In other words, the appreciator finds the harmony of *sungsang* and *hyungsang* in the work.

Finally, the *hyungsang* requisites for the appreciator refer to the appreciator's own physical condition. The appreciator must have healthy sense organs for sight and hearing, and his or her brain and nervous system should be in good condition. Since a human being is a united being of *sungsang* and *hyungsang*, a healthy condition of one's physical body is required for the appreciation of beauty, which is an activity of the *sungsang*.

Requisites for the Object in Appreciation

With regard to the requisites for the object (art work), first, the elements of beauty, namely, all the physical elements of the art work must be well-harmonized, centering on the purpose of creation. Second, there should be harmony between the *sungsang* (motif, purpose, theme, conception) and the *hyungsang* (physical elements) of the art work.

In appreciation, since a work of art is a completed piece appearing before the appreciator, those qualities which the art work already has can not be changed at will by the appreciator. Yet, as was pointed out earlier, the appreciator's resemblance to the art work can be enhanced through the subjective action of the appreciator. When displaying works of art, it is also important to prepare the environment in terms of location, background and lighting, in order to create an appropriate atmosphere for appreciation.

Judgment of Beauty

Based on the principle that "value is determined through a correlative relationship (the relationship of give and receive) between subject and object," beauty is judged or determined through the give and receive action between the appreciator (a subject with the above-mentioned requisites for the subject) and an art work (an object with the above-mentioned requisites for the object). This means that beauty is judged when the appreciator's desire to seek beauty is fulfilled by the emotional stimulation coming from the art work. The emotional stimulation coming from the art work refers to these elements of beauty within the work which stimulate the emotion of the subject. This means that beauty itself does not exist objectively. Only when the elements of beauty which exist in the art work stimulate the emotional function of the appreciator, and the appreciator judges that they are beautiful, do they manifest as actual beauty.

Let us consider for a moment the difference between an aesthetic judgment and a cognitive judgment. A cognitive judgment is made through collation between the subject (internal elements—prototypes) and the object (external elements—sense content). An aesthetic judgment is also made through the collation between subject and object. What is the difference between the two?

If, during collation, the faculty of intellect is more active than the other faculties, then it becomes a cognitive judgment; but if the faculty of emotion is more active, then it becomes an aesthetic judgment. In other words, when the physical elements of an object are perceived intellectually, it is a cognitive judgment, but when they are perceived emotionally, it is an aesthetic judgment. However, since the intellectual and emotional faculties can not be totally separated from each other, an aesthetic judgment is always accompanied by cognition. For example, the aesthetic judgment that "this flower is beautiful" is accompanied by the cognition that "this is a rose." The relationship between an aesthetic judgment and a cognitive

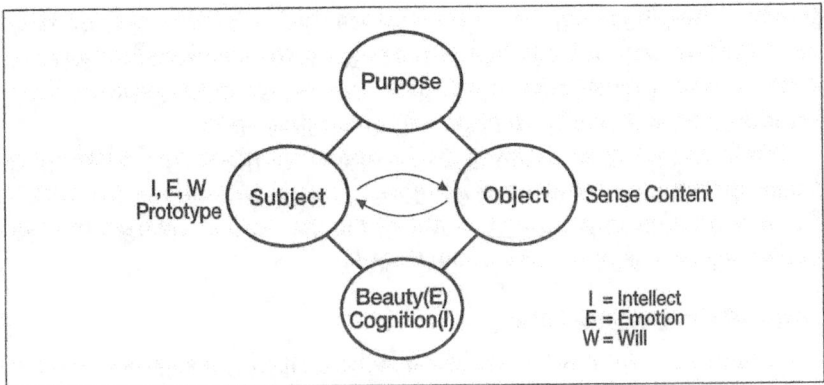

Fig. 7.4. Aesthetic Judgment and Cognitive Judgment

judgment is illustrated in fig. 7.4.

VII. Unity in Art

There are several pairs of correlative aspects (elements) involved in artistic activities, including creation and appreciation, content and form, universality and individuality, and eternity and temporality. Originally, these correlative aspects were not separated, but united. In artistic activities up to the present, however, there has been a tendency to separate these correlative elements, or to emphasize only one element or the other. Thus, the Unification Theory of Art clarifies the nature of the unity of these correlative aspects.

Unity of Creation and Appreciation

Usually it might be thought that creation is an activity primarily undertaken by the artist, whereas appreciation is undertaken separately by the general public. In the view of Unification Thought, however, both are essential modes of the activity of dominion. In order to exercise dominion over something, the correlative aspects of cognition and practice are nece-ssary, and the cognition and practice that take place centering on emotion are precisely the activities of appreciation and creation in the field of art. Cognition and practice form the two reciprocal circuits of give and receive action between the subject (human being) and the object (all things). Thus, there can be no practice without cognition, nor can there be cognition without practice. Therefore, in the relationship between creation and appreciation in art, there can be no appreciation without creation, nor can there be creation without appreciation.

While engaging in creation, artists appreciate their own work; also, while appreciating the art work of others, appreciators engage in creation. Creation in appreciation refers to the additional way of creation through one's subjective action, as mentioned above.

Unity of Content and Form

Certain schools of art, such as classicism, attach importance to form, whereas other schools disregard form and attach importance to content. Since content and form in art are in the relationship of *sungsang* and *hyungsang*, however, they should originally be united. That is to say, the *sungsang* content (such as motif, theme, and conception) and the form in which they are expressed with materials (*hyungsang*) should be in accord with each other. Tsutomu Ijima, a Japanese aesthetician, appropriately said, "Form is actually the form of content, and content is the content of form." [14] This means precisely that content and form should be united.

Unity of Universality and Individuality

Just as in all created beings the universal image and the individual image are united, likewise, in art, universality and individuality are united. First, there is the unity of universality and individuality within the artists themselves. Artists have their own unique individualities, and at the same time they belong to a certain school or have a certain method of creation in common with their specific region or period of time. The former is their individuality, the latter, their universality.

Since artists have universality and individuality united within themselves in this way, their works necessarily come to manifest this same unity of universality and individuality. Thus, in an art work, individual beauty and universal beauty are always manifested in a united manner.

In culture as well, there is unity between universality and individuality. That is to say, while the culture of a certain region has the special characteristics of that region, it also has characteristics common to the culture of the wider region to which it belongs. For example, the statue of Buddha in the Sŏkkuram grotto in Korea is a representative work of Shilla culture. It is also known that this work has the elements of the international fine art of Gandhara, which fused Greek art and Buddhist culture. Hence, in the Buddha statue of the Sŏkkuram grotto, both national elements (Shilla culture) and transnational elements (Gandhara fine art) are united, manifesting the unity of universality and individuality.

Here a question arises concerning national culture and the Unification culture. What will become of the traditional national cultures of each nation when the Unification culture is formed in the future? The Marxist theory of art, which claimed the partisanship of art and the basis-superstructure theory, neglected traditional national cultures. But that will not be the case with Unificationism, which seeks to form a unified culture while preserving national cultures. Unification culture will be formed through a universal spirituality and expression of art on a higher dimension, while at the same time preserving the essences of different national cultures, each with its own individuality.

Unity of Eternity and Temporality

Every created being is a being uniting the identity-maintaining (static) four position foundation and a developmental (dynamic) four position foundation; therefore, each created being exists as a being uniting immutability and mutability—hence, as the unity of eternity and temporarity. Likewise, in an art work, the eternal and temporal elements are united.

For example, the *Angelus* by Millet pictures a church, a farmer and his wife in prayer, and a countryside landscape, which we can regard as the unity of eternity and temporality. The church and the image of people in prayer transcend the ages and are eternal, but the countryside landscape and the clothes worn by the husband and wife are temporary, unique to that particular period of time.

As another example, we can cite the flowers arranged in a vase. The flowers themselves represent something eternal, which has existed from time immemorial, but the way of arranging the flowers and the vase itself are characteristic of a given period. Accordingly, the unity of eternity and temporality is manifested there. The beauty of an art work will become even more striking if we are able to grasp and appreciate a "moment in eternity," or "eternity in a moment," as thus described.

VIII. Art and Ethics

Recently, the vulgarization of art has often been discussed, even in the news media, and the relationship between art and ethics has become an issue. Art is one form of human dominion over the creation. Dominion over the creation, from the original standpoint, is intended to be carried out only by those who have reached perfection after passing through the growth process, which includes the three stages of formation, growth, and completion. Perfection means the perfection of love and the perfection of character. Therefore, one is meant first to become a loving person or an ethical person, and upon that foundation, to have dominion over all things. This means that an artist should first be an ethical person before he or she is an artist.

We can understand the relationship between ethics and art from the perspective of the relationship between love and beauty. Love is an emotional force that the subject gives to the object, and beauty is an emotional stimulation that the subject receives from the object. Thus, love and beauty are so closely related that they are like the two sides of a coin. Hence, we can understand that ethics, which deals with love, and art, which deals with beauty, are inseparably related. When we look at art and ethics in this way, we come to the conclusion that true beauty can only be established on the basis of true love.

Up to the present, however, such has not been the case with many artists. This is because there has not been any firm philosophical explanation as to why artists must be ethical. As a result, even though many artists, especially writers, have dealt with love as their theme, in most cases the love they dealt with was the non-principled love of the fallen world.

History is filled with such examples. Oscar Wilde (1854–1900), who advocated aestheticism (art-for-art's sake), was imprisoned on charges of homosexuality and died in disappointment and poverty. The romanticist poet Lord Byron (1788–1824) engaged in creative activity while carrying on licentious affairs with many women, and led a dissipated life. The works of such artists are little more than expressions of their fallen love, or their agony.

On the other hand, there have been writers who tried to express the ideal of true love. Leo Tolstoy (1828–1910) was one of these. While exposing fallen life in the upper class of Russian society of his time, he expressed true love. That is to say, while employing realism to express reality, he employed the style of idealism, pursuing the ideal. However, there have been very few artists, like Tolstoy, who have engaged in creative activity while pursuing true love.

IX. Types of Beauty

Let us now consider the various types of beauty. Since traditional aesthetics have discussed the types of beauty, I would like to consider this topic from the Unification Thought perspective.

A. Types of Love and Beauty from the Perspective of Unification Thought

Beauty is determined when a subject and an object engage in give and receive action centering on purpose. Accordingly, beauty varies depending on the observer (subject), and also depending on the type of object (an art work, a natural thing). Accordingly, there is a virtually infinite diversity in beauty; however, the various types of beauty can be categorized by grouping similar kinds of beauty. So, some scholars have tried to present what they regard as the basic types of beauty and to characterize the special qualities of each type.

From the Unification Thought viewpoint, as already mentioned, love and beauty are inseparable, and beauty can not exist apart from love. The more parents love their children, the more beautiful the children appear. Thus, as love increases in quantity, beauty is also felt to increase in quantity. This is because love and beauty form a reciprocal circuit in the give and receive action between subject and object partners. That is to say, the giver gives love, and the receiver receives it as beauty. In this way love and beauty are two sides of a coin. Accordingly, in thinking about the types of beauty, the first thing to do is to consider the various types of love.

God's love is manifested in the family as the three divisional forms of parents' love, husband and wife's love, and children's love (If brothers and sisters' love which is included in children's love is dealt with separately, there are four forms of divisional love). These three forms of divisional love are the basic patterns of love, which can further be divided into (1) fatherly love, (2) motherly love, (3) husband's love, (4) wife's love, (5) son's love, and (6) daughter's love.

Thus, the three basic types of divisional love are further divided into the pairs of unilateral love of both genders. These six kinds of unilateral love can be further divided into more subtly detailed kinds of love, manifesting more diverse types of love. For example, fatherly love has the qualities of strictness, magnanimity, broadness, solemnity, profoundness, awesomeness, and so on. Accordingly, fatherly love is manifested in the forms of strict love, magnanimous love, broad love, solemn love, profound love, awesome love, and so on. On the other hand, motherly love is mild and peaceful, and is manifested as graceful love, noble love, warm love, delicate love, gentle love, passionate love, and so on.

Next is conjugal love. A husband's love is masculine love, and so it is manifested to the wife as active love, trustworthy love, courageous love, resolute love, and so on. A wife's love is feminine love, and appears to her husband as passive love, supportive love, obedient love, reserved love, and so on.

Children's love appears to their parents as filial love, obedient love, dependent love, cute love, comical love, and so on. In addition, there are an elder brother's love for his younger brothers and sisters, an elder sister's love for her younger brothers and sisters, a younger brother's love for his elder brothers and sisters, and a younger sister's love for her elder brothers and sisters—all these various modes of love are included in the concept of children's love. Thus, the three basic forms of love are divided into pairs of unilateral loves, and further diversified, appearing as innumerable "colors" of love.

In correspondence to these various types of love, the different types of beauty are manifested. First, corresponding to the three basic forms of love, three basic forms of beauty are established, namely, parental beauty, conjugal beauty, and children's beauty. These can be further diversified as unilateral forms of beauty: (1) fatherly beauty, (2) motherly beauty, (3) husband's beauty, (4) wife's beauty, (5) son's beauty, and (6) daughter's beauty. These can be further sub-divided into the beauties of the accompanying diverse characteristics. They are as follows:

Fatherly beauty: strict beauty, magnanimous beauty, broad beauty, solemn beauty, profound beauty, awesome beauty, etc.

Motherly beauty: graceful beauty, noble beauty, warm-hearted beauty, delicate beauty, gentle beauty, passionate beauty, etc.

Husband's beauty: masculine beauty, active beauty, trustworthy beauty, courageous beauty, resolute beauty, brave beauty, prudent beauty, etc.

Wife's beauty: feminine beauty, passive beauty, supportive beauty, obedient beauty, calm beauty, tender beauty, cheerful beauty, reserved beauty, etc.

Son's beauty: filial beauty, obedient beauty, dependent beauty, youthful beauty, comical beauty, cute beauty, all of which have boyish characteristics, etc.

Daughter's beauty: filial beauty, obedient beauty, dependent beauty, youthful beauty, comical beauty, cute beauty, all of which have girlish characteristics, etc.

The love a father gives to his children is not always mild and warm. When his children do something wrong, he may scold them severely. On such occasions, children may feel bad, but later they feel grateful. Not only spring-like, warm love but also winter-like, strict love is a form of love. Such strict love can be felt by children as beauty, which can be called a strict kind of beauty. Or suppose a child has made a mistake and comes back home seriously expecting to be scolded severely by his or her father. Then, suppose the father unexpectedly forgives the child saying, "That's all right." That child would feel an ocean-like, broad beauty from the father on such an occasion. This is a kind of magnanimous beauty. Thus, when children receive various kinds of love from their father, they feel various kinds of beauty, with various nuances accordingly. In contrast, a mother's love is different from a father's love. A mother's love is mild and peaceful. Children feel such love from their mother as a graceful and gentle beauty. A husband's love is felt by the wife as masculine and sturdy. This is masculine beauty. In return, a wife's love is felt by the husband as feminine and tender. This is feminine beauty.

It is the original nature of children to try to please their parents. Children try to somehow please their parents by, for example, studying hard, drawing pictures, dancing around, or doing other things. This is children's love, and parents can perceive their actions as cute beauty. Or sometimes parents may feel it is very comical. This is comical beauty. Moreover, as children grow up, beauty corresponding to their age comes to be felt by their parents. Also, children's love is felt differently, depending on whether it is expressed by sons or daughters, as a son's beauty and a daughter's beauty. Also, unique kinds of beauty—namely, brotherly beauty and sisterly beauty—are manifested among children (brothers and sisters), corresponding to brotherly love or sisterly love. In this way, we experience various kinds or nuances of beauty as we grow up in our own family.

The various above-mentioned types of beauty can be further compounded, divided, or transformed, and innumerable kinds of beauty manifested. The feelings of beauty that we feel when we encounter nature and works of art are all derived from the types of beauty experienced in the family. In other words, the various forms of beauty experienced in human relationships based on the family are projected onto nature and works of art and are felt as the beauty of nature and art works. We thus have a basis for categorizing the various types of beauty experienced in nature and in works of art.

For example, when seeing a towering mountain or watching a waterfall descending from a lofty cliff, a person can feel a solemn kind of beauty, which is an extension and transformation of fatherly beauty. When admiring a quiet lake or a calm meadow, the beauty we feel is an extension and transformation of motherly beauty. The loveliness of the offspring of animals or sprouting plants is the extension or transformation of children's beauty. The same can be said about works of art. Paintings and statues of the Holy Mother Mary are the expression of motherly beauty, and Gothic architecture can be seen as the extension or transformation of fatherly beauty.

B. Traditional Types of Beauty

In the history of aesthetics, the basic types of beauty were regarded as being grace (*Grazie*) and the sublime (*Erhabenheit*). Grace is the type of beauty that gives us pleasure quite affirmatively and directly; we feel it expressed as a well-balanced beauty of harmony. On the other hand, the sublime is the type of beauty that gives us a sense of wonder, or a feeling of awe—as the feeling one has when looking at a tall mountain or a surging wave.

Kant, for example, held that in beauty (grace) there are the components of free beauty (*freie Schönheit*) and dependent beauty (*anhängende Schönheit*). Free beauty refers to the beauty felt in common by anybody, and not restricted by any particular concept. Dependent beauty refers to a beauty that depends on a certain purpose (or concept), and which is felt as being beautiful because of its appropriateness, such as its appropriateness for wearing or appropriateness as a place in which to live. In addition, pure beauty (*Reinschöne*), tragic beauty (*Tragische*), comical beauty (*Komische*), and other types are generally mentioned in theories of art.

These traditional types of beauty have merely been specified through human experience, however, and any criteria for their classification have been ambiguous. In contrast, the types of beauty set forth in the Unification Theory of Art are based on clear principles, namely, on the various types of love.

X. A Critique and Counterproposal to Socialist Realism

A. Socialist Realism

Among the various Communist revolutionary activities, one which played an important role was artistic activity, whose style of creation was called "socialist realism." What, then, was socialist realism? Lenin said that art should stand on the side of the proletariat, as follows:

> Art belongs to the people. The deepest wellspring of art must be found among the wide-ranging class of laborers····. Art should be based on their feelings, thoughts, and demands, and should grow along with them.[15]

> [Literature] must become party literature····. Down with non-partisan writers! Down with literary supermen! Literature must become *part* of the common cause of the proletariat, "a cog and a screw" of one single great Social-Democratic mechanism set in motion by the entire politically-conscious vanguard of the entire working class.[16]

Also, the founder of socialist realism in literature, Maxim Gorky (1868 –1936), stated the following about socialist realism:

> For us writers, it is necessary in our life and in our creative work to stand on the high viewpoint—and only on that viewpoint that can see clearly all of the filthy crimes of capitalism, all of its mean and bloody

intentions, and all of the greatness of the heroic activities of the proletariat.[17]

In the contemporary age, writers assume the mission to play two roles at the same time, that of a midwife [to socialism] and a grave digger [to capitalism].[18]

The main goal of socialist realism lies in inspiring a socialistic, revolutionary world view, or world sense.[19]

To state these sentiments in another way, writing poetry and novels, painting, and so forth, should all be carried out for the sole purpose of exposing the crimes of capitalism and praising socialism, and works should be created to inspire readers and viewers to stand up for revolution, with a righteously burning mind.

Socialist realism was formulated by Soviet artists under the guidance of Stalin in 1932, and came to be applied to all artistic fields, including literature, drama, cinema, painting, sculpture, music, and architecture. It advocated the following:

(1) To describe reality accurately with historic concreteness in its revolutionary development.

(2) To match one's artistic expression with the themes of ideological reform and the education of the workers in the socialist spirit.

What is the theoretical ground that gave rise to such socialist realism? This ground can be found in the Marxist theory of "basis and superstructure." Marx stated in the Introduction to *A Contribution to the Critique of Political Economy* as follows:

> The totality of these relations of production constitutes the economic structure of society, the real foundation, on which arises a legal and political superstructure and to which correspond definite forms of social consciousness [including art].[20]

Stalin further elaborated the theory of "basis and superstructure" as follows:

> Having come into being, it [the superstructure] becomes an exceedingly active force, actively assisting its base to take shape and consolidate

itself···. The superstructure is created by the base precisely in order to serve it, to actively help it to take shape and consolidate itself.[21]

The superstructure is the product of one epoch, the epoch in which the given economic base exists and operates. The superstructure is therefore short-lived; it is eliminated and disappears with the elimination and disappearance of the given base.[22]

To synthesize and summarize, the above quotes are saying that "Communist art must actively cooperate in eliminating the capitalist system and its superstructure, whereas in Communist society [socialist society], it must actively serve to maintain and strengthen its economic system, while educating the working people." Based upon this theory, socialist realism was established.

B. Critiques of Socialist Realism

As indicated by Lenin's words, "Literature must belong to the Party"; by Stalin's words, "Writers are the engineers of the human spirit"; and by Gorky's words, "Writers are the midwife to socialism, and the gravedigger to capitalism," artists and writers were required to obey the Party's directives absolutely, and their individuality and freedom were totally disregarded. As a result, since the beginning of the Revolution, artists and writers lived under surveillance and oppression in the Soviet Union until its collapse. Especially in the late 1930s, when Stalin promoted socialist realism, a great number of artists and writers were arrested and purged as heretics.[23] Even after Stalin's death, socialist realism continued to reign as the accepted theory of art, and consequently many artists and writers became dissidents.

Criticizing socialist realism, art critic Herbert Read said, "Socialist realism is nothing but an attempt to stuff intellectual or dogmatic objectives into art." [24] Ilya G. Ehrenburg (1891–1967), a Soviet journalist and novelist who was awarded the Stalin Prize for two of his novels, but later became critical of Stalin, said, "What is described in a book depicting weaving women in a spinning mill is not a human being but a machine, and not human feelings but merely the process of production." [25] Thus, he criticized the image of the human being depicted in socialist realism. The Korean art critic Yohan Cho also criticized the image of the human being in socialist realism, as follows:

> The farmers and workers whom they [the Soviet writers] described were wonderful heroes and heroines who did not show even the faintest sign of uneasiness. It was all the more so since a theory of no conflict was spread. That is, they do not seem to have any kind of anxiety whatsoever. They were the ones who had no life of their own····. Therefore, that writing could never express a person's internal world.[26]

In April 1986, an accident occurred at the nuclear power plant of Chernobyl in the Ukraine Republic of the U.S.S.R. Concerning the accident, Mikhail Gorbachev confirmed that the Soviet bureaucracy was responsible for the disaster, and said, "This is a tragedy. The nuclear accident was a great disaster, but it is even more regrettable to confirm that bureaucracy is deeply rooted in our society." Then, at the end of June, 1986, he attended a meeting of the Writers' Union and appealed to the writers, saying, "At the time of the Revolution, Gorky exposed and condemned the corruption and crimes of public officials. In the same way, Soviet public officials today have lapsed into bureaucratism, and there is a lot of vice. So, you writers should not hesitate to criticize them through your works." Then, a group of writers allegedly requested the Soviet government to stop its censorship of literary works. They did so because to date Soviet artists and writers have been deprived of freedom, in the name of socialist realism.

In Communist China, Mao Ze-dong granted freedom to intellectuals for a while, with his policy of "letting a hundred schools of thought contend," prior to the Great Proletarian Cultural Revolution. When that happened, most intellectuals criticized the socialist policies. Later, they were severely persecuted. When Deng Ziaoping grasped the political power and adopted pragmatic policies, he began to grant freedom to intellectuals bit by bit. As a result, a renowned theorist of Communist China, Wang Ruo, revealed that in socialism there is human alienation just as there is in capitalism.

When we consider these facts, we realize that socialist realism, as art for the proletarian revolution and as art that is subservient to party policy, has proved itself to be totally false art.

C. An Indictment of Communism by Notable Writers

Communist leaders compelled artists and writers to praise Communism from the viewpoint of socialist realism. Even under the Communist regime, however, the artists and writers who pursued true art, at home and abroad, indicted Communism for its falsehood.

André Gide (1869–1951), a French writer who had been fascinated by Communism, attended Gorky's funeral in 1936, and afterwards traveled in the Soviet Union for a month. He candidly expressed, in his book *Back From the U.S.S.R.*, his disappointment with the Soviet society he saw on that occasion. He said in the introduction,

> Three years ago I declared my admiration, my love, for the U.S.S.R. An unprecedented experiment was being attempted there, which filled our hearts with hope and from which we expected an immense advance, an impetus capable of carrying forward in its stride the whole human race···. In our hearts and in our minds we resolutely linked the future of culture itself with the glorious destiny of the U.S.S.R.[27]

However, after coming in contact with the Soviet people during his one-month trip, he wrote the following impressions:

> In the U.S.S.R. everybody knows beforehand, once and for all, that on any and every subject there can be only one opinion···. So that every time you talk to one Russian you feel as if you were talking to them all.[28]

Finally, he fiercely denounced the Soviet Union as follows:

> What is desired and demanded is approval of all that is done in the U.S.S.R.,···. And I doubt whether in any other country in the world, even Hitler's Germany, thought be less free, more bowed down, more fearful (terrorized), more vassalized.[29]

The Soviet writer Boris L. Pasternak (1829–1960) secretly wrote *Doctor Zhivago*, in which he expressed his disappointment with the Russian Revolution, and advocated the philosophy of love. That book was published, not in the Soviet Union but in foreign countries, and was received favorably. It was decided to award Pasternak the Nobel Prize but, as a result, at home he was expelled from the Writer's Union and denounced as a reactionary anti- Socialist writer. Pasternak stated in that book, through Zhivago, who represented his own conscience, the following:

> Marxism a science?... Marxism is too uncertain of its ground to be a science. Sciences are more balanced, more objective. I do not know a movement more self-centered and further removed from the facts than Marxism.[30]

He also denounced the attitude taken by the revolutionaries toward intellectuals, saying,

> At first everything was splendid. "Come along. We welcome good, honest work, we welcome ideas, especially new ideas. What could please us better? Do your work, struggle, and carry on." Then, you find in practice that what they meant by ideas is nothing but words—claptrap in praise of the revolution and the regime.[31]

D. Errors in the Communist Theory of Art Seen from the Perspective of Unification Thought

What are the causes of the errors of socialist realism?

First, socialist realism does not regard art as the "activity of creating beauty and joy for the whole (creation) as well as for oneself (appreciation) while respecting the individuality of the artist," but as a means of educating the people, while conforming to Party policy. Artists should manifest their individuality in their work to the utmost degree. By so doing, they please God and other people. Socialist realism, however, has deprived artists of their individual expression and has standardized all works of art. Therefore, there is no way for true art to be born out of it.

Second, socialist realism denies God; therefore, it has lost the fundamental standard of artistic activity. It establishes, instead, arbitrary standards based on Party policy, forcing artists and writers to conform to them.

Third, since beauty and love are as closely related as two sides of a coin, art and ethics must also be in an inseparable relationship. Yet, since Communism ignores this fact and denies the ethics of love, it has transformed art into art without love, or art as a tool of the Communist Party to rule the people.

Fourth, art is not a part of the superstructure. Nevertheless, socialist realism regards art as such and reduces it to the status of a servant of the economic system (the "base"). In reality, however, art is not determined by the economic system. Marx himself made the following confession in the latter part of his *Contribution to the Critique of Political Economy*:

> The difficulty we are confronted with is not, however, that of understanding how Greek art and epic poetry are associated with certain forms of social development. The difficulty is that they still give us aesthetic pleasure and are in certain respects regarded as a standard and unattainable ideal.[32]

According to the materialist conception of history, Greek culture (part of the superstructure) should have disappeared by the time of Marx without leaving a trace, and contemporary people should have felt no interest in it. But Marx felt difficulty in the fact that Greek art and epic poetry, such as *The Iliad and The Odyssey*, not only gave contemporary people joy, but had even become the models of art. This is nothing but Marx's own testimony to the error of his theory of "basis and superstructure."

Human beings have the fundamental desire to pursue the values of truth, goodness, and beauty. Even though fallen, all people possess it at all times and in all places. Therefore, if the values of truth, goodness, and beauty are expressed in a work of art, that work moves everyone's heart. The fact that Greek art has continued to be enjoyed by people even until today means that it contains eternal values of truth, goodness, and beauty.

Finally, let us consider the writers Gorky and Tolstoy, both of whom, though totally different in style, in the same way and in almost the same period, condemned the corruption of Russian society prior to the Revolution.

Gorky conformed with Communism, which sought to violently overthrow capitalism, and asserted that the mission of the artist lay in inspiring revolutions. Thus, he wrote works that glorified the revolutionary movement. *Mother*, by Gorky, has been regarded as a literary masterpiece of socialist realism. It depicts the image of a mother who, although she is an uneducated working woman, is strongly motivated by a desire to protect her only son, a son thrown into prison on charges of revolutionary activities, and becomes gradually awakened to the class nature of society. Finally, she herself becomes an active participant in the revolutionary movement.

On the other hand, while condemning social evils, Tolstoy advocated that the way to resolve them lay in the recovery of true human nature through love. One of Tolstoy's masterpieces is *Resurrection*. An aristocratic young man, appearing in court as a member of a jury, comes to learn that a young woman whom he seduced by mistake in his younger days has become degraded, and is being judged. He becomes conscience-stricken, repents, and decides to save her. Finally, she is rehabilitated, and the young man also starts a new life.

The way Gorky chose was the external way of social revolution, whereas that of Tolstoy was the internal way of spiritual revolution. Which was the correct way? The way of violent revolution, chosen by Gorky, was the wrong way, as the realities of the socialist countries following revolution—the oppression of human nature and the corruption of bureaucrats—indicates. On the other hand, the way Tolstoy chose was the true way, in that it was the way to recover human nature. It must be pointed out, however, that it still had its limits in saving society as a whole.

Unification Thought pursues the way for both humankind and society to be reformed into what they were originally intended to be. This becomes possible by understanding God correctly. In other words, by knowing correctly the attributes of God, who created humankind and the world, we can learn the ideal state of humankind and society as they were originally intended to be. All that must be done then is to begin to reform humankind and society in that direction. The new art advocated by Unification Thought is Unificationism, in which idealism and realism are unified, centering on God's Heart (love). Unificationism seeks to reform reality toward the original ideal of humankind and society.

8

Theory of History

The theory of history presented here is not merely a description of historical facts; rather, it is a way of viewing history, including the questions of how human history started, by what laws it is guided, and in what direction it is proceeding. It is an interpretation of history on the basis of Unification Thought. In short, it is a philosophy of history. Accordingly, this theory of history is called the Unification Theory of History or Unification view of history.

Why is this Unification theory of history necessary? It is necessary in order to establish the correct direction for history by clarifying the image of the future of humankind. From such a theory, a method for resolving actual problems can be drawn. In fact, finding fundamental solutions for today's complicated world problems is impossible without a clear and correct view of history, possessing a clear vision of the future.

Thus far, many scholars have presented various views of history, but none of them was as influential as the materialist, or Communist view of history. The Communist view of history defines human history as the history of class struggles. Based on this, the materialist view of history asserted that capitalist society would be overthrown through the struggle between bourgeoisie and proletariat, namely, through revolution, and that Communist society would inevitably come. Thus, it presented a clear vision of the future. To Communists, the materialist view of history served as the driving force for their revolutionary fervor. Accordingly, it would not be an exaggeration to say that the confrontation between the Communist sphere and the democratic sphere was a confrontation between views of history.

Yet, in the free world today we can not find any existing view of history that can contend with the materialist view of history. For that reason, the free world had been constantly on the defensive in the face of the Communist offensive and threat. In the end, however, the materialist view of history lost favor. It would not be an exaggeration to say that this is largely because of the Unification view of history advocated by Rev. Sun Myung Moon.

For half a century, during the period of its theoretical confrontation with Communism, the Unification view of history, a view grounded in a new theology, clearly revealed the flaws in the materialist view of history. The Unification view interprets history based on historical facts, and shows that human history is directed toward the world of God's original ideal of creation.

I. Basic Positions of the Unification View of History

The Unification view of history is based on the principle of restoration in the Divine Principle. It interprets history from three fundamental perspectives: first, as a sinful history; second, as the history of re-creation; and third, as the history of restoration. Also, it addresses such questions as whether or not laws operate in history, how history started, in which direction history has proceeded, and so on.

Sinful History

From the Unification view history has been a history of sin: it was initiated by the human fall. Because of the fall, it was not possible for human history to become a principled, peaceful history; instead, it became a history of confusion filled with conflicts, struggles, wars, pain, sorrow, misery, and the like. Accordingly, finding fundamental solutions to the various problems in history is impossible without solving the problem of the human fall, that is, the problem of sin.

History of Re-creation

Due to the fall of the first human ancestors, the original human beings and the ideal of the original world were lost, and humans fell into a state of spiritual death. The original human beings and the original world were lost while they were still incomplete. Therefore, throughout history,

God has carried out the dispensation of re-creating and reconstructing human beings and the world. Accordingly, history became a history of re-creation.

In this process, the laws (laws of creation) and the Word (Logos) through which God had created human beings and the universe come to be applied in human history as well. God's creation was carried out through the Word. Therefore, re-creation is also being carried out through the Word. Re-creation does not mean creating the universe all over again. Since the fall involved only human beings, the only being that needs to be re-created is the human being, who must be re-created through the Word. This is why God sent saints, righteous people, prophets, and other spiritual leaders to spread truth (Word) and guide people spiritually.

History of Restoration

Due to the fall of the first human ancestors, human beings were expelled from what was to become the original world (the Garden of Eden), and the ideal of the original human beings and original world were lost; therefore, non-principled (non-original) human beings came to live in a non-principled world. Thus, original human beings and the original world were left as an ideal still to be attained.

As for God, He has had to restore the non-principled world and human beings back to their original states in such a way that His creation would not remain a failure. Accordingly, since the dawn of human history, God has conducted His dispensation (providence of restoration) to restore sinful people and the sinful world back to their original state. Consequently, human history became the history of the providence of restoration. Since God is a God of principle, and the human fall resulted from human beings' failure to observe certain conditions, the providence of restoration, also, was carried out according to certain laws. These laws are referred to as the "laws of restoration."

The Law-Governed Nature of History

In establishing a theory of history, one of the most important requisites is to discern the laws which have been operating in history. To date, however, there have been few religious leaders or scholars who could show, clearly, the law-governed nature of history. For example, the Christian providential view of history has not presented persuasive laws.

As a result, the Christian view of history has been dismissed by the academic world, rejected as unscientific. In modern times, Hegel applied the dialectic (i.e., idealistic dialectic) to historical development, and asserted that history is the process of actualizing freedom through reason, and that, in the end, a rational state would be reached in which freedom would be fully realized. In Prussia, however, which Hegel regarded as an ideal state, freedom remained elusive, and history continued just as it always had. The historical laws described by Hegel were unrelated to reality. In the twentieth century, Arnold Toynbee established his "cultural view of history," which was an expansive, all-embracing view of history, through which he analyzed in detail the genesis, growth, breakdown, and disintegration of civilizations. Yet, Toynbee did not clearly present the laws of history. Under these circumstances, only Marx's materialistic view of history remained as allegedly showing the laws of history, calling itself a scientific view of history.

The Unification view of history asserts that history has been developing according to certain laws and clarifies that these laws are of two types, namely, the laws of creation and the laws of restoration. These laws are what are truly at work in history. When these genuine laws of history are pointed out, the falseness of the materialist view of history is exposed. It becomes clear that the laws advocated by the materialist view of history are in reality pseudo laws; that is, they are nothing more than dogmatic assertions. Furthermore, the Unification view of history, by clarifying the laws of history from a theological basis, has revived the traditional providential view, which had been regarded as unscientific, and has made it possible to treat the providential view as more of a social science.

The Origin, Direction, and Goal of History

As for the question of when and how history started, namely, its origin, the Unification view of history regards the creation of human beings and the human fall as the origin of history, just as does the Christian providential view of history. There is also a question concerning the origin of the human race itself, namely, whether the human race had a single origin (monogenetic) or multiple origins (polygenetic). The Unification view of history advocates a monogenetic view in asserting that the first human ancestors were Adam and Eve. This is because there is a law based on the principle of creation which holds that "creation starts from one."

Then, what is the goal of history? The Unification view of history regards the goal of history as being the restoration of the ideal world of creation on a higher dimension. The direction of history is such that it is moving or developing toward that goal. Therefore, the origin and goal of history are fixed and determined. However, how that goal is eventually reached is not determined. Each step in the forward progress of history is successfully completed only when the human portion of responsibility—especially the portion of responsibility of providential central figures—is fulfilled in accordance with God's providence. Therefore, the process that history actually takes—that is, whether history proceeds in a straight line or makes a detour; whether it is shortened or prolonged—depends entirely on the efforts of human beings. This means that the process of history is undetermined and is entrusted to the free will of human beings. In particular, it depends on whether or not providential figures fulfill their mission. This is called fulfillment of responsibility, or simply, portion of responsibility.

The view that the goal is determined but the process is undetermined, and that the progress of history depends on the human portion of responsibility, or free will, is referred to as the "theory of responsibility."

II. Laws of Creation

Let me now explain the laws of history in more detail. As already stated, human history is the history of re-creation and at the same time it is the history of restoration. Accordingly, historical changes have taken place in accordance with the "laws of creation" and the "laws of restoration." I will first explain the laws of creation. These laws include (1) the law of correlativity, (2) the law of give and receive action, (3) the law of repulsion, (4) the law of dominion by the center, (5) the law of completion through three stages, (6) the law of the period of the number six, and (7) the law of responsibility.

A. Law of Correlativity

Every created being has within itself two elements which form a correlative relationship. They are the principal element and the subordinate element. Also, each individual being externally forms another correlative relationship of subject and object between itself and another individual being, whereby it exists and develops. Living beings exist, multiply, and develop through such relationships. The formation of a relationship of subject and object means that they face each other; namely, that they are related with each other. Subject and object are related to each other either with or without a common purpose. When subject and object form a reciprocal relationship with a common purpose, it is said that they form a "correlative standard."

The fact that an individual being necessarily engages in a correlative relationship of subject and object with another being is called the "law of correlativity." Accordingly, the first requirement a society (or historical process) must fulfill in order to develop is that correlative elements (correlatives) of subject and object must form a correlative relationship in every field, such as politics, economy, culture, and science. No development can take place without correlative relationships. Correlative elements of subject and object refer to *sungsang* and *hyungsang*, yang and yin, or principal and subordinate elements (or principal and subordinate beings).

Examples of correlatives are spirit and body (mind and body), ideology and economic conditions (material conditions), spiritual culture and material civilization, government and people, managers and workers, workers and instruments of production, principal parts and subordinate parts in a machine, and so on. There are many other examples. As these correlative elements engage in the relationship of subject and object, development is achieved in all fields such as politics, economy, culture, science, and so on.

B. Law of Give and Receive Action

When the correlative elements of subject and object within a thing form a correlative relationship, the action of giving and receiving certain elements or forces takes place. Such interaction between subject and object is called "give and receive action." Any development, including development in history, is made through give and receive action. Thus, in history, the development of each field occurs when the correlative elements (correlatives) of subject and object form a correlative relationship and perform harmonious give and receive action, centering on a common purpose.

For example, in order for a nation to maintain its existence, and to prosper, its government and people must form a relationship of subject and object centered on the purpose of the nation's prosperity, and must engage in harmonious give and receive action. In order for an enterprise to prosper, investors, managers, workers, engineers, and machinery must have mutual relationships of subject and object, and perform harmonious give and receive actions. Therefore, the "law of correlativity" and the "law of give and receive action" are like two sides of a coin, and we can combine them together and call them the "law of give and receive action" in a broader sense.

Give and receive action is harmonious, and is never oppositional or conflictive. Yet, the materialist view of history asserts that history develops through the struggle of opposites. Struggles may become an impetus for development, but while the struggle is going on, development will come to a standstill or may even retrogress. Accordingly, as far as development is concerned, the assertion of the materialist view of history is quite erroneous; it proved to be a false theory concocted solely for the purpose of justifying class struggle.

C. Law of Repulsion

Give and receive action takes place between the correlative elements (or correlative individuals) of subject and object. Subject and subject (or object and object), however, repel each other. We call this repelling phenomenon the "action of repulsion." The action of repulsion in the natural world is originally latent and does not surface. It plays the role of strengthening or complementing the proper give and receive action between subject and object.

For example, in the natural world, positive electricity and positive electricity (or negative electricity and negative electricity) repel each other, but such phenomena serve to strengthen or complement the proper give and receive action between subject (positive electricity) and object (negative electricity), and never surfaces as itself. Therefore, in the natural world, proper order is not disturbed by the action of repulsion.

In human society, however, the action of repulsion between subject and subject appears in the form of conflict between two leaders. An instance of this is the conflict between an established leader and a new leader at the time of a revolution. During such actions of repulsion, or rivalry, the two conflicting subjects (the subject of conservative forces and the subject of reform forces) engage in give and receive action with their respective objects (groups of people in the object position), whereby they increase their respective forces. As a result, the two forces come into conflict with each other. In this case, one of the two camps is in a position closer to the direction of God's dispensation, whereas the other is in a position farther from it. The former is referred to as the "good side," the latter, the "evil side." Accordingly, in human society the action of repulsion between one subject and another subject appears fundamentally as a struggle between good and evil. When the side of goodness achieves victory in such a struggle, the direction of history is changed a little toward the direction of goodness.

Also, even in fallen societies, there have been cases where the action of repulsion demonstrates its original nature of complementing give and receive action. An example is the case where one country and another, or the people of one country and those of another, compete with each other in a peaceful manner. As a result, both develop culturally and economically.

D. Law of Dominion by the Center

In the give and receive action between subject and object, the subject becomes the center, and the object receives the dominion of the subject. As a result, the object comes to perform circular motion centering on the subject. For this reason, physical circular motion in the natural world is performed. For example, the earth revolves around the sun, and electrons revolve around the nucleus. In human society, since the relationship of subject and object is that of mind and body, circular motion takes place in the sense that the object follows orders, instructions, and requests from the subject.

In the history of restoration God establishes central figures and, through them, leads society in a direction in accord with His providence, namely, in the direction of goodness. In this case, He first forms a social environment, and then inspires the central figure to lead that environment in a direction in accord with His providence. For that to happen, the central figure is charged with their (portion of) responsibility to control the environment. In this way, there is a law that central figures in the providence of God have dominion over the environment. We call this the "law of dominion by the center." This law applies not only to the chosen people; it applies to all other peoples and countries, as well.

God has been promoting the history of the chosen people as the central history of humankind. The central history has been the history of the Israelites in the Old Testament Age and the history of the Western nations centered on Christianity in the New Testament Age. In the central history, God carries out His providence by establishing central figures. Examples of the central figures of different periods are such figures in the Old Testament Age as Noah, Abraham, Jacob, Moses, the kings, and the prophets, and such figures in the New Testament Age as Augustine, the popes, Martin Luther, and John Calvin, and such political leaders as Charlemagne of the Kingdom of the Franks, Henry VIII of England, and George Washington and Abraham Lincoln of the United States of America.

On the other hand, Satan, who seeks to oppose God's providence, has sought to establish a sphere of dominion centered on himself. By establishing central figures on his side, Satan sought to have dominion over the environment through them. Kaiser Wilhelm II and Adolf Hitler, who sought world domination by advocating Pan-Germanism, and Marx, Lenin, Stalin, and Mao Ze-dong, who aimed at the conquest of the world through Communism, were such central figures. Without their thought and leadership, the rise of totalitarianism and the Communist revolutions would never have occurred.

Toynbee said, "The growths of civilizations are the work of creative individuals or creative minorities." [1] The masses are guided by creative individuals or creative minorities, and follow them. This assertion by Toynbee points to the law of dominion by the center.

The materialist view of history theoretically attaches greater importance to the environment (i.e., the social environment) than to leaders, and asserts that the masses, which are the basis of the social environment, play the decisive role in social development. This view also claims that the leaders act only under the conditions determined by the specific social environment. This way of thinking is based on materialism, according to which, just as spirit is generated from, and determined by matter, so too, is the spirit of a leader determined by the social environment. In this way, Communism deals with the social environment (masses) as a material category, and with central figures (leaders) as a spiritual category. This is not a correct view, however. The leaders are the subject, and the masses, the object; the leaders guide the masses, or society, in a certain direction on the basis of their religious or political ideologies.

E. Law of Completion through Three Stages

According to the Principle of Creation, the growth or development of all things is attained through a process of three stages: formation, growth, and completion. For example, plants mature and perfect themselves through the three stages of germinating, growing stems and putting forth green leaves, and producing flowers and bearing fruit. This law applies to history as well; often the providence of re-creation has been carried out through a process of three stages. For example, it is a law that, if a certain providential event ends in failure, that providence can be prolonged up to a third time (or a third stage), but will necessarily be accomplished at the third stage.

For example, the providence to lay the foundation for the providence of restoration was not fulfilled in Adam's family due to the failure of Cain and Abel in the substantial offering, and it was accomplished for the first time in Abraham's family only after an unsuccessful attempt in Noah's family. Even so, the providence to lay the foundation for restoration which was to be fulfilled during Abraham's generation was not accomplished at first due to Abraham's failure in his offering. It was finally fulfilled for the first time at the time of Jacob, who was Abraham's third generation. The same thing can be said about the coming of the Messiah, the second Adam. Since God could not fulfill the purpose of creation due to the fall of Adam, He sent Jesus as the second Adam. But since Jesus was crucified and could not fulfill the purpose of creation completely, God sends Christ at the Second Advent as the third Adam to fulfill the purpose of creation.

In the modern era, which is the period of preparation to receive Christ at the Second Advent, movements for the revival of Hellenism and Hebraism arose, each developing through a process of three stages. The movement for the revival of Hellenism refers to a humanistic movement. Following the Renaissance, the first humanistic movement, there arose the Enlightenment, the second humanistic movement. The Enlightenment bore fruit in the form of the Communist ideological movement, the third humanistic movement. The movement for the revival of Hebraism refers to a God-centered movement, or a religious reformation. Following the first religious reformation, centered on Martin Luther and John Calvin, there arose the second religious reformation, centered on John Wesley, George Fox, and others; and today, the third religious reformation movement, centering on the Unification movement, is taking place.

The revival of Hebraism (the God-centered movement) was a movement on God's side, while the revival of Hellenism was a humanistic movement, a movement on Satan's side, which tended to gradually separate human beings from God. It is for that reason that this movement finally became atheistic Communism. If the God-centered movement becomes successful through the three stages, the humanistic movement, which is based on Satanic ideology, will inevitably come to decline and come under the God-centered movement. Accordingly, the law of completion through three stages for God's side becomes the law of inevitable fall through three stages for Satan's side. Thus, the success of the Unification movement, which is the third God-centered movement, and the collapse of Communism, which is the third humanistic movement, are both inevitable.

F. Law of the Period of the Number Six

According to the Bible, in the creation of the universe by God, Adam was created on the sixth day. In other words, the creation of Adam was achieved on the basis of a six-day period, as planned. That was the period of preparation for the creation of Adam. By the same token, in the history of re-creation as well, God began the preparation to receive the Messiah at the start of a period of the number six before the coming of the Messiah, the second Adam (Jesus).

That period began from the sixth century BC. God had the Jewish people taken captive to Babylon so that they might repent and turn away from their faithlessness. It was their preparation to receive the Messiah who was to come six centuries later. Around the sixth century BC, Confucius (ca. 551–479 BC) appeared in China and established Confucianism. Subsequent to Confucius, during these six centuries, many philosophers appeared in China, and the golden age of Chinese thought was established. In India, Gautama Buddha (ca. 563–483 BC) appeared in the sixth century BC and established Buddhism. Around the sixth century BC as well, the ancient Indian philosophical books called the *Upanishads* came into being. Also, at about the same time, Zoroastrianism arose in the Middle East. In Greece, philosophy, art, and science developed greatly from the sixth century BC. All of these developments were preparations to receive the Messiah. God made preparations in this way by guiding various peoples on earth in the direction of goodness through the methods appropriate to the people in each region.

Karl Jaspers, an existentialist philosopher, noticed the fact that remarkable spiritual leaders (founders of religions and philosophies) all appeared at about the same time in different regions of the world, such as China, India, Iran, Palestine, and Greece. He called it the "Axial Period."[2] What is the reason those spiritual leaders appeared in many parts of the world at about the same time, as if according to some signal or cue? Jaspers had no explanation, and he held it to be a historic mystery and an insoluble riddle.[3] This riddle can be solved for the first time, in light of the law of the period of the number six.

The same thing can be said with regard to the coming of the Second Advent of the Messiah. In order to send the Second Advent of the Messiah, who is the Third Adam, God made preparations at the start of a period of the number six. Good examples are the Reformation and the Renaissance, which started around the fourteenth century and blossomed in the sixteenth century.[4] During this time period of the number six (i.e., six centuries), the Industrial Revolution, which took place in the late eighteenth century, and the subsequent rapid progress of science and economy occurred. These were all preparations for the coming of the Messiah. God prepared in this way in order to send the Second Advent of the Messiah in the twentieth century.

The religious leaders and philosophers who appeared six centuries before the birth of Jesus were in the position of archangels, whose mission was to pave the way for the Messiah. Accordingly, the love and truth they taught were not perfect, but only partial. It is only the Messiah, the Son of God, who is capable of practicing true love, preaching the absolute truth, and, through such love and truth, solving the unresolved questions of religions and philosophies for the first time. When the time of the advent of the Messiah comes, the unresolved questions of religions and philosophies all come to the fore and the incapacity of traditional religions and philosophies to resolve them becomes clear, since traditional religions and philosophies were given by God through the angels, and their teachings of love and truth are imperfect. Then, in the Last Days, the Messiah appears and, with absolute love and truth, revives and strengthens traditional religions and philosophies, which had become incapacitated, thus realizing the unified world through the unification of all religions and philosophies.

However, since Jesus died on the cross, the realization of the unified world in his time did not take place, and his mission was entrusted to Christ at the Second Advent. As a result, Confucianism, Buddhism, Oriental philosophy, Greek philosophy, and other thoughts were left to subsist until the time of the Second Advent. Therefore, the unity of religions and all thought systems will come to be accomplished, for the first time, at the time of the Second Advent. That is to say, Christ at the Second Advent will solve all the unresolved questions of traditional religions and thoughts by means of the true love and truth of God. He will unify religions and thoughts, and will finally realize the unified world.

It should be noted that it was not necessary to establish totally new religions and philosophies six centuries before Christ at the Second Advent, as happened six centuries before Jesus. We need only to revive the already existing religions and philosophies. It is for that reason that such religions as Buddhism and Confucianism have survived until today. Zoroastrianism, which was a religion holding to a belief in two gods, one of light and one of darkness, was replaced by monotheistic Islam in the seventh century.

G. Law of Responsibility

The first human ancestors, Adam and Eve, were given a portion of responsibility to fulfill; with that responsibility no one could interfere, not even God. The purpose for this was to enable them to qualify to be the lords of dominion over all things. In other words, Adam and Eve were to become able to have dominion over all things by fulfilling their portion of responsibility, in addition to the portion of responsibility taken by God. Yet, due to their fall, they failed to fulfill that portion of responsibility.

The providence of re-creation is to be accomplished in the same way, that is, when the human portion of responsibility (especially that of providential central persons) is fulfilled in addition to God's portion of responsibility. Here, to fulfill the human portion of responsibility means to accomplish the mission given to human beings (providential persons) by exercising their own free will and taking responsibility for their actions.

Accordingly, if the providential persons fulfill their portions of responsibility, through their own wisdom and effort, in accordance with God's will, the providence moves to a new stage. If, on the contrary, those persons do not fulfill their portions of responsibility, the providence centered on them ends in failure and is thus prolonged. After a certain numerologically significant period of time, a new person is called by God to carry out the same providence.

The reason that sinful human history has been prolonged until today is that the providential persons have continually failed in fulfilling their portions of responsibility. Jesus was crucified and was unable to realize the unified world because the leaders of his time, including John the Baptist, the priests, and the lawyers, failed to fulfill their portions of responsibility. The reason why Communism caused conflicts and confusion all over the world is that, after the Industrial Revolution, the leaders of the Christian nations failed to fulfill their portions of responsibility.

Today, the leaders of democracy must be awakened to the need to fulfill their responsibility in accordance with God's will. In other words, they must guide all people, including the people in Communist countries, to God's true word and true love so that they may stand by God. By so doing, a truly peaceful world, namely, the Kingdom of Heaven on earth can be realized.

III. Laws of Restoration

Human history is a history of re-creation, and at the same time a history of restoration; that is, it is the process of recovering the original ideal world, which was lost due to the human fall. Accordingly, a series of laws, different from the laws of creation, are also at work in history. These are the laws of restoration. These laws include (1) the law of indemnity, (2) the law of separation, (3) the law of the restoration of the number four, (4) the law of conditioning providence, (5) the law of the false preceding the true, (6) the law of the horizontal reappearance of the vertical, and (7) the law of synchronous providence.

A. Law of Indemnity

The human fall refers to the fact that human beings lost their original position and state. Restoration is the process of regaining that lost position and state. Yet, in order to regain that original position and state, certain conditions have to be established. The conditions for this purpose are called "conditions of indemnity." The conditions of indemnity that human beings have to establish are, first, the "foundation of faith" and, second, the "foundation of substance." Establishing the foundation of faith means that the people must meet a leader (central figure) chosen by God and offer some object for the condition, centering on that leader, during a specified numerological period of indemnity. Establishing the foundation of substance means that the people obediently follow that leader chosen by God.

When we examine history, however, we see that people in sinful societies very seldom obeyed the leaders appointed by God; instead, most of the time they persecuted them. Accordingly, the paths of righteous people, sages, and saints continually turned into courses of hardship. Yet, God regarded the hardships undergone by those righteous leaders as sacrificial indemnity conditions, and gradually restored the people of the sinful world back to His side by subjugating them. In other words, with the hardships of righteous leaders as a condition, God could guide the sinful people to repent. This is the law of indemnity. A representative example is Jesus' crucifixion. Through Jesus' crucifixion, many people in the sinful world have awakened to their sinfulness and repented.

Up to the present time, Communists and other dictators have persecuted and killed numerous religious people, righteous people, and good people. Taking the suffering of those people as a condition, however, God finally made the dictatorial regimes surrender, and liberated their people. Therefore, from the viewpoint of the law of indemnity the fall of the Communist regimes, as well as other dictatorial regimes, was inevitable.

B. Law of Separation

Since the Creator is the one and only God, the originally created man and woman were supposed to always relate only to Him. Due to the sinful action of the fall, however, Adam came to be related also to Satan.

As a result, Adam came to stand in a midway position where he had to relate both to God and Satan. For that reason, when God tried to relate to Adam, the condition existed for Satan to relate to Adam as well. In such an unprincipled situation God was unable to conduct any kind of providence through Adam. Accordingly, God gave Adam two sons, and placed one of them in the position towards which only God could relate, and the other in a position towards which only Satan could relate. The one separated to God's side was Abel, the younger brother, and the one separated to Satan's side was Cain, the elder brother.[5]

God intended to restore both Cain and Abel to His side by having Cain obey Abel. The fall occurred when the human being (Adam), who was to deal only with God, was subjugated by Satan's temptation. In the principle, in order to achieve restoration through indemnity, Cain, who was on Satan's side, was required to obey Abel, who was on God's side. Thus, when Cain and Abel made offerings, God wanted Cain to make his offering not to Him directly, but rather through Abel. Instead, however, Cain resented Abel to the point of murdering him. Consequently, human history started as a sinful history.[6] However, there still existed the foundation of heart with which Abel, who had been positioned on God's side, remained loyal to the end. So, with that foundation as a condition, God was able, throughout history, to separate people from the Satanic world over to God's side.[7]

By first establishing an individual on the side of goodness, God gradually expanded the sphere of the good side by next establishing a family on the good side, then a tribe, a people, a nation, and finally a world on the good side. Yet Satan, who was working in opposition to God's provi-dence, has preceded God's work by starting with an individual on the side of evil, and expanding the sphere of evil by establishing a family, a tribe, a people, a nation, and a world on the evil side. By so doing, Satan has continually obstructed God's providence.

Usually, the people on the good side (such as saints and sages) tried to convey God's Word to the people on the evil side. The evil side, however, refused to accept that Word and instead persecuted and attacked the good people of God. Thus, struggles were carried out as the good side responded to those attacks. Therefore, throughout history, struggles on different levels have taken place: between an individual on the good side and an individual on the evil side, between families, tribes peoples, nations, and finally, between the world on the good side and the world on the evil side. These struggles have been continuing until today. Thus, history became a history of struggle between good and evil. In the process of restoration history, however, the good side and the evil side are not good and evil in an absolute sense. The side relatively closer to God's providence was separated to the good side, and the side relatively farther from God's providence was separated to the evil side.

Until recently, the world has been separated into two large blocs, namely, the bloc on the side of good and the bloc on the side of evil. These were the free world and the Communist world, respectively. More precisely, they were the group of countries that recognized religion (especially Christianity) and the group of countries that denied religion. The purpose for which God separated the world into a good side and an evil side was to restore both sides by having the good side subjugate the evil side. In the end, due to God's providence, the good side will win in the struggle between the two blocks. This is exactly what we see happening in the world today. The unification of the free world and the Communist world will be accomplished, ultimately, when the Messiah is received. Since the separation between Cain and Abel came into being because of the faithlessness of Adam, unification between Cain and Abel will be accomplished through the Messiah, who comes as the third Adam.

C. Law of the Restoration of the Number Four

God's purpose of creation was to realize His love through the family four position foundation. That is to say, if Adam and Eve had grown according to God's Word and had perfected themselves, they would have become husband and wife centering on God, and would have given birth to good children. Then, the family four position foundation, consisting of God, Adam (husband), Eve (wife), and their children, would have been formed, and a family filled with God's love would have been realized. Due to the fall of Adam and Eve, however, such a family four position foundation centered on God could not be formed; instead, a family four position foundation centered on Satan was formed, and the entire created world was put under the dominion of Satan. From that point on, it became the central purpose of history to restore the family four position foundation centered on God's vertical love.

In order to restore the four position foundation, God first conducted symbolic, conditional providences, the goal of which was to establish a period of time with a duration symbolizing the number four. This is called the law of the restoration of the number four. The restoration of the number four was a condition of indemnity to restore the family four position foundation numerologically. The period of the number four is realized through periods of forty days, forty years, four hundred years, and so on, during which time confusion is brought about by Satan, and the people on God's side usually undergo hardships.

Examples include Noah's forty-day flood, Moses' forty years in the wilderness, four hundred years of persecution of the Christians under the Roman Empire, and so on. When such periods of indemnity were over, the confusion was brought under control in the sense that the four position foundation was restored conditionally, and God's providence was able to proceed to a new stage. The law of the restoration of the number four applied not only to the history of the Israelites, but also to the history of other peoples and countries as well.

Arnold Toynbee noted that there were many cases in history where unification was accomplished after a period of four centuries of confusion (period of turmoil). We can cite some examples: the four centuries in the Hellenic World from the Peloponnesian War to the unification by the Roman Empire (431–31 BC); about four centuries from the period of "the Contending States" to the unification by the Ch'in and Han Empires in Chinese history (634–221 BC); and about four centuries of feudal anarchy from the Kamakura-Ashikaga period to the unification of all of Japan by Toyotomi Hideyoshi and the establishment of the Tokugawa Shogunate in Japanese history (1185–1597). Toynbee could not clarify, however, the reason why such periods of four centuries appeared in history.[8] A similar case is the forty-year rule by the Japanese over Korea, starting with the Eul-sa Treaty of Protection in 1905 and ending with the liberation of Korea in 1945.

D. Law of Conditioning Providence

The law of conditioning providence refers to the fact that, if a central person fulfills, or fails to fulfill his or her human portion of responsibility in accordance with God's will in a providential event, that will condition a specific providential event of a later period. This means that a providential event not only has an important significance in and of itself, at that time, but also becomes a condition that will determine the characteristics of providential events that will follow later in history.

For example, we know of the case in which Moses struck the rock twice in the wilderness (Deut. 20). Moses' action had, in itself, an actual necessity due to the particular circumstances of that time, namely, to enable the thirsty Israelites in the wilderness to have water to drink. At the same time, however, it also had the significance of symbolizing, and conditioning, God's providence at Jesus' coming, at a later date. About this matter, the content of the Divine Principle may be paraphrased as follows:[9]

The rock symbolized Adam. Specifically, the waterless rock, before being struck by Moses, symbolized the first (fallen) Adam; in contrast, the rock bringing forth water, after being struck once by Moses, symbolized Jesus, the second Adam. Since water symbolizes life, the first Adam, who was in the state of spiritual death due to the fall, could be symbolized as a rock that does not bring forth water; and Jesus, the second Adam, who would come in order to give life to spiritually dead people, could be symbolized as the water-giving rock. Yet, Moses struck the rock twice in anger at the faithlessness of the Israelites; and in so doing, he struck the rock bringing forth water, which symbolized Jesus. Through that act, the condition was established whereby, if later, when Jesus came, the Israelites were to turn faithless, Satan would have the condition to be able to strike Jesus, the fulfillment of the rock. Jesus was, in fact, crucified due to the faithlessness of the Israelites. This was in part because the double striking of the rock by Moses conditioned the providence at the time of the coming of the Messiah.

This is one example from history as recorded in the Old Testament. The law of conditioning providence was at work not only in this incident, but also in other historical events that were significant in God's providence. This means that providential events did not simply happen in their time, for no particular reason, but rather they were conditioned, to a certain degree, by various factors which preceded them. How a particular event in a certain age developed, in turn, has influenced later historical events. This is what the law of conditioning providence tells us.

E. Law of the False Preceding the True

This is a law under which the false appears before the true. Satan dominated the world, which had been created by God, by inducing the first human ancestors to fall away from God. Therefore, Satan created an unprincipled world of a pseudo-principle type, in advance of, and imitating God's providence. God could not but allow it because Adam had fallen without fulfilling his portion of responsibility. So, God has had to carry forward His providence, following the footsteps of Satan, to restore the unprincipled world built by Satan back to the principled world. The unprincipled world created by Satan is false; thus, even though it may prosper, its prosperity is only temporary. As God's providence progresses, Satan's unprincipled world can not but eventually collapse.

The ultimate goal of the providence of restoration is to actualize, on earth, a world in which the ideal of creation centered on God is realized, that is, one world in which all humanity is united. That is the kingdom of God, or the Kingdom of Heaven on earth, where all people attend God, or the True Parents of humankind as God's representatives, as the supreme sovereign. That world can be realized only through the coming of the Messiah. Satan, however, knowing God's plan, stole the contents of the providence in advance, established Messianic persons on the Satanic side before the coming (and before the second coming) of the Messiah, and attempted to create ideal states on the Satanic side. That is why a false Messiah and a false unified world have appeared first.

A good example of this is the appearance of the Roman Empire prior to the coming of Jesus. Julius Caesar appeared in the Roman Empire, conquered Gaul, incorporated it into the Roman Empire, and accomplished the unification of the Roman Empire (45 BC). After he was assassinated, Augustus (Octavian) brought the civil war under control (31 BC), and unified the Mediterranean area, building what was virtually a world empire. The peaceful and prosperous period of the Roman Empire was called the *Pax Romana* and lasted about two centuries. Julius Caesar and Augustus were messianic figures on the Satanic side. They created a false unified world of peace and prosperity in advance of the great unified world of everlasting love, peace, and prosperity that was to have been built through the coming of the true Messiah (Jesus). As it turned out, Jesus was crucified with his mission uncompleted, and therefore the true unified world, or true ideal world, could not appear at that time.

At the time of the Second Advent as well, in accordance with this law, a false Messiah and a false unified world appeared in advance of the providence of the Second Advent. That false Messiah was Stalin, and the false unified world was the Communist world. Stalin, in fact, was revered as "the sun of humankind," like a Messiah, and aimed to unify the world through Communism. Stalin died in 1953, and from the providential viewpoint, that was the time when the official course of the providence of the Second Advent was to start. The subsequent splintering of international Communism has been a foreshadowing of the collapse of the false unified world and the beginning of the realization of the true unified world.

F. Law of the Horizontal Reappearance of the Vertical

This law means that at the time of the consummation of the history of restoration, vertical (past) historical events reappear horizontally (in the present). "Vertical" refers to the passage of time, and "horizontal" refers to spatial expansion. In other words, the vertical refers to past history, and the horizontal refers to the present, actual world. Accordingly, the "horizontal reappearance of the vertical" means that God conducts His providence so that at the consummation of history all the past providential events and persons in history will reappear in the present in some form on the worldwide level. In this manner, God seeks to resolve, at one time, all the various problems or events that ended unresolved due to the failures of providential figures at various times in history up to this time. This is done in accord with God's providence, and to complete the history of the providence of restoration.

For example, in the two-thousand-year period of the providence of restoration from Adam to Abraham, the vertical indemnity conditions that had been invaded by Satan were restored through indemnity by the three generations of Abraham, Isaac, and Jacob. However, this was only conditional. In other words, the providence of Adam's family and the providence of Noah's family, which had ended in failure without proper completion, were conditionally completed through the providence of Abraham's family. At the time of Jesus, the providential events that had ended in failure due to the invasion of Satan during the four thousand years from Adam to Jesus were made to reappear horizontally so that they might be restored through indemnity at one time. Yet, due to the crucifixion of Jesus, this providence was not successful.

At the time of the providence of the Second Advent, all the events during the six-thousand-year history from Adam, which had been concluded only conditionally because of invasion by Satan, must reappear again horizontally so that they may be totally and fundamentally restored through indemnity, centering on the Second Advent of the Messiah. Thus, the providence of sinful history will be fully consummated. As long as these historical events remain unresolved, there can be no true peace on earth. Only by resolving all of these historical events fundamentally in the Last Days, can the problems of today's actual society be resolved completely, and the world of true peace realized.

For example, the root cause of the conflicts between Israel and the Arab nations today can be understood as the reappearance of the struggles between the Israelites and their surrounding peoples in the Old Testament days. Accordingly, it is very difficult to resolve the present-day conflict between Israel and the Arabs merely by dealing with it as a political problem. In other words, without tracing the history back to its root cause and resolving it fundamentally, the conflicts between the Israelites and the Arabs will never come to a complete end.

When it comes to the consummation of history in the Last Days, many vertical historical events reappear, and unexpected events happen one after another, thus throwing the world into great confusion. This is because, in accordance with the law of the horizontal reappearance of the vertical, various unresolved problems from past history all reappear in the Last Days. That is why Jesus referred to a "great tribulation": "For then there will be great tribulation, such as has not been from the beginning of the world until now, no, and never will be" (Matt. 24:21). Such confusion and conflict will come to be fundamentally resolved only when humankind welcomes the Second Advent of the Messiah and follows his word of truth and his teaching of true love.

The reason why God causes the events of history to reappear in the Last Days, whereby they become fundamentally resolved by the Second Advent of the Messiah, is that God wishes to achieve two purposes: first, to make human beings establish the condition that they have achieved victory in the six-thousand-year history without making mistakes, thus sweeping away the memories of the numerous miserable events in history once and for all; and second, to subjugate Satan completely by eliminating all the conditions for his accusation, and to eventually save even the Archangel, eternally.

G. Law of Synchronous Providence

The law of synchronous providence refers to a law under which a certain providential event which occurred in the past is repeated in some form in a later period. Such providential periods, the two of which are in the relationship of time-identity, display similar aspects in terms of central figures, main events, numerological time periods, and so on. This is because, in case a certain providential central figure did not fulfill his or her portion of responsibility, the providential period centered on that particular person would come to an end, and after a certain period of time, another person, who is similar to the previous person, would be established to restore through indemnity the historical course of the previous period. Thus, a providential event which is similar to that of the previous period is repeated. In such cases, since conditions of indemnity are gradually compounded together with the prolongation of the providence of restoration, the previous period would not be repeated precisely as before, but rather would be repeated on a higher dimension. Consequently, history develops in a spiral.

Then, how did the law of synchronous providence work in history? In the providence of restoration centered on the family level, during the two-thousand-year period from Adam to Abraham (the Age of the Providence to Lay the Foundation for Restoration), the Messiah was unable to come due to the failure of the providence. As a result, the two-thousand-year period of the providence of restoration centered on the Israelites, from Abraham to Jesus (the Age of the Providence of Restoration), appeared as the synchronous providence. Also, since the two-thousand-year period from Abraham to Jesus, the providence of restoration centered on the Israelites, also ended in failure due to the crucifixion of Jesus, the two-thousand-year period of the providence of restoration centered on Christianity from Jesus until today (the Age of the Prolongation of the Providence of Restoration) appeared as its synchronous providence. Arranging the characteristics of synchronism of the two periods of the two thousand years from Abraham to Jesus and the two thousand years from Jesus until today, we have the diagram as seen in table. 8.1.

Synchronism in history was noticed by Oswald Spengler. He said that

Table 8.1 The Providential Synchronism of the Age of the Providence of Restoration and the Age of the Prolongation of the Providence of Restoration

The Age of the Providence of Restoration	The Age of the Prolongation of the Providence of Restoration
Period of Slavery in Egypt (400 years)	Period of Persecution under the Roman Empire (400 years)
Period of the Judges (400 years)	Period of Regional Church Leadership (400 years)
Period of the United Kingdom (120 years)	Period of the Christian Empire (120 years)
Period of the Divided Kingdoms of North and South (400 years)	Period of the Divided Kingdoms of East and West (400 years)
Israel's Exile (70 years) Israel's Return (140 years)	Papal Exile (70 years) Papal Return (140 years)
Period of Preparation for the Advent of the Messiah (400 years) Renovation of Faith	Period of Preparation for the Second Advent of the Messiah (400 years) Religious Reformation

all cultures develop according to the same formula, and therefore, similar events appear in any two cultures of the world. He described these corresponding events as "synchronous." [10]

Arnold Toynbee noticed synchronism in history at about the same time as Spengler. While lecturing on Thucydides, Toynbee explained how he had realized that the history of ancient Greece and modern Western history are synchronous:

The year 1914 caught me at the University of Oxford, teaching the history of classical Greece. In August 1914, it flashed on my mind that the fifth-century BC historian Thucydides had had already the experience that was now overtaking me. He, like me, had been overtaken by a fratricidal great war between the states into which his world had been divided politically. Thucydides had foreseen that his generation's great war would be epoch-making for his world, and the sequel had proved him right. I now saw that classical Greek history and modern Western history were, in terms of experience, *contemporary* with each other. Their courses ran parallel. They could be studied comparatively.[11] (italics added)

Toynbee dealt with ancient Greek history and modern Western history as synchronous. In the Unification View of History, ancient Greek history was the period for the preparation for the coming of the Messiah, and modern Western history is the period for the preparation for the Second Coming of the Messiah. These two periods are, indeed, synchronous, and the essential significance of their synchronism is that each is a preparation period for receiving the Messiah.

IV. Changes in History

The laws of creation and the laws of restoration, which have been discussed above, have all been at work in history, but the most important laws are the law of give and receive, the law of repulsion, the law of indemnity, and the law of separation. Among these, the law of give and receive becomes the "law of development" in historical change, while the other three together become the "law of turning." (The law of turning is also called the "law of the struggle between good and evil.")

It has already been explained that history has been developing through give and receive action; that is, developments in the political, economic, cultural, and all other fields take place through harmonious give and receive action between various pairs of subject and object, such as spirit and matter, people and the environment (society and nature), government and people, organization and organization, individual and individual, people and machinery, and so on.

Development refers to growth, progress, improvement, and appearance of a new quality—all of which are irreversible types of forward motion. These phenomena appear when correlative elements of subject and object engage in give and receive action centering on a common purpose. On the other hand, struggle occurs between subject and subject, the two subjects having different purposes and different interests. When a struggle takes place, development or progress will be either suspended or reversed. Accordingly, any development or progress appearing in history took place, without exception, through give and receive action.

Subject and subject oppose and struggle with each other according to the law of repulsion. In human history repulsion between one subject and another refers to the conflict between one leader and another. One example is the struggle between the leaders of the bourgeoisie and the royalist aristocrats under Louis XVI, namely, the struggle between new leaders and old leaders at the time of the French Revolution. The two parties were separated according to the law of separation, with one party on the relatively good side (the position that was relatively closer to God's providence) and the other party on the relatively evil side (the position that obstructed God's providence). The subjects formed good and evil camps, respectively, by attracting people, who were in the object position to their respective sides (separating the people into two parts), and fought each other. The question of which leader is good and which is evil is a matter to be decided on the basis of the extent to which a leader is in accordance with God's providence. In many cases, however, the leaders in an existing society carried out tyrannical rule, leaning toward self-centered desire, and so God would often establish new leaders on the good side and would promote His providence through them.

In the struggle between good and evil, if the good side wins, history turns toward a better direction. Subsequently, when history reaches yet another new stage, another leader, who is even better, appears. Then, the old leader comes to stand in a relatively evil position, and a new struggle between good and evil starts. Again, if the good side wins, history turns once more to an even better direction. Finally, through this process, history reaches the stage of perfect goodness, that is, the stage of the ideal of creation. Only then will the struggle between good and evil come to an end. Thus, struggle does not actually bring about development; rather, it effects changes in the direction of history.

In a struggle between a good subject and an evil subject, if the evil side happened to be stronger, God would attempt to bring the evil side to surrender by using the law of indemnity. To explain further, God would guide the leaders on the good side to walk the path of suffering under persecution by the evil side. With that as a condition, He would work to have the leader on the evil side submit in surrender. In case the leader on the evil side would not surrender, He would influence the people on the evil side to isolate their leader. That way, the leaders on the evil side could not but surrender in the end. That is the working of the law of the struggle between good and evil. Accordingly, this law may also be called the "law of taking back by being struck," or the "tactic of taking back by being struck." It has been by virtue of this law of indemnity that religions have been propagated throughout the world until the present time, even through persecution.

In the ongoing struggle between good and evil, when the good side does not fully accomplish its responsibility and the evil side wins a

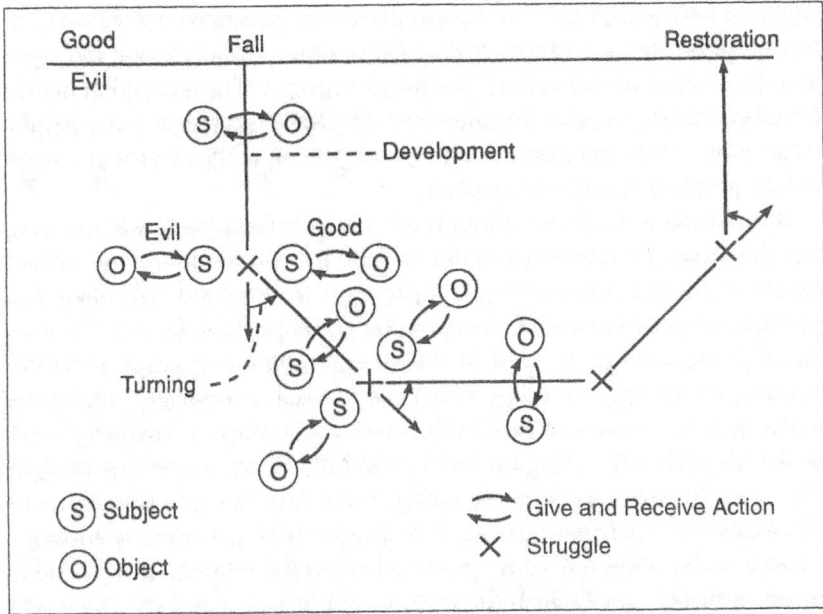

Fig. 8.1. Changes in Historical Direction through Give and Receive Action and the Struggle of Good and Evil

victory, then naturally history does not turn to a better direction but is, instead, prolonged in its existing direction, remaining as it is. After a specified length of time, God again raises a good leader and works to win victory over the evil side. This is the way God has been guiding history, from behind the scenes, toward a better direction. Therefore, human history has not been the history of class struggle, but rather the history of the struggle between good and evil.

In this way, history has developed through the give and receive action between subject and object, and has changed its direction through the struggle between good and evil. In other words, history has undergone changes in direction through the repetition of the process of development and turning. The process of historical changes can be illustrated in fig. 8.1.

From what has been said above, we can understand that history has undergone changes in two respects, namely, in the direction of development (progress), and in the direction of restoration (turning). Development here refers to the development of science, economy, culture, etc.; restoration refers to the recovery of the lost ideal world originally intended—the world of love and peace. The reason these two directions have existed in history is that human history is the history of re-creation and at the same time the history of restoration. The future world will be a world of highly developed science, and at the same time a highly ethical society. A scientific civilization will be attained through development, while an ethical society will be attained through restoration.

Restoration is achieved through the struggle between good and evil, but this does not necessarily refer to military conflict involving armed forces. If the evil side obediently surrenders to the good side, then it is possible for peaceful social change to be accomplished. In fact, the final struggle for putting an end to the struggle between good and evil, namely, the struggle through which the Messiah completely subjugates Satan, will be carried out peacefully, even if it is called a "struggle." That is, the Messiah will subjugate Satan peacefully by means of true love. In this way, history has been changing, following the two directions of development and restoration. Development will continue forever, whereas restoration will come to an end when the original ideal world is finally restored, after which the ideal world of peace and true love will continue forever.

V. Traditional Views of History

I would like now to present an overview of the representative traditional views of history in order to compare them with the Unification view of history.

Cyclical View of History (Fatalist View of History)

The ancient Greeks believed that just as the four seasons of spring, summer, autumn, and winter repeat themselves year after year, so does history follow a cyclical course. For them, the birth and fall of historical events were destined, and they could not be affected by human power, so that history had no meaning or goal. This view of history is called the "cyclical view of history," or the "fatalist view of history." Representative historians taking this view were Herodotus (ca. 484–425 BC), who is called the father of history and wrote *History*, and Thucydides (ca. 460–400 BC), who wrote *History of the Peloponnesian War*. Herodotus depicted the Persian war in the epic manner, whereas Thucydides depicted the

Peloponnesian War from beginning to end in a manner that was faithful to the historical facts. What these two men had in common, though, was the idea that history repeats itself.[12]

The cyclical view of history understands the course of history as being destined. It does not admit to the possibility that the development of history might be affected by human effort. Furthermore, because it does not see any goal to history it has no concern about offering a future image of the world.

Providential View of History

In contrast to the Greek view of history, which asserted that history has no beginning or end, or goal, but only repeats itself in a cyclical manner, Christianity presents a fundamentally different view of history, which asserts that history does have a beginning and advances in a direct manner toward a definite goal. In other words, it asserts that history started with the Creation and the human Fall, that it is a salvation history leading to the Last Judgment, and that what drives history is God's Providence. Such a view of history is called the "providential view of history," or the "Christian view of history."

It was St. Augustine (354–430) who, in his classic *The City of God*, systematized the Christian view of history. Augustine depicted history as a history of struggle between the City of God (*Civitas Dei*), where God-loving people live, and the City of the World (*Civitas terrena*), where those people who have yielded to the temptation of Satan reside. He asserted that the City of God would finally win victory in the end and would establish eternal peace. The course of history occurred according to the plan predestined by God, according to this view. Augustive divided human history, from the Fall to its consummation, into six periods: (1) from Adam to Noah's flood, (2) from Noah to Abraham, (3) from Abraham to David, (4) from David to the Babylonian captivity, (5) from the Babylonian captivity to the birth of Christ, and (6) from the first coming to the Second Coming of Christ. How long the sixth period would last was left unstated.

Through this Christian view, history became meaningful in the sense that it aims at a certain goal; still, the human being was no more than an instrument moved by God. This view possesses many ambiguities and is lacking both in logic and in any sense of historical lawfulness. As such, today it is generally regarded as unacceptable as a social science.

Spiritual View of History (Progressive View of History)

During the Renaissance, theological views of history gradually faded away, and in the Enlightenment of the eighteenth century, a new kind of view of history appeared. According to this new view, it was the human being, rather than God's providence, that drove history. This view held that history was progressing in a linear fashion, and necessarily, according to the progress of the human spirit. This view of history is called the "spiritual view of history," or the "progressive view of history."

Giambattista Vico (1668–1744) recognized God's providence in history, but he considered that the secular world was formed by human beings, and asserted that history should not be explained only by God's will alone. In his understanding of history, God was relegated to the background, and human beings were brought to the fore.[13]

Voltaire (1694–1778) excluded God's power working upon history. He asserted that history is driven not by God but rather by those people with higher education, those who had mastered science, namely, enlightened people.

Marquis de Condorcet (1743–94) asserted that, if human reason were awakened, history would progress with harmony between science and ethics.

Immanuel Kant (1724–1804) said that the purpose of history is to develop all noble human capacities in an international society consisting of a league of nations. He advocated seeing a universal history from a cosmopolitan point of view.

The romanticist philosopher J. G. Herder (1744–1803) asserted that the development of human nature is the goal of history.

Hegel (1770–1831) understood history as the process of the "self-realization of the spirit," or the "self-realization of the Idea." According to his view, reason rules the world, and world history progresses rationally. The reason that rules the world is called the "world spirit." He held that reason manipulates human beings, and called this the "trick by reason." Hegel's view of history is called a "spiritual view of history," or the "idealistic view of history." He believed that a rational state, where the Idea of freedom would be realized, was to come into being in Prussia; in reality, however, that did not take place. Instead, anti-rational social problems such as exploitation and human alienation became even more serious. Thus, Marx's historical materialism appeared in part as a revolt against Hegel's philosophy of history.

Historical Materialism

In contrast to Hegel, who advocated a spiritual view of history and asserted that it is Idea that drives history, Marx asserted that it is material forces that drive history, and argued for the "materialist view of history," or "historical materialism" (also called the "revolutionary view of history").

According to the materialist view of history, what drives history is the development of the productive forces, rather than the development of the Idea or spirit. Corresponding to the development of productive forces, certain relations of production are established. Whereas the productive forces develop steadily, however, the relations of production, once established, become fixed, and eventually turn into fetters against the further development of productive forces. Therefore, class struggle takes place between the class that seeks to maintain the old relations of production (ruling class) and the class that seeks new relations of production (ruled class). Accordingly, history has been a history of class struggle. In capitalist society, where this class struggle reaches its peak, revolution occurs in which the proletariat, the ruled class, overthrows the bourgeoisie, the ruling class. As a result, the classless Communist society, which is the "kingdom of freedom" without classes, is realized.

As shown by the fall of Communism, it becomes obvious that the materialist view of history was completely erroneous. When one closely examines this theory, all the laws of history presented by this view are found to be no more than sheer dogma. For example, the development of productive forces is regarded as a material development, but no materialistic dialectical explanation is given concerning how the productive forces develop. Also, according to this view, human history is the history of social changes through class struggles. Nevertheless, there was not a single case in which a society was actually changed by a class struggle. Thus, the materialist view of history has proved to be completely false.

Philosophy-of-Life View of History

Wilhelm Dilthey (1833–1911) and Georg Simmel (1858–1918) asserted that history grows together with the growth of life. This view is called the "philosophy-of-life view of history."

According to Dilthey, life is a human experience, and the experience is always expressed, and manifests itself in the external world. The manifestation of experience is the world of history and culture. Therefore, the cultural system of human beings, including religion, philosophy, art, science, politics, and law is the objectification of life. Simmel, similarly, asserted that history is the expression of life. Life is a stream that continues infinitely, and life's "stream of becoming" makes history.[14]

According to the philosophy-of-life view of history, the pain and unhappiness of humankind, as recorded in history, are regarded as inevitable phenomena that accompany the growth of life. Accordingly, the question of how people could be liberated from such pain and unhappiness remained unsolved in the philosophy-of-life view.

Cultural View of History

In Europe before World War I, trust in the progress and development of history was basically unshakable. People believed that history was developing, centering on Europe. It was Oswald Spengler (1880–1936) who questioned this linear, Eurocentric image of history.

Spengler advocated a cultural view of history, asserting that the foundation of history is culture. He regarded a culture to be an organism, and thus considered, a culture is born, grows, and dies, and therefore its death is inevitable. In Western civilization, he found symptoms of this impending decline, which corresponded to the decline of Greece and Rome, and predicted the decline of the West. He advocated that, knowing in advance of this decline of the West, one should live in acceptance of this inevitable destiny, without falling into pessimism. There was a strong tie with Nietzsche on this point. Spengler's view of history was deterministic.

Under the strong influence of Spengler, Arnold J. Toynbee (1889–1975) propounded his unique cultural view of history. According to Toynbee, the essential entity that constitutes world history is not a region, an ethnic people, or a nation, but a civilization. He considered that each civilization passes through the stages of genesis, growth, breakdown, disintegration, and dissolution.

The cause of the genesis of a civilization can be found in the human response to the challenges from the natural or social environment. Creative minorities foster a new civilization while guiding the masses of people, but when the creative minorities themselves eventually lose creativity, the civilization breaks down. Then, the creative minorities turn into the ruling minorities, and the "internal proletariat" within the civilization and the "external proletariat" surrounding it are born and separate themselves from the ruling minorities. As a result, society falls into confusion. After a while, however, the strongest among the ruling minorities establishes a "universal state," bringing an end to the period of turmoil. Under the oppressive rule by the universal state, the internal proletariat nurtures a "higher religion" and the external proletariat (savages surrounding it) forms the "barbarian war-bands" (aggressive forces). Thus, the universal state, the higher religion, and the war-bands constitute three factions. Eventually the higher religion becomes a "universal church" by converting the ruling classes, but the universal state soon collapses, and together with it, the civilization meets its death.

After the first civilization has disappeared, the external proletariat invades and becomes converted to the higher religion, giving birth to a civilization of the new generation. The relationship of such old and new civilizations is called "apparentation-and-affiliation." There were twenty-one fully grown civilizations in world history. All the present civilizations are in their third generation, and are separated into the four lineages of Christian (the West, Greek orthodoxy), Islamic, Hindu, and Far East civilizations. It can be said that the succession of civilizations through three generations, as advocated by Toynbee, correspond to the providential synchronism in three generations in the Unification view of history (the Age of the Providence to Lay the Foundation for Restoration, the Age of the Providence of Restoration, and the Age of the Prolongation of the Providence of Restoration).

It is characteristic of Toynbee's view of history that it excludes determinism and asserts non-determinism and the theory of free will: how human beings respond to challenges depends on their free will. Therefore, the way in which history proceeds is never predetermined, but human beings can choose their future.

Toynbee clearly envisioned the City of God (*Civitas Dei*) as a future image of human history. Yet, based on his non-deterministic position, he considered that the choice of the "Kingdom of God" or the "kingdom of night" would depend on human free will. He wrote as follows:

> Under a law of love which is the law of God's own Being, God's self-sacrifice challenges Man by setting before him an ideal of spiritual perfection; and Man has perfect freedom to accept or reject this. The law of love leaves Man as free to be a sinner as to be a saint; it leaves him free to choose whether his personal and his social life shall be a

progress towards the Kingdom of God or the kingdom of night.[15]

Another characteristic of Toynbee's view of history is the introduction of God into his view of history which, he says, modern society seems to have forgotten.

What do we mean by History? And the writer ··· would reply that he meant by History a vision—dim and partial, yet (he believed) true to reality as far as it went—of God revealing Himself in action to souls that were sincerely seeking Him.[16]

Traditional Views of History Seen from the Unification View of History

Having presented outlines of some traditional views of history, I will now compare them with the Unification view of history, and will attempt to show that the Unification view of history is able to unify traditional views.

First, there is the question whether history should be seen as a circular or as a linear movement. The Greek cyclical view and Spengler's cultural view grasped history as a circular movement, whereas the Christian view, the progressive view, and the materialist view regard history as a linear movement. The philosophy-of-life view held that history develops with the growth of the stream of life. That view could be seen as a modification of the progressive view.

If history is grasped as a linear movement, we can have hope in the development of history, but we are left without a good understanding of the breakdowns and revivals in human history. On the other hand, when we regard history as a circular movement, nations and cultures become destined to perish, and we are left without any hope.

The Unification view of history grasps history from the two aspects of re-creation and restoration and understands its development as a spiral movement that has both aspects, namely, a linear forward movement and a circular movement. In other words, it views history as a spiral movement that has both the forward-moving nature of development toward a goal (realization of the original ideal world of creation) and the circular-movement nature of restoring the lost original ideal world through the law of indemnity by establishing providential figures.

Second, there is the question of determinism and non-determinism. Such views of history as the Greek fatalist view, which holds that history moves inevitably towards a given destiny, and Spengler's cultural view, were deterministic. The providential view, which holds that history proceeds according to God's providence, can also be regarded as deterministic. Hegel's view, which holds that reason, or the world spirit, drives history, and the materialist view, which holds that history inevitably reaches the Communist society according to the development of productive forces, are also deterministic. All these views assert that some super-human power drives history. Under such types of determinism, the human being is no more than a being dragged along by history, and it is impossible to change history through efforts based on people's free will.

On the other hand, Toynbee advocated non-determinism from his position of the theory of free will. That is, he asserted that the way in which history proceeds is chosen by people's free will. In Toynbee's non-deterministic position, however, the future image of history remains ambiguous, and therefore we are left without a sure hope for the future.

In contrast, the Unification view of history takes the position that the goal of history is determined, but that the process of history is not determined because the accomplishment of providential events requires the fulfillment of the human portion of responsibility in addition to God's portion of responsibility. In other words, the Unification view of history has aspects both of determinism and non-determinism. This theory is called the "theory of responsibility."

When we compare the traditional views of history with the Unification view of history, we find that the traditional views have each emphasized a portion of the Unification view, and that the Unification view is the most comprehensive, unifying view of history. Also, Toynbee's view of history is similar in many ways to the Unification view of history. From a providential viewpoint, Toynbee's view can be regarded as being a preparation for the appearance of the Unification view of history. That is to say, Toynbee's view had the mission of serving as a bridge linking traditional views of history with the Unification view of history.

VI. Comparative Analysis of Providential View, Materialist View, and Unification View

Finally, I will present a comparison from various perspectives concerning the providential view and the materialist view, which are representatives of the traditional views of history, together with the Unification view. I will compare these three views of history on such points as their beginning, characteristics, driving force for development, laws of change in history, struggle, phenomena in the Last Days, events at the consummation of history, and the ideal world to come. This will help us deepen our understanding of the characteristics of each view of history.

1. Beginning of History

The providential view of history holds that human history began with the Creation and the Fall of the first human ancestors. Accordingly, human history started as a sinful history. In contrast, the materialist view of history holds that human history began when human beings separated from the animal kingdom, and that the first society was a primitive communal society. The Unification view of history, like the providential view, holds that history started with the Creation and the Fall of the first human ancestors and that human history began as a sinful history.

2. Characteristics of History

The providential view regards history as a history of salvation by God. The materialist view regards history as a history of class struggle. In contrast, the Unification view grasps history from the two aspects of re-creation and restoration.

3. Driving Force for the Development of History

According to the providential view, the driving force for the development of history is God's providence. According to the materialist view, the development of the productive forces, which are material forces, is the driving force of history. In contrast, the Unification view holds that it was both God's providence and the human portion of responsibility working in tandem that has moved history. According to the providential view, God moves all of history, and it therefore follows that even tragic events in history were allowed by God. From the standpoint of the Unification view, however, things did not turn out in accordance with God's will because human beings did not fulfill their portion of responsibility. Thus, human beings are responsible for all the tragic events in history.

4. Laws of Change in History

The providential view merely asserts that the Kingdom of God, consisting of those who believe in God, and the kingdom of the world, consisting of those who obey Satan, fight each other, but that in the end the Kingdom of God will be victorious. It fails to offer any other law of history. On the other hand, the materialist view of history applies the materialist dialectic to history and presents its laws of history: Human beings in their social life enter into certain relations of production, which are independent of their will; the relations of production correspond to a given stage in the development of the productive forces; the relations of production are the basis, and the forms of consciousness are the superstructure; people's social existence determines their consciousness; when the relations of production become fetters to the development of productive forces, revolution takes place; and so on. In contrast, the Unification view of history sets forth the laws of creation and the laws of restoration as the laws that have been at work in history.

5. Struggles at the Consummation of History

The providential view holds that a final struggle will take place between the Kingdom of God and the kingdom of the world. The Bible says that an angel (Michael), who serves God, and Satan will fight in Heaven. The materialist view holds that a fierce struggle between the bourgeoisie and the proletariat will take place in capitalist society, which is the last stage of class society in history. The Unification view holds that history is the struggle between good and evil, and that the struggle between good and evil at the consummation of history is the struggle between the democratic world and the Communist world, which takes place on a worldwide scale. In this struggle, the Communist world is subjugated by, and surrenders to, the free democratic world. Ultimately, both sides are reconciled and are united through the Messiah.

6. Phenomena of the Last Days

The providential view holds that extraordinary natural phenomena will take place in the Last Days, that is, at the consummation of human history. About such phenomena, the Bible says, "Immediately after the tribulation of those days the sun will be darkened, and the moon will not give its light, and the stars will fall from heaven, and the powers of the heavens will be shaken" (Matt. 24:29). The materialist view holds that in capitalist society such phenomena as misery, oppression, slavery, degradation, and exploitation will increase and economic collapse and social confusion will arise. The Unification view holds that at the consummation of history existing values will be neglected and collapse—especially, sexual morality will sharply decline—and that profound social confusion will be widespreod.

7. Events at the Consummation of History

The providential view of history holds that the Last Judgment will take place in the Last Days. According to the Bible, the sheep will be placed at the right hand of Christ and the goats at the left (Matt. 25:33), and those on the right side, namely, the sheep, those who obeyed God, will be given blessings (Matt. 25:34), whereas those on the left side, the goats, namely, those who followed Satan, will be thrown into eternal fire (Matt. 25:41). The materialist view asserts that the prehistory of humankind comes to an end as the proletariat, the ruled class, overthrows the bourgeoisie, the ruling class, through violent revolution. The Unification view asserts that in the Last Days the good side and evil side will be separated on a worldwide scale, and that the good side will convey God's truth and love to the evil side and naturally subjugate the evil side.

8. The History that Terminates

What comes to an end at the consummation of history, or what history comes to an end at the consummation of history? The providential view asserts that the sinful history of man will come to an end when the Kingdom of God wins victory over the kingdom of the world. The materialist view asserts that the history of class struggle comes to an end when the proletariat overthrows the bourgeoisie. The Unification view asserts that sinful history and the history of the struggle between good and evil will come to an end when the good side persuades the evil side to surrender naturally.

9. The Ideal World to Come

What will the world be like after history comes to an end? According to the providential view of history, the age of a new heaven and a new earth will come after the judgment of the last days is over (Rev. 21–22). It is not at all clear, however, what the age of the new heaven and the new earth will be like, specifically. The materialist view asserts that after the revolution, Communist society, which is the classless kingdom of freedom, will be realized. The Unification view of history asserts that the original ideal world of creation, namely, the Kingdom of Heaven on earth, where all humankind will become one family, will be realized by receiving the Messiah, the true parents of humankind.

A summary of the three views of history in terms of the above-mentioned nine points is shown in table 8.2. We find, unfortunately, that the Christian view of history is rather mysterious and so irrational that it hardly has any persuasive power today. It simply asserts that God promotes His providence in history. Since concrete laws of history are not presented, however, it is not at all clear how He conducts His providence. It is also hard to understand that in the Last Days those people represented by the goats on the left side will receive eternal punishment. Further, it does not clarify what the new heaven and the new earth will concretely be like.

The materialist view of history, when compared with the Christian view of history, seems more realistic and rational, and therefore it carries more persuasiveness. Consequently, it has captivated the minds of many intellectual young people. At its height, nearly half the world came to be ruled under Communism. Today, however, it has become clear that Communist society would not be the kingdom of freedom nor an affluent society, but rather the opposite. Thus, the idea of a Communist society has perished from the earth. Originally, as Toynbee said, Communism appeared as an accusation or a prosecution from Satan's side, because Christianity failed to fulfill its mission and suffered degeneration. That is why the materialist view of history had the external appearance of a Christian view of history which had been turned upside down. In this connection, Karl Löwith stated as follows:

> What explains the idealistic foundation of historical materialism is ··· old Jewish messianism, prophetism, and the untiring Jewish persistence

to absolute righteousness. *The Communist Manifesto* clearly has a feature of faith, the firm belief in "what one hopes for" in a reversed form of scientific prophesy. Thus, it is not at all accidental that the final hostility between the bourgeoisie and the proletariat corresponds to the faith in the ultimate conflict between Christ and the anti-Christ in the last period of history, and that the task of the proletariat resembles the world-historic mission of the chosen people. The role of the oppressed class for global salvation corresponds to the religious dialectic of the crucifixion and resurrection, and the transformation of the kingdom of necessity into the kingdom of freedom corresponds to the transformation of an old àeon into a new aeon. The process of history as described in *The Communist Manifesto*, reflects the well-known Judeo-Christian pattern of interpreting history as the events of salvation through the providence toward a significant final goal. The historical materialism is the salvation history in terms of political economy.[17]

The Unification view of history emerged as an elaboration of the Christian view of history; yet it is presented as a view that overcomes the mysteriousness and irrationality of the Christian view of history. It is a view of history that can successfully overcome the Communist accusation against Christianity. The Christian view of history asserts that the people in the kingdom of the world who obeyed Satan will receive eternal punishment. The materialist view of history asserts that the proletariat will overthrow the bourgeoisie by violent means. Yet, the Unification view of history asserts that the good side will induce the evil side naturally to surrender by means of true love and eventually will save all humankind by restoring the evil side to the good side. In the true ideal world all humankind must become happy. That is guaranteed by the Unification view of history.

The materialist view of history attacks the Christian view of history as being mere superstition or myth, and boasts, on the other hand, that it itself is a scientific view of history, with rational laws. Nevertheless, the laws presented by the materialist view of history have turned out to be nothing but arbitrary, pseudo laws, advocated for the sole purpose of rationalizing revolution. In contrast, the laws presented by the Unification view of history are genuine laws, fully supported by historical facts.

Table. 8.2 A Comparative Overview of the Providential, the Materialist, and the Unification Views of History

	Providential View of History	Materialist View of History	Unification View of History
Beginning of History	Creation & Fall of Humankind	Primitive Community	Creation & Fall of Humankind
Characteristics of History	History of Salvation	History of Class Struggle	History of Recreation & Restoration
Driving Force of History	God's Providence	Development of the Productive Forces	God's Providence & Human Portion of Responsibility
Laws of Change	None	Materialist Dialectic	Laws of Creation Laws of Restoration
Struggle in the Last Days	Struggle between Kingdom of God & Kingdom of the World (between Angels & Satan)	Struggle between Bourgeoisie & Proletariat	Struggle between Good & Evil
Phenomena in the Last Days	Fall of Heavenly Bodies, Earthquakes, etc	Economic Collapse, Social Disorder	Collapse of Values, Great Social Disorder
Grand Event in the Last Days	Last Judgment (Separation of Sheep & Goats)	Violent Revolution	Dissemination of God's Truth & Love (Separation of Good & Evil)
History that Terminates	Sinful History	History of Class Struggle	Sinful History (History of Struggle between Good & Evil)
Ideal World to Come	New Heaven and New Earth	Communist Society	Original Ideal World (Kingdom of Heaven on Earth)

9

Epistemology

Epistemology is that field of philosophy which seeks to solve the various fundamental problems about cognition (*Erkenntnis*). It is the theory of how the correct knowledge of an object can be obtained. Its goal is to bring to light the origin, method, and development of cognition. The English word epistemology is a combination of the Greek words *episteme*, which means knowledge, and *logia*, which means logic. It is said to have been used for the first time by J. F. Ferrier (1808–64). The German word *Erkenntnistheorie* is said to have been coined by K. L. Reinhold (1758–1823).

Epistemology already existed in ancient and medieval philosophies, but only in the modern period did it emerge as a central topic in philosophy. Unification Thought sees it as part of the call for the restoration of human nature and humankind's dominion over all things. Epistemology and ontology came to form the two major branches of philosophy.

As already mentioned, Unification Thought advocates the standard which claims to be able to fundamentally solve all actual problems. Today, enthusiasm about the study of epistemology has waned, and attention has instead moved to medical science. Yet, medical science has not given a complete solution to the problems of epistemology.

Undoubtedly, medical science has contributed to solving the problems of epistemology by giving a physiological foundation to the process of cognition. Yet, there are still unsolved problems in the work of medical research as regards cognition. Unification epistemology has solved these problems, as well as many traditional ones.

Epistemology is related to the fundamental problem of ontology, namely, the conflict between idealism and materialism. Cognition, or knowledge, is closely related to one's practical activities. Therefore, unless we can establish a correct view of epistemology, we can not solve actual problems effectively. Thus, it follows that a new theory of epistemology—one that can solve the problems of all traditional epistemologies—is needed. In order to respond to this call, Unification epistemology is presented here, based on Unification Thought.

I will begin with an outline of traditional epistemologies, pointing out their weaknesses. Then, I will present Unification epistemology, clarifying the following points: (1) Unification epistemology is capable of solving the problems that remain unresolved in traditional epistemologies; and (2) this epistemology is, literally, a Unification epistemology, in the sense that it has the capacity to unify all epistemologies. It should also be clarified that this epistemology was systematized under the instruction of Rev. Sun Myung Moon, in the same way as was done in the other sections of this book.

I. Traditional Epistemologies

Epistemological studies have been carried out since ancient times. It was only in the modern period, however, that epistemology became a central theme of philosophy. The philosopher who first explained epistemology systematically was John Locke, whose *An Essay Concerning Human Understanding* became known as an epoch-making work.

The most important questions with regard to the cognition of an object have been those of the *origin*, the *object*, and the *method* of cognition, each of which has two opposing positions. In terms of the origin of cognition, two opposing schools of thought have arisen: empiricism, which asserted that cognition could only be obtained through one's sensations, and rationalism, which asserted that cognition could be obtained only through one's thinking about ideas, innate in the mind. With regard to the object of cognition, two views have come into opposition: realism, which asserted that the object of cognition existed independently from the human being, and subjective idealism, which asserted that the object of cognition was merely those ideas or representations present in the mind of the subject. Concerning the method of cognition: the transcendental method and the dialectical method were both proposed.

Let me offer a brief review of some major historical developments in the realm of epistemology. As the conflict between empiricism and rationalism developed, empiricism finally fell into skepticism, and rationalism lapsed into dogmatism. Immanuel Kant made an effort to synthesize these two opposing positions by means of his critical method, or transcendental method.[1] This was his theory of an "a priori synthetic judgment," which holds that the object of cognition is synthesized by the subject. Later, plagiarizing Hegel's dialectic materialistically, Marx presented his materialist dialectic. Epistemology based on the materialist dialectic is Marxist epistemology, or dialectical epistemology. This is a "copy theory," or "reflection theory," which asserts that the content and form of cognition are no more than reflections on the mind of things in the external world.

I would like to clarify at this point that it is not my intention to introduce in any concrete or academic detail the contents of traditional epistemologies. This section is presented simply for the readers' reference; I will introduce briefly the relevant problems in a traditional epistemology for the sole purpose of showing how the Unification epistemology is able to solve the unresolved problems of traditional epistemologies. Therefore, in terms of an understanding of the Unification epistemology itself, this section can be skipped.

A. Origin of Cognition

Empiricism holds that all knowledge is obtained from one's experience, whereas rationalism claims that true cognition can be gained only through the operation of one's reason, independently from experience. During the seventeenth and eighteenth centuries, empiricism was advocated in Great Britain, and rationalism was advocated in continental Europe.

1. Empiricsm

a) Bacon (1561-1626)

Francis Bacon established the foundation for empiricism. In his renowned work, *Novum Organun* (1620), he considered traditional learning to be merely a series of useless words, empty in content, and that correct cognition is obtained through observation of nature, and experimentation. According to him, in order to obtain correct cognition, one must first renounce one's pre-conceived prejudices. As prejudices, he listed four Idols (*idola*).

The first is the *Idols of the Tribe*. This refers to the prejudice into which people in general are likely to fall, namely, the prejudice whereby the real nature of things are reflected distortedly, because the human intellect is like an uneven mirror. An example is the inclination to view nature as personalized.

The second is the *Idols of the Cave*. This prejudice arises due to an individual's unique nature, habits, or narrow preconceptions as if one were looking at the world from inside a cave.

The third is the *Idols of the Market Place*. This refers to the kind of prejudice that derives from one's intellect becoming influenced by words. For example, words may be created for things that do not exist, which could lead to empty arguments.

The fourth is the *Idols of the Theatre*. This is the prejudice that arises from blindly accepting authority or tradition. In other words, it is the prejudice that arises from relying on an authoritative thought or philosophy.

Bacon said that we should first remove these four Idols, and then observe nature to find the essence within each individual phenomenon. For that end, he proposed the inductive method.

b) Locke (1632-1704)

John Locke systematized empiricism, and in his major work, *An Essay concerning Human Understanding*, he developed his views. Locke denied what Descartes called "innate ideas," and considered the human mind to be like a blank sheet of paper (*tabula rasa*): All the ideas coming into the mind are drawn on the blank paper of the mind just as a picture or letters are drawn on a white paper. Thus, all ideas come from experience.[2]

Ideas come into the mind from two sources: one source is sensation, and the other is reflection. For Locke, experiences through sensation and reflection are the origin of cognition. Sensation refers to one's ability to perceive external objects through one's sense organs. The ideas of yellow, white, hot, cold, soft, hard, bitter, sweet, and so on, derive from sensation. Reflection refers to our perception of the operations of our mind such as thinking, doubting, believing, reasoning and willing.

Ideas consist of "simple ideas" and "complex ideas." Simple ideas are those obtained individually and separately from sensation and reflection. When simple ideas become higher ideas through combination, comparison and abstraction under the operations of our understanding, they become complex ideas.

Simple ideas include those with objective validity, namely, solidity, extension, figure, motion, rest, number, and the like; in addition, simple ideas include qualities with subjective validity, namely, color, smell, taste, sound, and the like. The former qualities are called "primary qualities," and the latter are called "secondary qualities."

There are three kinds of complex ideas, namely, mode, substance and relation. Mode refers to an idea expressing the state or quality of things, that is, the attributes of things, such as the mode of space (distance, immensity, figure), the mode of time (succession, duration, eternity), the mode of thinking (perception, recollection, contemplation), the mode of number, and the mode of power. Substance refers to an idea concerning the substratum that carries the various qualities. Finally, relation refers to the idea that comes into being by comparing two ideas, like the ideas of cause and effect, identity, and diversity.

Locke regarded knowledge as *"the perception of the connection and agreement, or disagreement and repugnancy of any of our Ideas."* [3] He also said, *"Truth* is the marking down in Words, the agreement or disagreement of *Ideas* as it is." [4] He sought to answer the question concerning the origin of cognition by analyzing ideas.

Locke considered certain the existence of the spirit, which is recognized intuitively, and the existence of God, which is recognized through logical proof. But he considered that there can not be certainty regarding the existence of material things in the external world, because they can be perceived only through sensation.

c) Berkeley (1685-1753)

George Berkeley rejected Locke's distinction between primary qualities and secondary qualities, and described both primary and secondary qualities as subjective. For example, distance seems to exist objectively as extension; namely, it seems to be an idea of the primary qualities. According to Berkeley, however, it is a subjective idea. The idea of distance is obtained as follows. We perceive a certain object from a distance with our eyes, and then we approach it and touch it with our hands. When we repeat this process, a certain visual sensation leads us to expect that it will be accompanied by certain tactile sensations of walking. Thus arises the idea of distance. In other words, we do not look at distance as extension itself.

Locke affirmed substance as being the carrier of qualities, but Berkley rejected this view and instead, viewed things as being mere collections of ideas. He asserted that "to be is to be perceived" (*esse est percipi*). Thus, Berkeley denied the existence of the substance of material objects, but he had no doubt as regards the existence of spirit as the substance that perceives.

d) Hume (1711–76)

David Hume developed empiricism to its logical conclusion. He considered our knowledge as being based on "impressions" and "ideas." An impression is a direct representation based on sensation and reflection, whereas an idea is a representation that appears in the mind through memory or imagination, after the impression has disappeared. Impressions and ideas make up what he called "perceptions."

Hume enumerated resemblance, contiguity, and cause and effect as the three laws of the association of ideas. He held the cognition of resemblance and of contiguity as being certain and posing no problem, but there is a problem with cause and effect, he said. With regard to cause and effect, Hume gave the following example: when one hears thunder after a bolt of lightning, one usually thinks that the lightning is the cause and the thunder the effect. Hume, however, claimed that there is no reason to connect the two as cause and effect, for they are merely impressions; the idea of cause and effect is established on the basis of people's subjective customs and beliefs, he asserted. As another example, the phenomenon of the sun rising shortly after a rooster crows is empirically well known. But we can not say that the rooster's crowing is the cause, and the sun's rising is the effect. Knowledge accepted as cause and effect is thus based on subjective human customs and beliefs.

In this way, empiricism, with Hume, became transformed into skepticism. Concerning the idea of substantiality, Hume, like Berkeley, doubted the existence of substance in material objects. He went even further by doubting the very existence of the spiritual substance, considering it to be nothing more than a bundle of perceptions.

2. Rationalism

In contrast to empiricism, which developed in Britain, and discussed above, rationalism expanded over continental Europe, represented by Descartes, Spinoza, Leibniz, Wolff, and others. Rationalism held that it is not through our experience that we can obtain correct cognition, but only through our thinking. Correct cognition can be obtained only through deductive logical reasoning. This is the position of Continental rationalism.

a) Descartes (1596–1650)

René Descartes, regarded as the founder of rationalism, began by doubting everything, as a method of obtaining true knowledge. This technique has been called "methodic doubt." Descartes believed that our sensations can deceive us, and so he doubted everything related to sensation. Why did he adopt such a method? He did so in order to obtain genuine truth. If there remains something that can not be doubted after we have doubted the existence of all things in the world and even ourselves, it is because it is indeed truth. Thus, he doubted everything. As a result, he came to realize that there is one thing which can not be doubted: the fact that I am engaged in the act of doubting. Hence, he established his famous proposition, "I think; therefore, I am" (*Cogito, ergo sum*).

For Descartes, the proposition "I think, therefore I am" is the first principle of philosophy.[5] That proposition is certain, he argued, because one's perception of it is clear and distinct. He then derived the general rule (the second principle) that, "things we perceive very clearly and very distinctly are all true."[6] "Clear" implies that something is present and obvious to the spirit, and "distinct" implies that it is distinguishable from other objects.[7] The opposite of "clear" is "obscure," and the opposite of "distinct" is "confused."

The existence of the spiritual substance, an attribute of which is thought, and the existence of the material substance, an attribute of which is extension, can be recognized as certain. In other words, the Cartesian dualism of matter and spirit is established from the first and second principles: The existence of mind (thought) is proved from the first principle, and the existence of matter (extension) is proved from the second principle.

In order to guarantee a clear and distinct cognition, one must not allow cases in which evil spirits secretly deceive people. In order to prevent such a thing, one must assume the existence of God. If God exists, no mistake can occur in our cognition, because the honest God can never deceive us.

Descartes is said to have proved the existence of God as follows: First, the idea of God is innate within us. In order for this idea to exist, the cause of this idea must exist. Second, the fact that we, who are imperfect, have the idea of a perfect Being proves the existence of God. Third, since the idea of the most perfect Being necessarily contains existence as its essence, the existence of God is proved. In this way the existence of God was proved. Therefore, God's essences, namely, infinity, omniscience, and omnipotence, become clear; honesty (*veracitas*), as one of God's attributes, is secured. Accordingly, clear and distinct cognition is guaranteed.

Descartes ascertained the existence of God and the existence of spiritual and corporeal substance, or mind and body; among these, the only independent being, in the true sense, is God, for mind and body are both dependent on God. Descartes also held that mind and body—with the attributes of thought and extension, respectively—are substances independent from each other; thus, he advocated dualism. Descartes proved the certainty of clear and distinct cognition, thereby asserting the certainty of rational cognition based on the mathematical method.

b) Spinoza (1632–77)

Baruch de Spinoza, like Descartes, thought that truth can be cognized through rigorous proofs, and tried to develop logical reasoning, particularly by applying the geometrical method to philosophy. The premise of Spinoza's philosophy was that all truth can be cognized through reason. That is, when one perceives things "in their eternal aspects" (*sub specie eternitatis*) through reason and also perceives them wholly and intuitively in their necessary relationship with God, true cognition can be obtained.

To perceive things "in their eternal aspects" means to understand all things in the process of necessity. Let me explain. When we look at things from such a standpoint, we need not be attached to or disturbed by transient things or passing phenomena, but rather we can come to comprehend things, phenomena, and even ourselves as being expressions of God's eternal truth, hence, as precious things. Then, we can reach our perfection, and obtain true life, boundless joy, and true happiness. This is what is meant by perceiving things in their eternal aspects. Such perception can be obtained through clear and distinct reason and our spiritual sense.

Spinoza divided cognition into three types: imagination, scientific knowledge (which is on the level of reason), and intuitive knowledge. Among these three, he held that if imagination is not properly ordered by reason, it is imperfect. He thought that true cognition can be obtained through scientific knowledge and intuitive knowledge. For Spinoza, intuitive knowledge is not separated from reason, but rather it is based on reason.

Descartes considered mind, with thought as an attribute, and body, with extension as an attribute, to be substances independent from each other. In contrast, Spinoza held that God alone is substance; and that both extension and thinking are God's attributes. Spinoza asserted that God and nature are in the relationship of *natura naturans* (the origin of all things) and *natura naturata* (everything which follows, by necessity, from the nature of God), and are inseparable. Thus he developed a pantheistic thought, claiming that "God is nature."

c) Leibnitz (1646–1716)

Gottfried Wilhelm von Leibniz placed great importance on the mathematical method, and considered that the ideal was to derive every proposition from a few fundamental principles. He classified truth into two kinds: first, there is truth that can be arrived at logically through reason, and second, there is truth that can be obtained through experience. He labeled the former as "eternal truths," or "truths of reason," and the latter as "truths of fact," or "contingent truths." He held that that which guarantees truths of reason is the principle of identity and the principle of contradiction, and that which guarantees truths of fact is the principle of sufficient reason, which says that nothing can exist without sufficient reason.

Yet, such distinctions among kinds of truths apply only to the human intellect. This is because God can cognize, through logical necessity, even that which is regarded by humans as truths of fact. Therefore, ultimately, truth of reason was held to be the ideal truth.

Leibniz also held that the true substance is the "monad," or a living mirror of the universe. He explained the monad as being a non-spatial substance having perception and appetite, whereby apperception arises as a collection of minute unconscious perceptions. Monads were classified into three stages: sleeping monads (or naked monads) in the material stage; souls (or dreaming monads) in the animal stage, possessing sensation and memory; and spirits (or rational souls) in the human stage, possessing universal cognition. In addition, there is the monad on the highest stage, which is God.

d) Wolff (1679–1754)

Based on Leibniz's philosophy, Christian Wolff further systematized the rationalistic position. Yet, in the process of this systematization, Leibniz's original spirit was lost or distorted, and so the main part of Leibniz's theory is missing from Wolff's system. Especially, the theory of monads and the doctrine of pre-established harmony were distorted. Kant belonged to the Wolffian school at first, but later strongly criticized him as representative of rational dogmatism.

Wolff held that true knowledge is the truth of reason, derived logically from fundamental principles. He proposed that all truths be established solely on the basis of the principles of identity and contradiction. He accepted the existence of empirical truths as fact, but according to him, truths of reason have nothing to do with empirical truths, and empirical truths are not necessarily true, but only contingently so. In this way, Continental rationalism attached little importance to the cognition of facts, considering that everything must be cognized rationally, and ultimately ended in dogmatism.[8]

B. Essence of the Object of Cognition

We must next consider the question of the object of cognition. Realism asserts that the object of cognition exists objectively, and independently of the subject, whereas subjective idealism states that the object of cognition does not exist in the objective world, but exists only as an idea within the consciousness of the subject.

1. Realism

Realism is a general perspective, which includes naive realism, scientific realism, idealistic realism and dialectical realism. Naive realism, also called natural realism, is the common sense view that the object is composed of matter and exists independently from the subject; moreover it exists just as we see it. In other words, our perception is a faithful copy of the object. Scientific realism is the view that the object exists independently of the subject, but sensory cognition, as it is, is not necessarily true. True existence can be correctly known only by adding our scientific reflection to the empirical facts already obtained from the object, and this is done through the function of understanding, which transcends mere sensory cognition.

For example, the sense of color is a visual phenomenon. Science examines this phenomenon and clarifies that color (say, red color) is the sensation caused by an electromagnetic wave with a definite wave length. Also, lightning and thunder which are sensed by our eyes and ears are regarded as caused by the electrical discharge taking place in the air. Thus, scientific realism adds scientific reflection to the common sense view of realism.

Idealistic realism, which is also called objective idealism, is the view that the essence of the object is spiritual and objective, transcending human consciousness. Specifically, this view holds that the spirit not only exists in human beings, but existed at the origin of the world even before the appearance of humankind, and that this original spirit is the true reality of the world, and is the prototype of the universe. In this view, all things are the various expressions of the spirit. For example, Plato regarded Ideas, which are the essences of things, as true reality, and asserted that this world is nothing but the shadow of the world of Ideas. Hegel asserted that the world is the self-development of the Absolute Spirit.

Dialectical materialism holds that an object exists independently of human consciousness, and that it is an objective reality that is reflected in our consciousness. Thus dialectical materialism, also, is realism. It asserts that cognition is the reflection from things outside, on human consciousness, just as things are reflected in a mirror. It does not, however, assert, as does naive realism, that an object exists as it is reflected on the subject's consciousness; rather, it asserts that true reality can only be cognized by verification through practice. That is the position of the dialectical epistemology, namely, Communist epistemology.

2. Subjective Idealism

Realism, as was mentioned, views the object of cognition as existing independently from the subject, whether the object is a material being or an idea. Subjective idealism, on the other hand, holds that the object does not exist independently of the human mind and that its existence can be recognized only to the extent that the object appears in the human mind. Berkeley was its representative exponent, and his proposition "to be is to be perceived" (*esse est percipi*) eloquently expresses this position. In addition, Johann G. Fichte (1762–1814) held that no one can ever say for sure whether or not non-ego (the object) exists apart from the function of ego, and Arthur Schopenhauer (1788–1860) said "The world is my representation" (*Die Welt ist mein Vorstellung*), both taking similar positions.

C. Epistemologies in Terms of Method

As we have seen, empiricism, which saw experience as the origin of cognition, developed into skepticism, whereas rationalism, which saw reason as the origin of cognition, developed into dogmatism. They reached these conclusions because they did not examine the questions of how experience becomes truth, and how cognition is made through reason, in other words, the method of cognition. It was Hegel, Marx and Kant who attached importance to the method of cognition. I will introduce here the main points of the Kantian and Marxian methods.

1. Kant's Transcendental Method

British empiricism fell into skepticism, and Continental rationalism fell into dogmatism, but Immanuel Kant (1724-1804) synthesized these two positions and established a new viewpoint. He considered empiricism to be mistaken because it ascribed cognition to experience, disregarding the function of reason, whereas on the other hand, rationalism was mistaken because it regarded reason as almighty. Thus, Kant held that in order to obtain true knowledge, one has to start from an analysis of how experience can become knowledge. To achieve this, one has to examine, or critique, the function of reason.

Kant wrote three books of critique, namely, *Critique of Pure Reason*, *Critique of Practical Reason*, and *Critique of Judgment*, which, respectively, deal with how truth is possible, how good is possible, and how judgment of taste is possible. Accordingly, Kant dealt with the realization of the values of truth, goodness, and beauty. Among his works, the one concerned with epistemology is his *Critique of Pure Reason*.

Main Points of the *Critique of Pure Reason*

Kant tried to unify empiricism and rationalism on the basis of the fact that knowledge increases through experience, and that correct knowledge must have universal validity. It is self-evident that cognition starts from experience. Then, Kant proposed that there existed within the subject of cognition "certain *a priori* forms of cognition." In other words, the object of cognition is established when the sense content (which is also called material, sensation, manifold of sense, or sense data) coming from the object is put in order by the a priori forms of the subject.

All former philosophies had held that the object is grasped as it is; in contrast, Kant said that the object of cognition is actually synthesized by the subject. Through this insight, Kant believed he had effected a Copernican revolution in philosophy. Thus, Kant's epistemology did not seek to obtain knowledge of the object itself, but sought to clarify how objective truthfulness might be obtained. He called it the "transcendental method."

For Kant, cognition is a judgment. A judgment is made in terms of a proposition, and in a proposition there are subject and predicate. Knowledge increases through a judgment (a proposition), in which a new concept that is not contained in the subject appears in the predicate. Kant called such a judgment a "synthetic judgment." In contrast, a judgment in which the concept of the predicate is already contained in the concept of the subject is called an "analytical judgment." Hence, new knowledge is obtained only through a synthetic judgment.

Among the examples given by Kant of analytical and synthetic judgments, there are the following: the judgment that "all bodies are extended" is an analytical judgment, for the concept of body already includes the meaning that it has extension. On the other hand, the judgment that "between two points, the straight line is the shortest line" is a synthetic judgment, for the concept of a straight line indicates only the feature of straightness without containing the quantity of length or shortness. Therefore, the concept of the shortest line is a completely new addition.

Yet, even though new knowledge can be obtained through synthetic judgment, it can not become correct knowledge if it does not have universal validity. In order for knowledge to have universal validity, it should not be merely empirical knowledge, but should have some a priori element independent of experience. That is, in order for a synthetic judgment to have universal validity, it must be an a priori cognition, namely, an a priori synthetic judgment. So, Kant had to cope with the question: "How are *a priori* synthetic judgments possible?"[9]

Content and Form

Kant tried to accomplish the synthesis of empiricism and rationalism through the unity of content and form. "Content" refers to the representations given to our senses through the stimuli from the things in the external world, namely, the content of our mind. Since the content is material coming from the outside, it is an a posteriori, empirical element. On the other hand, "form" refers to the framework, or determinative, that synthesizes or unifies the material, or the manifold of sense. It is the framework that unifies various materials formed in the stage of sensation. In other words, sense content is synthesized by a priori forms. A priori forms consist of the forms of intuition that arrange the manifold of sense in the frame of time and space, and the forms of thought that gives the frame to cognition in the stage of understanding. He argued that, through these a priori forms, synthetic judgments with universal validity become possible.

The forms of intuition are frameworks that perceive the manifold of sense in space and time. Cognition, however, does not take place through intuition alone. Kant said that it is necessary for the object to be thought through understanding, and asserted that a priori concepts, the forms of thought, exist within understanding. In other words, he held that cognition takes place when the content, which is perceived intuitively, and the forms of thought are combined. Kant described it in the following way: "Thoughts without content are empty; intuitions without concepts are blind."[10] Kant named the a priori concepts within the understanding "pure concepts of understanding" or "categories." Based on the judgment forms used in general logic since Aristotle, Kant derived the following twelve categories:

1. Quantity	{ Unity Plurality Totality	3. Relation	{ Substance Causality Reciprocity
2. Quality	{ Reality Negation Limitation	4. Modality	{ Possibility Actuality Necessity

In this way, Kant asserted that cognition becomes possible as the sense content is perceived through the forms of intuition and is thought through the forms of thought (categories).Yet, the sense content in the stage of sensation and the forms of thought in the stage of the understanding are not combined automatically. Sensation and understanding are both faculties of cognition, but they are essentially different. A third force common to the two faculties is necessary. That is the power of imagination (*Einbildingkraft*), with which sense content and the forms of thought are unified, whereby fragmented manifold of sense is synthesized and unified.

Thus, the object of cognition, as Kant says, is the result of the synthesis of the sense content and the forms of thought through the power of imagination. Hence, the object of cognition is not what exists objectively in the external world, but rather it is synthesized in the process of cognition.

We can understand, therefore, that the object of cognition, as Kant says, is something in which the a posteriori element of empiricism and the a priori element of rationalism are unified. The consciousness at the time of cognition should not be empirical or fragmentary, but there must be a pure consciousness underlying empirical consciousness, which has the power to unify. Kant called it "consciousness in general," "pure apperception," or "transcendental apperception." As for the question of how the functions of sensation and understanding are connected, Kant said that imagination serves as the mediator between the two, as mentioned above.

Denial of Metaphysics and the Thing-in-itself

In this way, Kant discussed how certain knowledge is possible in the phenomenal world, namely, in the natural sciences or mathematics, and then examined whether or not metaphysics is possible. Since a metaphysical entity has no sense content, and therefore, can not become an object of perception, it can not be perceived. Since, however, the function of our reason is related to understanding alone and not directly to sensation, there are some cases in which one has an illusion whereby something that does not really exist appears to exist. Kant called this type of illusion "transcendental illusion." The transcendental illusion consist of three types: the idea of the soul, the idea of the world, and the idea of God.[11]

Among these, he called the idea of the world, namely, the cosmological illusion, the antinomy of pure reason. This means that when reason pursues the infinite being (the infinite world), it will reach two entirely opposite conclusions from the same basis of argument. An example of this is the two contradictory propositions: "the world has a beginning in time and is also limited in regard to space" (the thesis) and "the world has no beginning in time and no limits in space, but is infinite in respect to both time and space" (the antithesis). Kant held this to be an error derived from trying to grasp the sense content as the world itself.

Kant held that cognition takes place only to the extent that the sense content coming from the object is synthesized through the a priori forms of the subject, and that the object itself, namely, the "thing-in-itself," can never be cognized. This is the agnosticism of Kant. The world of "things-in-themselves" is the reality lying behind phenomena, and is called the "noumenal reality." Nevertheless, Kant did not totally deny the world of things-in-themselves. In his *Critique of Practical Reason*, he held that noumenal reality is to be postulated in order to establish morality. He also claimed that, in order for noumenal reality to exist, freedom, the immortality of soul, and the existence of God must be postulated.

2. Marxist Epistemology

Next, I will explain the epistemology that is based on the materialist dialectic. This is called Marxist epistemology, or the dialectical materialist theory of knowledge.

Theory of Reflection (Copy Theory)

According to the materialist dialectic, the spirit (consciousness) is a product or a function of the brain,[12] and cognition takes place as objective reality is reflected (copied) onto consciousness. This theory is called the "theory of reflection" or "copy theory" (*teoriya otrazhenia*). Of this, Engels said, "we comprehended the concepts in our heads once more materialistically—as images [*Abbilder*] of real things." [13] Lenin stated that, "From Engels' point of view, the only immutability is the reflection by the human mind (when there is a human mind) of an external world existing and developing independently of the mind."[14] In Marxist epistemology, what Kant called sense content is not the only reflection of the objective world upon consciousness. The forms of thought are also the reflection of the objective world; they are the reflection of the forms of existence.

Sensory Cognition, Rational Cognition, and Practice

Cognition is not merely a reflection of the objective world, but it has to be verified through practice, according to Marxist epistemology. Lenin explains this process as follows: "From living perception to abstract thought, *and from this to practice,*—such is the dialectical path of the cognition of *truth*, of the cognition of objective reality."¹⁵ Mao Ze-dong explained the process of dialectical materialist cognition more concretely in the following quotes:

> This dialectical-materialist theory of the process of development of knowledge, basing itself on practice and proceeding from the shallower to the deeper, was never worked out by anybody before the rise of Marxism···. Marxism-Leninism holds that each of the two stages in the process of cognition has its own characteristics, with knowledge manifesting itself as perceptual at the lower stage and logical at the higher stage, but that both are stages in an integrated process of cognition. The perceptual and the rational are qualitatively different, but are not divorced from each other; they are unified on the basis of practice.¹⁶

> The first step in the process of cognition is contact with the objects of the external world; this belongs to the stage of perception [sensory stage of cognition]. The second step is to synthesize the data of perception by arranging and reconstructing them; this belongs to the stage of conception, judgment and inference [rational stage of cognition].¹⁷

In this way, cognition proceeds from sensory cognition to rational cognition (or logical cognition), and from rational cognition to practice. Now, cognition and practice are not something that take place only once. Mao Ze-dong said "Practice, knowledge, again practice, and again knowledge. This form repeats itself in endless cycles, and with each cycle the content of practice and knowledge rises to a higher level."¹⁸

Kant said that cognition takes place insofar as the subject synthesizes the object, and that it is impossible to cognize the "things-in-themselves" behind the phenomena, advocating agnosticism. In contrast, Marxism asserted that the essence of things can be known only through phenomena, and that things can be known fully through practice, thus rejecting Kant's notion of "things-in-themselves." About Kant, Engels said the following:

> In Kant's time, our knowledge of natural objects was indeed so fragmentary that he might well suspect, behind the little we knew about each of them, a mysterious "thing-in-itself." But one after another

these ungraspable things have been grasped, analyzed, and, what is more, *reproduced* by the giant progress of science; and what we can produce we certainly can not consider as unknowable.[19]

Now, in the continuing process of cognition and practice, practice is held to be of greater importance. Mao Ze-dong said, "The dialectical-materialist theory of knowledge places practice in the primary position, holding that human knowledge can in no way be separated from practice." [20] Practice usually refers to human action on nature and social activities, but in Marxism, revolution is held to be the supreme form of practice among all kinds of practice. Therefore, it can be said that the ultimate purpose of cognition is revolution. In fact, Mao Ze-dong said, "The active function of knowledge manifests itself not only in the active leap from perceptual to rational knowledge, but—and this is more important—it must manifest itself in the leap from rational knowledge to revolutionary practice." [21]

Let us next consider the forms of thought in logical cognition (rational cognition). Logical cognition refers to such acts of thinking as judgment and inference, which are mediated by concepts, and in which the forms of thought play an important role. Marxism, which advocates copy theory, regards the forms of thought as the reflection of the processes in the objective world upon the consciousness, that is, as the reflection of existing forms. Among the categories (forms of existence, forms of thought) in Marxism, there are the following: [22]

matter	proportion
motion	contradiction
space	the individual, particular, and universal
time	cause and effect
the finite and the infinite	necessity and chance
consciousness	possibility and reality
quantity	content and form
quality	essence and appearance

Absolute Truth and Relative Truth

Knowledge, according to Marx, grows through the successive repetition of cognition and practice. That knowledge grows means that the content of knowledge is enriched, and that the accuracy of knowledge is enhanced. Therefore, the relativity and absoluteness of knowledge becomes an issue.

Marxism says that truth is what reflects objective reality correctly. It says that, "If our sensations, perceptions, notions, concepts and theories correspond to objective reality, if they reflect it faithfully, we say that they are *true*, while true statements, judgments or theories are called the *truth*."[23]

Furthermore, Marxism asserts that practice—ultimately revolutionary practice—is the standard of truth. In order to know whether or not cognition is true, all one needs to do is to compare it with reality and ascertain that cognition concurs with reality. Of this, Marx said, "Man must prove the truth, i.e., the reality and power, the this-worldliness of his thinking in practice,"[24] and Mao Ze-dong said, "Man's social practice [class struggle in particular] alone is the criterion of the truth of his knowledge of the external world."[25] In sum, revolutionary practice is the criterion of the truth of knowledge.

According to Marxism, knowledge in a particular period is partial, imperfect, and remains as only relative truth, but with the progress of science, knowledge approaches absolute truth to an infinite degree. Thus, Marxism affirms the existence of absolute truth. Concerning this, Lenin says, "There is no impassable boundary between relative and absolute truth."[26] Also, the elements which are absolutely true are contained within relative truths, and as they are accumulated steadily, they become absolute truth, according to Marxism.[27]

This concludes my explanation about the traditional epistemologies. As mentioned earlier, I introduced, in summary form, certain traditional epistemologies for the reader's reference.

II. Unification Epistemology

We have surveyed an outline of previous epistemologies; now I wish to explain the epistemology of Unification Thought, or Unification epistemology. Unification epistemology has been established on the basis of concepts about cognition in the Divine Principle, Rev. Sun Myung Moon's speeches and sermons, Rev. Moon's responses to direct questions by the author, and so on.[28]

A. Outline of Unification Epistemology

Unification epistemology has, among its other features, the characteristic of being an alternative to traditional epistemologies. Thus, I will introduce Unification epistemology in terms of the topics dealt with by traditional epistemologies, such as the origin, object, and method of cognition.

1. The Origin of Cognition

As already explained, in the seventeenth and eighteenth centuries, empiricism, holding that the origin of cognition lies in one's experience, and rationalism, holding that the origin of cognition lies in one's thinking, emerged. Empiricism fell into skepticism in the hands of Hume, and rationalism ended in dogmatism with the work of Wolff. In order to overcome this impasse, Kant tried to unify empiricism and rationalism through his transcendental method, but he was left with an agnostic world of things-in-themselves. It is in the context of such a background that I will introduce the position of Unification epistemology.

In the former epistemologies, the relationship between the subject of cognition (human being) and the object of cognition (all things) was not well-clarified. Since they did not know the relationship between the human being and all things, emphasis was placed either on the subject of cognition, as in rationalism, asserting that cognition is achieved exactly as reason (or understanding) infers, or else emphasis was placed on the object of cognition, as in empiricism, asserting that cognition is achieved by grasping the object as it is, through sensation.

Kant held that cognition is achieved when the sense content coming from the object and the forms of thought of the subject are synthesized and unified by means of imagination, whereby an object of cognition is finally formed. He was not aware, however, of the necessary relationship between the subject and the object. So for Kant, cognition can be made only within the framework of the categories of the subject, and in the end, he held that the things-in-themselves are unknowable.

Hegel held that in the self-development of the absolute spirit, Idea becomes nature by alienating itself, but eventually restores itself through the human spirit. In this system, nature is merely an intermediate step leading up to the rise of the human spirit, and has no positive meaning as a permanent existence. Finally, in Marxism, the human being and nature are in an accidental relationship of opposition.

When we look at the problem in this way, how to understand correctly the relationship between the subject of cognition (human being) and the object of cognition (all things) becomes a crucial issue. From an atheistic position, the necessary relationship between human beings and nature can not be established. Even in the theory of the natural generation of the universe, human beings and nature are no more than accidental beings to each other. Only when the significance of God's creation of human beings and all things has been clarified, can the necessary relationship between human beings and all things become clear.

From the perspective of Unification Thought, human beings and all things are beings created in the relationship of subject and object. That is to say, the human being is the lord of dominion, or the subject of dominion over all things, and all things are objects of joy, beauty, and dominion for human beings. Subject and object are in an inseparable relationship. This might be compared to the relationship between the motor and the working parts in a machine. The working parts are meaningless without a motor, and vice-versa. The two components are designed to form a necessary relationship of subject and object. By the same token, human beings and all things have been created in such a way that both exist in a necessary relationship.

Cognition is the judgment of a human subject on all things, which are the objects of joy, beauty, and dominion. In this connection, cognition (i.e., judgment) involves "experience," and judgment is carried out through the function of "reason." Therefore, experience and reason are both necessary. Thus, in Unification epistemology, experience and reason are both indispensable, and cognition takes place through the unified operation of the two. Furthermore, since the human being and all things are in the relationship of subject and object, we can know all things fully and correctly.

2. The Object of Cognition

Unification Thought, first of all, acknowledges that all things exist objectively, outside the human being; that is, it accepts realism. As the subject of all things, the human being exercises dominion over all things—activities such as cultivating, raising, dealing with, processing, and making use of all things—and also cognizes all things. For that reason, all things must exist outside and independently of the human being, as objects of cognition and of dominion.

Furthermore, Unification Thought holds that the human being is the integration of all things, a microcosm—and therefore, that the human being is equipped with all the structures, elements, and qualities of all things. This is so because all things of the natural world have been created in symbolic resemblance to the human being, with the human body as the model. Therefore, the human being and all things have a mutual resemblance. Moreover, within the human being, the body is created in resemblance to the mind.

Cognition is always accompanied by judgment, and judgment is an act of measurement. For this measurement, standards (*criteria*) are necessary, and there are ideas existing within the human mind which serve as the standards of cognition. These ideas are called "prototypes." Each prototype is an image within the mind, and it is an internal object. Cognition takes place as a prototype within the mind (internal image) and an image coming from an external object (external image) are collated.

Realism insisted on the objective existence of the object of cognition, independently of human consciousness. Marxism, which advocates copy theory, is its representative exponent. Subjective idealism, as represented by Berkeley, asserted, on the contrary, that the object of cognition is nothing but ideas in human consciousness. In Unification epistemology, realism and idealism (subjective idealism) are unified.

3. The Method of Cognition

The method in Unification epistemology differs both from Kant's transcendental method, and also from Marx's dialectical method. The give and receive method, that is, the principle of give and receive action between subject and object, is the method in Unification epistemology. Accordingly, in terms of method, Unification epistemology can be called a "give and receive epistemology."

In the give and receive action between the subject (human being) and object (all things) in cognition, both subject and object must have certain requisites. As already explained in the Theory of Art, for example, subject and object must possess certain requisites in appreciation. In the appreciation of a work of art, the conditions that the subject (appreciator) must possess are: a concern for, or an interest in, the object, a desire to seek value, and the subjective elements of education, taste, and so on.

The object (work of art) should be equipped with a purpose of creation, and should possess harmony among its various elements. In cognition, the condition for the subject is to have a prototype and a concern for the object, and the condition for the object is to have content (i.e., attributes) and form.

In accordance with the two-stage structure, give and receive action in cognition consists of both inner and outer give and receive actions. Cognition takes place first as outer give and receive action, and then as inner give and receive action. Again, we mention that this theory of cognition is called a "give and receive epistemology."

Give and receive action takes place between a subject (human being) possessing the necessary requisites and an object (all things) possessing the necessary requisites. First, the content (attributes) and form (forms of existence) of the object are reflected in the human mind at the sensory stage, forming sensory content and form, which may be called an "external image," since it is brought about by the outer give and receive action. Then, give and receive action (of the collation type) takes place between the external content and form (external image) and the prototype (internal image) which the human subject possesses a priori. This is the inner give and receive action, or the formation of the inner four position foundation. Cognition is accomplished through this inner give and receive action.

Here, I can explain the differences between the method of Unification epistemology, the Kantian transcendental method, and the Marxist dialectical method. In Kant's method, the content (sense content) comes from the external world (object), and the forms (the forms of intuition and forms of thought) are a priori and subjective elements within the subject. Thus, the content belongs to the object, and the form belongs to the subject. In contrast, in the Unification Thought give and receive epistemology, content and form both belong to both subject and object. That is, both subject and object possess content and form.

In the Marxist method, content and form both belong to the object in the external world, and the consciousness of the subject simply reflects them. Thus, it can rightfully be said that the elements of both Kantian and Marxian epistemologies are contained in Unification epistemology. In other words, in Unification epistemology, there is an element of copy theory in the outer give and receive action, and there is an element of the transcendental method in the inner give and receive action. Thus, within

Unification epistemology the dialectical method (copy theory) and transcendental method (Kantian method) are unified.

B. Content and Form in Cognition

Usually, in speaking of content and form, we call what is contained inside a thing its content, and its external appearance, its form. The content dealt with in epistemology, however, refers to the attributes of a thing, while the form refers to a certain framework through which those attributes are manifested.

Content of the Object and Content of the Subject

Since the object of cognition is all things, the content of an object refers to the various attributes it possesses, namely, shape, weight, length, motion, color, sound, smell, taste, and so on. These are material content (or *hyungsang* content). On the other hand, the subject of cognition is a human being; therefore, the content of the subject refers to the various attributes that a human being possesses, which actually are the same as the attributes of all things, that is, material content, such as, shape, weight, length, motion, color, sound, smell, taste, and so on.

Usually when we talk about human attributes, in many cases we are referring to reason, freedom, spirituality, etc., but in epistemology, since we are dealing with the resemblance in content, we focus on the same attributes as those of the object (all things). As the integration of the universe (microcosm), the human being possesses, in miniature, all the structures, elements, qualities, and so on, that all things possess. Therefore, the human being is equipped with the same attributes as all things.

Give and receive action in cognition, however, does not take place merely because the subject (human being) and the object (all things) possess the same attributes. Since cognition is a phenomenon of thinking, the mind of the subject should also possess a certain content. The content in the mind of the subject is the prototype, or more accurately, that part of the prototype that corresponds to the content. This refers to the "protoimage," which appears in the protoconsciousness (subconsciousness in the living being, which will be further explained below). The protoimage is a mental image that exists in correspondence with the attributes of the human body.

The attributes of the human body are in correspondence with the attributes (material content) of all things in the external world. Therefore, the mental image (protoimage), or prototype, becomes the mental content that corresponds to the attributes of all things. Thus, the attributes of the human body correspond to the attributes of all things, and the mental image (protoimage) of the human mind corresponds to the attributes of the human body. Then, accordingly, the human mental image corresponds to the attributes of all things. Therefore, in cognition, the mental image (protoimage) of the subject (human being) and the material content (sense content) of the object are in correspondence with each other; give and receive action takes place between them, thus giving rise to cognition.

Form of the Object and Form of the Subject

The attributes of all things, which are the object of cognition, always appear in a certain framework. This framework is the form of existence. The form of existence is the form of relation among the attributes of those things. This form of existence, or form of relation, becomes the form of the object in cognition. The human body is a miniature of the universe (microcosm), and the integration of all things; therefore, the human body has the same form of existence as that of all things. The form in cognition is the form within the mind, that is, the form of thought. This is a reflection of the form of existence of the human body in the protoconsciousness, in other words, the image of form (or the image of relation), forming a part of the prototype.

Elements Making Up a Prototype

The mental image within the subject, which becomes the standard of judgment in cognition, is called the prototype. The prototype is made up of the following elements.

First, there is the protoimage. This is the image of the attributes of the cells and tissues (elements making up the human body) reflected in the protoconsciousness. In other words, the protoimage is the image of the attributes of the cells and tissues reflected in the "mirror" of the protoconsciousness.

The second element is the image of relation, that is, the form of thought. Not only the attributes of cells and tissues of the human body, but also the form of existence (form of relation) of those attributes are reflected in the protoconsciousness, forming the image of relation. This image of relation gives certain restrictions to the action of thinking, forming the form of thought.

The above-mentioned protoimage and image of relation (form of thought) are ideas that have nothing to do with experience, that is, they are a priori ideas; but in prototypes, there are also acquired ideas that are added through our experiences. The ideas obtained through experiences (i.e., prior to the current cognition) are empirical ideas and form a part of the prototypes in subsequent cognition. Therefore, when we encounter things that are similar to what we learned before, we can easily recognize them. Thus, a prototype consists of the protoimage, the image of relation (form of thought) and empirical ideas.

As stated above, a prototype consists of an a priori element, which exists prior to experiences, and an element acquired through experience, namely, the empirical element. The a priori element is the prototype which consists of the protoimage and the image of relation within protoconsciousness. This is an "a priori prototype" that has nothing to do with external experiences. It is also called an "original prototype." The empirical element refers to the empirical ideas that have been acquired through our daily life experiences, and once they have been acquired they become a part of the prototype. This is called an "empirical prototype." A prototype which consists of an a priori prototype and an empirical prototype is called a "complex prototype." As a matter of fact, all the prototypes in our daily life are actually complex prototypes.

Pre-existence of the Prototype, and Its Development

In any instance of cognition, a prototype that has been formed prior to it, namely, a complex prototype, functions as a standard of judgment. This means that, in any cognition, a standard of judgment (a prototype) already exists. Kant maintained that the forms possessed by the subject of cognition are a priori, whereas Unification epistemology asserts the pre-existence of the prototype which is possessed by the subject.

The original prototypes (protoimages and images of relation) with which people are born are imperfect in the case of a newborn baby because the cells, tissues, organs, nerves, sense organs, brain and so on, of the infant, are not well developed yet; therefore, the infant's cognition can not but be vague. However, as the infant's body develops and grows, the protoimages and images of relation gradually become clearer and clearer.

Furthermore, new ideas acquired through experience are added one by one. In this way, the prototype grows in quality and in quantity, which means that there is an increase in the amount of memory and an increase in new knowledge; namely, the progress of the empirical prototype and the complex prototype.

C. Protoconsciousness, Image in Protoconsciousness, and Category

Protoconsciousness

According to the Divine Principle, "all beings in the creation grow by virtue of the autonomy and governance given by God's Principle" (*DP*, 43). Autonomy and governance (or dominion) are characteristics of the life force. Life is the subconsciousness existing within the cells and tissues of living beings, and it has the capacity of sensitivity, perceptiveness, and purposiveness. Sensitivity is the ability to perceive the information of things intuitively; perceptiveness is the ability to maintain the state of perception; and purposiveness is the will-power to maintain and actualize a certain purpose.

"Protoconsciousness" here means original consciousness, and refers to that cosmic consciousness which has entered into a cell or tissue. From the perspective of the function of the mind, the protoconsciousness is the mind functioning on a lower level.[29] Therefore, it may be said to be a lower level function of the cosmic mind, or a lower level of God's mind. Protoconsciousness is also life. Once the cosmic consciousness enters cells and tissues, it becomes individualized and we can call it protoconsciousness or life. In other words, life is that cosmic consciousness which has entered cells or tissues. Just as an electric wave enters a radio and produces sound, so, too, does cosmic consciousness enter cells and tissues and give them life.[30] In short, then, protoconsciousness is life, and it is subconsciousness with sensitivity, perceptiveness, and purposiveness.

In Unification Thought it is asserted that when God created the universe through Logos, He inscribed all the information pertaining to each living being (i.e., Logos) in the cells of that being in the material form of a code. This code is the genetic code, which is a specific arrangement of the four kinds of bases (adenine, guanine, thymine, and cytosine) in DNA (deoxyribonucleic acid). This is because God wanted each living being to be able to multiply and maintain its species from generation to generation.

It is written in Genesis 2:7 that "the Lord God formed man of dust from the ground, and breathed into his nostrils the breath of life." With regard to things in the natural world, it could also be said that "God formed cells out of dust and poured life into them. So the cells became living cells." The cosmic consciousness which has entered into the cell is protoconsciousness, or life. Living beings become alive once cosmic consciousness has entered into their cells, tissues, and organs.

Function of Protoconsciousness

Let me explain the function of protoconsciousness. Protoconsciousness has various functions, including the reading of the genetic information (code), acting according to the direction of the information, and transmitting the information.

Let me explain these in turn. First, when cosmic consciousness enters into a cell, it reads the genetic code of the DNA of that cell. Following its reading of the genetic code, the protoconsciousness then causes the cells and tissues to act according to the instructions contained in the code. It acts to make cells and tissues develop, and these and new organs to grow and to form relationships with other cells, tissues, and organs. All this information about the cells and tissues is transmitted to the central nerves along the peripheral nerves (centripetal nerves), and the central nerves send directions to the cells and tissues through the peripheral nerves (centrifugal nerves). It is the protoconsciousness that transmits all this information; that is to say, the protoconsciousness plays the role of the giving and receiving of information between the center and cells and tissues. These are some of the functions of the protoconsciousness. All of these functions are based on the sensitivity, perceptivity, and purposiveness of the protoconsciousness. As the protoconsciousness carries these functions out over time, the protoimage and the image of relations develop, and become clearer.

Formation of the Image in Protoconsciousness

The subconsciousness within living beings, namely, the protoconsciousness, possesses sensitivity. Therefore, the protoconsciousness senses intuitively the structure, constituents, qualities, and so on, of the cells and tissues. Furthermore, the protoconsciousness even senses changes in the situation existing inside the cells and tissues. This content sensed by the protoconsciousness, that is, the image that is thus reflected onto the protoconsciousness, is the "protoimage." The idea that a protoimage is produced in the protoconsciousness can be compared to the phenomenon wherein a material object is reflected in a mirror, or in the way a material object is caught on film through exposure. Protoconsciousness has perceptiveness, which is the ability to maintain the state of perception, in other words, continuing to keep the protoimage. Thus, perceptiveness might also be regarded as a kind of memory.

The various elements within a human body, such as cells, tissues, and organs, exist, function, and grow through performing inner and outer give and receive actions as individual truth beings and as connected beings. In the case of a cell, for example, give and receive action between various elements (such as nucleus and cytoplasm) within the cell is inner give and receive action, and give and receive action between the cell and other cells is outer give and receive action. In these give and receive actions, various relationships are established. The condition or framework allowing for such relationship is called the "form of relation." All things, without exception, can exist only in accordance with this condition; therefore, the form of relation can also be called the "form of existence." The form of existence is the framework that was established when all things came to exist.

The form of existence is reflected on the protoconsciousness, forming a certain image there; we call this image an "image of relation" or an "image of form." Protoconsciousness thus has protoimage and image of relation (image of form), which together we call the "image in protoconsciousness."

Formation of the Forms of Thought

As already explained, the content possessed by the subject of cognition (human being) includes material content (*hyungsang* content) and mental content (*sungsang* content). The material content is the same as the attributes of the object (things), and the mental content is the protoimage. The material content is related to the mental content, as its corresponding element.

Here, a corresponding element refers to the partner element among the paired elements that are in the relationship of one-to-one. The relationship between a material object and its shadow is an example. When the material object moves, the shadow also moves, and when the material object stops, the shadow also stops. In this case, the material object is called the corresponding element to the shadow.

In the relationship between body and mind, when the body is healthy, the mind becomes healthy, and when the body is weak, the mind also becomes weak. Hence, the body is the corresponding element to the mind. Similarly, in the relationship of the material form (*hyungsang* form) and the mental form (*sungsang* form) of the subject of cognition, the former is the corresponding element to the latter. The material form is the form of existence of the object.

As already mentioned, the human body is the integration of the universe; therefore, the attributes of all things become directly the attributes of the human body, and the attributes of the human body are reflected on the protoconsciousness, forming protoimages, namely, the mental content. In the same way, the form of existence of all things is the same as the form of existence of the human body, which is itself reflected on the protoconsciousness, thus forming the mental form, namely, the image of relation. The mental form is the form of thought. That is, the root of the form of thought is the form of existence. Thus, the corresponding element of the form of thought is the form of existence.

The forms of relation (forms of existence) in cells and tissues are reflected on the protoconsciousness, forming the images of relation. The images of relation in the protoconsciousness are passed from the peripheral nerves to the lower nerve centers as bits of information and gather together at the upper center (cortex center). In this process, the images of relation are synthesized and arranged to shape the forms of thought at the cortex center. Forms of thought, therefore, come to exist as mental forms corresponding to the forms of existence in the external world.

When we engage in thinking, these forms of thought function as the framework which our thinking follows. That is, thinking is carried out according to the forms of thought. In other words, the forms of thought guide, restrict, or limit our thinking. Forms of thought are the same as categories, which are, in any philosophy, the most fundamental, general basic concepts.

Forms of Existence and Forms of Thought

Since the element corresponding to the form of thought is the form of existence, in order for us to understand the form of thought, we must first understand the form of existence. In order for things to exist, individual beings (or elements) should be related to each other, whereby the form of relation is the form of existence. From the Unification Thought perspective, there are ten basic forms of existence, as follows:

(1) *Existence and Force*: The existence of every being is always accompanied by the operation of force. There is no force apart from existence, and no existence apart from force. This is because the Prime Force from God makes all things exist by exerting power on them.

(2) *Sungsang and Hyungsang*: Every being consists of an inner, invisible, functional aspect and an outer, visible mass, structure, and shape.

(3) *Yang and Yin*: Every being has the characteristics of yang and yin as attributes of *sungsang* and *hyungsang*. Yang and yin are at work both in space and in time. Beauty is manifested through the harmony of yang and yin.

(4) *Subject and Object*: Every being exists through performing give and receive action between correlative elements within itself and between itself and another being in the relationship of subject and object.

(5) *Position and Settlement*: Every being exists in a certain position. That is, an appropriate being is settled in each position.

(6) *Unchangeability and Changeability*: Every being has both unchanging and changing aspects. This is because every created being embodies the unity between the identity-maintaining four position foundation (static four position foundation) and the developmental four position foundation (dynamic four position foundation).

(7) *Action and Effect*: Whenever the correlative elements of subject and object in a being enter into give and receive action, an effect always appears. That is, through give and receive action those elements form a united being, or give rise to a new being (multiplied being).

(8) *Time and Space*: Every being is a temporal and spatial being, existing in time and space. This is because to exist is to form a four position foundation (a foundation in space) and to engage in the Origin-Division-Union Action (an action in time).

(9) *Number and Principle*: Every being is a mathematical being, and at the same time a law-governed being. In other words, in every being, numbers are always united with laws, or principles.[31]

(10) *Finite and Infinite*: Every being has the aspect of being finite while at same time possessing an aspect of being infinite: Every being is a momentary being and at the same time endures by carrying out circular movement.

These ten are the most basic forms of existence and are established on the basis of the four position foundation, give and receive action, and Origin-Division-Union Action as explained in the Divine Principle. These are the forms of existence of all things, which are the objects of cognition, and at the same time they are the forms of existence of the components of the physical body of the human being, who is the subject of cognition.

The mental forms corresponding to these forms of existence are the forms of thought. That is, (1) existence and force, (2) *sungsang* and *hyungsang*, (3) yang and yin, (4) subject and object, (5) position and settlement, (6) unchangeability and changeability, (7) action and effect, (8) time and space, (9) number and principle, and (10) finite and infinite are, just as they are, the forms of thought. The forms of existence are material forms of relation, whereas the forms of thought (mental) are basic concepts, which are the forms of relationships among ideas.

Of course, there can be other forms of existence and forms of thought in addition to those mentioned above, which are the most basic in the Unification Thought perspective. It is not true that the forms of thought are, as Kant maintained, unrelated to existence; also, it is not at all the case that the forms of existence of the external world reflect, or give rise to, the forms of thought, as is stated in Marxism. Human beings, themselves, from the very beginning, are equipped with forms of thought, which correspond to the forms of existence appearing in the external world. For example, because human beings are themselves beings with temporal and spatial natures from the very beginning, they possess the forms of thought of time and space, and because they are themselves beings with subjectivity and objectivity, they possess the forms of thought of subject and object. Thus, human beings are endowed with forms of thought, which precisely correspond to the forms of existence.

D. Method of Cognition

Give and Receive Action

In the Divine Principle it is stated that when subject and object elements of an entity are engaged in give and receive action, forming a common base, this action generates "all the forces the entity needs for existence, multiplication and action" (*DP*, 22). Here "multiplication," in a broader sense of the term, means coming into being, generation, increase, and development. "Action" means movement, change, reaction, and so on.

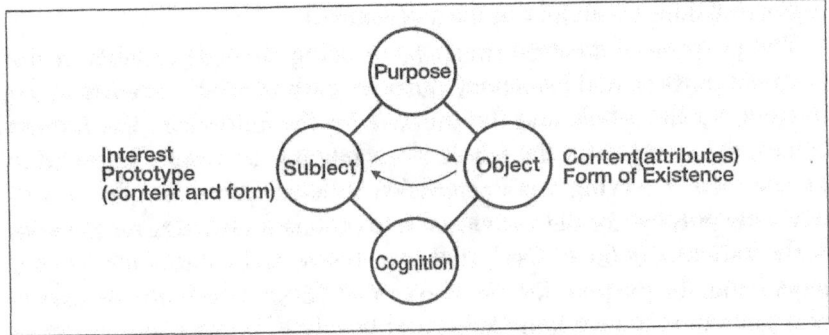

Fig. 9.1. Formation of a Four Position Foundation in Cognition

Since cognition means the acquisition or increase of knowledge, it can be included in the concept of "multiplication" through give and receive action. Accordingly, the proposition can be established that cognition takes place through give and receive action between subject and object.

"Subject" in cognition refers to a person with certain conditions, namely, an interest in the object and appropriate prototypes; "object," on the other hand, refers to all things having content (attributes) and form (forms of existence). Cognition takes place through the give and receive action between these two parties.

Formation of Four Position Foundation

Give and receive action between subject and object always takes place centering on a purpose, and cognition occurs as a result of give and receive action. Therefore, cognition is accomplished through the formation of a four position foundation (fig. 9.1).

The four position foundation is composed of four positions, namely, the center, subject, object, and result. Each of these will be explained next.

(1) Center

It is purpose that becomes the center of give and receive action. In purpose one can find the principle purpose and the daily, more ordinary purpose. The principle purpose refers to the purpose of creation for which God created humankind and all things. From the perspective of created beings, this is the purpose for which they were created. In God's purpose of creation, Heart (love) was the motivation for creation. Therefore, the original way of cognition for human beings is, also, to cognize all things with love as the motivation.

The purpose of creation (purpose of being created) consists of the *sungsang* purpose and *hyungsang* purpose, each of which consists of the purpose for the whole and the purpose for the individual. For human beings, the purpose for the whole in cognition is to acquire knowledge for the sake of serving one's neighbors, society, nation, and the world, while the purpose for the individual is to acquire knowledge for the sake of the individual's life of food, clothing, shelter, and cultural life. On the other hand, the purpose for the whole of all things, which are the objects of cognition, is to give knowledge and beauty to human beings and to give them joy by receiving dominion from them, whereas the purpose for the individual of all things is to be recognized and loved by human beings, as well as to maintain their existence and growth. However, due to the human fall, things can not fully fulfill their purpose of creation (the purpose for being created), and have been "groaning in travail together until now" (Rom. 8:22).

The daily (or actual) purpose refers to the individual purpose based on the principle purpose, namely, the purpose of each person in his or her daily life. For example, a botanist observing nature will acquire knowledge from the perspective of occupying an academic position; a painter observing this same nature will probably acquire knowledge from the position of pursuing beauty. Also, an economist may try to acquire knowledge about nature from the viewpoint of conducting business by developing nature. All of them do so in order to obtain joy. In this way, even though the principle purpose may be the same, the daily purpose for each individual person differs from person to person.

(2) Subject

In cognition, the subject's interest in the object is one of the requisites for the subject. Without interest, no common base can be established, and no give and receive action can take place. Consider, for instance, the case of a person walking down the street who happens to cross the path of a friend. If the person's mind is deeply absorbed in thought, the friend may pass by totally unnoticed. Also, the wife of a lighthouse attendant may not be awakened by the noise of the waves, but she can easily be awakened by the sound of a crying child, which may actually be much softer than the sound of the waves. The reason the noise of the waves is not perceived is that the wife has no real interest in that; in contrast, the sound of the crying child is more easily perceived because she is always concerned about it.

On the other hand, it is also often the case that we recognize things by chance. An obvious example is that, even though we may not expect it, we may suddenly see lightning and hear the sound of thunder. In such a case, it might seem that cognition takes place even if the subject has no interest. Even in this case, however, interest is always at work, though perhaps only unconsciously (or subconsciously). All of us remember, in the years of childhood, when we faced everything with a fresh sense of wonder and curiosity. This wonder and curiosity derive from our interest. When we visit a new place for the first time, we usually look at everything with a great deal of interest. As time goes by, however, we become familiar with the place, and our interest recedes to the subconscious mind. Yet, even then, interest is not gone completely, but is at work in the subconscious mind.

Another requisite for the subject is to possess prototypes. No matter how much interest one may have in a given object, if one does not have appropriate prototypes, cognition will not take place. For example, when listening to an unknown foreign language for the first time, we will not understand what is being said. Also, when meeting a person never seen before, we will just feel that the person is a "stranger"; but if we have seen that person before but forgotten him or her, that person will seem familiar. Accordingly, in order for cognition to take place, the subject must always be in possession of prototypes, which serve as the standards of judgment.

(3) Object

According to the Divine Principle, all things were created as objects to the human being, and the human being was created as the subject (the ruler) over all things. The human being, who is the subject, exerts dominion with love over all things, the objects, whereby he or she engages in appreciation and cognition of them. Therefore, all things are equipped with elements that enable them to become objects of beauty and objects of cognition. Those elements are the attributes of all things (which are the *content*) and the forms of existence of all things (which are the *form*). Such "content" and "form" are requisites that all things must have. They are not something that all things have acquired by themselves; rather, they have been endowed by God with these elements.

The human being is the integration of all things and a miniature of the universe (or microcosm); therefore, as a microcosm, the human being is equipped with the content and form that corresponds to the content and form of all things. As objects of cognition, there are all things in nature, as well as things, events, and persons in human society.

(4) Result

When a subject and an object engage in give and receive action, centering on a purpose, a result comes into being. In order to understand the nature of this result, we need to understand the nature of the four position foundation. As is explained in the Theory of the Original Image, the four position foundation can be classified into four kinds: inner identity-maintaining four position foundation, outer identity-maintaining four position foundation, inner developmental four position foundation, and outer developmental four position foundation. Cognition is basically the process of collating and uniting, through give and receive action, the "content and form" of the subject and the "content and form" of the object. When that happens, an identity-maintaining four position foundation is formed. On the other hand, a developmental four position foundation is formed in the case of the human activity of dominion.

Cognition is closely associated with dominion. There is no dominion without cognition, and there is no cognition without dominion. Cognition and dominion form reciprocal circuits of give and receive action between human beings and all things. That is to say, the process of cognition is one circuit (from the object to the subject), and the process of dominion is the other circuit (from the subject to the object). Then, let us examine the relationship between the developmental four position foundation in dominion and the identity-maintaining four position foundation in cognition. Dominion here refers to the exercise of one's creativity; therefore, the four position foundation in dominion is the same as the four position foundation in creation.

As explained in the Theory of the Original Image, God created all things through the two stages of creation, namely, the formation of the inner developmental four position foundation (i.e., the formation of Logos) and the formation of the outer developmental four position foundation. In this sequential process, first the inner developmental four position foundation was formed, and then the outer developmental four position foundation was formed. Thus, all things were created in

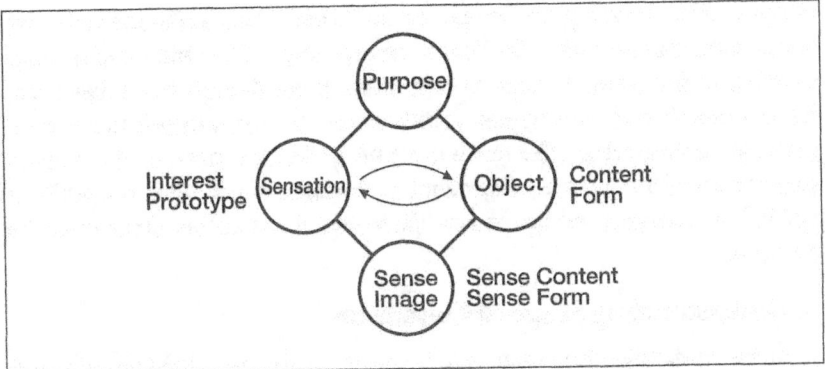

Fig. 9.2. Formation of the Outer Identity-Maintaining Four Position Foundation

sequence, "from the inner to the outer four position foundations." In contrast, in the formation of the identity-maintaining four position foundation for cognition, first, the outer identity-maintaining four position foundation is formed, and then the inner identity-maintaining four position foundation is formed. Thus, cognition takes place in sequence, "from the outer to the inner four position foundations."

Hence, cognition is accomplished as the result of the formation of the inner identity-maintaining four position foundation, whereby the external element and the internal element are collated. Then, more concretely, what is cognition? This will be clarified next.

E. Process of Cognition

We acquire various bits of knowledge through cognition, whereby cognition is accomplished through the three stages of formation, growth and completion, namely, a sensory stage, an understanding stage, and a rational stage, in the same manner as that in which all things grow through the three stages of formation, growth, and completion.

1. Sensory Stage of Cognition

This is the formation stage of cognition. In this stage the outer identity-maintaining four position foundation is first formed. Centering on either a conscious or an unconscious purpose, give and receive action between the subject (human being) and the object (all things) takes place, and the content and form of the object are reflected in the sensory centers of the subject, thus forming an image, or an "idea." This sense content and sense form can be called the "sense image" (fig. 9.2), which is the image existing in the sensory stage of cognition. Even though the subject may have interest and prototypes at this stage, the prototypes are not yet actively participating. The sense content and sense form at the sensory stage of cognition are only fragmentary images, which have not yet been unified as cognition of the object. Therefore, it is not yet clear what the object is.

2. Understanding Stage of Cognition

In the understanding stage of cognition, or the growth stage of cognition, the inner identity-maintaining four position foundation is formed through the inner identity-maintaining give and receive action, and the fragmentary images transmitted in the sensory stage of cognition become a unified image of the object.

The purpose at the center of the inner identity-maintaining four position foundation is the same as the purpose at the center of the outer identity-maintaining four position foundation at the sensory stage of cognition. This is a principle purpose or an actual regular purpose. What comes into the position of subject here is the inner *sungsang*, namely, the functional part of the mind, which, in cognition, is the unity of intellect, emotion, and will. Mind refers to the union of the spirit mind and the physical mind, which is the "original mind" of human beings; this is different in dimension from the instinct in animals.

In cognition, the spirit mind makes a judgment of value, while the physical mind manages sensation, and they jointly engage in the work of memory. Thus, the original mind, which is the unity of the spirit mind and physical mind, manages sensation and memory while oriented to values (truth, goodness, and beauty).

Here, we use the special term "spiritual apperception" to refer to the functional part of the mind in cognition.[32] In cognition, the spiritual apperception, or inner *sungsang*, functions as the power to apperceive, the power to make a comparison, the power to make a judgment of values, and the power to memorize, while in practice, it also functions as subjectivity and works as the power to realize values.

Next, what comes in the position of object in the inner four position foundation? First, the sense image, namely, the sense content and sense form that have been formed in the outer four position foundation in the

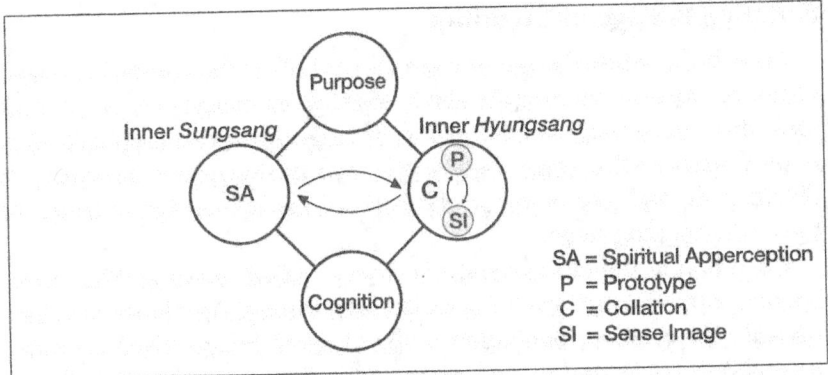

Fig. 9.3. Formation of the Inner Identity-Maintaining Four Position Foundation

sensory stage of cognition, is transmitted to the position of the object in the inner four position foundation, that is, to the inner *hyungsang*. Then the protoimage and the form of thought (that is, the prototype) corresponding to the sense content and sense form are drawn by the spiritual apperception from within the memory. These two elements, namely, the sense image and the prototype are held in the inner *hyungsang*.

Under these circumstances, give and receive action of the collation type takes place. This is so because the spiritual apperception, which is the subject, compares the two elements (i.e., the prototype and the sense image) and makes a judgment as to their agreement or disagreement, whereby the inner identity-maintaining four position foundation is formed as shown in fig. 9.3. Cognition takes place through this judgment, which is called "collation" in Unification epistemology. Thus, we come to the conclusion that cognition, per se, takes place through collation. Consequently, Unification epistemology is a "theory of collation" in terms of method, whereas Marxist epistemology was a "theory of reflection" and Kant's epistemology was a "theory of synthesis."

Sometimes, however, cognition may not be sufficiently well established through a single cognitive process (inner give and receive action) at the understanding stage.[33] In such a case, inner give and receive action continues together with practice (i.e., experiments, observations, experiences, etc.) until a new, and sufficiently clear, cognition is obtained.

3. Rational Stage of Cognition

Next is the rational stage of cognition, which is the completion stage cognition. Reason refers to the ability to think by means of concepts and ideas. Reason operates as the function of judgment and conceptualization in the understanding stage, while in the rational stage, new knowledge is obtained through reasoning on the basis of the knowledge obtained in the understanding stage.

Cognition in the rational stage is what is called thinking. This corresponds to the formation of Logos (a plan) through the inner developmental four position foundation in the Original Image. Thinking takes place through give and receive action within the mind, which is collation type give and receive action. That is, necessary elements are chosen from among the various ideas, concepts, mathematical principles, laws, and so on, already existing in the inner *hyungsang*, and under the influence of the inner *sungsang*, various mental operations, such as association, separation, synthesis, and analysis, are performed, utilizing those elements.

These operations are all performed on the foundation of give and receive action of the collation type; in other words, the inner *sungsang* compares idea and idea, concept and concept, and so forth, whereby new ideas or concepts are acquired. For example, one might compare the idea of "man" and the idea of "boy," and if they are related to each other, one arrives at the new idea of "father and son." For another example, one compares the idea of "society" and the idea of "system," and if they are related to each other, one can arrive at a new concept, "social system." Thus, operations using ideas refers to the acquisition of a new idea or a new concept from the various ideas and concepts contained within the inner *hyungsang*. Knowledge increases through the repetition of such operations. In these operations (inner give and receive actions) as well, the inner *sungsang* functions as spiritual apperception. Cognition in the rational stage is the formation of the inner developmental four position foundation (fig. 9.4).

In the rational state of cognition, acquisition of new knowledge takes place continually through completing each stage of judgment. That is to say, each new bit of knowledge that is obtained (completed judgment) is transmitted, in turn, to the inner *hyungsang*, and can be used in the formation of new knowledge at the next stage. This is the way knowledge develops. That is, knowledge develops by repeating the formation of the

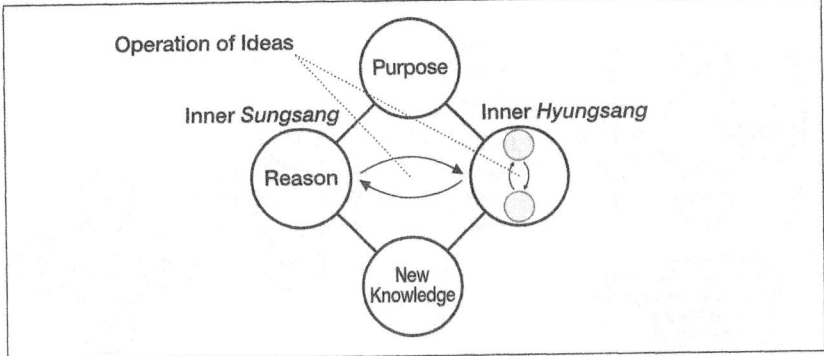

Fig. 9.4. Formation of the Inner Developmental Four Position Foundation

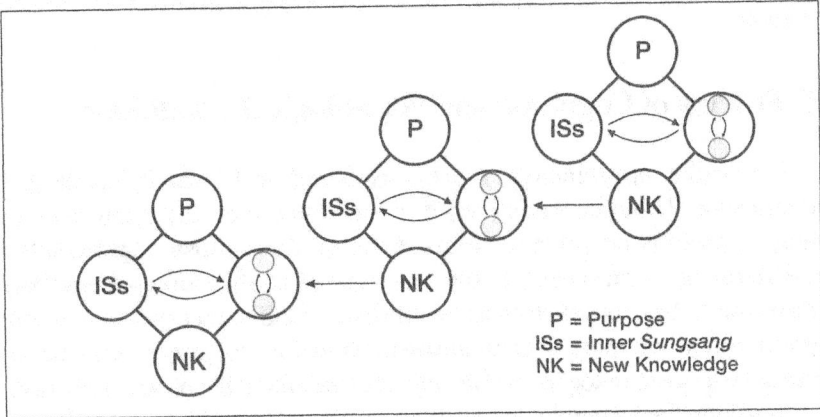

Fig. 9.5. Formation of Repetitive Inner Four Position Foundations through Reasoning

inner four position foundation (fig. 9.5).

Development of this kind of inner four position foundation takes place together with practice. The result (new being) obtained through practice is passed on to the inner *hyungsang* of the *sungsang* (inner four position foundation), and is used for the acquisition of new knowledge. When new knowledge is obtained, its truth can be tested through yet another instance of practice. In this way, repetitive instances of practice, that is, repetitive formations of outer four position foundations, take place together with the development of inner four position foundations for cognition (fig. 9.6).

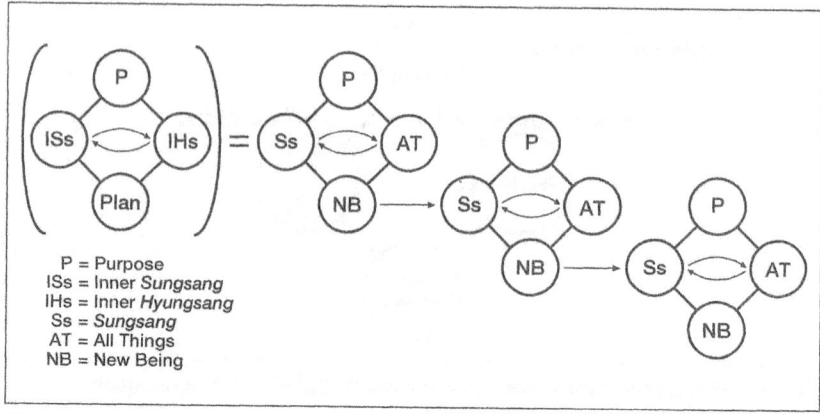

Fig. 9.6. Formation of Repetitive Outer Four Position Foundations through Practice

F. Process of Cognition and Physiological Conditions

Unification epistemology is a theory based on Divine Principle and Unification Thought. Therefore, it is inevitable that this epistemology may contain concepts and terms different from those of traditional epistemologies. However, if any assertion of Unification epistemology turns out to be contradictory to established scientific theories, then it will stand as nothing more than an unsubstantiated claim, just as was true for many past epistemologies, and its universal validity will not be ascertained.

Traditional epistemologies, such as empirical, rational, transcendental, and materialist epistemologies, have shown themselves to be theories having little if anything to do with accepted scientific knowledge; in other words, it has been proven that they are in disagreement with established scientific views. Consequently, they have little persuasiveness today, in view of the great development the sciences have achieved. This section offers evidence to show that Unification epistemology is, in fact, a valid theory, and that it is supported by scientific knowledge. Let me elaborate on this.

Parallels between Psychological Processes and Physiological Processes

Unification Thought asserts that all things have dual characteristics, namely, *sungsang* and *hyungsang*, since they are created in the likeness of the dual characteristics of the Original Image. The human being is a dual

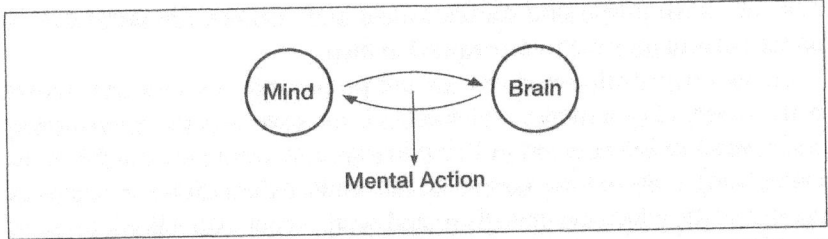

Fig. 9.7. Mental Action through the Give and Receive Action between Mind and Brain

being of mind and body; and cells, tissues, and organs making up the human body are united beings of mental and physical elements as well. Furthermore, all human actions and operations are dual—which means that psychological and physiological actions are always at work in parallel. Therefore, from the perspective of Unification Thought, in cognition as well, psychological and physiological processes are always at work in parallel. This means that mental action occurs through the give and receive action between mind and brain (fig. 9.7). Here, mind refers to the union of the spirit mind (mind of the spirit self) and the physical mind (mind of the physical self).

Wilder Penfield (1891–1976), a world-renowned authority in the study of the brain, compared the brain to a computer, saying that "the brain is a computer, and the mind is a programmer."[34] Another renowned researcher of the brain, John C. Eccles (1903–1997), also said that the mind and the brain are different things, and that it is necessary to grasp the mind-brain problem as the interaction between the mind and the brain.[35] Their assertions are in accord with the view of Unification Thought that mental activities are made through the give and receive action between the mind and the brain.

The Elements that Correspond to Protoconsciousness and Protoimage

Next, certain scientific views can be cited that arguably support the concepts of protoconsciousness and protoimage, concepts unique to Unification epistemology. As explained before, protoconsciousness is the cosmic consciousness which has permeated the cells and tissues of living things, that is to say, it is life; and protoimage is the image reflected on the protoconsciousness, which is a film of consciousness. Protoconsciousness is purposeful consciousness, and protoimage is information. This means that cells have purposeful consciousness and perform certain functions on the basis of information contained in them.

Let us verify protoconsciousness and protoimage from the standpoint of the theory of cybernetics. Cybernetics is the science of the transmission and control of information in living beings and automatic machines. In living beings, bits of information are transmitted through sense organs to nerve centers, which integrate them and send proper instructions, through peripheral nerves, to effectors (muscles). This is regarded as one of the phenomena of cybernetics in living beings, which is similar to the automatic operation of a machine.

When we look at even a single cell, we can see cybernetic phenomena taking place within it. That is to say, a continuous repetition of the transmission of information from the cytoplasm to the nucleus and a response back to it from the nucleus is made autonomously in a cell, whereby the cell exists and multiplies. Accordingly, based on these phenomena of cybernetics, we can find autonomy even in a single cell. The autonomy of a cell is none other than life and protoconsciousness.

The French physiologist Andrée Goudet-Perrot, for example, explains in *Cybernétique et Biologie* that the cell nucleus, which contains the source of the cell's information, gives instructions to the cytoplasmic organelles (mitochondria, Golgi complex, etc.) so that they may carry out the chemical reactions necessary for the life of the cell.[36] The cell's information includes all the information concerning the anatomical shapes and essential functions of living beings.[37]

Here, the following questions may arise. First, the code (information) must be decoded and memorized, but what is the subject that decodes and memorizes these codes? Second, in order for the cell nucleus to issue instructions to cause the chemical reactions necessary for the life of the cell, the nucleus must be accurately aware of the situation inside the cell. What is the subject of this awareness?

These questions can not be answered exclusively from the position of science (physiology) alone, since science deals only with phenomenological aspects. Unification Thought, however, with its theory of dual characteristics, can clearly state that there is a purposeful element of *sungsang*, namely, consciousness, working within the cell. The consciousness within the cell is protoconsciousness (inner *sungsang*), and the information is the protoimage (inner *hyungsang*).

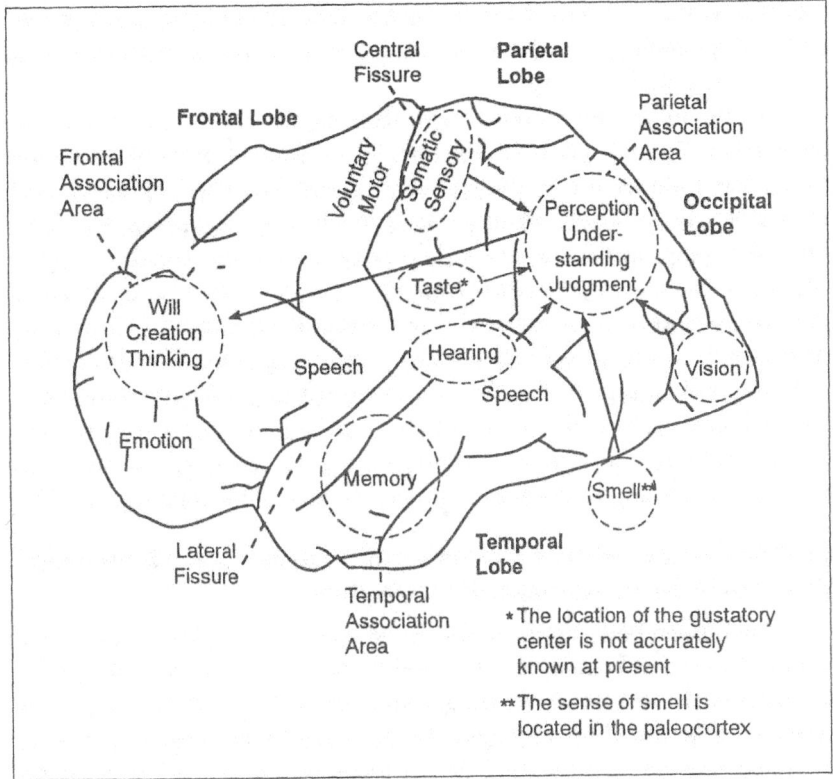

Fig. 9.8. Functional Areas in the Cerebral Cortex and the Three Stages of Cognition

Correspondence of Psychological and Physiological Processes in the Three Stages of Cognition

As discussed above, the three stages of cognition are the sensory stage, the understanding stage, and the rational stage. According to cerebral physiology, there are physiological processes corresponding to these three stages of cognition.

The cerebral cortex can roughly be divided into three areas, namely, the sensory area, which receives signals from the sense organs; the motor area, which sends out the signals related to voluntary movements; and the association areas, which are divided into frontal, parietal, and temporal association areas. It is believed that the frontal association area is concerned with the functions of will, creation, thinking, and emotion; the parietal association area is concerned with the functions of perception, judgment, and understanding; and the temporal association area is connected with the mechanism of memory.

First, the information about sight, hearing, taste, smell, and touch is transmitted through peripheral nerves to the sensory areas of the visual sense, the auditory sense, the gustatory sense, the olfactory sense, and the tactile sense (somatic sensory), respectively. The physiological process that takes place in the sensory area corresponds to the sensory stage of cognition. Next, the information from the sensory areas is gathered in the parietal association area, where it is understood and judged. This process corresponds to cognition in the understanding stage. Based on this understanding and judgment, thinking is carried out in the frontal association area, where creative activities are carried out. This process corresponds to the rational stage of cognition. In this way, the three stages of cognition have corresponding physiological processes within the brain (fig. 9.8).[38]

Correspondence between Psychological Processes and Physiological Processes in the Transmission of Information

In the human body there are functions operating constantly to receive various bits of information from both the outside and inside of the body, to process these bits of information, and to respond to them. The stimulation received by a receptor (sense organ such as eyes, ears, skin, etc.) becomes an impulse and passes through the afferent path of the nerve fiber to reach the central nerves. The central nerves process that information and send out an instruction, which is transmitted as an impulse through the efferent path of the nerve fiber to the effector which responds to it (fig. 9.9).

When a response toward the stimulation takes place in a manner that is unrelated to consciousness at the higher center, it is called a reflex. The spinal cord, medulla oblongata, and midbrain, are reflex centers, sending appropriate orders in response to stimulation.

Once a bit of information has entered the body through a receptor, how is it transmitted? The information that has entered through a receptor becomes a nerve impulse, which is an electrical impulse. A nerve impulse is a change in the electrical potential across the membrane between the excited and non-excited parts of the nerve fiber. The nerve impulse moves along the nerve fiber. The change in the electrical potential that takes place at that moment is called an "action potential."

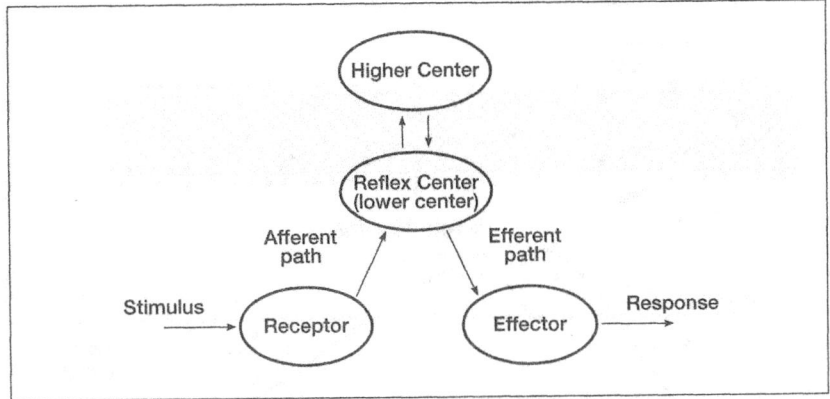

Fig. 9.9. Paths for the Transmission of Information in the Human Body

The inside of the membrane of a nerve fiber is negatively charged in an unstimulated state, but when an impulse passes through it, this charge is reversed, and the inside becomes positively charged. This phenomenon takes place when sodium ions (Na^+) flow into the membrane from the outside. Then, when potassium ions (K^+) flow out from the inside of the membrane, the balance of charge is restored to its former state (i.e., a negatively charged state). In this way, a change in the electrical potential across the membrane takes place and moves along the nerve fiber (fig. 9.10).

Next, how is a nerve impulse transmitted across the gap between neurons, namely, at a synapse? There the electrical impulse is converted into a discharge of chemical transmitter substances and moves through the gap of the synapse. When these substances reach the next neuron, the chemical process is again converted into an electrical process. In other words, an electrical signal in the nerve fiber is converted into a chemical signal at the synapse, and when it reaches the next neuron it is converted back into an electrical signal. The transmitter substance in the synapse is said to be acetylcholine in motor and parasympathetic nerves, and noradrenaline in sympathetic nerves. The mechanism for the transmission of information explained here may be expressed in a diagram as in fig. 9.11.

The above explanation is the physiological process of the transmission of information, but from the perspective of Unification Thought, there is always a conscious process in parallel with a physiological one. That is,

428 / EPISTEMOLOGY

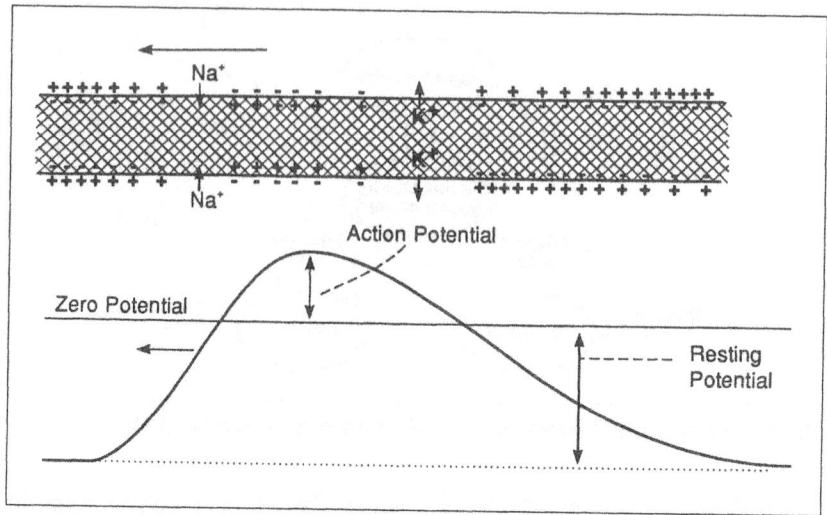

Fig. 9.10. Transmission of a Nerve Impulse
Source: J. C. Eccles. *The Understanding of the Brain* (New York: McGraw-Hill Book Company, 1977), p. 23.

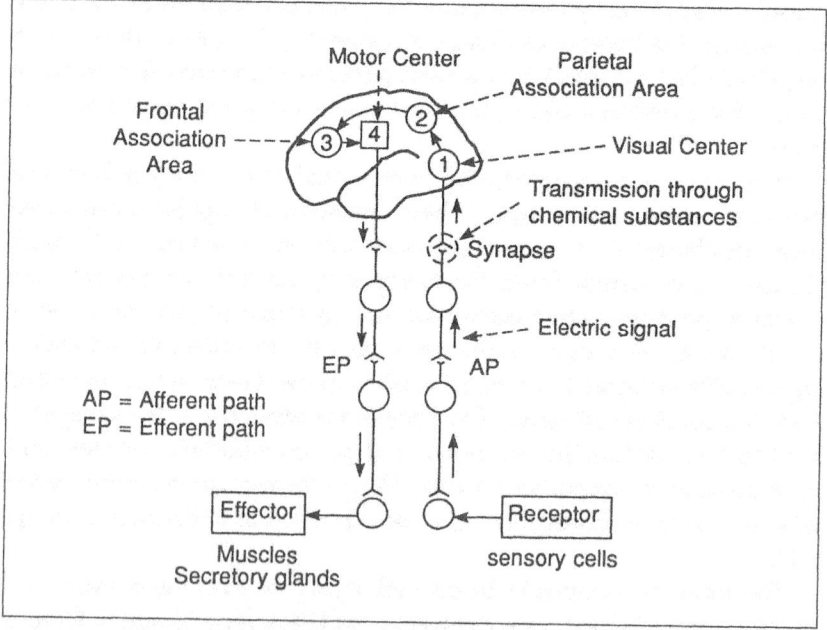

Fig. 9.11. Mechanism for the Transmission of Information between Neurons

associated with the movement of the action current in the nerve fiber and the transmitter substances at the synapse, there is always protoconsciousness at work, perceiving the content of the information and transmitting it to the center. In other words, protoconsciousness can be seen as the bearer of information. In sum, it can be understood that the occurrence of the action current in the nerve fiber and the chemical material at the synapse are accompanied by protoconsciousness, which is the bearer of information.

Corresponding Aspects in the Formation of Prototypes

It has already been explained that the corresponding elements of protoimage and image of relation are the content of cells and tissues and the mutual relationships among these elements. We call the protoimage and image of relation in the cell and the tissue the "terminal protoimage" and the "terminal image of relation," respectively. On the other hand, we can call the protoimage and the image of relation that arise at the understanding stage of cognition the "central protoimage" and the "central image of relation," respectively.

In the process whereby the terminal protoimages reach the higher center through nerve paths, they undergo selection at each level of the central nervous system and are combined, associated, and arranged, to form central protoimages. In the case of the terminal images of relation as well, they undergo selection at each level of the central nervous system and are combined, associated, and arranged, to form the central images of relation, which, when they reach the cerebral cortex, become the forms of thought. Here, each level of the central nervous system stores the protoimages and images of relation appropriate to its own level.

Among the elements from which prototypes are composed, there are also the empirical images (or ideas), in addition to the protoimages and forms of thought. These empirical images are the images (ideas) gained through past experiences and stored in the memory center. They constitute a part of the prototypes, which can be used for later cognition. As mentioned before, protoimages and images of relation together are called a priori prototypes, or original prototypes, and the empirical images are called the empirical prototypes.

As information is passed upwards from the lower to the higher levels, the amount of information received in the central nervous system (input), and the amount given out (output) increases. At the same time, the ways of processing information become more inclusive and universal. This is similar to an administrative organization: the higher the level, the greater the amount of information dealt with and the more inclusive and universal the way of processing that information.

In the highest center, namely, the cerebral cortex, the reception of information is cognition; the storage of information is memory; and the output of information is thinking (conception), creation, and practice. Although it is different in dimension, the integration at the lower centers is similar to that at the cerebral cortex. Purposive integration by consciousness is exercised at each center. The purposive integration consists of physiological and mental integrations. To put this in another way, at each level of the central nervous system, physiological integration is accompanied by mental integration. In other words, the physiological process of transmitting information (nerve impulses) in the central nerves is always accompanied by psychological processes of judgment, memory, conception, and so on.

As for the transmission of the images of relation (images of form), the fact that the processing of information becomes increasingly universal as it goes from the lower to the higher centers means that, as particular terminal images of relation are passed on to the higher centers (whereby various types of information are simplified and classified), those images of relation gradually become universalized and generalized. At the point of reaching the cerebral cortex, they have been completely conceptualized into the forms of thought, or categories. This is also similar to administrative organizations: the lower the level, the more individual and particular the information is; the higher the level, the more general and universal it becomes.

Prototypes and Physiology

Prototypes are the ideas and concepts possessed in advance by the subject at the time of cognition, and can also be called memory. It has previously been explained that the human being possesses a priori prototypes (original prototypes) and empirical prototypes, which can also be expressed—borrowing physiological expressions—as "hereditary memory" and "acquired memory," the latter gained through experience. [39]

The "hereditary memory" which is the information concerning the cells and tissues of a human being as a living being, is believed to be stored in the limbic system—that part of the cerebrum that consists of the older cortex, covered by the new cortex, according to cerebrophysiology. Then, how and where is the "acquired memory" stored?

Memory can be divided into short-term memory, which lasts only a few seconds, and long-term memory, which lasts from several hours to several years. Short-term memory is believed to be based on an electrical reverberating circuit. With regard to long-term memory, two theories have been proposed, i.e., the "neuron circuit theory" and the "memory substance theory." The neuron circuit theory is the view that each memory is stored in a particular network of neuron circuits, whose junctions (synapses) receive changes through the repeated nerve impulse. The memory substance theory is the view that such memory substances as RNA, peptides, etc., have something to do with each memory. Recently, however, the number of researchers who advocate the memory substance theory is decreasing.[40]

As for the area in which the long-term memory is stored, it is considered to be as follows: There is a part of the limbic system called the hippocampus, which is located within the cerebrum. This hippocampus first plays a role in the initial processing of the information to be memorized, and then the memory is thought to be stored in the new cortex (temporal lobe) for a long time.[41] That is, memory is believed to be stored in the temporal lobe through the hippocampus.

Goudet-Perrot explains that in cognition, such memory (stored knowledge) is collated with the information of an object in the external world coming through the sense organs, and is judged: "The information received by the sensory receptors is collated with the knowledge that was acquired by the sensory center in the cerebral cortex and was stored in memory, and judgment is made."[42] This view is in accord with the position of Unification Thought whereby information coming from the external world is collated with prototypes (inner images), and is judged as to whether it is in agreement or in disagreement with the prototypes.[43]

Encoding of Ideas and Ideation of Codes

In the process whereby a human subject cognizes an object, the information coming from the object, upon contacting the sense organs, becomes an impulse, which is a kind of code. This impulse is then ideated in the sensory center in the cerebral cortex and is reflected on the mirror of the consciousness as an image (an idea). This is the "ideation of a code." On the other hand, in the case of practice, an action is taken based on a certain idea. In this case, the idea becomes an impulse, passes through motor nerves, and moves an effector (muscle). This is the "encoding of an idea," since an impulse is a kind of code.

According to cerebrophysiology, an idea comes into being through cognition and is stored in a specific area of the brain as memory, encoded as a particular pattern of combinations of neurons. In order to recall a particular memory thus encoded, consciousness decodes the code and understands it as an idea. That is, in the storage and the recollection of memory, the "encoding of ideas" and the "ideation of codes" seem to be carried out. With regard to this matter, neurophysiologists M. S. Gazzaniga and J. E. LeDoux have stated the following:

> Our experiences are indeed multifaceted, and it is our view that different aspects of experience are differentially stored in the brain····. We may be faced with the fact that memory storage, encoding, and decoding is a multifaceted process that is multiply represented in the brain.[44]

This kind of mutual conversion between an idea and a code can be regarded as a type of induction phenomenon arising between the *sungsang*-type mental coil, which carries the idea, and the *hyungsang*-type physical coil (neurons), which carries the code, just as electricity moves between the first coil and the second coil through induction. The mutual conversion of an idea and a code provides support for the assertion that cognition is carried out through give and receive action between psychological and physiological processes.

III. Kantian and Marxist Epistemologies Seen from the Perspective of Unification Thought

Next, Kantian and Marxist epistemologies, which are the most important ones among traditional epistemologies, in view of the method of cognition, will be evaluated from the perspective of Unification Thought.

A. A Critique of Kantian Epistemology

Critique of the Transcendental Method

Kant asserted that the subject is endowed with a priori forms of thought (categories). However, when we examine things closely, we realize that there are forms of existence that correspond to the forms of thought. For example, all things in the objective world exist and perform their motion in the context of time and space. Also, scientists can accurately replicate certain phenomena in the form of time and space in the objective world. Therefore, the form of time and space is not only a subjective form, but an objective form as well. The same can be said of the form of causality. Scientists have discovered numerous relations of cause and effect in the phenomena of the natural world and have been able to reproduce similar phenomena on the basis of the relations of cause and effect. This indicates that there are indeed relations of cause and effect in the objective world.

Also, Kant asserted that an object of cognition is established through the combination of the form of the subject and the content coming from the object. From the perspective of Unification Thought, the subject (person) as well as the object (all things) have both content and form. What the subject possesses is not what Kant called "a priori forms" alone; rather, they are previously existing prototypes, which have both content and form and, therefore, include the forms mentioned by Kant. Also, what comes from the object is not a chaotic manifold of sense, but rather sense content organized by the forms of existence.

Furthermore, the subject (person) and object (all things) are in a correlative relationship and bear resemblance to each other. Therefore, cognition is not carried out through mere synthesis of the object; rather, cognition is carried out as the "content and form" (the prototype) of the subject, and the "content and form" of the object are collated through the give and receive action between them, with a judgment being made.

Critique of Kantian Agnosticism

Kant held that only natural, scientific knowledge in the phenomenal world is true, and he considered the world of things-in-themselves (the noumenal reality) uncognizable. Consequently, he entirely separated the phenomenal reality from the noumenal reality. This led to the separation between pure reason and practical reason, and between science and religion. From the perspective of Unification Thought, the thing-in-itself is the *sungsang* of a thing, while the sense content is its *hyungsang*. *Sungsang* and *hyungsang* are unified in all things, and since *sungsang* is expressed through *hyungsang*, we can know the *sungsang* of a thing through its *hyungsang*.

In addition, according to Unification Thought, the human being is the lord of dominion over all things, or the lord of creation, and all things were created in resemblance to the human being, as objects of joy for human beings. This means that the human being and all things resemble each other in structure and in elements; accordingly, they resemble each other in content and in form as well. Therefore, in cognition, the content and form possessed by the subject (human being) are similar to the content and form possessed by all things, and they can be collated. In addition, since through its content the thing-in-itself, namely, the *sungsang* of the object, is expressed, the subject can cognize not only the *hyungsang* (sense content and sense form) of the object, but also its *sungsang* (the thing-in-itself). Since Kant was not aware of the principled relationship between humans and all things, nor of the fact that a human being is the united being of spirit self and physical self, he could stray into agnosticism.

B. A Critique of Marxist Epistemology

Critique of the Theory of Reflection

As explained in the section on Unification epistemology, if there is no prototype within the subject of cognition that corresponds to the things in the external world as criteria for judgment, cognition can not be made, even if the external world is reflected on the consciousness. Moreover, since cognition is carried out through give and receive action between subject and object, it is necessary for the subject to have interest in the object. Even though an object in the external world is reflected on the consciousness of the subject, if the subject has no interest in the object, cognition will not take place. This means that cognition is not carried out through a passive material process like reflection, but becomes possible only through the participation of an active mental process (i.e., interest in the object and the function of collation).

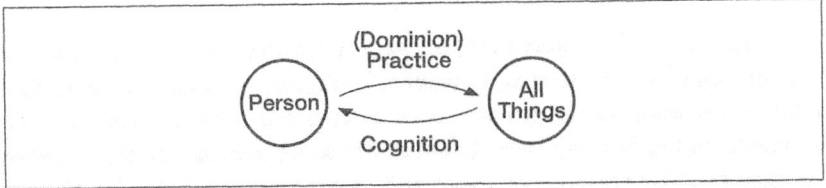

Fig. 9.12. Correlativity of Cognition and Practice

Critique of Sensory Cognition, Rational Cognition, and Practice

In Marxist epistemology, the process of cognition consists of three stages, namely, sensory cognition, rational cognition, and practice. The important question here is how consciousness, which is held to be a product or a function of the brain and to merely reflect the objective world, can achieve rational (logical) cognition (i.e., abstraction, judgment, inference), and moreover, how it can direct practice (revolutionary practice). Even though there exists a wide gap between the passive process of reflecting the external world on the one hand, and rational cognition and the active process of practice on the other, no reasonable explanation is given. This means that here there is a logical gap in the Marxist view.

From the perspective of Unification Thought, logical cognition and practice can never be made based solely on the physiological processes of the brain. This is because cognitive action takes place through give and receive action between mind and brain. In other words, logical cognition and practice are carried out through the give and receive action between the mind, which possesses the function of understanding and reason, and the brain.

Another question concerns the role of practice in cognition. Lenin said that cognition proceeds to practice, and Mao Ze-dong asserted that cognition and practice are inseparable. On this point, Unification Thought has no objection. All things were created as objects of joy for human beings, and we are to exercise dominion (practice) over all things according to the purpose of creation. Accordingly, we cognize all things in order to exercise dominion (practice). Cognition and practice form a correlative circuit of give and receive between human beings and all things (fig. 9.12). Thus, there is no cognition apart from practice (dominion), and no practice (dominion) apart from cognition.

Practice, as advocated by Marxism, is ultimately directed toward revolution. Contrary to this, however, Unification Thought asserts that neither cognition nor practice is ever carried out with revolution as its objective, but rather, they are carried out in order to actualize the purpose of creation. The purpose of creation is actualized when God exercises dominion over human beings with love, and human beings exercise dominion over all things with love, whereby joy is realized in God and human beings. Therefore, both cognition and practice are carried out for the purpose of obtaining joy through love.

Critique of the Marxist Concepts of Absolute Truth and Relative Truth

Lenin and Mao Ze-dong acknowledged the existence of absolute truth, saying that human beings infinitely approach absolute truth by repeating cognition and practice. Yet, their concept of "absolute" is ambiguous. Lenin said that the sum-total of relative truths is the absolute truth. No matter how we may sum up relative truths, however, the result is simply relative truths summed up, and can not become absolute truth.

Absolute truth refers to the universal, eternal truth. Therefore, without having the Absolute Being as the standard, the concept of absolute can not be established. Absolute truth is one with, and inseparable from, the absolute love of God, as explained in Axiology. This is the same as the way in which the warmth and brightness of sunlight are one and inseparable. Therefore, there can be no absolute truth apart from God's absolute love. Consequently, only when centered on God's love, will the human being understand the purpose of creation of all things and obtain true knowledge of them. Therefore, if God is denied, there is no way to obtain absolute truth, no matter how strenuously one may engage in practice.

10
Logic

Logic is the study of the laws and forms of thinking. A human being is a dual being of mind and body, which are both governed by certain laws and forms. The body maintains its healthy condition through its physiological functions, which are under the rule of certain laws and forms.

Blood, for example, circulates throughout the whole body, supplying nutrients and oxygen to the terminal cells and tissues under these laws and forms. This means that blood supplies nutritious elements and oxygen to the whole body through the "form" of circulation. Perception and response in the human body are carried out with the signals transmitted through the centripetal and centrifugal nerves. This means that perception and response is carried out through the "form" of transmission of signals in the nerves. In the blood, chemical reactions are always taking place with the catalytic action of oxygen. These reactions are taking place under certain laws. The blood flow is also under the fluid dynamic. Thus, the physiological functions in the human body are carried out under certain laws and forms.

In a similar manner, our thinking is carried out under certain laws and forms. It may seem that we think freely without being restricted by any forms or laws, but this is not the case. Since the time of Aristotle, who is considered to be its founder, formal logic has dealt with the laws and forms commonly associated with thinking, which contains various contents. In contrast to this, the dialectic of Hegel and Marx dealt with the laws and forms in the process of development both of thinking and of nature.

In this chapter, I will first outline certain traditional systems of logic, focusing especially on formal logic and Hegelian logic. Then, I will introduce the system of logic as established on the basis of Unification Thought.

Finally, I will examine traditional systems of logic from the perspective of Unification Thought.

I. Traditional Systems of Logic

In this section I will deal with formal logic, Hegelian logic, Marxist logic, symbolic logic, and transcendental logic. Among these, I will explain formal logic in some detail, since it is closely related to Unification Logic. I will explain other systems more briefly, since I merely want to show that Unification Logic is able to solve the difficult problems in traditional logic. Therefore, only certain relevant points are dealt with, as was done in the chapter on epistemology. Among the systems of logic, Hegel's logic is treated somewhat in detail, since there are many arguable points in it, and its explanation necessarily becomes a little longer. It may be noted that to understand Unification logic itself, this section can be skipped.

A. Formal Logic

Formal logic, which was established by Aristotle, is more the study of the forms and laws of thinking, and it does not deal so much with the content of thinking. According to Kant, "That logic has already, from the earliest times, proceeded upon this sure path is evidenced by the fact that since Aristotle it has not required to retrace a single step···. It is remarkable also that to the present day this logic has not been able to advance a single step, and is thus to all appearance a closed and completed body of doctrine."[1] Formal logic has existed, almost without change, for two thousand years since Aristotle. This is because formal logic contains considerable truth, in so far as it is concerned with thinking. Let me now introduce the main points of formal logic, and point out which parts are valid, and which are insufficient.

1. The Laws of Thought

Formal logic enumerates the following four laws as the laws of thought.

(1) The Law of Identity
(2) The Law of Contradiction
(3) The Law of the Excluded Middle
(4) The Law of Sufficient Reason

The law of identity can be expressed by the form "A is A," as in the statement, "A flower is a flower." This implies that, in spite of changes in phenomena, the substance of the flower remains unchanging. This also implies identity in thinking itself. That is to say, the concept of "flower" has one and the same meaning in every case. Furthermore, this principle can also imply that two concepts are in agreement, as in the statement, "A bird is an animal."

The law of contradiction can be expressed by the form "A is not not-A." This can be regarded as the principle of identity stated in reverse. In saying that "a flower is not a non-flower," one is actually saying that "a flower is a flower." Likewise, in saying that "a bird is not a non-animal," one is actually saying that "a bird is an animal." One is an affirmative way of expression, and the other is a negative way of expression, but the content remains the same.

The law of the excluded middle can be expressed as, "Everything is either A or not-A." This means that there can be no third or middle judgment.

The law of sufficient reason was first advocated by Leibniz. Its meaning is that every act of thinking comes into being due to necessary reasons. Expressed in a more general way, it becomes the law of cause and effect, which states that everything has a sufficient reason for its existence. Reason here has two meanings: namely, basis and cause. Basis is the opposite concept to conclusion, and cause is the opposite concept to result. Therefore, this law means that thought always has its basis, and that existence always has its cause. There are many other laws, but all of them are derived from these four fundamental ones. Formal logic also consists of three fundamental elements, that is, three elements of thought: concept, judgment, and inference. I will explain each of these next.

	Extension	
Living beings	life	plants, animals
Animals	life, senses	mollusks, arthropods, vertebrates, etc.
Vertebrates	life, senses, backbone	reptiles, birds, mammals, etc.
Mammals	life, senses, backbone, suckle their young	primates, carnivores, etc.
Primates	life, senses, backbone, suckle their young, ability to grasp	apes, human beings
Humankind	life, senses, backbone, suckle their young, ability to grasp, reason	individual persons
	Intension	

Fig. 10.1. Intension and Extension

2. Concept

A concept is a general representation (or idea) through which the essential characteristics of a thing are grasped. A concept has two aspects, namely, intension and extension. Intension refers to the qualities, or properties, common to a certain concept, and extension refers to a set of beings to which the concept is applied. To explain these, let me take living beings as an example.

Living beings can be classified into concepts on various levels, such as animals, vertebrates, mammals, primates, and human beings. Living beings are those beings that have life. Animals, in addition to life, have sense organs. Vertebrates have a backbone. Mammals have the nature of suckling their young. Primates have the ability to grasp things. Human beings have reason. In this way, the living beings of each level, represented by a certain concept, possess a certain common nature. The qualities, or properties, common to a certain concept are called the intension of that concept.

Among living beings, there are animals and plants, and among animals there are mollusks, arthropods, vertebrates, etc. Among vertebrates, there are reptiles, birds, mammals, etc. Among mammals, there are primates, carnivores, etc. Finally, among primates there are the various kinds of apes and human beings. A set of beings to which a certain concept is applied is called the extension of that concept (see fig. 10.1).

When we compare any two concepts, that concept whose intension is broader and extension narrower is called a "specific concept" (or subordinate concept), and that concept whose intension is narrower and extension

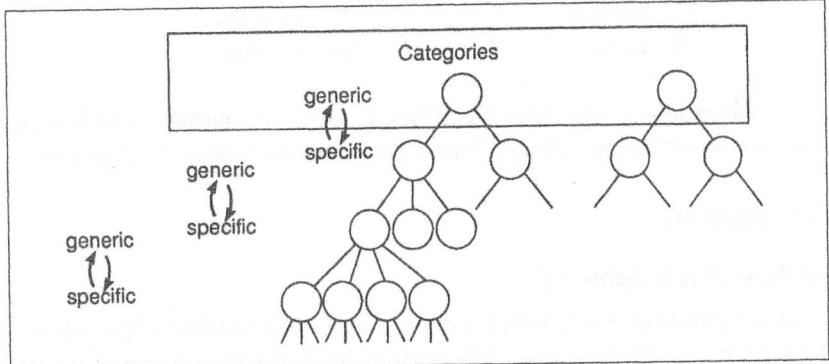

Fig. 10.2. Progressive Series Reaching up to Categories

broader is called a "generic concept" (or superordinate concept). For example, when we compare the concept of vertebrate with the concepts of reptile, bird, or mammal, the former is a generic concept in relationship to the latter; and the latter are specific concepts in relationship to the former.

Also, when we compare the concept of animal with the concepts of mollusks, arthropods, or vertebrates, the former is a generic concept, and the latter are specific concepts. Further, when we compare the concept of living beings with the concepts of plants or animals, the former is a generic concept, and the latter are specific concepts. If we repeat this operation over and over again, we will eventually reach the highest generic concept, beyond which no other concept can be traced. Such concepts are called "categories" (see fig. 10.2).

In addition, the pure concepts that reason possesses by nature (rather than through experiences) are also called categories. These categories vary from philosopher to philosopher. The reason for this is that the most important and fundamental concepts in each thought system are considered categories. Accordingly, the definition of categories varies from philosopher to philosopher.

Aristotle was the first philosopher to establish categories. He set up the following ten categories, taking clues from grammar:

(1) substance   (2) quantity
(3) quality   (4) relation
(5) place   (6) time

(7) position   (8) condition
(9) action   (10) passivity

In the modern age, Kant established twelve categories, which were mentioned in "Epistemology," based on the twelve forms of judgment.

3. Judgment

a) What is a Judgment?

An assertion of something about a certain object is called a "judgment." Logically, a judgment is an affirmation or denial of a relation among certain concepts. When expressed in language, a judgment is called a proposition. A judgment consists of the three elements of subject, predicate, and copula. The object to which thinking is directed is the subject; the predicate describes its content; and the copula connects the two. Generally, the subject is expressed as 'S,' predicate as 'P,' and copula as '—'. A judgment is formulated as "S—P."

b) Kinds of Judgment

As for the kinds of judgment, the twelve forms of judgment proposed by Kant are still employed in formal logic today. The Kantian twelve forms of judgment refer to the four main headings of quantity, quality, relation and modality, each of which is divided into three subdivisions. They are as follows:

Quantity	Universal Judgment:	Every S is P.
	Particular Judgment:	Some S is P.
	Singular Judgment:	This S is P.
Quality	Affirmative Judgment:	S is P.
	Negative Judgment:	S is not P.
	Infinite Judgment:	S is not-P.
Relation	Categorical Judgment:	S is P.
	Hypothetical Judgment:	If A is B, C is D.
	Disjunctive Judgment:	A is either B or C.

Modality Problematic Judgment: S may be P.
Assertive Judgment: S is in fact P.
Apodictic Judgment: S must be P.

As explained above, Kant established three forms of judgment in each of four headings of quantity, quality, relation, and modality. In our daily life, we face various incidents and situations, and in order to cope with them, we think in various ways. Needless to say, the content of thinking is different from person to person. However, as far as judgment is concerned, it is in accordance with the above-mentioned forms of judgment. That is, a judgment is either a judgment of quantity (much or little, many or few), a judgment of quality (is or is not), a judgment of relation (among concepts), or a judgment of modality (How is it certain?).

c) Basic Forms of Judgment

Of the above forms of judgment, the most basic is the categorical judgment. If the universal and particular forms of judgment concerning quantity, and the affirmative and negative forms of judgment concerning quality are combined with the categorical judgment, the following four kinds of judgment can be obtained:

Universal Affirmative Judgment: Every S is a P. ············ (A)
Universal Negative Judgment: No S is a P. ············ (E)
Particular Affirmative Judgment: Some S is a P. ············ (I)
Particular Negative Judgment: Some S is not a P. ······ (O)

The twelve forms of judgment, with the exceptions of disjunctive and hypothetical judgments, can be treated as categorical judgments. Then, if we arrange these categorical judgments in terms of quantity (a singular judgment can be treated as a universal judgment) and quality (an infinite judgment is included in the affirmative judgment), we arrive at the four basic forms of judgment, A, E, I, and O. The code letters A, E, I, and O derive from the first two vowels of the Latin words *affirmo* ('I affirm'—A, I) and *nego* ('I negate'—E, O).

d) Distributed and Undistributed Terms

In order not to fall into error in making a categorical judgment, one must examine the relationship between the extension of the subject and

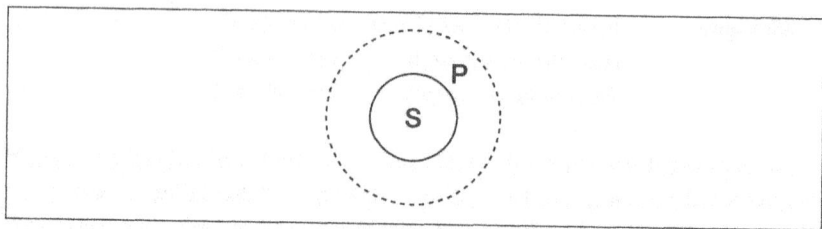

Fig. 10.3. Universal Affirmative Judgment

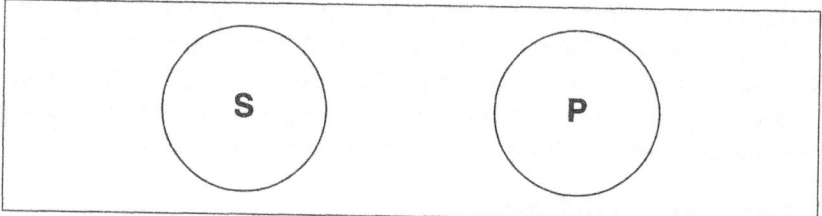

Fig. 10.4. Universal Negative Judgment

that of the predicate. In one case, a term (subject or predicate) in a judgment applies to an entire extension, but in other cases, it does not. When a term in a judgment applies to an entire extension, that term is said to be "distributed." When a term applies to only a part of its extension, that term is said to be "undistributed."

Distribution and undistribution of subject and of predicate are important concepts in a judgment. In a judgment, there is a case where both subject and predict are distributed, but there is a case also where subject and predicate can not both be distributed, and there is yet another case where only one of either subject or predicate can be distributed.

For example, in the universal affirmative judgment "every man (S) is an animal (P)" (judgment A), the subject is distributed while the predicate is undistributed (see fig. 10.3). In other words, the term 'man' applies to the proposition "every man is an animal," throughout its entire extension, but the same is not true about the term 'animal'.

In the universal negative judgment "every bird (S) is a non-mammal (P)," subject and predicate are both distributed (see fig.10.4).

In the particular affirmative judgment "some flowers (S) are red (P)," both subject and predicate are undistributed (see fig. 10.5).

In the particular negative judgment "some birds (S) are non-carnivorous animals (P)," the subject is undistributed, since some S does

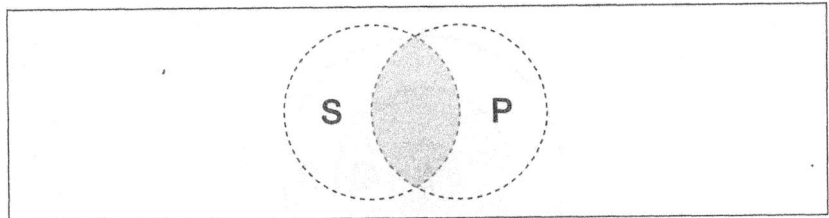

Fig. 10.5. Particular Affirmative Judgment

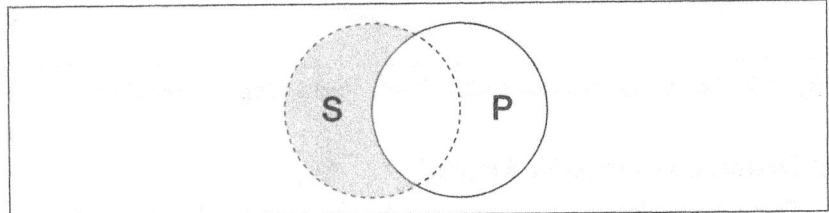

Fig. 10.6. Particular Negative Judgment

not belong to P, while the predicate is distributed (see fig. 10.6).

In the above judgments A, E, I, and O, the distribution of terms is a rule of judgment. If one violates the rule, one's judgment will fall into error. If, for example, one draws the conclusion "every lover of mountains is a hermit" from the judgment "every hermit is a lover of mountains," one will fall into undue distribution; thus, the judgment is a fallacy. In a universal affirmative judgment, S should be distributed, whereas P should be undistributed. In this example, however, both S and P are regarded as distributed.

4. Inference

Inference refers to the process of reasoning whereby a conclusion is derived from one or more propositions. In other words, a conclusion "therefore, S—P" is derived from already known judgments, which are called premises. When there is only one proposition as the premise, the inference is called a "direct inference." When there are two or more propositions as premises, it is called an "indirect inference." Indirect inference includes syllogism, induction, and analogy. Let me briefly explain each of these.

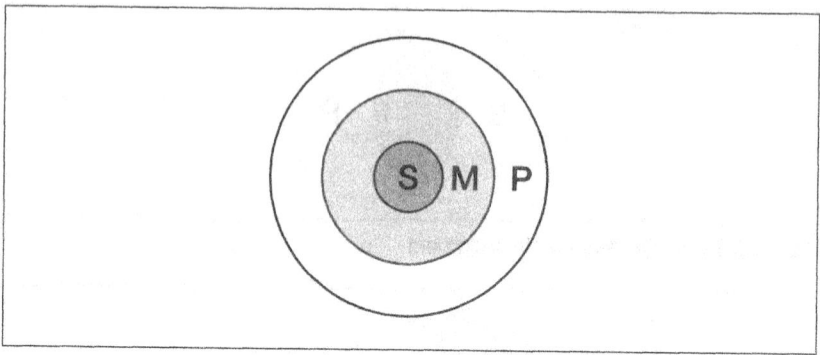

Fig. 10.7. The Relationship among Major Term, Middle Term and Minor Term

a) Deduction (Deductive Method)

Deduction refers to an inference wherein a particular conclusion is drawn from more than one universal, general premise. The representative deduction is the syllogism, as indirect inference, which draws a conclusion from two premises.

The first premise in the syllogism is called the major premise, and the second premise is called the minor premise. In the categorical syllogism, the major premise contains the major term (P) and the middle term (M), and the minor premise contains the minor term (S) and the middle term (M). The conclusion contains the minor term (S) and the major term (P). The following is an example of the categorical syllogism.

> Major premise: Every man (M) is mortal (P).
> Minor premise: Every hero (S) is a man (M).
> Conclusion: Therefore, every hero (S) is mortal (P).

The above can be expressed with signs as:

> M is P.
> S is M.
> Therefore, S is P.

In this syllogism, the extension of the major term (P) is larger than that of the middle term (M), which is larger than that of the minor term (S), as illustrated in figure 10.7.

b) Induction

The method by which one attempts to reach a general assertion from a number of observed particular facts is called inductive inference, or induction. It is regarded as an application of the syllogism. The following is an example of induction:

> Horses, dogs, chickens, and cows are mortal.
> Horses, dogs, chickens, and cows are animals.
> Therefore, all animals are mortal.

Is the conclusion "therefore, all animals are mortal" correct? This conclusion is a universal affirmative judgment. The term "animal," therefore, has to be distributed. In this inference, however, it is undistributed, since horses, dogs, chickens and cows are a part of animals. The conclusion is stated in the form of a universal affirmative judgment as shown in fig. 10.3. However, this conclusion is, in fact, a particular affirmative judgment as shown in fig. 10.5.

Thus, strictly speaking, this inference is erroneous. However, such an inductive inference is possible in natural science because of the application of the "principle of uniformity in nature" and the "law of causality." The former means that all phenomena in the natural world have the same form, and the latter means that the same effect is always brought about by the same cause. Accordingly, from our experiences the induction is considered to be correct.

c) Analogy

Another important mode of inference is analogy. Suppose there are two objects of observation, A and B, and it is known, through our observations, that A and B both have common natures (a), (b), (c), and (d). Furthermore, suppose that A has another nature (e), and it is difficult to observe whether B has the nature (e). In this situation, one may conclude that B also has the nature (e), which A does. This is an analogy. For example, through observations of the earth and Mars, it is known that the two planets have the following common natures:

> (a) Both are planets, revolving around the sun while rotating on their axes.
> (b) They have air.

(c) They have almost the same temperature.
(d) They have the changes of four seasons, and they have water.

Then, based on these facts, one may conclude that there are living beings on Mars, since such beings exist on the earth.

Analogy is often used in our daily lives. For example, present-day advanced scientific knowledge has been acquired through analogy, especially in the early stages of the development of science. Also, analogy plays an important role in our family life, group life, school life, business life, and creative activities. Therefore, the accuracy of analogy becomes an important issue. The requisites for the accuracy of analogy are:

(a) There should be as many similarities as possible in the objects to be compared.
(b) Those similarities should not be accidental, but rather essential.
(c) There should be no incompatible qualities in these similarities.

In formal logic, there are several other kinds of inferences to be dealt with, such as direct inference, hypothetical syllogism, disjunctive syllogism, the theory of fallacy, and so forth, but I will conclude here, since my intention was only to introduce the main points of formal logic.

B. Hegel's Logic

Characteristics of Hegel's Logic

The characteristics of Hegel's logic are that it is not a theory about the laws and forms of thought, but rather it is a theory about the laws and forms of the development of thought. Furthermore, his theory is not about human thought, but about God's thought. Accordingly, Hegel's logic is the study of those laws and forms with which God's thinking developed. God's thinking developed from thinking about Himself to thinking about nature, and then to thinking about history and the state, and finally into thinking about art, religion and philosophy. The laws and forms concerning the development of such thinking are characteristics of Hegel's logic.

As Hegel himself stated, his logic treats the development of God's thinking prior to His creation of the world, and it is thus "heavenly logic," or a description of *"God as He is in His eternal essence before the creation."*[2] However, unlike formal logic, it does not deal merely with the formal laws of thought. Although it holds itself forth to be the development of God's thinking, it attempts to deal also with the most universal definitions and laws of the real world.

Outline of Hegel's Logic

Hegel's logic consists of three branches, namely, the Doctrine of Being, the Doctrine of Essence, and the Doctrine of Notion. These three branches are each subdivided, such that the Doctrine of Being consists of Quality, Quantity, and Measure; the Doctrine of Essence consists of Essence, Appearance, and Actuality; and the Doctrine of Notion consists of Subjective Notion, Objective Notion and Idea, and these are each further subdivided. For example, Quality in the Doctrine of Being consists of Being, Determinate Being, and Being-for-Itself; and Being further consists of Being, Nothing, and Becoming.

The starting point for the development of Hegel's logic is the dialectic of Being, Nothing, and Becoming. After passing through these three stages, Being moves on to Determinate Being. This Determinate Being has three further stages, and after passing through these, the Determinate Being moves on to Being-for-self. Being-for-self has three additional stages, and when they are passed through, it moves on to Quantity.

Quantity moves on to Measure by passing through its own three stages, and when Measure has passed through its three stages, the theory concerning Being comes to an end.

Next is the theory concerning Essence. Hegel's logic moves from Essence to Appearance and from Appearance to Actuality. Then comes the theory concerning Notion. Notion moves from Subjective Notion to Objective Notion and from Objective Notion to Idea. Within Idea, there are three stages, namely, Life, Cognition, and Absolute Idea. Absolute Idea is the final destination in the development within logic.

Then the world of logic or the world of Idea negates itself, in order to realize itself truly, and moves on to the realm of Nature. According to Hegel, Idea moves on to become external to itself, in other words, Nature is the self-alienation of Idea, the negative of Idea, and Idea in the form of otherness. There are three stages of Mechanics, Physics and Organics in the realm of Nature.

Further, Idea, which externalizes itself by negating itself, returns to its

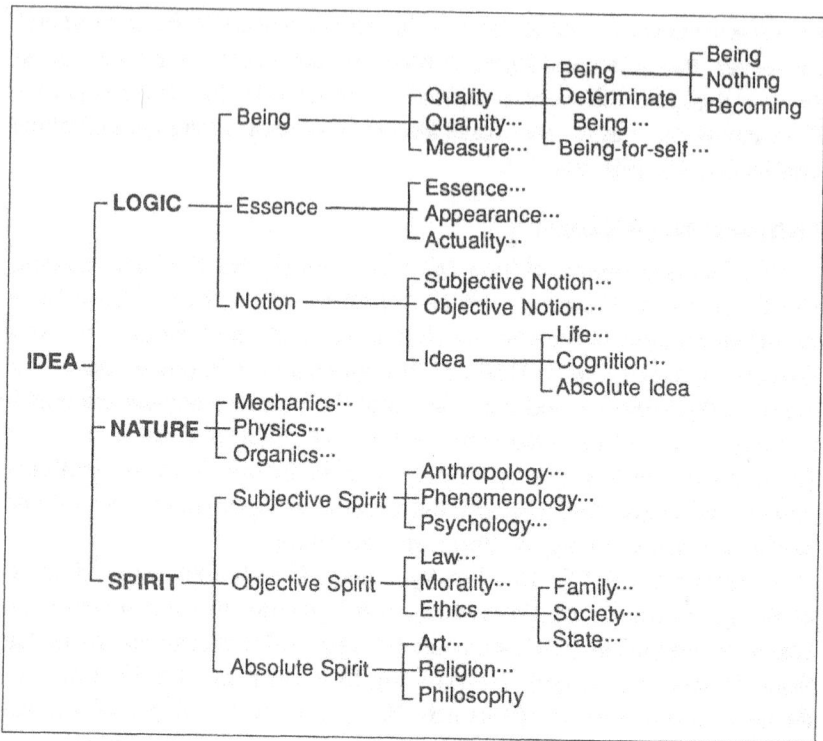

Fig. 10.8. Hegel's System

original self by further negating the negation. Idea as having recovered itself through human being is Spirit. Spirit passes through the three stages of Subjective Spirit, Objective Spirit, and Absolute Spirit. Absolute Spirit stands at the highest point in the development of Spirit. Absolute Spirit develops itself by passing through the three stages of Art, Religion, and Philosophy. The above description of Hegel's system can be illustrated in the following diagram (see fig. 10.8).

The Dialectic of Being, Nothing, and Becoming

Hegel's logic, starting with Being, deals with the process of reaching the Absolute Idea. Being is discussed in the Doctrine of Being, where he begins with the dialectic which consists of Being, Nothing, and Becoming. Hence, I will examine the dialectic of Being, Nothing, and Becoming, because this portion constitutes the core of Hegel's logic.

Hegel's logic starts with Being.[3] Being means simply that which exists, but this is the most abstract of all concepts, and is an entirely indeterminate, empty thought. Therefore, he says it is negative, namely, Nothing. For Hegel, Being and Nothing are both empty concepts, and there is little distinction between the two.[4] Next, Hegel says that the unity of Being and Nothing is Becoming. Both Being and Nothing are empty abstractions, but Becoming, which is the unity of the two opposites, is the first concrete thought.[5]

With this logic of Being, Nothing, and Becoming as the basis, the logical developments of thesis, antithesis, and synthesis; and affirmation, negation, and negation of negation, etc., which are usually regarded as Hegel's method, came to be established.

Determinate Being

Having examined Being, Nothing, and Becoming, we move on to the examination of the Determinate Being. Determinate Being is Being with a certain form, Being considered concretely. While Being means simply that which exists, Determinate Being means that which is something. Moving from Being, Nothing, and Becoming to Determinate Being, in short, means moving from the abstract to the concrete. Becoming is a contradiction containing Being and Nothing within itself, and through this contradiction, Becoming transcends itself to become Determinate Being.

In this way, Determinate Being is a definite Being, a qualified Being. This determinateness of Determinate Being was called Quality by Hegel. However, even though we may say determinate, what is considered here is simple determination. The determination that makes Being a Determinate Being implies the affirmative content of something, and at the same time, it implies limitation. Therefore, the quality that makes something what it is, is reality, when seen from the affirmative aspect of something, and at the same time it is negation when seen from the aspect of not being another thing.

Therefore, in Determinate Being, reality and negation, or affirmation and negation, are united. Next, Determinate Being proceeds to Being-for-self. Being-for-self refers to the Being that is neither in relationship to another thing, nor changing into another thing, but staying as itself in every way.

Being, Essence, and Notion

In the Doctrine of Being, starting from an analysis of what it is to exist, Hegel discussed the logic of change, or the logic of generation and disappearance. Next, the Doctrine of Being proceeds to the Doctrine of Essence. Here, the unchangeable aspect within things and the interconnectedness among all things are discussed. Next, it proceeds to the Doctrine of the Notion as the unity of the Doctrine of Being and the Doctrine of Essence. Here, the fact that things do not cease to be themselves while changing into other beings—that is, self-development—is discussed. The driving force of this development is the notion and life.

Then, can one say that God's thinking proceeded in the way of Being, Essence, and Notion? We can understand this if we watch the process of our cognition as we perceive things from the external to the internal, he says. In the case of perceiving a flower, for example, we first perceive the existence of the flower phenomenally. Next, we perceive the essence of the flower. Then, the notion of the flower is formed, in which the existence of the flower and the essence of the flower are united.

Logic, Nature, and Spirit

As mentioned before, according to Hegel, nature is Idea in the form of otherness, or Idea as self-alienated. Therefore, if Logic is made to be the thesis, then the philosophy of Nature becomes the antithesis. Next, Idea regains consciousness and freedom through the human being and becomes Spirit. Accordingly, the philosophy of Spirit becomes the synthesis.

The natural world, also, performs the dialectical development of thesis, antithesis, and synthesis, that is, the three stages of Mechanics, Physics, and Organics. This does not mean, however, that nature itself develops, but rather, this is the process through which the Idea behind the natural world manifests itself. First, the concept of force appears; next, the concept of physical phenomena; and then, the concept of living beings, he says.

Finally, the human being appears, and the Spirit develops itself through humankind. This development takes place in the three stages of Subjective Spirit, Objective Spirit, and Absolute Spirit. Subjective Spirit refers to the spirit of the individual; Objective Spirit refers to the socialized spirit, or the objectified spirit transcending the individual.

Objective Spirit has the three stages of Law, Morality, and Ethics. Law

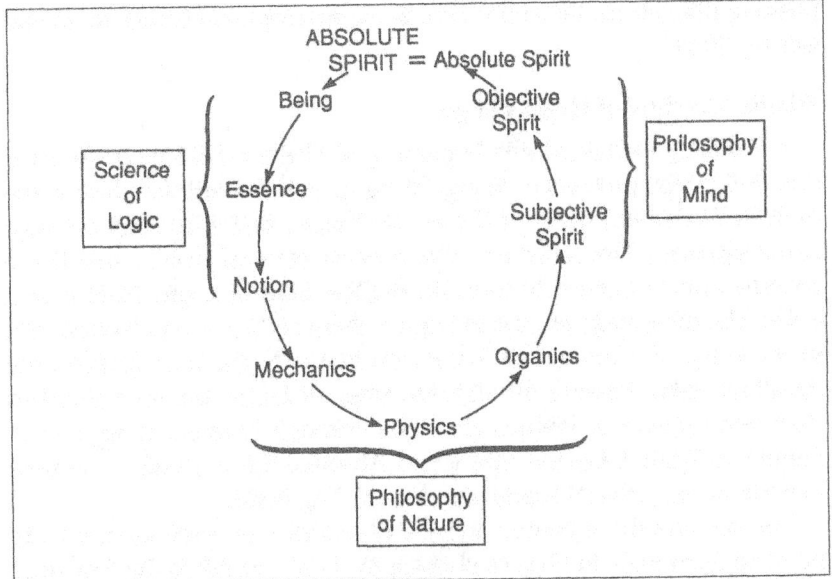

Fig. 10.9. The Returning Nature of Hegel's Dialectic

refers not to something systematized like the constitution of a state, but to elementary forms in human relationships, like a group of people. Next, man comes to respect the rights of others and to lead a moral life. However, there are still many subjective aspects (individual aspects) there. Thus, ethics appears as the norms that everyone should communally observe. The first stage in ethics is the family. In a family, members are linked with one another through love, and there is freedom there. However, in the second stage, namely, civil society, the interests of individuals conflict with one another, and freedom becomes restricted. Thus, in the third stage, the state, which integrates the family and civil society, appears. Hegel considered that Idea would manifest itself fully through the state. The state in which the Idea is actualized is the rational state. Human freedom will be fully actualized in that state.

Finally, there appears Absolute Spirit. Absolute Spirit manifests itself through the three stages of art, religion, and philosophy. When it comes to the stage of philosophy, Idea regains itself completely. The dialectical movement of Idea returns to the origin in this way. Nature appears; the human being appears; the state appears; art, religion, and philosophy appear; and finally Idea returns to the Absolute Idea (God).[6] By accomplishing this return, the entire process of development comes to an end (see fig. 10.9).[7]

Triadic Structure of Hegel's Logic

As already explained, the beginning of Hegel's dialectic is the triad (the three stage process) of Being, Nothing, and Becoming, which is the dialectical development of thesis, antithesis, and synthesis through contradiction. The triad process repeats several times, and these processes are combined to form the highest triad of Logic, Nature, and Spirit. The three stage process in Logic is Being, Essence, and Notion, and in the stage of Notion, God's thought becomes the Idea (finally, the Absolute Idea). Passing through the stage of Logic, the Idea alienates itself and appears as Nature, and then, through humans, it appears as Subjective Spirit, Objective Spirit, and Absolute Spirit. Finally, it returns to itself, namely, the Absolute Idea, the starting point.

The philosophy of Nature and the philosophy of Spirit are not independent from logic in Hegel's philosophy. Logic, which is the first stage of the triad, contains the philosophy of Nature and the philosophy of Spirit as prototypes. As already explained, God's thought becomes Idea in the stage of Notion in the triadic process of Being, Essence, and Notion. The Idea is the prototype of the philosophy of Nature and the philosophy of Spirit. In other words, it has the blueprint of the universe. Hence, the philosophy of Nature and the philosophy of Spirit are but the manifestations of the prototype within the Idea, in the same way as the moving pictures on a screen are the reflection of the pictures in a role of film. In other words, Hegel's logic, which is the first stage of the triad, is the prototype of the philosophy of Nature and the philosophy of Spirit. Therefore, Hegel's entire philosophical system is contained in his logic. The dialectic of Hegel, which deals with the development of God's thinking, is usually called an idealistic dialectic.

The Circular Nature, Laws, and Forms in Hegel's Dialectic

As already explained, Hegel's dialectic is a returning and circular movement whereby the original stage is restored at a higher standard through the repetition of the three stages of thesis, antithesis, and synthesis. This nature applies to the lower level triads as well as to the higher level triads. In addition to this, Hegel's dialectic has a completing nature, since there is no more development when the Absolute Spirit has restored itself.

Let us briefly compare the laws and forms in Hegel's logic with those of formal logic. The laws in formal logic are the law of identity, the law of contradiction, and so forth, and the forms are the forms of judgment, and the forms of inference. In contrast, the laws in Hegel's logic are dialectical laws, such as the law of development through contradiction, the law of the transformation of quantity into quality, the law of negation of the negation, and so forth; the form is that of a dialectical development, namely, the three stages of thesis, antithesis, and synthesis. A logic with such a form of development is called a dialectical logic.

C. Dialectical Logic (Marxist Logic)

According to Hegel, Idea manifests itself as nature in the clothing of matter; therefore, objective reality is Idea. Marx, however, asserted that objective reality is matter, and that ideas are merely the reflections of the material world on human consciousness. Yet Marx accepted, without change, Hegel's dialectic of thesis, antithesis, and synthesis, and asserted that it is in fact the form of material development. Accordingly, in opposition to Hegel's "idealistic dialectic," Marx's dialectic is called a "materialist dialectic."

Based on such a materialist dialectic, Marxist logic was established. The materialist dialectic is the same as the idealistic dialectic in that both have the three-stage process of thesis, antithesis, and synthesis; therefore, Marxist logic is also called a dialectical logic. Its original characteristic is its opposition to formal logic, especially to the law of identity and the law of contradiction;[8] that is because, according to dialectical logic, in order for things to develop, A should be A and at the same time it should be not-A; and because the laws of thought should be the reflection of the material development of things. From the position of a materialist conception of history, Marxists assume that the forms and laws of thinking advocated by formal logic belong to the superstructure and have a class nature, so they should be rejected and a new dialectical logic created, in opposition to formal logic.[9] However, if formal logic was to be rejected, then one would inevitably run into difficulty: without formal logic, it is impossible to conduct coherent and correct thinking.

Linguistics also faced a similar difficulty. Based on the assertion that language belongs to the superstructure, and has a class character, it was argued that a new Soviet language should be created in place of the old Russian language.[10] However, this was almost impossible. Therefore, in 1950, Stalin published a paper entitled "Marxism and the Problems of Linguistics," asserting that language does not belong to the superstructure nor does it have a class nature. With this thesis as the starting point, a series of discussions took place in the Soviet Union from 1950 to 1951 on the subject of how to evaluate formal logic. From those discussions, the conclusion was reached that the forms and laws of formal logic do not belong to the superstructure and do not have class nature. Concerning the relation between formal logic and dialectic logic, it was decided that, "while formal logic deals with the elementary laws and forms of thinking, dialectical logic is a higher logic concerning the laws of development of objective reality and of thinking, which is the reflection of objective reality."[11] Yet, logic based on a materialist dialectic, namely, dialectical logic, makes only basic assertions, such as criticizing the laws of identity and the law of contradiction. As a matter of fact, it has not been systematized as of yet.[12]

D. Symbolic Logic

Symbolic logic, which is a development of formal logic, is an attempt to apply the correct method of judgment by using mathematical symbols. Symbolic logic contrasts with formal logic in certain important ways. In formal logic, the subject matter is the relationship of implications between terms, that is, the relationship of implications between the subject and the predicate in a proposition. In contrast, symbolic logic focuses on the connection between terms, or between propositions, and its subject-matter is the study of the laws of thought through the use of mathematical symbols.

The five basic forms of connection between propositions are as follows (where p and q are two propositions):

i) Negation   "not-p"······ $\sim p$ (or $\bar{p}$)
ii) Disjunction   "p or q"······ $p \vee q$
iii) Conjunction   "p and q"······ $p \cdot q$
iv) Implication   "If p then q"······ $p \supset q$
v) Equivalence   "p equals q"······ $p \equiv q$

Through the combination of these five basic forms, any complicated deductive inference can be accurately expressed. For example, the basic laws of formal logic, namely, the law of identity, law of contradiction, and law of the excluded middle, can be symbolized as follows:

Law of identity	$p \supset q$ or $p \equiv q$
Law of contradiction	$\sim(p \cdot \sim p)$ or $\overline{(p \cdot \overline{p})}$
Law of excluded middle	$p \vee \sim p$ or $p \vee \overline{p}$

Philosophers often proposed extensive thought systems, but the question is whether or not their logical constructions are correct. In order to ascertain their correctness, we need to use mathematical symbols and make calculations. Symbolic logic came into being from such a point of view.

E. Transcendental Logic

Kant's logic is called a transcendental logic. Concerning the question of how objective knowledge can be obtained, Kant held that objective knowledge can be obtained by thinking, through one's forms of thought, about the sense content gained through forms of intuition.

As already explained, thinking follows certain forms: the judgment forms and inference forms in formal logic; the three stages of dialectical form in Hegel's logic; the forms of intuition and twelve forms of thought in Kant. Kant divided judgment into four headings: quantity, quality, relation, and mode. Further, he divided each of these into three kinds, establishing twelve forms. Based upon these forms, he established twelve forms of thought, or twelve categories. A category is the most basic framework through which we think. Categories are also called a priori concepts.

Kant held that the forms of intuition and the forms of thought are a priori, and not related to experience. His logic is called a transcendental logic. Cognition, however, can not be achieved with only a priori forms. Cognition takes place when the a priori forms are connected to the sense content from an outside object, whereby an object of cognition is finally synthesized. Kant's forms of thought are forms for cognition. They are concepts, or categories. A concept is something like an empty container. It is meaningless if there is no content. For example, the concept of "animal" has no substance (content) and it is merely a concept, whereas individual beings that really exist such as chicken, dog, horse, shark, and so on are beings with concrete content.

For Kant, things-in-themselves can not be known. The things themselves send various stimuli to our sense organs, whereby this manifold of sense—sense content, or sense qualities—is perceived. When the sense content and the concept of an "animal" are united the object of cognition is synthesized, for example a chicken or a dog. Thus, the forms of thought themselves are only an empty framework, and only when they are filled with the qualities from the outside, is the object of cognition synthesized. Thus, in Kant, cognition is that of the synthesized object.

Formal logic since Aristotle has dealt with the general forms and laws of thought, without considering the object of thought. Kant's logic, however, was epistemological logic, aiming to verify how knowledge about the object is achieved.

II. Unification Logic

A. Basic Postulates

The Starting Point and Direction of Thinking

Traditional systems of logic have focused primarily on the laws and forms of thought, but Unification logic begins by considering, first of all, the starting point of thinking itself. Unification logic starts from the question as to why thinking takes place at all, and then examines the forms and laws of thought. Why does a human being think? The reason is that, prior to the creation of the universe, God engaged in thinking. That is, prior to the creation of the universe, God established the purpose of actualizing love based on Heart, and then made plans in accordance with that purpose. That constituted His thinking, or Logos (Word).

Accordingly, a human being, who is created in God's likeness, establishes the purpose of actualizing love based on heart, and then proceeds to think in order to accomplish that purpose; that is the original way of human thinking. Purpose here refers to the "purpose for being created" which consists of the "purpose for the whole" and the "purpose for the individual." The purpose for the whole is to serve, with love, one's family, neighbors, nation, and all humankind, to please them, and moreover, to please God. The purpose for the individual is to satisfy one's own desires. Ultimately, these dual purposes are the purposes for which the human being should live and for these purposes, the human being engages in thinking. Between the purpose for the whole and the purpose for the individual, the former should be given priority.

Therefore, thinking is to be carried out primarily to actualize the purpose for the whole, and secondarily to actualize the purpose for the individual. Hence, the purpose for the individual is for the purpose for the whole. Thus, originally human beings are supposed to think not for the purpose of satisfying their own individual purpose, but for the purpose of loving others. This is the starting point, and the direction, of original thinking.

The Standard of Thinking

What is the standard of thinking? Just as Unification ontology and Unification epistemology find their foundation in the Original Image, so too, the system of Unification logic has its foundation in the original Image. Therefore, the standard of thinking is in the Original Image, and that is the logical structure of the Original Image; namely, the inner developmental four position foundation and the formation of Logos (plan). In other words, the standard of thinking is the harmonious give and receive action that takes place between the Inner *Sungsang* and Inner *Hyungsang* centering on the purpose based on Heart.

Related Fields

Another point that should be mentioned before proceeding to the main topic is the relationship between logic and other fields. Formal logic does not deal with the relationship with other fields. Then, in order to correct its deficiency, dialectical logic and transcendental logic appeared as its alternatives. In Unification logic, the starting point of thinking is the actualization of the purpose of creation based on God's love, and its standard is the logical structure of the Original Image; therefore, there is a wide range of related fields. This is because the origin of thinking is God's Word (Logos), or God's plan, and every field of culture is established based on this plan.

In the Original Image, the inner developmental four position foundation, through which Logos is formed, is the first part of the "two-stage structure of creation." Consequently, Logos, which is the Word, and at the same time a set of universal laws, functions in all created things. Similarly, logic is related to all other fields, since the inner developmental four position foundation (the logical structure) is related to the outer developmental four position foundation, in the formation of the two-stage structure of creation.

The inner four position foundation in the two-stage structure of creation becomes the logical structure, and the outer four position foundation becomes the structure of cognition, and the structure of dominion. The structure of cognition, which is the four position foundation in the acquisition of knowledge from nature, is formed in scientific research, and the structure of dominion is the four position foundation formed in production and practice, such as in industry, government, education, art, and so on. Thus, logic, which is based on the logical structure, is closely related to all other cultural fields, which are based on the structures of cognition and dominion.

Structure of the Original Image

Here, I can briefly review the structure of the Original Image. As explained before, the Original Image consists of the two stages of the inner and outer four position foundations. This structure is called the "two-stage structure of the Original Image." The similar two-stage structure in created beings is called the "two-stage structure of existence." Further, each of the inner and outer four position foundations assumes an identity-maintaining nature and a developmental nature, thus forming the identity-maintaining and developmental four position foundations. The inner and outer developmental four position foundations are called the "two-stage structure of creation."

Since every created being is made in the likeness of these two-stage structures, every individual truth being possesses the "two-stage structure of existence" and the "two-stage structure of creation." Therefore, in human beings, the structure of logic, structure of cognition, structure of existence, and structure of dominion all assume the two-stage structures; thus, every four position foundation formed in our daily lives necessarily assumes the two-stage four position foundation, or two-stage structure.

This also means that any field in which the formation of the inner four position foundation is emphasized, and any area in which the formation of the outer four position foundation is emphasized are in a complementary relationship to each other. For example, logic, which is mainly related

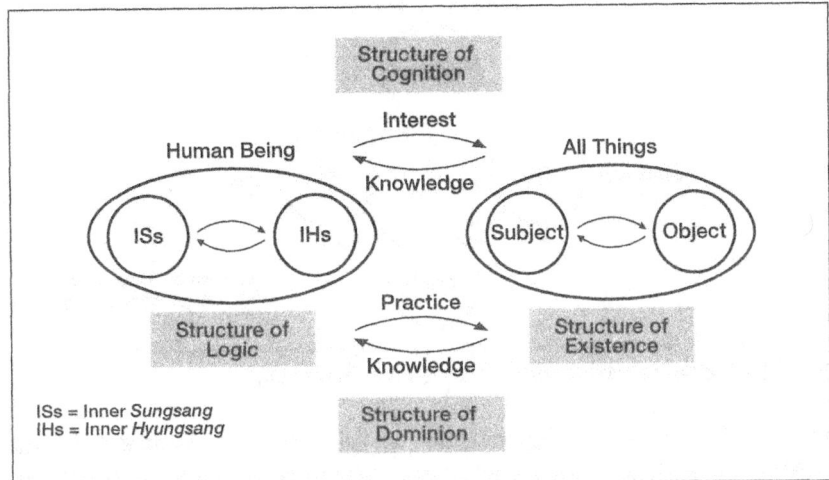

Fig. 10.10. Interconnectedness between the Structures of Logic, Cognition, Existence, and Dominion

to the inner structure, and pedagogy, and others, which are mainly related to the activity of dominion, thus focusing on the outer structure, are in a mutually complementary relationship. In conclusion, all the two-stage structures in human society derive from the two-stage Structure of the Original Image; therefore they are all interrelated (see fig. 10.10).

B. Logical Structure of the Original Image

Let me now proceed to the main topic.

Structure of the Formation of Logos and the Inner Developmental Four Position Foundation

As already explained, logic is the science concerning the laws and forms of thinking. The foundation of Unification logic lies in the inner four position foundation in the Original *Sungsang* of God, especially the inner developmental four position foundation. Therefore, we have to examine how thinking is made in the inner developmental four position foundation.

As explained in the Theory of the Original Image, the Inner *Sungsang* of the inner developmental four position foundation refers to intellect, emotion, and will, and the Inner *Hyungsang* refers to ideas, concepts,

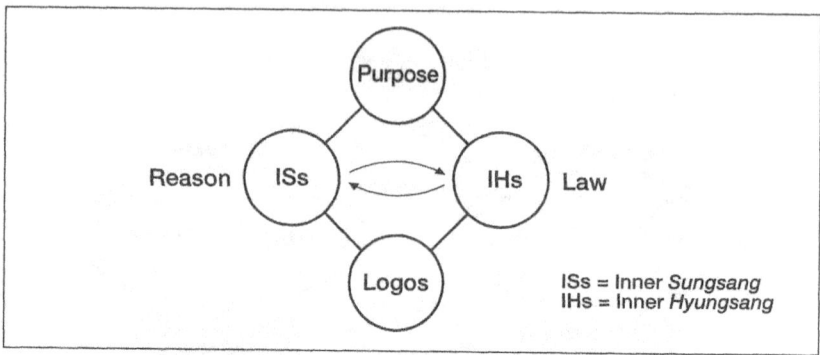

Fig. 10.11. Inner Developmental Four Position Foundation

laws and mathematical principles. In the inner developmental four position foundation, give and receive action takes place centering on purpose, which is established centering on Heart (love). That is to say, give and receive action takes place in order to actualize the purpose of Heart, whereby Logos or a plan is formed. Therefore, the plan formed is the plan for actualizing the purpose of love. This is the logical structure. Thus, the logical structure refers to the inner four position foundation of Logos which is formed through the inner give and receive action to actualize the purpose of love (see fig. 10.11).

Human beings should also form inner four position foundations for the sake of actualizing the purpose of love, in likeness to the logical structure of the Original Image. Thus, thinking should be carried out in order to realize love.

Original Way of Human Thinking

Originally, human thinking is motivated by heart or love. That is, thinking is for the practice of love. Freedom is for the practice of love as well. If someone does evil acts or hates others in the name of freedom, it is actually an abuse of freedom. The practice of love is to realize the world of love, or the world of the ideal of creation. If people think more and more for the sake of the realization of love, the world of love can soon be realized.

The Two-Stage Structure of Creation

Here, I will explain the relationship between logic and the two-stage structure of creation, which I have often mentioned. The two-stage

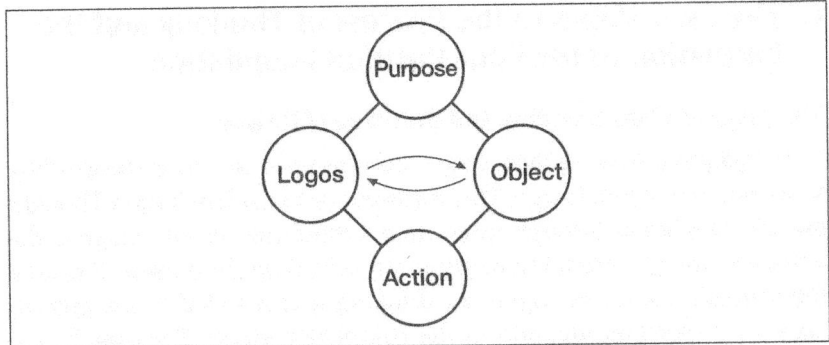

Fig. 10.12. Outer Developmental Four Position Foundation

structure of creation consists of the inner developmental four position foundation and the outer developmental four position foundation that are formed successively. At that moment, Logos is formed as the inner developmental four position foundation, which is the logical structure.

Then, what is the relationship between logic and the outer developmental four position foundation? Is the outer developmental four position foundation necessary for logic? Yes, it is absolutely necessary. This is because in Unification logic thinking is carried out in order to actualize the purpose of creation, or actualize love; therefore, the practice of love is the requisite for loving. Practice refers to the actualization of what one has thought in his or her mind; in other words, it is the formation of the outer developmental four position foundation. The object of one's practice is all things and human beings. That is, practice is to love all things and human beings. Thus, thinking is necessarily accompanied with motivation, purpose, and direction; and it should be practiced as an action (see fig. 10.12).

This unity of thinking and practice has its origin in God. God first made plans or formed Logos, and then began to create all things and human beings. That is, God planned (formed Logos), and started creation. This is the "two-stage structure of creation." Formal logic only deals with the forms and laws of thinking. From the viewpoint of Unification logic, formal logic is not incorrect, but it is incomplete. A unity of knowledge and action or the unity of theory and practice is necessary. Its theoretical foundation is the two-stage structure of creation.

C. The Two Stages in the Process of Thinking and the Formation of the Four Position Foundation

The Stage of Understanding and the Stage of Reason

In cognition, there are three stages: the sensory stage, the understanding stage, and the rational stage. This corresponds to the Unification Thought law of completion through three stages. Since the sensory stage is the entrance through which information comes in from the outside, it is only the formation stage of cognition; thinking is conducted in the growth stage of understanding, and in the completion stage of reason. In the understanding stage, thinking is affected by the information coming from the outside; in the rational stage, however, thinking is carried out freely.

Kant, also, speaks of three stages of cognition. The stage in which one receives the sense content coming from the outside through the forms of intuition is the sensory stage; the stage in which one thinks through the forms of thought is the stage of understanding, and that which unifies and arranges the knowledge acquired in the stage of understanding is the stage of reason.[13]

In the case of Marxism, the stage in which the sense content is reflected on the brain is the sensory stage. Next is the logical stage, or the rational stage, in which judgment and inference take place. Beyond that there is the stage of practice in which truth is confirmed through practice. For Marxists, forms of thought are reflections of forms of existence in the external world.

In terms of cerebral physiology, as was explained in the chapter on epistemology, it is considered that the sensory stage of thinking takes place in the sensory centers; the understanding stage, in the parietal association area; and the rational stage, in the frontal association area.

In the understanding stage and also in the rational stage, a logical structure resembling the structure of the Original Image is formed. In the understanding stage, thinking is restricted by the sense content entering from the outside. This content, from the external world, and the prototype of the internal world, are collated, completing cognition up to that point. Here, an internal, completed (identity-maintaining) four position foundation is formed as the cognitive or logical structure. In the rational stage, thinking is free to develop on the basis of knowledge obtained in the understanding stage; here, a new conception, or a plan (a multiplied being), can be established. The structure at this point is the inner developmental four position foundation.

Figuratively speaking, the sensory center (sensibility) corresponds to the entrance of a house; the parietal association area (understanding) corresponds to the reception room; and the frontal association area (reason) corresponds to the living room or study room. When informed of the visit of a guest, the host receives the guest in the reception room. This can be compared to the sensory stage. Then, the host tries to understand what the guest says while meeting the guest face to face. At that time, the host is not in a position to think freely about just anything he chooses, because his thinking is shaped by his conversation with his guest. This can be compared to the understanding stage. But when the visit is over, the host can retire to a private room and think freely, referring back to what the guest has said. This can be compared to the rational stage.

The Development of Thinking in the Stage of Reason

In the stage of reason, how does thinking develop? Thinking is made through give and receive action. First, through give and receive action between the inner *sungsang* and the inner *hyungsang*, a first step logos, or plan (a multiplied being) is formed as the conclusion of the thinking. This sometimes concludes the process, but in most cases, it is necessary to form a second step logos (plan) based upon that conclusion. The logos formed at the first step has been stored in the inner *hyungsang* as an idea or a concept and is mobilized as a datum for the next step of thinking, together with many other data (ideas, concepts, etc). In this way, the logos of the second step is formed, which is again stored in the inner *hyungsang* to be mobilized in further thinking. Then the third step logos comes to be formed. Subsequently, thinking proceeds to fourth and fifth stages, etc. Thus, in many cases, even simple thinking does not end in the first stage but continues many times. This is the process of forming the four position foundation in the rational stage. It is called the development of thinking in a spiral form (see fig. 10.13).

Thus, thinking continues to develop infinitely in the rational stage, since it is a developmental four position process. However, in the development of thinking, a new step begins after the previous step is completed; thus, the development of thinking consists of the successive formations of completed four position foundations. Therefore, thinking develops by repeating these completed steps.

466 / LOGIC

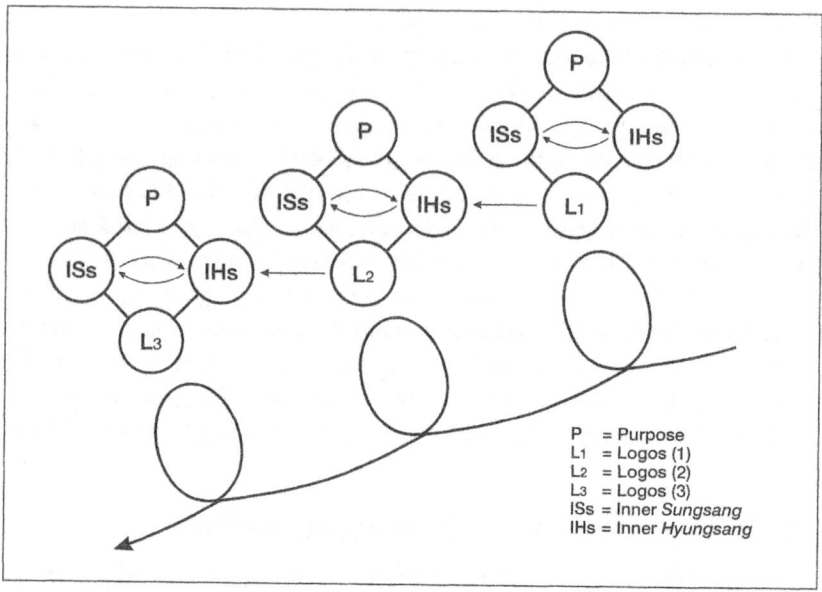

Fig. 10.13. The Development of Thinking in a Spiral Form in the Stage of Reason

Basic Forms of Thought

Thinking (or cognition) at the stage of understanding takes place with the sense content and prototype entering into give and receive action centering on purpose. First, the purpose must be properly established. The correct purpose refers to the purpose of creation based on heart (love).

As explained in Unification epistemology, the protoimages and the images of relation formed in the protoconsciousness of cells and tissues are transferred to the subconsciousness within the lower center through the peripheral nerves, and they are integrated and stored there. These are a priori prototypes (original prototypes) with which human beings are born. The images of relation become forms of thought, which put certain restrictions on cognition and thinking.

The subconsciousness in the lower center has certain forms (images of form). Suppose, for example, that an individual has appendicitis. The lower center, which integrates protoconsciousness, knows in advance the information concerning the *sungsang* and *hyungsang* (functions and structure) peculiar to the appendix. Therefore, the lower center immediately perceives an abnormality. Thus, the lower center sends an appropriate instruction for the appendix to return to its original, normal condition.

When the movement of the stomach is too strong, it can cause convulsions, and when the movement is too weak, it can cause gastric ptosis; the lower center knows the information concerning the strength of the stomach movement. When the movement is too strong or too weak, the lower center adjusts the strength properly. This kind of information is related to yang and yin.

The cell has a nucleus and cytoplasm; the nucleus controls the cytoplasm. The nucleus and cytoplasm are in the relationship of subject and object. The subconsciousness of the lower center has information concerning subject and object within the cell.

The subconsciousness also has the sense of time and space. Thus, when an infection occurs somewhere within the physical body, the subconsciousness sends white blood corpuscles to that location, and tries to cure it.

The subconsciousness also knows the relationship between finite and infinite. For example, red blood corpuscles die after they have lived for a certain period of time and new red blood corpuscles are created. In that way, new cells are continually being created within the body, and old cells die away. The subconsciousness is aware of this finitude. In the body, there are also cells and organs that exist and function while maintaining their durability, perpetuity, and cyclic nature. The subconsciousness knows about this infinity of cells and organs as well.

In this way, the subconsciousness of the lower center knows the forms of *sungsang* and *hyungsang*, yang and yin, subject and object, time and space, finitude and infinitude, etc. The images of these correlations reflected in the subconsciousness are the images of form, which are sent to the cerebral center and become the forms of thought in thinking.

The role that the forms of thought play in thinking can be explained by comparing it with a soccer game. In a soccer game, players run and kick the ball as they please; yet, they do it while following certain rules. Likewise, reason freely proceeds with thinking, but thinking is made with certain forms, which are under the influence of the images of form; in other words, thinking follows certain rules.

Forms of thought are otherwise called categories which are the highest generic concepts. In Unification Thought, categories are established on the basis of the principles of the four position foundation and give and receive action. This is because the four position foundation and give and receive action are the core principles of Unification Thought. First, ten basic categories are established, the meaning of which has been explained in the chapter on Epistemology.

In the past, many thinkers established various categories, and among those categories, there are many that are related to the categories of Unification Thought. For example, there is the category of essence and phenomenon, which corresponds to the Unification Thought category of *sungsang* and *hyungsang*.

Categories are divided into primary and secondary. The primary categories are the ten basic forms peculiar to Unification Thought. The secondary categories are developed on the basis of the primary categories. Among these, there are some that correspond to the categories of traditional philosophy. The following is a list of the primary and secondary categories. There is no particular limit to the number of secondary categories: here, only a few are mentioned.

Primary Categories
   (1) Existence & Force   (2) *Sungsang* & *Hyungsang*
   (3) Yang & Yin   (4) Subject & Object
   (5) Position & Settlement   (6) Unchangeability & Changeability
   (7) Action & Effect   (8) Time & Space
   (9) Number & Principle   (10) Finitude & Infinity

Secondary Categories
   (1) Quality & Quantity   (2) Content & Form
   (3) Essence & Phenomenon   (4) Cause & Effect
   (5) Whole & Individual   (6) Abstract & Concrete
   (7) Substance & Attribute

Since *sungsang* & *hyungsang*, among the primary categories, resemble essence & phenomenon or content & form, why use such a new, uncommon term? Those concepts which constitute the fundamentals of Unification Thought are such concepts as four position foundation, Origin, Division, and Union Action, give and receive action, and so on. If these were to be taken away, it would mean that Unification Thought would lose its skeleton. Therefore, we can not but use these terms as categories of Unification Thought.

Categories and thought systems are closely related. It can be said that when one sees the categories of a thought system, one knows the thought system itself, and when one grasps a thought system, one knows its categories. Categories are the signboard of a thought system. Since Unification Thought is a new thought, it is natural to establish categories with new terms appropriate to this new thought. Marx's thought has Marxist categories; Kant's thought has Kantian categories; and Hegel's thought has Hegelian categories. Likewise, Unification Thought must have Unification Thought categories, showing the characteristics of Unification Thought. These are the ten basic forms constituting its primary categories.

Basic Laws of Thought

In formal logic, the basic laws of thought are the law of identity, the law of contradiction, the law of excluded middle, and the law of sufficient reason. From the perspective of Unification Thought, there is an even more basic law, namely, the law of give and receive action. This law is not only the law of logic, but it also applies to all fields including politics, economics, society, science, history, art, religion, education, ethics, morality, speech, law, sports, business and natural sciences (physics, chemistry, physiology, astronomy, and so forth).

This law also applies to the entire created world; namely, the entire physical world (universe) and the whole spirit world. To be sure, it also applies to epistemology, which is closely related to logic. The reason why the give and receive law is so ubiquitously at work is that it is God's law of creation, which derives from the give and receive action between God's Original *Sungsang* and Original *Hyungsang*. God created all things in the likeness of His attributes; therefore, give and receive action in God becomes the law of the created world.

The law of give and receive action is the most fundamental law, governing all other laws. In other words, the basis of physical laws, chemical laws, astronomic laws, etc. is the law of give and receive action. The laws and forms of traditional systems of logic, including formal logic, are also based, ultimately, on the law of give and receive action. Thus, the law of give and receive action is the basic law of thought. In order to show this, I will make some comparisons between a syllogism and the law of give and receive action.

Syllogism and the Law of Give and Receive Action

A syllogism is an inference in formal logic. In order to show that the law of give and receive action is the foundation of the forms and laws of formal logic, let us consider, for instance, the following syllogism:

Man is mortal.
Socrates is a man.
Therefore, Socrates is mortal.

The conclusion is drawn as a result of the give and receive action between the major premise and the minor premise, centering on purpose; namely, the conclusion is drawn through the comparison of the two propositions: "Man is mortal" and "Socrates is a man" (see fig. 10.14). Furthermore, the proposition itself is established through the comparison of two concepts (subject and predicate) as shown in figure 10.15. The same thing can be said of the following example:

(a) One meter is 3.28 feet.
(b) The width of this desk is 2 meters.
(c) Therefore, the width of this desk is 6.56 feet.

In this case, the conclusion is obtained through a comparison of propositions (a) and (b).

The Law of Identity and the Law of Give and Receive Action

The same thing can be said of the law of identity. Consider, for example, the proposition, "This flower is a rose." This is a judgment in which "this flower" and "a rose" are compared in one's mind and it is concluded that they are the same. Comparison is a contrast type of give and receive action. Thus, the law of identity is based on the law of give and receive action. The same thing can be said of the law of contradiction. In this way, the forms and laws of formal logic are all based on the law of give and receive action.

Thinking and Freedom

Logic emphasizes the forms and laws of thinking. Then, one may think, "Are we restricted by laws and forms in our thinking?" or "I wish I could think freely without any restriction." In fact, however, forms and

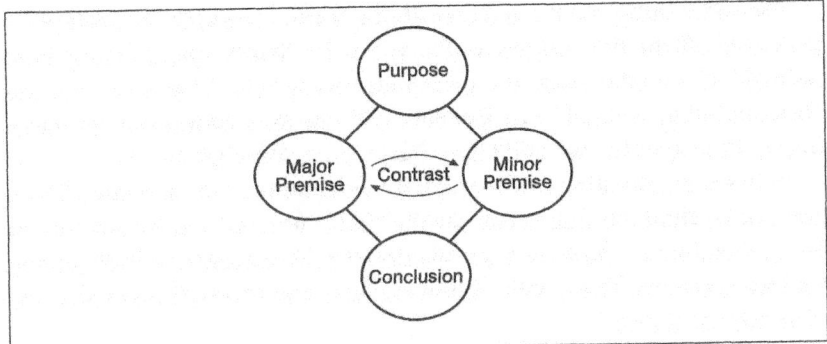

Fig. 10.14. Contrast-Type Give and Receive Action between Proposition and Proposition

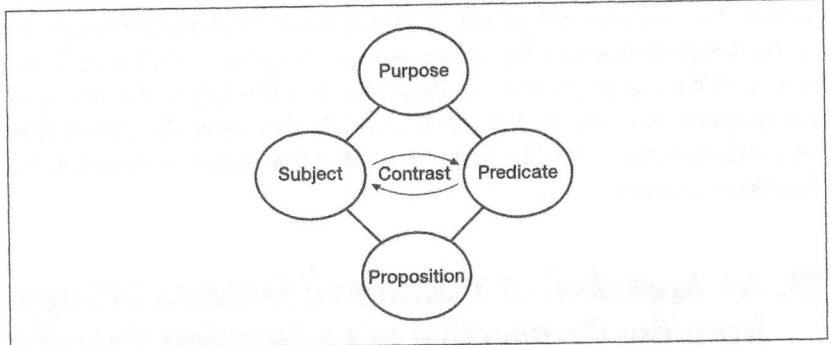

Fig. 10.15. Contrast-Type Give and Receive Action between Subject and Object

laws in thinking give us freedom in thinking. Thinking without laws and forms will break down. It is the same thing as a train unable to move without rails. Only when both our mind and body are in accordance with laws, can they work normally.

All the physiological functions of our body work in accordance with natural law: respiration, digestion, blood circulation, and transmission of information in the nerves are all under certain physiological laws. If physiological functions deviate from natural laws, our body will become ill right away. The same thing can be said of our thinking. Consider, for example, the law of identity, "A is A." If we do not use the logical term "is," we can not understand the meaning: If someone says "This flower, a rose" instead of "This flower is a rose," it is not completely clear what he or she means.

The same thing can be said concerning form. Consider, for example, a universal affirmative judgment (Every S is P): "Every human being is an animal." If we take away the form that "every S is P," and we just say "human being, animal," our listeners will not understand our meaning, and as time goes by, we will forget the meaning of what we say.

In this way, thinking necessarily follows certain forms and laws. There can not be thinking that is completely "free," unrestricted by any law or form. Freedom of thinking is the freedom to choose any one from among various concepts. Thus, while following laws and forms, thinking has the "freedom of choice."

When people think about love, for example, they have the common purpose or common direction of the actualization of love. In their specific thinking, however, purposes and directions are different from person to person. It is because each person has the freedom of choice; therefore, he or she freely determines his or her specific purpose or direction. Then, how is thinking made freely? Freedom in thinking is the spiritual apperception to freely synthesize or associate ideas and concepts within the inner *hyungsang*. It is the freedom of planning, which is based on the freedom of reason.

III. An Appraisal of Traditional Systems of Logic from the Perspective of Unification Thought

Formal Logic

Concerning formal logic itself, Unification logic finds nothing to criticize, and so Unification logic is in agreement with the laws and forms of thought dealt with in formal logic just as they are. Nevertheless, human thinking has not only the aspect of form, but also the aspect of content. Also, thinking has purpose, direction, and relations with other fields. Therefore, thinking is not to be done just for the sake of thinking itself, but rather for the sake of cognition and practice (dominion), and for the sake of actualizing the purpose of creation. That is, the laws of thought are merely conditions wherein thinking can take place.

Hegel's Logic

Hegel's logic tried to interpret philosophically the way God had created the universe. Hegel understood God as Logos, or Idea, and considered Idea to be the starting point of the creation of the universe. Hegel first explained the development of Being, Nothing, and Becoming in the world of Idea. Since Being as it is contains no development, he thought of Nothing as something to be opposed to Being. Then, according to him, as the unity of the opposition between Being and Nothing, Becoming comes into being. There is a problem in this view, however. For Hegel, Nothing originally is merely an interpretation of Being, and Being and Nothing are not separated.[14] However, Hegel separated Being and Nothing, and explained it as if Being and Nothing were opposed to each other.

Another problem is that he held that Idea develops by itself. From the perspective of Unification Thought, idea belongs to the Inner *Hyungsang* in the structure of the Original Image, and develops as follows: As the functions of intellect, emotion, and will—particularly reason within the function of intellect—act upon the idea centering on purpose, the Logos (conception or plan) is formed, which becomes a new idea. Accordingly, Logos, or Idea, is something formed within the mind of God, and there can never be the case that Idea develops by itself. Criticizing the "self-development of the Idea" advocated by Hegel, Max von Rumelin, of Tubingen University, said:

> The amount of effort we have made to understand the meaning that Hegel's so-called speculative method had for its founder, Hegel, is beyond description. Every person thinking of other people and shaking his head, would ask, "Do you understand? Without your doing anything, will the Idea move by itself within your mind?" We were told that those who answer yes are people with a speculative brain. We, who were different from them, merely stood at the stage of thinking in the category of limited understanding···. In our minds, the reason we had failed fully to understand that method was the dullness of our own talents; we did not have enough courage to consider that the reason lay in the very lack of clarity and in the defects of the method itself.[15]

Further, Hegel held nature to be the self-alienation, or the form of otherness, of Idea. As was pointed out in the Theory of the Original

Image, this view regards nature as the expression of God, and is a view that can lead to pantheism, making no distinction between nature and God. Thus, it has the potential to easily turn into materialism.

In Hegel's dialectic, nature was merely an intermediate step in the process leading to the appearance of humankind. Nature is like the scaffolding of a building under construction. Once the building is completed, the scaffolding, which was used as a means of constructing the building, is taken away. Likewise, once humankind came into being, nature in itself became meaningless from the philosophical point of view.

He also said that the human being is manipulated by reason in the development of history. Consequently, the human being actually is a being to be manipulated like a puppet by the Absolute Spirit. From the perspective of Unification Thought, however, God is not unilaterally moving history. History is made through the combination of the human being's portion of responsibility and God's portion of responsibility.

Furthermore, Hegel's dialectic has a cyclical, returning, and completing nature. According to Hegel, Prussia was supposed to become the rational state that had emerged at the end of history. In actuality, however, Prussia disappeared from history without becoming the rational state. Therefore, it follows that Hegel's philosophy came to an end with the end of Prussia. Problems such as these are abundant in Hegel's philosophy. We must say that the cause of these mistakes can be found in his logic. Let us examine this point further.

Hegel grasped the development of Idea as the dialectical development of thesis, antithesis, and synthesis. The Idea alienates itself and becomes nature; and later, by becoming spirit through humankind, it recovers itself. According to Hans Leisegang, this way of thinking is unique to Hegel, and is based on his study of the Bible. Specifically, Hegel's philosophy of opposition, which is transcended by a higher synthesis, is said to be based on the theme of certain passages from the Gospel according to John, such as "Unless a grain of wheat falls into the earth and dies, it remains alone; but if it dies, it bears much fruit" (John 12:24), and "I am the resurrection and the life; he who believes in me, though he dies, yet shall he live" (John 11:25).[16] From this position, Hegel conceived of God as Logos, or Idea, and held that God manifests Himself in the external world just as the life of a seed sown on the earth manifests itself on the outside. Here lies the fundamental cause of Hegel's errors.

From the perspective of Unification Thought, God is a God of Heart (love), and having established the purpose of creation motivated by Heart—an emotional impulse to be joyful by loving an object—He created the universe with Logos. Logos was the plan for creation in God's mind, and was not God Himself. In Hegel's idealistic dialectic, however, God's Heart (love) or His purpose of creation are not mentioned. In Hegel, God is not explained as God the Creator, but rather as a kind of life that germinates and grows.

At this point, let us compare Hegel's logic and Unification Thought logic. There are similarities between them, though the meanings are different. What Hegel calls Logos corresponds, in Unification Thought, to God's conception of, or plan for, creation. Hegel's process described as the dialectic of Logos corresponds in Unification Thought, to give and receive action in the Original Image. Hegel's thesis, antithesis, and synthesis correspond to the Origin, Division, and Union Action in Unification Thought. Hegel's dialectic, which has a returning and completing nature, can be understood, according to Unification Thought, as the spiral developmental movement in nature through give and receive action centered on the purpose of creation, and in history, as the history of re-creation and restoration. Hegel tried to find the Idea through nature, but Unification Thought holds that one can perceive the Original Image (Divine Image and Divine Character) through all things symbolically. Therefore, the problem of Hegel's pantheistic nature can be solved by the Unification Thought Theory of Pan-Divine Image, the view that the Divine Image is manifested in all created beings.

Dialectical Logic

As mentioned before, Stalin published a paper entitled "Marxism and the Problems of Linguistics," in order to settle the controversy which arose in the academic society of the Soviet Union. He concluded in it that linguistics does not belong to the superstructure and therefore it has no class nature. As a result, the law of identity and the law of contradiction in formal logic came to be recognized.

However, in the framework of Marxism, the law of identity and the law of contradiction are considered only as laws of thinking and are not laws of development of the objective world. Hence, even if they accept the law of identity and the law of contradiction in thinking, they claim that the objective world follows the dialectical law of contradiction (the law of the unity and struggle of opposites). This, however, is not in agreement with the basic tenet of materialist dialectic that thinking is a reflection of the objective world. Such a difficulty, or an aporia, occurred.[17]

In this way, after the publication of Stalin's paper, the law of the objective world (the dialectical law of contradiction) and the law of thought (the law of identity) became separated. In contrast, it is the assertion of Unification Thought that changeability (developmental nature) and unchangeability are united in the objective world as well as in thinking.

Thinking (or cognition) in the stage of understanding has mainly the identity-maintaining nature, because cognition is completed for the time being by collating the sense content coming from the external world with the prototypes from within. However, thinking becomes developmental in the rational stage. Still, thinking develops step by step; therefore, thinking has an aspect of completion (that is, an identity-maintaining aspect) in each of these steps. Accordingly, the law of identity and the law of contradiction are naturally recognized in Unification Thought.

More precisely, what does it mean that the materialist dialectic has come to recognize formal logic, that is to say, that the laws of identity and of contradiction have come to be recognized by the materialist dialectic? Originally, the basic assertion by the materialist dialectic was that things should be understood as continually changing and developing. However, the fact that the materialist dialectic has recognized the laws of identity and of contradiction means that it has come to affirm the unchanging nature of things, even if only with regard to thinking. That has brought about a change in the essential nature of the materialist dialectic. This is the same as a revision, or even collapse, of the materialist dialectic. At the same time, it goes to show that the assertion of Unification Thought, which views things as the unity of identity-maintenance and development, is the correct one.

Symbolic Logic

It is important to pursue accuracy or rigor in thinking, and, from that perspective, there is no reason why we should oppose symbolic logic. No one, however, can fully grasp human thinking by mere mathematical rigor alone.

In the Original Image, Logos is formed through the give and receive action between the Inner *Sungsang* and the Inner *Hyungsang*. Since laws and mathematical principles exist within the Inner *Hyungsang*, it follows that laws and mathematical principles are contained in Logos; therefore, all things created through Logos manifest laws and mathematical principles. That is why scientists are able to study nature mathematically.

Human thinking has God's Logos as its pattern. Therefore, human thinking naturally involves mathematical principles as well. In other words, it is desirable for thinking to be made with mathematical precision. Here we can recognize the significance of symbolic logic engaging in the mathematical study of thinking. We should keep in mind, however, that in the give and receive action between the Inner *Sungsang* and Inner *Hyungsang*, Heart is the center. This means that in the formation of Logos (Word), Heart stands in a position higher than reason and mathematical principles. Therefore, originally, a human being is not merely a being of logos (i.e., a rational or law-abiding being), but is more essentially a being with emotion (i.e., a being with heart, or an emotional being). Thus, even if one's thinking does not have mathematical strictness, if love or emotion is contained in one's thinking, the speaker's meaning can still be conveyed sufficiently well to others.

For example, when someone sees a fire and shouts, "Fire!", one can not know whether he meant to say, "This is a fire" or "There is a fire burning." In an emergency, however, if enough emotion calling for help is poured into the utterance, even if there is no grammatical accuracy in the words, people instantly understand the meaning of the utterance.

The human being is originally the union of logos and emotion. Therefore, by following only logos, a human being expresses only half of his or her true value. By being only rational, a human being is not fully human; only together with his or her emotional aspect can a human being be truly human. Therefore, sometimes words that have less accuracy can be more human. That is, there is an aspect in human thinking that requires strictness, but a human being does not always have to express everything accurately and logically. If we examine Jesus' words, we may find many illogical aspects there. And yet, why are his words great? It is because God's love is contained in them. Thus, even if our words may not precisely follow correct logic, we can still fully convey our meaning to others if the emotional element is properly included.

Transcendental Logic

Kant asserted that knowledge is acquired by thinking about an object (sense content) through a priori forms of thought. However, from the

TABLE 10.1 A Comparison between Unification Logic and Traditional Systems of Logic

	Unification Logic	Formal Logic	Dialectical Logic	Transcendental Logic
Forms of Thought	Objective & Subjective	Subjective	Objective	Subjective
Content of Thought	Objective & Subjective	None	Objective	Objective
Laws of Thought	Give and Receive Law	Law of Identity & Law of Contradiction	Dialectical Method	Transcendental Method
Standard of Thought	Structure of the Original Image	None	None	None
Characteristics	Theory of Collation	Theory of Form	Theory of Reflection	Theory of Synthesis

perspective of Unification Thought, the object has not only content (sense content) but also form (forms of existence), and the subject of cognition also has not only form (forms of thought) but also content (image of content). The truthfulness of thinking can not be guaranteed only by what Kant called the a priori forms and sense content. In contradistinction to that, in Unification Thought, the necessary relationship between human beings and all things leads to the correspondence between the laws and forms of thinking and the laws and forms of the external world, and thus the truthfulness of thinking about the object can be guaranteed.

A Comparison between Unification Logic and Traditional Systems of Logic

Finally, a diagram presenting a comparative view of Unification logic, formal logic, dialectical logic, and transcendental logic is presented above (see table. 10.1).

11

Methodology

Methodology is the study of how one can reach objective truth. In fact, the English word method is derived from the Greek word *meta* (following) and *hodos* (the way). Thus, "method" implies that in order to attain some purpose, one should follow a certain way. From the time of ancient Greece until today, many philosophers developed their own unique methodologies to find the truth. Here we will first take up some representative traditional methodologies, and then present the methodology of Unification Thought, that is Unification methodology. Finally, we will examine some of the traditional methodologies from the standpoint of Unification Thought. What I should add here is that it is not my intention to introduce the traditional methodologies in all of their academic detail. I will only introduce certain main points of those methodologies in order to clarify that Unification methodology can solve their problems.

I. Historical Review

Heraclitus' Dialectic—A Dynamic Method

Heraclitus (ca. 535–475 BC), called the founder of the dialectic by Hegel, considered the fundamental matter of the universe to be fire and regarded fire as constantly changing. Stating that "everything is in a state of flux," he held that nothing is eternal; rather, everything is in a state of generation and movement. Further, stating that "war is the father and the king of all," he considered everything to be generating and changing through the conflict of opposites. In that way, Heraclitus grasped all things in the aspects of generation, change, and flux; thus, his method was called dialectic by Hegel. Nevertheless, he held that there is something unchangeable in generation and change, namely, law, which he called Logos. Also, he held that in all things, harmony arises through conflict. Heraclitus' methodology deals with the way nature is, and with its development. His dialectic, which seeks to grasp the dynamic aspect of things in this way, could be called a dynamic method.

Zeno's Dialectic—A Static Method

Contrary to Heraclitus, who asserted that everything is in a state of flux, Parmenides (ca. 510 BC) of the Eleatic school held that there is neither generation nor destruction; neither motion or change. Inheriting Parmenides' idea, Zeno of Elea (ca. 490–430 BC) denied movement, and tried to prove that there are only motionless beings.

Zeno cited four proofs for his view that material bodies, though appearing to be moving, are, in fact, not moving at all. One of his proofs is that Achilles can not ever overtake a tortoise. Achilles was a hero who distinguished himself during the Trojan War. Though a very fast runner, still he could not overtake a tortoise, Zeno maintained. Suppose the tortoise starts first; after the tortoise has advanced to a certain point, Achilles starts running after it. When Achilles arrives at the place where the tortoise was when he started, the tortoise has already gone ahead a certain distance. When Achilles arrives at that next place, the tortoise has already advanced again by a certain distance. Consequently, the tortoise is always ahead of Achilles.

Another proof offered by Zeno was that a flying arrow is always at rest. Suppose an arrow is flying from point A toward point C. Between A and C, the arrow passes the pints B_1, B_2, B_3, $\cdots$. To pass through these points means to stop at each point for a moment. Since the distance between A and C is a continuum of an innumerable number of points, the arrow is continuously at rest. Therefore, the arrow is always at rest.

Zeno's method is the art of dispute through question and answer, whereby one refutes his opponent by exposing contradictions in his argument, while examining his assertions. Aristotle called him the founder of the dialectic. Zeno's dialectic, which denied movement and proved that there are only motionless beings, could be called a static method.

Socrates' Dialectic—A Method of Dialogue

In the latter half of the fifth century BC, democratic politics was developed in Athens. During that time, young people made an effort to learn the art of persuasion in order to succeed in politics. Therefore, there appeared professionals who specialized in teaching young people the art of persuasion. They were called sophists.

Early Greek philosophy dealt with nature as its object of study; but the sophists turned away from the philosophy of nature to discuss human and social problems. They realized, however, that, while nature has objectivity and necessity, human matters are relative; as a result, relativism, which claimed that the understanding of human matters is different according to one's subjective view, and skepticism which gave up the effort in finding solutions to human problems, gained influence. Sophists, who walked around the polis, could witness the fact that the standard of judgment differed from place to place, and so they came to assert that no truth exists with regard to human beings. As a result, the art of persuasion that they taught attached importance only to the method of refuting one's opponents, and came to use even sophistry for that purpose.

Socrates (470–399 BC) deplored the fact that sophists were confusing people in that way and asserted that what is important is the virtue with which one should live, rather than any technical knowledge designed for political success. For him, only true knowledge can show what virtue really is. He held that in order to attain truth, what is necessary, first of all, is to accept one's own ignorance, and stated, "Know thyself." Also, he asserted that, with a humble heart, one could reach the truth by engaging in dialogue with another person. Then, starting from the particular, we can be led to universal conclusions. To attain the truth is to evoke, through asking questions, the truth dormant in the mind of a person and, in this way, to draw forth the truth already inherent in the person's mind. Socrates named this process midwifery. His method of pursuing the truth is called a dialectic, and it takes place through discussion.

Plato's Dialectic—A Method of Division

Plato (427–347 BC), a disciple of Socrates, tried to explain how true knowledge, concerning the virtue referred to by Socrates, comes to be obtained. Plato maintained the existence of non-material being, which is the essence of a thing, and he called it Idea, or form (*eidos*). Among scores of Ideas he regarded the Idea of the Good as supreme, and asserted that only when people intuit the Idea of the Good can they lead the supreme life. According to Plato, that which truly exists is Idea, and the phenomenal world is but a copy of the world of Ideas. Accordingly, a knowledge of the Ideas is indeed true knowledge. He also called his method, the cognition of Ideas, the dialectic.

Plato's dialectic sought to determine the relationships between Ideas and to explain the structure of Ideas, which placed the Idea of the Good at the apex. In the cognition of Ideas, there are two directions: The first progresses from the upper to the lower through the division of the generic concepts into specific concepts; the second progresses from the lower to the upper through synthesizing the concepts of individual things, aiming at the supreme concept. Between the two methods, the direction of synthesis corresponds to Socrates' dialectic; the direction of division is most typically Plato's. Thus, when we refer to Plato's dialectic, we usually mean the method by division.

In contrast to Socrates, who held that knowledge could be obtained through a dialogue between persons, Plato proposed his dialectic as a method of classifying concepts, or a method of self-questioning and self-answering, namely, a method of questioning and answering taking place in one's own mind.

Aristotle's Deductive Method

The study of how correct knowledge can be obtained was systematized by Aristotle (384–322 BC) as the science of knowledge, that is, logic. Logic, which was compiled in his *Organon*, was regarded as an instrument for reaching truth through proper thinking, as a science preliminary to the various other sciences.

According to Aristotle, true knowledge should be obtained through logical proof. He recognized the inductive method as well, in which one proceeds from the particular to the universal; but Aristotle regarded it as less than perfect. He thought that the deductive method, in which the particulars are deduced from the universal, would provide surer knowledge. The fundamental tool of this method is the syllogism, a representative example of which is as follows:

All men are mortal. (Major Premise)
Socrates is a man. (Minor Premise)

Therefore, Socrates is mortal. (Conclusion)

In the Middle Ages, great importance was attached to Aristotle's logic as an instrument for proving the propositions of theology and philosophy deductively. The Aristotelian syllogism has been recognized for two thousand years, hardly undergoing any change.

Bacon's Inductive Method

Throughout the Middle Ages God was regarded as being transcendental, but during the Renaissance, the perception of the transcendental character of God was gradually lost among philosophers. Moreover, there arose a pantheistic philosophy of nature, which regarded God as inherent in nature. At the time when the Middle Ages came to an end and the Modern Age began, a philosopher proposed a new methodology with which to study nature. His name was Francis Bacon (1561–1626).

According to Bacon, previous studies, based on metaphysics, were "sterile and like a virgin consecrated to God, producing nothing," mainly because they employed Aristotle's method. Aristotle's logic was a method for the sake of logical proof. With such logic, one might persuade others. With it, however, one could not obtain truths from nature. Thus, Bacon advocated the inductive method as the logic for finding new truth. He named his own discourse on logic *New Organon*, in contrast to Aristotle's *Organon*.

Asserting that traditional studies, which were based on Aristotle's logic, had been nothing but logical arguments of useless words, Bacon held that in order to obtain sure knowledge, we must first eliminate those prejudices to which we are liable, and then directly explore nature itself. Those prejudices he called the four Idols (see "Epistemology"). After eliminating these Idols, we will be able to observe nature with a clear mind and make observations and experiments. In that way, we can find universal essences existing within individual phenomena. Inductive methods before Bacon had sought to derive general laws from a small number of observations and experiments; Bacon, however, tried to present a true inductive method in order to obtain sure knowledge by collecting as many cases as possible, even attaching importance to negative instances.

Descartes' Methodic Doubt

Due to the remarkable achievements made in the natural sciences since the Renaissance period, seventeenth century philosophy regarded the mechanistic view of nature as absolute truth, and tried not to contradict it. Rationalism tried to provide a foundation for the mechanistic view of nature from a fundamental standpoint. Its representative proponent was René Descartes (1596–1650). Descartes considered the mathematical method to be the only true method; thus, as in mathematics, he first looked for an intuitive truth that was obvious to everyone, and then based upon that, he sought to develop a new, certain truth deductively.

Thus, there arose the question of how one could seek an intuitive truth that could become the starting point of philosophy. Descartes' method was to doubt as much as he could in order to pursue an absolutely reliable truth, which could then become the principle for all knowledge. Even though he doubted everything, however, he noticed that the fact that he, who doubted, existed could not be doubted. He expressed this in his famous proposition, "I think, therefore I am" (*Cogito ergo sum*). Next, he asked why that proposition was certain without any proof, and he answered that it was because that proposition was clear and distinct. From that point he derived the general rule that "things we conceive very clearly and very distinctly are all true." Cartesian doubt is not for the sake of doubt, but for the sake of discovering truth. It is called methodic doubt. Descartes tried to obtain sure knowledge by following the mathematical method, with which one starts with axioms that can be intuited clearly and distinctly, and then goes on to prove various propositions.

Hume's Empiricism

Contrary to rationalism, represented by Descartes, empiricism, emerging in Britain, took the position of explaining mental phenomena on the basis of natural laws discovered empirically. In order to find a complete system of sciences, David Hume (1711–76) analyzed the mental processes of the human mind objectively, with a new method of finding truth. Through his search for the unchanging, natural laws in the human mind, Hume tried to clarify the foundation of all the sciences, wherein the human mind is involved.

Hume analyzed ideas, which are the elements of the human mind. According to Hume, when simple ideas are associated with each other to bring about complex ideas, there are three principles of association: resemblance, contiguity in time and space, and cause and effect. Among these three, he held that the resemblance of ideas and the contiguity of ideas are sure knowledge, whereas cause and effect is merely a subjective belief. As a result, Hume's empiricism fell into skepticism, which asserted that objective knowledge can not be obtained even through inductive inference based on experience and observation. He came to deny all forms of metaphysics and even regarded the natural sciences as insecure.

Kant's Transcendental Method

Immanuel Kant (1724–1804) started from the position of rationalism and natural science. He proclaimed that Hume had awakened him from his "dogmatic slumber,"[1] by which he meant that he felt obliged by Hume's criticism of causality to deal with the question of how causality could have objective validity.[2] If causality remains a subjective belief, as Hume has stated, the law of cause and effect naturally loses its objective validity, and natural science, which is established on the basis of the law of cause and effect, ceases to be a system of truth with objective validity. Thus, Kant questioned how experience in general is possible, and how objective truth can be obtained. With his transcendental method he tried to solve these problems.

Kant reasoned that if, as Hume had said, cognition is wholly dependent on experience, we can never reach objective truth. So Kant, who pursued the question of how objective truth can be obtained, examined human reason critically and discovered that there exist a priori elements, or forms, within the subject. That is to say, Kant asserted that there exist a priori forms of cognition, common to every person, prior to experience. Those a priori forms are the intuitive forms of time and space and the pure concepts of understanding (categories). According to Kant, cognition is not achieved by grasping the actual object as it is, but the object of cognition is synthesized through the subject's a priori forms.

Hegel's Idealistic Dialectic

While Kant's method was aimed at discovering how objective truth could become possible, the method of Georg Wilhelm Friedrich Hegel (1770–1831) is the logic of thought, called dialectic, which is identified with the logic of reality.

Kant proposed a priori concepts in order to guarantee the objective truth. Hegel, on the other hand held that, while a concept is a priori, it moves by transcending itself. That is, from the position of affirming itself, the concept comes to know that there exists a determination incompatible with itself, and then transcends both these two contradictory determinations in order to develop to a position that synthesizes the two. Hegel named these three stages "in itself," "for itself," and "in and for itself." These three stages are also called affirmation, negation, and negation of negation; or thesis, antithesis, and synthesis.

Hegel regarded contradiction to be the driving force of the self-development of a concept. He said, "Contradiction is the root of all movement and vitality; it is only in so far as something has a contradiction within it that it moves, has an urge and activity."[3] In this way, the logic of self-development through contradiction is the root of Hegel's dialectic. Hegel states that a concept develops by itself to become an Idea; the concept (Idea) negates itself, is alienated and emerges as Nature; then develops through human being as Spirit. Thus, Hegel's dialectic is the method of development of a concept, and at the same time the method of development of the objective world.

Marx's Materialistic Dialectic

In the modern age, the dialectical method was developed by German idealists, and Hegel stood at its apex. Karl Marx (1818–83) held, however, that Hegel's dialectic was distorted due to its idealism, and reversed Hegel's idealistic dialectic from the materialist position, thereby reestablishing dialectic. According to Friedrich Engels (1820–95), Marx's dialectic is "nothing more than the science of the general laws of motion and development of nature, human society and thought,"[4] in which the development of nature and society is regarded as the basis upon which the development of thought is dependent.

Both Hegel's idealistic dialectic and Marx's materialistic dialectic are dialectics of contradiction that can be understood as processes of development through the three stages of thesis, antithesis, and synthesis. Contradiction is the state in which one element rejects (negates) another, while maintaining a mutual relationship at the same time. In the case of Hegel's dialectic, the emphasis is placed more on synthesis (unity), while in the case of Marx's dialectic, the idea of struggle, in which one party overthrows and annihilates the other, is added to the concept of contradiction.

According to Engels, the fundamental laws of the materialist dialectic consist of the following three laws: (1) the law of the transformation of quantity into quality; (2) the law of the unity and struggle of opposites (or the law of the interpenetration of opposites); and (3) the law of the negation of negation.

The first law states that qualitative change occurs only through quantitative change, and when quantitative change reaches a certain stage, a sudden qualitative change occurs. The second law states that all things contain elements that are in an inseparable relationship to each other, yet reject each other, that is, are opposites, and that all things develop through the unity and struggle of these opposites. The third law states that things develop as the old stage passes to a new stage by being negated, and then passes to the third stage by again being negated. This passing over to the third stage is said to be the return to the initial stage, but on a higher dimension. (This is called "development in a spiral form.") When Engels explained these three laws, he referred to Hegel's *Science of Logic* and regarded the first law as being discussed in the Doctrine of Being, the second law in the Doctrine of Essence, and the third law in the Doctrine of Notion.

Among the three laws, the most central is the second one, namely, the law of the unity and struggle of opposites. It is said that the unity and struggle of opposites is the essence of contradiction; but in actuality, Marxists emphasize struggle more than unity. In fact, Lenin said, "The unity (coincidence, identity, equal action) of opposites is conditional, temporary, transitory, relative. The struggle of mutually exclusive opposites is absolute, just as development and motion are absolute."[5] He even went as far as to say that "development is the 'struggle' of opposites."[6]

Husserl's Phenomenological Method

Edmund Husserl (1859–1938) advocated phenomenology as the first philosophy, a universal science that provides a basis for all sciences. Phenomenology deals with consciousness, which makes up theories of the sciences and with which an object is cognized. He starts with the absolute certainty of Descartes' "I think," and while excluding the metaphysical dogmas underlying traditional philosophies, he examined consciousness as a strict science. He tried to clarify pure consciousness intuitively, rejecting all preconceptions.

In so doing, he made "To things themselves!" his motto. The word

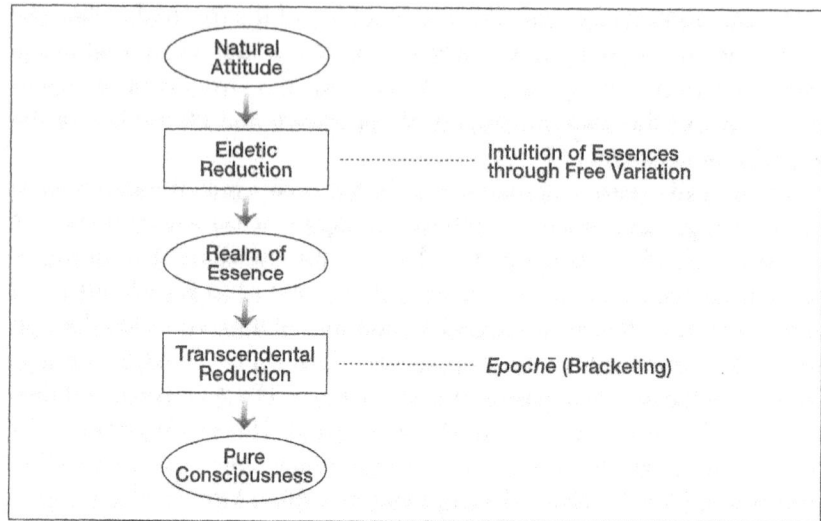

Fig. 11.1. From Natural Attitude to Phenomenological Attitude

"things" here, does not refer to empirical facts, but rather to pure phenomena that manifest themselves within pure consciousness. He sought to describe these phenomena intuitively, just as they are. According to Husserl, first we should exclude empirical elements from things, and then we grasp the essence intuitively and then grasp the internal essence of consciousness, and finally analyze the structure of a priori pure consciousness.

Our everyday view regarding the natural world lying before us as self-evident is called the "natural attitude." In this natural attitude there are, however, deep-rooted habits and preconceptions at work, and therefore, the world thus cognized can not be the true world. Thus, the "natural attitude" must change to a "phenomenological attitude," Husserl stated. For that purpose, we need to pass through the two stages of "eidetic reduction" and "transcendental reduction."

The term "eidetic reduction," for Husserl, refers to entering from the factual world into the world of essence. What takes place at this point is the intuition of essences through "free variation." In other words, when one changes existing individual beings through free imagination, and when something universal and unchanging, regardless of the variation, is intuited, one has reached the essence. For example, the essence of flower can be obtained by examining a rose, a tulip, a bud, a withering flower, etc., and extracting something unchangeable from all of these observations.

The next step that takes place is that of "transcendental reduction." This is carried out by stopping our judgment about whether the world does or does not exist. This does not mean to deny or doubt the existence of the external world, but to "suspend," or "bracket," our judgment. This process is called phenomenological *epochē*. What remains after being bracketed (excluded) is "pure consciousness," or "transcendental consciousness." What appears in this consciousness is "pure phenomena." This kind of attitude of seeking to comprehend pure phenomena is the phenomenological attitude (see fig. 11.1).

When we inquire into the general structure of pure consciousness, we find that it consists of *noesis*, which is the intentional act, and *noema*, which is the objective content the act refers to. The relationship between them is as that between "to think" and "to be thought." In this way, phenomenology tries faithfully to describe pure consciousness.

Analytical Philosophy—Method of Linguistic Analysis

Analytical philosophy forms one of the mainstreams of philosophy in the contemporary Western world. Analytical philosophy is the position that generally considers that the main task of philosophy lies in the logical analysis of linguistic structures. This position can be divided into two schools, namely, logical positivism in the early period, and the ordinary language school in the later period.

Logical positivism was formed centering around the philosophers of the Vienna Circle, namely, Moritz Schlick (1882–1936) and Rudolf Carnap (1891–1970). Logical positivism was influenced by "logical atomism," proposed by Bertrand Russell (1872–1970) and Ludwig Wittgenstein (1889–1951). According to logical atomism, the world is an agglomeration of atomic facts, which are the ultimate logical units. Logical positivism asserts that only knowledge that is verified through empirical perception is correct, and that all studies of facts should be done by science. Thus, the task of philosophy is to make a logical analysis of language so as to eliminate the ambiguities of ordinary language expressions. Renouncing conventional languages, they aimed at establishing one ideal, artificial language common to all sciences. This is the mathematical language employed by physics, or the language of physics. They sought to unify the sciences through this ideal language. The mottos of logical positivism were anti-metaphysics, the analysis of language, and scientism.

It was realized, however, that even scientific knowledge is based on unverified propositions, and that the assertions of logical positivism themselves were a form of dogma; thus, the limitations of logical positivism became clear. So, an ordinary language school, centering on George Edward Moore (1873–1958) and Gilbert Ryle (1900–1976), came to be established. The ordinary language school also holds that the task of philosophy is the logical analysis of language, but it abandoned the idea of forming a single, ideal, artificial language, and considered its task to be that of clarifying the meaning of concepts and discovering the logical structure within ordinary languages. Along with this, the anti-metaphysical outlook in analytical philosophy was eased considerably.

II. Unification Methodology—Give and Receive Method

The methodology of Unification Thought is based on the Divine Principle, and is called Unification methodology. This has also the meaning that it unifies traditional methodologies. The fundamental law of Unification methodology is the "method of give and receive action," which is simply called the "give and receive method."

A. Kinds of Give and Receive Action

Give and receive action refers to the interaction between subject and object, and this action has a center, which serves as the motive for this action. The nature of give and receive action is determined by the nature of the center. When give and receive action is carried out centering on Heart, subject and object become united, and the result of the give and receive action is a union. When a purpose is set up by Heart, however, and give and receive action takes place centering on that purpose, a multiplied being, or a new being, is produced.

The four position foundation in the Original Image is a notion dealing with the structure of God's attributes, which is the structure of four positions consisting of Heart (or purpose) as the center, subject, object, and a union (or a multiplied being). Seen from the viewpoint of time,

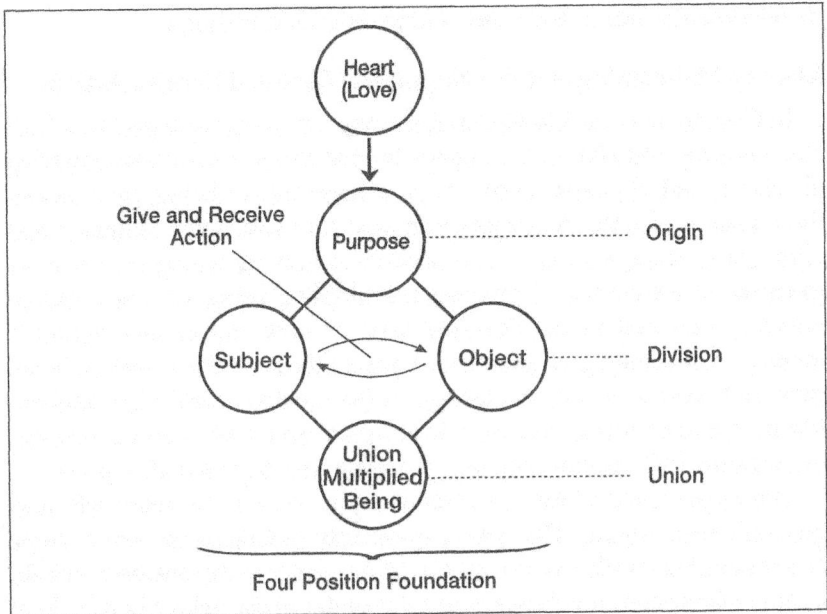

Fig. 11.2. Four Position Foundation and Origin-Division-Union Action

Heart (or purpose), which is the center, exists first; then, with that as the starting point, subject and object enter into give and receive action; as a result, a union or a multiplied being is formed. Here, Heart, which is the center, stands as Origin (*Chung*); subject and object stand as Division (*Boon*), in the sense that they are separated and placed face-to-face with each other; and union or multiplied being, namely, a result, stands as Union (*Hap*). The whole process of this give and receive action is called Origin, Division, and Union Action (*Chung-Boon-Hap Action*) (see fig. 11.2).

Division, in Origin-Division-Union Action means not that the Origin is divided into two halves, but that two elements are separated and placed face-to-face with each other, centering on the Origin. Division (*Boon*) in God means that each of the two attributes of one God are related to each other. Those two correlative attributes enter into give and receive action centering on Origin (*Chung*) and form Union (*Hap*). There are four kinds of give and receive action: identity-maintaining, developmental, inner, and outer give and receive actions. Corresponding to these, four kinds of four position foundation are formed, namely, identity-maintaining, developmental, inner, and outer four position foundations.

Identity-Maintaining and Developmental Give and Receive Actions

In God, there is the identity-maintaining, unchanging aspect in which His *Sungsang* and *Hyungsang* engage in give and receive action centering on Heart, and He exists eternally as a harmonized being, or a union; then, there is also the developmental aspect, in which His *Sungsang* and *Hyungsang* engage in give and receive action centering on purpose (purpose of creation) and produce a multiplied being, or a new being, namely, a created being. The first form of give and receive action is identity-maintaining give and receive action; the second is developmental give and receive action. All beings in the created world also perform identity-maintaining and developmental give and receive actions, maintaining both unchanging and changing (developmental) aspects.

The appearance of the universe is considered to be relatively and generally unchanging. The galaxy constantly maintains the same shape of a convex lens while revolving around the center of the universe. Within it, our solar system revolves around the center of the galaxy in a cycle of 250 million years, but is always located at the same distance from the center of the galaxy. Moreover, the disk shape of the solar system is also unchanging. The solar system has nine planets, each of which maintains its unchanged orbit while revolving around the sun. Each planet maintains its definite characteristics. In this way, the universe has unchanging, or identity-maintaining, aspects.

Yet, when seen in terms of the long period of about fifteen billion years, the universe is also found to be developing and growing. Scientists explain this fact by saying that the universe is expanding, or evolving. The universe has changed from a gaseous state into a solid state, whereby innumerable large and small heavenly bodies were formed; and on the surface of one of the planets (earth), plants, animals, and humans appeared. This process of the universe can be regarded as a kind of process of growth or development. In this way, the universe has both the aspect of identity-maintenance and that of development.

Living beings, as well, develop while maintaining their identity. In plants, seeds sprout, trunks grow, leaves develop, flowers blossom and bear fruits; in this way, they grow constantly. Still, they maintain their unchanging aspect in that they continue to exist as the same species of plant. Particular kinds of plants continue to produce the same kinds of flowers, the same kinds of fruits, etc. In other words, a plant has both the aspect of identity-maintenance and the aspect of development. Likewise, animals develop and grow while maintaining their own identity.

The same can be said of human society. In history, the rise and fall of states was continually repeated. Yet, everywhere and always the basic pattern of a state, in which the sovereign and the people are in the relationship of subject and object, remains identical. The same can be said of a family. While there were variations in the appearances of families according to the environment and the age, the relationships between parents and children, husband and wife, and so on, are unchanging. Also, individual persons constantly grow while maintaining their own characteristics as individuals. In this way, according to the law of give and receive action, in every being, unchanging characteristics (identity-maintenance) and changing characteristics (development) are united.

Inner and Outer Give and Receive Actions

Within God's Original *Sungsang*, the Inner *Sungsang* and the Inner *Hyungsang* engage in give and receive action centering on Heart, forming a union. Through that, the inner four position foundation is formed, which is the internal structure of God's *Sungsang*. Next, the Original *Sungsang* and the Original *Hyungsang* engage in give and receive action, forming a union. At this point, it is the outer four position foundation that is formed. When purpose is established in Heart, give and receive action assumes a dynamic, developmental nature. In the inner four position foundation, Logos (conception) is formed as a multiplied being, and in the outer four position foundation, created beings are formed as multiplied beings.

This two-stage structure of inner and outer four position foundations in God is applied without change to the creation. In the relationships between human being and all things (nature), through an inner give and receive action, the human being thinks and establishes conceptions (plans); while at the same time, through an outer give and receive action, human beings cognize and have dominion over all things. In humans, if we designate the give and receive action between spirit mind and physical mind within the human mind as the inner give and receive action, then the give and receive action between one person and another person (e.g., the give and receive action between husband and wife in a family) is the outer give and receive action. If we designate the exchanges among family members in a household as inner give and receive actions, then

494 / METHODOLOGY

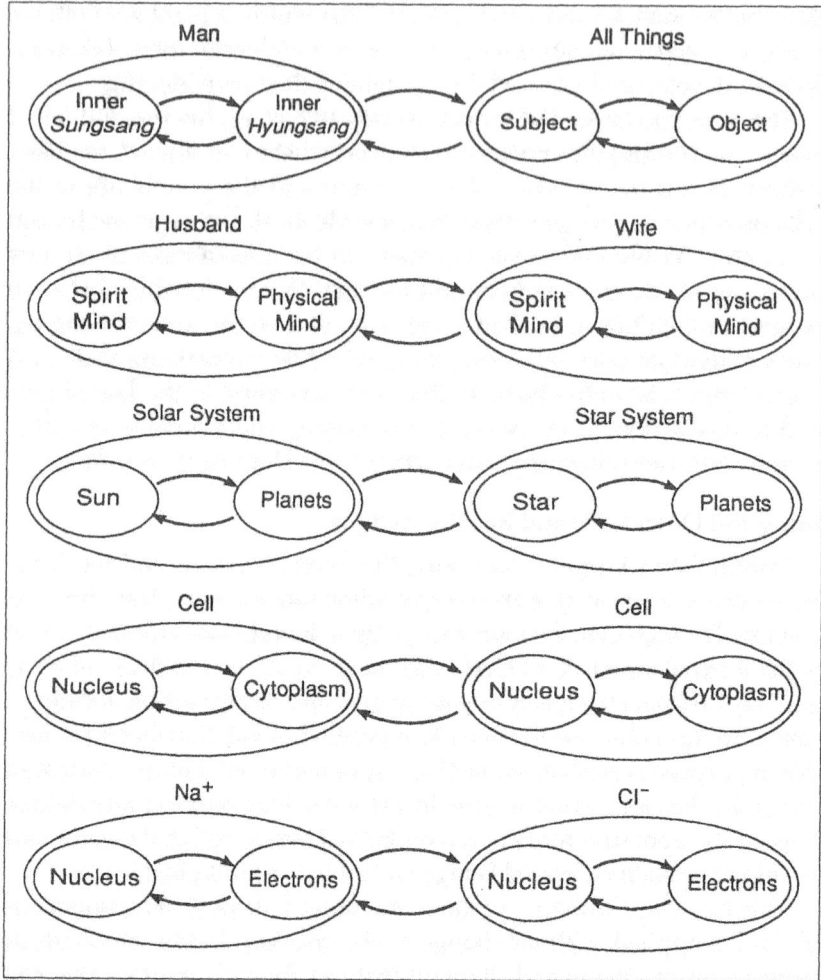

Fig. 11.3. Examples of Inner and Outer Give and Receive Actions

their exchanges with other people in society become outer give and receive actions.

Even a state has inner and outer give and receive actions. Within a state, the government and the people engage in relationships of subject and object, and thereby politics and economics are carried out. This is inner give and receive action. At the same time, political and economic relations are formed with other states; this is outer give and receive action.

In the world of nature as well, there are inner and outer give and receive actions. In the solar system, inner give and receive action takes place between the sun and the planets; at the same time, the solar system is performing outer give and receive action with other stars. Also, if we designate the give and receive action within the earth the inner give and receive action, then the give and receive action between the sun and the earth is called outer give and receive action. In living beings, inner give and receive action occurs between the nucleus and the cytoplasm in each cell, while cells perform outer give and receive action with one another.

In this way, in the relationships between human beings and all things, as well as in the relationships in human society and even in the creation, inner and outer give and receive actions take place in unity. As these inner and outer give and receive actions are carried out smoothly and harmoniously, things maintain their existence and continue to develop. Examples of inner and outer give and receive actions are shown in figure 11.3.

Now, let us consider the deductive and inductive methods of reasoning in relation to inner and outer give and receive actions. The deductive method is a method of logical development through inner give and receive action that takes place within the human mind. In contrast, the inductive method is the method of examining things in the external world—therefore, it is a method based on outer give and receive action. In Unification methodology, inner and outer give and receive actions take place in unity. Therefore, in Unification methodology, the inductive and deductive methods are united.

B. Scope of Give and Receive Action

The give and receive method is the fundamental method for existence and development in God, human beings, and nature. God, while maintaining His eternal nature through inner and outer identity-maintaining give and receive actions, created humankind and all things through inner and outer developmental give and receive actions.

In humankind, and in all things, each individual (individual truth being) maintains its existence and develops as the correlative elements within it perform inner give and receive action, and at the same time each individual performs outer give and receive action with other individuals.

Give and receive action between individuals includes give and receive action between human beings, between human beings and all things, and between all things.

First, there is give and receive action between one human being and another, which includes individual interaction in family life and in social life. Educational, ethical, political, economic, and all other activities are carried out through this give and receive action.

Next is the give and receive action between human beings and all things. In this type of give and receive action, there are two cases, namely, those cases in which a human being exercises dominion over all things, and those cases in which a human being cognizes all things. The cognition of all things includes the basic study of the natural sciences, the exploration and appreciation of nature, and so forth. Dominion over all things includes applied research in the natural sciences, business and economic activities, creative activities in art, and so forth.

Finally, there is the give and receive action between one thing and another. In nature, numerous elements form an orderly organic world as they engage in give and receive actions through their respective positions —such as the give and receive action among atoms, among cells, and among stars. The interaction between parts of a machine is another example of this case.

Thinking and conversation are also carried out based on the give and receive action. That is to say, as the subjective part in thinking (inner *sungsang*), namely, the functions of intellect, emotion, and will, and the objective part (inner *hyungsang*), namely, ideas, concepts, laws, mathematical principles, etc., enter into give and receive action, human thinking is conducted.

Judgment in thinking is also based on give and receive action. For example, in the judgment, "this flower is a rose," a contrast-type of give and receive action takes place, wherein one compares the idea "this flower" with the idea "rose." Conversation, also, is carried out through give and receive action. I can understand what another person is saying because the notions and concepts of that person are in accord with mine, and also because the laws of thinking of the other person are in accord with mine. However, if a person talks nonsense, I can not understand what that person is saying.

C. Types of Give and Receive Action

Give and receive action has the following five types, which were explained in Ontology:
(1) Bi-Conscious Type
(2) Uni-Conscious Type
(3) Unconscious Type
(4) Heteronomous Type
(5) Contrast Type (Collation Type)

D. Characteristics of Give and Receive Action

Give and receive action has the following seven characteristics, which were also explained in Ontology:
(1) Correlativity
(2) Purposefulness and Centrality
(3) Order and Position
(4) Harmony
(5) Individuality and Connectedness
(6) Identity-Maintaining Nature and Developmental Nature
(7) Circular Motion

III. An Appraisal of Conventional Methodologies from the Perspective of Unification Thought

Heraclitus

Heraclitus said that "everything is in a state of flux." It can be said that he grasped only the developmental aspect of the created world, neglecting the identity-maintaining aspect. He also said, "War is the father of all," ascribing the cause of the development of things to the struggle of opposites. Yet, in the Unification Thought view, things develop only through a harmonious give and receive action between correlative elements.

Zeno

First, let us consider his theory that a flying arrow is at rest. When Zeno says that an arrow is at rest at a certain point, he is referring to a mathematical point which has no space. The actual movement of an arrow occurs within time and space. The velocity of a body in motion (v) is the distance traveled (s) divided by the time elapsed (t), and is expressed with the equation $v = s / t$. Therefore, the movement of an object must be considered within a definite distance (space) and within a definite period of time. The movement of an object can not be discussed in relation to a point that has only position but no space (a mathematical point). Therefore, when we speak of the movement of an object at a certain point in space, no matter how small that point may be, we must consider it within a definite space, and when we speak of movement at a certain moment, no matter how short that moment may be, we must consider it within a definite period of time. If we do so, we can say, definitely, that a moving object is not at rest, but rather moving through a certain point of time and space.

Concerning this issue, the materialist dialectic asserts that an object is, and at the same time is not, at a certain place at a certain moment, claiming that it has resolved Zeno's paradox and has explained motion. This, however, is the same kind of sophistry as is found in Zeno's claim. The position of an object in motion is expressed as a function of time; therefore, a certain moment corresponds to a certain position on a one-to-one basis. It can not happen that something is, and at the same time is not, at a certain place at a certain moment. In conclusion, (1) an object in motion passes through a certain space without resting in it; and (2) an object in motion is at a certain place at a certain moment of time.

The next issue is "Achilles and the tortoise." Zeno argued only in terms of space, disregarding time; therefore, he drew the wrong conclusion in saying that Achilles is unable to pass the tortoise. If it is seen in terms of the passage of a certain time, Achilles can definitely go ahead of the tortoise.

Zeno tried to prove that there is no motion or change, that there is no generation or destruction. To that end, he resorted to sophistry. It can be said that, contrary to Heraclitus, Zeno grasped only the identity-maintaining aspect of things, disregarding the developmental aspect.

Socrates

Socrates thought that people could reach the truth by means of dialogue, with a humble heart. This is the multiplication of truth through outer give and receive action between person and person. It can be said

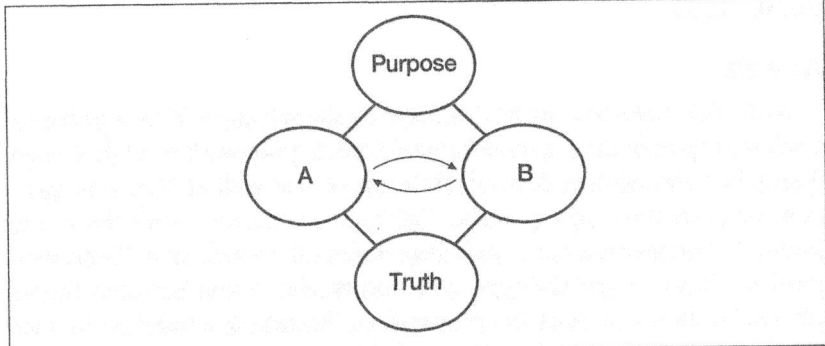

Fig. 11.4. The Socratic Method of Dialogue

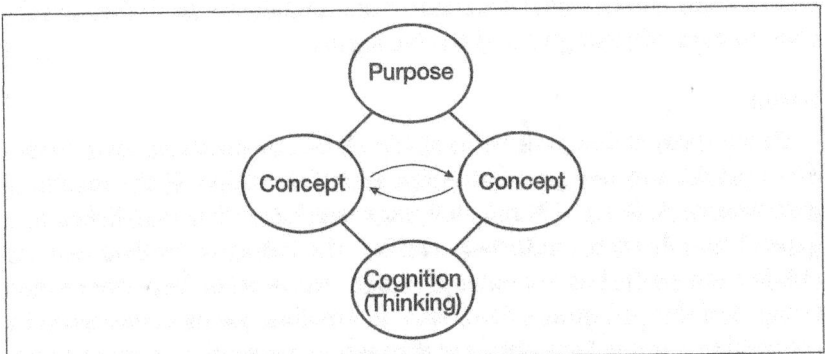

Fig. 11.5. Plato's Dialectic

that Socrates advocated the proper way of give and receive action between person and person (see fig. 11.4).

Plato

Plato studied the world of Ideas. As is explained in the Theory of the Original Image, there are various ideas and concepts in God's Inner *Hyungsang*. Plato considered them as belonging to the world of Ideas, and by analyzing and synthesizing them, he tried to clarify a hierarchy of Ideas. Analysis and synthesis of concepts are carried out through a comparison of concepts. This is a contrast-type of give and receive action. Since this is carried out within the mind, it is inner give and receive action. Accordingly, it can be said that Plato's method of searching for truth corresponds to the contrast-type of inner give and receive action (see fig. 11.5).

Aristotle

Aristotle's deductive method is based on the syllogism. First, a universal truth is proposed; then, a more limited truth is proposed; from these two, a specific conclusion is derived. In terms of one well-known syllogism, one contrasts the major premise, "all men are mortal" with the minor premise, "Socrates is a man," and thus derives the conclusion, "Socrates is mortal." This is a contrast-type give and receive action between propositions. Furthermore, since the proposition, "Socrates is a man" is obtained by contrasting "Socrates" and "man," this, also, is a contrast-type give and receive action. Accordingly, Aristotle's deductive method, as in the case of Plato, can be called the method of searching for truth through the contrast-type of inner give and receive action.

Bacon

Bacon claimed that in order to obtain truth, one must cast away prejudices (Idols) and rely on experiment and observation. If the results of experiments A, B, C, ⋯ N are all P, then conclusion P is established as a general law; this is the inductive method. The inductive method seeks to obtain truth on the basis of outer give and receive action between human beings and things (nature). Also, since this method yields a conclusion by contrasting various facts obtained through experiment and observation, it is also give and receive action of the contrast-type. Therefore, Bacon's inductive method is the method of pursuing truth through the contrast-type of outer give and receive action (see fig. 11.6).

Descartes

Descartes attempted to doubt everything and, as a result, he claimed to have reached a certain first principle: "I think, therefore I am." Here, the fact that Descartes doubted everything means that he denied everything and every phenomenon, and therefore, seen from the viewpoint of Unification Thought, it is the same as his tracing back to the stage prior to God's creation of the universe. The observation, "I think" corresponds to God's "plan," or "thought," before His creation of the universe. At this point, Descartes asserted, "I think; therefore I am." If he had instead asked "Why do I think?," his rationalism would not have led to dogmatism in his successors. In any case, his awareness of the truth of

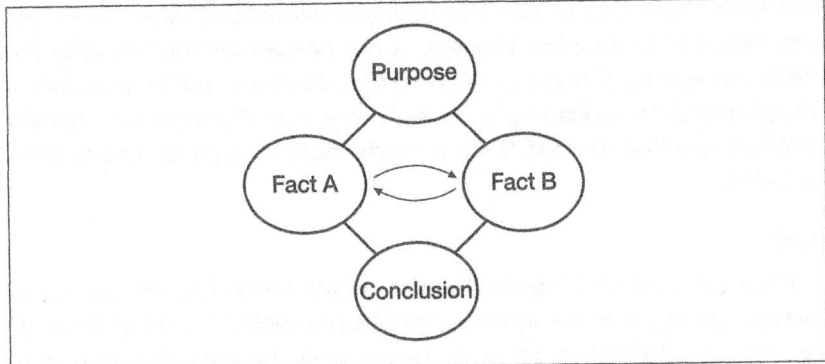

Fig. 11.6. Bacon's Inductive Method

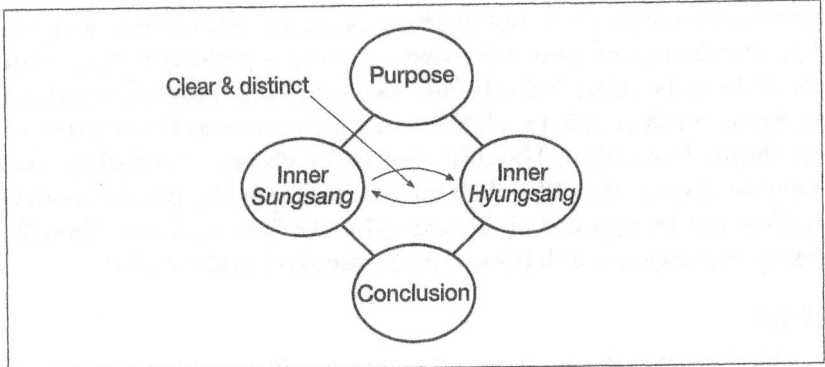

Fig. 11.7. Descartes' Methodic Doubt

"I think; therefore, I am" means, from the viewpoint of Unification Thought, that he acknowledged the certainty of the inner give and receive action within the human mind. After that, he established the general rule that "things we conceive very clearly and very distinctly are true," which guarantees the multiplication of truth through the formation of the inner four position foundation (see fig. 11.7).

Hume

Hume considered causality merely a subjective belief. However, causality is not merely subjective, but is both subjective and objective, as already explained in the chapter on epistemology. Moreover, Hume denied both material substance and spiritual substance (self), holding that there exist merely bundles of impressions and ideas. From the perspective of Unification Thought, it can be said that he saw only the inner *hyungsang* (ideas) as sure things. Hume tried to establish a complete system of philosophy by analyzing mental phenomena, but the problem was that he tried to do it on the basis of separate impressions and ideas.

Kant

Kant claimed that cognition takes place when the chaotic sense content coming from the object is synthesized with the a priori forms of the subject. Unification Thought agrees with the view that cognition occurs through the interaction between the human subject and the object. However, from the perspective of Unification Thought, the subject possesses not only forms (forms of thought), but also content (images). The combination of form and content is called a prototype. Also, what comes from the object is not chaotic sense content, but content organized by forms of existence in the objective world. Contrary to Kant's theory of synthesis, Unification Thought asserts the theory of collation. The Kantian theory of synthesis, which is based on the transcendental method can be regarded as one expression of the Unification Thought theory of collation, which is based on the give and receive method.

Hegel

Hegel grasped the development of Idea and the world as a process of transcendence and the unity of contradiction—or the process of thesis, antithesis, and synthesis. From the perspective of Unification Thought, however, development does not occur through contradiction.

Development occurs when correlatives, in the relationship of subject and object, enter into give and receive action centering on purpose. This process is called Origin, Division, and Union Action. Origin here means purpose, Division means correlatives, and Union means multiplied being. Idea does not develop by itself through an inner contradiction, as Hegel claimed. Thinking is carried out as the inner *sungsang*—namely, the functions of intellect, emotion, and will—acts upon the inner *hyungsang* (including ideas), forming new ideas. This is called the development of thinking in a spiral form, as was explained in the chapter on logic. It can be seen that Hegel grasped development—which, according to Unification Thought, is give and receive action between correlatives—as an interaction between opposing elements.

Marx

Marx held that spiritual processes are merely the reflection of material processes. From the perspective of Unification Thought, however, *sungsang* (spirit) and *hyungsang* (matter) are in the relationship of subject and object; therefore, there is a relationship of correspondence between spiritual laws (laws of value) and material laws.

As a counterproposal to the "law of the transformation of quantity into quality," Unification Thought offers the "law of the balanced development of quality and quantity." It is not correct to say that quantity is transformed into quality. Also, a sudden qualitative change does not occur when the quantitative change reaches a certain point. Quality and quantity are in the relationship of *sungsang* and *hyungsang*, and they change simultaneously, gradually, and stage by stage.

As a counterproposal to the "law of the unity and struggle of opposites," Unification Thought proposes the "law of the give and receive action between correlatives." A struggle of opposites gives rise only to destruction and ruin, and never brings about development. All things develop through the harmonious give and receive action between correlatives centered on a common purpose.

To the "law of negation of the negation," Unification Thought proposes, as a counterproposal, the "law of affirmative development." In nature, as well as in society, development takes place as the correlative elements of subject and object within nature and society perform harmonious give and receive action. In nature, inorganic beings perform circular motion in space and living beings perform circular motion in space and in time (spiral motion).

Among the methodologies in the past, none was more influential than the Marxist materialistic dialectic. Trying to prove that Marx's dialectic was valid in nature as well, Engels studied natural sciences for eight years. As a result, he concluded that "nature is the proof of dialectics."[7] The errors of the materialist dialectic are now evident, however. Natural phenomena are, if examined carefully, not the "proof of dialectics," but instead they are the "proof of the law of give and receive action" (see fig. 11.8).

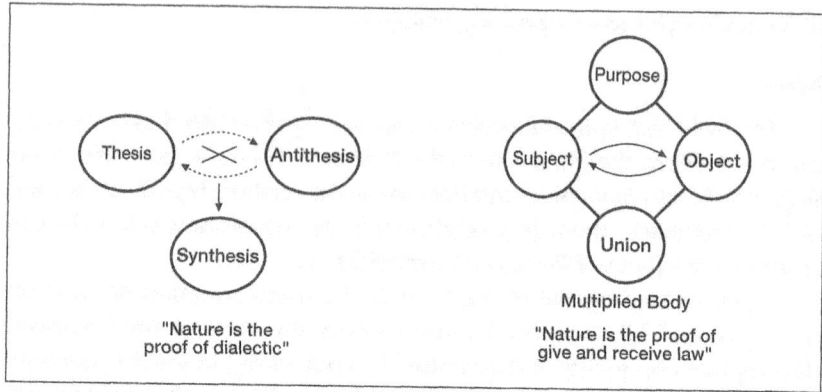

Fig. 11.8. The Way of Dialectic vs the Way of Give and Receive Action

Husserl

Husserl first started with things of the natural world. Things are, when seen from the perspective of Unification Thought, unified beings of *sungsang* and *hyungsang*. Next, he advocated the intuition of essences through eidetic reduction. Essence here corresponds to the *sungsang* of existing beings. In addition, Husserl claimed that when judgment is suspended and consciousness (pure consciousness) is analyzed, there is a structure of *noesis* and *noema*. This, when seen from the perspective of Unification Thought, corresponds to the internal structure of *sungsang* (mind), which consists of inner *sungsang* and inner *hyungsang*. A comparison between Husserl's phenomenological method and the viewpoint of Unification Thought would be as in figure 11.9. Husserl, like Descartes, unconsciously considered as important that which actually corresponds to the Unification Thought concept of the inner four position foundation. In other words, he tried to unify all sciences through an analysis of the inner four position foundation.

Analytical Philosophy

Language is formed through inner developmental give and receive action, which has an intellectual aspect (logos) centered on reason, and an emotional aspect (pathos) centered on emotional feeling. Analytical philosophy grasped only the aspect of logos, and pursued only logicalness.

From the perspective of Unification Thought, language originally exists in order to actualize love, and the logical structure of language is

	Object	Essence of object	Mind of subject
Husserl	Things	Essence	Noesis ⇌ Noema
Unification Thought	Sung-sang ⇌ Hyung-sang	Sungsang	Inner Sung-sang ⇌ Inner Hyung-sang

Fig. 11.9. Comparison between Husserl's Phenomenological Method and Unification Thought

merely a necessary condition for that purpose. The use of language is the expression of thought, and is a kind of creative activity. The center of creative activity is heart. Therefore, an emotional element centered on love plays the subjective role in the formation of thought. Analytical philosophy engaged so much in the logical analysis of language from beginning to end, however, that it came to disregard the creative aspect and the value-created aspect of thought formed through language.

Appendix

During the time in which I was arranging Rev. Sun Myung Moon's many ideas, he continued to express many new teachings and insights. So I would like to explain here "the principle of mutual existence, mutual prosperity, and mutual righteousness," which are introduced in the Divine Principle. I would also like to introduce certain especially important topics: the "three great subjects thought," the "four great realms of heart," and the "three great kingships."

I. Principle of Mutual Existence, Mutual Prosperity and Mutual Righteousness

The principle of mutual existence, mutual prosperity and mutual righteousness is a principle addressing a certain dimension of Rev. Moon's concept of Godism, namely, the dimension including economics, politics and ethics. It is a compound principle consisting actually of three concepts: mutual existence, mutual prosperity, and mutual righteousness. In order to understand the meaning of the principle of mutual existence, mutual prosperity and mutual righteousness correctly, it is helpful to understand each concept in turn. Thus, I will explain one by one.

A. Principle of Mutual Existence

The principle of mutual existence is a concept dealing with the economic aspects of an ideal society, especially the aspect of ownership.

In terms of ownership, in capitalist economy there is private (individual) ownership, while in socialist economy there is social (national) ownership. Yet, in both economies the element of love is totally excluded. That is to say, whether private or socialist (public), economy is simply materialistic ownership, without regard to the mental aspect.

In contrast, in the principle of mutual existence, joint ownership is based on God's true love. In other words, it is first, the joint ownership of God and myself; second, the joint ownership of the whole and myself; and third, the joint ownership of my neighbors and myself. It is not simply a materialistic ownership, but rather it is an ownership based on God's true love. This means that, through God's infinite love, we (myself, my neighbors, and the whole) are entrusted to jointly take care of God's property, which is given to us as His loving gift.

According to the principle of creation, the created world is God's possession, and it was created to be governed by Him through love (*DP*, 64). It is written in the Bible that God, the Creator, let birds fly above the earth, and He let the waters swarm with fish, and He made the beasts of the earth (Gen. 1:20–25). This means that the sky is the joint possession of all birds, the waters are the joint possession of all fish, and that the ground is the joint possession of all beasts, all based on God's love.

Even birds of prey, like eagles, will not monopolize the sky. Even beasts of prey, like tigers, will not monopolize the ground. Even violent sharks will not monopolize the sea. Since God endowed human beings with the right to have dominion over all things with love, all human beings were to jointly possess the sky, the sea, and the land, as well as all living beings, including birds, fish and beasts, with a heart of gratitude, based on God's true love. Thus, nature is the joint possession of God and human beings.

Nevertheless, due to the fall, human beings fell into self-centered individualism, and came to monopolize land and property. Today, under the banner of liberal democracy, people legally possess vast lands and enormous amounts of property. Yet, they are not usually very grateful; they seldom experience any pangs of a guilty conscience. Even when they see their neighbors starving, they often do not seem to care, and just continue to live arrogantly; this is characteristic of capitalist society. They are basically living their lives against the Way of Heaven.

The relationship between God and human beings is that of parent and children, the basic form of which is realized in a family. In a family, all property—such as the house, the garden, the yard, cattle, and so on—belongs to the parents, and at the same time to the children. In other words, in a family, even if the property is legally possessed by the parents, in fact, it is jointly possessed by both parents and children. In the original world, parents always love their children; therefore, children always have a heart of gratitude towards their parents and take good care of the family property.

In the basic form of the family the three generations of grandparents, parents and children (brothers and sisters) live together. Therefore, joint ownership is, strictly speaking, joint ownership of the three generations: namely, the joint ownership of grandparents, parents and children, all based on true love. Here, since the grandparents are in the position representing God, the joint ownership of the three generations can be expressed as the joint ownership of God, who is the subject of true love, parents, and children. The family joint ownership in which three generations possess things together, is the prototype for various other kinds of joint ownership. Thus, joint ownership in the principle of mutual existence is the joint ownership of God and I, the whole and I, and my neighbors and I, all based on God's true love. It is the joint ownership of all three levels of the other and I. In short, it may be called "the joint ownership of God, the whole, my neighbors, and I."

An extension of this joint family ownership is the joint ownership of various other organizations. For example, the joint ownership of a company is the joint ownership of three parties: God, who is the subject of true love, the executives, who are in the position of parents, and employees, who are in the position of children. Therefore, it is the joint ownership of the three levels of "the other and I," namely, "God and I," "executives and I," and "my fellow employees and I."

In the original world, even when a company is founded by entrepreneurs, it should first be offered to God. After it is offered to God, thus becoming God's possession, it is returned to the entrepreneurs with God's true love; then, it will be possessed jointly by the entrepreneurs and God. Such a procedure is more than a mere formality. Only through such a procedure can God's true love, protection and help effectively come to a company. The same thing can be said of other organizations as well.

Next, let me explain about joint ownership on a national level. In the case of a state-owned enterprise, for example, all properties are under the joint possession of the state and the people. It is the joint possession of the three parties of God, who is the subject of true love, the president or the sovereign of the country, and the employees of the enterprise; also it is the joint possession of the three levels of "the other and I," namely, "God and I," "the president and I," and "the employees and I." Here, God's love, protection and help can be given; the president will give affectionate concern and assistance; and the employees will be thankful to God and to the president, and they will take good care of all property with a consciousness of joint ownership. This is the concept of "joint ownership on a national level."

Here, one might raise the question; "Is not there any private ownership in the ideal world?" Yes, there is, and it is proper that there should be. This is because a human being, in resemblance to God, has both a universal image and an individual image. That is to say, a human being has a common attribute (universality) and at the same time, an attribute peculiar to himself or herself (individual image). A human being has dual purposes: the purpose for the individual and the purpose for the whole, as well as the desire and freedom to practice love. Thus, private ownership is allowed. I will explain this using the case of joint family ownership, which is the prototype for various other joint ownerships.

Let's take the example of the family of a farmer. It is for pursuing the purpose for the whole that family members jointly take care of, and keep, the family property, i.e., house, garden, field, cattle, and so on. In other words, all the family members jointly seek the life of food, clothing, and shelter. They do so, living under the same roof, spending the same budget. Yet, each member of the family has his or her own unique individuality (individual image). Thus, he or she will lead his or her own way of life according to his or her situation, tastes, and so on. Also, in many cases, children need a room, clothes, or other living necessities for their exclusive use in the same way that parents do. So, parents will give allowances to their children. This kind of personal possession is necessary for them to accomplish their individual purpose.

Private possession is necessary to accomplish the purpose for the individual, and at the same time, it is necessary to accomplish the purpose for the whole as well. The purpose for the whole is accomplished through a community life or a family life, by using the jointly owned property; at the same time, it is accomplished through personal ways by using personal property.

When children try to comfort and please their parents, they are fulfilling the purpose for the whole. For example, in order to please parents, an elder brother reads many books, which are his possessions, and gets good grades at school; a younger brother paints a beautiful picture using painting instruments, which are his possessions, and gets a special prize at an art exhibition; an elder sister plays the violin, which she possesses, and receives the highest praise from the audience at a concert. In these cases, they fulfill the purpose for the whole through their personal possessions.

In this way, private possessions are necessary not only for accomplishing the purpose for the individual but also for accomplishing the purpose for the whole. Thus, human beings are endowed with desire, love, and freedom in order to love others (to realize the purpose for the whole) according to their free will, investing their unique individualities and personal possessions.

Then, to what extent is personal possession reasonable? This is determined according to the appropriate necessity of each person. This kind of possession is called appropriate possession. The proper quantity and quality will be determined according to one's own conscience. Rather differently from the case of fallen people, an original person will easily understand the quantity, quality, and kinds of his or her necessary personal posses-sions.

We often express the psychological amount—the amount of desire, gratitude, satisfaction and so on—through material means. For example, when we receive kindness from others, we often express gratitude with a kind of gift, or a sum of money. Similarly, in the case of private possessions, a psychological amount which one feels appropriate to oneself can be expressed through a material amount. No one other than oneself, can best express one's psychological amount in a material amount. Thus, a psychological amount which is appropriate to oneself can easily be determined by oneself. When we have meals, we know our condition well: if we eat little, our physical strength will become weak, and if we eat too much, our stomach will have trouble. Similarly, if our conscience is pure, God will show us through our conscience the psychological amount appropriate for our personal possessions. Thus, the appropriate possession of private property can be easily determined.

It should be clarified here that even if the proper quantity and quality of one's private possessions are determined through one's conscience, that quantity and quality may vary from person to person. There are certain reasons for that. First, each person has his or her unique individual image, and therefore unique character, taste, and so on. Second, every person is an individual truth being and at the same time a connected being. A connected being refers to an individual person who is related to others in the six directions of high and low, front and back, and right and left. In order to have such relations, a person, as a connected being, requires at least a certain necessary quantity of personal possessions. Usually, the higher the position a person occupies, the greater the quantity and quality of his or her necessary possessions become. Therefore, the proper quantity and quality of personal possessions will differ from person to person. Thus, if a person has adequate personal possessions necessary to love others, then, those possessions are appropriate, even if the amount of his or her personal possessions is substantially higher or lower than the average.

In this way, the principle of mutual existence is the theory of joint economy based on joint ownership. The concept of economy here refers, first, to the totality of activities related to the production, exchange, distribution, and consumption of goods through primary, secondary, and tertiary industries, in the same way as it does in conventional economic theory. However, since the economy in the future world is based on joint ownership centered on God's true love, as already explained, economic activity in the future world will be quite different from the economic activity up until today. To explain briefly, all economic activities are the unity of spiritual processes, which are the flow of heart, love, gratitude, and so on, and the material process, which is the circulation of commodities. The commodity itself is a united being of spirit and matter where love and sincere heart dwell, and the circulation of commodities is also the unity of spiritual processes and material processes where love and a sincere heart circulate.

Since the future world will be a unified world without national boundaries, the future economy will be one global economy in which regional bloc economies are organically and harmoniously united. In other words, a unified industry will be established, in which local, special industries fitted for particular regions and non-local, universal industries are harmonized and unified. This is a conclusion derived from Unification Thought, which states that every being is a united being in which the universal image (universality) and individual image (individuality) are unified.

In future industry, an enterprise will seek to contribute to the progress of the welfare of all humankind rather than aiming only for the interest of the entrepreneurs. Therefore, the overall result of industrial activity will be the multiplication of beneficial goods for humankind.

In the future, society's most serious economic problem, which must be solved, is the food problem, since the population is increasing in a geometric progression. Thomas Malthus expressed concern about this problem in his *An Essay on the Principle of Population as It Affects the Future Improvement of Society*, and the Club of Rome also warned about this problem back in the 1970's. However, this difficult problem will be solved through the development of the marine industry—based on the development of aquaculture, and so on. This is a conclusion which is derived from the Divine Principle, according to which the ocean symbolizes a woman, and a woman's important mission is fertility or production.

B. Principle of Mutual Prosperity

The principle of mutual prosperity is concerned with the political aspects of the future ideal society. Especially, the principle of mutual prosperity is proposed as an alternative to democracy, which is the political ideology of capitalism. As is well known, democracy in capitalist society is a liberal democracy, a political ideology associated with the slogan "life, liberty, and the pursuit of happiness" in the Declaration of Independence of America and the slogan "freedom, equality, and fraternity," which derives from the French Revolution.

Democracy is an ideology wherein "sovereignty rests with the people." This is well-expressed in his famous Gettysburg Address by Abraham Lincoln, the sixteenth President of the United States, as the "government of the people, by the people, and for the people." Essentially, democracy is an ideology seeking to realize freedom and equality for all people. In other words, the ultimate purpose of democracy, which claims majority rule and parliamentary government, is the realization of freedom and equality for people. Freedom and equality are like two sides of a coin: there is no equality without freedom, nor is there freedom without equality.

Then, what is meant by the "people"? In the days of bourgeois revolutions, the people were the ruled class under an absolute monarchy. Today, however, "people" generally refers to the masses, transcending social classes. The ruling class is often dictatorial; therefore, it can be said that people means "the majority of the people," those apart from the ruling class, and the wealthy, privileged class as well.

Over two hundred years have passed since democracy was established. Have freedom and equality of the people been realized? It certainly seems that they have not been. Due to its structural contradiction, capitalism, which was established based on liberal democracy, has brought about economic inequality and the restriction of economic freedom, along with an uneven distribution of wealth. We have also witnessed in history many cases in which economic inequality and the restriction of economic freedom were directly connected to political inequality and the restriction of political freedom.

Especially the freedom and human rights of the majority of the people —the lower class—are often apt to be trampled upon under the name of democracy. Therefore, the sovereignty of the people exists only in name. Actually, freedom and human rights are utilized for the special interests of politicians, who spend enormous amounts of money to get elected. Today, an election campaign is hardly more than a political contest for concessions. Thus, democracy has failed to become a genuine "government of the people, by the people, and for the people"; rather, it has become almost like a "government of the party members, by the party members, for the party members." Due to this deficiency of liberal democracy, Communists accused it saying, "it is no more than a bourgeois democracy for the ruling and wealthy classes, rather than for the people." Since World War II, they maintained that Communism for laborers and farmers is the true people's democracy.

What is the reason why democracy, which aimed at the realization of true liberty, equality and fraternity, has failed to realize its purpose for more than two hundred years? The main reason is that democracy, which was established by overthrowing absolute monarchy through bourgeois revolution, was closely united with individualism; it has claimed the rights, freedom, and equality of an individual person. Individualism is to be respected in that it emphasizes the importance of individuality, personality, and individual values. Due to the policy of the separation of church and state, however, Christianity, as a guiding principle for the human spirit, became unable to function, and as a result individualism degenerated into egoism. Thus, democracy came to be established on the basis of egoistic individualism.

Since egoistic individualism rules the minds of economists and politicians, capitalists perpetually pursue the maximization of profit, and politicians regard political power as their concessions. Today, politicians invest enormous amounts of money for elections with the spirit of investing to acquire concessions, in the name of fair elections. So, due to entrepreneurs' persistent pursuit of profit, and politicians' insatiable desire for power, corruption, and various kinds of injustices and crimes are rampant in democratic society today.

This means that democracy had, from its very beginning, inherent limitations on the realization of its slogan of liberty, equality, and fraternity. Democracy, in which religion and politics are separated, has the inevitable tendency for individualism to degenerate into egoism. However, it is not that liberal democracy has failed in every respect. Clearly, it has played an important role in securing freedom of faith. In fact, in liberal democratic countries, the flowers of religion and faith are in full bloom, in the same way that many flowers bloom in the spring time.

Here, let me explain about the significance of the emergence of democracy, as seen from the viewpoint of God's providence. It is in accordance with God's providence that democracy has secured freedom of faith, since democracy is a political system that emerged prior to the Messianic Kingdom. It should be noted that democracy was established by the bourgeois revolution, which overthrew the existing absolute monarchy. If the political system of those days had not been an absolute monarchy, but had been the Messianic Kingdom, realizing God's true love, the bourgeois revolution would not have occurred, and humankind would have lived happily, enjoying true liberty, equality and fraternity. The above-mentioned presupposition that "if it had not been an absolute monarchy but had been the Messianic Kingdom" is not a mere assumption. Seen from the viewpoint of God's providence, the Messianic Kingdom was already supposed to have been established by that time. Let me explain this point more concretely.

Charlemagne (Charles the Great) developed the Frankish Kingdom and revived the Western Roman Empire from the end of the eighth century through the early ninth century. Seen from God's providence, Charlemagne, in the New Testament Age, is the figure who corresponds to King Saul of the Jewish United Kingdom, in the Old Testament Age.

The prophet Samuel anointed Saul with oil as the first king of Israel about 800 years after Abraham. Similarly, Charlemagne was crowned by Pope Leo III as the emperor of the Western Roman Empire about 800 years after Jesus. According to the Divine Principle, the Frankish Kingdom, from Charlemagne's enthronement until the end of the Carolingian reign, is called the Christian Empire, which corresponds to the Jewish Kingdom in the Old Testament Age.

It was God's providential will that the First Coming of Christ come to the Jewish Kingdom in the Old Testament Age to unify the world and establish the Kingdom of the Messiah, centered on God's true love. In the New Testament Age, it was God's providence that Christ at the Second Advent come to the Christian Empire to establish the Kingdom of the Messiah, centered on God's true love.

In the Jewish United Kingdom of the Old Testament Age, the kings failed, throughout the three generations, to establish providential conditions in accord with God's will; therefore, God divided that kingdom into two: Israel in the north and Judah in the south. Eventually, God allowed the northern kingdom to be occupied by Assyria, a Satanic kingdom, and the southern kingdom to be occupied by New Babylonia. The Jewish kings were made prisoners. Thus, God's providence for establishing the Messianic Kingdom through the Jewish Kingdom ended in failure.

Likewise, since the kings of the Christian Empire, in the New Testament Age, failed to establish providential conditions in accord with God's will, the Christian Empire was divided into Eastern and Western Kingdoms, and finally came to endure the hardships of the Crusades, and the Popes' captivity in Avignon. Also, due to the failure of the kings of the Christian Empire, Satanic absolute monarchies appeared.

Thus, God's providence to establish the Kingdom of the Messiah on earth by receiving the Messiah at the time of the Christian Empire failed in the same way as it had in the Old Testament Age. However, God's providence to establish the Kingdom of the Messiah continued in force, and a new providence to receive the Messiah was initiated. That was the providence to receive the Messiah through the will of the people—from the bottom. This kind of providence appeared in both the Old Testament Age and the New Testament Age. In order to receive the Messiah through the will of the people, Satanic kingdoms and monarchies which obstructed God's providence had to be overthrown, and a social environment created, in which the people's will could freely be manifested. Thus, God universalized democracy, wherein each person would be respected.

In the Old Testament Age, God established Persia, a gentile nation on Abel's side, and let it overthrow New Babylonia, which had captured the Israelites, and thus enabled the Israelites to return home. Then God, sending the prophet Malachi, started the providence of the preparation to receive the Messiah. At the same time, He left the throne of the king of Israel vacant and put the Israelites under the Hellenistic cultural sphere from the end of the fourth century BC. Since the Hellenistic culture was based on democracy, which respects individualities, the Israelites were able to express their own opinions freely under this culture. Thus, it became possible to receive the Messiah through the will of the people. According to the Divine Principle, this type of society is called a "society in the form of democracy" (*DP*, 332).

God conducted a similar providence in the New Testament Age: He arranged for the Satanic forces, which were obstructing God's providence, to disintegrate and decline. At the beginning of the sixteenth century God inspired Martin Luther to initiate the Protestant Reformation in order to awaken Christianity, which had been secularized by Satan. Then, from the end of the sixteenth century through the end of the eighteenth century, He allowed the Enlightenment to spread throughout Europe. This was a movement against the authority, privileges, social restrictions, and inequalities of the old regime, while yet maintaining respect for human reason. On the basis of the Enlightenment, God allowed the French Revolution, the slogan of which was "liberty, equality and fraternity," to occur, and He arranged for the Satanic absolute monarchies to decline. Thus, in this way modern democracy was established. Yet, as mentioned above, democracy is a political ideology established in order to receive the Second Advent of the Messiah through the will of the people; it is not an ideology able to actualize true liberty, equality, and fraternity.

Historically, religions had certain shortcomings, including a disregard for the individuality, freedom, and rights of human beings. Therefore, democratic governments felt it necessary to implement the policy of the separation of religion and politics. As a result, the absolute standard of value which the human spirit should follow came to be lost, and as a matter of course, democracy degenerated into egoistic democracy. Thus, in democratic society, the great confusion which we see today came about.

Actual problems of all kinds can be solved fundamentally only with God's truth and true love. Therefore, it will be possible to solve all problems fundamentally only when the Kingdom of the Second Advent of the Messiah, who will come with truth and true love, is established. I have so far pointed out the limitations of liberal democracy when seen from the viewpoint of God's providence. I have also noted the fact that democracy, to its great merit, has fulfilled its responsibility in guaranteeing freedom of faith, so that people can freely receive the Second Advent of the Messiah, according to their will.

The principle of mutual prosperity is, in short, a theory concerning joint government. Joint government refers to a government achieved through "the joint participation of all people." The joint participation of all people is an ideal which represents the ideology of democracy in the true sense. The joint participation of all people is, in fact, a people's participation through their election of their representatives. Then, if participation in politics through elected representatives is joint politics according to the principle of mutual prosperity, one may ask the following question: "How is this different from present democracy?" There is one basic difference between them, which we must now consider.

A joint government under the principle of mutual prosperity would have the following characteristics. First, the relationship among the candidates would not be that of rivalry, but that of brothers and sisters attending the Messiah, the representative of God, as the true parents of humankind. Second, the candidates would run for election not by their own will, but rather with the recommendation of many neighbors (brothers and sisters), namely, by the will of others, since those who are in the relationship of brothers and sisters centered on true love will make mutual recommendations. Third, an election would not take place in a way that would require an enormous expenditure of money, with all the accompanying side effects. After a preliminary election in the first stage, an election by lottery would be made in the second stage, accompanied by solemn prayer and appropriate formality. With the assurance and confidence that the outcome was in accord with God's will, those elected, those not elected, and, in fact, all the people, would be thankful to God, and could accept the result happily and sincerely.

In this way, a joint government under the principle of mutual prosperity is a government conducted through the joint participation of the people, based on God's true love. It would be the government of the Kingdom of the Messiah, in which the entire world can be unified. Also, since all people would attend the Messiah, the representative of God, as the True Parents of humankind, and participate in the joint government as brothers and sisters who have inherited the love of True Parents, a joint government will be a "government of the brothers and sisters, by the brothers and sisters, and for the brothers and sisters, centered on the True Parents of humankind," rather than "government of the people, by the people, and for the people." To be specific, a government under the principle of mutual prosperity is not a democracy, but rather a government of brothers and sisters centered on Heavenly Father.

True liberty, equality, respect for human rights, fraternity, and so on, all of which are the aims of democracy, but unrealized even today, can be realized completely through a government of brothers and sisters centered on Heavenly Father. In this sense, joint government under the principle of mutual prosperity can be expressed as a fraternal democracy. It should be noted that the sense of brotherhood described here has a different meaning from the common sense meaning: we are not referring to a brotherhood confined within a national boundary, thus creating regional brothers and sisters, as we see today. The brotherhood I am talking about is a universal brotherhood, in the true sense, wherein the entire world is united into one nation of brothers and sisters, and all humankind, as children, attend the True Parents, the center of humankind.

The reason why the idea of universal brotherhood has not been realized even today is that, first, the unification of the world has not yet been accomplished, and second, the True Parents of humankind had not appeared. The same thing can be said of democracy. The reason why democracy has not yet been fully realized is that—other than the reasons mentioned above—democracy, which is originally a supra-ethnic and supranational idea, is, in reality, restricted by ethnic and national characteristics.

A similar thing can be said concerning the Kingdom of the Messiah. The Kingdom of the Messiah is not a regional kingdom, but rather it is a supra-ethnic and supranational kingdom. The advent of the Messiah takes place in one elected nation, which is a regional nation, whereas the establishment of the Kingdom of the Messiah is possible only after the world is unified. It needs to be said, however, that the principle of mutual existence, mutual prosperity and mutual righteousness can be realized to some extent, even before the actual unification of the world, if the leaders of the world are willing to make an effort, attending God as the True Parents. By their doing so, a temporary solution of various kinds of confusion we experience today would be possible. Thus, I would say that the actual society functioning fully under the principle of mutual existence, mutual prosperity and mutual righteousness, will be established only after the present time of capitalism.

Finally, let me explain about the relationship between such a joint government functioning under the principle of mutual prosperity, and the separation of three powers. Democracy is a constitutional government, whose essence is the separation of the three branches of government: the legislative, the judicial, and the executive. Following this tradition, a joint government under the principle of mutual prosperity is a government by the representatives wherein the separation of the three powers is practiced.

However, the separation of three powers under the principle of mutual prosperity is not exactly the same concept as that proposed by Montesquieu, who sought to avoid any abuse of power. Under the principle of mutual prosperity, a separation of the three powers is proposed, but more in the sense of a division of the work of the three branches, legislation, judicial, and administrative, all working in harmony. The concept of power in the principle of mutual prosperity is also different from the traditional understanding. The traditional concept of power refers to physical force with which to subjugate people; but in the principle of mutual prosperity, power refers to an authority with true love, which inspires the object (people) to gratefully and willingly obey the will of the subject (sovereign).

While exercising their own physiological functions in harmony with each other, the various organs in a human body cooperate for the common purpose of supporting the life of the human body. Similarly, based on the common ideal of the country, the three branches will form an organic and harmonious system of cooperation, as they carry out the three functions of legislation, judicature and administration for the existence of the country.

According to the Divine Principle, the legislative, judiciary, and executive branches, which are all in a cooperative relationship with one another, are compared respectively to the lungs, heart, and stomach of the human body. The peripheral nerves connected to various organs in the human body cooperate with one another, harmoniously fulfilling the physiological functions of the human body, according to the commands of the brain. Similarly, in the ideal society, the will of God, who is the true subject of love, will be conveyed to the legislative, judicial, and executive branches through the organs of communication, and these three branches will cooperate harmoniously.

It should be clarified here that in God's creation the ideal image of the Kingdom of Heaven on earth was conceived in God's mind by taking the human body as a model. Therefore, the structure of the state in the ideal world resembles the structure of the human body. I explained above that the legislative, judicial, and executive branches are compared respectively to the lungs, heart and stomach; as a matter of fact, these three branches were established by imitating the lungs, heart, and stomach.

Due to the human fall, nations lost their original character, and became non-principled nations. Yet, the framework of a nation still resembles the structure of the human body. Thus, in the same way that the structure and function of the organs (lungs, heart, and stomach) of the human body are unchangeable, the structure and the function of the three branches of legislation, judicature and administration are unchangeable in the principled world. What should be added here is that the realities of the three branches in the ideal world are not identical to today's non-principled ones. In fact, principled power and non-principled power are very different in that the former is based on an emotional force of true love, whereas the latter is based on a compulsory force of physical power.

C. Principle of Mutual Righteousness

The principle of mutual righteousness refers to joint ethics. This is the perspective needed for the realization of an ethical society, namely, a society of joint ethics, in which everyone observes and practices morality and ethics, both publicly and privately. Today, regardless of there being a capitalist or Communist society (including the ex-Communist societies), morality and ethics, which people should observe, have all but collapsed. As a result, various injustices and social crimes are rampant, and the world is now sunk in great confusion. Many people deplore this collapse of values, but no one seems to be able to offer any effective measures for revitalizing those values.

The principle of mutual righteousness is an ideology capable of terminating this collapse of values, and of establishing a healthy society on earth, wherein everybody freely observes morality and ethics everywhere and at all times. The ideal society, which is to come after both the capitalist and communist societies, will be the society of mutual existence and mutual prosperity as explained above and, at the same time, it will be the society of joint ethics, where all people, regardless of their positions, will live with the same ethical attitudes. The principle of mutual righteousness is the very core of the future society of mutual existence, mutual prosperity and mutual righteousness. More concretely, and this will be explained shortly, the society of mutual righteousness will be the society in which the three great subjects thought is fully practiced.

In the future ideal society, religion will not be necessary, since the purpose of religion will have been completely realized. The purpose of Christian teaching is to empower an individual to firmly maintain faith until he or she receives the Second Advent of the Messiah. The purpose of Confucianism is to empower people to practice virtue until the ideal world of universal brotherhood arrives. The purpose of Buddhism is to empower people to train themselves and observe the law (*Dharma*) until the ideal world—the Realm of the Lotus-store (the World illuminated by the Buddha of Perfect Enlightenment) as taught in the Hua-yen (*Kegon*) School—arrives. Islam seeks a theocracy centering on the sovereignty of Allah. Therefore, the purpose of Christianity will be achieved when the ideal world of creation is realized by receiving the Second Advent of the Messiah; the purpose of Confucianism will be accomplished when the world of universal brotherhood is realized; the purpose of Buddhism will be accomplished when the Realm of the Lotus-store is realized; and the purpose of Islam will be realized when the theocracy centering on the sovereignty of Allah is realized.

The world in which the purpose of all religions has been accomplished is the society of mutual existence, mutual prosperity and mutual righteousness, namely, the society centered on the Second Advent of the Messiah. The teachings of the Second Advent of the Messiah embrace the core teachings of Christianity, Confucianism, Buddhism, and Islam. Therefore, there is no further need for any religion to persist. The society of mutual existence, mutual prosperity and mutual righteousness is not merely an instructive, ideal society, as traditional religions have taught, but rather the society in which people will lead a life of true love; a heavenly life in the midst of reality together with the Messiah. In that society, all people will live with the same values; therefore, religious doctrines centered on faith will be transformed into, and consummated as, living ethics centered on practice. This aspect of the future society is called the society of joint ethics, namely, the society of mutual righteousness

Then, what will be the characteristics of the society of joint ethics— First, social life will be reinforced by the true love of the three great subjects based on the three great subjects thought. Primarily, the three great subjects—namely, parents, who are the center of the family, teachers, who are the center of the school, and managers or leaders (company presidents, leaders of organizations, heads of state), who are the center of dominion—give God's true love continuously and limitlessly to their object partners, namely, children, students, employees or the people of their country, all based on the three great subjects thought. Subsequently, mutual love among object partners will be induced, and the entire society, a highly ethical society, will resemble, metaphorically speaking, a garden of love.

Various inequalities will disappear with the practice of true love. Poverty will disappear through the true love of those who have more. Those who are thirsty for knowledge will be satisfied through the true love of those who have knowledge. Those who were alienated in the workplace will be consoled by the true love of the manager. Inspired by God's true love, we can not but feel like helping those in need. This is what it means to say that the society will resemble a garden of love, and will be an ethical society.

A school filled with the teacher's true love, and a workplace filled with the manager's true love will both become ethical systems, which are the extended forms of an ethical family. That is to say, a school filled with the true love of a teacher is how a family filled with the true love of parents is extended in the aspect of education; a workplace filled with the true love of a manager is an extended family in the aspect of management. Thus, the entire society will be filled with God's love. This is the society of mutual righteousness. Thus, the society of mutual existence, mutual prosperity and mutual righteousness will be the social system based on the three great subjects thought.

Second, the basic unit of the society of mutual existence, mutual prosperity and mutual righteousness is the family. In other words, the practice of the loves of the three great subjects is first realized in a family.

There are four positions in the family, i.e., the positions of grandparents, parents (husband and wife), children (brothers and sisters), and grandchildren. God's love is given and received between the various members of a family who are in these four positions. Thus, grandparents' love, parents' love, husband and wife's love, brothers and sisters' love, and children's love are all fully realized in the family. When these kinds of love are given and received in the family, family law and family order will naturally be established. With the establishment of family law and family order (norm), a peaceful family, filled with compassion and harmony, will be realized. Such a family is indeed an ideal family.

The economical, political and ethical society based on the ideal family is the society of mutual existence, mutual prosperity and mutual righteousness. In this way, the long-cherished desire of humankind and the ideal of many thinkers and religious believers will finally be realized, and the world of the ideal of creation which has been fervently desired by God for over six thousand biblical years will be realized.

Conclusion

I have explained the basic concepts of the principle of mutual existence, the principle of mutual prosperity and the principle of mutual righteousness. My explanations have hopefully clarified that the principle of mutual existence, the principle of mutual prosperity, and the principle of mutual righteousness are not separate ideas but rather they are integrated as one. When this one, integrated idea is realized, the world of the ideal of creation, which God originally envisioned, will be realized for the first time. Thus, we call this one idea the "principle of mutual existence, mutual prosperity and mutual righteousness," using this single phrase. This concludes my explanation about the principle of mutual existence, mutual prosperity and mutual righteousness. Next, I will explain the concept of the three great subjects thought, the ideology of the ideal family, which is the core of the principle of mutual righteousness.

II. Three Great Subjects Thought

The three great subjects thought is an expression coined by Rev. Sun Myung Moon. The three great subjects refer to parents, teacher, and leader. In other words, the three great subjects mean the three great centers: the parents, who are the center of a family; the teacher, who is the center of a school; and the leader, who is the center of dominion. Here, the center of dominion refers to the center of a group, an enterprise, a country, and so on, namely, the central person who is responsible for management or leadership. Hence, the head of a group (a union, a political party, a federation, etc.), the president of an enterprise, the governor of a province, the president of a country, and so on, all fall under this category of leader. In this way, we call the three centers of parents, teacher and leader the three great subjects. The three great subjects thought emphasizes that these three great subjects should all practice God's true love.

God's True Love

God's love is absolute, since He is the absolute being. The term "absolute" in the sense used here, has a meaning different from any kind of sense carrying a secular meaning. The term "absolute," as it is used here, connotes the qualities of eternal, unchangeable, limitless, and universal. God is eternal, and omnipresent, existing all the time and everywhere. Accordingly, God's love is also eternal, and omnipresent. Such love is absolute love, or true love.

True love can be compared to sunlight. There is no place upon which the sun does not shine, and the sun is always shining eternally without rest. Similarly, true love is a comprehensive love, given to all humankind as well as to all things. All created beings are object partners of true love, and nothing in the universe is excluded from the realm of true love. Love was sometimes taken as referring to the intimacy between people, but true love is love given to all humankind, including enemies, and also to all things.

A person is related with other people in the six directions of above and below, front and back, and right and left. Taking oneself as the center, one is related above with one's parents, superiors, and elder persons; below with children, subordinates, and younger persons; to the front, with teachers, senior colleagues, and leaders; to the back, with students, junior colleagues, and followers; to the right, with brothers and sisters, intimate friends, and intimate colleagues; to the left, with competitors, strangers, and opponents. True love covers all these persons in all six directions. Furthermore, true love extends to all things. The three great subjects thought asserts that we should practice such true love at all times and in all places.

What is love? Love is to seek to care for one's object partners, while expressing to them a warm heart. With true love, one wants to give what one has to others, rather than to receive things from others. Secular love is a more selfish love, with which one looks after one's own interests. In contrast, the true love which Rev. Sun Myung Moon teaches is a love with which one expects nothing in return and only wishes to give to others. Thus, in true love, one wishes to continuously give to others, with a warm heart. Then, in what concrete way should we express love to others? There are many ways to love: "to talk gently," "to understand one's circumstances," "to give financial aid," "to extend cooperation," "to serve," "to support," "to help someone get out of difficulties," "to embrace," "to forgive one's enemies," "to teach kindly," and so on. To give, and then to give again to others with a warm heart in this way is the practice of true love. The spirit of this way of life is called altruism, or the spirit of "living for the sake of others."

True Love of the Three Great Subjects

As explained above, the true love of God is a love with which one wishes to give, and give again, endlessly to others. Just as hot water flows endlessly from a hot spring, so, too, one should endlessly embrace others with the hot-spring-like-water of true love from a warm heart. The three great subjects should always practice such love in their daily life. This is the core of the three great subjects thought. That is to say, parents should express such love to their children; a teacher should express such love to his or her students; and a leader should express such love to his or her subordinates or followers. Then, how do we express true love in the practice of our daily life?

We should practice true love through acting in the role of a subject. The role of parents is to bring up their children. The Korean term for raising children is *yangyuk*(養育), which consists of two Chinese characters, *yang* and *yuk*. *Yang* means to raise children by giving them food, clothing and shelter. While performing the duty of parents—namely, giving food, clothing and shelter—parents love their children with a warm heart. *Yuk* means to educate: parents teach their children family law, manners, ethics, morality, and any necessary knowledge, with a deep and warm heart.

In this way, parents can convey to their children the true love of God in the process of raising them. Parents should not love their children merely for the purpose of receiving something back when they have grown up. In other words, parents should not have the idea that they can make money or achieve power through their children. Wishing wholeheartedly that their children will become good, praiseworthy persons, they should raise them with a warm heart. This is the role of the parents. The expression of love when raising their children is the parents' practice of true love.

The role of a teacher is to teach his or her students through the education of knowledge, technical education, artistic education, physical education, and so on. A teacher should teach students kindly and sincerely. If students raise questions, the teacher should answer sincerely, and if they have any difficult problems, the teacher should help them as much as possible. In this way, a teacher can practice God's true love. This is the practice of true love in the role of a teacher. To teach only for the sake of wages is simply to sell and buy knowledge. This kind of education is not a correct education, since there is no love invested. A teacher should focus primarily on teaching students with sincerity, setting aside their receiving a salary as a secondary concern. Teaching should aim at the cultivation of the personality of students so that they will be empowered to serve society once they have matured. In order to do this, the teacher him or herself should first of all have a noble personality and a spirit of serving others. It is with the true love of a teacher that the teacher seeks to teach students with such a spirit of service and with a sincere and warm heart. Thus, the true love of a teacher is to practice love in one's role as a teacher.

Finally, let me explain the true love of a leader as expressed through the role of being a leader. What is the proper role of a leader? The role of the president of a country is to govern the people well and empower them to live well. The role of the governor of a province is to harmoniously govern the province, and the role of the manager of a company is to offer good welfare to employees. Let me briefly explain about the case of a company more concretely. The manager of a company should not have the idea of making employees engage in hard work in order to make money for himself or herself. Of course, a company should make money. However, once the company has made money, managers should return an appropriate share of it to the employees. In the future society, the spirit of making money will be united with the spirit of giving.

The manager of a company should have an altruistic spirit of service.

He or she should love the employees and have the spirit of giving with a warm heart. The manager should be concerned about the circumstances of the employees, and whether or not they have any difficulties with regard to food, clothing, and shelter. This is a dominion with love. In many cases, however, dominion includes giving orders to subordinates. An order in itself can feel cold; but when a leader gives an order with a warm and sincere heart, subordinates can receive it with gratitude because the order carries with it such a warm feeling.

The Bible says that God gave human beings the three great blessings. In the third blessing, God ordered human beings to dominate all things with love. The primary, secondary, and tertiary industries, as well as all other activities which deal with materials, fall under the category of dominion over all things. Dominion should be done with love. Thus, we should manage buildings and facilities, regarding them as belonging to all people and to God rather than to ourselves.

Thus, the management and maintenance of properties and facilities should be carried out with a sincere heart. This is the spirit of management as an exercise of loving dominion over all things. Pollution, which recently has become a serious problem, is the inevitable result arising from the loss of the spirit of dominion or the spirit of management with love. The spirit of dominion with love is the practice of the true love of a leader. In summary, the idea that the three great subjects should practice God's true love through their respective roles is the three great subjects thought.

Three Subjectivities with One Center

Three subjectivities with one center refers to the idea that a central figure serves in the roles of, and practices simultaneously the loves of, the three great subjects, i.e., parents, teacher, and leader. In other words, although parents, teacher, and leader are different roles, nevertheless, parents should be at the same time a teacher and a leader. In other words, parents practice true love through the roles of the three subjects: While parents are primarily fulfilling their role as parents to love their children with a warm heart, they also carry out the roles of teacher and leader.

While engaging primarily in teaching, a teacher also stands in the position of a parent and raises students as if they were his or her own children, and at the same time, the teacher stands in the position of a leader to guide the students.

While engaging primarily in the management of an organization, a leader should also accomplish the roles of parent and teacher. A manager, in addition to the work of management, should express a warm heart to his or her employees with the heart of a parent in raising children, having constant concern for their eating, sleeping and welfare. Also, a leader, standing in the position of a teacher, should teach his or her subordinates social norms and knowledge.

Thus, it is the assertion of the three great subjects thought that one subject, or one center, simultaneously plays the role of three subjects. In other words, the three great subjects thought is the thought concerning the practice of a parent's three subjectivities, a teacher's three subjectivities and a leader's three subjectivities. Since the love of parents to children, the love of a teacher to students, and the love of a leader to subordinates are downward-oriented loves, the three great subjects thought claims that one subject should practice three downward loves through the roles of the three subjects.

As mentioned previously, true love does not seek one's self-interest but rather it wishes to give limitlessly. With true love you want to invest totally and forget what you have done. You want to give and give again, and you forget completely what you have given. No matter how much you have loved someone, you release it, and you do not carry with you any idea that you have loved.

When you forget the extent to which you have loved, your heart can become empty and humble. If you think that "I have loved him so much, but he did not respond. What a rude person he is," then you can become arrogant. Once you become arrogant, it becomes difficult for you to truly love anymore. Therefore, when you give, you must forget it; and when you forget, you can feel like loving again, since God's true love will fill your empty heart. Thus, always love with a fresh mind, and you will be empowered to love again. Parents, teachers, and leaders should all do this. This is the way of true love.

The Spread of Love

If parents truly love their children, children can not merely remain still, since love causes an inductive effect. Children will be moved by their parents' love and, gratefully, they will serve their parents. Since parents love their children with all their heart, children, with all their hearts, feel like serving their parents with filial piety. This is the upward-directed love of children.

Also, when children receive the true love of their parents, not only does a filial heart toward their parents emerge, but also, the children themselves, namely, brothers and sisters, will come to love one another. This is horizontal love. In addition to that, a son and his wife (daughter-in-law) will also love each other in conjugal love, which is a horizontal love. Thus, based on parents' love, both upward love and horizontal love are brought about, and the family is filled with love. Consequently, in a family the parents' downward love is most important.

The same thing can be said about the love of a teacher at a school. Students who receive the true love of their teacher (downward love) will automatically respect their teacher from the bottom of their heart. They will think that their teacher is great. While satisfied intellectually, they are also impressed by the sincerity of the teaching; they naturally bow their heads toward the teacher. Then, students can not but respect their teacher. This is the upward love of students to the teacher. Not only that, but being impressed by the true love of their teacher, students themselves will come to love one another. This is a horizontal love among students. Thus, the love of the teacher (downward love) causes an inductive effect.

A few years ago, there was an unsavory incident at a certain university in Korea: Students struck a teacher. At that time, every newspaper condemned the students. The criticism of the students was not wrong in itself, but it was a misdirected criticism, in terms of solving the problem. The responsibility for the mishap rested primarily with the teacher and only secondarily with the students. The students reacted as they did because the teacher did not teach them properly. Would there be any valid reason for the students to strike the teacher if the teacher had regularly practiced the roles of the three subjects with true love, and followed the way of a teacher? The students' violence can, in one sense, be understood as an expression of their complaint, "why did you not teach us properly?" Furthermore, the parents also share the blame. The students' parents must not have given downward love to their children in daily life. Therefore, there was no base for the students to respect the teacher, whose position is not different from their parents. Hence, the solution to the problem of student violence against teachers can be found through the three great subjects thought.

As mentioned above, the loves of the three great subjects are downward loves: parents' love toward children, teacher's love toward students, and a leader's love toward followers. The downward love is primary, and upward and horizontal loves are then induced by such downward love.

Since there is an inductive effect and a reciprocal reaction in love, there are certain cases where the upward love of the subordinate is given first, and that is followed by the induced downward love of the superior. When children show filial piety to their parents, students respect their teacher, and subordinates are loyal to their leaders, parents' love, a teacher's love, and a leader's love are all induced. In principle, however, the downward love is primary, and upward and horizontal loves are secondary. When downward love is prior, upward love and horizontal love can be induced one hundred per cent, whereas when upward love is prior, there is no guarantee that downward love will be induced one hundred percent. The same thing can be said of horizontal love. The starting point of true love is the downward love, since the origin of true love is in God, and everything comes downward from God in the first place.

If the manager of a company truly loves the employees, they will not simply be satisfied with receiving salaries, but they will want to reward the manager. That is to say, when the manager makes constant efforts with a warm heart to give the employees as much as possible from the income of the company, then the employees will respect and be thankful to the manager. In this situation, if the company should face difficulty, the employees might say, "We do not need an increase in salary. Please invest a portion of our salary increase back into the company, and manage it well." In this way, if the manager of a company shows true love, the employees will love the manager, and at the same time love will spread among the employees. In addition, the employees will love and care for the facilities and properties of the company. Thus, the subject's downward love, namely parents' love, teacher's love and leader's love, should be given first.

If, in this way, true love spreads to a family, to a school, and to a company, and then to a nation, and to the entire world, the global village will eventually be filled with God's love. As a result, all crimes on earth will disappear without any trace, and true and everlasting peace can be actualized.

The Origin of the Three Great Subjects Is God

What is the origin of the three great subjects in the three great subjects thought? It is God. The origin of all subjects is God. The most representative subjects among all subjects are the three great subjects, and the origin of the three great subjects is God.

God is, first of all, the Parents of humankind. In prayer, someone may call God "Father," while someone else may call God "Mother." In fact, God possesses Yang and Yin dual characteristics; therefore, God is the Parents of humankind. God created human beings as His (Her) sons and daughters. Originally human beings are not sinners, but are God's sons and daughters; due to the human fall, however, human beings became sinners. Thus, God is the Parents of humankind, and at the same time the subject of true love. God created the universe with Logos, as is written in the Gospel according to John, chapter 1. Logos is truth and God's Word. Therefore, God is the subject of truth. The subject of truth is basically a teacher. Thus God is the teacher of truth. Also God is the master, since the Creator is the master of dominion.

The traditional Korean term *Kun-Sa-Bu*(君師父) refers to the ideal of parents, teacher and leader. *Kun* means the master, *Sa* means the teacher, and *Bu* means father (who represents parents). The Korean people possessed this *Kun-Sa-Bu* thought from their ancient times, and the origin of *Kun-Sa-Bu* is God. Hence, God is father (parents), teacher, and leader. *Kun-Sa-Bu* is, indeed, the same as the three great subjects, there being only a difference in the order of the words.

In the Korean national anthem there is a passage: "Long live our country, which *Hanunim* protects!" *Hanunim* is the same as *Hananim*, or the Creator, God. How does God protect Korea? He protects it with the true love of parents, teacher and master. The origin of parents, teacher, and master, or the origin of *Kun-Sa-Bu* is God. Therefore, the love of the three great subjects is in accordance with the Way of Heaven, which is absolute. Thus, the three great subjects thought is absolute and it will never fail. Those who disobey the Way of Heaven, or those who do not live according to this thought, can only decline, or perish.

Why is today's society in such confusion? It is because we did not practice the love of the three great subjects, and we did not observe the Way of Heaven. If we disobey natural law, we will suffer physically; therefore, we lead our lives, observing natural law. Similarly, we should spiritually lead our lives according to the Way of Heaven. Since the three great subjects thought is in accordance with the Way of Heaven, which is based on God, we can not but observe it. If we observe it, peace can be realized, and if we do not, confusion will prevail. This is the very reason why traditional religions have all emphasized love.

Buddhism taught us to practice mercy; Confucianism, *jen*; Islam, compassion, and Christianity, love. However, the reason why we should do so has never before been clarified. Now, it can be clarified that the origin of mercy, *jen*, compassion, and love is the true love of God, which is also the origin of the love of the three great subjects. The three bonds (ruler and ruled, father and son, and husband and wife) and five moral duties (between father and son, husband and wife, elder brother and younger brother, one friend with another, and ruler and ruled) in Confucianism, the main teaching of which is the relationship between parents and children, is in agreement with the three great subjects thought. The same thing can be said about the virtues of Buddhism, the virtues of Islam and the virtues of Christianity. All the teachings of the saints and sages, about love, are also included, without exception, in this category of the love of the three great subjects.

The reason why traditional values have been declining is that people do not realize that mercy in Buddhism, *jen* in Confucianism, compassion in Islam, and love in Christianity all originate from the true love of God, and they are precisely the various expressions of the love of the three great subjects. To put it in another way, when it becomes clear that the origin of all these traditional religious virtues is the true love of God and, therefore, based on the love of the three great subjects, then all the traditional virtues will be revitalized, and they will recover the ability to guide and empower the minds of humankind today.

The Three Great Subjects Thought, the Principle of Mutual Existence, Mutual Prosperity and Mutual Righteousness, and the Principle of the Ideal Family

The principle of mutual existence, mutual prosperity and mutual righteousness is the concept which describes the characteristics of the economic, political, and ethical system of our future ideal society. That is, the future society will be an economic and political system which is managed under the principle of mutual righteousness (joint ethics). The content of the principle of mutual righteousness is the practice of the three great subjects thought, and the essence of the three great subjects thought is the principle of the ideal family. In sum, the future society will be an economic and political system that is managed under the principle of mutual righteousness; concretely, it will be managed by the three great subjects thought whose essence is the principle of the ideal family.

Establishment of a New Value Perspective

Finally, let me explain how a new value perspective can be firmly established on the basis of the three great subjects thought. When, from the ethical aspect, we see the actions, which are the expression of the three great subject's true love, and the consequent love of the object partners which is thereby induced, namely, the downward love of the subject partners and the upward and horizontal loves of the object partners, we accept them as truly good. When those same deeds are seen from the intellectual and educational aspect, we accept them as genuine trueness, and when they are seen from the artistic aspect, we experience them as true beauty. Truth, goodness, and beauty are not separated in one's actions. A deed of true love is accepted as truth, goodness, or beauty according to the mental aspect with which we perceive it. All traditional values will be revitalized and enlivened when they embrace this new value perspective of the three great subjects thought.

III. Significance of the Four Great Realms of Heart and the Three Great Kingships

Rev. Sun Myung Moon proposed the concepts of "the four great realms of heart" and "the three great kingships" at the beginning of the Completed Testament Age. It is important for us to understand these concepts clearly in order to realize the ideal family which is the basic unit of the ideal society. First, let me explain the four great realms of heart.

A. Four Great Realms of Heart

Concept of Heart

In order to understand the concept of the four great realms of heart, it is first necessary to understand the concept of heart. Heart refers to "the emotional impulse to seek joy through love." In other words, heart is "the emotional impulse that can not but love." It was due to His emotional impulse that can not help but love, that God created human beings as His object partners, and all things as the object partners of joy for human beings.

Realm of Heart

The realm of heart means the sphere of influence of one's heart. The realm of culture means the sphere of influence of a culture, and the realm of sovereign power means the sphere of influence of one's power. So, again, the realm of heart means the sphere of influence of one's heart. Since heart is the emotional impulse to love, it necessarily accompanies the practice of love. Heart and love are two sides of a coin, and the sphere of influence of one's heart is the sphere of influence of one's love.

The four great hearts refer to the four kinds of hearts: heart of parents, heart of husband and wife, heart of brothers and sisters, and heart of children. Since heart and love are two sides of a coin, the four great hearts are the same as the four great loves: parents' love, husband and wife's love, brothers and sisters' love, and children's love.

Vertical Love, Horizontal Love, and Family Love

In order to understand the four great hearts or four great loves correctly, it is necessary to understand the direction of love, that is, the vertical and horizontal directions of love. Vertical love refers to a downward-oriented love, one which flows from above downwards, such as God's love to human beings, and parents' love to their children, and to an upward-oriented love, one which flows from below upwards, such as human beings' love to God, and children's love to parents. Horizontal love, on the other hand, refers to the love that flows horizontally, such as brothers and sisters' love and husband and wife's love. The brothers and sisters' love includes love between brothers, love between sisters, and love between brother and sister. Parents' love, husband and wife's love, brothers and sisters' love, and children's love are all practiced in a family; therefore they are family loves.

Parents' love, husband and wife's love, and children's love, are called the three object partners' loves in the Divine Principle. When God is seen as the subject, parents, husband and wife, and children are His three object partners; therefore, parents' love, husband and wife's love, and children's love are called the three object partners' loves. The four great loves, which are based on the four great hearts, are the three object partners' loves plus brothers and sisters' love.

Four Great Realms of Heart and the Growth of Love

Rev. Sun Myung Moon teaches that love grows as one develops from childhood. An infant does not know well what love is like; but as he or she grows in parents' love, his or her love for his or her parents will gradually grow. This is children's love. The word infant here refers not to a son or daughter possessing particular sex characteristics, but to a child who does not yet have any consciousness of sexuality. In other words, the relation between children is not yet that of boy and girl, but that between children (for example, like twins) without any sexual consciousness.

Then, brothers and sisters' love, namely, the love between brothers, the love between sisters, and the love between brother and sister, begins to grow among children, as it is stimulated by the love of parents. In the same way, as children's love grows under parents' love, so too, does brothers and sisters' love grow under the parents' downward love, along with the simultaneous growth of their physical bodies. This is accomplished in accordance with the inductive effect of love.

When brothers and sisters mature to the appropriate point, a brother will become engaged with the sister of another family or a sister will become engaged with the brother of another family; then, they will get married and become husband and wife. The love between them is a husband and wife's love, which is also practiced under the inducement of parents' love.

When children have thus grown, and have completed themselves, they finally become parents. The concept of parents here is not a concept imbued with any sexual character; rather, it is the more simple concept of those who are "opposite" of children. Parents practice parents' love toward their children.

So far, I have explained husband and wife's love and parents' love as well as the growth of children's love and brothers and sisters' love. It should be noted here that husband and wife's love does not appear all of a sudden once a brother and a sister have matured and get married; rather, as they grow, their love for the opposite sex, which is a stage prior to that of conjugal love, grows in them little by little. In fact, as brothers and sisters grow, they only gradually become qualified to become husband and wife. Thus, as their physical bodies grow, a love for the opposite sex (namely, the stage prior to conjugal love) grows unconsciously in them, in a vague form.

The same thing can be said about parents' love. It is not the case that children grow to become parents and then all of a sudden parents' love appears, but rather they already experience parents' love unconsciously while they grow. Since children grow under parents' love, they experience what parents' love is like. Thus, there is a growing of love not only in children's love and brothers and sisters' love but also in husband and wife's love and parents' love.

Inclusiveness of Love

Inclusiveness means that something is included in another thing. Therefore, the inclusiveness of love means that a certain love is included in another love. Those including other loves are brothers and sisters' love, husband and wife's love, and parents' love.

Brothers and sisters' love includes children's love, since brothers and sisters are related with each other in a family where they grow as children. Next, husband and wife's love includes both brothers and sisters' love, and children's love, since a brother and a sister have grown up from childhood to become husband and wife. Of course, it is not the case that a brother and sister within the same family become husband and wife, but that a brother in one family and a sister in another, different, family become husband and wife. Finally, parents' love includes all those loves, namely, children's love, brothers and sisters' love and husband and wife's love.

Seen from the aspect of heart, brothers and sisters' heart includes the children's heart; husband and wife's heart includes children's heart and brothers and sisters' heart; and parents' heart includes all these hearts. To put it another way, the realm of children's heart is the narrowest, the realm of brothers and sisters' heart is broader, the realm of husband and wife's heart is even broader, and the realm of parents' heart is the broadest.

Concretely speaking, for children's love (or heart), there is one object partner, the parents. For brothers and sisters' love (or heart), there are at least the two object partners of parents and siblings. It may seem that conjugal love (or heart) has only one object partner (the spouse), but this is not the case. In the Divine Principle view, a husband represents all the men in the family, and a wife represents all the women in the family. In other words, the husband represents the grandfather, the father, and a

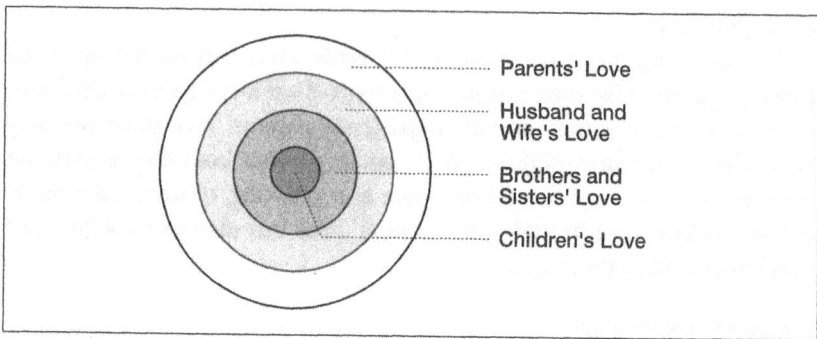

Fig. 12.1. Concentric Circles of Love

brother, and the wife represents the grandmother, the mother, and a sister. Hence, for husband and wife's love, there are at least three object partners of parents, spouse, and siblings.

Next, the realm of parents' love is broader than the realm of husband and wife's love since parents are parents to their children and at the same they are husband and wife. Here must be added the fact that these four kinds of love, namely children's love, brothers and sisters' love, husband and wife's love, and parents' love, are all practiced under God's love; therefore, all the family members can be grateful to God and, at the same time, they can regard God as their object partner of love consciously or unconsciously. The breadth of the realm of the four loves can be shown by four concentric circles as in fig. 12.1.

Husband and Wife's Love as a Representative Love

Among the four loves mentioned above, the most representative one is the husband and wife's love. This is because, as already mentioned, the husband represents all the men in a family and the wife represents all the women in a family; moreover, each represents one of God's dual characteristics. Furthermore, the husband represents all men, half of humankind, and the wife represents all women, the other half of humankind; the husband represents the yang aspects of all things in the universe, and the wife represents the yin aspects of all things in the universe.

Husband and wife's love, therefore, represents the masculine and feminine loves in a family, in all humankind, and in all things, as well as the masculine and feminine loves in God. In other words, husband and wife's love includes all the kinds of love in the created world as well as God's love. Thus, husband and wife's love is the representative love in a family.

Center of the Cosmos and the Fruit of Love

I have clarified above that the husband and wife's love is not only the love between a man and woman, but rather it is a synthesized love wherein God's love, family love, and the love in all things are united. When such love is synthesized, there is a multiplying effect, which engenders a strong impulse which can not be repressed. The position of conjugal union represents the cosmos, namely, it is the center of the cosmos, and at the same time it is the position of the second Creator where the ideal of creation is accomplished. The True Parents of humankind (messiah) are the model, the second Creator. Thus, the position of conjugal union is very precious and holy; it is the position wherein human beings most resemble God.

The foundation for all the various types of love beyond the family—one's love for the nation, love for humankind, love for all things, love for one's fatherland, and so on—is conjugal love. This is because conjugal love is not only the love between a man and woman, but rather it represents all the different types of love between all subjects and objects. That is to say, conjugal love represents the love between principal element (or individual) and subordinate element (or individual) as well as the love between subject and object in the sense of *sungsang* and *hyungsang*.

As a matter of fact, a husband (man) represents heaven, and a wife (woman) represents the earth. In other words, the relationship between husband and wife is like that between God and the created world. Accordingly, conjugal love represents the love between God and created beings (human beings).

In principle, the husband takes the initiative and his wife acts according to his directive; therefore, the relationship between husband and wife is that of subject and object, in the sense of *sungsang* and *hyungsang*. Furthermore, conjugal love represents the love between spiritual beings, and physical beings in the world.

Also, in principle, the husband is the head of the family, and his wife is his support. Hence, the relationship between husband and wife is that of subject and object in the sense of superordinate and subordinate. Teacher and student, government and people, the sun and the earth, a cell nucleus and cell cytoplasm are all examples of such a relationship.

Furthermore, the husband is the representative of all men, half of humankind, and his wife is the representative of all women, the other half. Accordingly, the union of man and woman relates to the unification of humankind, and thus conjugal love is a love for all humankind. Also, the husband represents the yang aspect of the universe and spirit world, and the woman represents the yin aspect of the universe and spirit world. Hence, the conjugal union is the representative center of the cosmos.

It can be concluded that conjugal love represents all the types of love in the created world. They are all manifestations of God's love. Therefore, husband and wife's love, which is the representative love and synthesized love, is none other than God's love. Hence, the position of the union of husband and wife, where such synthesized love appears, is the center of the cosmos, the position of the second Creator, and the position of the perfection of the ideal of creation.

Original conjugal love is indeed boundlessly broad and deep, and the children born through such a conjugal love are the fruit of this holy, synthesized love. Since conjugal love is the love that synthesizes God's love and the love of the whole world, the children (new beings) who are born through that love are God's children, who are the integration of the universe and, therefore, they are microcosms.

It is important to realize here that all phenomena take place first in the heavenly world, or the spirit world, and then manifest on the earth. Hence, the image of children being born and growing as brothers and sisters, and becoming husband and wife and then parents, namely, the phenomena that human beings are born and grow, while experiencing love step by step, take place first in heaven or, more precisely, within God's mind. That is to say, the growth of children, growth of brothers and sisters, becoming husband and wife, and then becoming parents first takes place in an ideal form in God's mind before they appear on earth.

To put it another way, before creating Adam and Eve, God envisioned such a content in His mind, and then, in accordance with that vision, Adam and Eve were to be created as His children, and were to grow as brother and sister, become husband and wife, and then parents. Thus, the "envisioned" Adam and Eve, children, brother and sister, husband and wife, and parents within God's plan can be called mental Adam and Eve, mental children, mental brother and mental sister, mental husband and wife, and mental parents respectively. This is illustrated in fig. 12.2.

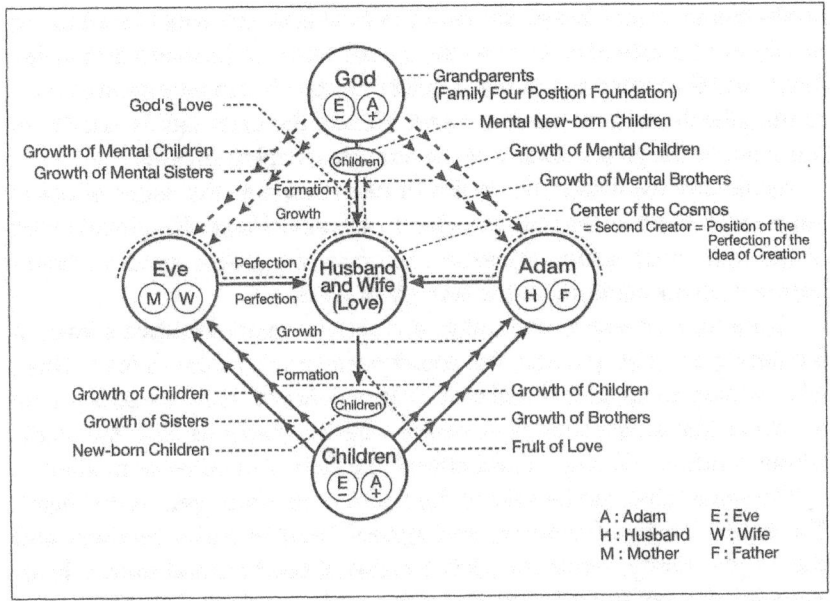

Fig. 12.2. Development of Conjugal Love based on the Four Great Hearts (Four Great Loves)

A Global Realm of Heart as the Extended Form of the Four Great Realms of Heart

The four great loves are family loves, and the four great hearts are family hearts. The realm of children's heart, the realm of brothers and sisters' heart, the realm of husband and wife's heart, and the realm of parents' heart are all the realms of heart in the family. Thus, the basic form of the four great realms of heart is that of the family.

According to the Divine Principle, in the original society all human beings attend the True Parents of humankind. That is to say, in the original society all humankind becomes one great family centering on the True Parents. In other words, in the ideal world of creation, human society is a great family society existing as an extended form of a family, and each family is a miniature of the great family society, namely, it is a small family society.

Therefore, the realm of children's heart in the family can be extended even to the global realm of children's heart; the realm of brothers and sisters' heart in the family can be extended even to the global realm of brothers and sisters' heart; the realm of husband and wife's heart in the family can be extended even to the global realm of husband and wife's heart; and the realm of parents' heart in the family can be extended even to the global realm of parents' heart. Hence, the great family society of humanity is the global society of the four great realms of heart.

As already explained, the realm of heart refers to the realm of object partners of heart, or the realm of object partners of love. The global realm of the four great hearts, therefore, refers to the global realm of object partners (all humankind) of the four great loves.

Those who belong to the realm of children's heart (children's love) in the family are their parents, the object partners of children's love. Then, who belongs to the global realm of children's heart? They are adults who are about the same age as their parents: those persons all over the world whom children will respect and attend like their own father or mother.

The same thing can be said of the realm of brothers and sisters' heart. The family realm of brothers and sisters' heart includes brothers and sisters in a family, while the global realm of brothers and sisters' heart includes all men and women about the same age as one's brothers and sisters. Accordingly, wherever you may go and happen to meet men and women of about the same age as your own brothers and sisters, you can express love to them as if they were your real brothers and sisters, and you can receive love from them as well.

The same thing can not be said about the realm of husband and wife's heart, however. The realm of husband and wife's heart is different in character from the other realms of heart in this regard. When a woman meets a man of the same age as her husband, or when a man meets a woman of the same age as his wife, can she give him a love similar to that which she gives to her husband? Can he give her a love similar to that which he gives to his wife? Absolutely not! This is because the husband and wife relationship is a monogamous relationship incorporating a sexual life. Since husband and wife's love is necessarily accompanied by their sexual life, conjugal love can not be allowed beyond the parameters of their relationship. Instead, one should express brothers and sisters' love toward men or women of the same age as your husband or wife, in the same way that you love your brothers and sisters in your family.

As for the realm of parents' heart, the same thing can be said as regards the realms of children's heart and brothers and sisters' heart. Wherever you may meet children of the same age as your sons or daughters, you should relate to them with a parents' heart or parents' love in the same way as you do to your own children.

B. Three Great Kingships

Significance of the Three Great Kingships

In speaking of the three great kingships, one may wonder what difference exists between the three great kingships and the three great subjects. As already explained, the three great subjects in the three great subjects thought refer to the centers of the family, the school, and the workplace. The king of a country is the center of the country, and therefore, he is the subject. Then, one may think that the three great kings of the world are the three great subjects, but this is not the case.

The king in the three great kingships does not mean the king of a country as it is understood in the mundane world. The kings in the three great kingships are the centers or the heads of a family. The heads of a family are the parents, and the three great kings in the three great kingships refer to the parents of the three generations: grandparents, parents and children.

Kingship means possessing the authority of a king. In the secular sense, the king is the central figure who governs the people with kingship, or, the figure in the highest position. In contrast, in the Kingdom of Heaven, as mentioned above, the king is the center and the head of a family, namely, the parents. Thus, the parents of the family are the parents and the king and queen of the family. The king of the country is the parent and the king of the country. In an enterprise, which is an extended form of a family, the president and his or her spouse are the parents and the king and queen of the enterprise.

In a family, there is only one set of parents. Then, why is it said that there are three kings in the family? Because there are three kings: the king of the past, the king of the present, and the king of the future; namely, the parents of the past, the parents of the present, and the parents of the future. Thus, three kings in a family refer to grandparents, parents, and children. The grandparents are the king and queen of the past; the parents are the king and queen of the present; and children are the kings and queens of the future. Since the grandparents, parents, and children are all kings and queens, the authority of king is given to all of them; namely, the three great kingships. Yet, the three kingships are different from each other in character.

Characteristics of the Three Great Kingships

Grandparents belong to the past and they are the king and queen of the past. It means that they were king and queen on earth in the past. Then, what is their status now? They are still king and queen. However, they are no longer a king and queen representing the earth, but a king and queen representing the spirit world. Furthermore, they are a king and queen representing God. In other words, grandparents represent the spirit world and God. Accordingly, the four position foundation centered on God as explained in the Divine Principle is also the four position foundation centered on grandparents in the original world. Therefore, from now on, grandparents will be the center of the family four position foundation, representing God and the True Parents of humankind. Hence, the position of grandparents is that of God, which is the highest in the family and, therefore, children and grandchildren have to attend their grandparents in the most respectful manner.

Parents are the king and queen representing the present world, while grandparents are the king and queen representing the spirit world. Also, parents are the king and queen in the family. Children are the future head of the family. At present, they are princes and princesses, and in the future they will be kings and queens of the family, and of the world. Children also represent all the descendants, namely, grandchildren and great-grandchildren and so on, who are also future kings and queens.

The Reason Why the Term "Three Great Kingships" Is Necessary

One may raise the following question: Why do we need to call them kings instead of just saying grandparents, parents and children? It is because the position of king is the most noble and respectable position. The conventional concepts of grandparents, parents and children are quite different from those in the original world. Through the Divine Principle, we have learned the preciousness of the family, namely, the preciousness of grandparents, parents and children. However, there is still a great difference between those concepts as conceived by God, and those which are conceived by human beings. We express the most supreme nobility with the term king or prince. Originally, every human being was to be a noble being like a king. With the study of the Divine Principle, however, we may not yet have fully realized the true nobility of the human being.

Suppose there is a prince of a country who is hiding himself in a village in a remote mountain area and wearing shabby clothes, separated from his father, the king, due to the betrayal of his men. If the elders of the village realized the truth, they would apologize to him saying, "What has happened to Your Highness? We did not know that you are such a noble person, and we have committed a great crime. Please forgive our disloyalty." Then, with the greatest sincerity, they would respect him and attend him, placing him in the highest position. The greatest sincerity, the highest position and the best attendance that the prince would receive all express the nobility of his position as prince. The value of a human being in God's eyes is much like this, or even greater.

Thus, the original concepts of grandparents, parents and children are very precious, and the conventional concepts are not able to convey the same noble sense as do the original concepts. There is no better means of expression than to use the concept of king in order to express their nobility, importance and gloriousness, since the king occupies the most supreme of all positions on earth. Thus, in the original world, where humans are so precious, the nobility of grandparents, parents, and children is expressed through the concepts of the three great kingships.

Parents should not treat their children casually, even when their children are young. Rather, they should treat their children just as a king would treat his prince and princess. Once the king has decided on his son as his successor, no matter how young he may be, the king will not ignore the prince's words. Therefore, from now, parents should not neglect their children. And children should attend their parents, regarding them as king and queen, and attend their grandparents, regarding them as honorable king and queen mother (king and queen of the spirit world).

Kingship and Its Concept

A king possesses the authority of a king, namely, kingship. The kingships of grandparents, parents, and children are together called the three great kingships. In other words, authority is given to the three great kings. From this viewpoint, we should look at the members of our family, and other families, as those who are as precious as kings and queens. Hence, a home is a royal palace.

After bequeathing his throne to his child, the king becomes the grandfather in the royal palace, and stays in the central position as the great king, representing the spirit world and God. A home is as precious as a royal palace. A family constitution therefore is the constitution of a royal palace. The family of the True Parents is its model. When the ideal world is realized, all the families of the world will resemble the True Parents' family.

Finally, let me explain about the power of kingship. Conventional power is what makes people in the object position obey the sovereign subject, usually through fear and reverence. Secular power is enforced physically. It has the authority to make people obey the sovereign compulsorily by using police or military force. In contrast, power in the Kingdom of Heaven will be that which inspires the object to obey the subject with a grateful heart, and it will be based on God's true love.

Power in the Kingdom of Heaven, however, also has a certain authority which gives people, as objects, a certain feeling of fear. This is the fear which arises from the intuition one possesses of the spiritual death which would accrue with one's separation from or one's opposition to God's true love. Since love is the source of life, and the loss of love is connected with the loss of true life, or the death of true life, should one disregard or oppose the love of the subject figure, one's subconsciousness would perceive its inevitable result (that is, the death of life) and feel fear. This is why one would feel fear even while feeling happiness in God's limitless love.

There is a difference between the obedience of people to the subject (the dictator) in the Communist world and the obedience of people to the subject in the Kingdom of Heaven. The dictators in the Communist world made the people obey compulsorily, threatening them with death. In the Kingdom of Heaven, however, people will want to obey the sovereign, centered on true love. This is the precise point of difference between the two worlds.

However, both worlds are the same in that the people suffer if they do not unite with the sovereign. In the Communist world, if one does not obey the dictator, one is risking one's life, or risking being purged at once. In contrast, in the Kingdom of Heaven, if one disobeys the subject's order which is based on love, one feels a shrinkage or risk of one's life, to a greater or lesser degree, at once or after a certain period of time, depending on the degree of disobedience. Thus, love is accompanied with authority.

In the Bible, there is written an expression conveying the authority of

God: When Abraham was prepared to offer his only begotten son, Isaac, in order to indemnify his failure in his earlier, symbolic, offering, God said, "now I know that you fear God" (Gen. 22:12). This passage makes plain that God's love is accompanied with a certain authority and fear. Thus, secular power is enforcement with compulsory power, while power in the Kingdom of Heaven is the power of true love which induces people to obey voluntarily. Kingship is to be exercised. The exercise of the three great kingships is that the grandparents, parents, and children demonstrate such power of love over their object partners.

Notes

1. Theory of the Original Image

1. A representative example of the reciprocal relationship is yang and yin, or man and woman. *Exposition of the Divine Principle* (hereafter cited as *DP*) explains that the relationship between *Sungsang* and *Hyungsang* is, in a way, the same as that between Yang and Yin, or man and woman, as follows: i) "In this case, the yang and yin of God were manifested in masculinity and femininity" (*DP*, 19). ii) "Because God exists as the subject partner having the qualities of internal nature and masculinity, He created the universe as His object partner with the qualities of external form and femininity" (*DP*, 19). iii) God is the Subject in whom the dual characteristics of original internal nature and original external form are in harmony. At the same time, God is the harmonious union of masculinity and femininity, which manifests the qualities of original internal nature and original external form, respectively. In relation to the universe, God is the subject partner having the qualities of internal nature and masculinity" (*DP*, 19). Consequently, the relationship of *Sungsang* and *Hyungsang*, and the relationship between God and the creation are also the reciprocal relationships of yang and yin.
2. The Holy Spirit Association for the Unification of World Christianity, *Exposition of the Divine Principle* (New York: HSA-UWC, 1996).
3. Paul A. Dirac, et al., Scientific American Resource Library: *Readings in the Physical Sciences* (Japanese version) (Tokyo: Kodansha), 1972, 79.
4. The Holy Spirit Association for the Unification of World Christianity, *Divine Principle* (Korean version) (Seoul: Sunghwa-sa, 1987).
5. From around 1951, Werner Heisenberg (1901–76), the founder of quantum physics, dealt with the unified theory of elementary particles

and advocated the idea of "prime-matter." This theory asserts that the elementary particles that have been observed, of which there are approximately 300, have come into being from a prime-matter, the ultimate matter, following a cosmic equation expressed in a certain mathematical form. Heisenberg also said that "prime-matter" is the same as "prime-energy," and that all the various kinds of elementary particles (therefore, all matter) of the universe consists of prime-energy. The prime-matter, or prime-energy, advocated by Heisenberg can be regarded as pointing to pre-matter, or pre-energy, as advocated by Unification Thought. Today it is known that all matter consists of quarks and leptons. Recently the "sub-quark" model has been advocated. This model states that quarks and leptons are made of even more basic particles, and active research is being conducted into that area. Specifically, the sub-quark model states that all matter is made of sub-quarks, and that there are three kinds of sub-quarks, which can be regarded as different states of a single sub-quark. If this theory is correct, it follows that all matter is made of a single, basic substance. This can be seen as a contemporary version of Heisenberg's monistic unified model. For further reference, see Hidezumi Terasawa's *Sub-quark Physics and Original Geometry* (in Japanese) (Tokyo, Kyoritsu Shuppan Sha,1982), 17–21.

6. The Universal Prime Force is acting on the created world, and the force of give and receive action is working between existing beings as the result of the operation of the Universal Prime Force. Therefore, the Universal Prime Force is the causal force operating on the created world; in other words, the Universal Prime Force and the force of give and receive action are in the relationship of cause and effect. (This note is added by the editor.)

7. Let me concretely explain about homogeneous elements and absolute attributes. One may raise the question: "Even though *Sungsang* and *Hyungsang* are two expressions of the homogeneous element, *Sungsang* itself and *Hyungsang* itself are different, aren't they? For example, steam and ice are the two expressions of water (H_2O). They are supposed to be essentially the same in that both have in themselves the relative relationship between attraction and repulsion of water molecules. However, attraction and repulsion are different from each other. Likewise, even if it is claimed that *Sungsang* and *Hyungsang* are homogeneous in that *Sungsang* contains *Hyungsang* and *Hyungsang*

contains *Sungsang*, aren't *Sungsang* and *Hyungsang* themselves different from each other?"

This question seems reasonable but, nevertheless, is shortsighted. It arises from one's being unaware of the fact that the phenomenal world is somewhat different from the causal world. In fact, there is a difference between macroscopic phenomena and microscopic phenomena. For example, the principle of uncertainty says that, in the microscopic world, the position of the particle and its momentum can not be exactly determined at the same time through our observation. Also, light, or the photon, is known to have the two discrepant attributes of particle and wave at the same time. Such phenomena are not seen in the macroscopic world. In other words, there are certain cases in which we can not understand microscopic phenomena in the same manner as we do when we think of the macroscopic world. This means that there are cases when we have to abandon our ideas and concepts formed in the macroscopic world in order to understand the microscopic world properly.

A similar thing can be said about our knowledge of the attributes of God, the ultimate Cause. It is not always appropriate to apply our concepts of the phenomenal world to the causal world. In the above-mentioned example of ice and steam, I explained that the common element between them is the relative relationship between attraction and repulsion of water molecules. As for the question whether the attractive force and the repulsive force are essentially different or not, it will be properly answered if it is proven that both forces originate from a single force.

Though it is not yet proven that the attractive force and the repulsive force originate from a single force, we will assume that the separation into two attributes from one attribute is possible in the causal world. For example, a photon, which belongs to the microscopic world, manifests itself as particle and wave. The photon, or light quantum, as named by A. Einstein, is "light" which has the united attributes. When a photon operates in the actual world, it shows one of the two characters according to the circumstances. In other words, the substance of light is one, but only manifests itself as one of its attributes.

Light gives us brightness and heat. This does not mean that brightness and heat, which are separate qualities, are united in the light. Rather, a light is perceived as brightness and warmth through our sense of sight and sense of touch respectively. Likewise, we should understand that God's *Sungsang* and *Hyungsang* are not essentially different attributes, but rather are one absolute attribute which has become separated into two correlative attributes in His creation. If *Sungsang* and *Hyungsang* were essentially heterogeneous attributes, give and receive action between them would not be possible.

When I explain *Sungsang* and *Hyungsang* in this way, one may think that this is the same as the Identity-philosophy. The Identity-philosophy claims that the correlative elements in the phenomenal world—spirit and matter, or subject and object—originate from one and the same entity (the absolute). In contrast, the theory of homogeneity of *Sungsang* and *Hyungsang* is an argument in the realm of the Causal Being, namely, God. In God, there is no time; therefore, the relationship between the absolute and the relative attributes is not cause and effect. Hence, in God, the absolute attribute is at the same time a relative attribute. In this respect, it is quite different from the Identity-philosophy.

8. Unification Thought ontology is "Unification Theory" or "Theory of Oneness," which is a kind of monism, a monism with dual characteristics. The Theory of Oneness is different in its character from the monisms of materialism and spiritualism (idealism). Materialism is a monism in the sense that it considers matter to be prior to spirit, and spiritualism is a monism in the sense that it considers spirit to be prior to matter. Hence, both materialism and spiritualism are relative monisms. In contrast, the Theory of Oneness claims that the origin of spirit and matter is one; therefore, it is an absolute monism.

9. A famous British theoretical physicist, David Bohm, explored the realm of consciousness and formulated his unique cosmology. He said, "If the immanence is pursued more and more deeply in matter, I believe we may eventually reach the stream which we also experience as mind, so that mind and matter fuse." *The Holographic Paradigm and Other Paradoxes*, ed. Ken Wilber (Shambhala/Boston & London: New Science Library, 1985), 193. We can see that Bohm, while exploring the realm of consciousness from the perspective of a natural scientist, has reached the same conclusion as that of the Theory of Oneness advocated by Unification Thought.

10. Nicolas de Malebranche (1638–1715) applied Geulincx's occasionalistic idea to epistemological questions. If spirit and matter are kinds of substances that are totally different from each other, how can spirit

recognize matter? Malebranche explained that in God there are eternal ideas as the prototypes of things and that in recognizing things, we do not recognize things directly, but rather we recognize the ideas within God. On this point he said, "We see all things in God." The consequence of this view is that we are relating ourselves ultimately to God, and the significance of the existence of matter diminishes. See Takeo Iwasaki's *History of Western Philosophy* (in Japanese) (Tokyo, Yuhikaku, 1975), 147.

11. Confucius, *Confucian Analects, The Great Learning & The Doctrine of the Mean*, trans. James Legge (New York: Dover Publications, 1971), 359.

12. In humans, the actualization of love means to show a warm heart to others, or to please others, and ultimately, to return joy to God. In order to show our warm heart to others, intellectual, emotional, and volitional activities are necessary in our real life. In other words, the goal of our intellectual, emotional, and volitional activities is the actualization of love.

13. In *Exposition of the Divine Principle*, the Universal Prime Force is explained as belonging to God (*DP*, 21), while in *Explaining the Divine Principle* (in Korean) (Seoul: Sejong Moonhwa-sa, 1957), Universal Prime Force is explained as belonging to the created world (p. 35). Between these, Unification Thought chooses the latter in order to more clearly distinguish between the force from God and the force among all things.

14. When we say that the Prime Force is a vertical force and the Universal Prime Force is a horizontal force, the concept of vertical and horizontal refers to the relation of cause and effect. Accordingly, the Universal Prime Force is a horizontal force in relation to the Prime Force, while it is a vertical force in relation to the force of give and receive action. (This note is added by the editor.)

15. The force of God's love is manifested differently according to the hierarchical ranking of created beings. For human beings, God's love manifests on a full scale.

16. Inner *Sungsang* and Inner *Hyungsang* may jointly be called "inner dual characteristics." Also, if necessary, *Sungsang* and *Hyungsang* may be jointly called "outer dual characteristics." Similarly, such concepts as "inner subject and object" and "outer subject and object" may also be established.

17. When a driver observes traffic rules, the driver does not do so obliged by force, but rather does so according to his or her free will and decision. Therefore, the relationship of freedom and necessity is one of subject and object.
18. A galvanometer is a machine used to detect a weak electric current. By attaching it to a human body, the change in a person's thought or emotion can be detected through the measurement of the human body's electrical potential, which is recorded on a graph. One day, on impulse, Cleve Backster, America's foremost lie-detector examiner attached the electrodes of a polygraph (lie detector) to a leaf of his dracaena (a foliage plant) in his laboratory, and tried to observe any change which might occur in the galvanometer as a result of threatening the plant as he might threaten a human suspect. To his surprise, a dramatic change occurred in the movement of the needle of the galvanometer. The dracaena perceived Backster's threat and responded to it. Later he made the same test on more than twenty-five different varieties of plants and fruits, and all the results were the same. It is concluded, therefore, that plants are sentient. Peter Tompkins & Christopher Bird, *The Secret Life of Plants* (New York: Harper and Row Publishers, 1973), 3–6.
19. Based on his theory of complex relativity, Jean E. Charon, theoretical physicist at the University of Paris, explained that electrons and photons themselves are microcosms equipped with mechanisms of memory and thinking. The theory of complex relativity, in which complex numbers are used, refers to an extension of the theory of relativity. A complex number consists of a real number and an imaginary number. In physics, natural phenomena are usually described within a four dimensional world of time and space using real numbers. In the theory of relativity as well, phenomena are described in the four dimensional world of time and space using real numbers. Yet, in the theory of complex relativity, the four dimensional world of time and space in imaginary numbers is added. Hence, phenomena are described in an eight dimensional world of time and space. It is possible for us to observe the real world of time and space, since it has a definite extension. On the contrary, the imaginary world of time and space is a "closed world" without extension; therefore, it is impossible to observe this world from the real world. However, Charon says that this imaginary world actually exists in the same

way that our consciousness does. Thus, the universe consists of the real, material existence and the imaginary, spiritual existence, and we are beings that can perceive these two existences. Mitsuo Ishikawa, *The Worldview of New Science* (in Japanese) (Tokyo: Tama Shuppan, 1985), 176–79.

20. Dominion is, in principle, human dominion over all things in nature, but the concept of dominion can also be applied to human relationships, in which the subject rules or leads the object; for example, the relationship between a government and the people. In human relationships, the subject exercises dominion over the object with creativity and love.

21. When we mention the "reciprocal relationship between *Sungsang* and *Hyungsang*," how can we reconcile it with the "essential homogeneity of *Sungsang* and *Hyungsang*"? In the section "Content of the Original Image" I explained about "the difference and homogeneity between *Sungsang* and *Hyungsang*," and said that *Sungsang* and *Hyungsang*, as the correlative attributes in God's creation, are essentially homogeneous, since they are the two correlative attributes into which the absolute attribute has separated. Here, another question may be raised: If *Sungsang* and *Hyungsang* are essentially homogeneous, *Sungsang* is *Hyungsang*, and *Hyungsang* is *Sungsang*, and the formation of the reciprocal relationship, and the give and receive action between them would become impossible, wouldn't it? This is not the case, however. When *Sungsang* and *Hyungsang* are separated from the absolute attribute and become correlative attributes, *Sungsang* and *Hyungsang* assume different attributes in addition to having common aspects; therefore, reciprocal relationships, and give and receive action between them, are possible.

22. It should be noted here that, as already explained, there are two kinds of result, union and a multiplied being. Union is realized when *Sungsang* and *Hyungsang* enter into give and receive action to be united into oneness; and a multiplied being is realized when *Sungsang* and *Hyungsang* enter into give and receive action, giving rise to a new individual or element.

23. The four position foundation was originally to be used as a spatial concept similar to the four directions of north, south, east and west. In actuality, however, it is also used as an abstract mental concept.

24. For example, the earth revolves around the sun while rotating itself,

and an electron revolves around the nucleus while rotating itself. Here, rotation originates in the inner give and receive action, and revolution originates in the outer give and receive action.

25. In the Original Image, the center in the identity-maintaining four position foundation, or the center of the give and receive action whereby union is realized, is Heart, while the center in the developmental four position foundation, or the center of the give and receive action whereby a multiplied being is formed, is purpose (purpose of creation). In the created world, however, the center is purpose both in forming a union (identity-maintaining four position foundation) and in forming a multiplied being (developmental four position foundation). This is because, in created beings, both the formation of unity and the formation of a multiplied being are made in order to accomplish the purpose of creation. Needless to say, the purpose of creation is based on heart; therefore, the center is purpose and, at the same time, it is heart.

26. The inner identity-maintaining four position foundation and outer identity-maintaining four position foundation together form the two stage four position foundations, which is the "two-stage structure of the Original Image."

27. From the viewpoint of the Divine Principle, development means the multiplication of an individual of new quality (namely, a new being). Development is equivalent to creation when creation is seen from the result. In fact, economic development is the multiplication of economic properties; cultural development is the multiplication of cultural properties, and scientific development is the multiplication of inventions and discoveries. All of these are productions made by give and receive actions based on four position foundations.

28. Not a few animals have creativity, though their creative abilities are of a lower level compared to those of humans. Bees, ants, spiders and magpies are such examples. Their creativity is instinctive, yet they also have the ability to form the inner developmental four position foundation, though at a lower level. In contrast, human creativity consists of instinctive and rational creativity.

29. The Inner *Sungsang*, as the union of intellect, emotion, and will also becomes a standard for the solution of an actual problem related to the problem of freedom: Is freedom a freedom of reason, of emotion, or of will? Divine Principle mentions "free will" or "free action" (*DP*,

74); therefore freedom is a freedom of will. In philosophy, freedom is often referred to as a freedom of will in the sense of a freedom of choice. Yet freedom, as Hegel claimed, is a freedom of reason; and freedom, as Kant claimed, is that humans obey moral laws unrestricted by sensuous desires; and the freedom of the late eighteenth century German philosophy of feeling is a freedom of feeling and faith.

Thus, freedom seems to be a freedom of reason, or of emotion, or of will. Which one is correct? The Unification Thought view of the unity of intellect, emotion, and will, provides an answer to this problem. In this view, a freedom of reason is, and should be, at the same time a freedom of will, and a freedom of emotion. Let's discuss freedom of choice. This is a freedom to decide by one's own will; therefore, it is a freedom of will. (In this sense, "free will" as mentioned in the Divine Principle is correct.) When we choose something, however, we make a judgment as to which one is better. This is a freedom of reason. Also, when we choose something, we do so in such a way that we become pleased and do not become unhappy; therefore, freedom of choice is at the same time a freedom of emotion.

Among the three views of freedom above, the most essential freedom is that of reason. This is because one has to understand an object before one makes a choice, and then one gives a direction to one's will, so that one may follow one's decision. The ability to understand an object and the ability to give a direction to one's will lies in one's reason. As for emotional freedom, it is accompanied by esthetic judgment, which is also accompanied by factual and logical judgments. Therefore, the work of reason is also required.

30. What should be clarified here is that complex ideas (which are formed through the synthesis of various simple ideas), as well as simple ideas in the Inner *Hyungsang*, play the role of a spiritual mold. In human creative activity, a lot of moldings are made from a single mold, while in God's creation of human beings, the role of each mold in His Inner *Hyungsang* ends when a person is created. Each mold is, in other words, an individual image in God.

31. This becomes the standard in solving another problem in logic. Traditional logic regards thinking as an established fact, and does not take into consideration such questions as why we should think, or in what direction we should think, in spite of the importance of such questions. As a result, traditional logic has come to a deadlock. These

problems of logic can be solved through the theory of the inner developmental four position foundation in the Original *Sungsang*.

32. Here, the difference between pantheism and the Pan-Divine-Image Theory is explained in order to clarify that Unification Thought is not pantheism, but rather it is the Pan-Divine-Image Theory. Pantheism is the religious or philosophical view that regards all things in nature as being identical to or the representations of God; hence, it does not distinguish God from nature. Spinoza's philosophy, Brahminist philosophy in ancient India, Buddhist philosophy, and some Egyptian or Greek philosophies are examples of pantheism. Pantheism gave rise to optimism, which recognizes divine nature in all things and regards all phenomena as good. On the other hand, pantheism gave rise to pessimism, since pantheism regards all things indiscriminately as the manifestations of God, and therefore any distinction between good and evil, or between true and false became meaningless, and thus the foundation for moral effort was lost. Needless to say, both optimism and pessimism are powerless in solving actual problems.

It is because of the ignorance of God's personality and His creation that pantheism is powerless in solving actual problems. Pantheists never considered such an idea as that of "Heart motivation" in God's creation. As explained already, Unification Thought proposes "Heart motivation" and "creation in likeness"; therefore, it is possible for Unification Thought to fundamentally solve any difficult actual problem.Then, what is the Unification Thought view about pantheism? As mentioned above, Unification Thought is not pantheistic, but rather a Pan-Divine-Image theory. In Unification Thought, all things were created according to the law of likeness, centered on the purpose of creation. Hence, all things are not the direct manifestations of God, but rather they are created in the image of God, in other words, in the Divine Image of God. Hence, Unification Thought regards the relationship between God and all things as the relationship between the Creator and the created, the infinite and the finite, and the original being and the imitation; furthermore, Unification Thought regards the relationship between God and human beings as the relationship between parents and children.

33. In the Divine Principle it is written: The universe is formed by the multiplication of myriad substantial manifestations of God's original internal nature and original external form through their give and

take action in the pursuit of the purpose of creation (*DP*, 31).
34. Here, I can explain more concretely about the meaning of a living "idea-mold" or a "living mold." An idea-mold is an idea which serves as a mold, or a model, in God's creation. But, what does it mean to say that an idea is living? A living idea may be compared to the animation on a screen. However, an animation is not an actual living image; it is only a series of still images, for example, in a roll of film, projected onto a screen. However, a living idea-mold has life; therefore, it is literally alive. Let me offer a figurative explanation here as to a living idea-mold, although it may not be a completely appropriate example.

We sometimes meet a person who claims to have met someone in his dream whom he had never seen before, and consequently, he actually meets the person about whom he dreamed. In this case, the person in the dream corresponds to a living idea-mold, and the real person corresponds to a being created in the way matter (pre-energy) is put into the idea-mold. Also, one might observe a scene including mountains, rivers, animals, and plants in their dream, and to their surprise, a few days later, he or she sees exactly the same scene on their actual trip. This may also serve as a helpful example enabling us to understand that there are, at first, idea-molds for all things, and then all real things are created when matter is put into them.
35. The Holy Spirit Association for the Unification of World Christianity, *Explaining the Divine Principle* (in Korean) (Seoul: Sejong Moonhwa-sa, 1957).
36. What should be clarified here is that there is a difference in the nature of the Inner *Sungsang* of Logos between the two cases: Logos with which human beings were created and the Logos with which all things were created. In the creation of all things, the Inner *Sungsang* of Logos consists of the lower level faculties of intellect, emotion, and will, whereas in the creation of human beings, the Inner *Sungsang* of Logos consists of both the higher level and lower level faculties of intellect, emotion, and will. When a human being is created, the lower level faculties of intellect, emotion, and will appear as the "physical mind," the mind of the physical self, and the higher level faculties of intellect, emotion, and will, appear as the "spirit mind," the mind of the spirit self.
37. It is written in the Divine Principle that everything reaches perfection

by passing through three ordered stages of growth: the formation stage, the growth stage, and the completion stage (*DP*, 41–42). The three stages of growth originated from the number three in God, as it is written in the Divine Principle that "God is the one absolute reality in whom the dual characteristics interact in harmony; therefore, He is a Being of the number three" (*DP*, 41). This statement is the prototype for the four position foundation in which the center is the absolute, or Heart, the correlative elements of subject and object are engaged in the give and receive action, and the result is harmony or union; at the same time it is the prototype for the origin, division, and union action (*Chung-Boon-Hap action*) in which the absolute reality corresponds to origin, the dual characteristics correspond to division, and harmony corresponds to union.

38. Hirschberger states, "People like to call this pan-logism, and in relation to this pan-logism, they have regarded Hegel as the advocate of the mystical, pantheistic theory that all is one. Philosophers with scholastic inclinations have generally uniformly regarded Hegel as a philosopher of a pantheistic identity." *Geschichte der Philosophie* (Freiburg: Verlag Herder, 1984), II., 419.

39. Here, I will explain further about a proof for the existence of God. Since Unification Thought is a theory based on God, we should necessarily offer some proof of His existence.

   A. Traditional Arguments to Prove the Existence of God
   (1) Ontological Argument
   This is a method of proving God's existence based on the concept of God held by human beings. For example, Anselm (1033–1109) in his *Proslogium* (Words toward God) asserted that "It is because God exists that human beings understand God as the most perfect being. If God does not possess the attribute of existence, then He can not be seen as the most perfect being. Therefore, God must exist." This method of proof was also used by René Descartes. However, with this proof, it is difficult to overcome the refutation of atheists like Feuerbach that "God is nothing but the objectification of the human species-essence and desire for perfection."

   (2) Cosmological Argument
   This refers to a proof proposed by Thomas Aquinas (1224–75). He asserted that if we trace back the causal relationships of the movements of the physical world, we will finally reach the ultimate cause,

namely, the first cause, which is the original mover, or self cause. He recognized this as God. This method of proof was established based on Aristotle's methodology, in which he recognized an unmoved mover. Nonetheless, it is difficult to persuade atheists and materialists using this method. They argue that there is no compelling reason why the first cause, as the ultimate cause of the material causal relationships, must be God. Materialists (atheists) make the point that regardless of how one traces the cause of matter back, it can never be anything other than matter. They assert that even if the first cause of the universe is said to be God, then God must be a material being.

(3) Teleological Argument

This is a method of proving the existence of God using the following argument: "Just as the structure and physiology of the human body seemingly assume purposefulness, so too the universe, which is composed of innumerable heavenly bodies, is a huge system of order formed in accordance with a specific purposive plan. When we consider it in this way, the planner must be God." Another argument is that "From the beauty and solemnity of the natural world, we can not but admit that God with His supreme wisdom created the world." However, this method of proof also faces difficulty in overcoming atheism or materialism, because atheists believe that the movement of the universe can be explained solely through the inevitability of laws. It is the atheistic viewpoint that for teleology to consider the phenomena of the universe to be purposive simply because the structure and movements of the human body are purposive, is a jump in logic. Atheists hold that the movement of the universe is completely law-governed.

(4) Moral Argument

This is a method of proof by way of recognizing God's existence as the source of the moral laws that human beings follow in their daily life, and as the source of moral world order. It is also the method, used especially by Kant, of proving the existence of God based on the moral imperative, that is, the necessary criterion for a moral life. The standpoint whereby one regards the conscience as being God's voice also falls into this category. However, this kind of theory also fails to persuade atheists, especially Marxists, because they consider traditional morality and ethics as mere carry-overs from a previous feudal society, or feudal norms created by the ruling class in order to maintain and consolidate their class rule. When considered in this way, these traditional proofs for God's existence are seen to be little more than logical fortifications for belief in God's existence, valid only when there is a prior belief in God. In other words, they are proofs assuming a theistic position to start with. Therefore, such proofs of God can not make a common base with atheism and these two positions will remain as far apart as ever. In other words, in order to persuade atheists to recognize God's existence, it is essential to develop one's logic in such a way that they can relate to it. This requirement is met, I believe, by the effort to prove God's existence using the hypothetical method. Let me explain about this method.

B. Hypothetical Method

A hypothesis has to do with an assumption or speculation formulated in order to explain a certain thing or phenomenon, the certainty of the truth or falsehood of which has not yet been proven through any empirical method. The hypothetical method, then, refers to a way or method of proving that the hypothesis is true by verifying it through scientific observations or experiments. A very common example of this is when a medical doctor cures a patient's illness. First, he will speculate as to what the cause of that illness might be (for example, in assuming an illness with a high fever to be influenza, based on observed symptoms), and then he will prescribe a cure for that illness (influenza) based upon his assumption. If the patient's illness is cured, that diagnosis will have been proven to be a correct diagnosis, and if not, that diagnosis will have been shown to be a wrong diagnosis. The same thing can be said about the hypothetical method.

Let me cite an example from natural science. The ancient Greek philosopher Democritus (ca.460–370 BC) claimed that all matter is composed of minute particles called atoms that can not be further divided. This claim was not obtained from any natural scientific observation or experimentation, but was merely a hypothesis. However, in the contemporary period, now that science is so developed, even the weight and internal structure of the minute particles composing matter are being clarified; thereby, his atomic theory has come to be officially recognized as a true theory, verified scientifically.

This kind of example can also be found in the discovery of the atomic elements. D. I. Mendeleev (1834–1907), who first laid out the periodic table of the elements, predicted through this table the atomic weights, atomic numbers, and characteristics of several atoms that had not yet been discovered. Later, in 1886, C. A. Winkler actually discovered germanium, one of the atoms predicted by Mendeleev. This is another example in which a hypothesis is first set up, and then becomes an established theory through consequent verification.

Thus, a hypothesis is first established concerning something which is not yet recognized scientifically. If the conclusion derived from that hypothesis can be verified through scientific observations and experiments, then that hypothesis can be considered as a recognized, true theory. In many cases in the history of the development of science, theories have been affirmed as correct through the hypothetical method. The atomic theory is one such example.

In this way, the hypothetical method can be regarded as a way, recognized by natural science, to inquire after truth, one that can be, or should be, acknowledged by atheists as well. This same principle can be applied to the hypothetical deductive method of the proof of the existence of God. In other words, if a proof for God's existence were offered using this hypothetical method, and subsequent investigation confirmed its veracity, then atheists would be obliged to seriously consider it.

In order to prove the existence of God through the hypothetical method in Unification Thought, we may first propose that an atheist consider the theory concerning the attributes of God (the Theory of the Original Image) as a hypothesis, then they can be challenged to participate in the attempt at verification, namely, a comparison of the conclusion obtained from the hypothesis with the results of various experiments and observations made by natural scientists. If they can then find themselves in complete agreement with the experimental results, then the Theory of the Original Image should be recognized as a true, established theory and they would be obligated to lend their consent. This is the hypothetical method. Let me explain it with some examples.

The essential parts of the Theory of the Original Image are, first, that "God is the harmonious Subject of the dual characteristics of *Sungsang* and *Hyungsang*, and at the same time the harmonious Subject of the dual characteristics of Yang and Yin, where Yang and

Yin are the attributes of *Sungsang* and *Hyungsang*." A second part is that "centering on the purpose of creation, God created all things through give and receive action, and this takes place on the basis of the four position foundation, which consists of four types: inner and outer four position foundations, and identity-maintaining and developmental four position foundations."

Atheists will not accept this theory concerning the attributes of God, if it is simply presented as dogma. Therefore, especially for them, the Theory of the Original Image may be treated as a hypothesis, and they can be asked to consider the verification of the hypothesis. That is, together we can examine whether the conclusion derived from the hypothesis is in agreement with the results of scientific experiments and observations. As mentioned above, the hypothetical method is a scientific method of pursuing truth; therefore, if atheists refuse even the verification of the hypothesis, that will mean that they are abandoning or evading the pursuit of truth, thus revealing their unscientific attitude. Therefore, they would be obliged to acknowledge the verification.

Strictly speaking, any verification of the hypothesis should be carried out through direct scientific experiments and observations by the advocate of the hypothesis. Today, however, with our highly developed natural sciences, such efforts are not necessary. All we have to do is compare already established scientific achievements with the conclusion of the hypothesis, and make a judgment as to whether or not they are in agreement. To invite atheists to attend to the verification of the hypothesis means to consider, together with them, whether or not natural scientific facts and the hypothetical conclusions are in agreement. If it can be conclusively shown that scientific facts and the propositions of the Theory of the Original Image are in agreement, then even atheists would be obliged to accept the Theory of the Original Image as a plausible counterproposal to atheism.

In this way, if the conclusion obtained from a hypothesis is in accord with the experiments and observations of the natural sciences, then that hypothesis can become a true, established theory. Next, let me explain how the Theory of the Original Image, once accepted as a hypothesis, can become an established theory through verification, citing some examples.

(1) Verification of the Dual Characteristics of *Sungsang* and *Hyungsang*

i) *Hypothesis*

Let us accept the following assertion of the Theory of the Original Image as a hypothesis for the time being: "God is the harmonious Subject of *Sungsang* and *Hyungsang*. All things, which were created according to the law of likeness, resemble God; therefore, they are united beings of the dual characteristics of *sungsang* and *hyungsang*."

ii) *Conclusion*

From this hypothesis, the following conclusion can be obtained: "All created beings resemble God's dual characteristics of *Sungsang* and *Hyungsang*; therefore, they are endowed, without exception, with an invisible *sungsang* aspect and a visible *hyungsang* aspect. That is to say, all created beings, including minerals, plants, animals, and human beings, possess these *sungsang* and *hyungsang* aspects without exception." Accordingly, what is required next is to verify whether or not this conclusion is in accord with the facts of the natural sciences, namely, the results of experiments and observations.

iii) *Verification*

Verification in this case is to confirm through scientific analysis whether or not human beings, animals, plants, and minerals all do have the correlative aspects of *sungsang* and *hyungsang*. In fact, we can see that this conclusion is in complete agreement with scientific facts.

In present-day medical science, a human being is regarded as a union of mind and body, and research is being conducted on the mutual relationship between the two aspects. This field is being covered by psychosomatic medicine, psychophysics, psychic physiology, and so on. Spirit or mind is *sungsang*, and the body is *hyungsang*. In this way, medical science today is showing that a human being is, in fact, a union of *sungsang* and *hyungsang*, thus resembling the dual characteristics of God.

It has been clarified by such sciences as animal psychology, that there is a part in animals which corresponds to the human mind. A neurophysiologist, John Eccles, said, based on his experiments, that animals (mammals) also have consciousness in the same way that humans do, and that the only difference between humans and animals is that humans have self-consciousness, whereas animals do not. This scientifically proves that animals have minds, even though it may be of a lower dimension. It goes without saying that animals have bodies, as do humans. Thus, animals are also the unions of *sungsang* and *hyungsang*, resembling the dual characteristics of God.

Plants are also living beings, as are animals. Life activity is a physiological phenomenon, and the science which studies this phenomenon is physiology. The physiology which deals with plants is called plant physiology. Life is not material, but has the invisible function of responding to environmental stimuli; therefore, it is similar to animal instinct in its function of responding to environmental stimuli. The two functions are different only in dimension. Botany includes such fields as plant anatomy, morphological botany, and so on, which deal with the physical, visible aspects of plants, including cells, tissues, and structures. Thus, we see that plants also have a functional, invisible aspect and a visible, physical aspect. Therefore, we can verify, through science, that plants also have the two aspects of *sungsang* and *hyungsang*, resembling the dual characteristics of God.

Since minerals are inorganic and lifeless material beings, they may seem to have no *sungsang* aspect. But this is not so at all. The *sungsang* aspect in minerals refers to their properties or functions. In order to find out whether minerals have invisible properties or functions, what we have to do is examine the scientific achievements concerning the constituents of minerals, in other words, atoms and molecules. Every atom has its definite atomic weight and definite chemical properties. The periodic table of the elements illustrates this graphically. Also, every atom or molecule has the potential to exert a definite force. This potential is the function of an atom or a molecule. For example, an atomic nucleus has the potential to cause a nuclear reaction. The energy emitted at this time is the atomic force. A molecule also has its potential to exert an intermolecular force. A potential or a function is invisible; therefore, it is the *sungsang* element. On the other hand, an atom or a molecule has its visible aspect. The visible aspect of an atom is its atomic structure, which is dealt with in atomic theory. Also, a molecule has a molecular structure as its visible aspect, which is dealt with in the theory of molecular structure. Thus, an atom or a molecule has its *hyungsang* aspect as well. Atoms and molecules combine together to form minerals. It is confirmed, therefore, through scientific achievements that minerals are also unions of *sungsang* and *hyungsang*, resembling the dual characteristics of God.

From the above explanation, I think it should be quite clear that even though God is invisible, and thus can not, per se, become an object of research for the natural sciences, the existence of God can be persuasively argued for through the hypothetical method, which is a scientific method.

(2) Verification of the Dual Characteristics of Yang and Yin

i) *Hypothesis*

In the Theory of the Original Image, there is an assertion that "God is the harmonious Subject of the dual characteristics of Yang and Yin, and all things created according to the law of likeness exist in a correlative relationship of Yang and Yin, resembling the dual characteristics of God." If this is regarded as a hypothesis, the following conclusion can be derived.

ii) *Conclusion*

It may be concluded that "every created being is endowed with the correlative attributes of yang and yin, and it is engaged in correlative relationships of yang and yin with other created beings, in resem-blance to the dual characteristics of Yang and Yin of God." Therefore, whether this conclusion agrees with scientific facts or not should be examined.

iii) *Verification*

Let us see to the verification of the conclusion which is based on our hypothesis. We concluded that "every created being exists with another created being in a correlative relationship of yang and yin." In human beings, for instance, yang is a man, and yin is a woman. The difference between man and woman is clearly expressed anatomically (skull, pelvis, sexual organs, etc.), physiologically (voice, hormones, etc.), and in appearance (face, breasts, hips, etc.). The yang and yin in animals are male and female animals, and the difference between male and female animals is well expressed anatomically and physiologically. The yang and yin in plants are expressed as stamen and pistil, a male type tree and a female type tree, namely, a tree bearing fruit and a tree bearing no fruit (in the case of a ginkgo), and a male type flower and a female type flower.

Let me offer another example. In the DNA (deoxyribonucleic

acid) molecule, which contains the genes of a living being, there are two pairs of nitrogenous bases: the A−T pair and the G−C pair. The two base pairs serve as the connections or rungs between the two chains of the double helix, which is made of sugars and phosphates. It is known that the relationship between A and T, or G and C is a complementary relationship, as if one were a positive picture, and the other a negative picture. This can easily be understood as a relationship of yang and yin.

Next, let us examine minerals. As I have mentioned, the constituents of minerals are atoms, which, as atomic physics has made clear, are composed of the nucleus (which consists of protons and neutrons) which carries positive charges, and electrons, revolving around the nucleus, which carry negative charges. That is, minerals exist with yang and yin elements within themselves.

Thus, it seems that the hypothetical conclusion that "every created being exists with another created being in the correlative relationship of yang and yin" is in agreement with the results of research in the natural sciences (medical science, zoology, botany, atomic physics, etc.), and that, therefore, the hypothesis that "God exists as the harmonious Subject of Yang and Yin dual characteristics," and "all things created according to the law of likeness exist in a correlative relationship of yang and yin, resembling the dual characteristics of God," receives solid support in being considered as a true, established theory.

The same thing can be said with regard to the other central tenets of the Theory of the Original Image: "Centering on the purpose of creation, God created all things through the give and receive action between *Sungsang* and *Hyungsang*. This give and receive action takes place on the basis of the four position foundation, which can be divided into four kinds, namely, inner and outer, identity-maintaining and developmental four position foundations." First, this assertion is regarded as a hypothesis, then a conclusion may be derived from it, and finally the conclusion may be verified with scientific facts. Due to spatial limitations, and since one can easily understand the argument if one examines the explanation of the "Structure of the Original Image" in the Theory of the Original Image, I will here omit the verification of this hypothesis. With this, nevertheless, I am convinced that it has been clarified that the "existence of God" can be asserted most correctly using the hypothetical method of Unification Thought.

I would like to add one final point here before I end and that is that no matter what kind of atheist one may claim to be, once a theory concerning God has been verified as being in accord with scientific fact through the hypothetical method, the proper scientific attitude commensurate with that would be to accept the theory as true with a humble heart. Since Communists and materialists, in particular, have long denied God, it would seem that they are steeped in a mindset which opposes or rejects "God" unconditionally. However, they should come to realize that such an inflexible attitude of unconditional rejection is highly unscientific.

The way to fundamentally solve the great confusion of today's world is to pull down the banners of atheism from the face of the earth and raise high the banner of God. As human beings become one under the banner of God, an ideal world of love, freedom, prosperity and peace, which has long been the dream of humankind, can finally become a reality.

2. Ontology

1. Hiroshi Motoyama, *Yoga and Parapsychology* (in Japanese) (Tokyo: Shukyo-shinri Shuppan, 1972), 109.
2. The phenomenon of the direct influence of the will over matter is called "psychokinesis." Through psychokinesis the will can move a distant object, can bend, extend, or harden a metal, and can even make a random-number generator lose its randomness. See Michel Cazenave, ed., *Science et Conscience*, trans. A. Hall and E. Callander (Oxford: Pergamon Press, 1984), 49.
3. In 1966 Cleve Backster, an American lie-detector technician, examined the reactions of a plant by attaching the electrodes of a lie-detector to its leaves. To his surprise, Backster found that the plant was able to read his mind. For instance, when he pictured burning the leaves, the instant he pictured the flame in his mind, even before he moved to get matches, the plant reacted strongly. Subsequently, he conducted various experiments and concluded that plants seem to have consciousness and sense. This discovery by Backster is called the "Backster Effect."

See Peter Tompkins & Christopher Bird, *The Secret Life of Plants* (New York: Harper and Row, Publishers, 1973), 3–5.
Attempts to reproduce the kinds of communication between human beings and plants that Backster reported were also made in the Soviet Union. V. N. Pushkin and other researchers confirmed that plants react to the emotion of a person in a hypnotic state. See A. P. Dubrov & V. N. Pushkin, *Parapsychology and Contemporary Natural Science* (Moscow, 1983).

4. On this matter, David Bohm of London University said, "There may be a sort of living energy in all matter that manifests in us in certain ways which it does not do in the rock. If that were the case, if a sort of intelligence were generalized throughout nature, then the speculative proposal that inanimate matter might respond to our thought is not so illogical." *The Holographic Paradigm and Other Paradoxes*, ed. Ken Wilber (Shambhala/Boston & London: New Science Library, 1985), 211.

    Also, Jean E. Charon, a theoretical physicist at Paris University, said that electrons and photons themselves are microcosms, equipped with mechanisms of memory and thinking. See Mitsuo Ishikawa, *The World View of New Science* (in Japanese) (Tokyo: Tama Shuppan, 1985), 178-79.

5. Traditionally, it had been considered that single-cell organisms (bacteria) were sexless; but in 1946, J. Lederberg and E. L. Tatum demonstrated that even bacteria engage in sexual reproduction. Concerning the sex of bacteria and paramecia, see, for example, Koichi Hiwatashi, *The Search for the Origin of the Sex* (in Japanese) (Tokyo: Iwanami Shoten, 1986).

6. The Big Bang theory is still in the hypothetical stage, with the possibility that it may be revised in the future.

7. Joseph V. Stalin, *Dialectical and Historical Materialism* (New York: International Publishers, 1940), 7.

8. Friedrich Engels, *Anti-Dühring* (Moscow: Progress Publishers, 1969), 33.

9. Sang Hun Lee, *The End of Communism* (New York: Unification Thought Institute, 1985), chapter 3.

10. Here, let me explain the types of time for your reference. Divine Principle often mentions the providential periods of 21 days, 40 days, 210 years, 400 years, and so forth, in the providential history of restoration. Such providential periods are different from ordinary time-periods. In order to clarify this fact, the different types of time

should be examined. There are five types of time as follows:

(1) *Physical Time*: This is the time observed in repetitive circular motion in non-living beings, caused by physical force.

(2) *Biological Time*: This is the time observed during the growth of living beings, and the repetition of the life cycle (the succession of generations), brought about by the life force.

(3) *Historical Time*: This is the time required in the formation and development of a culture, brought about by the human spirit.

(4) *Providential Time*: This is the time assigned for providential figures, in pursuit of their mission, to accomplish the providence of restoration with faith and through accomplishing their portion of responsibility.

(5) *Ideal Time*: This is the time necessary for the realization of true love, which is God's ideal of creation. It is the time in which people are to realize the three great blessings.

Thus, there are five types of time. It can be said that most human beings living on earth, live in one or two, at the most, of these five types of time. The people who live without a sense of purpose or mission, but only for the sake of food, clothing, and shelter, and to feed their children, are living in biological time in much the same way that animals do. Those who are contributing to cultural development with their spirit are people who live in historical time. Those who are dedicating themselves to the realization of God's providence to save humankind are the people who live in providential time. In the future, when God's providence of restoration has been completed, and the ideal world has come, the whole of humankind will live in ideal time.

11. David Bohm speaks about the influence of a seed upon its environment as follows: "According to the implicate order, the seed is continually providing inanimate matter in the environment with new information that leads it to produce the living plant or animal. Who is to say, then, that life is not immanent, even before the seed is planted?" *The Holographic Paradigm and Other Paradoxes*, 193.
12. Engels, *Anti-Dühring*, 75-76.
13. V.I. Lenin, "On the Question of Dialectics," *Collected Works*, Vol. 38 (Moscow: Progress Publishers, 1976), 358.
14. Ibid.
15. If perfected human beings have a dominion of love over all things, even the phenomena of "the strong preying upon the weak" in the

animal world will vanish.

3. Theory of the Original Human Nature

1. The Rev. Sun Myung Moon has stated this idea as follows: "For a man, his wife represents mother, elder sisters, younger sisters, and, indeed, all women of the world. To love a wife who has such significance means to love all races of humanity, all women, and one's mother, elder sister, and younger sister in the home. Accordingly, the family is the 'basic training' center that educates people in human love. Therefore, to be trusted and to live a happy life in a family means to live a happy life as the center of the universe and to be situated at the center of happy love. There is nothing meaningful without love. Likewise for a woman, her husband represents father, elder brothers, younger brothers, and all men on earth. This is our ideal of the family." *God's Will and the World* (New York: The Holy Spirit Association for the Unification of World Christianity, 1985), 446.
2. Confucius, *The Analects*, trans. D. C. Lau (Harmondsworth: Penguin Books, 1979), 63.
3. Rev. Sun Myung Moon, "Founder's Address (Fourteenth ICUS)," in *Absolute Values and the New Cultural Revolution* (New York: The International Cultural Foundation, 1985), 16.
4. F. Engels, "Socialism: Utopian and Scientific," in Karl Marx and Frederick Engels, *Selected Works*, vol. 3 (Moscow: Progress Publishers, 1970), 149.
5. John Locke states as follows: "Man being born, as has been proved, with a Title to perfect Freedom and an uncontrolled enjoyment of all the Rights and Privileges of the Law of Nature, equally with any other Man, or Number of Men in the World, hath by Nature a Power, not only to preserve his Property, that is, his Life, Liberty and Estate, against the Injuries and Attempts of other Men; but to judge of, and to punish the breaches of that Law in others, ··· even with Death itself." *Two Treatises of Government*, ed. Peter Laslett (New York: Cambridge University Press, 1988), 323–324.
6. Søren Kierkegaard, *The Sickness Unto Death* (Princeton: Princeton University Press, 1980), 13.

7. Søren Kierkegaard, *The Present Age* (New York: Harper and Row Publishers, 1962), 63.
8. Friedrich Nietzsche, "Thus Spake Zarathustra" in *The Portable Nietzsche*, ed. and trans., Walter Kaufmann (New York: Penguin Books, 1982), 226.
9. Friedrich Nietzsche, "The Antichrist" in *The Portable Nietzshe*, 570.
10. Friedrich Nietzsche, "Thus Spake Zarathustra" in *The Portable Nietzsche*, 329.
11. Nietzsche asserted in "The Antichrist" that Paul had changed "evangel" into "dysangel," and Jesus' teachings into a kind of teaching for after death. Nietzsche said as follows: "I tell the *genuine* history of Christianity. The very word 'Christianity' is a misunderstanding: in truth, there was only *one* Christian, and he *died* on the cross. The 'evangel' *died* on the cross. What has been called 'evangel' from that moment was actually the opposite of that which *he* had lived: *'ill tidings,'* a *dysangel*" (*The Portable Nietzshe*, 612). He also said the following: "Paul simply transposed the center of gravity of that whole existence *after* this existence—in the *lie* of the 'resurrected' Jesus" (Ibid., 617).
12. Karl Jaspers, *Philosophy*, vol.1, trans. E. B. Ashton (Chicago: The University of Chicago Press, 1969), 56.
13. Karl Jaspers, *Philosophy*, vol. 2, 193–215.
14. Karl Jaspers, *What is Philosophy?* (Japanese version) (Tokyo: Hakusuisha, 1978), 22. Originally published as *Was ist Philosophie? Ein Lesebuch*, ed. Hans Sauer (Munich: R. Piper & Co. Verlag, 1976).
15. Ibid., 26.
16. Jaspers explains "the loving struggle" as follows: "The love in this communication is not blind love regardless of its object. It is the fighting, clear-sighted love of possible Existenz tackling another possible Existenz, questioning it, challenging it, making things hard for it." *Philosophy*, vol. 2, 59-60.
17. Heidegger spoke of "they" (*Das Man*) as follows: "The 'who' is not this one, not that one, not oneself [man selbst], not some people [einige], and not the sum of them all. The 'who' is the neuter, the 'they' [*Das Man*]." *Being and Time*, trans. John Macquarrie and Edward Robinson (Southampton: Basil Blackwell, 1962), 164.
18. Ibid., 320.
19. Jean-Paul Sartre, "Existentialism is a Humanism" in *The Fabric of*

Existentialism, ed. R. Gill & E. Sherman (New York: Meredith Corporation, 1973), 523.
20. Ibid., 521.
21. Ibid., 522.
22. Jean-Paul Sartre, "Existentialism is a Humanism" in *The Fabric of Existentialism*, 523–524.
23. Jean-Paul Sartre, *Being and Nothingness*, trans. H. E. Barnes (New York: Washington Square Press, 1956), 373.
24. Ibid., 555.

4. Axiology: A Theory of Value

1. The Society for the Research of Teaching Materials of Philosophy, *New Lectures on Philosophy* (in Korean) (Seoul: Hakusa, 1978), 132.
2. Rev. Sun Myung Moon, *New Hope—Twelve Talks by Sun Myung Moon*, ed. Rebecca Salonen (New York: HSA-UWC, 1973), 55.
3. In Buddhism, the Three Realms refer to the three stages of the world where people live, die, and change, namely, the realm of desire, the realm of matter, and the realm of non-matter. The realm of desire is the lowest one; those who inhabit it are consumed by desires of carnal pleasure, food, and sleep. The realm of matter is located above the realm of desire and refers to the realm consisting of exquisite matter for those who have rid themselves of desire. The realm of non-matter refers to the highest stage and is a highly spiritual realm, transcending matter.
4. With regard to the universal standard, Rev. Sun Myung Moon said, "We must recognize that there is a universal principle involved, regardless of what race you are. You can see that the universe has certain fundamental laws, and anyone who violates them will be judged accordingly, regardless of his race or stature. What is the spirit of that constitution of the universe? It aims to preserve or uphold the men and women who try to live for others. It would also try to eliminate people who take advantage of others and seek to benefit only themselves. This is why we can say that good people are those who exist for the sake of others, and good deeds are those actions which benefit others." *God's Will and the World* (New York: HSA-UWC,

1985), 497.
5. The Rev. Moon's consistent assertion at the International Conferences on the Unity of the Sciences is that absolute values should be pursued on the basis of absolute love.
6. Liberation Theology is a new theology that emerged in the less developed world. It departs from the traditional Christian view of salvation, and insists on active participation in resolving actual problems. Theology's most important problem among actual problems is the dehumanization of people, and Liberation Theology asserts that the cause of this dehumanization lies in the structural contradictions and social evils of capitalist society. Accordingly, it asserts, in order to liberate human nature, that capitalist society must be overthrown; thus, it affiliates itself with Communism.
7. After World War II, the less developed world obtained independence politically; economically, however, it still depends on the developed world and can not get out of the state of underdevelopment. Dependency Theory grasps this situation as a relationship between central and peripheral nations, and interprets it as a projection, on an international scale, of the class confrontation of capitalist society. That is to say, just as the working class is exploited by the capitalist class, so the less developed countries are exploited by the developed countries—exploitation carried out through multinational corporations—it asserts. Therefore, in order for the less developed world to get out of its underdeveloped state, it must liberate itself from the developed countries and become socialist—and the way to do that is to expel multinational corporations, abolish all forms of dependency relations, and overthrow comprador capital and the authoritarian class.
8. Confucius says in *The Great Learning*: "Things being investigated, knowledge became complete. Their knowledge being complete, their thoughts were sincere. Their thoughts being sincere, their hearts were then rectified. Their hearts being rectified, their persons were cultivated. Their persons being cultivated, their families were regulated. Their families being regulated, their States were rightly governed. Their States being rightly governed, the whole kingdom was made tranquil and happy." *Confucian Analects, The Great Learning and The Doctrine of the Mean*, trans. James Legge (New York: Dover Publications, 1971), 358–59. *The Great Learning* was part of *The Book of Rites*. Zhu Xi (Chu Hsi) characterized the *Analects, Mencius, The Doctrine of the Mean*, and

The Great Learning as *The Four Chinese Classics*. It is said that *The Great Learning* is the work of one of Confucius' disciples.
9. Confucius says in *Confucian Analects*, "Heaven produced the virtue that is in me" (*Confucian Analects, The Great Learning and The Doctrine of the Mean*, 202), which means that virtues are given by Heaven. Tung Chung-shu said that Heaven is *jen* (benevolence).
10. It is said that *Tathagata* is the "one who comes from *Tathatā*." Also, one of the Buddhist sūtras says that *Tathagata* has the great merciful heart that is found in every living being. Therefore, *Tathatā* can be regarded as the root of mercy, which is the fundamental virtue of Buddhism.
11. The Koran says: "Say: We belive in Allah and that which is revealed to us; in what was revealed to Abraham, Ishmael, Isaac, Jacob, and the tribes; to Moses and Jesus and the other prophets by their Lord. We make no distinction amongst any of them, and to Allah we have surrendered ourselves." *THE KORAN*, trans. with notes. N.J. Dawood (New York: Penguin Books, 1974), 346.
12. The Exordium of the Koran, which is the Opening Chapter, contains the Seven Verses, which are called "the essence of the Koran," as follows (Ibid., 15):

IN THE NAME OF ALLAH
THE COMPASSIONATE
THE MERCIFUL
Praise be to Allah, Lord of the Creation,
The Compassionate, the Merciful,
King of Judgement-day!
You alone we worship, and to You alone
we pray for help.
Guide us to the straight path
The path of those whom You have favoured,
Not of those who have incurred Your wrath,
Nor of those who have gone astray.

13. Pascal wrote as follows: "Man without faith can know neither true good nor justice. All men seek happiness. There are no exceptions···. What else does this craving, and this helplessness, proclaim but that there was once in man a true happiness, of which all that now remains is empty print and trace? ··· None can help [him], since this infinite

576 / NOTES

abyss can be filled only with an infinite and immutable object; in other words, God himself." *Pensées*, trans. A. J. Krailsheimer (New York: Penguin Books, 1966), 74–75. He also wrote, "It is the heart which perceives God and not the reason. That is what faith is: God perceived by the heart, not by the reason" (Ibid., 154).
14. *Dictionary of Philosophy* (in Japanese), ed. Koichi Mori (Tokyo: Aoki Shoten, 1974), 61.

5. Theory of Education

1. Comenius gave the following subtitle to his book *The Great Didactic*:

> The whole Art of Teaching
> all Things to all Men
> or
> A certain Inducement to found such Schools in all
> the Parishes, Towns, and Villages of every
> Christian Kingdom, that the entire
> Youth of both Sexes, none
> being excepted, shall
> **Quickly, Pleasantly, and Thoroughly**
> Become learned in the Sciences, pure in Morals,
> trained to Piety, and in this manner
> instructed in all things necessary
> for the present and for
> the future life,

K-John Amos Comenius, *The Great Didactic*, trans. M. W. Keatinge (New York: Russell and Russell, 1967), 1.
2. J. J. Rousseau, trans. Barbara Foxley, *Émile* (London: L.M. Dent & Sons Ltd., 1974), 5.
3. Immanuel Kant, *Education*, trans. Annette Churton (The University of Michigan Press, 1960), 1.
4. Ibid., 6.
5. On intellectual education (mental education) and moral-religious education (heart education), Pestalozzi wrote the following:

"Originally, intellectual education is not at all suitable for producing innocence and child-like feelings within ourselves, which produce all the methods that enhance ourselves to higher, divine feelings. As a thorn does not bear figs and a thistle does not bear grapes, so mere spiritual education, separate from heart education, does not bear the fruit of love. Since spiritual education is a victim of the selfishness and weakness that arise as a result of this separation, it has the cause of degradation in itself, and exhausts itself by its own power, just as a flame burns out as soon as it is taken out of the fuel container." *Spirit and Heart in the Method* (Japanese version) (Meiji-Tosho: Tokyo, 1980), 122. In *Swans' Song* (1826), which he wrote just before his death, he explained spiritual power, heart power, and technical power, and clarified that love is the force that unites them.

6. F. Froebel, *The Education of Man* (Clifton: Augustus M. Kelley, Publishers, 1974), 10.
7. John Dewey, *Democracy and Education, An Introduction to the Philosophy of Education* (New York: The Free Press, 1944), 53.
8. Ibid., 9.
9. Ibid., 77.
10. K. Marx, "The Class Struggles in France, 1848 to 1850," in K. Marx and F. Engels, *Selected Works* (Moscow: Progress Publishers, 1969), 1:278.
11. K. Marx, *Capital* (New York: International Publishers, 1967), 1:477.
12. V. I. Lenin, *Collected Works* (Moscow: Progress Publishers, 1965), 28:86 (hereafter cited as CWL).
13. *CWL*, 28:407–408.
14. *CWL*, 29:132.
15. *CWL*, 31:368.
16. Yoshimatsu Shibata and Satoru Kawanobe, eds., *Material on Soviet Pedagogy* (in Japanese) (Tokyo: Shin-dokusho Sha, 1976), 708.
17. *CWL*, 31:50. See also K. Marx, *Capital*, 1:454.
18. The instruction was given by the Americans for the reconstruction of Japan after its defeat in World War II. In 1946, an education mission was sent from the United States in order to offer advice on reforming education in Japan. "Report of the United States Education Mission to Japan" was the proposal for democratic education for the reconstruction of Japan. That report is quoted here because it contains a good summary of the educational ideals of democracy.

19. *Report of the United States Education Mission to Japan—Submitted to the Supreme Commander for the Allied Powers* (Tokyo: March 30, 1946), Introduction, x.
20. Ibid., 3–4.

6. Ethics

1. At this point, I can explain "vertical love and horizontal love." I can also explain certain other terms that Rev. Sun Myung Moon, in referring to love, has often used, such as the "vertical and horizontal axes of love."

    Since the relationship between God and human beings is like that between heaven and earth, or that between parents and children, it can be described as a relationship between above and below—in other words, it is a vertical relationship. On the other hand, since the relationship between husband and wife is that between man and woman of the same generation, it is a horizontal relationship. Accordingly, God's love is vertical, and the love between husband and wife is horizontal.

    God's love derives from the impulsive, emotional force of His Heart; once it starts, it travels in a straight line—much in the same way as light travels in a straight line. This means that God's love does not travel in a roundabout or curved manner. This characteristic of love is called "the axis of God's love." So, the form of God's vertical love moving in a straight line is expressed as "the vertical axis of love." Love between husband and wife also moves in a straight line. So, the form of conjugal, horizontal love moving in a straight line is expressed as "the horizontal axis of love."

    In the same way as the light traveling in a straight line is expressed as a "beam of light," the love moving in a straight line is expressed as a "beam of love" or "axis of love." The vertical beam of love is the "vertical axis of love," and the horizontal beam of love is the "horizontal axis of love."

2. The concept of "object" in the term "three object purpose" and the concept of "object" in the relationship of subject and object are slightly different. In a subject-object relationship, "object" refers to a being that

stands as an object toward a subject; in the three object purpose, "object" refers to a being that stands in a position correlative to another being.
3. I. Kant, *Critique of Practical Reason*, trans. and ed. Mary Gregor (Cambridge: Cambridge University Press, 1997), 28.
4. Ibid., 73.
5. J. Bentham, *The Principles of Morals and Legislation* (New York: Prometheus, 1988), 1.
6. Ibid., 24.
7. G. E. Moore, *Principia Ethica* (Cambridge: Cambridge University Press, 1959), 7.
8. Ibid., 6.
9. William James, *Pragmatism* (Cambridge: Harvard University Press, 1975), 97.
10. John Dewey, *Theory on the Moral Life* (New York: Holt, Rinehart & Winston, Inc., 1960), 141.

7. Theory of Art

1. The Holy Spirit Association for the Unification of World Christianity, *Exposition of the Divine Principle* (New York: HSA-UWC, 1996), 33.
2. Ibid., 20.
3. It is written in the Divine Principle as follows: "God is the Subject in whom the dual characteristics of original internal nature and original external form are in harmony. At the same time, God is the harmonious union of masculinity and femininity, manifesting the qualities of original internal nature and original external form, respectively. In relation to the universe God is the subject partner having the qualities of internal nature and masculinity." *Exposition of the Divine Principle*, 19. And also, "It may be said that the universe is formed by the multiplication of myriad substantial manifestations of God's original internal nature and original external form through their give and take action in the pursuit of the purpose of creation" (Ibid., 31).
4. H. Read, *The Meaning of Art* (London: Faber and Faber Ltd., 1972), 18.
5. Complementarity, wherein one feels joy through finding in one's object partner the aspect one lacks, applies not only to one's *hyungsang* but also to one's *sungsang*. For example, there is a case in which one who

has a delicate mind likes someone who has a bold mind, and also there is a case in which one who has a hasty and rough character likes someone who has a quiet and calm character.
6. Plato, *Early Socratic Dialogues* (New York: Penguin Books, 1987), 256.
7. Immanuel Kant, *The Critique of Judgment*, trans. J. H. Bernard (New York: Prometheus Books, 2000), 69.
8. Albert Hofstadter and Richard Kuhns, ed., *Philosophies of Art and Beauty* (Chicago: The University of Chicago Press, 1964), 96.
9. H. Read, *The Meaning of Art*, 35.
10. Romain Rolland wrote: Beethoven said, "There is nothing finer than to approach the Divine and to shed its rays on the human race." *Beethoven*, trans. B. Constance Hull (New York: Books for Libraries Press, 1969), 101. Romain Rolland also said in a lecture commemorating Beethoven, "His [Beethoven's] thought to put his art to the use of others was constantly repeated in his letters····. He determined just two objects in his life. They are his dedication to holy art and a conduct intended to make others happy." *Life of Beethoven* (Japanese version) (Tokyo: Iwanami-shoten, 1965), 159.
11. Generally, in aesthetics the process of creation is divided into the following four stages: (1) *Creative feeling*: the state of the fermentation of vague feelings; (2) *Conception*: the stage where a plan of a work of art looms; (3) *Internal refinement*: the stage where a clear plan is developed; (4) *External perfection, finishing*: the stage where a work of art is concretely produced with specific materials and techniques. *The Encyclopedia of Aesthetics* (in Japanese), ed. Toshio Takeuchi (Tokyo: Iwanami-shoten, 1965), 159. Looking from the viewpoint of Unification Thought, (1), (2), and (3) correspond to the formation of the inner four position foundation, and (4), to the formation of the outer four position foundation.
12. Romain Rolland said that Millet had in mind the following: "The mission of fine art is one of love, rather than hatred. Also, even when fine art describes the pain of the poor, it should not aim at stimulating jealousy toward the rich class." *Millet* (Japanese version) (Tokyo: Iwanami-Bunko, 1959), 9. "It was the ultimate objective of Millet's creed and art to express the poetry and beauty of human life in the pain of labor as much as possible" (Ibid., 11–12).
13. Theodore Lipps (1851–1914) calls it "empathy" (*Einfühling*) when the subject projects onto the object the feelings inspired by the object, and

experiences those feelings as though belonging to the object itself.
14. Tsutomu Ijima, *Aesthetics* (in Japanese) (Tokyo: Sobunsha, 1958), 213
15. Clara Zetkin, *Reminiscences of Lenin* (in German) (Berlin: Dietz Verlag, 1957), 17.
16. V. I. Lenin, *Collected Works*, 10:45.
17. Maxim Gorky, "Marshlands and Highlands" in *Mother* (Japanese version) (Tokyo: Shin-Nippon Bunko, 1976), 2:335.
18. Maxim Gorky, "On Socialist Realism," in *An Introduction to Literature* (Japanese version) (Tokyo: Aoki-Shoten, 1962), 136.
19. Ibid., 148–149.
20. Karl Marx, *A Contribution to the Critique of Political Economy* (Moscow: Progress Publishers, 1970), 20.
21. Joseph Stalin, "Concerning Marxism in Linguistics" (Pravda, 1950), in *Marxism and Problems of Linguistics* (Peking: Foreign Languages Press, 1972), 5.
22. Ibid., 7.
23. R. A. Medvedev, who criticized Stalin, depicts how Soviet writers and artists were oppressed in the late 1930s. Medvedev explains the reality of socialist realism by saying that, as it turned out, social realism did not describe the truth of reality, but on the contrary embellished reality in order to embellish Communism. He said that "[In the forties], the embellishment of reality became the hallmark of many writers; the desirable was often indistinguishable from the real." *Let History Judge: Origins and Consequences of Stalinism* (London: Macmillan, 1972), 531. He also said that "Artistic quality was bound to be very low. A vast quantity of gray, uninteresting works appeared in all fields of literature and art" (Ibid. 532).
24. Herbert Read, "Art and Society," in *The Philosophy of Art*, by Yohan Choe (in Korean) (Seoul: Kyungmun-sa, 1974), 169.
25. Ilya Ehrenburg, "The Work of a Writer," in *The Philosophy of Art*, by Yohan Choe, 169.
26. Yohan Choe, *The Philosophy of Art* (in Korean) (Seoul: Kyungmun-sa, 1974), 168–69.
27. André Gide, *Back from the U.S.S.R.* (London: Martin Secker & Warburg, Ltd., 1937), 11.
28. Ibid., 45.
29. Ibid., 62–63.
30. Boris Pasternak, *Doctor Zhivago*, trans. Max Hayward and Manya

Harari (New York: Ballantine Books, 1981), 259.
31. Ibid., 408.
32. Karl Marx, *A Contribution to the Critique of Political Economy*, 217.

8. Theory of History

1. Arnold Toynbee, *A Study of History*, abridgement of I-VI by D. C. Somervell (Oxford: Oxford University Press, 1974), 214.
2. Karl Jaspers wrote: "It would seem that this axis of history is to be found in the period around 500 B.C., in the spiritual process that occurred between 800 and 200 BC. It is there that we meet with the most deepcut dividing line in history. Man, as we know him today, came into being. For short, we may style this the 'Axial Period.'" *The Origin and Goal of History*, trans. Michael Bullock (Westport: Greenwood Press, 1976), 1.
3. Jaspers also wrote: "But it is an historical mystery which progressive research into the facts of the situation renders increasingly great. The Axial Period, with its overwhelming plenitude of spiritual creations, which has determined all human history down to the present day, is accompanied by the enigma of the occurrence, in these three mutually independent regions, of an analogous and inseparably connected process" (Ibid., 13).
4. In the fourteenth century, John Wycliffe (ca. 1320–84) of Great Britain translated the Bible into English, and asserted that the standard of faith should be placed, not on the pope or the clergy, but on the Bible itself, and fiercely denounced the corruption of the Church. Jan Huss (ca. 1374–1415) of Bohemia believed in Wycliffe's teachings and started a reform movement of Christianity, but was declared a heretic and burnt at the stake. In fifteenth century Florence, Girolamo Savonarola (1452–98) conducted a church reform movement, but was likewise suppressed and burnt at the stake. Then, in the sixteenth century, the Reformation sparked by Martin Luther (1483–1546) and John Calvin (1509–64) was carried forth. The Renaissance was a cultural movement that started in Italy and spread to the Western European nations in the fourteenth to sixteenth centuries. Dante (1265–1321), Petrarca (1304–74), and Boccaccio (1313–75) of Florence were the precursors of the

Renaissance Movement. The center of the Renaissance in its golden age moved from Florence to Rome, during which time the representative figures were Leonardo da Vinci (1452–1519), Raphael (1483–1520), and Michelangelo (1475–1564).
5. *DP*, 191.
6. *DP*, 197.
7. *DP*, 198.
8. Toynbee attributes the 400-year period of turmoil until the rise of the Roman Empire to the following effect: "The historian sees that the Graeco-Roman world achieved a rally in the generation of Augustus after the Battle at Actium. He also sees that the preceding breakdown began with the outbreak of the Peloponnesian War, four centuries earlier. For him, the vitally interesting problem is: What was it that went wrong in the fifth century and continued to go wrong until the last century B.C.? Now, the solution of this problem can only be found by studying Greek and Roman history as a continuing story with a plot that is one and indivisible." *Civilization on Trial* (New York: Oxford University Press, 1948), 46. He said, however, "if one does succeed in obtaining this light from it, it proves, *experto crede*, to be most amazingly illuminating" (Ibid., 61)—concluding that, if this question is solved, it would be as if we had obtained a revelation.
9. *DP*, 255, 271. This is a summary of the content of *Exposition of the Divine Principle*.
10. Oswald Spengler stated as follows: "The application of the 'homology' principle to historical phenomena brings with it an entirely new connotation for the word 'contemporary.' I designate as contemporary two historical facts that occur in exactly the same—relative—positions in their respective Cultures, and therefore possess exactly equivalent importance···. I hope to show that without exception all great creations and forms in religion, art, politics, social life, economy and science appear, fulfill themselves and die down *contemporaneously* in all the Cultures; that the inner structure of one corresponds strictly with that of all the others." *The Decline of the West*, trans. Charles Francis Atkinson (London: George Allen & Unwin, Ltd., 1961), 112.

He cites as examples the relationship between ancient Graeco-Roman culture and Western culture, Alexander the Great and Napoleon in the political field, Pythagoras and Descartes in the mathematical field, and so on.

11. Arnold Toynbee, *A Study of History*, Illustrated (Oxford: Oxford University Press, 1972), 11.
12. Herodotus was a fatalist who described history in the epic manner as manipulated by the thread of fate. On the other hand, Thucydides described historical facts realistically and scientifically. Yet, Thucydides also considered, according to the ordinary Greek way of thinking, that history repeats itself. He wrote, "The absence of romance in my history will, I fear, detract somewhat from its interest; but if it be judged useful by those inquirers who desire an exact knowledge of the past as an aid to the interpretation of the future, which in the course of human things must resemble if it does not reflect it, I shall be content. In fine, I have written my work, not as an essay which is to win the applause of the moment, but as a possession for all time." *The History of the Peloponnesian War* (London: J. M. Dent and Sons, Ltd., 1948), 11.
13. According to the view of history of Enlightenment thought, God's power was excluded from history because history was thought to be made by man. But Vico thought that even though history was made by man, still it is under God's providence. This means that history is the product of human power and God's providence. That view is in accord with the Unification view of history. Also, Vico thought that, although history is mainly in the process of progress or development, there are patterns of development and decline in history, and thus he grasped history as spiral progress. In that respect, he was a forerunner for the appearance of the cultural view of history advocated by Spengler and Toynbee.
14. Simmel stated in the introduction to the third edition of *The Problems of History* that "the spirit describes its coast and the rhythm of wave, in the stream of becoming, whereby it finds itself, and by doing so, it makes the stream of becoming a history." *Die Probleme der Geschichte* (Munchen: Verlag Dunker and Humblot, 1923), VII; my translation.
15. Arnold Toynbee, *A Study of History*, Illustrated, 488.
16. Arnold Toynbee, *A Study of History* (London: Oxford University Press, 1954), vol. 10, 1.
17. Karl Löwith, *Weltgeschichte und Heilsgeschehen* (Stuttgart: W. Kohlhammer Verlag, 1953), 48; my translation.

9. Epistemology

1. Masaaki Kohsaka, a Japanese scholar, states the following: "As a result of ten years of silence and study beginning in 1770, Kant's critical philosophy, which synthesized rationalism and empiricism, was established, and in 1781, he published *Critique of Pure Reason*." *History of Western Philosophy* (in Japanese) (Tokyo: Sobunsha, 1971), 322.
2. Locke wrote, "How comes it [the mind] to be furnished? ··· Whence has it all the materials of Reason and Knowledge? To this I answer, in one word, From *Experience*: In that, all our Knowledge is founded; and from that, it ultimately derives itself." *An Essay concerning Human Understanding* (Oxford: Oxford University Press, 1979), 104.
3. Ibid., 525.
4. Ibid., 578.
5. René Descartes, "Discourse Concerning Method," in John J. Blom, *René Descartes: The Essential Writings* (New York: Harper Torchbooks, 1977), 134.
6. Ibid., 135.
7. René Descartes, "Principles of Philosophy," in *The Philosophical Works of Descartes*, (Cambridge: At the University Press, 1911, reprinted 1977), vol. 1, 237.
8. Kant, who regarded Wolff as the representative philosopher of dogmatism, said in the preface to the second edition of his *Critique of Pure Reason*: "Dogmatism is thus the dogmatic procedure of pure reason, *without previous criticism of its own powers*." *Critique of Pure Reason*, trans. Norman Kemp Smith (London: The Macmillan Press Ltd., 1933), 32.
9. Ibid., 55.
10. Ibid., 93.
11. Here, the idea refers to the rational concept.
12. Engels said, "But if the further question is raised: what then are thought and consciousness, and whence they come, it becomes apparent that they are products of the human brain and that man himself is a product of Nature, which has developed in and along with its environment." *Anti-Dühring* (Moscow: Progress Publishers, 1969), 49. Lenin also said, "The mind does not exist independently of the body, ··· mind is secondary, a function of the brain, a reflection of the external world." *Materialism and Empirio-criticism* (Peking: Foreign

Language Press, 1972), 95.
13. Frederick Engels, "Ludwig Feuerbach and the End of Classical German Philosophy," in K. Marx and F. Engels, *Selected Works* (Moscow: Progress Publishers, 1970), 3:362 (hereafter *MESW*).
14. V. I. Lenin, *Materialism and Empirio-criticism*, 313.
15. V. I. Lenin, "Conspectus of Hegel's Science of Logic," in V. I. Lenin, *Collected Works* (Moscow: Progress Publishers, 1976), 38:171.
16. Mao Tse-tung, "On Practice," in *Selected Works of Mao Tse-tung* (Peking: Foreign Languages Press, 1975), 1:298-99 (hereafter *SWM*).
17. Ibid., 1:302.
18. Ibid., 1:308.
19. Engels, "Socialism: Utopian and Scientific," in *MESW* 3:102.
20. Mao Tse-tung, "On Practice," in *SWM* 1:297.
21. Ibid., 1:304.
22. F. V. Konstantinov, ed., *The Fundamentals of Marxist-Leninist Philosophy* (Moscow: Progress Publishers, 1982), 123–46.
23. O. W. Kuusinen, et al., *Fundamentals of Marxism-Leninism* (Moscow: Foreign Language Publishing House, 1961), 119.
24. K. Marx, "Thesis on Feuerbach," in K. Marx and F. Engels, *Collected Works* (New York: International Publishers, 1976), 5:6.
25. Mao Tse-tung, "On Practice," *SWM* 1:296.
26. V. I. Lenin, *Materialism and Empirio-criticism*, 152.
27. Lenin said, "Human thought then by its nature is capable of giving, and does give, absolute truth, which is compounded of a sum-total of relative truths. Each step in the development of science adds new grains to the sum of absolute truth." *Materialism and Empirio-criticism*, 151.
28. Some of the major points of Divine Principle, on which Unification epistemology is based, are the following:

(1) "The process of God's creation begins when the dual characteristics within God form a common base through the prompting of His universal prime energy. As they engage in give and take action, they generate a force which engenders multiplication. This force projects the dual characteristics into discrete substantial object partners, each relating to God as its center" (*DP*, 24). "Multiplication takes place through origin-division-union action which is built upon good interactions [give and receive actions]" (*DP*, 31). The phenomenon of the increase in new knowledge can be explained through

this principle.

(2) "The spirit can grow only while it abides in the flesh" (*DP*, 48). "All the sensibilities of a spirit are cultivated through the reciprocal relationship with the physical self during earthly life" (*DP*, 49). "Good or evil in the conduct of the physical self is the main determinant of whether the spirit self becomes good or evil" (*DP*, 48). Through these points of Divine Principle, we can come to understand that cognition through the five physical senses necessarily corresponds to cognition through the five spiritual senses, and that cognition and action (practice) originally are intended to fulfill the purpose of good.

(3) "The natural world returns beauty as an object partner" (*DP*, 38). "They [human beings] must earn certain qualifications to gain their God-given mandate to govern" (*DP*, 78). "The purpose for which the universe was created is to have man feel joy and peace." *Explaining the Principle* (in Korean) (Seoul: Sejong Moonhwa-sa, 1957), 50. From these points of the Principle, we can understand that cognition and dominion (practice) are in an inseparable relationship, and that the purpose of cognition and dominion lies in the realization of joy and peace.

(4) "Every human being embodies all the elements in the cosmos" (*DP*, 30). "In a human cell, there is life and consciousness, and the mystery of the universe is contained there" (a sermon by Rev. Sun Myung Moon). From these points we can derive the concepts of protoconsciousness and protoimage as the criteria through which all things in the external world can be cognized.

(5) "In give and receive action, there are various types, and among them there is also a contrast type" (Rev. Moon's answer to a question from the author). From this teaching, it was possible to obtain the concept of "collation" in cognition.

(6) "The body resembles the mind and moves according to its commands in such a way as to sustain life and pursue the mind's purposes" (*DP*, 17). "Thinking is also a kind of give and receive action"; "There are give and receive actions between mind and body, and give and receive actions within the mind" (Rev. Moon's response to the author's questions). Through these points of Divine Principle and Rev. Moon's teachings, it was possible to come to understand such phenomena as the correspondence between the invisible mind and the visible body, that is, the will and the movement of the body,

and the cognition (judgment) of the mind about the information (codes) coming through the body (nerves).

(7) "God created human beings to be the rulers of the universe" (*DP*, 46). "What will the world be like when the natural world abides under the direct dominion of human beings? When a fully mature person relates with the diverse things in nature as his object partners, they come together to form a four position foundation" (*DP*, 45). "God created the invisible substantial world and the visible substantial world, and He created man as the ruler over them" (*Explaining the Principle*, 44). "The universe was created as the substantial object to the subjective *sungsang* of man" (Ibid., 50). From these principles, we can realize that human beings are created as the subject of cognition as well as the subject of dominion (practice) over all things, and that all things are created as the object of cognition and the object of dominion by human beings, and that, therefore, the relationship between human beings and all things is a necessary relationship, similar to the relationship between mind and body.

29. The functions of the mind include intuition (sensibility), perception, cognition, thinking, inference, conception, planning, memory, pursuit of purpose, recollection, and aesthetic appreciation. Protoconsciousness possesses only some of these functions, such as the functions of sensibility, perception, and pursuit of purpose (purposiveness). Accordingly, protoconsciousness is the mind on a lower dimension. Cosmic consciousness is the expression of the cosmic mind on a lower dimension, that is, the expression of God's mind (*sungsang*) on a lower dimension.

30. Cosmic consciousness is contained not only in living beings, but also in minerals. However, in minerals it surfaces only as physicochemical functions, because of the structural character of minerals.

31. Numbers and laws are in inseparable relationships, as shown in the following:

One	= absolute	Six	= number of creation
Two	= relative	Seven	= perfection, Sabbath
Three	= Origin-Division-Union	Eight	= new start
Four	= Four Position Foundation	Nine	= 3 multiplied by 3
Five	= metal, wood, water, fire, and soil	Ten	= Return

The following examples also show that numbers exist with laws or principles.

the number of human vertebra
the breathing rate
the pulse rate
body temperature
the four seasons of the year
the three months of a season
the thirty (or thirty one) days of a month
the twenty four hours of a day
the sixty minutes in an hour
the sixty seconds in a minute
the ratio of a circle's circumference to its diameter ($\pi = 3.14$).

32. The spirit mind is the mind of the spirit self and contains spiritual elements. Thus, the functional part of the union of the spirit mind and physical mind is called "spiritual apperception" in epistemology.

33. When, in the formation of an inner four position foundation of the understanding stage, cognition does not take place, the sense image becomes an undetermined image. Then, the following options are available: (1) Create a new image (a new prototype) and repeat the process of collation; (2) Ask someone else for a judgment (this is called "judgment by another," or "educational judgment"); (3) Abort the judgment (in this case, the sense image will be erased); (4) Suspend the judgment (in this case, the sense image will be stored in memory).

34. Wilder Penfield states: "The brain is a kind of computer in which an automatic mechanism acquired anew is at work. Every computer becomes useful only after it is given a program and is operated by someone existing separately from the computer. Let us consider the case where we observe a certain thing. It seems that the decision to do so is the function of the mind, which exists separately from the brain." *The Mystery of the Mind* (Japanese version) (Tokyo: Hosei University Press, 1978), 110.

35. Eccles states the following: "These considerations lead me to the alternative hypothesis of dualist-interactionism, which has been expanded at length in *The Self and its Brain*. It is really the commonsense view, namely, that we are a combination of two things or entities: our brains on the one hand; and our conscious selves on the other. The self is central to the totality of our conscious experiences as persons through our whole waking life. We link it in memory from our earliest

conscious experiences. The self has a subconscious existence during sleep, except for dreams, and on waking the conscious self is resumed and linked with the past by the continuity of memory." J. C. Eccles and D. N. Robinson, *The Wonder of Being Human* (New York: The Free Press, 1984), 33.

36. Andrée Goudet-Perrot, *Cybernétique et Biologie* (Japanese version) (Tokyo: Hakusuisha, 1970), 15.
37. Ibid., 105.
38. This does not exclude, however, the possibility that future development in cerebrophysiology may lead to the appearance of a new physiological theory of epistemology. Here I have only provided evidence for the point that natural science, as it develops more and more, will support the positions of Unification Thought.
39. According to Goudet-Perrot, memory can be divided into two kinds: (1) *Hereditary memory*, which is received before birth, like the information contained in genes; (2) *Acquired memory*, which is acquired after birth and constitutes consciousness. *Cybernétique et Biologie*, 105.
40. Shigeru Kobayashi, et al., *Introduction to Brain Science* (in Japanese) (Tokyo: Ohmusha, 1987), 134.
41. Masao Ito, *Brain and Behavior* (in Japanese) (Tokyo: NHK Press Association, 1990), 125.
42. Goudet-Perrot, *Cybernétique et Biologie*, 89.
43. Hisashi Oshima's view supports the concept of prototype and the theory of collation of Unification Epistemology. Oshima states the following: "During our long-time contact and interaction with the environment, we come to form numerous prototypes in our mind. The structure of our knowledge is built centering on those prototypes···. Knowledge has a structure in which, centering on prototypes, things are ordered···. When we try to understand someone's speech, we compare and collate it with the knowledge that is structured in this way. The portions that accord with it are integrated in the structure of knowledge, but those that do not accord are not understood, and even if they appear somehow to be understood, in reality they will be misunderstood." *The Science of Knowledge* (in Japanese) (Tokyo: Shinyosha, 1986), 68–69.
44. M. S. Gazzaniga and J. E. Ledoux, *The Integrated Mind* (New York: Plenum Press, 1978), 132–135.

10. Logic

1. Immanuel Kant, *Critique of Pure Reason*, trans. Norman Kemp Smith (London: The Macmillan Press Ltd. 1933), 17.
2. Hegel stated the following in the introduction to *The Science of Logic*: "One may therefore express it thus: that this content *shows forth God as He is in His eternal essence before the creation of nature and of a finite spirit.*" "The Science of Logic," in *The Philosophy of Hegel*, trans. W. H. Johnson and L. G. Struthers, ed. Carl J. Friedrich (New York: The Modern Library, 1954), 186.
3. In the section dealing with "Quality," in "The Doctrine of Being," Hegel stated, "Pure **Being** makes the beginning: because it is on one hand pure thought, and on the other immediacy itself, simple and indeterminate; and the first beginning can not be mediated by anything, or be further determined." *Hegel's Logic*, trans. William Wallace (Oxford: Oxford University Press, 1975), 124.
4. Hegel stated, "But this mere Being, as it is mere abstraction, is therefore the absolutely negative; which, in a similarly immediate aspect, is just **Nothing**" (Ibid., 127).
5. Hegel stated, "Becoming is the first concrete thought, and therefore the first notion; whereas Being and Nought are empty abstractions···. Becoming is only the explicit statement of what Being is in its truth" (Ibid., 132).
6. The Absolute Idea at the end of the philosophy of Spirit is actual while the Absolute Idea at the end of the Logic is abstract. W. T. Stace writes as follows: "The Idea is thus both subject and object here. The whole development of spirit from its earliest stages has been motivated by this one impulse,—to bridge the gulf between subject and object, and this is now complete, and with this the development of spirit is complete. Subject and object are now identical. Absolute reconciliation is reached. And since the Idea now has itself for object, it is seen as what it is, self-consciousness, the Absolute Idea. This is the same result as we reached at the end of the Logic. But the Absolute Idea as found at the end of the Logic was still abstract to this extent that it was merely a category. Absolute spirit is the same thing which has now given itself actuality, has passed from the sphere of pure thought, of categories, into actual existence." *The Philosophy of Hegel: A Systematic Exposition* (New York: Dover Publications, Inc., 1955), 516.

7. At the end of *The Phenomenology of Mind*, Hegel stated, "This transforming process is a cycle that returns into itself, a cycle that presupposes its beginning, and reaches its beginning only at the end." *The Phenomenology of Mind*, trans. J. B. Baillie (New York: Harper Torchbooks, 1967), 801.

Concerning the circular nature of Hegel's philosophy, W. T. Stace explains as follows: "The sphere of absolute spirit ends the Hegelian system. It appears as the final result of all development. In accordance, however, with Hegelian principles, it is also the absolute foundation, the beginning. Thus the end of philosophy is also the beginning. This is what Hegel means when he says that philosophy is a circle which returns into itself. Here at the end of the system of philosophy we reach philosophy. If we ask what is this philosophy which we have reached the only answer possible is to begin again at the beginning of the Logic. Thus having reached the end, we must, to explain it, begin again at the beginning. This is the circle of philosophy. The Logic, with which we began, treated of the Idea. Here at the end of the philosophy of spirit we again reach the Idea, the Idea now as actual, existent in the philosophic mind. It is here that the world-process is consummated. 'The eternal Idea, in full fruition of its essence, eternally sets itself to work, engenders and enjoys itself as absolute mind (spirit)'." *The philosophy of Hegel: A systematic Exposition*, 517–518.

8. Engels, satirizing the laws of identity and contradiction in formal logic, wrote, "To the metaphysician, things and their mental reflexes, ideas, are isolated, are to be considered one after the other and apart from each other, are objects of investigation fixed, rigid, given once and for all. He thinks in absolutely irreconcilable antitheses. 'His communication is yea, yea; nay, nay; for whatsoever is more than these cometh of evil.' For him a thing either exists or does not exist; a thing can not at the same time be itself and something else. Positive and negative absolutely exclude one another; cause and effect stand in a rigid antithesis one to the other." *Anti-Dühring* (Moscow: Progress Publishers, 1969), 31.

9. Masatane Iwasaki, *Contemporary Logic* (in Japanese) (Chiba: Azusa Shuppansha, 1979), 31.

10. In response to the question "Is it true that language is a superstructure on the base?", Stalin clearly denied the view that a new language will be established in place of the Russian language as follows: "In this respect language radically differs from the superstructure. Take, for

example, Russian society and the Russian language. In the course of the past thirty years the old, capitalist base has been eliminated in Russia and a new, socialist base has been built⋯. But in spite of this the Russian language has remained basically what it was before the October Revolution⋯. As to the basic stock of words and the grammatical system of the Russian language, which constitute the foundation of a language, they, after the elimination of the capitalist base, far from having been eliminated and supplanted by a new basic word stock and a new grammatical system of the language, have been preserved in their entirety and have not undergone any serious changes—they have been preserved precisely as the foundation of the modern Russian language." *Marxism and Problems of Linguistics* (Peking: Foreign Languages Press, 1972), 3–5.

11. Masatane Iwasaki, *Contemporary Logic*, 37.
12. Concerning dialectical logic, the Japanese author Tsunenobu Terasawa wrote in the preface of his *An Essay on Dialectical Logic*, "About 150 years have passed since Hegel wrote *Science of Logic* (1812–1816), and in the meantime, no system of dialectical logic to replace it has been written by anyone. Even though the need for dialectical logic from a materialist position has often been emphasized, it has not as yet been written systematically by anyone." *Science of Logic* (in Japanese) (Tokyo: Otsuki Shoten, 1957), p. i. And even after Terasawa wrote that, no systematized dialectical logic seems to have appeared.
13. Kant wrote, "All our knowledge starts with the senses, proceeds from thence to understanding, and ends with reason, beyond which there is no higher faculty to be found in us⋯. Reason, like understanding, can be employed in a merely formal, that is, logical manner, wherein it abstracts from all content of knowledge." *Critique of Pure Reason*, trans. Kemp Smith (London: The Macmillan Press Ltd., 1950), 300.
14. Hegel stated the following: "But every additional and more concrete characterization causes Being to lose that integrity and simplicity it has in the beginning. Only in, and by virtue of, this mere generality is it Nothing, something inexpressible, whereof the distinction from Nothing is a mere intention or *meaning*. All that is wanted is to realize that these beginnings are nothing but these empty abstractions, one as empty as the other." *Hegel's Logic*, 127.
15. Kazuto Matsumura, *Hegel's Logic* (in Japanese) (Tokyo: Keiso Shobo,

1959), 40.
16. Johannes Hirschberger, *History of Philosophy III: The Modern Period* (Japanese edition) (Tokyo: Risosha, 1976), 509–10.
17. According to Akira Seto, the following difficulties arose as a result of the debate on Logic in the fifties:

(i) Difficulty in the Reflection Theory of Logic: It was asserted that the law of identity and the law of contradiction are on the one hand relative, as they are reflections of the relative unchangeability of objective reality, while on the other hand they are absolute as the rules of operation of thought, or the forms of thought. However, the refutation was made that if the law of identity and the law of contradiction are merely relative reflections of reality, then they can naturally have only relative validity.

(ii) Difficulty in the Operation Theory of Logic: Formal logic is the logic of operation in the sense that it is not concerned with the truthfulness of thinking, but with the validity of thinking. Therefore, it was asserted that the law of identity and the law of contradiction are not reflections of reality but they are purely the laws and norms of thinking. However, to recognize independent laws of thinking without any relationship to existence would imply losing the materialistic foundation, falling into Kantian a priorism. *Contemporary Epistemology and Dialectic* (in Japanese) (Tokyo: Sekibunsha, 1976), 234–237.

The difficulty pointed out in my book refers to part (ii) above. As a method of solving the two difficulties above, Seto suggests that we should recognize that the two contradictions in the law of contradiction, namely, the dialectical contradiction and the contradiction in the formal logic are originally different in nature. However, to regard the two contradictions as essentially different would be to lose the materi-alistic foundation. After all, the problems are not solved at all, as Seto himself points out: "This does not solve all problems····. A question is raised as to the reason why the situation has arisen that the two essentially different contradictions are expressed in the law of contradiction at the same time" (Ibid., 250).

11. Methodology

1. Immanuel Kant, "Prolegomena," in *The Philosophy of Kant—Immanuel Kant's Moral and Political Writings*, ed. and trans. Carl J. Friedrich (New York: The Modern Library, 1977), 45.
2. Kant stated: "That had not even occurred to anyone except him [Hume], although everyone unconcernedly used these concepts (without asking on what their objective validity rested)" (Ibid., 46).
3. *Hegel's Science of Logic*, trans. A.V. Miller (London: George Allen & Unwin Ltd., 1969), 439.
4. Frederick Engels, *Anti-Dühring* (Moscow: Progress Publishers, 1969), 168-9.
5. V. I. Lenin, *Collected Works*, vol. 38 (Moscow: Progress Publishers, 1976), 358.
6. Ibid.
7. F. Engels, *Anti-Dühring*, 33.

Bibliography

Bentham, J. *The Principles of Morals and Legislation*. New York: Prometheus, 1988.
Casenave, Michel, ed. *Science and Consciousness: Two Views of the Universe*. Translated by A. Hall and E. Callander. Oxford Press, Pergamon, 1984.
Choe, Yohan. *The Philosophy of Art* (in Korean). Seoul: Kyungmun-sa, 1974.
Comenius, John Amos. *The Great Didactic*. Translated by M. W. Keatinge. New York: Russell and Russell, 1967.
Confucius. *The Analects*. Translated by D. C. Lau. Harmondsworth: Penguin Books, 1979.
―――. *Confucian Analects, The Great Learning, and the Doctrine of the Mean*. Translated by James Legge. New York: Dover Publications, 1971.
Descartes, René. "Discourse Concerning Method." In *René Descartes: The Essential Writings*, translated by John J. Blom. New York: Harper Torchbooks, 1977.
―――. "Principles of Philosophy." In *The Philosophical Works of Descartes*, vol. 1. Cambridge: University Press, 1911, reprinted 1977.
Dewey, John. *Democracy and Education: An Introduction to the Philosophy of Education*. New York: The Free Press, 1944.
―――. *Theory on the Moral Life*. New York: Holt, Rinehart & Winston, Inc., 1960.
Dirac, Paul A., et al. *Scientific American Resource Library: Readings in the Physical Sciences* (Japanese version). Tokyo: Kodansha, 1972.
Dubrov, A. P. and V. N. Pushkin. *Parapsychology and Contemporary Natural Science* (Japanese version). Tokyo; Kodansha, 1985.
Eccles, John C. and D. N. Robinson. *The Wonder of Being Human*. New York: The Free Press, 1984.
Engels, Friedrich. *Anti-Dühring*. Moscow: Progress Publishers, 1969.
―――. "Ludwig Feuerbach and the End of Classical German Philosophy."

In Karl Marx and Friedrich Engels, *Selected Works* (hereafter *MESW*). vol. 3. Moscow: Progress Publishers, 1970.
―――. "Socialism: Utopian and Scientific." *MESW*, vol. 3. Moscow: Progress Publishers, 1970.
Feuerbach, Ludwig. *The Essence of Christianity*. Translated by George Eliot. New York: Harper and Row, 1957.
Froebel, Friedrich. *The Education of Man*. Clifton: Augustus M. Kelley, Publishers, 1974.
Gazzaniga, M. S. and J. E. Ledoux. *The Integrated Mind*. New York: Plenum Press, 1978.
Gide, André. *Back from the U.S.S.R*. London: Martin Decker and Warburg, Ltd., 1937.
Gorky, Maxim. "On Socialist Realism." In *An Introduction to Literature* (Japanese version). Tokyo: Aoki Shoten, 1962.
―――. "Marshlands and Highlands." In *Mother* (Japanese version), Tokyo: Shin-nippon Shuppansha, 1976.
Goudet-Perrot, Andrée. *Cybernétique et Biologie* (Japanese version). Translated by Jun Okuda, et al. Tokyo: Hakusuisha, 1970.
Hegel, G.W.F. *Hegel's Logic*. Translated by William Wallace. Oxford: Oxford University Press, 1975.
―――. *The Phenomenology of Mind*. Translated by J. B. Baillie. New York: Harper Torchbooks, 1967.
―――. *The Philosophy of Hegel*. Edited by Carl J. Friedrich. New York: The Modern Library, 1954.
―――. *The Science of Logic*. 4 vols (Japanese version). Translated by Tatehito Takeichi. Tokyo: Iwanami Shoten, 1956-61.
―――. *The Science of Logic*. Translated by A. V. Miller. London: George Allen & Unwin, Ltd., 1969.
Heidegger, Martin. *Being and Time*. Translated by John Macquarrie and Edward Robinson. Southampton: Basil Blackwell, 1962.
Hirschberger, Johannes. *History of Western Philosophy III: The Modern Period* (Japanese version). Tokyo: Risosha, 1976. Originally published as *Geschichte der Philosophie*, vol. 2. Freiburg: Verlag Herder, 1965.
Hiwatashi, Koichi. *Search for the Origin of the Sex* in Japanese. Tokyo: Iwanami Shoten, 1986.
Hofstadter, A. and Kuhns, R., eds. *Philosophies of Art and Beauty*. Chicago: The University of Chicago Press, 1964.
Hokekyo (The Lotus Sutra) (Japanese version). Translated by Y. Sakamoto

and Y. Iwamoto. 3Vols. Tokyo: Iwanami Shoten, 1962-67.
Holy Spirit Association for the Unification of World Christianity. *Divine Principle* (in Korean). Seoul: Sunghwa-sa, 1987.
Holy Spirit Association for the Unification of World Christianity. *Explaining the Divine Principle* (in Korean). Seoul: Sejong Moonhwa-sa, 1957.
Holy Spirit Association for the Unification of World Christianity. *Exposition of the Divine Principle*. New York: HSA-UWC, 1996.
Ijima, Tsutomu. *Aesthetics* (in Japanese). Tokyo: Sobunsha, 1958.
Ishikawa, Mitsuo. *The World View of New Science* (in Japanese). Tokyo: Tama Shuppan, 1985.
Ito, Masao. *Brain and Behavior* (in Japanese). Tokyo: NHK Press Association, 1990.
Iwasaki, Masatane. *Contemporary Logic* (in Japanese). Chiba: Azusa Shuppansha, 1979.
Iwasaki, Takeo. *History of Western Philosophy* (in Japanese). Tokyo: Yuhikaku, 1975.
James, William. *Pragmatism*. Cambridge: Harvard University Press, 1975.
Jaspers, Karl. *The Origin and Goal of History*. Westport: Greenwood Press Publishers, 1953.
———. *Philosophy*. 3vols. Translated by E. B. Ashton. Chicago: The University of Chicago Press, 1969–71.
———. *What is Philosophy?* (Japanese version). Tokyo: Hakusuisha, 1978. Originally published as *Was ist Philosophie?* Edited by Hans Sayer. Munich: R. Piper & Co. Verlag, 1976.
Kant, Immanuel. *Critique of Judgment*. Translated by James Creed Meredith. Chicago: Encyclopedia Britannica, Inc., 1952.
———. *Critique of Pure Reason*. Translated by Norman Kemp Smith. London: The Macmillan Press Ltd., 1933.
———. *Critique of Practical Reason*. Translated by T. K. Abbott. Chicago: Encyclopedia Britannica, Inc., 1952.
———. *Education*. Translated by Annette Churton. Chicago: The University of Michigan Press, 1960.
———. "Prolegomena." In *The Philosophy of Kant—Immanuel Kant's Moral and Political Writings*, edited by Carl J. Friedrich. New York: The Modern Library, 1977.
Kierkegaard, Søren. *The Present Age*. New York: Harper and Row Publishers, 1962.
———. *The Sickness unto Death*. Princeton: Princeton University Press,

1980.
The Koran, Translated with notes by N. J. Dawood. New York: Penguin Books, 1974.
Kobayashi, Shigeru, et al. *Introduction to Brain Science* (in Japanese). Tokyo: NHK Press Association, 1990.
Konstantinov, F. V., et al. *The Fundamentals of Marxist-Leninist Philosophy*. Moscow: Progress Publishers, 1982.
Kohsaka, Masa-aki. *History of Western Philosophy* (in Japanese). Tokyo: Sobunsha, 1971.
Kuusinen, O. W., et al. *The Fundamentals of Marxism-Leninism*. Moscow: Foreign Language Publishing House, 1961.
Lenin, V. I. *Collected Works* (hereafter *CWL*). 45 vols. Moscow: Progress Publishers, 1960–1970.
———. "Conspectus of Hegel's Science and Logic." *CWL*, vol. 38. Moscow: Progress Publishers, 1965.
———. *Materialism and Empirio-criticism*. Peking: Foreign Language Press, 1972.
———. "On the Question of Dialectics." *CWL*, Vol. 39. Moscow: Progress Publishers, 1976.
Locke, John. *An Essay concerning Human Understanding*. Oxford: Oxford University Press, 1979.
———. *Two Treatises of Government*, edited by Peter Laslett. New York: Cambridge University Press, 1988.
Löwith, Karl. *World History and the History of Salvation* (Japanese version). Translated by Sinoda et al. Tokyo: Sobunsha, 1964. Originally published as *Weltgeschichte und Heilsgeschehen*. Stuttgart: Verlag W. Kohlhammer, 1953.
Mao, Tse-tung. *Selected Works of Mao Tse-tung* (hereafter *SWM*). 5 vols. Peking: Foreign Language Press, 1975–1997.
———. "On Practice." *SWM*, vol.1.
Marx, Karl and Friedrich Engels. *Collected Works* (hereafter *MECW*). 50 vols. New York: International Publishers, 1975–.
Marx, Karl and Friedrich Engels, *Selected Works* (hereafter *MESW*). 3 vols. Moscow: Progress Publishers, 1969–70.
Marx, Karl. *Capital*. 3 vols. New York: International Publishers, 1967.
———. "The Class Struggle in France, 1848 to 1885." *MESW*, vol. 1.
———. "Thesis on Feuerbach." *MECW*, vol. 5.
Matsumura, Kazuto. *Hegel's Logic* (in Japanese). Tokyo: Keiso Shobo,

1959.

Medvedev, R. A. *Let History Judge: Origins and Consequences of Stalinism.* New York: Alfred Knopf, Inc., 1972.

Moon, Sun Myung. *New Hope—Twelve Talks by Sun Myung Moon,* edited by Rebecca Salonen. New York: HSA-UWC, 1973.

———. *God's Will and the World.* New York: HSA-UWC, 1985.

———. "Founder's Address (Fourteenth ICUS)." In *Absolute Values and the New Cultural Revolution.* New York: The International Cultural Foundation, 1986.

Moore, G. E. *Principia Ethica.* Cambridge: Cambridge University Press, 1959.

Mori, Koichi, ed., *Dictionary of Philosophy* (in Japanese). Tokyo: Aoki Shoten, 1974.

Motoyama, Hiroshi. *Yoga and Parapsychology* (in Japanese). Tokyo: Shukyo-shinri Shuppan, 1972.

Nietzsche, Friedrich. "The Antichrist." In *Nietzshe.* edited and translated by Walter Kaufmann. New York: Penguin Books, 1982.

———. "Thus Spake Zarathustra." In *Nietzshe.* edited and translated by Walter Kaufmann. New York: Penguin Books, 1982.

Oshima, Hisashi. *The Science of Knowledge* (in Japanese). Tokyo: Shin-yosha, 1986.

Pascal, Blaise. *Pensees.* Translated by A. J. Krailsheimer. New York: Penguin Books, 1966.

Pasternak, Boris. *Doctor Zhivago.* Translated by M. Hayward and M. Harari. New York: Ballantine Books, 1981.

Penfield, Wilder. *The Mystery of the Mind* (Japanese version). Tokyo: Hosei University Press, 1978.

Pestalozzi, J. H. *Spirit and Heart in the Method* (Japanese version). Tokyo: Meiji Tosho, 1980.

Plato. "Hippias Major, Hippias Minor, Euthydemus." Translated by Robin Waterfield. In *Early Socratic Dialogues.* Harmondsworth: Penguin Books, 1987.

Read, Herbert. *The Meaning of Art.* London: Faber & Faber, 1972.

"Report of the United States Education Mission to Japan—Submitted to the Supreme Commander for the Allied Powers." Tokyo: March 30, 1946.

Rolland, Romain. *Millet* (Japanese version). Tokyo: Iwanami Bunko, 1959.

———. *Beethoven.* Translated by BC. Hull. New York: Books for Libraries

Press, 1969.
Rousseau, Jean-Jacques. *Émile*. Translated by Barbara Foxley. London: L. M. Dent & Sons, Ltd., 1974.
Sartre, Jean Paul, *Being and Nothingness*. New York: Washington Square Press, 1956.
―――. "Existentialism is a Humanism." In *The Fabric of Existentialism*, edited by R. Gill & E. Sherman. New York: Meredith Corporation, 1973.
Seto, Akira. *Contemporary Epistemology and Dialectic* (in Japanese). Tokyo: Sekibunsha, 1976.
Shibata, Yoshimatsu and Satoru Kawanobe, eds. *Materials on Soviet Pedagogy* (in Japanese). Tokyo: Shin-dokushosha, 1976.
Shoji, Masako, editorial supervisor. *The History of Contemporary Western Education*. Tokyo: Aki Shobo, 1969.
Simmel, Georg. *Die Probleme der Geschichtphilosophie. Eine erkenntnistheoretische Studie*, 4. Verlag von Duncker & Humblot, 1922.
The Society for the Research of the Teaching Materials of Philosophy. *New Lecture of Philosophy* (in Korean). Seoul: Hakusa, 1978.
Spengler, Oswald. *The Decline of the West*. Translated by C. F. Atkinson. London: George Allen Unwin, Ltd., 1961.
Stace, W. T. *The Philosophy of Hegel: A Systematic Exposition*. New York: Dover Publications. Inc., 1955.
Stalin, Joseph. *Dialectical and Historical Materialism*. New York: International Publishers, 1940.
―――. "Concerning Marxism in Linguistics" (Pravda, 1950). In *Marxism and Problems of Linguistics*. Peking: Foreign Languages Press, 1972.
Suzuki, Yoshijiro. "Tung Chung-shu." In *Lectures on Oriental Thought* (in Japanese), edited by Sei-ich Uno, et al, vol. 2. Tokyo: Tokyo University Press, 1967.
Takeuchi, Toshio, ed. *Encyclopedia of Aesthetics*. Tokyo: Kobundo, 1974.
Terasawa, Hidezumi. *Subquark Physics and Original Geometry* (in Japanese). Tokyo: Kyoritsu Shuppansha, 1982.
Terasawa, Tsunenobu. *An Essay on Dialectical Logic* (in Japanese). Tokyo: Otsuki Shoten, 1957.
Thucydides, H. S. *The History of the Peloponnesian War*. London: J. M. Dent & Sons, Ltd., 1948.
Tompkins, Peter and Christopher Bird. *The Secret Life of Plants*. New York: Harper and Row, 1973.

Toynbee, Arnold J. *Civilization on Trial*. New York: Oxford University Press, 1948.

———. *A Study of History*. vol. 10. London: Oxford University Press, 1954.

———. *A Study of History*. 2 vols. Abridged by D.C. Somervell. Oxford: Oxford University Press, 1974.

———. *A Study of History, Illustrated*. New York: Weathervane Books, 1972.

Tugarinov, B. P. "The Problems of Value in Philosophy." In *Dictionary of Philosophy* (in Japanese), edited by Koichi Mori. Tokyo: Aoki Shoten, 1974.

Wilber, Ken, ed. *The Holographic Paradigm and Other Paradoxes*. Boston: Shambhala, 1985.

Zetkin, Clara. *Reminiscences of Lenin* (in German). Berlin: Dietz Verlag, 1950.

www.ingramcontent.com/pod-product-compliance
Lightning Source LLC
Chambersburg PA
CBHW060906300426
44112CB00011B/1361